I0879124

Citizenship in Heaven and on Earth

Citizenship in Heaven and on Earth

Karl Barth's Ethics

Alexander Massmann

Fortress Press
Minneapolis

CITIZENSHIP IN HEAVEN AND ON EARTH

Karl Barth's Ethics

Cover design: Joe Reinke

Library of Congress Cataloging-in-Publication Data

Print ISBN: 978-1-4514-7814-3

eBook ISBN: 978-1-5064-0146-1

The paper used in this publication meets the minimum requirements of American National Standard for Information Sciences — Permanence of Paper for Printed Library Materials, ANSI Z329.48-1984.

Manufactured in the U.S.A.

This book was produced using Pressbooks.com, and PDF rendering was done by PrinceXML.

Contents

Acknowledgments

This book is a reworked translation of my *Bürgerrecht im Himmel und auf Erden: Karl Barth's Ethik*, which was published in German in 2013, in the series Öffentliche Theologie ("Public Theology," by Evangelische Verlagsanstalt in Leipzig). That book goes back to my PhD dissertation at Heidelberg University, Germany, which was graciously supervised by Michael Welker. Apart from him, many people have contributed helpfully during the work on this publication, among them the participants of Michael Welker's doctoral colloquia as well as Gregor Etzelmüller, Bruce McCormack, George Hunsinger, Daniel Migliore, and Michael Plathow. The staff at Fortress Press, especially Michael Gibson, Esther Diley, Lisa Gruenisen, and Layne Meyer, has been supportive and helpful throughout the publication process. Jennifer Adams-Massmann has not only been extremely patient about the enduring presence of a certain Swiss theologian in our lives, but she has also contributed significantly during the reworking and translation of the book. A special word of thanks is due to my parents for their continuing support and interest. I dedicate it to them.

A note on language is appropriate at this point. Barth's original writing in German may be called gender neutral as far as grammar is concerned. In German, the words for God and the human person require male pronouns grammatically, and while the grammatical gender is male in both cases, *Mensch* (person) differs from *Mann* (male person). By contrast, the published English translations of Barth's work opt for male terminology beyond grammatical requirements. One may wish to correct this usage in quotations, but then again the fact that the relevant German terminology is male grammatically does not reflect complete gender inclusiveness, either. Whenever I have translated passages from the German originals myself, I have tried to keep the language gender neutral.

Quotations from Barth's writings published with Wipf & Stock Publishers are used by permission (www.wipfandstock.com). Permission to quote from the Barth-Gesamtausgabe by Theologischer Verlag Zurich (TVZ) is gratefully acknowledged, as well as fair use policies by William B. Eerdmans Publishing Co. and Ignatius Press. Permissions have also been obtained from Bloomsbury/T&T Clark.

Abbreviations

"CCCC"

Karl Barth. "The Christian Community and Civil Community." In *Community, Church, and State: Three Essays*. Edited by David Haddorff. Translated by Will Herberg. Eugene, OR: Wipf & Stock, 2004, 149–89. ("Christengemeinde und Bürgergemeinde")

CD

Karl Barth. *Church Dogmatics*. Edited by Geoffrey W. Bromiley and Thomas F. Torrance. Translated by Geoffrey W. Bromiley, George Thomas Thomson, et al. Edinburgh: T&T Clark, 1936–69. (*Die Kirchliche Dogmatik*)

"ChrSoc"

Karl Barth. "The Christian in Society." In *The Word of God and Theology*. Translated by Amy Marga. London and New York: T&T Clark, 2011, 31–70. ("Der Christ in der Gesellschaft")

CL

Karl Barth. *The Christian Life: Church Dogmatics IV,4; Lecture*

Fragments. Edited by Hans-Anton Drewes and Eberhard Jüngel. Translated by Geoffrey W. Bromiley. Grand Rapids: Eerdmans, 1981. (*Das christliche Leben*)

"CS"

Karl Barth. "Church and State." In *Community, Church, and State: Three Essays*. Edited by David Haddorff. Translated by Will Herberg. Eugene, OR: Wipf & Stock, 2004, 101–4. ("Rechtfertigung und Recht")

"Das Erste Gebot"

Karl Barth. "Das erste Gebot als theologisches Axiom." In *Vorträge und kleinere Arbeiten 1930–1933*. Edited by Michael Beintker, Michael Hüttenhoff, and Peter Zocher. Barth-Gesamtausgabe. Zurich: Theologischer Verlag, 2013, 209–41.

***GD* I**

Karl Barth. *The Göttingen Dogmatics: Instruction in the Christian Religion*. Edited by Hannelotte Reiffen. Translated by Geoffrey W. Bromiley. Vol. 1. Grand Rapids: Eerdmans, 1991. (*Unterricht in der christlichen Religion*. Vol. 1)

***GD* II–III**

Karl Barth. *Unterricht in der christlichen Religion*. Vol. 2: *Die Lehre von Gott/Die Lehre vom Menschen 1924/25*. Edited by Hinrich Stoevesandt. Barth-Gesamtausgabe. Zurich: Theologischer Verlag, 1990. Vol. 3: *Die Lehre von der Versöhnung/Die Lehre von der Erlösung*

1925/26. Edited by Hinrich Stoevesandt. Barth-Gesamtausgabe. Zurich: Theologischer Verlag, 2003.

"GL"

Karl Barth. "Gospel and Law." In *Community, Church, and State: Three Essays*. Edited by David Haddorff. Translated by Will Herberg. Eugene, OR: Wipf & Stock, 2004, 71–100. ("Gesetz und Evangelium")

KD

Karl Barth. *Die Kirchliche Dogmatik*. Vols. I/1–IV/4. Munich: Kaiser; Zurich: Theologischer Verlag, 1932–81.

MD

Karl Barth. *Die christliche Dogmatik im Entwurf: Die Lehre vom Worte Gottes: Prolegomena zur christlichen Dogmatik: 1927*. Edited by Gerhard Sauter. Barth-Gesamtausgabe. Zurich: Theologischer Verlag, 1982.

Rom **I**

Karl Barth. *Der Römerbrief (Erste Fassung): 1919*. Edited by Hermann Schmidt. Barth-Gesamtausgabe. Zurich: Theologischer Verlag, 1985.

Rom **II**

Karl Barth. *Der Römerbrief (Zweite Fassung): 1922*. Edited by Cornelis van der Kooi and Katja Tolstaja. Barth-Gesamtausgabe. Zurich: Theologischer Verlag, 2010.

Introduction

In order to get a sense of the multifaceted nature of Karl Barth's ethics, one thing to do is to conjure up before the inner eye images that western societies commonly associate with a long interval of the twentieth century such as the years between 1932 and 1967. This was the time it took Barth to publish his multi-volume *Church Dogmatics* (*CD*),[1] which comprises both theology and ethics. Moreover, the various social, ecclesial and political contexts of his work are reflected in the fact that the critical edition of Barth's works includes five volumes of individual smaller texts, written for particular occasions, as well as three volumes of open letters. The particular contexts of his work not only help us gain a better sense of where Barth is coming from in a given text. The fact that Barth often engaged contemporary public issues—be it in a more academic or a slightly more popular fashion—also provides us with clues about his own understanding of the ethical dimension of his work. While its multifaceted character does not make the descriptive and interpretive task easier, it also adds to the power inherent in Barth's work to speak to different times and contexts.

1. Barth, *Church Dogmatics* (Edinburgh: T&T Clark, 1936–61).

Barth's Ethics: Appreciative and Critical Stances

Karl Barth's influence in the church and the public sphere may well be unparalleled among his contemporaries in the German-speaking academy. The well-known issues that characterized his public activity include the role of the churches during Hitler's reign as well as political questions during the Cold War. Writing from exile, the philosopher Karl Löwith judged in 1940 that Barth's pamphlet *Theological Existence Today!* "was and remained the only serious expression of academic resistance against the raging time."[2] Barth critiqued the National Socialist transformation of a pluralistic society into a monohierarchical, totalitarian state when he addressed the problem of the so-called Aryan paragraph in church law and the unification of German Protestant churches under a national bishop. More dramatically, in 1938 Barth called on Czechoslovakians to resist an impending German invasion by force: "Every Czech soldier who would then fight and suffer will do so also for us, and he will do so—I am saying so today without reservation—even for the church of Jesus Christ."[3]

What may be less well-known is that, for example, his discussion of abortion in *CD* was the first thorough treatment of the issue in German after approximately 2 million German women suffered rape by members of the Red Army occupying east Germany.[4] Another little-known consequence of Barth's work is that shortly after his death, a German reform of criminal law was influenced also by

2. Karl Löwith, *My Life in Germany before and after 1933: A Report*, trans. Elisabeth King (Athlone: University of Illinois Press, 1994), 37.
3. Barth, "Brief an Prof. Dr. Josef L. Hromádka, Prag 1938," in *Offene Briefe 1935–42*, ed. Diether Koch, Barth-Gesamtausgabe (Zurich: Theologischer Verlag, 2001), 107–33, 114. Whenever the footnote provides a German title for an English quotation, the translation is my own.
4. John L. Gaddis, *The Cold War* (London: Penguin, 2005), 24; Christiane Kohler-Weiss, *Schutz der Menschwerdung: Schwangerschaft und Schwangerschaftskonflikt als Thema evangelischer Ethik*, Öffentliche Theologie 17 (Gütersloh: Kaiser and Gütersloher, 2003), 37.

his ethical thought.[5] There are even more examples of the public impact of Barth's thought in Germany. A politician and churchman who played an important role in the German policy of détente with the USSR under chancellor Willy Brandt, Erhard Eppler, recounts how his involvement in politics began when he heard Barth give the lecture "The Church between East and West."[6] Another notable politician and church man, Jürgen Schmude, named the Barmen Declaration, penned mainly by Barth himself, his source of continuing orientation,[7] as did the German constitutional judge Helmut Simon.[8]

All of these examples of Barth's impact on public life indicate that an important dimension of his ethics is eminently public in character. In all these examples of Barth's influence on German public life,

5. A key figure in the German reform of criminal law was Gustav Heinemann, former German secretary of justice and German president, who held the Barmen Declaration in high esteem and whose sister-in-law Gertrud Staewen was Barth's lifelong friend. A notable feature of the reform was, for instance, the abrogation of atonement as a category in criminal law. See Peter Borowsky, "Sozialliberale Koalition und innere Reformen," Informationen zur politischen Bildung 258 (1998): 31–40, www.bit.ly/JrG5iC; Gustav Walter Heinemann, *Einspruch: Ermutigung für entschiedene Demokraten*, ed. Diether Koch (Bonn: Dietz, 1999).

6. In Bern, Eppler attended Barth's original presentation of his lecture "Die Kirche zwischen Ost und West" (The church between east and west), published in *"Der Götze wackelt": Zeitkritische Aufsätze, Reden und Briefe von 1930 bis 1960*, ed. Karl Kupisch (Berlin: Vogt, 1961), 124–43. Eppler worked closely with Heinemann, became federal minister for development aid, and held high positions in the German Social Democratic Party. Rainer Burchardt, "Vom Minister zur Galionsfigur der Friedensbewegung: Zeitzeugen im Gespräch: Erhard Eppler," *Deutschlandradio*, Nov. 27th, 2008, http://tinyurl.com/nskt4c2. Jussi Hanhimäki, "Détente in Europe: 1969–1975," in *The Cambridge History of the Cold War: Crises and Détente*, ed. Melvyn P. Leffler and Odd Arne Westad (Cambridge: Cambridge University Press, 2010), 198–218. On Eppler, see Christine Simon, Erhard Epplers Deutschland- und Ostpolitik, PhD diss., University of Bonn, Germany, 2004, http://hss.ulb.uni-bonn.de/2004/0337/0337.htm.

7. Jürgen Schmude was secretary of education and science, of law, and of domestic affairs in West Germany (1978–82, successively), but also President of the Council of the Evangelical Church in Germany (EKD). From 1983–6, he chaired a commission of the Union of Evangelical Churches, Germany (EKU, part of EKD), with the task to articulate the contemporary meaning of the fifth thesis of the Barmen Declaration. He was awarded the Karl Barth Award of the EKU in 2008.

8. See Helmut Simon, "Die zweite und die fünfte These der Barmer Erklärung und der staatliche Gewaltgebrauch," in *Bekennende Kirche wagen: Barmen 1934–1984*, ed. Jürgen Moltmann, Kaiser Traktate (Munich: Kaiser, 1984), 199–222.

substantially theological reasons played a role in Barth's justification of his positions. He typically distinguished the church's characteristic standards of reasoning from "worldly" ones and challenged the church to cultivate the former. At the same time he rejected "Christian" public politics based primarily on religious justifications.[9] But he did not simply withdraw from public responsibility into sectarian particularism. In the instances just mentioned, his ethical argument was thoroughly discursive and public. These are tensions, but they are fruitful, productive tensions. It should be added, however, that Barth did not always make it easy for his contemporaries to understand how these tensions might eventually be resolved. Sometimes his assertiveness was even perceived as the erratic instinct of a would-be prophet rather than resting on scholarly argument.[10]

Barth may be seen as steering a course between the Scylla of an ethical argument that is driven by the facts available to everyone—which would require attention to so many empirical details that one would no longer know how to fit all of them into an interpretive framework—and the Charybdis of a cantankerousness that can always tell good and evil apart, but consistently fails to appeal to those not yet converted. Can we discern a helpful strategy of ethical argument in Barth's work? How did he combine his insistence that the church focus on its particular task in faith and theology with his theological concern for wider society? Moreover, how is Barth's thinking on specific moral issues connected to positions he took on

9. Barth, "The Christian Community and Civil Community," in *Community, Church, and State: Three Essays*, ed. David Haddorff, trans. Will Herberg (Eugene: Wipf & Stock, 2004), 149–89, 160–61. ("CCCC").

10. Eberhard Busch, *Karl Barth: His Life from Letters and Autobiographical Texts*, trans. John Bowden (Eugene: Wipf & Stock, 2005), 405. When asked why political disputes with him regularly seem to escalate into all-out personal judgments, Barth rather unhelpfully called such a confrontation exemplary Christian commitment. See also ibid., 395.

other moral questions, to his convictions in ethical methodology, and to his wider theological thought?

The question may arise whether the public role of the theologian is not in tension with the notion that Barth's standards of reasoning are strictly internal to the church. Is it true to the spirit of Barth's ethics, for example, to rely on empirical indications while arguing for faithful Christian action? It is very common to answer these questions in the negative. This seems to be in tension with the way Barth sought public attention, however, which then may very easily appear as authoritarian. By contrast, this volume argues that on the whole, the answer should be yes, even by standards internal to Barth's own theological thought. With this premise, what is Barth's conceptual strategy to attain wider resonance within society, while retaining his insistence on particular Christian commitments? I contend, as outlined below, that Barth's argument for a particular relationship between gospel and law is crucial in this regard, which will, however, require revision of certain aspects of textbook depictions of Barth's ethics.

In contrast to existing analyses of Barth's thought, the present work does not merely isolate a few exemplary material issues in ethics, nor does it suffice to extrapolate one strategy of ethical argument, such as "actualistic ethics" or "natural law." Indeed, while there are helpful and significant studies on Barth's ethics already, a serious attempt at a comprehensive look at Barth's ethical oeuvre still remains to be desired.[11] What must become clearer is not only if and how Barth

11. Since 1990, at least sixteen works dealing with Barth's ethics have been published in English, and, since 1968, about a dozen German monographs on individual aspects (see the overview below). Timothy Gorringe's *Karl Barth: Against Hegemony* stands out for its historico-genealogical approach, but Barth's substantial ethical sections in *CD* II/2 (273 pages) and III/4 (685 pages) are discussed on ten pages altogether. Gerald McKenny's *The Analogy of Grace* laments that an analysis of Barth's special ethics remains a desideratum of research. The following titles stand out in the English literature: Nigel Biggar, *The Hastening That Waits: Karl Barth's Ethics* (Oxford: Clarendon, 1993); John B. Webster, *Barth's Ethics of Reconciliation*

made a consistent argument for any one strategy through the years, but especially how such a strategy relates to the particular positions he took on specific moral questions.

Trying to answer these questions, the present book is the only one to examine Barth's ethics using a historico-genealogical approach. This method will reveal new aspects in several large sections of Barth's texts, a close reading of which has remained a desideratum of research for some time. It will not come as a surprise if a work the scope of *CD*, written over more than three decades in the context of dramatic ecclesial and political changes, implies tensions, at least in some parts. It is multifaceted even if considered only in its ethical parts, and indeed *CD* will turn out to advocate rival views of ethics at times, some aspects of which are more helpful for today's ethical reflections than others.

A conundrum in current Barth studies is that his thought is claimed for contradicting agendas in theological ethics. While Nigel Biggar makes a case that Barth emphasized orders of creation, Paul Nimmo

(Cambridge: Cambridge University Press, 1995); Webster, *Barth's Moral Theology: Human Action in Barth's Thought* (Edinburgh: T&T Clark, 1998), Timothy J. Gorringe, *Karl Barth: Against Hegemony*, Christian Theology in Context (Oxford: Oxford University Press, 1999); David Clough, *Ethics in Crisis: Interpreting Barth's Ethics*, Barth Studies (Farnham: Ashgate, 2005); Paul T. Nimmo, *Being in Action: The Theological Shape of Barth's Ethical Vision* (Edinburgh: T&T Clark, 2006); Gerald McKenny, *The Analogy of Grace: Karl Barth's Moral Theology* (Oxford: Oxford University Press, 2010); Matthew Rose, *Ethics with Barth: God, Metaphysics and Morals*, Barth Studies (Farnham: Ashgate, 2010); David Haddorff, *Christian Ethics as Witness: Barth's Ethics for a World at Risk* (Eugene: Wipf & Stock, 2011). As the most recent collection of interactions with Barth on ethics, see the forthcoming volume by Markus Höfner (ed.), *Theo-Politics? Conversing with Barth in Western and Asian Contexts* (Minneapolis: Fortress Press, 2016). In the German literature, Friedrich-Wilhelm Marquardt, Herbert Anzinger, and Frank Jehle have made helpful contributions, but the following titles deserve mention especially: Ulrich Dannemann, *Theologie und Politik im Denken Karl Barths*, Gesellschaft und Theologie 22 (München: Kaiser, 1977); Herbert Lindenlauf, *Karl Barth und die Lehre von der "Königsherrschaft Christi": Eine Untersuchung zum christozentrischen Ansatz der Ethik des Politischen im deutschsprachigen Protestantismus nach 1934* (Spardorf: Wilfer, 1988); Marco Hofheinz, *"Er ist unser Friede": Karl Barths christologische Grundlegung der Friedensethik im Gespräch mit John Howard Yoder*, Forschungen zur systematischen und ökumenischen Theologie 144 (Göttingen: Vandenhoeck & Ruprecht, 2014).

describes Barth's ethics in terms of a divine command that is unforeseeable and cannot be deduced. This latter concept, also known as actualism, views both God's command and God's self-determination of God's very nature as fundamentally contingent. Given the vast extent of Barth's writing, it is not surprising that current interpretations arrive at markedly different results. To some extent, there are difficulties in justifying the selection of key texts to guide one's overall argument. One of the goals of this book is to achieve a greater degree of objectivity in this descriptive task. For a more representative view, it is necessary to examine the correlation between Barth's conceptual approach and his judgments on specific moral questions. Nor are these aspects to be confined to just one period of Barth's work. In addition, greater attention needs to be paid to the historical circumstances in which Barth wrote his contributions to ethics.

According to a widespread critique, Barth evacuates ethics from critical discourse, which is closely connected with Barth's views about an ever "afresh" commanding of God that supersedes all previous ethical convictions. Barth's ethics are often criticized for a deficit in integrating experience into ethics, which is sometimes associated with a critique of the priority Barth assigns to the gospel over the law. By contrast, the priority of the *law* over the gospel in the Lutheran tradition is sometimes taken to forge a complementary, rather than a more critical, relationship between natural law traditions and christological traditions. The main document of Barth's actualistic ethics, *CD* II/2 (ch. 8), opens the ethical section opposing that prioritization.

The question has been raised, however, if, under the rubric of the gospel, a christological approach can incorporate all the empirical factors that enter into moral discernment for those involved in moral conflict. James M. Gustafson argues that Christians do not merely live a life characterized by religious commitments, but participate also in the worlds of politics, science, or business, for example, and a coherent, plausible way of life poses the difficult task of doing justice to many spheres of value. He considers a conception of ethics in which God simply hands down a command that requires obedience in all spheres of life insufficient.[12] Barth's reference to the gospel may also be said to bring the category of law under one-sided domination by ecclesial proclamation. The christological premises then confront the moral subject with drastic alternatives, furthering a contrast between church and world. This critique is voiced, among others, by Martin Honecker and Trutz Rendtorff.[13]

12. James M. Gustafson, *Can Ethics Be Christian?* (Chicago: University of Chicago Press, 1975), 156–57, and "The Sectarian Temptation: Reflections on Theology, the Church, and the University," in *Moral Discernment in the Christian Life: Essays on Theological Essays*, ed. Theo A. Boer and Paul E. Capetz, Library of Theological Ethics (Louisville and London: Westminster John Knox, 2007), 142–54, at 150–51.
13. Trutz Rendtorff, *Ethics: Basic Elements and Methodology in an Ethical Theology*, trans. Keith Crim (Philadelphia: Augsburg Fortress Press, 1986), 18, 61; Rendtorff, "Karl Barth und die Neuzeit," in *Theologie in der Moderne: Über Religion im Prozess der Aufklärung* (Gütersloh: Gütersloher, 1991), 127–45, at 142. On Rendtorff, see also McKenny, *Analogy of Grace*, 127. The charge of authoritarianism is also associated with the critique of actualism, the "category of a decision that cannot be deduced" (Rendtorff, "Barth und die Neuzeit," 142). See also Martin Honecker, "Weltliches Handeln unter der Herrschaft Christi: Zur Interpretation von Barmen II," *Zeitschrift für Theologie und Kirche* 96 (1972): 72–99, at 72–73 ("christological totalitarianism"), more moderately in *Einführung in die Theologische Ethik*, de Gruyter Lehrbuch (Berlin and New York: de Gruyter, 1990), 79–82; Hermann Ringeling, "Kritik der Moderne und kritische Modernität: Evangelische Ethik heute," *Zeitschrift für Evangelische Ethik* 40 (1996): 23–37, at 29; Georg Pfleiderer, *Karl Barths praktische Theologie: Zu Genese und Kontext eines paradigmatischen Entwurfs systematischer Theologie im 20. Jahrhundert* (Tübingen: Mohr Siebeck, 2000), 22. In his essay, "Die politische Verantwortung der Christengemeinde im Denken Barths," *Zeitschrift für dialektische Theologie* 12 (1996): 149–74, Michael Beintker presents Barth's actualistic ethics favorably as a "situational ethics" (155), which in its fundamental allegiance to Christ retains an openness and freedom vis-à-vis mere principles, the nontheological sciences (145–6), and ideologies. However, even its strict commitment to God's command in the present situation is "after all something like a 'principle' as well" (156n33). In addition, Christian ethics necessarily depends on empirical analysis (167, 171), which Barth, however, cannot incorporate with a consistent methodology. As a result, his stance toward the social sciences is eclectic. To the extent that the church's proclamation is supposed to "reflect back into society" (167), the question arises about the true constructive potential of the "prophetic [dimension] as a qualified expression of the present Christ, who asserts his presence in an actualistic way and proclaims himself" (166). Is there not a tension between Beintker's case for social analysis and

On the other hand, it has been noted—for example, in the works of ethicists Heinz Eduard Tödt and Wolfgang Huber—in favor of Barth's ethics that there are "significant cases of a rapprochement between an ethics indebted to Barth and Bonhoeffer and an 'ethics of responsibility' aware of the importance of consequences."[14] It is a sign of Barth's influence that since about 1990, significant contributions to "public theology" have been influenced by a priority of the gospel to the law.[15] It should be added, however, that this "brand" of theology is not typically associated with Barth's name, as public theology argues for greater public debate and interdisciplinary analysis than Barth's work is generally known for.[16]

The mattress will not be covered by too short a bed sheet. Attempts to describe Barth's ethical work in terms of one particular theological method should be resisted. No analysis of this extensive work can do without substantial critique at least of certain aspects. To some degree, the considerable influence that Barth's ethics has exercised rests on the fact that it inspired resistance against National Socialism and its totalitarian politics toward the churches. Although this remains a valid argument in favor of Barth's ethics, its effects can be ambiguous. The subordination of ethics to theology has enabled a critique of ideologies that helped German theologians gain a constructive stance toward the recent German past.[17] Even after 1945, it had an emancipatory effect in contexts other than National

"relationships of responsibility" (171), on the one hand, and the supposedly strictly situational character of Barth's ethics, on the other?

14. Ringeling, "Kritik der Moderne," 27.

15. Heinrich Bedford-Strohm, "Geschenkte Freiheit: Von welchen Voraussetzungen lebt der demokratische Staat?" *Zeitschrift für Evangelische Ethik* 49 (2005): 248–65, at 258–59.

16. Yet another ethics inspired by Barth is Hans Günther Ulrich, *Wie Geschöpfe leben: Konturen evangelischer Ethik*, Ethics in Theological Discourse 2, 2nd ed. (Berlin: LIT, 2007). It is closely related to Barth's actualism, but still differs from Barth's notion of God's contingent revelation of God's command. The book avoids Barth's name painstakingly, but might be said to transpose Barth's actualism into a Lutheran key.

17. This can be demonstrated in the case of the ethicist Heinz Eduard Tödt: Wolfgang Schuhmacher, *Theologische Ethik als Verantwortungsethik: Leben und Werk Heinz Eduard Tödts in*

Socialism.[18] In particular circumstances, however, the argument of a critique of ideologies can contribute to an unhelpful polarization of the discussion about Barth's ethics. Rather than mapping out entire forests, one must also distinguish between individual trees. With a word from Barth's *Epistle to the Romans* (2nd ed., 1922, henceforth: *Rom* II), we should hope that eventually, "calm reflection on 'justice' and 'injustice' may then replace the revolutionary spasm . . . 'reality' can be taken into account prudently, as the hubris of a war of the good ones against the evil ones has been overcome."[19] Critics doubt that the extent to which such realism captures the spirit of Barth's ethics is very large, however. If a working antidiscriminatory system of legal and social justice has been established, critics may still fear that Barth's ethics tends to treat moral decisions as a *status confessionis*, a situation that calls urgently for an exclusive Christian confession, precisely because it does not—supposedly—rest on empirical analysis, but on a mere judgment of faith.

In the face of these problems, it may help to set things in perspective historically. The most prominent document of Barth's ethical actualism, *CD* II/2 (ch. 8), appeared when the National Socialist regime was at the peak of its international power, with Nazi sympathizers becoming more vocal even in Switzerland.[20] This

ökumenischer Perspektive, Öffentliche Theologie 20 (Leipzig: Evangelische Verlagsanstalt, 2006), 90.

18. On Barth's reception in Eastern Germany, see Matthias Gockel and Martin Leiner, "Kritik und Versöhnung: Karl Barth und die DDR," in *Karl Barths Theologie als europäisches Ereignis*, eds. Martin Leiner and Michael Trowitzsch (Göttingen: Vandenhoeck & Ruprecht, 2008), 79–119, at 117–19; Heino Falcke, "Was hatte die Barmer Theologische Erklärung den Kirchen in der DDR zu sagen?" *Ökumenische Rundschau* 58 (2009): 28–37. For apartheid South Africa, see *On Reading Karl Barth in South Africa*, ed. Charles Villa-Vicencio (Grand Rapids: Eerdmans, 1988). See Dirkie Smit, "Paradigms of Radical Grace," in Villa-Vicencio, ibid., 17–43, at 20, and in the same volume John de Gruchy, "Racism, Reconciliation, and Resistance," 139–55, at 140–41. See also Nico N. Koopman, "*Status confessionis* im Blick auf Apartheid, *processus confessionis* zu Fragen der ungerechten Weltwirtschaft: zur Rezeption der Barmer Theologischen Erklärung in Südafrika," *Ökumenische Rundschau* 58 (2009): 167–80.
19. Barth, *Der Römerbrief (Zweite Fassung): 1922*, ed. Cornelis van der Kooi and Katja Tolstaja, Barth-Gesamtausgabe (Zurich: Theologischer Verlag, 2010), 653 (*Rom* II).

was a moment when an ideologically heated atmosphere was hardly conducive to a distanced and open-ended discourse according to shared standards of reasoning. On the other hand, the ensuing major ethical section, *CD* III/4, appeared in 1951, before the polarizing controversies about West Germany's joining NATO (1954) and the foundation of the army in West Germany (1955) took place. Germany and Switzerland had to find their own places in a newly emerging political order in the Northern Atlantic world. This background may be helpful in interpreting the fact that *CD* III/4 aims much more strongly than actualistic ethics at establishing ethical consensus by discursive means.

What to make of the emancipatory potential of the priority of the gospel to the law then? Deciding for the special ethics—that is, the discussion of relatively concrete ethical questions—of *CD* III/4 against the ethics of the doctrine of God in *CD* II/2 would merely short-circuit the problem. After all, the theory of God's sovereign commanding in *CD* II/2 follows on the heels of a section expounding the precedence of the gospel. Although Barth's ordering of gospel and law is controversial, it should not be overlooked that, of all things, critics take issue with a text according to which a course of action is moral only to the extent that it is rooted in the *liberation* of the human person by God. This should raise the question how far a course of action is in keeping with an emancipatory impulse. In turn, how does actualism relate to the priority of the gospel over the law?

Actualism and Election

To begin with, it is helpful to compare two major approaches in

20. Only toward the end of 1941 did it turn out that the German invasion of the Soviet Union suffered from fundamental logistical and strategic mistakes, if nothing else. In summer 1942, military events sealed the fate of the invasion. Kurt Bauer, *Nationalsozialismus: Ursprünge, Anfänge, Aufstieg und Fall* (Wien et al.: Böhlau, 2008), 382, 388.

research on Barth's ethical oeuvre. While Nimmo highlights Barth's actualistic ethics, especially in *CD* II/2, Biggar's account relies mainly on Barth's special ethics, as in *CD* III/4. Both interpretations hinge on a specific view of Barth's theological thought as a whole.

Nimmo's monograph *Being in Action* pursues the actualistic interpretation of Barth's ethics most resolutely. The significance of this interpretive approach is also highlighted by David Clough, who draws a parallel between the actualistic ethics of *Rom* II and *CD*.[21] Like Clough, Nimmo explicitly does not aim at a diachronic, historico-genealogical presentation of Barth's ethics. He restricts his monograph, moreover, to a synchronic, systematic presentation of the ethical sections in *CD* and the lectures *The Christian Life* from 1959–61 (edited posthumously, henceforth: *CL*). He understands Barth's actualistic concept of God's command as the consequence of a strictly "actualistic ontology." This notion objects to attempts to extrapolate general guidelines in God's commanding beyond an ever-fresh attending to God's new, incomparable commandment; God's very being is characterized by historical interaction.[22]

It is only in this encounter with God that truly good news can be experienced. The God of the gospel is not characterized by any steady, inert being. Rather than being in the manner of a simple fact, God "is" only insofar as God acts ever anew. For this view Nimmo points especially to Barth's doctrine of election in *CD* II/2, which Barth calls "the sum of the Gospel."[23] In eternity, God the Son elects humanity and resolves to bear the consequences of the creature's sin. In this Nimmo sees the theological culmination of the baseline

21. Clough, *Ethics in Crisis*, 107, 127–28, 131.

22. Nimmo echoes Barth's vague statement that God will issue God's commands in accordance with certain continuous lines that are open to discovery (Nimmo, *Being in Action*, 32–3). Yet Nimmo also agrees with Barth's statement that all moral convictions must be suspended in asking for God's commandment, so they do not eclipse God's actual, new command (ibid., 63).

23. *CD* II/2, 3.

conviction, "the history of Jesus Christ is identical with the history of God."[24] Not *all* theology is "ontotheology," Barth may be taken to imply in a gesture to an ongoing contemporary philosophical dispute.[25] In ethics, this focus on God's action and history is reacting against a general ontology, which might draw ethical conclusions from an order of nature, and against any attempt to pin God down to creaturely standards, which always orient themselves to being rather than opening themselves radically for God's ever-new action.[26] Christian ethics does its job best when arguing for the need to listen ever anew and making a theological case for this stance.[27] These statements rely especially on Barth's ethics of the doctrine of God in *CD* II/2, which follows on the heels of Barth's doctrine of election. The concept of God does not come full circle before the concept of God's commanding, as God not only elects the creatures, but also claims them, which constitutes their responsibility before God. Importantly, God's commanding even determines God's very being.

Doubts about the constancy of the commanding would be misplaced, Nimmo argues, as constancy plays an important role among God's perfections.[28] God's commanding takes place as

24. Ibid., 8.
25. When Martin Heidegger recast ontology in temporal terms, he was wary of metaphysics as a distraction from the challenge of facing *Sein* squarely. One response would be to recast theology accordingly. It is probably not a coincidence that Dietrich Braun begins his preface to Barth's ethics lectures with the reminder that Heidegger's *Being and Time* and Carl Schmitt's *The Concept of the Political* enjoyed wide currency when Barth wrote these lectures. Barth, *Ethics*, vii. See Heidegger, *Being and Time*, trans. John Macquarrie and Edward Robinson (Oxford: Basil Blackwell, 1986), 41: "Dasein's Being finds its meaning in temporality. But temporality is also the condition which makes historicality possible as a temporal kind of Being which Dasein itself possesses, regardless of whether or how Dasein is an entity 'in time'. Historicality, as a determinate character, is prior to what is called 'history' (world-historical [events])."
26. Nimmo, *Being in Action*, 62.
27. Ibid., 65. Ethics are about "the formation of a creaturely *habitus*" that attends to God ever anew. The only crucial thing is, in Barth's and Nimmo's words, "to dare" afresh, again and again, "the leap of choice, decision and action" (ibid., 66).
28. Nimmo concludes, using Barth's words, "The constancy of the command is guaranteed, for ... it has 'all the constancy of the divine faithfulness in contrast to our unfaithfulness'" (ibid., 21).

Scripture interprets itself, thus confronting the human person with God in its witness to God's action. At the same time this must not lead to any fixation on the letter of the Bible, which would be in contrast to God's free commanding.[29] While faithful to Scripture, God's command remains free vis-à-vis Scripture. This must be kept in mind when the ethics of the doctrine of creation *CD* III/4 seeks "assistance in listening to the command." Nimmo concedes that perhaps Barth does not fully sustain his polemics against casuistic deductions, coming too close to specifying what God's command truly says.[30] By contrast, Nimmo argues, if we do not learn from God's current commanding itself, we cannot know what God commands.

In great measure Nimmo's actualistic interpretation of Barth's ethics is in harmony with Bruce L. McCormack's influential historico-genealogical study, *Karl Barth's Critically Realistic Dialectical Theology* (1995).[31] Its detailed theological interpretations, which highlight the dialectical element in Barth's thought over against analogy, are important both for the purposes of this study and in gaining a better understanding of the interpretation of Barth's ethics so far. According to McCormack, a transition from Barth's critical thought in *Rom* II to a more constructive presentation of a dogmatics was manifest already in the 1924 dogmatics lectures at Göttingen (1924–5; part 3 held in Münster; henceforth *GD*).[32] In addition,

In a similar vein, see Clough, *Ethics in Crisis*, 129. What has been received as God's command is God's command in fact. To doubt if this command is in keeping with God's faithfulness is an expression of sin. Nimmo, *Being in Action*, 19; 36–37.

29. According to Nimmo, *Being in Action*, 33, 36, God's command is not bound by Scripture's witness to a previous command. God's freedom "dictates" this (33), which, then, seems to have a strong libertarian dimension.

30. Ibid., 58.

31. Bruce L. McCormack, *Karl Barth's Critically Realistic Dialectical Theology: Its Genesis and Development 1909–1936* (Oxford: Clarendon, 1997).

32. *The Göttingen Dogmatics: Instruction in the Christian Religion*, ed. Hannelotte Reiffen, trans. Geoffrey W. Bromiley (Grand Rapids: Eerdmans, 1991) (*GD* I).

Barth's theological change was far less drastic than typically assumed. While *Rom* II highlights the aspect of judgment perhaps too strongly, it also maintains the temporal reality of the resurrection.[33] Barth's critique of religion is compatible with constructive theological thought as the resurrection is that reality in history that constitutes its own worldly possibility. Understood as *actus purus*, or "pure event,"[34] revelation is also possible by the standards of *Rom* II, even while Jesus Christ represents a critical no vis-à-vis the world. Here actualism denotes God's action as it takes place in irreducibly contingent, historically real events, which thus place the addressees into a critical position vis-à-vis worldly realities. Thus God reveals God's self through a medium that also conceals God's self.[35] The point of this concept of revelation is that proclamation participates in an extraordinary, contingent "correlation of Spirit and Scripture."[36] McCormack also captures this with the terminology of *pneumatocentrism* and an *an–* or *enhypostatic* Christology: the revelation in Christ is nothing short of a miracle performed in the freedom of the Holy Spirit; Jesus Christ's humanity is nothing more and nothing less than the vehicle of revelation, and apart from revelation, there would be no human person Jesus Christ. Christ's humanity is strictly dependent on the eternal Son, for whom it is entirely transparent, both in the Son's self-revelation and his self-concealing.[37] This concept amounts to radical divine freedom both from and for the world. As the antithesis of revelation and

33. Ibid., 251–52.
34. Ibid., 253.
35. Ibid., 250. Thus still in *CD* II/1, 341 ("God is for us fully revealed and fully concealed in His self-disclosure").
36. McCormack, *Barth's Theology*, 342.
37. Barth, *Unterricht in der christlichen Religion: Die Lehre von Gott/Die Lehre vom Menschen 1924/25*, ed. Hinrich Stoevesandt, Barth-Gesamtausgabe (Zurich: Theologischer Verlag, 1990), 193–94; this volume, the successor of *Göttingen Dogmatics* vol. 1 (*GD* I), will be abbreviated *GD* II. Translations of quotations by A. M. See also McCormack, *Barth's Theology*, 362.

concealment is dialectically sublated in Jesus Christ, God's current revelation in Christ cannot be measured critically against the standard of a previous revelation.

McCormack thus objects to Hans Urs von Balthasar's influential interpretation of Barth's theology. Von Balthasar posited that Barth's *Christliche Dogmatik im Entwurf* (the *Münster Dogmatics* from 1927, relying upon Barth's 1926–28 lecture series, henceforth *MD*), in conjunction with Barth's book *Fides quaerens intellectum* (1931), represents a change of direction from a dialectical to an analogical mode of thought.[38] According to McCormack, both elements are already present, if in varying degrees, in *Rom* II and *GD*. Yet Barth highlights divine freedom over against the notion of an *analogia entis*, the notion that divine revelation relies on creaturely things that are thus imbued with an abiding theological purchasing power.

McCormack's last chapter, however, lays out a momentous new development, describing Barth's new interpretation of the doctrine of election around 1940.[39] A significant modification of Barth's actualism now takes place, as he argues critically that his brother Peter's interpretation of John Calvin's notion of divine election fails to do justice to the history of Jesus Christ as the true norm of theology. God's election takes place as God's revelation separates belief from unbelief every moment anew, Peter argued.[40] By contrast,

38. Barth's *Fides quaerens intellectum* argues that only the church's proclamation, rather than speculation apart from such witness, does justice to God's power and aseity. Barth, *Fides quaerens intellectum: Anselms Beweis für die Existenz Gottes, 1931*, ed. Eberhard Jüngel and Ingolf U. Dalferth, Barth-Gesamtausgabe (Zurich: Theologischer Verlag, 1981). God is truth as the "ground of all . . . that exists" (103). Thus, in the church, "that *summum bonum*" (highest good) must be "deduced" (*erschlossen*) "in 'ascending' from the relative, finite goods" (120).

39. On Barth's doctrine of election in *GD* and *CD*, see especially Matthias Gockel, *Barth and Schleiermacher on the Doctrine of Election: A Systematic-Theological Comparison* (Oxford: Oxford University Press, 2006).

40. McCormack, *Barth's Theology*, 455–56. Karl appreciates Peter's concept to the extent that it does not isolate God's eternal choice from history. Going beyond that, however, Maury views the history that figures prominently in God's election in christological terms. Karl intensifies this

Karl contends—based on a lecture by Pierre Maury—that with the eternal decree in Jesus Christ, a unique contingent act gains ontological importance for God's self.[41]

In consequence, Jesus Christ's story is God's own story.[42] In this new scheme, the statement "God's being is a 'being in act'" means God's one definite, eternal act, from which a distinct, 'crucial' historical course of action flows. This new approach to the doctrine of election is actualistic as it focuses on a contingent event. However, we are now dealing with a single, eternal event, which led to a particular historical event, or a coherent story of historical events, rather than many seemingly disparate historical events. McCormack in fact prefers the term *covenant ontology* to the term *actualistic ontology*, thus highlighting a theological concept with a more specific historical reference rather than the principle of contingency.[43]

In accordance with this usage, I will employ the term *actualistic* in the sense of a libertarian divine freedom leading to new, potentially incommensurate historical events that define God's being. This distinction between two varieties of actualism—perhaps one defended by Peter Barth and Karl's early work, the other by Karl's later

new take in 1936 and 1937 by calling Christ the electing God and the elected human person. Gockel, *Barth and Schleiermacher on the Doctrine of Election*, 160–64.

41. McCormack, *Barth's Theology*, 456.

42. Ibid., 461. For this reason, Gundlach raises "critical questions regarding the positioning of the doctrine of the Trinity in the overall structure of Barth's *CD*." Thies Gundlach, *Selbstbegrenzung Gottes und die Autonomie des Menschen: Karl Barths Kirchliche Dogmatik als Modernisierungsschritt evangelischer Theologie*, Europäische Hochschulschriften Theologie 471 (Frankfurt am Main and New York: Lang, 1992), 161–62. See also Raymund Schwager, *Der wunderbare Tausch. Zur Geschichte und Deutung der Erlösungslehre* (Munich: Kösel, 1986), 250, who calls God's election according to Barth "in the full sense God's decision about God's self." Hans Theodor Goebel argues: "Strikingly, Barth's doctrine of election has the same function as the doctrine of the Trinity, as laid out in the prolegomena of the *Church Dogmatics*." Goebel, "Trinitätslehre und Erwählungslehre bei Karl Barth: Eine Problemanzeige," in *Wahrheit und Versöhnung: Theologische und philosophische Beiträge zur Gotteslehre*, eds. Dietrich Korsch and Hartmut Ruddies (Gütersloh: Gütersloher Verlagshaus Mohn 1989), 147–66, at 159, see also 153–54.

43. Bruce L. McCormack, "Grace and Being: The Role of God's Gracious Election in Karl Barth's Theological Ontology," in *The Cambridge Companion to Karl Barth*, ed. John B. Webster (Cambridge: Cambridge University Press, 2000), 92–110, at 99.

work—is crucial for the present work. For a fundamental problem with the insistence on God's radical freedom is that the more things change, the more they stay the same. Moreover, novel ways of being faithful in novel situations require criteria, lest we project the mere freedom of license into God's command. But Jesus' story, with which God's story is taken to be identical, is a particular, definite story. Disputing the role of this story as a criterion for discussions in applied ethics, however, would appear to empty the legitimate and helpful notion that revelation inscribes historical contingency into God's very being, rendering contingency pointless by overemphasizing it. Already here we must ask whether God's revelation—of God's self, of God's command—may indeed always be correlated with a similar concealing on God's part, if indeed Barth's turn in the doctrine of election is directed against an ever-new electing and refusing, and if a correlation of divine revelation and concealment highlights a principle of historical contingency in such a way that it may introduce a certain degree of theological arbitrariness via an unspecific principle of historical contingency.

Orders of Creation

In contrast to the actualistic interpretation of Barth's ethics, Nigel Biggar's monograph *The Hastening That Waits* (1993) highlights continuity in the content of God's commandment.[44] Biggar points out that God revealed God's will in Jesus Christ, as the eternal election once and for all vouches for God's faithfulness toward humanity.[45] On the whole, however, Biggar's point is that Barth's

44. Nigel Biggar, *The Hastening the Waits: Karl Barth's Ethics*, Oxford Studies in Theological Ethics (Oxford: Clarendon, 1993). See also Biggar, "Barth's Trinitarian Ethic," in Webster, *Cambridge Companion to Barth*, 212–27 and Biggar, "Hearing God's Command and Thinking About What's Right: With and beyond Barth," in *Reckoning with Barth: Essays in Commemoration of the Centenary of Karl Barth's Birth* (London: Mowbray, 1988), 101–18.

45. Biggar, *Hastening That Waits*, 28–29, 42, 118. God's election is in view as well when Biggar

ethics aim at action according to orders of creation. Barth interprets the biblical witness to God's revelation as containing ethical rules that must be continually matched with and applied to the current situation.[46] By contrast, Biggar criticizes large parts of Barth's ethics, especially the actualistic ethics of the doctrine of God (*CD* II/2), as the arbitrary piety of a Christian intuitionism, as actualistic ethics does not recognize any criterion of a supposed commandment apart from God's self.[47] This would preclude, however, discussions in applied ethics.[48] While Biggar devotes very little space to Barth's notion of an incommensurate command that must be heard ever afresh, he argues that Barth's ethics of creation in *CD* III/4 offer a new approach. These sections discuss specific ethics.[49] Once Barth tackles specific moral problems, Biggar argues, he assumes that God's command works much in the way of general rules.[50]

Such moral rules do not, however, override the necessity of acting differently in very particular situations, which constitutes Barth's notion of the marginal case, or *Grenzfall.* In such cases God's command is not suspended, but takes on a new shape, reflecting the extraordinary nature of the situation. It amounts to an extraordinary

(ibid., 28n95) quotes Paul Ramsey: "While for Barth God is free (as Lehmann constantly stresses and hence is concerned with the exceptional all the time), He has also made Himself known quite historically in Jesus Christ. . . . In Him is all we know about the humanity of God (theology) and the humanity of man (anthropology). This is also all we are given to know about the freedom of God, i.e., His freedom to bind Himself to the world and the world to Himself. By contrast, God's freedom in Lehmann is simply an autonomous theological speculation drawn from this world of rapid change" (Ramsey's parentheses).

46. See also William Werpehowski, "Justification and Justice in the Theology of Karl Barth," *The Thomist* 50 (1986): 623–42. Wolf Krötke also highlights the closeness of Barth's thought in *CD* III/4 to the notion of orders of creation: Krötke, "Die Schöpfungsordnungen im Lichte der Christologie: Zu Karl Barths Umgang mit einem unabweisbaren Problem," in *Barmen—Barth—Bonhoeffer: Beiträge zu einer zeitgemäßen christozentrischen Theologie* (Bielefeld: Luther, 2009), 155–78, at 164–65.
47. Biggar, *Hastening That Waits*, 20–21.
48. Ibid., 19, 33.
49. Ibid., 25–26.
50. Ibid., 119.

instruction that may even be in tension with the shape God's command displays in regular cases. Barth thus practices a casuistry that, by way of both theological and empirical work, carves out a correlation between specific commandment and situation.[51] While a key category of this ethics is indeed creation, it also hinges on an important christological dimension, which says that in the eternal election in Christ, God committed God's self to absolute faithfulness toward creation. The command thus revealed remains reliable.

An important point of Barth's that Biggar does not mention, however, is that God's election of humanity corresponds to Jesus Christ's decision to bear the burden of the divine reprobation of sin. The drama of the cross indeed indicates that matters are more complicated than accidental human sin in the face of a good, intact creation. However, Biggar's chapter on the trinitarian structure of Barth's ethics relativizes revelation in Christ with the statement that a personal differentiation within the Godhead, and also within God's commanding, is merely of a logical, not of an ontological kind.[52] Of course this raises the doubt whether it is indeed God's grace that is enacted in Jesus of Nazareth.

On the whole, Biggar concedes, Barth's ethics strangely avoids an open confession of its nature as an ethics of the orders of creation. Yet both *MD* and *CD* III/4 consider "work, marriage, family, and the inseparable principles of equality and leadership" the fundamental orders, according to Biggar.[53]

Biggar's interpretation of Barth's ethical theory can be described with the classic adage *gratia non destruit sed supponit et perficit naturam*, "grace presupposes and perfects nature rather than destroying it."[54]

51. Ibid., 36–38 speaks of open systems, which can integrate data from the environment.
52. Ibid., 46. Of course Biggar's point that God is one is correct, but the well-known difficulties with the doctrine of the Trinity consist precisely in the fact that the differentiation between three divine persons is no less ontological. Ibid., 46.
53. Ibid., 57.

For the most part it is in harmony with von Balthasar's interpretation of Barth's thought. After describing an about-face of Barth's in favor of constructive theology in the late 1920s, von Balthasar goes on to flesh out how Barth's thought reaches full maturity in his doctrine of creation in *CD* III/1–3. The doctrine of God in *CD* II/1 and the prolegomena of *CD* I already shaped the theological argument in terms of analogy. Indeed, von Balthasar offers important examples of an *analogia entis* operative in *CD* III.[55] Just as Barth shies away from calling the ethics of orders in *CD* III/4 by its name according to Biggar, so von Balthasar calls Barth's reserve against the *analogia entis* a self-contradiction. Von Balthasar reconstructs the *analogia entis* to denote the correspondence of God's special revelation—to use the schematic concepts of this discourse—to general creaturely phenomena, which in turn render special revelation more plausible—without, however, abstracting from the heuristic starting point in special revelation and Christian faith. He agrees with Barth that God does not use general phenomena in revelation that are not themselves more closely determined in special revelation, and maintains a reciprocal reference between general and special revelation. According to von Balthasar, natural theology is a theology of revelation, and both are legitimate only in close conjunction.[56]

Von Balthasar highlights Barth's dialogistic personalism in his notion of heterosexual shared humanity. In this phenomenon he sees confirmation of the validity and significance of the personal encounter with God: "And above all, God has prepared the human

54. Ibid., 92; see Thomas Aquinas, *Summa theologiae* I, 1 a. 8 ad 2. Certainly it cannot be denied in theology that divine acts of grace presuppose and ennoble creation. It is doubtful, however, if the reliability of nature can be categorically asserted in the question to which general phenomena God's special grace thus refers and in what sense it transforms them.

55. Hans Urs von Balthasar, *The Theology of Karl Barth: Exposition and Interpretation*, trans. Edward T. Oakes, SJ, Communio Books (San Francisco: Ignatius, 1992), 110 and especially 116–20, 123–26.

56. Ibid., 110, 126.

race for communion with him; in fact he makes it possible in the first place, in the sign of man and woman."[57] At this point God's activity in reconciliation makes a presupposition (". . . *sed supponit* . . ."): "This brings us up against the central problem in Barth's theology in its most recent form: the concept of *presupposition*."[58] Reconciliation in Christ thus "perfects" its own presupposition. One must merely avoid confusing creation with the cause of creation—"despite this relationship whereby grace presupposes [*supponit*] and perfects nature."[59]

According to von Balthasar, Barth resolutely claims such thoughts in *CD* II/1, where he rejects his previous emphasis on the futility of creation,[60] arguing that the absolute God[61] affirms creation as a reality beyond God's self. This is preceded by von Balthasar's argument that *Rom* II identifies any stance vis-à-vis God with sin, thus rendering a genuine incarnation impossible.[62] Interestingly, this latter point about *Rom* II is openly conceded even by defenders of *Rom* II.[63] It is only once creation's existence is firmly rooted in God's self that there can be a legitimate ethics, which responds to God's grace.[64]

57. Ibid., 124. See 96, 134–36; Barth considers personal human fellowship a presupposition rather than merely a correspondence to God's grace in *CD* III/2, 274. The present work will discuss *CD* III/4 § 54.1, which is relevant in this context, in the context of *CD* IV.
58. Von Balthasar, *Theology of Karl Barth*, 119. The notion of *presupposition* achieves prominence once again in the chapter "Analogia Entis" (161). Von Balthasar, ibid., 167, quotes Barth, *CD* II/1, 411: "In this sense we must admit the truth of that maxim of Thomas Aquinas which is so often put to dangerous use and in the first instance was no doubt dangerously meant: *gratia non tollit (non destruit) sed (praesupponit et) perficit naturam.*"
59. Von Balthasar, *Theology of Karl Barth*, 123 (trans. rev.).
60. Ibid., 114. "The first volume of the *Church Dogmatics* was still speaking of the 'contrast,' the 'contradiction' between the Word of God and its configuration in the Bible, proclamation, theology" (trans. rev.).
61. For von Balthasar's characteristic notion of God's absoluteness see ibid., 111, 137, 145.
62. Ibid., 71.
63. Cornelis van der Kooi, "Karl Barths zweiter Römerbrief und seine Wirkungen," in *Karl Barth in Deutschland (1921–1935): Aufbruch—Klärung—Widerstand*, eds. Michael Beintker, Christian Link, and Michael Trowitzsch (Zurich: Theologischer Verlag, 2005), 57–75, at 75.
64. Von Balthasar, *Theology of Karl Barth*, 113.

Von Balthasar's thesis of an *analogia entis* implies not only justification through grace and works,[65] but also motivates him to reject Barth's doctrine of election explicitly in *CD* II/2 and to downplay Christ's cross. Occasional allusions to the doctrine of election do not mention damnation,[66] and the rare references to Jesus' cross often highlight its role as an example.[67] He hardly acknowledges Barth's conviction that the election of humanity is correlated with the damnation borne by Christ before his section on "Praedestinatio Gemina," which explicitly rejects Barth's doctrine of election. Von Balthasar sees Barth's doctrine of election culminate in universal salvation, which he calls overly daring, thus "gnosis, theosophy; in short, philosophy."[68] Moreover, according to von Balthasar, Barth's doctrine of election counters the notion *operari sequitur esse* ("action follows being") "with what to the Scholastic mind would be an absurdity: *esse sequitur operari*" ("being follows action").[69] By contrast, von Balthasar asserts that Barth usually affirms God's absolute nature in the sense "that God's absolute being and God's absolute truth [do] not become intermingled with the sphere of the relative, created being and its truth."[70]

Gospel and Law and the Public Dimension of Ethics

A theology of orders and actualism denote two fundamental foci

65. Ibid., 135.
66. Ibid., 118, 127.
67. Ibid., 375, portrays Christ as an example for another righteous person who undergoes suffering on account of someone else's guilt, by which "he shares an active portion in the holiness of the Redeemer." Ibid., 385, however, strikes an unexpected tone with the statement that Golgotha is synonymous with the murder of God. Yet ibid., 118, quotes Barth's portrayal of the dramatic extent of God's mercy (*CD* III/1, 50) tendentiously. Von Balthasar repeats Barth's reference to the cross, on which Christ bore the sins of the world, yet omits Barth's reference to the world's "lowliness and non-godliness, indeed its anti-godliness."
68. Ibid., 185.
69. Ibid., 191.
70. Ibid., 130.

of interpretation that each find some justification in particular parts of Barth's oeuvre. As far as the analysis of Barth's explicitly ethical writings is concerned, I will pay more attention to actualism. This concept has clearer roots in Barth's ethical works, especially the ethics of the doctrine of God in *CD* II/2. By contrast, an explicit ethics of orders is especially to be found in Barth's early ethics lectures,[71] which Biggar was one of the first to interpret in greater detail. Yet the importance of the orders for Barth's thought on the whole depends especially on the ethics of creation in *CD* III/4, as Barth never published the early ethics lectures. On the other hand, von Balthasar and Biggar argue for an about-face in Barth's thought that led Barth only later to take the created order seriously. The implications about Barth's earlier work are worth full attention. My analysis of *CD* III/4 will not confirm Biggar's notion of an ethics of orders. Nonetheless, Barth's interpreters often agree that the ethics of creation discusses various courses of action in a more discursive manner than warranted by the actualistic concept.[72] This may be a helpful effect of Barth's renewed attention to creation. However, it will also become clear that sometimes, some of von Balthasar's and Biggar's instincts in terms of a natural theology and God's absoluteness in Barth's work are not misplaced on a descriptive level.

While the concepts of actualism and an ethics of orders elucidate important parts of Barth's ethical thought, they do not do full justice to its full range. Presumably this is the reason why many discussions of Barth's ethics do not deal constructively with a prominent lecture such as "Church and State" ("Rechtfertigung und Recht" [or

71. Barth, *Ethics*, ed. Dietrich Braun, trans. Geoffrey W. Bromiley (Eugene: Wipf & Stock, 2013). Barth gave this ethics lecture cycle twice, in two consecutive semesters each time, in 1928–9 in Münster and in 1930–31 in Bonn. The lectures became widely available in print only with the critical German edition (2 vols.): ed. Dietrich Braun, Barth-Gesamtausgabe (Zurich: Theologischer Verlag, 1973 and 1978).

72. Biggar, *Hastening That Waits*, 23–25, Nimmo, *Being in Action*, 58.

Justification and Justice], 1938, henceforth "CS").[73] If not plainly negated as a contribution to social ethics, it is sometimes mischaracterized as drawing on a Lutheran theory of two kingdoms in clarifying the relation between the justification of the sinner and worldly justice.[74] A theory of God's two kingdoms distinguishes clearly between the two ways in which spiritual and worldly affairs are governed respectively, by the gospel and the word on the one hand, and law and worldly force on the other. Barth's own contribution to political ethics is then located in the theology of creation, where he devises a concept of shared humanity (*CD* III/2).[75] At first glance, the theory of two kingdoms can seem to provide the answer to Barth's questions, as the two distinct dimensions of the theory can be seen as united in God's sovereign agency.

> Take the problem of *order*, of that order, which is no longer, or not yet, the order of the Kingdom of God; or the problem of *peace*, which is no longer, or not yet, the eternal Peace of God; or the problem of *freedom*, which is no longer, or not yet, the eternal Peace of God—do all these problems belong to the realm of the "new creation" of man through the Word of God, do they all belong to the sanctification through the Spirit?[76]

The Reformers were clear that Christian faith and public

73. Barth, "Church and State," in *Community, State, and Church: Three Essays; With a New Introduction*, ed. David Haddorff, trans. Will Herberg (Eugene: Wipf & Stock, 2004), 101–48 ("CS").
74. According to George Hunsinger, the lecture does not keep its promise of presenting a social ethics. "Justification and Justice: Toward an Evangelical Social Ethic," in *Karl Barth im europäischen Zeitgeschehen (1935–1950): Widerstand—Bewährung—Orientierung*, eds. Michael Beintker, Christian Link, and Michael Trowitzsch (Zurich: Theologischer Verlag, 2010), 457–70, at 457. For the suggestion that "CS" presents a Lutheran theory of two reigns, see Werpehowski, "Justification," 628.
75. Werpehowski, "Justification," 632.
76. "CS," 101. See 102: "It should be noted that the interest in this question begins where the interest in the Reformation confessional writings and Reformation theology as a whole ceases." It is thus unlikely that Barth was after a Lutheran theory of God's two kingdoms. That theory deals with worldly order mainly on the basis of God's revelation of the law, or on the basis of natural law, not the gospel.

responsibility are not at odds, Barth argues. "But . . . they do not by all means tell us all that we might have expected. . . . Clearly we need to know not only that the two are not in conflict, but, first and foremost, to what extent they are connected."[77] But Barth has yet something else than a theory of two kingdoms in mind. As he discusses the relevance of the gospel for the public dimension of Protestant ethics, he distinguishes less clearly—or perhaps even less rigidly—between worldly order and the gospel. Barth insists on justice in a constitutional state:

> Of one thing in the New Testament there can be no doubt: namely, that the description of the order of the new age is that of a political order. . . . Wherever [the church] believes in, and proclaims here and now, the justification of the sinner through the blood of the lamb, it is faced with the city of eternal *justice*, "coming down out of heaven from God." . . . Could the church of divine justification hold the human state of justice [*dem Staate des Rechts*] in higher esteem than when it sees in that very State, in its heavenly reality, into which its terrestrial existence will finally be absorbed, the final predicate of its own grounds for hope?[78]

While the theory of two kingdoms views the political dimension of biblical law as a particular, contingent manifestation of natural law,[79] Barth argues here that the church should advocate for particular political goals and procedures regardless of natural law, based on its commitment to the gospel. "CS" stands thus in close proximity to Barth's lecture "Gospel and Law" (1935, henceforth: "GL"), which argued that the necessity of acting according to the law is constituted by the gospel. This is in contrast to a traditionally Lutheran account

77. "CS," 102.
78. Ibid., 124 (trans. rev.). Herberg's translation of *Recht* with *law*, which seems indebted to legal positivism, has been altered to *justice*. Notably, *Recht* can also mean *righteousness*. *Staat des Rechts* amounts to the same as *Rechtsstaat*, constitutional democracy or (just) rule of law.
79. Martin Luther, "How Christians Should Regard Moses, 1525," in *Word and Sacrament*, vol. 1, ed. and trans. E. Theodore Bachmann, Luther's Works vol. 35 (Philadelphia: Mühlenberg Press, 1960), 161–74.

of law and gospel, in which the judgment of the law destroys the illusion of works righteousness, but is not meant to orient Christian action. On the one hand, "CS" identifies legal justice as an essential element in the Christian proclamation of the cross and the kingdom of God; on the other, according to "GL," the nature of God's grace as a free gift makes a particular mode of life obligatory. Consequently, the church has a public responsibility to support legal justice. In accordance with the gospel, the church will strive for a "prophetic witness *for* the will of God *against* all of men's sinful presumption, *against* all their lawlessness and unrighteousness."[80]

As described above, Barth's concept of gospel and law has been singled out for critique. It has been said to bring ethical study under heteronomous dominance by ecclesial traditions, for example. By contrast, this study will argue that the most creative potential of Barth's new concept still remains to be tapped. The crucial point is that the freedom of the gospel seeks affirmation within particular empirical conditions. If, for example, ecclesial moral traditions cannot be articulated as good news within particular social constellations, the critical potential of the gospel must also reflect back upon those moral traditions. This does not, however, amount to an uncritical justification of the powers that be, but calls for ethical work that allows for transformation that is critical, creative, and constructive. It is this dynamic that allows Barth to engage the empirical dimension of life within which the gospel will take on the practical shape of the command with which it is correlated. The main reason for the new Christian ethos, however, can be described as thankfulness.

The main thesis of this study is that an essential strand in Barth's ethics aims at the church's public responsibility, which amounts, in broad terms, to a politically active sense of justice. As Barth

80. Barth, "Gospel and Law," in Haddorff, *Community, State, and Church*, 71–101, at 80 ("GL").

emphasizes a correspondence between ethics and the gospel, the present work is entitled *Citizenship in Heaven and on Earth.*

According to these broad outlines, the church is not conceived of primarily as a factor warranting a stable political order, of whatever political color; it is not supposed to focus either on personal morality—even the personal morality of faith—or natural law; nor is it meant to address an inner spiritual realm, distinguishing political affairs strictly from the gospel. Instead, as the import of the gospel cannot be separated from external forms of life, the church faces the challenge of how particular forms of practical correspondence to the gospel can be advocated for in a wider public—without monopolizing the public realm spiritually, morally, or any other way. Certainly, Barth does not disregard the question whether legal justice can be the only, or even the predominant, concern in the public role of the church. Instead, social and economic justice are as important. Such reflection will always need to ask self-critically if public ecclesial advocacy may be a mere "retreat to commitment,"[81] rather than being motivated and oriented by the gospel. This constellation leads Barth to seek theological clarification in questions of public relevance, such as the termination of pregnancy or war and peace (*CD* III/4). The thesis that requires justification is that this concept of gospel and law leads to a position capable of public defense, resting neither on an ever-new, incommensurate commanding nor supposedly universal orders of creation. At the same time, such an ethics will be eager to absorb new insight, regardless where it can be found.

This book's positive goal of presenting Barth's ethics of public responsibility will only emerge piecemeal from the historical reconstruction of Barth's ethical writings and the large body of relevant theological discussions. This detailed, at times even strenuous

81. See Wolfhart Pannenberg, *Systematic Theology*, trans. Geoffrey W. Bromiley, 3 vols. (New York: T&T Clark, 1992), 1:47.

historical pathway has been chosen in the hope of attaining greater descriptive accuracy. This seems advisable in the face of Barth's extensive and multifaceted oeuvre. A close reading of the ethics of the doctrine of God, for example, rather than a top-down eclectic access, has still been a desideratum of research. Faced with this difficulty, a more objective interpretation of Barth's work can be achieved not only with extensive reference to Barth's texts and secondary literature, but also with attention to the genesis and historical context of the text at hand. Barth's private letters often prove helpful.

The first major task is to reconstruct the genesis of Barth's actualistic concept of revelation. On the face of it, actualism seems to be the ground in which Barth's priority of the gospel over against the law is rooted. The actualistic ethics of an ever-new, incommensurate commanding in *CD* II/2, sections 38 and following follows on the heels of sections 36–7, in which Barth integrates the priority of the gospel into his magnum opus, *CD*.

For this reason proponents of actualism claim that it is the ethical theory that best captures Barth's concept of gospel and law. The rivalry with an ethics of ecclesial public responsibility is obvious once the church needs to give reasons—even if only internally—for a particular course of action. For example, in 1951, the motto of the German Evangelical Church Assembly proclaimed that "We Are All Brothers," while in 1963, the chosen theme was "Living With Conflicts."[82] Actualism, however, avoids arguing for a course of action supposedly commanded by God. Instead, God supposedly

82. The German Evangelical Church Assembly (*Deutscher Evangelischer Kirchentag*) is a biannual meeting of Protestants in Germany. Before the Berlin Wall excluded East German participants from meetings in the West such as the one in 1963, there were ca. forty-five thousand participants in 1961. Wolfgang Huber, "Streit um das rechte Handeln: Zwischen persönlicher Vergewisserung und gemeinsamer Aktion," in *Konflikt und Konsens: Studien zur Ethik der Verantwortung* (Munich: Kaiser, 1990), 272-90, at 280. See also Dirk Palm, *"Wir sind doch Brüder!" Der evangelische Kirchentag und die deutsche Frage 1949–1961*, Arbeiten zur Kirchlichen Zeitgeschichte B 36 (Göttingen: Vandenhoeck & Ruprecht, 2002).

commands every individual directly. Since pluralistic, constitutional democracies seek reasons, however, that may bolster up consensus in the long run—faced with a plurality of convictions—actualistic ethics is left with the choice between a supposedly prophetic path of mere appeals and admonitions that may at times border on the enigmatic, a withdrawal from the public realm, or a Lutheran theory of two kingdoms.

Gospel and Law in Historico-Genealogical Perspective

Due to the inherent difficulty of the actualistic concept of revelation, the first chapter of the present work will reconstruct its development from *Rom* I to *CD* I/1. The extensive focus on Barth's early work, which may at times even seem overly critical, requires justification. Interestingly, Barth research has not grasped the full theological implications of the emphasis *Rom* II puts on sacrifice and repentance. Yet these concepts are of fundamental importance for the actualistic concept of revelation as a whole. To be sure, *GD* does not leave the theology of *Rom* II unchanged but continues the constructive theological work. *GD*'s actualistic concept of revelation creates a dialectical relationship between the negative ethics of *Rom* II and a positive ethics. Yet it is precisely this dialectical synthesis that raises the question of the extent to which a Lutheran constellation of law and gospel has abiding importance even as we are dealing with what is often considered the beginnings of Barth's mature thought. This hunch is confirmed by the fact that even around 1930, Barth argues repeatedly for an ethics of orders. Not only has the precedence of the law over the gospel had a significant affinity to an ethics of orders historically, but the latter concept, as it was expounded in twentieth-century Protestantism, was taken to lend practical shape to the law's condemnation of sin. Moreover, one conceptual difficulty of actualism is that it is oriented toward God's command in the current moment rather than to larger political and cultural constellations, a difficulty that may appear to be remedied by resorting to an ethic of orders.

It may seem to be a surprising claim that there is a significant influence of a Lutheran understanding of law and gospel on Barth's ethical work, in spite of Barth's notable efforts to the contrary. He advocated for a new conceptualization of gospel and law in the lecture of the same name, which is sometimes taken as sufficient reason for the claim that this new concept obtains throughout his work after 1935, perhaps being foreshadowed already in *Rom* II. The significance of the issue can be illustrated by Barth's remarkable, albeit late, argument that "it cannot be denied . . . that the doctrine of Calvin obviously suffers from a curious over-emphasizing of *mortificatio* [mortification] at the expense of *vivificatio* [God's enlivening work]."[83] A strong emphasis on mortification, which precedes and prepares the ground for an embrace of the gospel, is a hallmark of the Lutheran constellation of law and gospel. Yet there is no slight irony in the fact that Barth attributes a position to Calvin that the Geneva reformer is usually credited with overcoming[84]—which is then taken as Barth's main inspiration in "GL." However, and again with a certain irony, in 1951, Barth himself attaches great importance to the negative aspect in Calvin's ethics that "our sanctification consists in the *mortificatio propriae voluntatis . . . ut propriis affectibus et operibus emortui, regnum Dei meditemur*" (killing of one's own will . . . so that we reflect on

83. *CD* IV/2 651; See Luther, *On the Bondage of the Will,* in *Career of the Reformer*, vol. 3, ed. and trans. Philip S. Watson, Luther's Works 33 (Philadelphia: Fortress Press, 1972), 62: "Thus when God makes alive he does it by killing."

84. See John Calvin, *Institutes of the Christian Religion*, ed. John T. McNeill, trans. John L. Battles, The Library of Christian Classics (Louisville: Westminster John Knox, 2006), 1:360–61 (II, 7, 12).

God's reign, having died to our own feelings and works).[85] Twenty years before that, Barth's early ethics lectures characteristically quote Calvin in calling faith an "exinanition (abasement)."[86] It must be added, of course, that Barth also refers to Calvin in arguing that positively, Christian action proceeds in "harmony" and "consensus" with God's will, and that Calvin's views on Christian participation in Christ influenced Barth as well. It is notably Barth's lecture on Calvin that plants the seeds for his later, new understanding of ethics. Regardless of the questions about the true shape of John Calvin's ethics and the extent to which Barth's early ethics were influenced by Calvin in particular, it is a negative aspect that characterizes Barth's early ethics very strongly, in a way that is not counterbalanced by a corresponding notion of liberation and empowerment in the gospel. When Barth, later in his life, critiques Calvin, of all people, for highlighting the negative aspect of human unrighteousness and, as a result, the importance of mortification, this is also an indirect critique of his own ethical work.

For these reasons, the first chapter leads to significant critical conclusions about Barth's ethics up to the early 1930s. Yet it is especially before this backdrop that the epochal nature of a new development in Barth's thought in the early 1930s can be properly appreciated. The second chapter deals with the new development of "gospel and law" in Barth's thought. It would indeed be to underestimate the significance and deeper logic of this new development to take the 1935 lecture, together with a few other prominent texts, as sufficient reason for a blanket assertion that Barth's theology on the whole argues for a new understanding of the relationship between gospel and law. In an influential interpretation of Barth's thought, Eberhard Jüngel called Barth's lecture "Gospel and

85. *CD* III/4, 58; Calvin, *Institutes*, 1:396 (II, 8, 29).

86. Barth, *Ethics*, 280, Calvin, *Institutes*, 1:733 (III, 11, 7).

Law" an important, if belated supplement to Barth's doctrine of the word of God, or the *prolegomena*, of *CD* I/1.[87]

Theologically, this is associated with the increasing significance of the doctrine of election. Barth previously insisted that God revealed God's self while at the same time remaining the unknown God—in the face of which the proper human posture is sacrifice and repentance. By contrast, the doctrine of election in *CD* II/2 pursues the implications of the priority of the gospel vis-à-vis the law into the realm of trinitarian theology, so that in the eternal election, God determines God's self to be the God of the gospel. Thus, a notion of an entire dimension in which God is not fundamentally committed to the gospel is radically disqualified in Christian theology. This also renders reliance on concepts of natural law—as in a theory of two kingdoms and a corresponding ethics of orders—problematic. However, even *CD* II/2 is not free of "theistic elements"[88] that contradict the doctrine of election. An extensive discussion of the ethics of the doctrine of God in *CD* II/2 will seek to demonstrate that its actualistic ethics rests precisely on those theistic elements that highlight God's unconditioned nature and God's omnipotence. This raises the question of how far Barth himself heeds his own call to subordinate ethics to dogmatics.

Chapter 3 deals with Barth's ethics of the doctrine of creation in *CD* III/4. Individual cases of actualistic reasoning collide with Barth's repeated categorical judgments about the content of God's command in certain situations, but also with his discussions about

87. Eberhard Jüngel, "Zum Verhältnis von Kirche und Staat nach Karl Barth," in *Zur Theologie Karl Barths: Beiträge aus Anlass seines 100. Geburtstags*, ed. E. Jüngel (Tübingen: Mohr Siebeck, 1986), 76–135, at 77. *CD* I/1 discussed the concept of God's word without reference to the relation between law and gospel. See also Jüngel, "Gospel and Law: The Relationship of Dogmatics to Ethics," in *Karl Barth: A Theological Legacy*, trans. Garrett E. Paul (Philadelphia: Westminster John Knox, 1986), 105–26, at 110.

88. Wilfried Härle, *Sein und Gnade: Die Ontologie in Karl Barths Kirchlicher Dogmatik*, Theologische Bibliothek Töpelmann 27 (Berlin and New York: de Gruyter, 1975), 24n66.

the particular empirical circumstances in which such a precedent cannot be specified. On the theological side, how serious would the subordination of the law to the gospel in fact be if it did not prompt greater specificity in ethical judgment? In addition, Barth considers the ethical status of some courses of action to depend on the implied consequences. Thus, *CD* III/4 fulfills an important criterion of an ethics of responsibility. These aspects are discussed during the analysis of various issues in applied ethics.

The ensuing chapter analyzes Barth's theological and ethical decisions in *CD* IV, where theological issues fundamental to different ethical concepts are discussed. His early ethics of repentance and sacrifice continues to have repercussions, such as the subordination of wives to their husbands, as presented in *CD* III/4, which culminates in *CD* IV in a vision of the hierarchical life of the Trinity, and which reinforces an ethical paradigm of cruciform discipleship. This is closely related to Barth's view that the humiliation and exaltation of the Son of God are correlated in such a way that his most drastic humiliation is simultaneously a triumph at an even deeper level. On a more technical level, the call for cruciform discipleship, justified by the assertion that the misery of torture was in fact Christ's coronation, can very easily be misused to undercut the significance of empirical issues in ethics and the moral conflicts they imply. Interestingly, Jesus' cry of godforsakenness (Mark 15:34; Matt. 27:46) is the scriptural verse Barth mentions most often in *CD* IV/1. However, in repeated attempts, Barth does not succeed in offering a consistent interpretation of the verse. On the constructive side, the resurrection also gains significantly in importance. That redemption from suffering, rather than gruesome torture, becomes the guiding vision in theology is highly significant from an ethical perspective as well. Finally, it is relevant also from an ethical point of view to see how Barth tackles pneumatology again.

The final chapter asks what inspiration this historical reconstruction of Barth's thought offers for contemporary ethics. Barth's new constellation of gospel and law stands out due to its biblical and theological roots as well as its emancipatory potential. This may raise the concern that Barth's ethics has sometimes been associated with an ethical tradition dubbed Christ's royal reign (*Königsherrschaft Christi*). From opposition to Luther's theory of two kingdoms, a dualism resulted that created a deadlock in the theological conversations in German Protestantism during the Cold War, bringing it to the brink of schism.[89] The claim advanced here is that rather than leading into such a deadlock, a particular perspective on Barth's ethics has a significant constructive potential. The discussion of *CD* III/4, for example, highlights Barth's empirical sensibility—a feature often claimed to distinguish a two kingdoms theory from a closer relationship between gospel and law. This conceptual strong point will need to be developed further, in contrast to abiding problems in Barth's work. A comparison between Barth's ethics and William Schweiker's ethics of responsibility will show repeated commonalities in the understanding of a theory of goods and human responsibility. For Barth, Christian responsibility for social and legal justice in society is based in Christ's work of reconciliation. Thus Barth approaches the issue of moral responsibility much more strongly from a christological point of view. A thinker who engages the christological dimension of Barth's work is Jüngel. The present work highlights his critique of an ontological isolation of God from humanity and his question of human godlessness, which he develops in constructive dialogue with Barth. My own suggestion is to mediate between a rejection of a

89. Lienemann, "Das Problem des gerechten Krieges im deutschen Protestantismus nach dem Zweiten Weltkrieg," in *Der gerechte Krieg: Christentum, Islam, Marxismus*, ed. Reiner Steinweg, Edition Suhrkamp 1017 (Frankfurt am Main: Suhrkamp, 1980), 125-62, 137–41.

worldlessness of God and the possibility of human godlessness in a way that draws on pneumatological aspects of Barth's work. This is also highly relevant with respect to ethics.

1

The Development of Barth's Ethics from the First *Epistle to the Romans* to *Church Dogmatics* I/1

In Barth's early thought, two major aspects are of particular ethical significance. To begin with, Barth attributes great significance to the notion of sacrifice and repentance, which the literature on Barth has not sufficiently noted.[1] In order to keep this critical, negative dimension from dominating ethics, Barth eventually developed the actualistic concept of revelation.[2] This is the roadmap for this

1. For example, the section on *Rom* II in David Clough, *Ethics in Crisis: Interpreting Barth's Ethics*, Barth Studies Series (Aldershot: Ashgate, 2005), 3–42 does not take note of the prominence of the term *sacrifice*. The textual basis for this overall claim consists especially of *Rom* II, *GD*, lectures such as "Der Heilige Geist und das christliche Leben" (1929) and Barth's lecture cycle on ethics (1928–9; 1930–1).
2. In contrast to this, the priority of the gospel over against the law was a new initiative, which is not part of this chapter. In *GD* and *Ethics*, there are at best hints of Barth's later rearrangement of the relationship between gospel and law.

chapter's discussion of Barth's major works from the first edition of *The Epistle to the Romans* (henceforth *Rom* I) to *CD* I/1.

From Sacrifice to Revelation: The Actualistic Concept of Revelation

The emphasis on sacrifice in Barth's early work is part of a charged issue in the political contexts of Barth's work. The notion of sacrifice was already very popular in the Weimar Republic, and the prominence of the term was about to increase in highly explosive contexts.[3]

On the one hand, Barth's call for sacrifice is directed against political ideologies. On the whole, the turbulent political background of the years 1917–20 are of particular importance for Barth's early work. The revolutionary ideologies and events in Russia, Switzerland, and Germany 1917–19 especially come to mind.[4] Barth's

3. See Emanuel Hirsch, "Kurzer Unterricht in der christlichen Religion," in *Das kirchliche Wollen der Deutschen Christen*, 2nd ed. (Berlin: Grevemeyer, 1933), 17–20, at 17: God "testifies for God's self in our sense of a call to unconditional obedience and unconditional service, to complete sacrifice and commitment." The "Church movement of German Christians in Thuringia" argued, "No era was more replete with parables of [Christ's] eternal sacrifice than our lineage, than the Third Reich. . . . Sacrifices by millions at the front." Gerhard Niemöller, *Die erste Bekenntnissynode der Deutschen Evangelischen Kirche zu Barmen: Geschichte, Kritik und Bedeutung der Synode*, 2nd ed. (Göttingen: Vandenhoeck & Ruprecht, 1984), 24. See also Paul Althaus, *Grundriß der Ethik* (Erlangen: Merkel, 1931), 108 (parentheses by Althaus): "In history as a vocation to *commitment* (being granted to die), we experience the parable and preparation for the Kingdom of God that demands our very selves; in history as the place of the *contrast* (obligation to kill) we look out for the coming of the Kingdom of God."

4. Timothy Gorringe, *Karl Barth: Against Hegemony*, Christian Theology in Context (Oxford: Oxford University Press, 1999), 292–7. Notable events included the October Revolution 1917, followed by unrest in Switzerland, and the general strike in Switzerland in 1918. Bruce L. McCormack, *Karl Barth's Critically Realistic Dialectical Theology: Its Genesis and Development 1909–1936* (Oxford: Clarendon/Oxford University Press, 1997), 185–9. The Weimar Republic was founded in 1919 amid revolutionary unrest: an uprising in Berlin (*Spartakusaufstand*), inspired by the Communist Party, was put down by violent means, with the ensuing murder of Communist leaders Rosa Luxemburg and Karl Liebknecht. The same year witnessed the initiation of the Third International in 1919, of the Bavarian Soviet Republic in 1919, the failure of a right wing coup d'état in Berlin in 1920 (*Kapp-Putsch*), as well as the suppression of a communist uprising in the Ruhrgebiet in western Germany. The Weimar Republic continued to be shaken by instability, in the assassination of foreign minister Walther Rathenau in 1922

explicit political statements from the early years are supportive of democracy, while the relation he draws between theology and politics is complex, even paradoxical. If the critique of ideologies is articulated as a general call to sacrifice public claims and supposedly higher justifications, however, the effect on political life in the Weimar Republic was the opposite from Barth's intention. His message was likely to weaken moderate, democratic forces. For example, Barth's categorical critique of anything vaguely resembling an ideology also affected the Tambach conference in 1919. The organizers sought to gain support for the German Democratic Party (DDP) among Christian circles, who often hankered for a restitution of the monarchy and its alliance of throne and altar.[5] Barth's critique of *any* religious element sustaining political conviction, however, contributed to a power vacuum that was capable of being exploited both by radicals and by those conservative Protestant circles for whom Barth's harsh critique of theopolitical attitudes was beyond the pale theologically. These Protestants would indeed turn out to be a crucial voting block for Hitler.[6]

Already in Barth's early theology, Christology is the key to how Christians are supposed to act. Especially *Rom* II portrays Christ as the crucified one, who manifests humanity's sin. The salvific event of the resurrection is beyond demonstration and can only be seen

and the so-called Beer Hall Putsch in 1923, a failed coup d'état in which Hitler played a leading role.

5. Barth presented the influential lecture "The Christian in Society" ("Der Christ in der Gesellschaft") at the Tambach conference. The organizer, Otto Herpel, also had socialist leanings, but the journal he edited, *The Christian Democrat: Weekly Journal for the Protestant Home*, was not yet geared in that direction. Barth, "Der Christ in der Gesellschaft. 1919," in *Vorträge und kleinere Arbeiten: 1914–1921*, ed. Hans-Anton Drewes, Barth-Gesamtausgabe (Zurich: Theologischer Verlag, 2012), 546–98, at 546 (editor's introduction). Founded in November 1918, the DDP is commonly characterized as both liberal and left-leaning, but even Max Weber was among its founding members. Together with the Social Democrats, it was the most outspoken advocate of the Weimar Republic among the political parties of the time.
6. Jürgen W. Falter, *Hitlers Wähler* (München: Beck, 1991), 169–88; 251–6. See Karl Löwith's statement to a similar effect below.

in the negation of all worldly entities. Barth vigorously highlights Jesus Christ's humiliation. In spite of inner developments, the ethics of *Rom* II results in a negative ethics of self-withdrawal. Believing in the crucified Christ, Christians ratify their condemnation as sinners, albeit justified sinners. In the face of this charge of sinfulness, ethics corresponds to a theology of the cross by instructing one to practice sacrifice and repentance. Although Barth also attempts to give relative theological justifications for a particular kind of political action, this is decisively overshadowed by the critical vigor of the message of the cross. What Barth has in mind specifically is restraint in the public debates in Germany and Switzerland. Barth's call for a sacrificial stance rooted in the cross emerges only as he revises the positions he took in previous prominent writings. *Rom* I and the Tambach lecture, "The Christian in Society" (1919, henceforth: "ChrSoc"), by contrast, highlight "the force of the resurrection." Admittedly, *Rom* I already warns against a "war of the good ones with the evil ones."[7] It is precisely the rejection of ideological thought that drives Barth's transformation of his previous positions. Yet even *Rom* II, his most influential work at the time, cannot be seen as a satisfactory conclusion in this regard.

In the mid-1920s, a modification of a one-sided ethics of sacrifice and repentance began to take shape, as he emphasized that the gospel works not only as a "power of death," but as Jesus Christ trumps this dynamic in an extraordinary act of revelation and command. As this event remains a radically contingent, elusive act, this concept both questions and affirms the negative view of creation and history.

This dialectical dynamic is only overcome with a consistent concept of the gospel's priority over the law. To begin with, developments in the 1920s point in this direction, but the plot

7. *Rom* I, 43.

thickens only with the lectures "Die Not der evangelischen Kirche" ("The Affliction of the Protestant Church," 1931) and "Das erste Gebot als theologisches Axiom" ("The First Commandment as a Theological Axiom," 1933). A milestone was then reached with the Barmen Declaration (1934) and "GL" (1935). This chapter focuses on the point before Barth's thought began to move in this new direction, his writings from *Rom* I to the ethics lectures (held in Münster in 1928–9 and in Bonn in 1930–31).

"The Christian in Society" and the First Edition of *The Epistle to the Romans*

Barth's lecture "ChrSoc," held in Tambach (1919),[8] is characterized by dialectical thought in ethics. Barth criticizes the practice of giving directly religious reasons for public action. It is especially what he calls the "hyphens," as in a "Christian-social" and "religious-social" orientation of ethics, that try to attenuate the ethics of autonomous secular systems in a Christian vein.[9] This leads to a tension between two positions: on the one hand, Barth's critique of religion considers directly Christian justifications for action "presumptuous."[10] On the other, a religiously motivated critique of ideologies refuses strictly secular ethical norms, as in the argument for strict autonomy of the economic and political spheres. Barth castigates the combination of spiritual and worldly concepts, as in the catchphrase "religious-social"[11] or in the intention "to employ the fundamental principles of

8. Barth, "The Christian in Society," in *The Word of God and Theology*, trans. Amy Marga (London and New York: T&T Clark, 2011), 31–70 ("ChrSoc"). The lecture was given for the Vereinigung der Freunde des Christlichen Demokraten (Association of the friends of the *Christian Democrat*), supporters of a political journal sympathetic to the German Democratic Party (Deutsche Demokratische Partei) that tried to win over Christian circles for the young Weimar Republic. Friedrich-Wilhelm Marquardt, *Der Christ in der Gesellschaft: 1919–1979: Geschichte, Analysen und aktuelle Bedeutung von Karl Barths Tambacher Vortrag* (Munich: Kaiser, 1980), 7.
9. "ChrSoc," 37.
10. Ibid., see 38.

Jesus' way of being as maxims for any and every public . . . formation of society"[12] as a secularization of Christ and a clericalization of society. It will be seen how this continues a concern Barth brought up in *Rom* I.[13] On the one hand, a strictly secular ethics is destined to perish.[14] On the other hand, partial Christian traditions cannot be pitted against a secular ethics: "Christ's death is always for the benefit of the others, for those on the outside as well."[15] As understandable as the intention guiding all "hyphenation" theologies in their attempt to overcome a strict "autonomy of culture, of the state, of economic life"[16] may be, it cannot be carried out in any straightforward way. By contrast, Barth calls for greater attention to God's current action in history, to which Christians should respond in appropriate secular activities. For appropriate, sober action has the capacity to be a parable of the kingdom of God.[17] Christian responsible action in society is supposed to ask what secular societal processes result in parables of the kingdom of God. There is a particular divine promise for such a task, for even while their action takes on a secular form, Christians are moved by the power of the resurrection.[18] For "the Christian" is active in society in such a way that it is not Christians, but Christ who works in them.[19] Christ's work in them is

11. Ibid., 37.
12. Ibid., 39, Marquardt, *Christ in der Gesellschaft*, 9.
13. Barth, "ChrSoc," 38, 40. See also *Rom* I, 517: "The same insight, which is supposed to keep you from rashly secularizing the divine, must now also keep you from rashly clericalizing yourselves, from pursuing a clear conscience in an escape from the world and an aloof isolationism."
14. "ChrSoc," 39.
15. For this translation see Barth, "Der Christ in der Gesellschaft," in *Vorträge und kleinere Arbeiten: 1914–1921*, 557. Revised translations of "ChrSoc" are indicated with reference to Barth, "Christ in der Gesellschaft."
16. Barth, "Christ in der Gesellschaft," 561.
17. "ChrSoc," 54–8.
18. "ChrSoc," 44.
19. Ibid., 36.

transcendent vis-à-vis their religion. This is the ambiguity of Christian action, its limitation and its authority.

The difficulty in Barth's ethical concept is that God's concealed action must be of such a kind that the necessities imposed by secular societal spheres, such as economics, politics, law, etc., are reconciled with Barth's skepticism toward the world. In order to do justice to his conviction that "*We* stand more deeply in the 'No' than in the 'Yes,'"[20] Barth must show how God's concealed action remains truthful to the eschatological difference between the kingdom of God and the world, while still being compatible with the demands of specialized spheres of secular society.

It is no accident that Barth's notion of God's action remains vague in "ChrSoc": it is not just "*another thing*, not just *any* other thing, but the *wholly other* thing of the kingdom, the kingdom of *God*."[21] God's action is not limited to a negation of the status quo, but free to affirm certain aspects in sovereign independence. But at the same time, "the kingdom of God approaches in its *attack* upon society."[22] The affirmation of worldly standards of excellence can be in agreement with God's transcendent action in the world, but there is nonetheless a great danger that "our gaze upon the Creator through the lens of an affirmation of the world can become the mere reflection of the creature upon itself."[23] Barth hopes to address this concern not with criteria of ethical agency, but by asserting self-evidence: "But isn't it actually evil to take this possibility—as possibility—much too seriously? . . . We draw our *life* from the power of the resurrection. . . . We *are* moved by God. We do know God. The history of God is happening in us and toward us. . . . The history of God is *a priori* a

20. Ibid., 60.
21. Ibid., 65.
22. "ChrSoc," 61.
23. Ibid., 54.

victorious history."[24] That raises the question, however, in what sense "*we* stand more deeply in the 'No' than in the 'Yes.'" Yet Barth draws the surprising conclusion: "After all, why should we not know what to do, *sub specie aeternitatis*? . . . We cannot do much, but we can do one thing. It is a thing not done by *us*. For, what can the Christian in society do except follow closely that which is done by *God*?"[25]

The affirmation of God's action in the world constitutes a commonality between "ChrSoc" and the preceding *Rom* I, to which the discussion will now turn. In both works the "power of the resurrection" features prominently.[26] The "dynamics" of the resurrection are "inexhaustibly active in our lives."[27] Due to this shared notion, *Rom* I and "ChrSoc" also equally affirm the self-evident character of the ethical. "'What am I to do?' Answer: first of all, stop asking!"[28] The misguided attempt to translate Christian theological concepts directly into a worldly agenda is already in view when *Rom* I warns of a "secularization" of eschatology and a "clericalization" of the world. Action is properly Christian, argues *Rom* I, if Christians act in a prereflexive way. The flip side of this account of moral agency is a restriction of the Christian ethos to the private realm, however.

By contrast, "ChrSoc" proposes a concept for a Christian social ethics. According to the Tambach lecture, God is also at work outside of the church, so that Christian ethics does not in principle enter a *terra incognita* when explicitly addressing moral issues in wider society. It is true that "ChrSoc" shares the rejection of an explicitly

24. Ibid., 50–51, see 66.
25. Ibid., 68–9.
26. *Rom* I, 14, 22, 54, 77, etc.
27. Ibid., 221; see 170, 203, 213, 219, 261, see McCormack, *Barth's Theology*, 201.
28. *Rom* I, 517. Ingrid Spieckermann, *Gotteserkenntnis: Ein Beitrag zur Grundfrage der neuen Theologie Karl Barths*, Beiträge zur evangelischen Theologie 97 (Munich: Kaiser, 1985), 103, calls a correspondence of Christian action to God's action a "dynamic, ambiguous prototype of the analogy of faith."

Christian politics of *Rom* I. Yet the social ethics of "ChrSoc," with its notion of a secular parable to the kingdom of God, attempts a dialectical solution to a problem that *Rom* I was unable to solve. While *Rom* I sees God's organic activity in the church overcoming the contrast between God and world, this approach cannot reconcile the Christian life with an ethics of the public life; politics and the economy, for example, follow a different logic than a religious one.[29]

According to *Rom* I, the power of the resurrection is clearly limited to the congregation. In the first place, *Rom* I attaches fundamental importance to baptism, which it calls a "stronghold of the new world."[30] Baptism is the "warrant that . . . the work of God's redemptive will is no human, all too human tower of Babel."[31] On the one hand, *Rom* I emphasizes that faith and life in the Holy Spirit are not human options by nature. On the other hand, this negative aspect can also appear in a positive way: while it is not true that Christians possess the Holy Spirit, the Holy Spirit does exercise power over Christians.[32] Describing the work of the Holy Spirit as the organic growth of the church presents little problem to Barth. For this reason, *Rom* I should not be read as the document of a *critical* actualism according to which faith is only a reality of the moment, while its lack would already be felt in the next moment.[33]

29. *Rom* I, 509.
30. Ibid., 214; see 212 about the sacraments: "It is the objective, creative word of God. . . . Due to this content, baptism is a sacrament, does not only signify, but is the new creation."
31. Ibid., 368.
32. Ibid., 307, 337.
33. That the deficit is experienced as such in the next moment is only the best case, which is a problem with the actualistic reading of *Rom* I advocated by McCormack, *Barth's Theology*, 145–7, 156–7, 164–5. Yet according to *Rom* I, 449, attaining belief in Christ in every new moment is nothing fundamentally difficult. Along these lines see *Rom* I, 344 (see Spieckermann, *Gotteserkenntnis*, 105). The certainty of the Spirit's presence also in the future creates new problems. Precisely for this reason, *Rom* I, 449 insists that Christians must not consider faith their own achievement. What human beings lack in natural habitual potential is made up for, almost too easily, by word and sacrament. See also Herbert Anzinger, *Glaube und kommunikative Praxis: Eine Studie zur 'vordialektischen' Theologie Karl Barths*, Beiträge zur evangelischen

The sacramentalist foundation of *Rom* I can lead, however, to quietism: if Christians engage in confrontation, they compromise the power of the resurrection.[34] Christians are beyond good and evil;[35] their hope of redemption "cannot become the subject of the discipline of 'ethics.'"[36] Barth is resolutely against a "tactics of the Kingdom of God" (*Gottesreichstaktik*), which would result in the "Godlessness of the good cause." *Rom* I thus adopts Hermann Kutter's polemics against Leonhard Ragaz's religious socialism.[37] The truth of Christianity degrades into the "idea of the 'war of the good against the evil'"[38] when translated directly into political action. There must not be any Christian "insistence on being right in principle" (*Rechthaberei*).[39] These critical thoughts constitute a fundamental cause in *Rom* I (which *Rom* II will maintain).[40] The sensitivity to problems in religious action is indeed clear-sighted. However, Barth combines it with a problematic response. Christians are not supposed to employ the "method of the world" instead of the "method of the Kingdom of God."[41] They should not deal with either political or legal questions.[42] Power is evil and politics is violence. Christians

Theologie 110 (Munich: Kaiser, 1991), 202. Moreover, an actualistic reading of *Rom* I leads to the problems of how to avoid the kind of religious individualism against which *Rom* I is directed.

34. *Rom* I, 492.
35. Ibid., 493.
36. Ibid., 507, see also 250.
37. According to ibid., 493 (editor's note), the expression "godlessness of the good cause" (*Gottlosigkeit im Guten*) is taken from another commentary on Romans: Hermann Kutter, *Das Bilderbuch Gottes für Groß und Klein* (Basel: Kober, 1917), 200. Kutter and Barth are critical of Leonhard Ragaz's religious socialism. Ragaz himself commented that the criticism of his position in *Rom* I hit "the center." Markus Mattmüller, *Leonhard Ragaz und der religiöse Sozialismus: Eine Biographie* (Zurich: Evangelischer Verlag, 1968), 2:251.
38. *Rom* I, 43.
39. Ibid., 394, see also 388: "The rejection of the Christ was not a deed of viciousness and passion, but a peak performance of Israelite religiosity and morality."
40. Spieckermann, *Gotteserkenntnis*, 107.
41. *Rom* I, 499. See also Timothy Gorringe, "Karl Barth on Romans," in *The Oxford Handbook of the Reception History of the Bible*, eds. Michael Lieb, Emma Mason, and Jonathan Roberts (Oxford: Oxford University Press, 2011), 590–608, at 597–8.

must be reminded that "your nation state is in heaven (Phil. 3:20)."[43] Christian political action can, at the most, consist in refusing any religious qualifications of the state[44] and in hoping for a silent "absorption of the divine atmosphere by all people (in the Christ!)."[45]

To be sure, *Rom* I is already markedly critical of religion. Christ was crucified, of all people, by the pious.[46] Nonetheless, the difference between church and world is fundamental for ethics in *Rom* I.[47] Barth highlights the power of God's action at the expense of human activity, thus replacing religious activism with quietism. Christians are, Barth asserts, crucified and risen with Christ, so that they are no longer characterized by religion and morals but by God's influence.[48] Thus they do not advocate particular Christian concerns in public debates.

Nevertheless, if any distinctly Christian public positioning is criticized as religion or morality, one must wonder if a blanket refusal of such positioning can escape Barth's charge. For a "tactics of the Kingdom of God" to be theologically superior to a "method of the world," a true dialectical sublation rather than a simple contrast would be necessary. However, *Rom* I reverses the leading sign that characterizes religious socialism, and what used to be a position similar to Ragaz's religious activism becomes quietism, and no less

42. Ibid., 504, 506.
43. Ibid., 503, see 501–2.
44. Ibid., 505.
45. Ibid., 508. On the political circumstances at the end of World War I, see McCormack, *Barth's Theology*, 186–9. In the interest of national safety, the Swiss parliament granted significant new powers to the administration in 1914. As a consequence, working hours were increased, child labor was facilitated, and the recruitment of the youth for the military was legalized. The Socialist Party called for a general strike in 1918, which, aiming at reform within the existing democratic system, remained peaceful, yet also created the danger of further political destabilization—which was also true of the intransigent action of the administration.
46. *Rom* I, 365, 388, 422.
47. Spieckermann, *Gotteserkenntnis*, 104 asks critically, too, "Is the '*organ of discernment*,' so boldly called '*feeling*,' . . . indeed entirely safe from confusion with religious feeling, the liberal, immediate synthesis 'starting from the human person'?" See also ibid., 108.
48. *Rom* I, 262.

religious at that. Admittedly, *Rom* I rejects any escalation of public debates through Christian claims to higher authority. Yet neither can Christian traditions, in Barth's new reading, contribute to a constructive solution to conflicts. As if theology and ethics could be cleanly separated, Barth counsels that the only meaningful political position is that of the "extreme left. But as for the details, you need to consult an ethics."[49]

In the meantime, when ethical decisions can no longer be deferred, he advises an "ethics of the stuck situation" (*Ethik der verfahrenen Situation*).[50] This concept resembles what Luther's theory of God's two kingdoms envisages for holders of public offices.[51] In the face of difficult public decisions, this ethics appears rather fatalistic: inevitably, practical necessities sometimes lead to problematic results.[52] Yet for political action, God's forgiveness can be factored in across the board: "Your sins, including your political sins, are forgiven then."[53] Certainly Barth is against religious support for violent ideologies—patriarchal authorities must be "*starved out with respect to religion*."[54] Yet the assurance of a blanket forgiveness of political sins does not inspire a critical spirit. Instead, it runs the risk of ideological collaboration when extreme political measures are presented as necessities of a sober realism. Advocacy for sustained social justice, peace, or democracy are not an issue in *Rom* I. Even the calmness of the problematic quietism is at risk when Barth asserts that believers would first "develop an organ that feels the action of the

49. Ibid., 508.
50. Ibid., 495.
51. See Wilfried Härle, "Luthers Zwei-Regimenten-Lehre als Lehre vom Handeln Gottes," *Marburger Jahrbuch Theologie* 1 (1987): 12–32, at 16.
52. See also *Rom* I, 493: "Unfortunately, some things are necessary that would not be necessary!"
53. Ibid., 510.
54. Ibid., 507–8.

Spirit and to respond. . . . You will obey the commandment of the moment . . . *now* the Spirit is speaking!"[55]

A concept of social ethics in *Rom* I that seems to offer an alternative to prereflexive action and the "ethics of the stuck situation" is the Christian admonition in intra-Christian affairs.[56] The question of right action shows the elusive character of the Spirit, which now constitutes the necessity of leaving all ideologies behind in favor of a sober admonition. This contradicts the fundamental approach of *Rom* I, however, even pointing out some of its shortcomings. After all, *Rom* I argues for a renewed gift of the Spirit in word and sacrament, so the only legitimate admonition would be to call for participation in the worship service.

In comparing *Rom* I and "ChrSoc," it is an innovation that "ChrSoc" calls extraecclesial activity capable of becoming a "parable." *Rom* I does mention parables but focuses on a piety within the church that, outside of this realm, takes on a prereflexive stance that is not explicitly Christian.[57] While action in worldly terms with a "parabolic" intention avoids the reduction of Christian ethics to the ecclesial realm, it remains open to discussion and correction. Christian ethics can thus enter into dialogue with other academic areas. Since Barth considers worldly events and rationalities capable

55. Ibid., 485–6.
56. Ibid., 463. On the "Christian admonition," see Anzinger, *Glaube*, 198–210. This passage is less than clear about the contrast between the intraecclesial function of the admonition—after all, in contrast to idealism, Christians must not create their own laws (cf. Anzinger, *Glaube*, 198–9)—and the statement that this admonition has the "recognition of unredeemed reality" in view (*Rom* I, 241; Anzinger, *Glaube*, 203). "Directed at people who do not yet fulfill the presuppositions of ch.s 5–8, but even with regard to ourselves—insofar as those presuppositions have perhaps not been actualized yet—this Christian admonition cannot appear any other way than as a very peculiar form of *law*" (*Rom* I, 464).
57. Link characterizes "ChrSoc" as a decisive turn in Barth's thought, as it is the first time that Barth refused, publicly and in principle, building theology on the foundations of religiosity. Christian Link, "Bleibende Einsichten von Tambach," in *Karl Barth in Deutschland (1921–1935): Aufbruch—Klärung—Widerstand*, eds. Michael Beintker, Christian Link, and Michael Trowitzsch (Zurich: Theologischer Verlag, 2005), 333–46, at 338–9.

of becoming a parable of God's reign, he leaves the ecclesiocentric approach of *Rom* I behind. In part, this change may be due to the fact that the village pastor of *Rom* I has suddenly attracted a lot of attention and is now, in "ChrSoc," challenged to address a specialized group of theologians, politicians, and social reformers. Neither will the genre of an exegetical commentary do in addressing the ethical topic "The Christian in Society." In this new and challenging context, it is a shrewd measure for "ChrSoc" to characterize God as "entirely different." This description of God's action is not entirely absent in *Rom* I,[58] yet there the contrast is with specific, individual phenomena of the pious life rather than with the entire realm of human experience. *Rom* I still argued that one might do justice to the one who is "entirely different . . . by an uncompromising commitment" in opposition to "what is important in the world."[59] It is only in "ChrSoc" that Barth characterizes God's activity as *totaliter aliter* (entirely different) or impinging "vertically from above."[60] Then again, "ChrSoc" does argue, "We *are* moved by God. We do know God,"[61] yet it negates a direct correspondence between human and divine action; the similarity does not extend beyond that of a parable.[62] This new approach in "ChrSoc" is also directed against the sacramentalism and the problematic ecclesiality of *Rom* I.

Much can be singled out for praise in the social ethics of "ChrSoc." The notion of worldly action serving as a parable of the kingdom helps Christian ethics to enter into a dialogue with the sciences

58. There are nine passages, which are not especially striking: *Rom* I, 131, 172, 190, 206, 361, 431, 443, 453, 468.

59. Ibid., 467.

60. "ChrSoc," 42. In *Rom* I, the expression "from above" twice refers to political authority in contrast to those thus governed (502, 512) and only once to God in clear distinction from creation (577). The expression "vertically from above" does not occur in *Rom* I.

61. "ChrSoc," 51.

62. "All that is transitory is *but* a parable" (ibid., 55): Johann Wolfgang von Goethe, *Faust*, part 2, act 5 (Barth's italics).

and other academic endeavors. The emphasis on worldly parables justifies its critique of a clericalization of the world with reference to the cross. This aspect will also characterize certain strands of Barth's later ethical work. "CS" (1938) deals, for example, with a correspondence between a just constitutional democracy and the very creation of justice and right in Christ's work of reconciliation. The lecture "The Christian Community and the Civil Community" ("CCCC," 1946) highlights the "analogical capacities and needs of political organization."[63] The notion of secular words being a parable resurfaces in the "doctrine of lights" (*CD* IV/3 §69.2 114–16). *CL* will (1959–61) argue that only a human "movement *analogous* to that which we ask and expect from God" is in accordance with the petition "Hallowed by thy name."[64] These statements do not, however, merely repeat the concept of a parable, but refine it in a way that reflects the gravity of human sin as revealed on the cross. Further, a dialectical mode of thought that either recommends the importance of worldly expertise or critiques it on theological grounds may help reduce prejudice in controversial ethical questions. This is in contrast to a partisanship that advocates in principle either a particular rationality and an ethos of a particular social sphere, or is fundamentally committed to a countercultural stance.

If we take a closer look, however, at the critique of religion that stands out in "ChrSoc," a greater difficulty emerges. To begin with, "ChrSoc" articulates a critique of a particular religiosity. Barth argues that human action must be oriented toward God's action, which is neither restricted to inspiring the human religious consciousness

63. "CCCC," 168. See also *CD* IV/2, §67.4: the legal system is a continuum that allows for a constructive dialogue between church and "world," in spite of all specific differences. Barth's objection to a clericalization of the world also causes him to critique all directly Christian justifications of political decisions as well as the establishment of Christian political parties: "CCCC," 182.

64. *CL*, 169.

nor an exclusively ecclesial stance.[65] Thus Barth's ethical approach relativizes a theology of consciousness often associated with Schleiermacher.[66]

Nonetheless, Barth does not leave behind the methodological orientation toward religiosity. After all it is a religious judgment that, according to "ChrSoc," discerns God's action in the world. Although the lecture reacts critically against a theology of consciousness, it is also in keeping with a theology of consciousness in describing the cross as "a critical 'No' and a creative 'Yes' upon the content of our consciousness."[67] Immediately after Barth's presentation of the lecture, his reaction against religious experience was faced with the objection that even Barth's own ethical concept rests on a religious foundation—"that is, at that moment at which Christians gain certainty *where* they had seen the living God at work."[68] Faced with this ambiguity in "ChrSoc," it is worth noting that the two theological concepts that Barth critiques, both the strongly ecclesial focus of *Rom* I and Schleiermacher's theology of consciousness—whatever else may be said about them—at least offer guideposts that help us discern a potential act of God. According to *Rom* I, God is not at work in the legal system or in politics, and is certainly outside of the realm of confrontation; according to

65. "Precisely for this reason, the *knowledge* of God is essentially the *history* of God and no mere event in our consciousness" ("ChrSoc," 45, see also 46).

66. Schleiermacher is one of the few theological authors "ChrSoc" names explicitly. Although God's action results in the subjective reaction on the human part, Barth argues, this must not be used as a new basis for theological insight about God. "And the movement of life unveiled in Jesus is not some kind of new piety" (Barth, "ChrSoc," 43–4). With this statement Barth draws the conclusion from another point he made, with which, however, Schleiermacher would indeed agree: "The Immediate, the Origin, will never be experienced as such" (ibid., 43). See Friedrich Schleiermacher, *The Christian Faith*, ed. Hugh R. MacKintosh and James S. Stewart (New York: T&T Clark, 1999), §4.1, 12–13.

67. Barth, "Christ in der Gesellschaft," 557.

68. Thus, one of the organizers of the Tambach conference, Otto Herpel, wrote about the lecture. O. H. [*sic*], "Berichte und Urteile über die Tambacher Konferenz vom 22.–25. September 1919, I.," quoted after Marquardt, *Christ in der Gesellschaft*, 27. See also ibid., 34–5.

Schleiermacher, theology is not dealing with an act of God that supposedly consists in anything other than the religious inspiration of consciousness.[69]

"ChrSoc," by contrast, hardly offers any guidance for discerning a historical act of God at all—even the rejection of sloppy work leaves the question for criteria open. The greatest problem of "ChrSoc" is therefore that God is portrayed in broad strokes as power within history, which, however, Barth describes only very vaguely as "entirely different." It is of course not a new thesis that Barth's early work speaks of God only vaguely, rather than deriving critical and constructive theological guidelines from the biblical testimonies to God's revelation in Christ. Yet in "ChrSoc," this risks confusing the most diverse historical developments with God's action. This problem is compounded by Barth's description of the cross as "the power that moves . . . the world."[70] As God is active in history in a way that cannot be clearly distinguished from any other human activity, Barth's emphasis on the marked difference between God and the world (*totaliter aliter*) no longer offers any leverage in the critique of events that are contrary to divine intentions. The characterization of God's work as "*a priori* a victorious history"[71] can increase the danger of identifying God with the powers that be.[72] Hans Bader, for example, perceived "ChrSoc" as an encouragement in his opinion that religious socialism is "not a human cause in which we are

69. See Schleiermacher, *The Christian Faith*, §4.4, 17: "Now our proposition is in no wise intended to dispute the existence of such an original knowledge [i.e., knowledge about God that precedes the 'feeling of absolute dependence'], but simply to set it aside as something with which, in a system of Christian doctrine, we could never have any concern."

70. "ChrSoc," 66.

71. Ibid., 51.

72. This interpretation emerged in Otto Herpel's paraphrase of the lecture; see Marquardt, *Christ in der Gesellschaft*, 25–6. Marquardt considers this a "misunderstanding in terms of a theology of history" (ibid., 26), but does not offer reasons for his dismissal. For an extreme variation on Herpel's understanding in terms of a theology of history, see Hans Ehrenberg's take on "ChrSoc" below.

engaged, but God's activity, to which we can only give ourselves up."[73] Even more explosive is Hans Ehrenberg's preface to "ChrSoc." The philosopher from Heidelberg was in fact the editor responsible for Barth's first contact to a wider readership.[74] His preface reflects on Barth's lecture: "How full of parables to the heavenly history worldly history is!"[75] He looks back to the war that just ended, interpreting the suffering of the German people as a parable of Jesus' suffering on the cross. In the same way that God once bought humanity for God's self by means of Jesus' blood, thus God bought the unfaithful German people once again through the bloodshed of World War I.[76] The commonwealth emerging from the ruins now promises "resurrection." Since the misery of the battlefield is a parable, according to Ehrenberg, the readers of Barth's lecture should bear in mind: "Thus we must indeed give ourselves up truly."

A crucial idea of the lecture thus remains worryingly vague. During World War II, for example, Heinz Eduard Tödt, who would, after a military career in World War II and some soul searching, go on to become an influential ethicist, found consolation in the

73. Bader wrote that religious socialism "is not a human affair in which we are involved, but God's action, to which we can only devote ourselves." *Vertrauliche Mitteilungen für die Freunde des 'Neuen Werks'* 3 (1919), 6, cited after Marquardt, *Christ in der Gesellschaft*, 31.

74. Hans Brakelmann, *Hans Ehrenberg: Ein judenchristliches Schicksal in Deutschland: Leben, Denken, Wirken 1883–1932* (Waltrop: Spenner, 1997), 95.

75. Hans Ehrenberg, "Geleitwort," (preface) in Barth, *Der Christ in der Gesellschaft: Eine Tambacher Rede: Mit einem Geleitwort von Hans Ehrenberg* (Würzburg: Patmos, 1920), iii–vi, at iii (dated November 1919). See Eberhard Busch, "Antworten, die zu Fragen wurden: Die Bedeutung des Tambacher Vortrags für K. Barths eigenen Weg," in *Der Christ in der Gesellschaft: Tambach 1919–1994*, ed. Wilhelm Ebting (Reinhardsbrunn, 1994), 9–21, http://tinyurl.com/lkmv2gm, ch. 2: "Hans Ehrenberg . . . felt that [Barth's lecture] gave wings to his identification of the turn from the old epoch to the new with the German 'now.'" Busch refers to a letter of Barth's to Thurneysen, in which Barth reported his disconcertedness about a statement of Ehrenberg that he does not mention. Karl Barth and Eduard Thurneysen, *Barth-Thurneysen-Briefwechsel 1913–1921*, ed. Eduard Thurneysen, Barth-Gesamtausgabe (Zurich: Evangelischer Verlag, 1973), 421. But still Barth's precise position on Ehrenberg's preface remains unclear. According to Barth, Ehrenberg wrote "a preface to my lecture, which I returned to him with urgent censoring notes" (Barth's letter to Thurneysen, Nov. 11, 1919, in *Barth-Thurneysen-Briefwechsel 1913–21*, 351).

76. Ehrenberg, "Geleitwort," iii; in the following see also ibid., iv.

prayer, "Thy will be done," after his brother had died in battle.[77] The positive evaluation of technical expertise in Barth's lecture in particular makes a theology of history especially explosive. It was this amalgam that contributed significantly to the destructive power of the Nazi regime.[78] I hasten to add that "ChrSoc" was not responsible for the failure of the Weimar Republic and much less for Nazi atrocities. But these events nevertheless illustrate the potential inherent in the lecture. Faced with this danger, Barth's assurance that the analogy always works "from above to below, and never the other way around"[79] is too abstract to be helpful. Many natural theologies—including Barth's own book *Fides quaerens intellectum*—in fact consider themselves theologies of revelation,[80] and the categories by which one interprets the biblical witness to revelation often seem to be plainly "in the text." Barth's reminder about the right "direction" of our understanding presupposes a clearer understanding of the divine that would render the necessity of worldly analogies unnecessary in the first place. Barth's later work would modify this understanding of God's action in history by speaking of God's commandment instead. At the same time this

77. Heinz Eduard Tödt, *Der verlorene Haufe: Fünf Jahre an den Fronten des Zweiten Weltkriegs* (typescript, 1991), 35, cited according to Wolfgang Schuhmacher, *Theologische Ethik als Verantwortungsethik: Leben und Werk Heinz Eduard Tödts in ökumenischer Perspektive,* Öffentliche Theologie 20 (Leipzig: Evangelische Verlagsanstalt, 2009), 59.

78. A characteristic of the National Socialist regime was the employment of young, technically talented specialists with a high degree of motivation and professionalism in their limited areas. See Götz Aly, *Hitler's Beneficiaries: Plunder, Racial War, and the Nazi Welfare State*, trans. Jefferson Chase (New York: Holt/Metropolitan, 2009), 14–16, William Sweet, "The Volksgerichtshof: 1934–45," *Journal of Modern History* 46 (1974): 314–29, at 321: "There is no need to assume that the Volksgericht's members were radical Nazis deliberately undermining traditional law." Yet the death penalty was their verdict in almost 50 percent of the cases (see ibid., 326). The problem of technically solid work under totalitarian conditions is also illustrated by a statement of former imperial arms minister Albert Speer: "It is part of history that in those days I was in all earnest convinced that as the Arms Minister my work was only technical, but not political." Stephan Schlak, "Ordnung und Revolte: Helmut Schelsky und Jean Améry," Intellektuelle Gegenpole, pt. 4, May 24, 2009, Deutschlandfunk, http://bit.ly/dCRt5o.

79. "ChrSoc," 67.

80. See Introduction, n39. This is von Balthasar's notion of *analogia entis.*

preserved a highly contingent factor in answering the question of how to judge the morality of Christian action. The present discussion of "ChrSoc" raises the question, however, of how Barth avoids the ideological abuse of the contingent factor in his thought. "ChrSoc" only mentions the cross twice; with such a reference, however, Barth might have emphasized much more strongly how controversial and contested God's action in the world can in fact be.[81] Certainly, the lecture does not intend to weaken the loyalty Barth himself felt for the young Weimar Republic, or even his political leanings toward the left.[82] Yet once one professes to be faithful to a perceived divine action in history without more precise theological criteria, one weakens the critique of the "war of the good against evil" that Barth articulated in *Rom* I.[83] However, *Rom* II will repeat the protest against a "war between good and evil."[84] This makes it necessary to ask for proper theological guidelines for action. This presupposes that—as significant as Barth's critique of religion is indeed—the religious character of Christian faith cannot be dismissed out of hand. One of Barth's texts most critical of religion, *CD* I/2, §17, does recognize the religious character of faith by calling Christianity the true religion, in the sense in which even sinners are justified by grace.[85] This is based on a theological orientation toward the incarnation: by becoming incarnate in Christ, God does not exclude the risk of being confused with other deities. "God's revelation is in fact God's presence and thus God's *hiddenness* in the world of human *religion*. Because God reveals himself, the divine particular is hidden in a human universal, . . . and

81. See the references to the cross in "ChrSoc," 36, as a critique of ecclesiocentrism and 51 as an indication of God's love of the world.

82. McCormack, *Barth's Theology*, 201.

83. *Rom* I, 43.

84. *Rom* II, 653.

85. See Garrett Green's new translation: Barth, *On Religion: The Revelation of God as the Sublimation of Religion*, ed. and trans. Garrett Green, T&T Clark Theology (New York: T&T Clark, 2006).

thus the *divinely unique* in something merely *humanly remarkable.*"[86] This makes a constructive discussion of potential religious illusions inescapable. By contrast, *Rom* II chooses a different path in trying to rule out a confusion of the true God with idols.

The Second Edition of *The Epistle to the Romans*

The second edition of *Romans* has been characterized as part of the new expressionist wave in German intellectual life, a description that does justice at least to its vigorous rhetoric, its use of paradox, and its harsh criticism of traditional authorities.[87] The mode of argumentation is indeed highly paradoxical, often gesturing toward the ineffable with the back and forth of a passionate argument. Since Barth kept sending on a constant flow of manuscript pages directly to the printer for publication while still writing,[88] there is a grain of truth even in his ironic comment: "The cornucopia of these dialectics will never be exhausted and emptied. The book will be unbearable, and already now I am having compassion with those readers that will have to follow all the windings of this meandering river."[89] In addition, a "tone of anger"[90] is apparent in many places. To what extent the book will develop a consistent thrust with which it might achieve a particular impact requires careful analysis.

When Barth presented some of the crucial new ideas in the lecture "Biblical Questions, Insights, and Vistas" in 1920, speaking of God as "completely different," of revelation as a "limit" to humanity and its impact as the "wisdom of death,"[91] Adolf von Harnack reacted with

86. Barth, *On Religion*, 35 (*CD* I/2, 282).
87. This is the motivation for Barth's theological stance in this period suggested between the lines by Wilhelm Pauck, *Karl Barth: Prophet of a New Christianity?* (New York: Harper, 1931), 18–19.
88. Eberhard Busch, *Karl Barth: His Life from Letters and Autobiographical Texts*, trans. John Bowden (Eugene: Wipf & Stock: 2005), 117.
89. *Barth-Thurneysen-Briefwechsel 1913–21*, 485 (May 13, 1921, Barth commenting on Romans 7).
90. McCormack, *Barth's Theology*, 243.

consternation.[92] An important contributor to the "Manifesto of the Ninety-Three German Intellectuals" (1914), which rallied German intellectuals around the German cause in World War I, Harnack personified, like few others, the scholarly achievements and creative energy, but also the ideological blinkers that characterized German liberal Protestantism in the Wilhelmine empire.[93]

Even against this backdrop, *Rom* II is more than merely a child of its time.[94] The trenchant critique of bourgeois theology dressing up the ideologies of the time should always remain a thorn in the flesh of theological ethics. Yet how far does the theological authority of its ethical vision reach in fact? To what degree is *Rom* II influenced by its perceived opponent, specifically in how its critique of ideology is calibrated?

The difference between "ChrSoc" and *Rom* II is obvious from a new understanding of a central term of the lecture: the parable. *Rom* II uses the concept in a new sense by highlighting Christ's cross, which goes hand in hand with a stronger critique of moral positions. In addition, *Rom* II quotes the statement of skepticism toward worldly rationality from "ChrSoc"—itself almost a literal

91. Barth, "Biblical Questions, Insights, and Vistas," in *Word of God and Theology*, 71–100, at 87, 74, 93.

92. Eberhard Busch, *Barth: His Life from Letters*, 115. Von Harnack appeared out of touch with reality to Barth, while other representatives of this generation of scholars treated him with condescension (ibid.). See Hans-Anton Drewes, "Die Auseinandersetzung mit Adolf von Harnack," in *Karl Barth in Deutschland*, eds. Beintker et al., 189–204.

93. On the "Manifesto" and its role in Barth's turning away from liberal Protestantism, see Wilfried Härle, "Der Aufruf der 93 Intellektuellen und Karl Barths Bruch mit der liberalen Theologie," *Zeitschrift für Theologie und Kirche* 72 (1975): 207–24, Drewes, "Die Auseinandersetzung," 191–2. Drewes (ibid., 193) illustrates in what sense *Rom* II was directed at the foundations of Wilhelmine intellectual life: "In reality, presumably we must understand the entire *Epistle to the Romans* as an open contradiction to the way historical texts and documents were dealt with, which in the generation before Barth nobody developed in such an impressive degree or practiced as brilliantly as Harnack did."

94. Paul D. Jones argues that "the conspicuous pressures of the time exerted less influence on his theological work than one might think." "The Rhetoric of War in Karl Barth's Epistle to the Romans: A Theological Analysis," *Journal for the History of Modern Theology* 17 (2010): 90–111, at 91.

quotation from *Rom* I, which *GD* II is going to repeat again: "*We* stand more deeply in the 'No' than in the 'Yes.'"[95] Yet in keeping with the special attention to the cross in *Rom* II, an even stronger critique of culture results. Jesus is a "purely negative entity for us."[96] While the effect of the resurrection power provides fresh orientation to Christian moral action according to *Rom* I, thus disqualifying the old human—all too human—behavior at the same time, *Rom* II retains merely this negative aspect: God is "the pure negation."[97] Nonetheless, the new edition elaborates consistently on the previous one insofar as the latter was unable to offer clear criteria for a distinction between the new ethos of the congregation and the morals of the old eon, putting in jeopardy the refusal of the old eon.[98] *Rom* II negates the positive interpretation of the analogy. The negation of a positive revelation and the revelation of God's abiding hiddenness now replace what previously Barth viewed as an "organic" growth of the congregation towards a fulfillment of God's will.[99] The new development has also been described as an analogy.[100]

95. "ChrSoc," 60; *Rom* II, 620: "*We* are standing more *deeply* in the 'No' than in the 'Yes.'" See already *Rom* I, 216: "Perhaps it is the case that now we are standing more deeply in the 'No' than in the 'Yes.'" See again *GD* II, 244: "Wir *stehen* tiefer *im Nein als im Ja.*"

96. *Rom* II, 147, see 147 ("in the secret of his greatness, which is entirely negative for us"), 150–51, 218 ("The doctrine of Christ's threefold office obscures and weakens the focus of the New Testament view [of Christ's death]. There is no independent second or third aspect *besides* this one and only, this exclusive meaning of Christ.") See also 524: "We must recall the most serious of all symptoms: it was the church—not the world, but the *church*—which crucified Christ."

97. Ibid., 194.

98. Thus also Spieckermann, *Gotteserkenntnis*, 108, 121–2. Eberhard Busch, *Karl Barth und die Pietisten: Die Pietismuskritik des jungen Karl Barth und ihre Erwiderung* (Munich: Kaiser, 1978), 88–90, lists further commonalities between *Rom* I and *Rom* II (God as the objective reality critically confronting the world; faced with this critique, all differences between pious and secular pale; the relationship between world and God is to be viewed in strictly eschatological terms).

99. See Busch, *Barth und die Pietisten*, 90–91. See *Rom* II, 194, *pace* McCormack, *Barth's Theology*, 255.

100. Spieckermann, *Gotteserkenntnis*, 143, calls this "*analogy of the cross*" the "primeval form" of the "*analogia fidei*, which Barth develops after 1930." McCormack, *Barth's Theology*, 12, observes that a differentiation between different kinds of dialectics in Barth's early work makes it impossible to maintain a blanket decrease of "the dialectics." On dialectics in the early Barth,

But the fallen world resembles God's new reality only insofar as the old world negates itself; there can be no positive analogy.

Arguing for an integration of even the deepest skepticism into a true dialectic, which would result in a relative analogy to the kingdom of God in *Rom* II, one might point to a statement like this: "To the extent that the religious or the anti-religious gesture puts the emphasis on pointing beyond itself, its questionable character is relativized and absolute skepticism loses its right."[101] But this statement requires careful analysis. Does Barth truly succeed in making a relative, constructive case against his vigorous denial of the human reality?

When arguing for the positive nature of God's relation to the world, an "absolute skepticism" cannot be reconciled dialectically with the kingdom of God. Barth argues it is negated and "loses its right." In making a positive case for a dialectic, any "absolute skepticism" must be watered down to mere ambiguity. Indeed, proponents of a dialectic discern a relative, not an absolute message of judgment in *Rom* II: "The 'No' is not absolute, even if it is total."[102]

If, in turn, God's judgment of the world is absolute, one cannot argue that it is outweighed by God's positive relation to the world, which would disregard the categorical nature of God's judgment. But then again the refutation of this world is so vigorous in *Rom* II that it is hard to see how anything might be salvaged to constitute, even in all relativity, a valid parable of the kingdom of God. Barth repeatedly calls the negation of this world "absolute,"[103] "pure,"[104] an

see Michael Beintker, *Die Dialektik in der 'dialektischen Theologie' Karl Barths* (Munich: Kaiser 1985), 25–31.

101. *Rom* II, 188.

102. Cornelis van der Kooi, "Karl Barths zweiter Römerbrief und seine Wirkungen," in *Barth in Deutschland*, eds. Beintker et al., 57–76, at 67.

103. *Rom* II, 112.

104. Ibid., 188, 194, 199.

"*absolute* assault."[105] God's judgment is the "most radical finishing off of history."[106] Thus the dialectic fails since Barth attempts to forge it by disregarding the categorical nature of the antithesis. Death is not grace "as long as it is merely a relative negation."[107] "But God's judgment is the end of history, not the beginning of a new, second history. History is finished off, it is not continued. What remains after judgment is not only distinguished and separated from the state of affairs before judgment in a relative way, but absolutely."[108] How could we fail to suspect that that which is deemed, in all relativity, an analogy or parable, is in fact just another religious illusion? After all, God is "absolutely different from all that is light, power, and good for us."[109] If God's judgment is absolute, we literally do not have the words to hint at a hope beyond judgment.

In a clear rejection of the old eon, Barth calls Jesus' death "the critical negation of all life concerns."[110] How can Barth's gesturing toward a new hope beyond be anything else than a "life concern" as well, if the critical edge of *Rom* II is to be taken seriously? Barth seemed to underestimate this fact, for example when "ChrSoc" polemicized against religious concerns, but still ended with the question, "What can the Christian in society do than follow closely that which is done by *God*?"[111] This quite rightly provoked the critique among his listeners that Barth's own positive vision also rested on a religious foundation—"that is, at that moment at which

105. Ibid., 581.
106. Ibid., 112.
107. Ibid., 268.
108. Ibid., 111. If, however, the dialectic were hypothetically consistent, what would be gained in the final synthesis? The quotation continues, "The final subjection to the wrath of God is faith in God's righteousness: and then God is known as the Unknown God."
109. Ibid., 157.
110. Ibid., 220. See 380–81: Jesus came "into this system which we can ultimately only interpret in biological categories, into this system which is ultimately only open to an understanding in economic and materialistic terms, which we call history."
111. "ChrSoc," 69.

Christians gain certainty *where* they have seen the living God at work."[112] Yet "ChrSoc" also advocated an "*absolute* criticism of life." However, this implies precisely the opposite of what the lecture then goes on to assert: "We can recognize the *analogy* of the *divine* in the *worldly* things that surround us."[113]

Rom I argued that this concern is indeed exempt from God's judgment: "Of that which we are in and of ourselves (Rom. 7:25b)—of that question ('The Christian and Sin') o let fiends of hell hold nightly converse!"[114] In *Rom* II, by contrast, precisely "that question" is of the utmost importance. Maintaining its critical edge, *Rom* II does not recognize a fundamental renewal of Christian morality in the power of the resurrection. Repeatedly, Jesus' cross is said to imply that a "parable" of the resurrection consists in nothing less than physical death.[115]

As religion does not lead us out of sin, God's sending God's Son "can only be circumscribed in the strongest negations."[116] Barth speaks of the "force with which the resurrection works death."[117] While he calls the resurrection "the positive entity in the most pronounced sense,"[118] under worldly circumstances, this position can only assert itself in its negative flip side. In the message of the resurrection, God reveals God's self as "the unknown God living in light so brilliant that no human can approach him."[119] Facing a

112. Thus, one of the organizers of the Tambach conference, Otto Herpel, about the lecture. O. H., "Berichte und Urteile über die Tambacher Konferenz," 1, quoted after Marquardt, *Christ in der Gesellschaft*, 27. See also ibid., 34–5.
113. "ChrSoc," 56.
114. *Rom* I, 308, an allusion to P. Wernle, *Der Christ und die Sünde bei Paulus* and a quotation derived from Johann Wolfgang von Goethe, *Iphigenia in Tauris*.
115. *Rom* II, 280: "'Death [becomes] the only (the only!) parable of the kingdom of heaven." See also 220, 230, 619.
116. Ibid., 381.
117. Ibid., 271. Barth attributes also to the resurrection what in 2 Corinthians Paul attributes to the perverted law as opposed to the Spirit. See also 293, 278–9.
118. Ibid., 270.
119. Ibid., 74.

radical alienation between God and world, Barth arrives at drastic statements: the human world is "chaos" in the pejorative sense, life is doomed and utterly senseless: "human life is an illusion," a "union with God" is real only "beyond birth and death."[120] God and world are in no sense positively related. The "righteousness of God" "is the denial of the human person."[121] More positive statements about the hope for the Spirit and redemption are categorically relativized in order to nip in the bud even a faint appearance of a worldly triumph: "The promise kills the human person and everything human, so that they live for God. The church, of all things, must not evade this dying. It is precisely the dying that really lives by this promise, in the reflection of the fulfillment that approaches eternally, beyond life and death."[122] Faced with the world in which Jesus appeared, the father of Jesus Christ is characterized by a radical worldlessness.[123] The contradiction that this God is present nonetheless in Christ is resolved with the statement that Christ embodies the radical critique and negation of the world. A divine presence in the world that is more than fleeting and paradoxical is beyond *Rom* II. Admittedly, *Rom* II does call God the origin (*Ursprung*) of the world. Yet its fall is so radical that even this origin is incommensurate to the world. Now God can face the world only as entirely different.[124] In comparison to

120. Ibid., 60. The affirmation of a relation with God "beyond birth and death" (see also 76) is a fundamental negation of creation. See also 284, 430, 630.

121. Ibid., 202.

122. Ibid., 470–71. Cornelis van der Kooi, *Anfängliche Theologie: Der Denkweg des jungen Karl Barth (1909–1927)*, Beiträge zur evangelischen Theologie 103 (Munich: Kaiser, 1987), 194 adduces *Rom* II, 470 to argue that Barth articulates a careful sense of hope. Yet the quotation above follows on the heels of that passage, negating any hope for this life.

123. McCormack, *Barth's Theology*, 244 approvingly cites Ruschke's judgment that a statement may be one-sided and still true. Werner M. Ruschke, *Entstehung und Ausführung der Diastasentheologie in Karl Barths zweitem 'Römerbrief'* (Neukirchen-Vluyn: Neukirchener, 1987), 6. Yet in the same breath, McCormack judges, "Above all, the second edition is radical in its one-sidedness," like "all heresies worth their salt."

124. This is not in contrast to Barth's statement, "God's judgment and righteousness warrant God's most authentic immanence precisely in God's true transcendence" (*Rom* II, 162; see Busch, *Barth und die Pietisten*, 92). God is immanent to the world only as its primal origin, from

the cross, mention of Christ's physical resurrection is rather disparate at best,[125] as is the view that "this is what *krisis* means: negation and affirmation, death and life of the human person."[126]

Although the main impulse of *Rom* II is aggressively negative, a helpful aspect can nonetheless be seen in Barth's typical nature metaphors. To begin with, *Rom* II virtually always highlights the negative side of the experience of nature:

> How come modern people have this strange longing to experience the glaciers . . . the desert, the North Pole . . . the abyss of the infinitely great and the infinitely small, the terrible events of the past millions of years . . . the longing to experience and know a thousand things, which human persons would indeed not wish to experience and know, if they are immediately concerned with life itself, in an unbroken spirit.[127]

Barth thus deals with the topic of the sublime, sensitive to what Friedrich Schiller saw evoking both "woefulness" and "joyfulness."[128] A partner in conversation with Schiller was another intellectual lodestar of the young Barth, Immanuel Kant.[129] The notion of the

which, however, the world has become alienated. The "radicalism" of God's negation of the world must be understood "entirely radically." The negation cannot subsist alongside anything positive (*Rom* II, 160). The concept of God as the origin of the world is so radical that even the most pronounced contrast between God and world does not alter this relation—which thus must be conceived of in *entirely* abstract terms. Christians "are not relieved from the obligation to carry the *entire* burden of sin and the *entire* curse of death" (61).

125. See, for example, *Rom* II, 280. But see also 283–4: "The concept of the *resurrection* emerges with the concept of *death*, which means, however, with the concept of the end of all historical things as such. Christ as the physically *risen* one is always face-to-face with the physically *crucified* Christ and nothing else. . . . He is revealed and visible as the new human person . . . to the extent that he has given up on all visible, human, historical possibilities . . . in order to die. ... His resurrection is the non-historical event par excellence. . . . Obviously, *we* are *not* the ones who call this life 'our' life; obviously, this knowledge can be concrete only as the knowledge of our death."

126. *Rom* II, 101. However, the "negation" of the world must be complete, as is made clear shortly before, see 99–100.

127. Ibid., 420–21.

128. Friedrich Schiller, "Concerning the Sublime," in *Essays*, trans. Walter Hinderer and Daniel O. Dahlstrom, The German Library (New York: Continuum, 1993), 70–85; Frederick Beiser, *Schiller as Philosopher: A Re-Examination* (Oxford: Clarendon Press, 2005), 257–62.

129. According to Kant, the sublime challenges the mind to abstract from inclinations, thus

sublime resurfaces in Rudolf Otto's influential phenomenology of religion *The Idea of the Holy* (1917), which Barth had read "with considerable pleasure" in 1919.[130] *Rom* II, by contrast, interprets the sublime exclusively as calling the human person into question: "The understanding of what is characteristic of God is lost: the awareness of the ice crevice, the polar zone, the zone of desolation."[131] A critical perspective on the sublime is relevant since, for example, fascination and terror have often been experienced simultaneously in war. Tödt, for instance, described his experience of World War II in such terms.[132]

Part of the reason that *Rom* II is especially preoccupied with negating the sense of awe arising out of the experience of terror in nature is that *Rom* II advocates a priority of the law over the gospel, as will be argued in greater detail below. We might ask whether the experience of terror in nature or in history opens the door to a "natural theology," if indeed God's judgment precedes God's mercy. Later in his theological development, Barth would respond by rejecting the priority of the law. *Rom* II, by contrast, negates any legitimacy of the interest in the terrors of nature or history in the first place.

On the whole, the worldview of *Rom* II—a renunciation of "every hope in *this* world and in *this* heaven"[133]—resembles that which Hans Jonas described as gnosis.[134] To what extent does the gnostic mindset

provoking freedom. Immanuel Kant, *Critique of Judgment*, trans. Werner S. Pluhar (Indianapolis and Cambridge: Hackett, 1987), 121.

130. Rudolf Otto, *The Idea of the Holy: An Inquiry into the Non-rational Factor in the Idea of the Divine and Its Relation to the Rational*, trans. John W. Harvey, 7th ed. (Oxford: Oxford University Press, 1936, German 1917). Barth, letter to Thurneysen (June 3, 1919) in *Barth-Thurneysen-Briefwechsel 1913–21*, 329–32, at 330.

131. *Rom* II, 76, see 291, 470.

132. Tödt, *Der verlorene Haufe,* in Schuhmacher, *Verantwortungsethik*, 53. See Tödt, 181/ Schuhmacher, 54: "Negating this 'aesthetic' side of the war would be unrealistic and, for those that have experienced it, hypocritical."

133. *Rom* II, 100.

considers sacraments, mysticism, and ethics meaningful in a dark world, or do they give way to nihilism? Jonas argues that these are

> secondary questions compared to the more urgent discovery that the fundamental approach of *any* existential ethics which might be possible in this area stipulates radical *negation* rather than the development within the natural and the human dimension. This creates . . . a lack of relationship, which does not tolerate any active subject of continuous self-realization to replace the passive subject of "dying" and "rebirth," of discontinuous transformation.[135]

It is certainly relevant at this point that Barth's categorical, critical language does not protect him from the impression that he negates the material world: "That which 'is' must be recognized as that which is not, so that that which is not can come into view as that which is."[136] The most striking parallel between *Rom* II and gnostic thought, however, is the gnostic notion of the transcendent redeemer who imparts knowledge by appearing in the world and then disappears into the transcendent realm—thus indicating God's worldlessness.[137]

134. See Benjamin Lazier, *God Interrupted: Heresy and the European Imagination between the World Wars* (Princeton: Princeton University Press, 2008), 41. Hans Urs von Balthasar, *The Theology of Karl Barth: Exposition and Interpretation*, trans. Edward T. Oakes, SJ, Communio Books (San Francisco: Ignatius, 1992), 71, also calls *Rom* II gnostic. Compared with Christoph Markschies's more historically minded typology of gnostic literature, there is no ontological hierarchy of divine figures, including a demiurge, and no distinction of classes among humans in *Rom* II. *Rom* II may even call God the Creator of the universe, although this remains highly abstract. See Christoph Markschies, *Die Gnosis*, Beck'sche Reihe (Munich: Beck, 2001), 25–6. By contrast, Hans Jonas characterizes the subsumption of both matter and spirit in the realm of futility as the difference between gnosis and Platonism (see below).

135. Hans Jonas, *Gnosis und spätantiker Geist: Die mythologische Gnosis*, 3rd ed. (Göttingen: Vandenhoeck & Ruprecht, 1964), 200; see 144–5: "The great equation 'world = darkness' (*kosmos—skotos*) arises out of a new experience of the world, of which it is the most condensed expression. It is of an entirely different, constitutive universality than the notion 'body = grave' (*sōma—sēma*) that emerged from Greek culture, in orphism, yet which nonetheless could be integrated into a positive worldview . . . 'psyche' itself, now understood no longer in contrast to the lowly matter of the body, is conceptualized with withering clarity as a function of that dark cosmos. Human will, once it is faced with the options presented by the world, feels that with any self-actualization through choosing one of them, repeatedly reveals nothing other than its slavery to the world as such."

136. *Rom* II, 194.

Hans Urs von Balthasar summarized the theological problem with *Rom* II thus: "We see how the very heart of Christianity, its most crucial doctrine, the Incarnation, becomes impossible."[138] Even sympathetic readers of *Rom* II such as Michael Beintker, Bruce McCormack, and Cornelis van der Kooi concede this latter point.[139]

At the same time von Balthasar's interpretation of *Rom* II is less than balanced in at least one respect. He argues that *Rom* II views the world in a fundamentally critical way, mostly as an independent entity vis-à-vis God. Yet von Balthasar takes Jesus' death on the cross fully into account only in the last section of his book on Barth, considering it the necessary consequence of the world's futility. *Rom* II, however, views the cross not only as the consequence of the world's futility, but primarily as its revelation: Christ "bridges the distance between God and the human person by ripping it open."[140] In spite of the one-sidedness of *Rom* II, it is a positive aspect that the cross is not romanticized and "adorned with roses."[141] Instead, the harshness of the cross is perceived as the blunt consequence and sign of alienation. Although the realization of scandalous suffering induces a reflex in Barth that negates the world that imposes such suffering, at the same time we are warned against belittling the passion. To be sure, this aspect is explicated in a one-sided way: Jesus

137. See Markschies, *Gnosis,* 25, 73, 92, Jonas, *Gnosis*, 124–6, 408.

138. Von Balthasar, *Theology of Karl Barth*, 72.

139. Cornelis van der Kooi, "Barths zweiter Römerbrief," 70, 75, McCormack, *Barth's Theology*, 264.

140. *Rom* II, 53. Von Balthasar's interpretation of *Rom* II alludes to the cross only on 70, 72.

141. This image by Goethe, which corresponds to ideas in Luther and Hegel, was picked up, for example, by Hans Joachim Iwand: "The cross is the absolutely incommensurate dimension in God's revelation. It has become too much used to us, we are hardly stumbling against it anymore. We adorned the scandal of the cross with roses. We turned it into a theory of salvation. But that is not the cross. . . . Hegel defined the cross, saying, 'God is dead.' Presumably he was right in identifying the night of true and ultimate separation from God, which cannot be interpreted." Hans Joachim Iwand, "Tod und Auferstehung: Christologie II, Bonn 1959," in *Christologie: Die Umkehrung des Menschen zur Menschlichkeit*, eds. Eduard Lempp and Eberhard Thaidigsmann (Gütersloh: Kaiser/Gütersloher Verlagshaus, 1999), 291–433, 407. See Johann Wolfgang von Goethe, "Die Geheimnisse: Ein Fragment": "Es steht das Kreuz mit Rosen dicht umschlungen. / Wer hat dem Kreuze Rosen zugesellt?"

"is the End of the human person."[142] While the crucified Christ is the "transparent image," the "incognito" of God's new world,[143] the cross is also the sign of the "the absolute (and not just a relative) otherness of God."[144] The hidden God is revealed in the Son and still remains the hidden God ("correcting here what was written in the first edition of this book"[145]). For the Son reveals the hidden God in a world that in the cross turns out to be the world of death. To be sure, it is theologically legitimate and necessary to speak of God's revelation of God's hiddenness.[146] The fundamental difficulty in *Rom* II, however, is that God's hiddenness, along with God's judgment on humanity, eclipses the revelation of the gospel. It is for this reason that von Balthasar's judgment about creation in *Rom* II is right after all: "Though the world (which is faced with the word of God) is certainly something and not nothing, it looks so forlorn and hopeless under this harsh glare [in *Rom* II] that one might as well wish it did not exist."[147] In the cross, the negation, the reality of God's salvation takes on worldly form, while in its nonworldly, eschatological form it is real in Christ's resurrection. In the face of the fundamental and definitive negation of the world, the salvific aspect

142. This phrase occurs in *Rom* II, 206, 258, 689. 50 calls Jesus the "end of time."

143. Ibid., 442.

144. Ibid., 222 (Barth's parenthesis).

145. Ibid., 595.

146. See Eberhard Jüngel's emphasis on human joy in God's revelation, which crucially includes an abiding hiddenness, in "The Revelation of the Hiddenness of God: A Contribution to the Protestant Understanding of the Hiddenness of Divine Action," in *Theological Essays* II, trans. Arnold Neufeldt-Fast (New York: Bloomsbury/T&T Clark, 2014), 120–44, "Die Offenbarung der Verborgenheit Gottes: Ein Beitrag zum evangelischen Verständnis der Verborgenheit des göttlichen Wirkens," in *Wertlose Wahrheit: Zur Identität und Relevanz des christlichen Glaubens*, Theologische Erörterungen III (München: Kaiser 1990), 163–82, at 169. In Jüngel's essay, however, the sense of joy about God's revelation, in which certain aspects remain hidden, is jeopardized by his adherence to Luther's fundamental conviction that God kills in order to make alive (ibid., 173; 1 Sam. 2:6), a statement that also plays an important role in *Rom* II. Jüngel seeks to redress the balance by negating a dark side in God (Jüngel, ibid., 195–6). This leaves God's undialectical being at variance with God's dialectical action, which emphatically includes "gruesome aspects" (ibid., 174, 175).

147. Von Balthasar, *Theology of Karl Barth*, 94 (trans. rev.).

of the cross can only be expressed in an escapist way. Thus one can only embrace salvation indirectly in accepting its shadow side, the cross, as the critical negation of oneself.[148] Ultimately, however, *Rom* II does not simply wish for the world to cease to exist, but argues that Christians, as part of the world, must symbolize the necessary passing away of the world in their own lives. For this reason, faith is not a positive testimony to another reality, but a "void."[149] Only in negating themselves and affirming the fundamental weakness of their epistemological powers can Christians assume a posture that is appropriate vis-à-vis God. With human self-negation, the proper correspondence to Christ's cross that acknowledges God's reality within the confines of what is radically distinct from God, *Rom* II transcends a mere antithesis of human opinions and God's reality, articulating a relationship that is, however, of an utterly critical kind.[150] This is what Barth calls the primary ethical activity.

148. *Rom* II, 217 goes to great lengths to argue for embracing salvation in spite of judgment: "Love of God is the impossible act in which the creature loves the creator; the condemned one loves the judge; the vanquished, even the slain one loves the enemy; the sacrifice loves the priest who sacrifices it—only because God, *as* all of this and *in* all of this, is God, and because it would be still more impossible not to love God."

149. Ibid., 49, 56, 59, 86, etc.

150. According to Spieckermann, *Gotteserkenntnis*, 129, it is Christ's cross that constitutes an analogy between world and God. Yet certainly the critical edge of the negation must not be overlooked: "No descriptive analogy can capture the holiness of the primal origin and end" (*Rom* II, 549). God's positive relation to the world is real, but it cannot take on concrete form in the world; the negation of all worldly possibilities points to this fact, which thus, in this negative form, might be said to point indirectly to something positive. McCormack highlights the analogy of the cross at times (McCormack, *Barth's Theology*, 8, 261, 340). Yet what he considers decisive (ibid., 252) is that the resurrection was a spatio-temporal event, even if not according to the standards of what is possible in this world. Thus, McCormack interprets *Rom* II in the sense that the *resurrection* creates an analogy between historical entities and God, in contrast to Spieckermann's preoccupation with the analogy of the *cross*. This former kind of analogy is, however, of an actualistic nature (ibid., 254; 262). The resurrection takes place in spite of the stark contrast between world and God. Indeed *Rom* II, 280 speaks of Christ as "the bodily, physically, personally risen one." In this *Rom* II breaks through the problematic contrast of immanence and transcendence. On the whole, however, the interest of *Rom* II is not in a positive relationship, but in the establishing of difference, calling the resurrection "the non-historical event par excellence" (284). Jesus' life is compatible with human history only in the sense of a "*futurum resurrectionis*" (270, see below). McCormack omits Barth's explicit restrictions

One crucial passage in which Barth argues for the utterly critical stance as the only appropriate one *coram Deo* (before God) is the interpretation of Romans 6. In a letter to Eduard Thurneysen, Barth called this chapter "the axle around which the entire letter revolves."[151] According to Rom. 6:4, Christians should "walk in newness of life" in order to correspond practically to being buried with Christ in baptism. Barth's previous interpretation in *Rom* I called baptism the warrant for the truth and the reality of the eschatological renewal of the present life. However, in a letter Barth now calls this view "surprisingly useless."[152] *Rom* II, by contrast, presents the aorist subjunctive *peripatēsōmen* ("[now] let us walk," Rom. 6:4) as a future subjunctive, which supposedly implies the strict transcendence of the new life.[153] In this world, the future will never become the present. This leads Barth to coin a new grammatical concept, a *futurum resurrectionis*, or *aeternum*, "future of the resurrection," or "eternal future."[154] In consequence, the new eschatological life does not have any temporal extension.

in quotations from *Rom* II (see *Rom* II, 271 in McCormack, *Barth's Theology*, 258; *Rom* II, 284 in McCormack, *Barth's Theology*, 257). As Jesus' resurrection is nonhistorical, so is the new ethos of Rom. 6:4 nonhistorical. This is the "deadly [*sic!*] and incommensurable power of the Resurrection," which "protrudes into my *continuing in sin*" (*Rom* II, 271). By contrast, van der Kooi, "Barths zweiter Römerbrief," interprets the new life in *Rom* II in a strictly forensic sense, but he argues that *Rom* II retreats to a different dimension than that of history, which has remained "a weakness" (ibid., 70).

151. *Barth-Thurneysen-Briefwechsel 1913–21*, 477 (March 18, 1921).

152. Ibid.

153. *Rom* II, 270. See Barth's letter to Thurneysen from March 18, 1921 (*Barth-Thurneysen-Briefwechsel 1913–21*, 477). By contrast, Ernst Käsemann comments on Rom. 6:4, "The aorist subjunctive possibly replaces a logical future. . . . Yet the eschatological futures in vv. 5b and 8b are against this. . . . The verb *peripatein* should call attention to the fact that the apostle expects our resurrection only in the future and, as vv. 12–23 show, sees in the new obedience an anticipation of it and the sign of the already present reality of its power." Ernst Käsemann, *Commentary on Romans*, trans. Geoffrey W. Bromiley (Grand Rapids: Eerdmans, 1980), 166–7.

154. *Rom* II, 270–72. Barth writes openly to Thurneysen that an exegetical predicament was the mother of invention (*Barth-Thurneysen-Briefwechsel 1913–21*, 477, March 18, 1921). See Beintker, *Die Dialektik*, 41–5: *Rom* II is characterized by a "dehistoricization of the salvific event, which is palpable throughout" (ibid., 44).

> The "walking in newness of life" characterizes of the new "I," which has been created anew in Christ, as being allowed, able, obliged and willing. It confirms my citizenship in heaven (Phil. 3:20) and constitutes the vitality of my life, which is hidden with Christ in God (Col. 3:3). The "walking in newness of life" is the invisible center of perspective and pole of relationship, the judgment which the invisible aspect of my life brings upon the visible aspect, the threat and promise, which—in a non-concrete, a-temporal manner—is valid beyond *all* concrete and temporal events of "my" life. It is valid *beyond* all of them because and to the extent that world is world, time is time, and the human person is human. The eternal future of my "walking in newness of life," which, in radical exclusivity, protrudes into my "continuing in sin" as the deadly and incommensurate power of the resurrection, is the meaning and, at the same time, the critique of my temporal being, thinking, and willing.[155]

Barth builds on this presupposition when he argues that Christians *are* new persons "only if the *futurum resurrectionis—we shall live*—presupposes a new 'we' as the reverse of dying with Christ."[156] Thus, the new ethos is not a positive presence, but objection to the old. In accordance, Barth understands Rom. 7:6—"But now we are discharged from the law" (*katērgēthēmen tou nomou*)—to say that the current ethos continues to be under categorical judgment; Christians are "liberated" from the law, however, insofar as they do not attribute any ultimate importance to the current state of affairs.[157]

His interpretation of Rom. 6:4 set the course for this view. In that verse, however, the question is less how plausible the "aspect" of a *futurum resurrectionis* may seem; the fundamental problem is that there is no such thing as a future subjunctive in Greek, whatever the

155. *Rom* II, 271. On the new life protruding (*hineinragen*) into life in sin like a rock, see Kant, *Critique of Judgment*, 120 ("On Nature as a [Force]"): "Consider bold, overhanging and, as it were, threatening rocks . . . the sight of them becomes all the more attractive the more fearful it is, provided we are in a safe place." On Barth's engagement with the subject of the sublime, see above. Barth's re-configuration of the sublime aims at subverting any theological import of the experience of nature, thus restoring God's judgment as the only sublime event in the theological sense of the term.

156. *Rom* II, 284.

157. Ibid., 327.

aspect.[158] The verb is an ingressive aorist. Paul chose this aspect to convey that the new "walking" is becoming a reality not in some future, much less in some unattainable future, but right now.

In the face of this "eternal future," there is a remarkable—and, ironically, oft-quoted—comment of Barth's from 1940 that looks back to *Rom* II:

> It was due to the inner and outer circumstances of these years that the divine No of judgment, now understood as a No directed both to the present position and to all possible and attempted religious and cultural developments, had to be expressed more loudly, and certainly more clearly heard, than the gracious Yes that we believed we genuinely heard, and genuinely wished to express, from the end, the real end, of all things.[159]

Rom II argued for a relation of God to time that seemed posttemporal, but was in fact supratemporal. By contrast, *CD* II/1 argues, "The conceptions of God's pre-temporality, supra-temporality, and post-temporality have all to be emphasised in their different ways. But they are not to be played off the one against the other, as if God could be better known and were to be taken more seriously under one of these forms and less so or not at all under another."[160]

It is remarkable, however, that, as late as 1940, even this self-critical comment fails to go to the heart of the matter. Barth now refines God's extratemporality, but he cannot bring himself to attribute temporal being itself to God. This is the decisive problem already in *Rom* II, according to which God is temporal in Christ only insofar as God leaves the temporal mode of existence behind in the cross.

This problem is also relevant in ethics, for *Rom* II calls for a

158. Friedrich Blass and Albert Debrunner, *A Greek Grammar of the New Testament and Other Early Christian Literature,* trans. Robert W. Funk (Chicago: Chicago University Press, 1961), 15. There is no textual variant to the aorist, according to *Novum Testamentum Graece*, 27th ed.

159. Barth, *CD* II/1, 634.

160. Ibid., 631.

correspondence to the negation of the world in an act of sacrifice.[161] "If an *ethics* is at issue, nothing else is possible than a *critique* of all ethos."[162] The cross does not, in justification, constitute the dignity of good action. While *Rom* I argued that the question for right action distracts from its being carried out—"'What am I to do?' Answer: First of all stop asking like this!"[163]—*Rom* II makes an about-face: "What, then, are we to do? . . . First and foremost, *ask this question*! May God preserve for us *this question*! May God encircle us with it, as a question, on every side and rob us of all answers that are anything else than, again, questions!"[164] While Barth previously spoke of a "guarantee that . . . the work of God's will for salvation is no tower of Babel of unredeemed humanity,"[165] *Rom* II calls the "organic growth," with which God creates a new ethos in the church, a "tower of Babel."[166] The prevailing emphasis on the cross in *Rom* II increases his skepticism against worldly reasoning and human epistemological powers: "When would our worst enemies have been concerned subjectively with anything but—doing what is objectively right?"[167]

161. Rowan Williams, "Barth, War and the State," in *Reckoning with Barth: Essays in Commemoration of the Centenary of Karl Barth's Birth*, ed. Nigel Biggar (London: Mowbray, 1988), 170–90, 176–7.

162. *Rom* II, 576. To some extent, this statement confirms Trutz Rendtorff's thesis that Barth wishes for a "suspension" of human action in general. Trutz Rendtorff, *Theorie des Christentums: Historisch-theologische Studien zu seiner neuzeitlichen Verfassung* (Gütersloh: Gütersloher Verlagshaus, 1972), 170. But in contrast to Rendtorff's interpretation, Barth's skepticism is less about God's radical autonomy under worldly conditions than about the world's passing away.

163. *Rom* I, 263.

164. *Rom* II, 348.

165. *Rom* I, 368: "*Kein alt-menschlicher Babelsturm.*"

166. *Rom* II, 582.

167. Ibid., 634, see 629: Barth portrays the human condition as entirely unfavorable ("obstinate," "extravagant quirks," "obdurate," "entirely unlovable"), so that people must be "restrained" by God with "no energy left," so they are unable to commit hostilities. Barth calls the human situation "always stuck," thus alluding to the "realist" ethics of the "stuck situation" ("*Ethik der verfahrenen Situation*") of *Rom* I, in which Christians were counseled to follow a pragmatic worldly ethics.

The legitimate interest in this statement is to question supposedly objective justifications of violence. In *CD* III/4, for example, Barth will confront supposedly noble moral justifications of war with the claim that usually war is about economic interest.[168] While moral justifications for the use of force are sometimes criticized as covertly following the maxim, "might is right," the question must also be raised how an alternative position can escape the same problem. As Socrates's sophist opponents once concluded in opposition to moral realism, and as, for example, Paul Althaus once indirectly admitted, if moral realism is as radically questioned as in *Rom* II, the surrogate of "right," to the extent that it is effective in society, will still turn out to be constituted by might.[169]

Moreover, Barth's skepticism of worldly reason is, again with a grain of truth, directed against a strict autonomy of functional spheres of society.[170] In "ChrSoc," the relative appreciation of secular action rested on the hope vested in God's hidden action within history. Thus Barth even argued that Christians cannot *not* know what to do. But while "ChrSoc" saw the potential of each secular sphere for serving as a parable of God's action, *Rom* II understands the notion of parable strictly in light of the cross. In contrast to "ChrSoc," *Rom* II argues that God's action can only be experienced negatively. "We must not overlook that the second edition of Romans, as critical as it is towards all sides, also amounts to such self-criticism to a considerable

168. *CD* III/4, 452. This discussion of war, however, is not as categorical in its critique of war.

169. Plato, *Gorgias* 492a–b (Callicles); Paul Althaus, *Grundriss der Ethik*, 2nd ed. (Erlangen: Merkel, 1931), 107. This critique of Barth corresponds to Eckhard Lessing's diagnosis in his *Das Problem der Gesellschaft in der Theologie Karl Barths und Friedrich Gogartens* (Gütersloh: Gütersloher Verlagshaus Mohn, 1972), 102–3: Barth's contrast between time and eternity leads to a critique of a rationality of value.

170. There is no autonomous ethics for "the public office, profession, and politics" (*Rom* II, 580, see 576–7), and the orders of "state, church, law, society, etc." are under God's judgment (621, 638).

extent."[171] The only legitimate parable to the kingdom of God now consists in a sacrifice.[172]

Due to the change in meaning of the central concepts, the notion of sacrifice gives a new meaning to the notion of parable in *Rom* II. Sacrifice and closely related terms appear increasingly in the chapter on the ethical section of Romans 12–15, "The Great Disturbance."[173] Romans 12:1, 15:7 indeed suggest speaking of sacrifice. Yet Barth inculcates the futility of all human action in a much more drastic way than demanded by Paul's texts. After all, Paul does not call for an absolute sacrifice of one's own demands and positions. Instead, Romans 12 is about being moderate in accordance with the "participation in faith as the estate of the Christian man, which God has given specifically to each as a grant-in-aid of grace, i.e., as *charisma*."[174]

There are other interpreters of Barth, however, who claim that *Rom* II already prepares the ground for Barth's later subordination of the law to the gospel.[175] If this is the case, Barth's critique should be considered less harsh than presented here. However, a recent examination of Barth's sermons from the early 1920s found his preaching to be in line with a Lutheran understanding of law and gospel, even though the analysis presupposed without further discussion that the theology of *Rom* II is in contrast to that.[176] This calls into question how deep the roots of Barth's later rearrangement

171. Busch, "Fragen," ch. 2, ninth paragraph. *Pace* McCormack, *Barth's Theology*, 253.

172. See van der Kooi, *Theologie*, 195.

173. This is the location of forty-two of the sixty-nine occurrences of the word *sacrifice* in *Rom* II.

174. Ernst Käsemann, "Worship and Everyday Life: A Note on Romans 12," in *New Testament Questions of Today*, trans. W. J. Montague (London: S.C.M., 1969), 188–95, at 192.

175. See especially Beintker's contributions mentioned below. For an overview, see Jones, "Rhetoric of War," 99.

176. André Demut, *Evangelium und Gesetz: Eine systematisch-theologische Reflexion zu Karl Barths Predigtwerk*, Theologische Bibliothek Töpelmann 145 (Berlin and New York: 2006), 348. Jones, "Rhetoric of War," 93 argues that *Rom* II exploits drastic, bellicose imagery to drive home its anthropology: the human person is "judged and saved by God."

of the law and gospel constellation really are. If *Rom* II prepared the ground for Barth's later reordering in terms of gospel and law, the commentary would have relativized God's judgment with God's grace. Occasionally, Barth does point to the *forgiveness* of sins in arguing for a new kind of ethics—albeit a very specific kind of ethics—which is a hallmark of the new position of gospel and law.[177] At these points, however, Barth does not speak about the law, and *Rom* II imposes strict limitations on a new constitution of moral agency. Even Lutherans such as Werner Elert or Paul Althaus argued that action should be based on justification.[178] Barth's view is in some ways similar to Luther's position that the living gospel, at least for the moment and in a particular sense, excludes the validity of the law.[179] *Rom* II portrays human piety as being close to the law, which is radically called into question by Christ, however. Law and religion are ambiguous: in the penultimate realm of the world, religion can and should point to the absolute, yet at the same time this leads to the confusion of relative and absolute things.[180] The law points to what is essentially good, yet conveys a false sense of security. Thus the effect of truly recognizing God is always an extremely harsh self-criticism in the first place. *Rom* II speaks of God's "assault" and "attack" on humanity, even of an "absolute assault."[181] "Our life in this world

177. *Rom* II, 580, see McCormack, *Barth's Theology*, 239; Ruschke, *Entstehung*, 73.

178. Wolf Krötke, *Das Problem 'Gesetz und Evangelium' bei W. Elert und P. Althaus*, (Zurich: Evangelischer Verlag, 1965), 17–18; 26–8. According to P. Althaus, the third use of the law is not in contrast to Luther's theology (ibid.).

179. For example, commenting on Rom. 7:6, *Rom* II, 326 voices the classic Lutheran position of an antagonism between gospel and law: "Still standing in the shadow of *the law,* we already see this 'but now!' (3:21) in the light (in the light of the uncreated light!), we see the law and its dialectics as that which is done away with." On Luther, see Albrecht Peters, *Gesetz und Evangelium*, Handbuch systematischer Theologie 2 (Gütersloh: Gütersloher Verlagshaus Mohn, 1981), 35–8; Eberhard Jüngel, "Gospel and Law: The Relationship of Dogmatics to Ethics," in *Barth: A Theological Legacy*, trans. Garrett E. Paul (Philadelphia: Westminster John Knox, 1986), 122–3.

180. See *Rom* II, esp. 323–8, 124, 454–5, 523.

181. Rom II speaks of God's "attack" on humans and God as an "attacker" in 104, 123, 245, 269,

has meaning only in its relation to the true God. But this relation can be established if our minds and hearts are broken . . . by the remembrance of eternity."[182] Such breaking of the heart had best take on cynical proportions:

> Is it not in an ultimate, worst skepticism perhaps, where nothing "noble" can find an entrance at all, where we are entirely unable to be impressed by anything at all that there may perhaps exist that *true brokenness* which is the sense for God, even for God's self?[183]

> The "work" that is pleasing to God is more likely to consist in the end, the complete end of all human righteousness in them [the justified

277, 298, 299 (six times), 262 ("lethal attack"), 268, 269 (twice), 288, 299, 303, 306, 311, 335, 394, 405, 505 ("absolute attack"), 523, 576 ("most radical attack"), 581 ("absolute attack"), 588, 625 ("fundamental attack"), 639, 645, 670, 674 (twice). See also Jones, "Rhetoric of War," 95–6. In Paul's Epistle to the Romans, by contrast, the language of attack is conspicuously absent. One may perhaps think of Gal. 5:17, but there the invasion of the Spirit in the congregation is said to have been transforming the congregation already, so that the "works of the flesh" are indeed "evident" —as listed in a rather conventional catalog of vices. Even in Galatians, "attack" would be an inappropriate category to summarize God's relation to the world on the whole. In comparison with the rhetorical immensity with which Barth portrays God's attack on humanity, little consolation can be drawn from the fact that in Jesus, God endured suffering first. Jones, "Rhetoric of War," 101 revises the translation of *Rom* II, 114 and points to Christ's solidarity with the world according to Barth. I doubt that Barth held this view, based on his original German phrasing (*Rom* II, 114: "*Die ganze Widergöttlichkeit des Geschichtsverlaufs*"; Jones: "the utter godforsakenness of the course of history"). But even if Christ's suffering works for salvation, it is crucial that at the same time it adds to the justification of God's attack, which in Barth's portrayal inflicts such severe wounds that neither must nor can be healed in this life. "The positive meaning of the Creator and the *eternal* meaning of the creature have never been recognized in any other way than in the negation of the creature" (*Rom* II, 124). The gospel may be described as "the negation of the negation" (for example, 194, 199, 214, 251, etc.), but in the face of God's abiding attack even this takes on a virtual character. A phenomenological priority of the law is often observed in scholarly descriptions of *Rom* II, for example in McCormack, *Barth's Theology*, 267: God "kills in order to make alive." This quotation from 1 Sam. 2:6 characteristically appears in Luther, *Bondage of the Will*, in *Career of the Reformer*, ed. Harold J. Grimm, Luther's Works 31 (Philadelphia: Muhlenberg Press: 1957), 3:62. Jüngel calls this verse Luther's standard reference for God's dual action of an alien and a proper work (Jüngel, "The Revelation of the Hiddenness": "Die Offenbarung der Verborgenheit," 173). See also Jones, "Rhetoric of War," 92–3. ("God's 'attack,' . . . a grace that kills and raises"). David Klemm, "Towards a Rhetoric of Postmodern Theology: Through Barth and Heidegger," *Journal of the American Academy of Religion* 55 (1987): 443–69, at 452–3; 463–4, sees in Barth's statement that hidden under God's no is God's yes, a parallel to Heidegger's notion that fear of death opens up the possibility of facing being properly.

182. *Rom* II, 47.

183. Ibid., 98.

> "pagans"], in the fact that they are certainly lost. . . . All that is left is perhaps really only naked humanity in its last stages (Dostoevsky!). Perhaps there is only one ultimate evil affliction, embarrassment, and destitution. Perhaps no more than some last terror before the mystery, in the hour of death, some indignant uprising against the inevitability of our subsistence and existence, a person falling silent in bitterness, leaving the venue in protest.[184]

To be sure, Barth's attention to misery and destitution is also motivated by a deep theological appreciation of the human factor in all its dignity, present even where dominant culture turns its back on people or reduces them to mere objects of condescension.[185] At the same time, however, Barth's description of God's special attention to the downtrodden acquires normative force in a different sense. The point is not to empower the downtrodden and to enable them to transform their misery. A legitimate sense of awe before the divine requires an absolute end to all human aspirations ("naked humanity in its last stages"). God's Son was emphatically not sent into this world in order "to change anything in this world of ours."[186]

As a result, misery itself appears in an advantageous light.[187] The aspect of transformation will require further consideration later on. But insisting on the vicarious nature of Christ's suffering would be contrary to Barth's intentions: "Persons suffer from God [*sic*], because they require to be healed by God."[188]

> The most radical finishing off of history, the negation under which all flesh comes to stand, the absolute judgment, which is the meaning

184. Ibid., 100.
185. See, for example, ibid., 494.
186. Ibid., 381 (trans. rev.).
187. Hong Liang argues in his dissertation on Dostoevsky's influence on the early Barth and early Thurneysen that Barth, while interpreting the Grand Inquisitor in a sense highly critical of the institutional church, misses the constructive role Dostoevsky attributes to the question of theodicy articulated by Ivan (*The Brothers Karamazov*, book 5, sections 4–5). Hong Liang, *Leben vor den letzten Dingen*, PhD diss., Tübingen: 2015, ch. 5, §1.
188. *Rom* II, 517 ("Weil sie an Gott genesen sollen, sind sie an Gott krank").

> of God for the world of humanity and time and things, is also the continuous theme which characterizes the entire subsistence and existence of the world. But when the corruptible is recognized as such, it *is* the parable of incorruption. To submit finally to God's wrath is to have faith in God's righteousness. For this is to *know* God as the *unknown* God.[189]

From the macro perspective as well, Barth's ecclesiological chapters on Romans 9–11 give classic expression to the Lutheran priority of the law over the gospel: "The Tribulation of the Church" (ch. 9), "The Guilt of the Church" (ch. 10), "The Hope of the Church" (ch. 11). Indeed, the law[190] fulfills the *usus elenchticus legis*, before which the church stands accused.[191] But then again, not even the notion of a recognition of sin induced by the cross differs significantly from Lutheran theology.[192] Although Luther argued against a recognition of sin induced by the *gospel*, the gospel by itself does not exhaust the meaning of the cross, which indeed Paul proclaimed as causing doubt among Jews and Greeks. As God does not work God's *opus proprium*

189. Ibid., 112. The approach of seeing temporal things as a parable even as they are condemned absolutely is vulnerable to objections of any sort. But even then Barth does not allow for knowledge of God but only brings himself to an affirmation of the Unknown God.
190. See ibid., 338.
191. Ibid., 523. Luther, *Temporal Authority: To What Extent It Should Be Obeyed*, trans. J. J. Schindel, in *The Christian in Society*, ed. Walther I. Brandt, Luther's Works 45 (Philadelphia: Muhlenberg Press: 1962), 2:75–130, at 89–90, speaks of a twofold function of the law: it puts limits on the misdeeds of the unjust, creating a certain external political stability, and it also humbles them before God subjectively by revealing their sins to them (see Romans 7; Galatians 2). See also Luther, *Lectures on Galatians 1535: Chapters 1–4*, ed. and trans. Jaroslav Pelikan, Luther's Works 26 (Saint Louis: Concordia Publishing: 1963), 308–10. According to *Rom* II, 335, 338, the law condemns human disobedience as, in Nietzsche's contemptuous words, a "rising of slaves against the authority of God," and 522 says that God must be obeyed even and precisely as this implies a heteronomous element, that of God as "the King, the Monarch, the Despot."
192. Wilfried Joest, "Karl Barth und das lutherische Verständnis von Gesetz und Evangelium: Gedanken und Fragen zur Wiederaufnahme einer stehen gebliebenen Diskussion," *Kerygma und Dogma* 24 (1978): 86–103, at 88 argues that the law even as it reveals and condemns particular sins, is properly recognized in God's revelation in Jesus Christ. "The shift of the recognition of the law into the area of historical institutions and movements must, in my opinion, be judged as an ideological super-elevation [i.e., of relative entities] that changes what Luther had in mind as a general recognition of the law, the '*usus civilis*'" (ibid., 91).

(the work proper to God), according to Luther, without God's *opus alienum* (the work foreign to God), God's salvific revelation thus takes place "in the humility and shame of the cross."[193] The difficulty with this position is that a destructive aspect in God's action receives undue attention, sidetracking the quest for transformative and liberating aspects of God's work. This is precisely what justifies the present interest in the rival scheme of assigning the gospel priority over the law.

As God is said to both reveal and conceal God's self in the cross, the cross implies consolation and despair. In a similar way, Barth's notion of the hidden and the revealed God are rooted in Luther's theology of the cross, which implies a priority of the law.[194] It is in contrast to *Rom* II, however, when "GL" (1935) will explain that the law's accusation of sin must not be highlighted too strongly, as the prime use of the law consists in guiding the way to a practical correspondence to the gospel.[195]

Rom II also does not speak of a priority of grace in the Christian worldly experience. In contrast to a Lutheran understanding of "law and gospel," the affirmation of the human person refers, according to *Rom* II, to an ahistorical condition. Nonetheless, *Rom* II is closer to a Lutheran understanding of "law and gospel" than to Barth's later reinterpretation of the relationship between gospel and law.

193. Luther, *Heidelberg Disputation*, in Grimm, *Career of the Reformer*, 1:35–70, at 53 (thesis 20). See also 51 (thesis 16): "Thus an action which is alien to God's nature [*opus alienum Dei*] results in a deed belonging to his very nature [*opus eius proprium*]: he makes a person a sinner so that he may make him righteous."

194. See ibid., 53 (thesis 20): "Truly, thou art a God who hidest thyself" ("*Vere absconditus tu es Deus*").

195. On the *usus legis in renatis*, or *tertius usus legis*, see John Calvin, *Institutes of the Christian Religion*, ed. John T. McNeill, trans. John L. Battles, The Library of Christian Classics (Louisville: Westminster John Knox, 2006), 360–61 (II, 7, 12). Calvin calls the third use of the law the most important one (*praecipuus usus legis*): it reveals God's will to believers and urges them on. In consequence, the *usus elenchticus* would not be called the *usus theologicus legis* as in the Lutheran tradition. The *Institutes* discuss the *usus elenchticus legis* in II, 7, 6–9 (ibid., 354–8) and the *usus civilis legis* in II, 7, 10–11 (ibid., 358–60).

According to Barth's own testimony, it was after discussion with the ostentatiously Lutheran thinker F. Gogarten that the new outlines of *Rom* II emerged from *Rom* I, and he associates the thrust of the new edition especially with Luther's name.[196]

By contrast, Michael Beintker argues that the crisis motif in *Rom* II describes an "attack motivated by love,"[197] which prepares the way for a subordination of the law to the gospel.[198] With respect to God's self, the affirmation of the world has priority; it is only under worldly conditions that it must be perceived differently, as a negation. If a typical Lutheran concept of law and gospel indeed assumes a priority of judgment and thus locates an antithesis of judgment and grace *within* God's *eternal* self, rather than merely in worldly experience, then *Rom* II might be in greater proximity

196. *Barth-Thurneysen-Briefwechsel 1913–21*, 435 (Oct. 27, 1920): "And now for a strange and terrifying piece of news: Once Gogarten (with whom, by the way, I had several good talks, both during the day and at night, besides these excursions) had left, all of a sudden the *Epistle to the Romans* began to cast its own skin, i.e., I received the inspiration that it must by no means simply be printed in its current state. Instead, it must be reformed from top to bottom." Ibid., 448 (Dec. 3, 1920): "The turn from Osiander to Luther asserts itself against the first edition like a disaster."

197. Michael Beintker, "Krisis und Gnade: Zur theologischen Deutung der Dialektik beim frühen Barth," in *Krisis und Gnade: Gesammelte Studien zu Karl Barth*, eds. Stefan Holtmann and Peter Zocher (Tübingen: Mohr Siebeck, 2013), 22–39, at 28.

198. Matthias Haudel, "Das Verhältnis von Gesetz und Evangelium als innerprotestantische und interkonfessionelle Herausforderung," *Kerygma und Dogma* (2007): 230–49, at 235 asserts that Beintker had already shown how *Rom* II thinks along the lines of "GL." Yet this view makes Beintker's case more ambitious than Beintker's original article is. Beintker, "Krisis und Gnade," argues that in *Rom* II, grace rules "between the lines" (ibid., 35); when God's yes would be carried through, it remains "strangely abstract," unable to be conceived of as a temporal event; nor does Barth succeed in "appropriately bringing to the fore the christological foundations of this 'Yes'" (ibid., 36). To begin with, Beintker states that *Rom* II is not a theology of mere crisis (ibid., 25–6), arguing that God's judgment is rooted in God's grace. The article interprets this in part as grace preceding judgment and in part as a simultaneity of grace and judgment, which points to Barth's development in the direction of the gospel's priority over the law. At the same time judgment can also be presented as preceding grace (ibid., 26: "Insofar as God negates the human person in his or her current sin, this person can become the object of God's 'Yes.'") The texts adduced in favor of the priority of grace are not always cogent, sometimes they call God's yes directed at a world that is negated categorically (*Rom* II, 277). Ibid., 123–4: the comprehensive yes, in which the comprehensive no is rooted, is never real in this world. According to 236, Adam "is accepted by being negated in the Christ."

to Barth's later understanding of gospel and law. But there are prominent statements by Luther that call an ultimate priority of grace within God's self precisely the reason for a priority of the law in temporal experience.[199] An "attack," however, is hard to reconcile with a priority of the gospel. The injuries thus sustained may well call into question the trustworthiness of the attacker.

Barth's ethics lectures and *CD* II/2 will—quite in the spirit of Kantian autonomy—rightly invoke the classical humanist heritage against the legitimacy of what must seem like sheer power to the one thus attacked: "[Even] if the broken world-disc crashes, the ruins will strike him undaunted [nonetheless]."[200] This undercuts the meaningfulness of an attack of the law paving the way for the gospel. *CD* II/2 adds,

> Prometheus is justified against Zeus. . . . Man as man is still free in face of power as power. He can sink under it; he can be annihilated by it. But he does not owe it obedience, and even the most preponderant power cannot as such compel him to obey. . . . Power as power does not have

199. See Luther, *Lectures on Galatians 1535*, 310: "The proclamation of free grace and the forgiveness of sins does not enter into [the proud person's] heart and understanding. . . . To break and crush [this presumption of righteousness], God needs a large and powerful hammer, that is, the Law, which is the hammer of death. . . . Then the heart is crushed to the point of despair. This use and function of the Law is felt by terrified and desperate consciences, who yearn for death or want to inflict death on themselves because of the anguish of conscience." See Luther, *Bondage of the Will*, 3:61–3. Thus Beintker's quotation from Luther's *Bondage of the Will*, which is cited also in *Rom* II, highlights the ultimately salvific meaning of judgment: "Faith has to do with things not seen. Hence in order that there may be room for faith, it is necessary that everything which is believed should be hidden" (Luther, *Bondage of the Will*, 62, Barth, *Rom* II, 62; Beintker, "Krisis," 32). The prominence of the "unobservable" and the *deus absconditus* in *Rom* II corresponds to this statement of Luther's. For an objection to a fundamental dualism of law and gospel in Luther's thought, see also Ernstpeter Maurer, "Barth-Rezeption bei lutherischen Theologen in Deutschland," in *Karl Barths Theologie als europäisches Ereignis*, eds. Martin Leiner and Michael Trowitzsch (Göttingen: Vandenhoeck & Ruprecht, 2008), 367–86, at 376–84. On the priority of the law in Luther, Beintker comments that God's action in judgment and in mercy are more clearly structured into two different acts in Luther's thought, while Barth highlights the unity of the two. That statement seems to compare Barth with the diastasis of law and gospel in certain strands of German Lutheranism in the first half of the twentieth century.

200. *Si fractus illabatur orbis impavidum ferient ruinae* (Horace). Barth, *Ethics*, 95, *CD* II/2, 554.

> any divine claim, no matter how imposing or effective it might be. . . . To reserve himself against power as power, even to his own undoing, is not merely a possibility for man. . . . It is the duty which he has to fulfil with his existence as man.[201]

If God's word were first destructive, it would only challenge and attempt to defeat genuine human freedom, a freedom that Barth later recognizes as the true freedom of the gospel. Barth's notion that "persons suffer from God, because they require to be healed by God"[202] underestimates the human resourcefulness—even dignity—in reinterpreting such suffering as a painful refinement of their faithfulness to long-standing convictions. By contrast, if *Rom* II assigned priority over the gospel, one would expect Barth to emphasize transformation and liberation instead of destruction. Barth's later writings will call for a discussion of such questions in further detail.

In sum, it depends on the interpretation of Luther's complex writings whether or not it is in keeping with a Reformation understanding of law and gospel to say the suffering caused by God's judgment is instrumental rather than happening for its own sake. However, a logical priority of grace in God's self—which the human person, in turn, can only experience after suffering under God's judgment—merely rejects an *eternal dualism* in the relationship between law and gospel, rather than subordinating the law to the gospel. The priority of judgment for worldly experience would nonetheless be legitimate, but such an intervention under the rubric of the law would face serious difficulties in shaking off the specter of authoritarianism. A simultaneity of grace and judgment, which Beintker also diagnoses in *Rom* II, might even speak for a dualism in God, too.[203] Occasionally Beintker argues that *Rom* II is characterized

201. *CD* II/2, 553 (trans. rev.). Note the Kantian terminology.
202. *Rom* II, 517.

by a dialectics in which thesis and antithesis are not sublated.[204] But what else can a dialectics without sublation be called than an antithesis?

As far as fundamental ethical schemes in Rom II are concerned, there may seem to be two options in *Rom* II for human action corresponding to God's will, while Barth does not argue for a *tertius usus legis*. On the one hand, Barth asserts that a theology of the cross constitutes a preferential option for the politically and socially marginalized, or for Social Democracy. In contrast to people in established and secure positions, the marginalized are closer to death, out of which Jesus was resurrected.[205] The destitute are closer to the position in which everything has already been sacrificed. "*We* are standing more *deeply* in the 'No' than in the 'Yes.'"[206] Middle class achievements—Barth recalls the functional spheres of "pure and applied science, the arts, morals, and religion"[207]—are in danger of leading away from God rather than to God, given how they are the supreme performances of the human spirit. By contrast, God is revealed in the disenfranchised, suffering Christ. Partiality for them is what Barth calls the secondary ethical activity.

203. The apparent diastasis of demand and gift constitutes two independent, opposed concerns within God's self without denouement in a higher synthesis. It is significant, moreover, that the antithesis between law and gospel can at the same time coincide with a teleology, in which law and gospel reinforce each other mutually in their tension-filled work. See Krötke, '*Gesetz und Evangelium*,' 15.

204. Beintker, "Krisis," 27–8.

205. *Rom* II, 622: Christianity "sees everywhere in the 'lowlands' at least the parable of life, for it cannot forget the meaning of the resurrection." Presumably, Barth thought of such moral orientation when he wrote in view of the interpretation of Romans 12–15 that the emphasis on ethics was a rather late idea: "How good that I ended up finding the trick in question after all last fall." Barth's letter to Thurneysen (May 22, 1922) in Karl Barth and Eduard Thurneysen, *Barth-Thurneysen-Briefwechsel 1921–1930*, ed. Eduard Thurneysen, Barth-Gesamtausgabe (Zurich: Evangelischer Verlag, 1974), 79; see Hinrich Stoevesandt, "Barths Calvinvorlesung als Station seiner theologischen Biographie," in *Karl Barth und Johannes Calvin: Karl Barths Göttinger Calvin-Vorlesung von 1922*, ed. Hans Scholl (Neukirchen: Neukirchen-Vluyn, 1995), 107–24, at 120.

206. *Rom* II, 620.

207. Ibid., 621.

But is this secondary ethical activity truly compatible with the primary one?[208] If taking sides with the marginalized means to take sides, indirectly, with Christ, a new theopolitical claim is introduced into Christian ethics, which contradicts the notion of sacrifice. Thus, the marginalized might, under the pretext of God's glory, seek their own. Given the contemporary impact of socialist and communist movements, Barth even argues that this is the specific temptation of the disenfranchised.[209] Yet there is a dangerous temptation even for moderate forces, such as Social Democrats. Even for a moderate cause, they have to argue with particular vigor, since they wish to prevail against ideologically charged forces.

In social ethics, Barth's stance of a sacrifice and his notion of the "eternal future" mean that the objection to the old worldly life is just as much a critique of one's own course of action as that of others. Indeed, it is not a coincidence that Barth's clearest discussion of a preferential option for the poor and his plea for Social Democracy[210] lead directly into an argument that ethics is not in fact about action but about a better understanding of the human situation vis-à-vis God. The cause of solidarity with the marginalized cannot maintain its own ground against Barth's cause of existential hermeneutics.[211]

> Are we perhaps startled to notice how very deeply all of our activity is involved in the sphere of relativity? That is precisely what we are supposed to notice. Yet again: relativity means being in relationship.

208. See McCormack, *Barth's Theology*, 275–80, who insists that the christological foundations of a positive ethics are in place in *Rom* II. He concedes, however (ibid., 279–80): "Given the purpose for which *Romans* II was written, it is understandable that Barth would lay the greatest stress possible on 'primary ethical activity'; understandable too that his treatment of 'secondary ethical activity' would have a highly negative feel (focused as it was upon protest and criticism). In *Romans* II, Barth had little incentive to provide positive descriptions of 'secondary ethical activities.'"

209. Ibid., 622, 638–9.

210. Ibid., 620–23.

211. See also Arthur Rich, *Wirtschaftsethik: Grundlagen in theologischer Perspektive* (Gütersloh: Gütersloher Verlagshaus Mohn, 1984), 139–40.

> Every *ethical* activity takes place in *relationship* to the primal origin, as a positive state of affairs, as a person's demeanor of this or that kind. That is precisely what "Christianity" can and should achieve: to bring *that* to our attention. The absolute character of Christian ethics is precisely this: to consist entirely and only in a *question*, and even to consist entirely in *questions* even in its explication, in such questions to which only God can be the answer. In point of fact, the clarity gained here is startling: all human ethos can *only* be a demonstration, *only* a reference, *only* a sacrifice.[212]

The emphasis on sacrifice might be helpful as it denies any justification to all ideologies. It calls for greater "objectivity" in a heated, radicalized climate. Barth's hope and plea is that "a prudent reckoning with 'reality' has left behind the hubris of war between good and evil."[213] At the same time, however, in *Rom* II "objectivity" means recognition of *universal* guilt and hubris.[214] This is especially directed against the appreciation of the ethics of particular functional spheres of society, within which "ChrSoc" hopes for a greater degree

212. *Rom* II, 623–4. For a related emphasis on the human question, see Martin Heidegger, *Being and Time*, trans. John Macquarrie and Edward Robinson (Oxford: Basil Blackwell, 1986), 26–7: "If the question about Being is to be explicitly formulated and carried through in such a manner as to be completely transparent to itself, then any treatment of it . . . requires us to explain how Being is to be looked at. . . . All these ways of behaving are constitutive for our inquiry, and therefore are modes of Being for those particular entities which we, the inquirers, are ourselves. Thus to work out the question of Being adequately, we must make an entity—the inquirer—transparent in his own Being. The very asking of this question is an entity's mode of *Being;* and as such it gets its essential character from what is inquired about—namely, Being. This entity which each of us is himself and which includes inquiring as one of the possibilities of its Being, we shall denote by the term '*Dasein.*' If we are to formulate our question explicitly and transparently, we must first give a proper explication of an entity (Dasein), with regard to its Being."

213. Ibid., 653.

214. Ibid., 72–3: "The divine 'No,' which reinforces our limits, thus making us transcend our limits, can be confirmed and comprehended 'since the creation of the world,' 'seen through the things God has made,' if our reflection is calm, objective, free from religious prejudice." "The positive reality of the Creator and the *eternal* meaning of the creature have never been recognized in any other way than in the negation of the creature. *That* is what history tells us." (ibid., 124). Ibid., 367: The real expert will "certainly show greater insight and objectivity sense for reality than the supposed virtuousos of piety (in reality they are the most cruel dilettantes!). . . . But the critical efforts [of the expert] will be in vain, since the capacity for religion is too deep-seated in the human person for us not to indulge in it." See also McCormack, *Barth's Theology*, 131.

of "objectivity."[215] In *Rom* II, however, Barth's call for "objectivity" can only offer a very limited degree of orientation, as he arrives only at a general notion of injustice, but not at a positive judgment about the legitimacy of a particular position. Faced with universal human injustice, Barth argues that in politics, "we are unable to speak of being objectively in the right"; politics must be seen "to be essentially a game."[216] This is indeed the problem with Barth's concept of a secondary ethical activity. *Rom* II can offer positive moral guidance only as long as the new moral orientation is neither self-consciously right nor affirmed in opposition to rival courses of action.[217] By implication, *Rom* II invites us to consider the fight against child abuse, racism, human trafficking, and other sorts of unbridled violence as a game, that is, as an activity following entirely conventional, and thus arbitrary, goals.

To claim politics as a game, Barth argues, offers the distance necessary "to recognize the *relative* possibilities to do good in the midst of evil."[218] Here a limited passage in *Rom* II might again begin to offer ethical guidance as an alternative to complete relativism. The question is whether this approach holds up against Barth's own relentless critique of any privileged knowledge. This problem becomes even more acute in the historical context of *Rom* II, as

215. Barth, "Christ in der Gesellschaft," 583: "One thing that does not occur in the parables is amateurishness, bungling, and half-baked jobs. . . . If a job is done properly, there is evidently—not the kingdom of heaven itself, but a great possibility that the kingdom of heaven breaks through its worldly foreground in order to be witnessed, to become apparent."

216. *Rom* II, 653.

217. Jüngel, for example, opens a chapter on Barth's "Dialectical Theology" by highlighting the potential for "analogy" even in Barth's message of judgment. His prime examples are from "ChrSoc." Barth claims Christians should "stand in *absolute* criticism of life" and "recognize the *analogy* of the *divine* in *worldly* things" ("ChrSoc," 56; Eberhard Jüngel, "Barth's Life and Work," in *Karl Barth: A Theological Legacy*, 22–52, at 34). The problem is that due to the lack of theological criteria, any identification of a particular analogy is under dispute. If the criticism is indeed "*absolute*," any sense of an "*analogy* of the *divine in worldly* things" is under illusions about the emperor's new clothes.

218. *Rom* II, 653.

it would confront ideological objections in concrete political discourse.[219] After all, Barth's political opponents would not include their own position in their judgment of widespread injustice. Against such positions, Barth would have to assert his own relative position again with greater vigor. Yet due to Christ's cross, he argues, any political zeal that offers religious justifications in politics and accepts a "mixing of heaven and earth in the sphere of morals"[220] is out of the question. Indeed, Barth clearly states that the distinct moral guidance that his commentary might provide in politics is certainly invalid in any situation of confrontation.[221] Barth certainly directs his call for sacrifice against militarism and Leninism, but also against religious socialism and strict pacifism.[222] To be serious about the moral orientation that might be drawn from *Rom* II in spite of its fight against all moral presumptuousness, Barth would need to turn

219. This is also true of the passage *Rom* II, 227–8, quoted by Jones, "Rhetoric of War," 103–4, who argues that *Rom* II opens up the possibility of a definite ethics after all. According to Barth's commentary, grace makes material ethics necessary. Yet Barth restricts this immediately, saying that such an ethics must definitely be aware of its preliminary, insecure status. What Barth gives with one hand he immediately takes away with the other: "The human knowledge which emerges is at once dissolved by the very criterion by which it was created. Only because of the power of obedience in which we stand are we able to comprehend and lay hold of the possibility of impossibility. And this power is the power of the Resurrection" (*Rom* II, 228). It should also be noted that *Rom* II calls the "power of resurrection" a power of death. In addition, the reference to "alliances" (ibid.), which might suggest greater ethical specificity, is a mistranslation of the highly formal "*Verhältnisse*" (ibid., 210).

220. Ibid., 582.

221. Ibid., 635–6.

222. *Rom* II, 588: "Nevertheless there are actions from which the light of sacrifice shines, the *sacrificed* person and thus *not the human person* in some new positive or negative human condition, but what is proper to God, God's own will, power, and claim—God the *Lord*. It is this light which disturbs people, the ideal person of the Ludendorff-Lenin type and the ideal person of the Foerster-Ragaz type. For it is an assault on the human person tout court." Foerster, professor of pedagogy and philosophy, had been sentenced to prison for speaking out against the critique of Social Democrats by emperor William II. He also critiqued the First World War from his pacifist perspective, for which he was beaten up by Munich students. Beginning in 1933 he was persecuted by the German authorities. His controversy with Barth and Thurneysen was based on his critique that their new theology subverted a humanistic, religious ethos. See "Foerster, Friedrich Wilhelm," *Munzinger-Biographie: Internationales Biographisches Archiv*, http://tinyurl.com/npfr87t, "Friedrich Wilhelm Foerster," *Der Spiegel* 20, no. 4 (1966): 90, http://tinyurl.com/pydj2wa.

his universal critique into a positive argument for one particular position, yet in his view any one particular position falls under the verdict of hubris before God.[223] In this way, Barth's interpretation of the cross critiques all ideologies just as much as all other positions that are pursued with the earnestness of a struggle against ideology.[224] Any "moral indignation against, for example, a Tirpitz or a Bethmann Hollweg, or even a Lenin" is declared irrelevant vis-à-vis "a wholly different problem before whose eeriness anyone must fall silent."[225] Barth was therefore opposed to a distinction between nationalistic militarism or a violent fight for the dictatorship of the proletariat and moderate political options, while the Weimar Republic faced serious attempts at extremist coups d'état.[226] If indeed adherents of *Rom* II were to avoid confronting any ideological positions, they would cede the political arena to partisans of a totalitarian order. After all, those are the least likely to take Barth's theological arguments to heart, and they would not consider politics "essentially a game." In effect, the emphasis on sacrifice in *Rom* II would weaken the church's support for a constitutional democracy. In 1940 Karl Löwith named *Rom* II in the same breath as Oswald Spengler's *Decline of the West,* stating that

223. *Rom* II, 455 with reference to Dostoevsky's Grand Inquisitor.

224. Ulrich Dannemann, *Theologie und Politik im Denken Karl Barths*, Gesellschaft und Theologie 22 (München: Kaiser, 1977), 99–102 highlights Barth's rejection of ideological reasoning in *Rom* II, but does not question Barth's ethical approach focusing on individual or personal ethics.

225. *Rom* II, 578–9. On the persons named by Barth, see the articles in the *Encyclopaedia Britannica*: "Theobald von Bethmann Hollweg," "Vladimir Ilich Lenin," "Alfred von Tirpitz," *Encyclopaedia Britannica: Encyclopaedia Britannica Online Academic Edition*, 2014, www.britannica.com.' As an advisor to the Emperor William II, Tirpitz contributed significantly to the escalation of the arms race within the German navy. While Bethmann Hollweg as imperial chancellor was a moderate by comparison, he also contributed to the outbreak of World War I.

226. Ruschke argues that the ethical merits of *Rom* II lie in an "ethics of the question," albeit not a question for good or right action, but for the human status before God (Ruschke, *Entstehung*, 74). As the main achievement of *Rom* II, Ruschke points to the negation of traditional orders (ibid., 76). Discussing numerous interpretations of *Rom* II that call the book authoritarian or antidemocratic, he concedes "that Barth's theology could have been read precisely like this *too*, and that this in fact happened" (ibid., 154).

these were the two most important books in his German intellectual circles in the 1920s and that both, at best, contributed to a paralysis in the political and cultural defense against National Socialism.[227]

In this context it is remarkable that in 1922, when *Rom* II appeared, the notorious lawyer and protagonist of the "Conservative Revolution," Carl Schmitt, noted with a certain acumen that "all significant concepts of the modern theory of the state are secularized theological concepts."[228] According to Schmitt, the state of emergency, which the Weimar constitution defined in article 48, ultimately rests on the traditional notion of a miraculous suspension of natural law by God. By contrast, modern constitutional democracy is rooted in the intellectual history of Deism and the Enlightenment, which in turn highlight natural law. The objection these traditions raised against "the sovereign's direct intervention in a valid legal order" is implied in their critique of all supernatural forms of political legitimation.[229]

This is an example of an influential political protagonist who took the theological nature of political conflict very seriously. Its

227. "Even Spengler—who promoted the ideology of National Socialism through his writings like no other—took fright and turned away from it at the moment of his actual victory. . . . Apart from Spengler's book, there was only one other of similar importance, albeit a less influential one: Karl Barth's *Römerbrief* . . . which was published at the same time. This work, too, subsisted on the negation of progress, in that it saw a theological advantage in the decay of culture. The lack of faith in all human solutions that had been promoted by the war drove Barth from Christian socialism to his radical theology, which rejects any 'development' of Christianity at its root. These two works by Spengler and Barth, which bore the imprint of the period at the end of the First World War, were the books that most excited us." Karl Löwith, *My Life in Germany before and after 1933: A Report*, trans. Elisabeth King (Athlone: University of Illinois Press, 1994), 26 (trans. rev.). Having finished a PhD dissertation on Nietzsche in 1923, Löwith was in a good position to evaluate Barth's fascination with Nietzsche, as when Barth contemptuously calls human piety a "rising of slaves" (*Rom* II, 335, 338). By contrast, when Löwith compared *Rom* II to Spengler's works in 1940, he was even quite appreciative of Barth's more recent stance (see ibid., 37). Ironically, Koshar quotes Löwith's last sentence about Barth and Spengler in trying to make a point in favor of Barth. Rudy Koshar, "Where Is Barth in Modern European History?" *Modern Intellectual History* 5 (2008): 333–62, at 350.

228. Carl Schmitt, *Political Theology: Four Chapters on the Concept of Sovereignty* (Chicago: University of Chicago Press, 1985), 36.

229. Ibid.

authoritarian intentions should be countered drawing on substantial theological traditions as well. To react with the proclamation that we are all sinners before God, to "attack" by undermining *any* theopolitical sense of responsibility,[230] undermines one's own responsibility in social ethics first. By contrast, Jeffrey Stout argues in his study about *Democracy and Tradition,*

> Under circumstances as . . . ours, with potentially anti-democratic forces assembling allies and attempting to divide or co-opt their foes, the question of character attains utmost importance for friends of democracy. It becomes the question of whether the people can summon the spiritual wherewithal, the moral fiber, to act on behalf of democracy before democracy itself gives way.[231]

Rom II may perhaps be said to contribute to the democratic tradition with its vigilant, iconoclastic spirit and its provocative critique that does not yield to any worldly authority. It does not tolerate civil religion being put to use for anyone's political gain. The problem is that not even the democratic tradition can be salvaged from Barth's harsh critique. From this sobering perspective, the decisive question is of a more pragmatic nature: in the end, who will profit from this stance? In the ideologically charged atmosphere of the Weimar Republic, the social ethics of *Rom* II amounted to a negative ethics and quietism, with harmful political consequences.[232] Christian faith

230. Gorringe, "Barth on Romans," 605–7.
231. Jeffrey Stout, *Democracy and Tradition* (Princeton: Princeton University Press, 2004), 23. In contrast to the critique of Barth in this chapter, Stout criticizes new Christian traditionalists who argue that the individualism of democracy undermines the cohesive force of authority and tradition. As far as the wider work of Barth is concerned, however, Stout is explicit in his appreciation of George Hunsinger's work as a prodemocratic, public contribution drawing chiefly on a theological thinker.
232. Timothy Gorringe contests Jüngel's interpretation of *Rom* II as strictly apolitical with the citation of Barth's "No revolution is the best preparation for the true revolution. But even that is not a recipe" (*Rom* II, 647). He sees the political nature of *Rom* II in the determination to undermine anyone's missionary zeal in politics, but does not discuss how that squares with Barth's indirect sympathies for Social Democratic politics. The results do not differ from a

may orient action in private life, where morality can perhaps be considered "essentially a game" played with a detached "humor."[233] It is indeed individual or personal ethics that Barth focuses on when, against the grain of *Rom* II, he comments on Rom. 12:9–15 that there may be good action "by virtue of the imperishable disposition of the cosmos, which gives it even in its 'current' state the capacity to be a parable."[234] Even that is said with several caveats: "We must, however, be [very] careful [in expressing this]." Barth concedes only with serious reservations that concrete human action—if only in the love ethos of an individual—can indeed become a parable of the good. Even here the moral judgment tentatively chooses between slight qualitative degrees, espousing options that seem "more easily" to come close to the divine will, to which they seem "more closely related" than others.[235]

On the positive side, Barth raises his voice for the marginalized, even though ultimately the theological integration of this theme into the whole of the commentary is haphazard. While the consequences are dubious in the final analysis, Barth's keen sense for the scandal of the unjust torture of the cross is remarkable. This aspect takes on the form of an indictment rather than being leveled in an innocuous message of mere forgiveness.

This analysis of *Rom* II has also argued that it is insufficient to react negatively, as *Rom* II mostly does, against attempts to co-opt particular political positions in the name of universal reason. The protection and care of those mechanisms that allow for freedom in religion and worldview—thus enabling the critique of religion in *Rom* II in the first place—require a more nuanced position. Moreover,

restriction of Christian ethics to the private sphere and an evacuation of the public realm from any constructive efforts inspired by the gospel. Gorringe, "Barth on Romans," 605–7.

233. Ibid., 653, 623.

234. Ibid., 607

235. Ibid.

as *Rom* II rejects attempts at universal accounts of salvation history and the divine, there are points of contact with postmodern thought.[236] To be sure, Barth's categorical call for sacrifice would be met with skepticism in postmodern discourse. Yet a critique of *Rom* II would face the question of the extent to which rejecting all "metanarratives" contributes too little to the maintenance of those levels of freedom attained in pluralistic societies.[237]

Sacrifice and Repentance after the Second Edition of the Romans Commentary

In his dogmatics lectures on "Sanctification" in *GD* (*GD* III §32, 1925),[238] Barth characterizes moral action as sacrifice and repentance. The thesis statement of §32 calls the life of the faithful an "object of Christ's action as king." However, Barth interprets this as avoidance of the Christian's own moral agency by highlighting "suffering from one's sin" and "struggle against oneself." When speaking of "hunger for righteousness," Barth emphasizes negatively one's own lack of righteousness before God.[239] When trying to bring the issue to life

236. See Klemm, "Rhetoric," 456–8; Philipp Stoellger, "Barth und die Postmoderne: Perspektiven auf eine prekäre Konstellation," in *Barths Theologie*, eds. Leiner and Trowitzsch, 397–432.
237. Ingolf Dalferth, "'Was Gott ist, bestimme ich!' Theologie im Zeitalter der 'Caféteria-Religion,'" in *Gedeutete Gegenwart: Zur Wahrnehmung Gottes in den Wahrnehmungen der Zeit* (Tübingen: Mohr Siebeck, 1997), 10–35, at 17, does not simply want to bolster up the postmodern "critique of the ideology of uniformity of Enlightenment reason," but to argue reasonably for the Christian faith, thus continuing the emancipatory Enlightenment cause; see ibid., 14, 23. Michael Welker, *Kirche im Pluralismus* (Gütersloh: Kaiser, 1995), 29–34 argues that the biblical traditions are closely related to the project of achieving a higher degree of freedom and justice in late modern pluralism. He views pluralism not as a mere plurality, but a differentiated relationship between particular social structures, which require both critique and protection. See his *God the Spirit*, trans. John Hoffmeyer, 2nd ed. (Minneapolis: Fortress Press, 2004), 21–7 on a "pluralism of the Spirit."
238. For lack of a published translation, quotations from *GD* II–III (1924/25, 1925/26) are translated by me with references to the German edition: *Unterricht in der christlichen Religion*, Barth-Gesamtausgabe (Zurich: Theologischer Verlag), vol. 2: *Die Lehre von Gott/Die Lehre vom Menschen 1924/25*, ed. Hinrich Stoevesandt (1990), vol. 3: *Die Lehre von der Versöhnung/Die Lehre von der Erlösung 1925/26*, ed. Hinrich Stoevesandt (2003). The abbreviations for all volumes, regardless of the difference in title and language, are *GD* I–III.

with positive qualifications, Barth mentions joy and thankfulness for justification, but on the whole, the negation of positive moral agency prevails. The new Christian life consists "exclusively in obedience, i.e., in repentance."[240] Contrary to the location of the section within the wider architecture of *GD*, the substance of §32 hearkens back more clearly to Christ's priestly office than the royal one.[241] This is in keeping with the statement from *Rom* II:

> Christ's life, his resurrection, on which faith is based, is concrete in his passive obedience, in his death on the cross, only, solely, and exclusively in his death on the cross. The doctrine of Christ's threefold office obscures and weakens the focus of the New Testament view. There is no independent second or third aspect *besides* this one and only, this exclusive meaning of Christ.[242]

Again this is in accordance with *GD* §7 ("Faith and Obedience"), which is Barth's first text to show signs of a priority of the gospel over the law. To begin with, this section says that God's will and God's glory require human sanctification—not as a precondition of, but as an important correspondence to God's grace. Thus Barth opts against the notion that faith in and of itself already brings about a renewal of the moral life. However, Barth also portrays the new obedience in terms of the abnegation of the self and repentance. He tends to conceive of God's glory and human flourishing in competitive terms, describing God's revelation to be about "primarily . . . *himself*—his will and power and glory."[243] God's communion with the creature is not in view here.

The abandonment of self in §§7, 32 is not the only word on ethics in *GD*. Section 29 will require a different treatment (see below).

239. *GD* III, 323–4.
240. Ibid., 304 (thesis statement §32), see 331.
241. Ibid., 151.
242. *Rom* II, 218.
243. *GD* I, 172.

Nonetheless, the overall negative character of the ethics in *GD* is not a coincidence. The danger of a vacuum in society that offers a foothold for extreme political forces constitutes a particular risk of a negative ethics, but presumably Barth was less than aware of this problem due to a notable theological factor. *GD* expressly attributes a key position to human religiosity. Admittedly this is in contrast to the first three sections that lay the foundations of theology in proclamation based on biblical texts (see §1: "The Word of God as the Problem of Dogmatics," §2: "Preaching as the Starting Point and Goal of Dogmatics," and §3: "Deus Dixit" ["And God said"]). Section 4, however, ("Man and His Question") subverts this approach: "God's revelation, which is the basis of Christian preaching, is the answer to our question how we can overcome the contradiction in our existence."[244] Human self-negation is a meaningful form of preparation for God's revelation, which, however, responds to a prior, nonthematic presence of God in all human lives. This response requires a religious stance that will be vindicated by the church's proclamation. The basic human situation prior to God's address in the sermon bears much promise. In light of this helpful natural human condition, even the risks of political life seem much less explosive.

A few years later, Barth would view his attempt to articulate dogmatic points in correlation to the existential questions of human life critically:

> Usually we attach great importance to being the one who is asking "the other" the questions and to retaining this role. As is well known, since Socrates this role has to be understood as the role of knowledge, that of the midwife helping further insight along. This position is superior to

244. Ibid., 69; see also 80. In a similar vein, on the premises of Barth's theology in the Göttingen years and its presuppositions about the "natural" human person, see Eberhard Busch, *Die Anfänge des Theologen Karl Barth in seinen Göttinger Jahren* (Göttingen: Vandenhoeck & Ruprecht, 1986), 10–11.

> really facing a question from "the other," to accepting that we have been asked a question, thus to assuming the less noble position of the pupil.[245]

The potentially explosive character of a correlation between existential concerns and God's revelation can be illustrated with a statement from Barth's private letters dating from the early crisis-torn years of the Weimar Republic: "German professors really are true masters in giving intellectual, moral, and Christian justifications for brutalities. You can't wipe that out! [Emanuel] Hirsch, too, was *disastrous*, talking about the una sancta [one and holy, i.e., church] (of the German people) and of course once again of 'conscience.'"[246] Barth had been a horrified witness to the aggressive nationalism and antisemitism among his Göttingen colleagues.[247]

In spite of the disillusioning illustrating material, the key position of existential questions in *GD* is not an exception in Barth's early work. Still in 1924 and again in 1928, Barth published two lectures from 1922 that argue for a hermeneutical function of the existential question.[248] The first is the lecture "The Need and Promise of

245. Barth, "Der römische Katholizismus als Frage an die protestantische Kirche. 1928," in *Vorträge und kleinere Arbeiten 1925–1930*, ed. Hermann Schmidt, Barth-Gesamtausgabe (Zurich: Theologischer Verlag, 1994), 303–43, at 309.

246. *Barth-Thurneysen-Briefwechsel 1921–30*, 131 (Jan 23, 1923); see Barth, *Offene Briefe 1909–1935*, ed. Diether Koch, Barth-Gesamtausgabe (Zurich: Theologischer Verlag, 2001), 184n3.

247. See *Barth-Thurneysen-Briefwechsel 1921–30*, 32–3 (Jan. 23, 1922): "It is the joy of the Germans to stand in proper marching order and to obey! . . . The German officer families have been at least as strong a cultural force as the German parsonage." See ibid., 88–9 (Jan. 28, 1922): after the assassination of foreign minister Walter Rathenau, Barth heard his colleagues say, "a Jew never has any patriotic loyalties and just simply must not be part of a German administration." See also Barth, "An Prof. Dr. Erich von Holst, Heidelberg, 1947," in *Offene Briefe 1945–1968*, ed. Diether Koch, Barth-Gesamtausgabe (Zurich: Theologischer Verlag, 1984), 121–34.

248. Barth, "The Need and Promise of Christian Proclamation, 1922" and "The Problem of Ethics Today, 1922," both in *Word of God and Theology*, 101–29; 131–69. Still in 1928, Barth comments on the first English translation of this anthology, *The Word of God and the Word of Man*, trans. Douglas Horton (Boston: Pilgrim Press, 1928): "May they [i.e., U. S. theologians] benefit from it. So far, everything one hears from there gives me a forlorn impression" (*Barth-Thurneysen-Briefwechsel 1921–30*, 565 [March 12, 1928]).

Christian Proclamation." The pattern of question and answer plays an important role here:

> While the congregation primarily *brings* to the church the great *question* of life and *seeks* an *answer* for it, on the contrary, the Bible primarily *brings* an *answer*, and it *seeks* the *question* to this answer. It seeks questioning *people* who want to seek and find this answer; who in so doing understand that its seeking of them is the very answer to their question.[249]

Barth considers the existential worries of churchgoers limited in comparison to Jesus' cry of dereliction on the cross. Significantly, existential questions are not simply given an answer, but in their quest, a merging of horizons occurs. The "*minor* questions" lead the way to Christ's "*major* question," and only in this way can the cross be appropriately understood.[250] Certainly the existential worries of parishioners are far from determining entirely the message they receive in proclamation. Yet a significant hermeneutical contribution to the particular theological shape that the biblical texts take in this two-way communication cannot be denied to the individual situation of the listener. According to this lecture, such correlation between proclamation and the addressee's concerns is theologically fully legitimate.

According to the lecture "The Problem of Ethics Today," the awareness of moral problems is theologically fundamental. Here the sensitive conscience assumes the role of a propaedeutics of justifying faith: "What awaits us in the problem of ethics is the mystery of the impossibility of humans as we know them, of the living and the perishing; the mystery that *this* human can only perish before God."[251] One important difference to *Rom* II is that the ethical crisis

249. Barth, "Need and Promise," 117.
250. Ibid., 119.
251. Barth, "Problem of Ethics," 137. Von Balthasar, *Theology of Karl Barth*, 100.

does not arise from some prior commitment to biblical traditions proclaiming God's mercy over the sinner and God's wrath over sin, but merely from a general moral concern, which supposedly coincides with God's moral concern. "The individual," "the human person" asks, and "we" ask, "what are we supposed to do," exposing "the ethical problem," and this is best exemplified by Kant's ethics.[252] All it takes on the human part is an "entirely sincere conscience."[253] The deeper meaning of this ethical crisis is that, ultimately, morals are not about action, but about an encounter with God. "It is necessary to immediately *bow* under the judgment that arises in the problem of ethics. Precisely in the inescapable sharpness of this judgment, we hit upon the reality of *God*."[254] The judgment of the law, which takes place in the general question of how to act, eventually results in justification through the gospel.[255]

Barth's emphasis on general ethics coincides with the interpretation of Luther by Emanuel Hirsch's teacher, Karl Holl. Like Hirsch after him,[256] Holl described Luther's religion as "'religion of the conscience' in the most pronounced sense of the word."[257]

252. "We can gain clarity about . . . this attack from the perspective of the questioning subject, and best orient ourselves to it based on the ethic of Kant. . . . What I am referring to here is Kant's basing of the concept of moral personality on the idea of the autonomous will. ... The seriousness with which the question is shot through is seldom spoken of more clearly" ("Problem of Ethics," 146–7). See 152–3.

253. Ibid., 158.

254. Ibid. Barth puts these assertions in perspective on the last four pages of this forty-page lecture. By itself, the crisis of consciousness does not lead to Jesus Christ (see 169). However, if Barth's overall position is compared to that of Karl Holl, it must be said that Holl would not have asserted such a thing either, for encountering God in judgment is not the same as encountering Jesus Christ for Holl.

255. See ibid., 159–60.

256. On Hirsch's understanding of law and gospel, see Gunther Wenz, "'...der Unterscheid des Gesetzes und Evangelii als ein besonder herrlich Licht' (BSLK 790, 21 f): Fallbeispiele zur Aufnahme des hermeneutischen Kriteriums der Wittenberger Reformation in der Dogmatik des 20. Jahrhunderts," in *Grundfragen ökumenischer Theologie: Gesammelte Aufsätze* (Göttingen: Vandenhoeck & Ruprecht, 2010), 2:116–59, at 133–8.

257. Karl Holl, *What Did Luther Understand by Religion?*, ed. James L. Adams and Walter F. Bense, trans. Fred W. Meuser and Walter R. Wietzke (Minneapolis: Augsburg Fortress Press, 1977), 48; 113. See also *Barth-Thurneysen-Briefwechsel 1921–30*, 36 (Feb. 11, 1922).

The human person falls into despair faced with God's "gift of moral apperception," which is the appropriately receptive stance vis-à-vis God's justification of the sinner.[258] The encounter with God is characterized, according to both Holl and Barth, by the dialectics of law and gospel.[259]

Against this backdrop, it may come as a surprise that Barth's lecture "Das Halten der Gebote" ("Keeping the Commandments," 1927) clearly articulates the priority of the gospel over the law. Here human action is not presented fundamentally under the judgment of the law. By contrast, the authority of the law is not even sufficiently justified merely with the absolute majesty of the legislator: "The law is inherently '*gratuitae adoptionis foedere vestita*'" ("clothed in the covenant of gracious adoption," John Calvin).[260] Election precedes the law, so the law can never be primarily a force of condemnation. Thus the law is not heteronomous coercion, but aims—again in Calvin's words—at "'*symmetria*' and '*consensus*'"[261] (correspondence/harmony and agreement) between God and the human person. The gospel does not, of all things, liberate from the commandment of the law,[262] but wins the human person over for thankful compliance; it even promises the keeping of the commandments.

258. Holl, *What Did Luther Understand by Religion?*, 44.

259. Barth, "Problem of Ethics," 160. The reference to a "unity" of law and gospel means that the law is God's instrument in bringing about communion with the creature, but "the ethical question . . . will remain *posed* as ever. There is no escape from the problematic of life." In other words, God will remain primarily the critical judge rather than, in acting through the law, the inspiration and power of the new ethos. That this is very much in keeping with Luther's conception of law and gospel is evident from Barth's reference to Luther's *Bondage of the Will*, which inculcates the preceding and abiding judgment of the law (ibid.).

260. Barth, "Das Halten der Gebote. 1927," in *Vorträge 1925–30*, 99–139, at 122; Calvin: when Paul "teaches that the law was given on account of transgressions," as a "guardian" over the Jews, he "is at times forced strictly to assume a naked law, although it is otherwise clothed in the covenant of gracious adoption." *Ioannis Calvini Institutionum Christianae Religionis Libri Quatuor: Editio Postrema,* Amsterdam: Schipper, 1671, 87 (II, 7, 2) (Alexander Street Press: The Digital Library of Classic Protestant Texts)/Calvin, *Institutes of the Christian Religion*, 1:351.

261. Ibid., 1:684 (III, 6, 1).

262. Barth, "Halten der Gebote," 133.

> The law receives truth and power only through the gospel. Without the gospel I would not have attended to the law as law, not as a binding word. Indeed, I only recognize the commandments as such in recognizing them as God's commandments. But I only recognize them as God's commandments in recognizing God's love in them, the love of the God who claims myself for God. And I only recognize God's love in them by accepting that God's love is unconditional, not conditioned by my decision, but preceding it, God's love in eternal election.[263]

Even in keeping the commandments, Christians cannot achieve any merits before God. Within the abiding power of sin, however, Christians attempt nothing more and nothing less than "creating a sign, demonstrating"[264] that they hear the commandment and strive to keep it.

Although this is a clear concept, this lecture is still not the decisive turn in Barth's wrestling with the relationship between gospel and law. The reason is primarily that Barth's ethics lectures, given in Münster and Bonn, highlight the accusation of sin much more strongly than the *usus practicus legis* (see below).[265] But even when Barth, in 1927, delivered the lecture "Das Halten der Gebote" for the second and third time, he continued the next day to deliver the lecture "Rechtfertigung und Heiligung" ("Justification and Sanctification," 1927), which again mostly considers human action under the aspect of sacrifice (see below). After presenting "Das Halten der Gebote" for the first time, he conceded a "defeat" in the ensuing open discussion, in which his critics had the last say. Ironically, "Das Halten der Gebote" was criticized for too negative an image of the human person and for too critical a view of the human capacity for positive action.[266] Thurneysen summarizes this reaction as a "concerted attack on us in the synergistic spirit."[267] This shows why,

263. Ibid., 122–3.
264. Ibid., 138.
265. On Barth's ethics lecture cycle, see below.
266. Barth, "Halten der Gebote," 101–4 (editor's introduction).

later on, Barth added the quietistic reminder of judgment and sin to the measured encouragement for action. In keeping with this, the ethics lecture only hints toward a priority of the gospel over against the law. *Rom* II already condemned an overly optimistic evaluation of one's moral capacities as hubris, and although an insistence on judgment and sin can be no less presumptuous, Barth returns to this position for the time being.

While Barth often presents the emphasis on sacrifice and fundamental self-restraint as a critique of religiosity, his positive evaluation of this attitude shows that sacrifice is a form of religiosity as well. For example, the lecture "Rechtfertigung und Heiligung" shows with drastic images that, of course, the category of sacrifice is taken from the history of religions. Sanctification consists in sacrificing an "intellectual, moral, pious humanity" for God. "There is fire below, wood on that, and then the human person on top, the entire 'I' with reason and everything the person received from God."[268] If, however, the certainty and energy with which theology and the church contribute to a humane society are not to suffer fundamental damage, it would be necessary for the relation with God not to be dominated by reduction and weakening, but that Christians are also called in positive terms, receiving orientation for constructive work.

The lecture "Der Heilige Geist und das christliche Leben" ("The Holy Spirit and the Christian Life," 1929) describes the activity of the Holy Spirit especially in relation to the justification of the *sinner*. From an ethical point of view, this results in a fundamental conservatism. The lecture argues that the Spirit renews human action in such a way that a confession of sins, repentance, and sacrifice result.

267. Thurneysen's letter to Barth from March 23, 1927, *Barth-Thurneysen-Briefwechsel 1921–30*, 475–8, at 476; see Barth's answer from April 7, 1927, ibid., 489–93, at 490–91.
268. Barth, "Rechtfertigung und Heiligung, 1927" in *Vorträge 1925–30*, 57–98, at 85.

It is precisely this attitude in which joy about justification is real.[269] The Holy Spirit is decidedly the Spirit "of the Son of God, who was crucified for us in the flesh."[270] To begin with, however, persons need to gain clarity about the crucial contribution human hostility to God makes to such humiliation. Barth's statement that the work particular to the Holy Spirit is "the office of punishment" (*Strafamt*) is due to this systematic interest, but certainly not due to biblical traditions of the Holy Spirit.[271]

The problem with such views is not that the gospel excluded an indictment of sin; the judgment must not, however, dominate. There is an irony in the fact that Barth does not ask what the consequences of sin are on human society by emphasizing the aspect of judgment. For the confession of sin, the lecture argues, must take the form of accepting "orders of creation." Such "orders" thus receive particular theological legitimation.[272] Admittedly, Barth does not pursue a theology of orders single-mindedly; he admits that subordination in such orders can indeed be perverted by sin.[273] He assigns legitimacy to a theology of orders, but what shape human action should take within such orders in particular is up to God's ever-new commandment.[274]

This caveat of Barth's is not strong enough, however. For contemporary theologies of order insisted on relationships of authority and subordination, and for the most part, Barth's theological means to relativize these in principle are underdeveloped. Thus, the lecture does not question the legitimacy of such relationships but presupposes such subaltern forms of life too

269. Barth, "Der heilige Geist und das christliche Leben, 1929," in *Vorträge 1925–30*, 458–520, at 493.
270. Ibid., 485.
271. Ibid., 488.
272. Ibid., 502.
273. Ibid., 505–6.
274. Ibid., 471.

uncritically. Barth's attention to punishment, sin, repentance, and sacrifice creates a prejudice in favor of authoritarianism. Moreover, the prominent role of repentance and sacrifice is in danger of leading to passive fatalism. For justification through faith means consolation in the face of adversity and grievances:

> And the hiddenness of faith takes on concrete form in a terrible way in temptation: that is, once it is obvious how much reason there is for us, precisely as Christians, for repentance, once suffering overcomes a Christian in a way that only Christians know, for only they know that God does not owe them anything.[275]

To rise up and protest against the "irredeemable emergency which ultimately characterizes humans all the time and which is obvious in 'tribulation'"[276] would seem a presumptuous resistance against the Spirit's "office of punishment,"[277] an act of resistance that seems driven by the view that justification is only an incomplete consolation.

The Dogmatic Concept of the Actualistic Commandment 1924–32: Personalism and Lordship

Barth's notion of sacrifice casts sanctification in terms of a particular interpretation of Christ's cross, which sees repentance rather than transformation as the prime implication of justification. The lecture cycle *The Theology of John Calvin* (1922) initially shares this concern. Barth argues that in contrast to Roman Catholicism, teaching universal sinfulness is the essence of Protestant theology.[278] This places Christ's cross at the center of theology:

275. Ibid., 496.
276. Ibid., 494.
277. Ibid., 488; 498: reconciliation works "against our existence."
278. Barth, *The Theology of John Calvin*, ed. Hans Scholl, trans. Geoffrey W. Bromiley (Grand Rapids: Eerdmans, 1995), 42–3.

> Initially Luther had no other concern than to refer to the forgotten cross at the beginning of our human way. . . . We are forced to say that this one concern in all its one-sidedness is indeed the true essence of the Reformation. Where people have this concern, there is Protestantism; where they do not, or have moved on past it, there is a prolongation of the Middle Ages![279]

Later on, however, Barth lays out a notable theology of the cross of a different kind. Luther's thought resembles a cross with a discontinuous horizontal line, which is thus not intersected by the vertical line. Luther's theology is thus all about God's condescension—the vertical line—to which, however, the Christian life does not sufficiently conform, which is symbolized by the discontinuity in the horizontal line. Barth calls it a "historical fact that Luther's heart concern was with the pure *foundation* for works and not the *will* for them, with fighting *against* papist works and not fighting *for* works of the Spirit and love."[280]

By contrast, Calvin is convinced that "*to God's glory* something must [be done] in faith."[281] The current task is to create a continuous line in the vertical dimension as well. However, human works are inappropriate when compared to something as dramatic as God's condescension,[282] or they question justification by faith alone. Such an entirely continuous "cross" can be found neither in the Bible nor in the works of the Reformers.[283] A concept in which works are not merely a spontaneous—and thus a slightly erratic—result of justification would be necessary for this, but at the same time it had

279. Ibid., 47–8.

280. Ibid., 76, (trans. rev.: "*Reinheit der Begründung*"). The purity of the foundation of action is also the concern of *Rom* II, 583: "The purity of the ethos demands (and indeed we consider ourselves in agreement with Kant at this point) that no mixing of heaven and earth takes place here. For the purity of the ethos depends on its primal origin . . . to call God God and the human person a human person."

281. Barth, *Theology of John Calvin*, 77; see also 143.

282. Ibid., 73–4.

283. Ibid., 82–3.

to be clear that justification is in no way due to human achievement. This dilemma is the reason why the concept of obedience stands out in Barth's discussion of Calvin's theology. Barth understands obedience in such a way that he also characterizes Calvin's ethics as an ethics of freedom.[284]

The notion that God's glory requires a certain human activity is remarkable. By contrast, Hinrich Stoevesandt notes that the call for a sacrifice in *Rom* II is clearly in keeping with the position that the Calvin lectures attribute to Luther.[285] The call for self-abnegation and the adamant refusal of even the most subtle forms of self-righteousness in *Rom* II thus correspond to Luther's struggle for the purity of the foundation of the ethos[286] and the fight against religious confidence in one's own works. In 1922, by contrast, Barth commends Calvin's ethics: "This, mark you, is what I would call a definite and unequivocal approach to ethics in contrast to Luther's."[287]

A lecture of 1923 describes the characteristically Reformed element in Protestant ethics as a practical, sober "act of *obedience*."[288] Indeed, the difference Barth observes between Luther and Calvin raises the question of how to justify a particular act of obedience. So far, Barth mostly assumed that obedience consists in the negation of the

284. Ibid., 195–6.

285. "Indeed, the theology of the *Epistle to the Romans* is, as clearly as possible, a theology of the vertical dimension—that vertical dimension which Barth's lecture attributes a fortiori to Luther" (Hinrich Stoevesandt, "Barths Calvinvorlesung," 119). While Luther commended a natural law ethos in public affairs, which may include the use of force, the parallel of *Rom* II with this approach is that Luther clearly ruled out any use of force in the ecclesial realm.

286. *Rom* II, 583: "The purity of the ethos demands (and indeed we consider ourselves in agreement with Kant at this point) that no mixing of heaven and earth takes place here." See Barth, *Theology of John Calvin*, 76 (trans. rev.): "It is a historical fact that Luther's heart concern was with the pure *foundation* of works and not the *will* for them, with fighting *against* papist works and not fighting *for* works of the Spirit and love."

287. Barth, *Theology of John Calvin*, 77.

288. Barth, "The Substance and Task of Reformed Doctrine, 1923," in *Word of God and Theology*, 191–237, at 215: "The question of the Reformation in *old* Geneva [is not] whether one wants to be inspired, impressed, excited, and carried away by this or that religious thing. Rather, it is whether one wants to 'live according to the Word of God.'"

particular value of one's course of action. How can there be, by contrast, a positive notion of action that does not sacrifice all claims in confrontation with others, but that "in faith" strives for something specific "*to God's glory*"?

To answer this question, Barth devises the actualistic concept of revelation. This concept will take us into Barth's well-known ethics of the divine command. The theological development leading up to that point takes place in several momentous theological decisions. Since the starting point and the result of this development of Barth's are highly important, a thorough theological reconstruction is called for.

Statements similar to Barth's comparison between Luther and Calvin that also aim at the theological foundations of a new moral agency can be found in Barth's *Göttingen Dogmatics* (*GD* I–III, especially *GD* III, 1925/26), although they do not come into their own in §32 ("Sanctification"). By contrast, the section on baptism and vocation (*GD* III §30) highlights the *insertio in Christum* (grafting into Christ) that presents "practically Calvin's core doctrine."[289] It emphasizes the new Christian agency. Reconciliation is said to consist in the event in which "Christ becomes *indirectly identical* with me and I with him. That is to say: Christ lives in me [Gal. 2:20]. Indirectly: for I do not cease to be *myself*, nor does he stop being himself. There is no elimination of persons. But still *identical*: in addition to his life, he lives mine, in addition to my life I live his, he in freedom as the one who gives, I in dependency as the one who receives."[290]

Rom II objected to a "mixing of heaven and earth in the sphere of morals."[291] *GD* III, by contrast, does not rest with this simple

289. *GD* III 245–6.
290. Ibid., 247.
291. *Rom* II, 583.

opposition. Becoming members of the church in baptism, Christians participate in the royal reign of Christ (*munus regium*), as laid out in the section on Christ's work, §29. In comparison to the manuals of Protestant Orthodoxy, which *GD* uses as influential works of reference, already the mere amount of text signals a strong appreciation of the royal office of Christ.[292] Christ's priestly sacrifice constitutes the church, which is in turn maintained, protected, and guided by Christ the king. In consequence, Christ guides his own so that their works correspond positively to how justification based on Christ's work grants communion with God. What is new in comparison with Barth's works discussed so far is that Christ's royal office complements the doctrines of Christ's prophetic and, first and foremost, priestly office.

> The fact that the Son of God has acquired his own people through his blood and that he addresses them as his own in his revelation does not say quite enough yet. Are they his own in fact? Is there indeed the church of the elect and the reconciled within the world—although everything, everything speaks against the notion that the church is real and no mere idea? Yes, answers the doctrine of the *munus regium* [Christ's royal office].[293]

Due to this fact, the church is viewed differently than in *Rom* II. The commentary was especially critical of the church, calling it the hubristic attempt of pouring the relationship with the holy God into an institutional form.[294] The church's striving for a continuous temporal correspondence to the eschatological truth of God is "no

292. Hinrich Stoevesandt, "Die Göttinger Dogmatikvorlesung: Grundriss der Theologie Barths," in Beintker et al., *Barth in Deutschland*, 77–98, at 91: While Heppe and Bizer's compendium of Reformed Orthodoxy presents significantly less material on Christ's royal office than on the priestly one, *GD* draws on both concepts in roughly equal measure.
293. *GD* III, 170 ("*in der Welt, in der Alles, Alles dagegen spricht*").
294. Barth, *Rom* II, 455: "The church is the place where people know all sorts of things about God and dispose of them, and thus where they do not know and do not dispose of them . . . where one no longer needs to count one's days any moment in order to gain a wise heart."

more than an extension" of "this world,"[295] and hence destined to fail. If, however, Christians avoid the "mixing of heaven and earth," their politics will rightly be "essentially a game."[296] By contrast, Barth argues in 1925 that since the church knows it is founded, maintained, and authorized by its eternal lord, it will be "more demanding, more aggressive, and more critical" in relation to "state, society, culture."[297]

Barth adds that even vis-à-vis the church, the *munus regium* also has "a critical import." At this point Barth only slightly modifies the statement from *Rom* II that the power of resurrection is at work as the power of death: "In the violent act of Christ's kingship, because of his sacrifice and in his word, Christ lets [the church's] life die again and again, he fundamentally questions the church as a factor in history again and again, and destroys the church's continuity again and again."[298] In keeping with the tenor of *Rom* II, Barth warns, "No Christian philosophies of history!"[299]

This does not mean, however, that Barth negates the positive reality of the new Christian ethos categorically. By contrast, he finds a way to reconcile the newly discovered grounds for a positive Christian ethos with the critical perspective of *Rom* II. For this purpose, he reacts against the notion of a knowledge of God and an inspiration of the church that might be so continuous as to be indistinguishable from the capacities of the believers themselves: "This is fundamentally questioned by Christ's death."[300] Barth describes knowledge of God and the inspiration of the church by the Holy Spirit as special events that take place anew each time in a contingent way.[301] "Being in the church essentially means being in

295. Ibid.
296. Ibid., 432, 489.
297. *GD* III, 168
298. Ibid., 173 ("*Gewaltakt . . . in den Tod gegeben . . . ihre geschichtliche Größe . . . Kontinuität immer wieder abgerissen*").
299. Ibid., 190.
300. Ibid., 191.

this new space and this new time in which the impossible (i.e., what is impossible in worldly space and worldly time) becomes possible: human participation in God's knowledge of God's self."[302] This event is not about a new cognitive act but about a new being, as Barth explains with reference to 2 Cor. 5:7.[303]

> Where the work of the son takes place, takes place entirely (and where it takes place, it always takes place entirely), precisely with this the work of the Spirit also takes place. The work of vocation and justification, of sanctification and perseverance is wrought by the Spirit who is God together with the Son and the Father from eternity to eternity.

This position offers a synthesis of *Rom* I and *Rom* II.[304] In the words of *Rom* II, the power of resurrection can work only as a power of death, as a unity of God and world is possible only "beyond birth and death."[305] But from that realm "beyond birth and death," Jesus Christ works in the power of the resurrection as such—under spatio-temporal conditions that, however, are not those of the world. These conditions are the church, not understood as an institution, but as the volatile, elusive event of revelation, an act that occurs entirely afresh whenever it happens. Revelation is virtually without temporal extension: "In the resurrection the new world of the Holy Spirit touches the old world of the flesh. But it touches it the way a tangent touches a circle, that is, without touching it, and precisely because it does *not* touch it, it touches it as its boundary, as a *new* world."[306]

301. Ibid., 191.
302. Ibid., 189 (Barth's parenthesis).
303. Ibid. The following quotation is from 175–6 (Barth's parentheses).
304. In 1947, Barth describes the genesis of his thought especially with regard to *The Epistle to the Romans* as a smooth development, not differentiating between the two editions. Barth, "Brechen und Bauen: Eine Diskussion," in "'*Der Götze wackelt': Zeitkritische Aufsätze, Reden und Briefe von 1930 bis 1960*, ed. Klaus Kupisch (Berlin: Käthe Vogt, 1961), 108–23, at 112–13.
305. *Rom* II, 60, 77, 319. Among the concepts from *Rom* II that assume fundamental importance in *GD* as well is especially the revelation of God's hiddenness: Daniel L. Migliore, "Karl Barth's First Lectures in Dogmatics: Instruction in the Christian Religion," in *GD* I, xv–lvii, at xxix–xxx.

Thus, Barth does not view baptism as a "stronghold of the new world" as in *Rom* I,[307] a "warrant" that "the work of [God's] redemptive will is no human, all too human tower of Babel."[308] Nonetheless, and in keeping with *Rom* I, *GD* views true baptism not as a "tower of Babel," but the effective act of being grafted into Christ. In baptism, God's action brings forth a real new being and a positive new ethos. Barth retains the critical edge of *Rom* II in pointing out that the divine event is not at anyone's disposal: in any moment, as long as it lasts, God prevails over against the fallen condition of the world.

In the worldly, human sphere, the critical questioning of any ethos is quite appropriate then: "What, then, are we to do? . . . First and foremost, *ask this question*! May God preserve for us *this question*! May God encircle us with it, as a question, on every side."[309] Acting in this worldly sphere means taking a stance appropriate to the power of death, to avoid all morality, and to negate oneself in true repentance. In the moment in which Christ does his work in the church, however—"and where it takes place, it always takes place entirely"—the situation has changed: "What are we to do? First and foremost, stop asking this question."[310] In that moment, Christians must not question revelation in a worldly manner. Questioning God critically in the moment of revelation would mean turning revelation into an object and thus rebelling against God's being active as the ultimate subject. On the one hand, Barth envisions revelation as God's powerful effect on Christians. Any hypothetical attempt of Christians to subvert their new reality is doomed to failure anyway.

306. *Rom* II, 51–2.
307. *Rom* I, 214.
308. Ibid., 368.
309. *Rom* II, 348.
310. *Rom* I, 517.

On the other hand, Christians, no less than anyone else, are dyed-in-the-wool rebels.

> The power of God's action abolishes the state of sin, making it a matter of the past. The state of grace is made present and valid. That does not mean that the human person is no longer a sinner. It does mean that as a sinner the human person is an entity of the past, something abolished. . . . The Holy Spirit calls people in complete, unlimited sovereignty. The fact of the matter is not at all that human persons might provoke or sabotage their vocation. They certainly want to sabotage their vocation, even with all their powers, with their entire existence.[311]

Barth notably calls God's revelation, along the lines of *Rom* II, an "impossibility," which becomes a "possibility" in every act of revelation anew, although "everything, everything"[312] speaks against it. If God's revelation becomes real in the church, however, things are turned around: in the moment of revelation, God's hiddenness is an impossibility. The contrast between §§29–30 and §32 ("Sanctification") lies in the fact that §32 does not yet make actualism the reigning principle in ethics, conjuring up the dark backdrop instead, against which God's contingent revelation stands out like a bolt of lightning in the night sky.[313] A similar dynamic is operative in the lecture "Rechtfertigung und Heiligung" (1927).

Thus, when Friedrich Gogarten's pamphlet *Gericht oder Skepsis* (Judgment or skepticism) criticizes Barth's preoccupation with judgment for reducing all action to doing no more than giving expression to its own worthlessness, he is partly right as far as Barth's texts from the 1920s are at issue.[314] Even if God's actualistic activity leads to some positive action, the judgment of futility is still looming

311. *GD* III, 241.
312. Ibid., 170.
313. For the image of "lightning" describing revelation, see *Rom* II, 390, *GD* II, 61.
314. On the criticism in "Gericht oder Skepsis" see Stefan Holtmann, *Karl Barth als Theologe der Neuzeit: Studien zur kritischen Deutung seiner Theologie*, Forschungen zur systematischen und ökumenischen Theologie 118 (Göttingen: Vandenhoeck & Ruprecht, 2007), 165–70.

large in the background. The shortcomings of *Rom* II still contribute significantly to Barth's new concept. For this reason even the new actualistic ethics does not rest on a solid foundation. However, since Gogarten's critique does not note the transformation of the human person in the fleeting event of revelation, according to Barth, and since Gogarten's critique also comes with a delay of ten years, and finally since Gogarten's striving for ecclesial power in a racist state in the late 30s is even worse, we must also conclude that Gogarten is not right, either.[315]

GD does not yet highlight as single-mindedly as some of Barth's later texts that revelation must be conceived of as the revelation of a lord who is the ineluctable active subject (in contrast to an object) within the encounter between an I and a Thou. Yet even if this view does not leap out at the reader of *GD*, it belongs, nonetheless, to its theological foundations. That the sermon is the medium of the divine address is crucial for *GD*.[316] In an oft-repeated expression of Goethe's, Barth lays clear emphasis on the purely spiritual character of revelation: "Spirit speaking to spirit through the Spirit."[317] Barth does not immediately draw attention to the immediate encounter with God's self, in which unreserved personal intimacy is supposedly the crucial aspect. The first time he does so pointedly is in a short paragraph in §3 under the heading "*Deus Dixit*" ("And God said"): "Only within this I-Thou relation, in which one speaks and another

315. In 1937, Gogarten called on the church to commit itself more strongly to the German people and the German state; see Holtmann, *Barth*, 168.

316. Barth, *GD* I, 14; 30–31.

317. Ibid., 62, 225, 227, 237 (twice), 253, 308. See also *GD* II, 69 (§16: "God's Essence"); *GD* III, 415. According to *MD* 88, 511, 578, "The Spirit speaks to the spirit." The quotation is from Johann Wolfgang von Goethe, *Wilhelm Meister's Apprenticeship*, book 8, ch. 5: "The person whom I am to speak with, I must see, because it is a solitary man, whose form and character gives worth or worthlessness to what he says: but, on the other hand, whoever sings to me must be invisible; his form must not confuse me, or corrupt my judgment. Here, it is but one human organ speaking to another; it is not spirit speaking to spirit, not a thousandfold world to the eye, not a heaven to the man."

is spoken to, in which there is communication and reception, only in full *action* is revelation revelation."[318] Thus, in a more actualistic manner, the section would have to be called *Deus Dicit*, "God speaks," while the perfect tense *Deus Dixit* obscures Barth's concern.

How does a personal encounter take place in which God still remains the lord? Barth does not describe this before the second-to-last sentence of the section on the Trinity, §5, in the conclusion to the pneumatological section. Before, Barth describes the conceptual task of doing justice to God's lordship in a way that is no mere abstraction. It must become clear "that the Lord who is over and in the world makes himself known to me, the person I am, as *my* Lord, that he stands in *my* life, that he is seen by *me* as a factor with which I have to reckon."[319] At the end of the section, Barth wishes to do justice to this demand with the typical vocabulary of dialogistic personalism:

> The unheard-of thing that we *believe* and *obey* . . . is not really posited by our thinking of God as Revealer and Revealed. We also have to think of something special in addition. God is God in another way as well. ... He is Lord not only *over* all things and *in* all things, but . . . God is *our* Lord, *mine* and *yours*, the God who stands related to us as I and Thou, as Thou and I, from eternity to eternity.[320]

Barth's premise that God must not be called Lord merely in the abstract shows Barth's interest in God's power and authority. This concern repeats what has been important in §5 all along. He spoke not only repeatedly of Christ as *kyrios* (Lord), but already the thesis statement points out that the Trinitarian persons are, in different respects, Lord over the human contradiction against God. Yet it is

318. *GD* I, 58
319. Ibid., 125.
320. Ibid., 130 (italics in the German original). Remarkably, in this passage, at the end of the section on the Trinity, Barth argues for the personhood of the Spirit, a notion he later disputed in *CD* I/1, interpreting the Spirit's epithet in the Nicene creed, *to kyrion*, as a neuter adjective. The previous quotation from *GD* I, 58 does not yet combine the title *Lord* with personalist thought.

only at the end of the section that he combines the title *Lord* with the notion of a personal encounter between God and the human person. Only in this combination can Barth do justice to his conviction that God is Lord not in abstraction, but "for me." Thus, the experience of an individual, personal, spiritual encounter becomes the crucial and exclusive criterion of anything worthy of being called revelation.

After von Balthasar had pointed out the theological importance of this concept, the relevant secondary literature again ignored the importance of this notion of Barth's. According to von Balthasar, the *Münster Dogmatics* (*MD*) asks,

> Is human nature a suitable medium for God's revelation? Barth affirms that it is: the I-Thou-relationship between two human beings presents two implications: (1) the reality of an I, which is a true subject . . . and (2) the reality of an authentic encounter . . . Barth will later call the I-Thou-relationship in man an "analogy" with that between God and man, which will then imply the possibility of a revelation.[321]

Barth does not yet draw a parallel between the personal encounter with God, on the one hand, and that between husband and wife, on the other, which will figure prominently in *CD* III and that is so important for von Balthasar as well. Yet against the backdrop of *GD*, the personal relationship between man and woman seems like a special case of the general notion of the personal encounter that is already highly charged theologically. Without this theological significance of personalism in *GD*, however, the statement is too vague that, in good preaching, a "correlation of Spirit and Scripture" takes place, which happens dialectically and is not warranted by a mere recitation of Scripture.[322] This raises the question of the

321. Von Balthasar, *Theology of Karl Barth*, 88–9. The fact that after *Rom* II, Barth comes to attach great importance to personalism is a light at the end of the tunnel for von Balthasar; finally, Barth comes closer to the truth of a rightly understood *analogia entis*.

322. McCormack, *Barth's Theology*, 342.

criterion to use to determine whether such correlation is not a mere illusion and that the Spirit active in that event is indeed the Holy Spirit.

By assigning personalism high systematic significance at this point, Barth moves closer to Gogarten, whose personalism Barth found highly fascinating. He reports how in a lively personal meeting with Barth in 1926, Gogarten explained to him what his theology was really after.

> The incarnation, hence truly Luther's core concern, neither the Trinity nor eschatology, but the doctrine of reconciliation in the form of God's becoming a human person. Where is God? In heaven? What is God in *heaven* to me! In Christ God is present for me, having become a human person, more precisely. . . . Christ's thus being human is what gives me the right and the possibility to view human beings indeed as such persons in whom I am encountered by Christ and his divine demand. This is where the Thou-I-dialectics step in.[323]

There is a significant commonality between *GD* and Gogarten's thought indeed. Barth shares with the Lutheran theologian at least the insistence on God's abiding character as the active subject and the personalist form of the encounter with God.[324] God transforms God's self into an object, while always remaining the active subject.

Yet the theological relationship between Barth and Gogarten had always been ambiguous. On the one hand, in a letter from 1926, Barth conceded in a problematic way that Gogarten's personalism is right in "rooting out anything object-like from revelation." On the other hand, Gogarten is "moving very closely alongside the most

323. *Barth-Thurneysen-Briefwechsel 1921–30*, 438–9 (Oct. 30, 1926). Barth refers to Gogarten's book *Ich glaube an den dreieinigen Gott: Eine Untersuchung über Glauben und Geschichte* (Jena: Diederichs, 1926).

324. Friedrich Gogarten, "Karl Barths Dogmatik," *Theologische Rundschau* 1 (1929): 60–80, at 60–61, 74. See also Holtmann, *Barth*, 162–4; Holtmann, "Dialektische Theologie im Streit um die Neuzeit: Zur Auseinandersetzung zwischen Karl Barth und Friedrich Gogarten," *Zeitschrift für Dialektische Theologie* 23 (2007): 246–62, at 260.

dangerous identifications between God and history."[325] Already *Rom* II had argued that the fellow human being as "the other" points to the "wholly other," a notion that later gained in prominence in the ethics lecture. Yet in the concept of revelation presented in *GD*, it is the Holy Spirit who plays the role that Gogarten assigns to Christ as the incarnate God. In proclamation, we are faced with God as a Thou, yet not a Thou incarnate in the flesh, but in the Spirit and thus as Lord.

Gogarten's interpretation of the incarnation is imprecise to be sure. God's becoming human does not mean per se that any human person reflects the authority of the incarnate God.[326] Nonetheless, Gogarten was on target with a point he made in a review of Barth's *MD*. This is his critical question whether Barth arrives at his theological conclusions "based on the event of the *incarnation* of the word."[327] Gogarten thinks that Barth fails to be consistent in his claim that God's "being human" is not a "second reality apart from God's divinity, an appearance, a piece of clothing, a dwelling place, a symbol, a mere parable of the word."[328] Admittedly, Barth is right in another viewpoint criticized by Gogarten, that theology should indeed speak of a "realm in which God is God in God's self."[329] Yet this notion does not suffice given Barth's further notion that God reveals God's self completely in a spiritual or mental way, as "Spirit speaking to spirit through the Spirit."[330] Barth's insistence on

325. *Barth-Thurneysen-Briefwechsel 1921–30*, 422 (June 10, 1926). Barth's lecture, "Das Erste Gebot als theologisches Axiom," will repeat the charge of confusing God and creaturely, historical entities. In Barth's *Theologische Fragen und Antworten* (Zollikon: Evangelischer Verlag, 1957), 127–43, at 141.

326. Gogarten, "Barths Dogmatik," 72–3.

327. Ibid., 72. Gogarten indeed fell for the *Zeitgeist* (McCormack, *Barth's Theology*, 409), yet his reasoning *seemed* thoroughly theological, even making an impression on Barth.

328. *MD*, 357; see also *GD* I, 147–8; see Gogarten, "Barths Dogmatik," 76.

329. *MD*, 311; see 310.

330. See n316 above. By contrast, Gogarten ("Barths Dogmatik," 75) criticizes in principle Barth's advocacy of the concept of an immanent Trinity.

the completeness and sufficiency of a spiritual or mental encounter between an I and a Thou makes God's revelation in the flesh merely a one-off trigger of a revelation that from then on takes place every time anew, yet in a purely spiritual event.

By contrast, Barth calls the incarnation an inappropriate vehicle for God's "pure" revelation, even a diminution and alienation: "No other creature can do what God in God's pure deity cannot do, namely, really *meet* us, become objective, perceptible, and comprehensible to us as one of ourselves."[331] With regard to the creature Jesus, Gogarten has a point in insisting on the incarnation against Barth.[332] Yet since Gogarten understands personalism in keeping with a supposedly general principle of divine incarnation exemplified in the incarnation of the Son, he tends toward a blanket "identification between God and history." In turn, since Barth understands personalism in keeping with a mentalist principle of spirituality, which he views as the work of the Holy Spirit, he still tends toward the notion of God's worldlessness. Von Balthasar comments, "The emphasis is not, as in the later volumes of the *Church Dogmatics*, on the fact of God becoming *human*, not even on God *becoming* human, but still and entirely on the actuosity of the word."[333]

In the two lecture cycles of *GD* after the summer term of 1924 (partly held in Münster), Barth's personalism becomes even more pronounced. For example, Barth asserts that to begin with, God assumes the form of an object in the encounter between the I and the Thou, so that God's unrestricted being as an active subject remains God's mystery. Yet since God does remain the active subject, God's mystery is revealed precisely in the moment in which God

331. *GD* I, 137.

332. According to Matthias Gockel, *Barth and Schleiermacher on the Doctrine of Election: A Systematic-Theological Comparison* (Oxford: Oxford University Press, 2006), 154–5, too, the actualism in *GD* works to the detriment of Christology.

333. Von Balthasar, *Barth*, 91 (trans. rev.).

encounters the Christian personally as a Thou.[334] If we do not take seriously that God takes the form of the object, revealing God's self directly as Lord,

> we slip willy-nilly into the neutral sphere where the I and Thou merge into one another. . . . When we do not think of revelation as such, that is, one person speaking and another spoken to, God revealing himself to us and we to whom God reveals himself; when revelation is seen from the standpoint of the noninvolved spectator, then it amounts to nonrevelation.[335]

The coincidence of opposites in God being active subject and object is the core of Barth's concept of revelation in these texts, which takes the form of the revelation of the Lord as a Thou.

It also follows from this concept that outside of the event of revelation, anything revealed by God becomes a mere object, which is thus no longer in keeping with revelation.[336] The attempt to make God merely a passive object of knowledge is doomed to failure, argues Barth, since this would miss God's lordship. God the Lord is necessarily characterized by unlimited power and authority. God can be known exclusively through God's own activity. This fact creates the mystery of revelation. In the act of revelation this mystery is revealed, yet it remains a mystery. At the same time God could not be revealed in any wider sense, as God's revelation is by necessity both direct and indirect. Neither of the two characterizations excludes the other or restricts it. In revelation, both characterizations are only what they are in being strictly correlated with the other. God is only perceived appropriately as a Thou and as Lord at the same time.[337] The fact of the church, Barth argues, rests on God's immediacy

334. *GD* II, 60–61.
335. *GD* I, 62, 58.
336. *GD* II, 60–61.
337. *CD* I/1, 43, 402.

becoming real only in God's indirect presence: "Precisely as witness, preaching is immediate not only to scripture but also to revelation."[338] Due to the volatile relation of God as subject and object, Barth calls revelation a simultaneous revealing and hiding.[339]

This is the so-called actualism in Barth's concept of revelation: God's free encounter with humanity as I and Thou must "be an event in new actuality every morning, if it truly is an occurrence between God and the human person."[340] In this sense, *GD* §§29–30 shows that an ethics that rests on the concept of revelation advocated in *GD* must be an actualistic ethics. The actualistic character of Barth's ethics lectures 1928–31 will be explored later on. But already according to *GD* §§29–30, all ethics must be actualistic, or God's revelation as Lord, as exclusive, active subject in the I-Thou-encounter is impossible.

The fundamentally actualistic character of Barth's theology in this phase, as well as the ensuing theological problems, are also clear from Barth's doctrine of election (*GD* I, §18).[341] God elects and rejects people not once and for all according to one absolute decree, but again and again anew in time. Significantly, the goal of the repeated choice does not, at least not per se, lie in increasing the number of the elect. For predestination takes place again and again "for every single person individually, in now electing, now rejecting."[342] Here Barth pays notable attention to God's negative judgment. On the positive side, election takes place unconditionally. The elect are thus led through judgment to repentance.[343] God's election makes God's

338. *GD* I, 36 (trans. rev.).

339. On this concept see McCormack, *Barth's Theology*, 18.

340. *GD* II, 61.

341. Section 18 is included in the English *GD* I, while in the German edition of *Unterricht in der christlichen Religion*, it is part of vol. 2. References are to the English translation (*GD* I).

342. *GD* I, 454 (trans. rev.). "Naturally, specific people are catastrophically affected by the divine electing and rejecting" (ibid.). See 471 ("all are at every moment under the divine either—or and can be either elected or rejected at any moment," trans. rev.). See Gockel, *Barth*, 146.

hiddenness take the form of judgment, and in this judgment, God promises salvation.[344] In reprobation, however, judgment takes on a different form. Rather than suffering from God's judgment, the reprobate remain blissfully unaware of their predicament. "In this case nothing special happens to us; without being aware of what it means we remain in contradiction, in guilt and need, and finally in the eternal damnation [*Verdammnis*] that is, without any hope, due to us anyway."[345]

God's actualistic predestination constitutes the "either—or of this twofold possibility with which each of us is faced at any moment."[346] By reinterpreting *election* in the eternal decree in a specific way, Barth is (the terminology of the Reformed tradition notwithstanding) in close proximity to a Lutheran doctrine of law and gospel. Barth agrees with a Lutheran notion of law and gospel in saying: "But the divine Word does not say No. It says Yes, for the Yes constantly breaks forth out of the No."[347] The sinner embraces God's free grace in the acute awareness that grace is not deserved—far from it. Barth makes a point to note the "teleology" in this dynamic, which, however, takes place in *one* aspect of double predestination, in election. It is an inconsistency when in this passage he calls the

343. *GD* I, 440 (thesis statement §18).

344. Ibid., 447–8. With regard to reprobation and election, *CD* II/1, 236 speaks of "an ordered dialectic, and indeed one which is teleologically ordered." According to McCormack's plausible judgment (*Theology*, 459–60), this is an innovation that Barth hit upon when he developed his doctrine of election further in the mid-1930s. Certainly, *GD* §18 already strove for a dialectical teleology of rejection and election, but it is questionable whether Barth succeeded in this endeavor.

345. *GD* II, 440, see 453, 456.

346. Ibid., 440 (trans. rev.).

347. *GD* I, 461; see 464–5. See also 471 (trans. rev.): the Christian's path leads through "condemnation—indeed, though hell itself—to salvation and life. In this *teleology* of *God* that is revealed in *Christ* (we must stress all three words) there is the source of our certainty of election and salvation." See Luther, *Bondage of the Will,* 3:62: "Thus when God makes alive he does it by killing. . . . The Lord kills and brings to life; he brings down to Sheol and raises up." See also Luther, *Heidelberg Disputation*, 1:51–2 (thesis 18).

judgment experienced by the elect "reprobation."[348] While this may cause confusion about the relation between reprobation and teleology at this point, reprobation is not, on the whole, part of this teleology, as Barth emphasizes otherwise that the reprobate do not experience judgment, remaining unaware of their sin. Grace as they know it is cheap grace, not God's grace. That, of all things, is the critical edge of reprobation. A teleology resulting from the interplay of law and gospel—two aspects Barth subsumes under *election*—is characteristic even for a hard-nosed conservative Lutheran such as Werner Elert.[349] For Barth, election results in the elect, of all people, facing God's hiddenness in all its harshness, as God's judgment. Nonetheless, hidden in God's no, they also discover God's 'Yes.'[350] But the analogy to the concept of law and gospel refers to the dynamic inherent in God's election and not to reprobation. When Barth calls Jesus Christ the mirror of election,[351] he uses Reformed terminology in order to articulate Luther's concern to point toward the proclamation of law and gospel, thus moving away from all speculation about God's sheer divinity. On the whole, the parallels between *GD* §18 and Luther's *On the Bondage of the Will* are significant.[352] They include a parallel between *reprobation* and Luther's *deus absconditus* (hidden God).

348. Ibid. (trans. rev.: "*Verwerfung*"). See n346.

349. Werner Elert, "Dialektik der Offenbarung," in *Gesetz und Evangelium: Beiträge zur gegenwärtigen theologischen Diskussion*, eds. Ernst Kinder and Klaus Haendler (Darmstadt: Wissenschaftliche Buchgesellschaft, 1968), 159 65, at 161.

350. *GD* I, 447–8. Ibid., 469, Barth quotes Rom. 11:32 in order to argue first for the possibility of rejection by God and then for a teleology towards election.

351. Ibid., 470.

352. For Luther's views on God's election and rejection, see Luther, *Bondage of the Will*, in *Career of the Reformer* 3:58–9, 146–7, 180, 199–200. Barth's rejecting God corresponds to Luther's *deus absconditus*, as God's erratic, even fearsome activity is not revealed in Christ. An exception to the correspondence is that for Luther, faith in Christ indicates that one will not be under the sway of this hidden God, while Barth's God changes God's mind freely (see below). In addition, Luther argues for a fundamental actualism, according to which the world would cease to exist if it were not for God's constantly renewed action, see ibid., 180–81, 64.

The crucial question that remains is how actualistic double predestination might aim teleologically at salvation. Barth asserts that it does,[353] but significant problems have remained overlooked in recent research. There is a significant inconsistency in §18. Certainly Barth does assert that we "know God in his revelation in Christ as the one whose will is to save and not to judge."[354] But such recognition presupposes election already, while it remains unclear how rejection, by itself, might contribute to salvation rather than damnation. Barth's argument that God only reprobates in order to elect can also suggest that reprobation is never God's last word. But then why does Barth highlight eternal damnation? "*Hell does exist, however*, even if we can say less about it than the forefathers did."[355]

353. Ibid., 460.
354. Ibid., 471.
355. *GD* II, 441–2. See *GD* I, 440 (cited below), 458–9, *GD* II, 289, 414, 425; *GD* III, 6. The full implications of the cited statement about hell require unpacking. Gockel's monograph on the doctrine of election, for example, offers no more than a vague gesture towards eternal damnation, omitting them from Barth's thesis statement (*GD* I, 440 in Gockel, *Barth*, 139; see also *GD* I, 459 in Gockel, *Barth*, 149). Thus, Barth's references to a teleology in double predestination suggest, mistakenly, that eternal damnation is not an issue for Barth. In consequence, Barth's critique of the traditional Reformed doctrine of predestination is open to a misunderstanding. Section 18 is said to disagree with H. Heidegger's statement that "certain human beings were not elected and remain in the general misery of damnation. In particular, Barth objects to the use of the phrase 'certain human beings,' which entails the existence of two strictly separate groups of individuals" (ibid., 145). However, regarding the last judgment itself, §18 agrees with Heidegger's view. Barth argues that at any one point, and thus—crucially—also on judgment day, there are indeed 'certain persons' who constitute 'strictly separate groups.' Before the last judgment—and this is the disagreement between Barth and Heidegger—God's renewed judgment renders the boundary between the two groups permeable. Nonetheless, a reprobate is *not* elect at that point, and in that sense the groups are strictly separate indeed. There may be a repeated transfer between the two groups *before* judgment day, in both directions. But the last judgment cements the boundary between the two groups for eternity, and we do not know which act of election or reprobation will be the last one. There will be no transfer between the saved and the damned. This results in a dilemma, however: the relation between a person's previous faith and the ultimate judgment is strictly arbitrary. In *contrast* to the traditional view, Calvin's argument that "Christ is thus the mirror" of election (*GD* I, 470) has no leverage in an actualistic scheme. The argument that people are elect if they believe in Christ now means nothing more than that a person will be granted eternal salvation if and only if she finds herself elect in the very moment of the last judgment, *regardless* of her previous status. Barth's actualism reduces his assertion that Christ is "the source of our certainty of election and salvation" (ibid., 471) to a commonplace, since God can reject even the elect at

Barth's thesis statement of §18 is programmatic in not positing a teleology towards salvation:

> If veiling is the content of God's unveiling and unveiling the point of his veiling, we are obviously set under a twofold possibility grounded in God himself. The hiddenness of God in his revelation might mean that with hearing ears we hear only offense or foolishness or nothing at all and are therefore under an illusion about God. In this case nothing special happens to us; without being aware of what it means we remain in contradiction, in guilt and need, and finally in the eternal damnation that, without any hope, is due to us anyway. Or else God's revelation in his hiddenness through the Holy Spirit becomes the basis of faith and obedience and therefore of knowledge of God. Something special then happens to us, for the darkness in which we find ourselves becomes the judgment of God, but we also participate therewith in the grace of God and the hope of eternal salvation. In the first case we are passed over or reprobated by God; in the second case we are elected or accepted by God. In the either—or of this twofold possibility which is actual for each of us at this moment, God's glory triumphs no matter how the decision goes.[356]

While rejection is abandonment to fatal indifference rather than the cause of suffering or worldly failure, election is the cause of a salvific crisis.[357] Yet Barth asserts that "all are at every moment

any one moment. A crucial commonality between Barth's actualistic concept and the traditional view of double predestination is however, that in deciding whether a particular person will serve God's glory either by being saved or by being damned eternally (on the operative notion of glory, see below), God is no better off than Buridan's ass.

356. *GD* I, 440 (trans. rev.). The first sentence might hint at the possibility of a teleology (God's unveiling as the point of veiling—but then again: veiling as the point of unveiling), but this remains inherent in election, not involving reprobation. After the quoted section, Barth adds that "at each moment this decision is to be sought where it has been taken from all eternity, that is, in God's wisdom and mercy." But of course the reprobate are fundamentally unable to find the answer to the question in God's wisdom or mercy—in their false self-confidence, they do not even seek an answer.

357. If reprobation implied the subjective experience of judgment by the one thus rejected, the teleology of reprobation and election would work out, as the assurance of the gospel would break forth from God's judgment—i.e., if law and gospel corresponded to reprobation and election, respectively. But according to Barth, the judgment of reprobation is not experienced as crisis. Thus, the question is how reprobation relates to election within the supposed teleology of double predestination. Since reprobation itself does not contribute to a teleology—which,

under the divine either—or and can be either elected or rejected at every moment."[358] Why would God choose to abandon a believer to be indifferent to sin, judgment, and undeserved grace, even if that person embraced salvation in Christ before? Does this not place God's faithfulness in jeopardy? Barth arrives at a dualism in God by failing to conceptualize the supposed teleology that God might achieve by both rejecting and electing. Thus, God's goal in double predestination is to manifest "his glory by manifesting mercy and *iustitia* (justice, righteousness)."[359] In this aspect, Barth is in full agreement with the traditional doctrine of predestination. God pursues God's glory also in a way excluding a creature's salvation. Since it contributes to God's glory for condemnation to be the eternal lot of some, libertarian freedom seems to be an important aspect of God's glory. Indeed it is entirely in God's hands whether a person

in the concept of law and gospel, the law does, relentlessly crushing all obstinacy—another mechanism for a potential teleology must be sought. Since Barth does highlight the eternal damnation of the reprobate and explicitly refers to God reprobating even the elect (see n357), there is no teleology towards salvation. In sum, the doctrine of election in *GD* is teleological only in the trivial sense that God's election, if sustained, works salvation and God's reprobation, if sustained, works condemnation, while God remains glorious both in working salvation for some and punishing others eternally. The latter aspect refers to a God who is not revealed in Christ. To the extent that Barth disputes that, §18 is inconsistent.

358. *GD* I, 471 (trans. rev.), see also 453 ("God's free, uninhibited sovereignty over Jews and Gentiles that now has mercy and now hardens," trans. rev.). Gockel, *Barth*, 147 also highlights "God's lasting freedom to say either Yes or No to a human being." The irresistibility of God's grace only applies as long as election lasts (*GD* I, 457). The possibility of rejecting even the elect is a criterion of God's true divinity: "To be granted, even obliged to believe, is seen as grace only when we perceive that we are, as it were, passed from one hand of God to the other hand of the same God; that he who now receives us could with the same power reprobate us . . . that we are in his hands whether for grace or its opposite" (ibid., 452, trans. rev.). God's grace is only grace because being merciless is always a 'living option' for God. But how could anyone put all trust in God, if there were, as §18 suggests, reason to suspect that God is not *faithful* in being merciful? People may think of alternatives. Even though he certainly does not trust God, we might, with Camus, "imagine Sisyphus happy."

359. *GD* I, 467 (trans. rev.). This also echoes the original traditional Reformed definition of reprobation, with which Barth is thus, to a large extent, in agreement (with qualifications pertaining to "certain," or "fixed men")—in H. Heidegger's words: "Reprobation is the decree of God, by which out of the mere good pleasure of His will he has resolved to leave fixed men, whom He does not elect, in the mass of corruption . . . in order to display the glory of His *iustitia* (justice, righteousness)" (*GD* I, 453, trans. rev.).

repents or not.[360] Section 18 portrays God's honor as God's free power of disposal over the creature, although the deeper legitimacy with which such disposal is exercised may remain obscure. To the extent that God's glory implies just condemnation, God is not revealed in Jesus Christ's cross and resurrection. Related to this is the unpredictable element in actualism in general, which will also characterize the actualistic ethics of Barth's later ethics lectures. This problem will only be solved with a new doctrine of election that sees God's fullness in no other way than as revealed in Christ.

In spite of such problems, the doctrine of election §18 presents more than merely a repetition of the ideas from *Rom* II. To begin with, Barth *attempts*—if unsuccessfully—to argue for a goal orientation in God's action, calling Christ the mirror of election. Although the theology fleshing out this notion remained to be developed, at least Barth does not highlight judgment as strongly as salvation when speaking of Christ.

Nonetheless, the actualism of revelation and the negation of the world are two sides of the same coin.[361] This is true although Barth remarks in 1924 that "God is *our* Lord, *mine* and *yours*, the God who stands related to us as I and Thou, as Thou and I, from eternity to eternity."[362] Even so, God's lordship appears against the backdrop of the condemnation of the world, from which it stands out as incommensurate and unworldly. The act of revelation takes the human person, as it were, out of herself.

360. Ibid., 451.
361. Von Balthasar, *Theology of Karl Barth*, 94 comments on *MD* that Barth was "still fascinated, overpowered even, by the philosophical ideology and schematism of *The Epistle to the Romans*. . . . Though the world (which stands vis-à-vis the Word of God) is certainly something and not nothing, it looks so harsh and forlorn under this glare that one might just as well wish it did not exist. . . . Barth finally came to see the unchristian tenor of such a panorama and strove with all his might to overcome it. From all sides he tried to deflect such consequences while keeping to his original table of consequences" (trans. rev.).
362. *GD* I, 130.

In a vague way, Barth's *MD* (1927) relativizes the fundamental importance of negative ethics that was still formative in the new concept of revelation. Section 19, "Faith and Obedience," asserts that the obedience of faith relativizes the human ignorance and disregard of God. Again, the fundamental hermeneutic function of a general, vague religiosity, observed already in *GD* I, reemerges when Barth speaks of a Thou that is hidden in history, yet meets us there and speaks.[363] Nonetheless, Barth at times presents "the conscious comprehension of God by the human person . . . as an unbiased and serious act of the human person."[364] This notion will also be the conclusion of *CD* I/1, §1.[365] Although knowledge of God, rather than ethics, is at issue here, Barth begins to relativize the dominance of self-negation by appreciating the human activity that remains needful of forgiveness, but participates in God's promise. *MD* also shows the great prominence of personalism in Barth's thought, especially in the context of the Trinitarian revelation. In revealing God's self in a Trinitarian act, God is both Lord and a Thou. In contrast to the section on the Trinity in *GD*, the thesis statement *MD* §10 now also highlights the elements *Thou* and *Lord* concisely as the essential notions:

> God reveals God's self as the one who is Lord in three modes that are as inseparably connected as they are irreducibly distinct: God the Father, the Son, and the Holy Spirit. Precisely in God's revelation, God proves and confirms God's self as the Thou that confronts the human person as an ineluctable active subject, precisely the act in which God is God to the human person.[366]

363. *MD*, §19, 419.
364. Ibid., 421; see 422; 424.
365. *CD* I/1 §1.3 can be summarized with the quotation of Calvin on 18: "Every proper knowledge of God is born out of obedience." Such obedience becomes possible in a prayer and faith that "justifies God and not [the Christian]" (23).
366. *MD*, 198: thesis statement §10, "The Triunity of God."

Both *MD* and *CD* I/1 retain the concept of the actualistic revelation of the Lord. In *MD* as in *CD* I/1, not only the thesis statements on the Trinity call God a Thou,[367] but Barth repeats and enhances the predication of God as Lord, which *GD* used of Father, Son, and Spirit. Beyond the usage in *GD,* all five thesis statements on the Trinitarian revelation in *MD* and *CD* I/1 use the title *Lord*.[368] "Barth's theological interpretation of the revelation thus rests on the *concept of God*, which is defined as *rule* (*Herrschaft*)."[369]

> Communion with the One who reveals Himself there always and in all circumstances means for man that this God meets him as a Thou meets an I and unites with him as a Thou unites with an I. Not otherwise! Totally excluded is a communion with this God of the kind that we can have with creatures, namely, of such a kind that the Thou can be changed by an I into an It or He over which or whom the I gains control. Also and particularly as Son and Spirit, the One who reveals Himself according to the witness of Scripture does not become an It or He, but remains Thou. And in remaining Thou He remains the Lord. The subject of revelation is the subject that remains indissolubly subject. One cannot get behind this subject. It cannot become object.[370]

367. Ibid., §10, 198; *CD* I/1 §9, 348.
368. *GD* I, §5, 105. *MD*, §§9–13, *CD* I/1, §§8–12: "God in His Revelation," "The Triunity of God," "God the Father," "God the Son," "God the Holy Spirit" (titles and order identical in *MD* and *CD*). *CD* I/1, §§8–12 constitute the first of three parts within *CD* ch. 2 ("The Revelation of God"): "The Triune God." This is followed by ch. 2 part 2, "The Incarnation of the Word" (*CD* I/2, §§13–15) and ch. 2, part 3, the doctrine of the appropriating grace in the work of the Holy Spirit ("The Outpouring of the Holy Spirit," *CD* I/2, §§16–18). This confirms the impression that in ch. 2, God the Father is conceived of as absolute, so the particular role of the first person within the Trinity remains obscure. A remark by John Webster is apposite here: "If the Spirit's work is merely applicatory, then it is difficult to envisage him as having as full a place in the divine economy of salvation as the other persons." John Webster, "The Identity of the Holy Spirit: A Problem in Trinitarian Theology," *Themelios* 9 (1983): 4–7, 6.
369. Wilfried Härle, *Sein und Gnade: Die Ontologie in Karl Barths Kirchlicher Dogmatik*, Theologische Bibliothek Töpelmann 27 (New York: de Gruyter, 1975), 28. Ibid., 29: "The *concept of God* turns out to be fundamental in Barth's noetics. . . . This is the key that determines the selection, emphasis, and interpretation of the witness to revelation up to all the details." It remains to be added that apart from the notion of God's lordly rule, personalism is also an important presupposition of Barth's concept of revelation in *GD*, *MD*, and *CD* I/1.
370. Ibid., 382. Barth again inculcates the fundamental significance of the coincidence of personal intimacy and sovereignty on 307, 381.

When Barth also insists in *CD* I/1 that God's word is "spiritual," the crucial antonyms are *natural, corporeal,* and *physical.*[371] This does not address a "discernment of spirits" and must thus be interpreted in the sense of "mental" or "intellectual": "Speech, including God's speech, is the form in which reason communicates with reason and person with person. To be sure it is the divine reason communicating with the human reason and the divine person with the human person."[372] Barth repeats explicitly that this is not to be misconstrued in a symbolic sense.[373] Neither does he have Scripture and proclamation only in view here, but God's word as such.[374]

But does Barth not, even at this stage, explore another theological dimension that is at least as relevant for his oeuvre, that is, the historical events themselves as perceived in the biblical traditions? Indeed: "Part of the concept of the biblically attested revelation is that it is a historical event."[375] Quite a different dimension than the personalist encounter is featured when Barth points out,

> When the Bible gives an account of revelation it means to narrate history, i.e., not to tell of a relation between God and man that exists generally in every time and place and that is always in process, but to tell of an event that takes place there and only there, then and only then, between God and certain very specific men.[376]

371. Ibid., 133. This passage adds that God always manifests God's self in conjunction with physical phenomena, yet these seem merely like instrumental vehicles rather than as contributing to the inherent essence of God.
372. Ibid., 135.
373. Ibid., 134, 204. See also 63, 183–4. Barth asserts, "We are not absolutising the human possibilities of the intellect." Yet this negation is doubtful. Barth declares that if the intellect is the crucial category for describing God's word, any skepticism is an irrelevant "private opinion" (ibid., 134).
374. See ibid., 128, thesis statement §5: "The Word of God in all its three forms is God's speech to man."
375. Ibid., 324.
376. Ibid., 326.

A crucial achievement of *CD* I/1 is that a tension arises here with dialogism and the abstract principle of sovereign rule.[377] Attention to the Old Testament stories between God and Israel, as with the Exodus, also constitutes decisive progress in comparison with *GD* and *MD*. In *CD* I/2, the theological importance of the Exodus, for example, will increase further.[378] This important development will be associated with a clearer reordering of the relationship between gospel and law in Barth's lecture, "Das Erste Gebot als theologisches Axiom" (1933, see below). At the same time *CD* I/1 is clearer in its rejection of a revelation inherent in any historical event, no matter how spiritual.

Certainly Barth's insistence on spirituality, reason, or mind contains a grain of truth insofar as these modes of life are important vehicles in which the testimonies to revelation are commonly shared and reflected.[379] From this vehicle, in which the testimonies to revelation are "brought to mind," however, the referent of the testimonies needs to be clearly distinguished. From *GD* to *CD* I/1, a fatal confusion occurs as Barth is focused on fending off an overemphasis on another anthropological dimension besides the mind.[380] A theological emphasis on pious feeling, Barth argues, grants too little attention to the biblical traditions giving testimony to God's revelation in Jesus Christ. By contrast, within the framework of strict personalism, proclamation and theology can only articulate corporeal, economic, political, legal, or social concerns of biblical

377. Rowan D. Williams, "Barth on the Triune God," in *Karl Barth: Studies of his Theological Method*, ed. Stephen W. Sykes (New York: Clarendon/Oxford University Press, 1979), 147–93, at 154, asks critically if the Exodus, the divine encounter at Sinai, and the resurrection were primarily God's self-concealing and revelation, i.e., a cognitive event, in comparison to which the historical particulars might be neglected.

378. *CD* I/2, 80–81, 91, 225, 274, 359, 377–8, 383, 585.

379. See *CD* I/1, 196–7.

380. For Barth's polemics against Schleiermacher's attention to feeling and direct self-consciousness during this period, see ibid., 36–7 and 202–4.

traditions, at best, under the condition that they are interpreted in a sense strictly subservient to a direct mental and personalistic encounter with God. Biblical texts thus have to be reduced to a strictly personalistic encounter between an individual person and God. Not only the Exodus story mentioned above and other narrative passages as well as Old Testament creation traditions, legal texts, cultic rules, and wisdom traditions need to be sacrificed to personalism. Even in several miracle stories in the Synoptic tradition, the personal encounter with Jesus is not in the foreground.[381] Certainly, saying that the Word became flesh means neither that the Word is manifest in any flesh nor that the Word ceases being the Word. Nonetheless, according to John 1:14 the Word did not become spirit, not even "Spirit speaking to the spirit"[382]—Goethe's genius not withstanding—but flesh.

CD I/1 attributes extraordinary theological importance, on the one hand, to biblical traditions that witness to particular historical events such as the Exodus or even the "incarnation," which are rather difficult to understand in accordance with Barth's mentalist characterization of the Word of God, as if "naturalness, corporeality, or any physical event" were at best to be considered a secondary, "lower" aspect serving the primary, "higher" aspect of spirit.[383] This tension within *CD* I/1, on the other hand, means that the criteriological significance of Barth's intellectual personalism comes dangerously close to what Barth himself calls natural theology, the attempt to reduce the biblical testimonies of revelation to foreign criteria. Barth's dualism of "spirit" and "nature" may obscure this

381. To confirm Barth's thesis in dialogue with biblical traditions, it would need to be shown that, for example, healings and miracles merely have a serving function in comparison to the personal encounter. That is not the case, for example, in Mark 5:21–43, 6:30–56, 7:24–8:26, 9:14–29, 10:1–45.

382. See n316.

383. *CD* I/1, 133.

problem, appearing to pit the "spiritual" encounter with God against "natural" theology. However, the intellectual notion of God's speech fits all too nicely into a general human form of speech, "the form in which reason communicates with reason and person with person."[384]

This is in keeping with part of the gist of the historical reconstruction above, according to which Barth's personalistic kyriology slowly replaces other theological concepts in which a general religious sense takes on a crucial role in the proclamation based on biblical traditions.[385] From this perspective, Barth's categorical theological personalism is merely a continuation of these concepts. Barth even admitted, if haphazardly, that his dialogic personalism is the attempt of a natural cognition of God. Emil Brunner charged Barth with merely transferring the human experience of spiritual or mental communication onto the relationship with God, setting it as absolute, and declaring an unexplained concept of human subjectivity the standard of any theological conception of God. Barth replied haphazardly, "Let the reader decide whether [Brunner] is right. It was certainly not done purposely or consciously."[386]

Barth stated in *MD* that it mattered less in theology which philosophy one feels inclined to, as long as one does not make it absolute.[387] This, however, is precisely what Barth's kyriological personalism does. The one-sided way in which Barth's intellectual personalism highlights Christ's dominion creates tensions in the

384. Ibid., 135.

385. See above, "The Dogmatic Concept of the Actualistic Commandment 1924–32: Personalism and Lordship."

386. Barth, "No! Response to Emil Brunner," in: *Natural Theology: Comprising "Natural Theology" by Emil Brunner and the Reply "No" by Karl Barth*, ed. and trans. Peter Fraenkel (Eugene: Wipf & Stock, 2002), 128.

387. *MD*, 526; *GD* II, 241: "The perfection of the world, the goodness imparted to it consists precisely in its creatureliness, in its limitations, in its relativity, on account of which it can be witness to and even instrument and medium of the word of God."

doctrine of God. This also becomes clear in the pneumatology of *CD* I/1, §12, which places Galatians 4 (or Romans 8) in the foreground. In an actualistic ethics, the Spirit does indeed play an important role, as it is conceived as the medium of God's commanding. The object of pneumatology consists, according to Barth, in "what the New Testament usually calls the Holy Spirit as the subjective side in the event of revelation."[388] This is an important part of the event of revelation that *CD* I/1 considers, if not the Trinity itself, the characteristic activity of the Trinitarian God: God the Father is revealed in the Son, which is revealed to humans, also "subjectively," in the Spirit.[389] In unfolding this, Barth highlights, in *CD* I/1 as before, both the personalistic element as well as God's sovereignty as the only criteria of revelation that are both necessary and, in combination, sufficient:

388. *CD* I/1, 449, see also ibid., 203, 242, 332. Barth defined the Holy Spirit as the "subjective side" of revelation also in *GD* I, 48, 168, 185, 198, 446; *MD*, 380, 385, 387. With Jesus as the "objective" side of revelation and the character of God as the "absolute," as discussed above, Barth's doctrine of the Trinity is fundamentally formalistic. Of course, this does not mean that the work of vocation must be avoided in pneumatology. A case against the dominance of this element, as it occurs not only in Barth but indeed in the most formative theologies of consciousness, is made by Michael Welker, *God the Spirit*, trans. John Hoffmeyer, 2nd ed. (Minneapolis: Fortress Press, 2004), 44, 78, 144.

389. On the doctrine of the Trinity in *CD* I/1 and the dominance of the concept of revelation, see Wolfhart Pannenberg, "Die Subjektivität Gottes und die Trinitätslehre: Ein Beitrag zur Beziehung zwischen Karl Barth und der Philosophie Hegels," in *Grundfragen systematischer Theologie: Gesammelte Aufsätze* (Göttingen: Vandenhoeck & Ruprecht, 1980), 2:96–111, with which Wolf Krötke, "Die Summe des Evangeliums: Karl Barths Erwählungslehre im Kontext der Kirchlichen Dogmatik," in *Karl Barth im europäischen Zeitgeschehen (1935–1950: Widerstand—Bewährung—Orientierung. Beiträge zum Internationalen Symposion vom 1. bis 4. Mai 2008 in der Johannes a Lasco Bibliothek, Emden)*, ed. Michael Beintker, Christian Link, and Michael Trowitzsch (Zurich: Theologischer Verlag, 2010), 67–82, at 77 also agrees. Barth's interpretation of the Trinity as an expression of God's being an active subject is very close to Hegel's thought and tends towards subordinationism, as he calls God the Father the revealer and the Son and the Spirit the medium of revelation (ibid., 100). That Barth reconstructs God's being in accordance with the structure of finite cognition suggests projectionism (ibid., 104–5, 107, 110). Pannenberg submits that Jesus' relationship to the Father would be a better starting point (ibid., 101). He also prefers to speak of three "persons" in God who "surrender their independence vis-à-vis each other" (ibid., 108).

> Godhead in the Bible means freedom, ontic and noetic autonomy. . . . The self-sufficiency or immediacy so characteristic of the biblical revelation is the very thing that characterises it as God's revelation on the one side and as the revelation of lordship on the other. But all this becomes fully characteristic only when we note that what we have here is . . . God Himself, who in this freedom speaks as an I and addresses by a Thou. . . . By the fact that He speaks as an I and addresses by a Thou God announces His kingdom. . . . As freedom, lordship and Godhead are real and true in God Himself and only in God Himself, being inaccessible and unknown if God Himself, this I, does not speak and address by a Thou. . . . He is God, He is the ground without grounds . . . we receive it from Him, that God, as Himself, is with us, with us as a man who says I and addresses us as Thou is with others, but with us as the One He is, as the Lord, as He who is free.[390]

Only the free gift of the Spirit makes the encounter with God possible. As the doctrine of God itself, so is the pneumatology of *CD* I/1 (§12: "God the Holy Spirit") a function of the doctrine of revelation. Whether this pneumatology indeed rests on biblical foundations is the theological test of Barth's doctrine of revelation.

According to the thesis statement of the section, revelation takes place when believers become "children of God" by receiving the Holy Spirit. In this event, God reveals God's self in personal intimacy, as a Thou. How does such personal intimacy with God come to be?

Calling believers "children of God," Barth draws on Galatians 4 and Romans 8. He wishes to vindicate his doctrine of revelation especially with reference to this tradition. This attempt may seem natural considering the Spirit-filled cry "Abba, father!" (Gal. 4:6). For Paul, however, the relationship between father and son denotes neither parental authority and strictness nor personal intimacy. By contrast, "sonship" in Romans 8 and Galatians 4 is about legal status and rights throughout, being associated with liberation from "slavery" and a future inheritance.[391] In addition, later on in Romans

390. *CD* I/1, 307.

8, the Spirit is intimately connected with nondialogistic dimensions, such as the constitution of a new Christian ethos and the resurrection (Rom. 8:4,13–14).[392]

According to Barth, being a child of God through faith is not merely a promise, but reality. The person who is given the Holy Spirit is *homo peccator capax verbi divini* (a person capable of receiving the Word of God although a sinner).[393] In the call of personal intimacy, the filial relationship with God is fulfilled, as tribulation is now encountered trusting in God, rather than despair.[394] In Barth's terminology, in the work of the Spirit, God as "Father" makes God's self an object for believers, a Thou in which they may trust. God remains sovereign Lord, yet does not remain, crucially, merely the ruler in an unreachable distance. In that sense, the Spirit is the subjective reality of the filial relationship with God, which nonetheless remains God's free gift rather than being an evident fact.[395]

Barth's theological approach to pneumatology is less appropriate, however, in the face of several exegetical observations in Romans 8. To begin with, the "first fruits of the Spirit" (Rom. 8:23) do not imply that believers call on God as children already. Instead, they *hope for* the filial relationship.[396] This relationship, in turn, denoted less

391. J. Louis Martyn, *Galatians: A New Translation with Introduction and Commentary*, The Anchor Bible 33A (New York: Doubleday, 1997), 386. Neither should mention of the "hearts" (Gal. 4:6) be taken to refer to the emotional aspect involved in personal closeness, while in fact its scope of meaning is much wider, encompassing "the will, the passion, the intellect" (ibid., 391).

392. Romans 8 is better suited to argue for Barth's notion of revelation in the Spirit than, for example, the sayings about the paraclete in John 14:16–17, 26; 15:26; 16:7b–11, 13–15 or the miracle of Pentecost, passages that mainly deal with a witness to Christ, but that lack the aspect of a personal encounter between God and the human person.

393. *CD* I/1, 457 and 458. This is in contrast to the notion *homo peccator non capax verbi divini* in the sections preceding §12 on God the Spirit, ibid., 220, 407. This transition constitutes the point of §12.

394. Ibid., 459.

395. Ibid., 464–5.

396. Having the Spirit in its first instantiations while only expecting the filial status is something other than being a child of God in a hidden manner already. For the futurity of childhood, see

personal intimacy for Paul than legal and political privilege. Further, Rom. 8:19 does not even restrict "creation" merely to human persons, who can have a conscious sense of personal intimacy. Redemption from the "suffering of the present times" must not be reduced to the pangs of conscience, but includes other dimensions such as the physical or the social with the same urgency.[397] This wider referent of salvation is in view three times in Romans 8.[398] Barth's silence on these matters is evidence for the detrimental effect of the intellectual reductionism operative in his concept of revelation, as it systematically occludes an entire dimension in the hope for salvation articulated in Rom. 8. By contrast, in *CD* IV/2, Barth changes course:

> Looking back, we may well ask with amazement how it was that the Reformation, and (apart from a few exceptions) the whole of earlier and especially more recent Protestantism as it followed both Luther and Calvin, could overlook this dimension of the Gospel which is so clearly attested in the New Testament—its power as a message of mercifully omnipotent and unconditionally complete liberation from *phthora* [transiency, physical destruction], death and wrong as the power of evil.[399]

Finally, there is no correlate to Barth's notion of immediacy to God in Romans 8. Certainly, Barth's understanding of the communication between God and the human person also implies an indirect element.

the parallel between having the Spirit (*tēn aparchēn tou pneumatos echontes*) and the expectation of childhood (*hyiothesian apekdechomenoi*) as well as the emphasis "even we ourselves among ourselves" in Rom. 8:23: *tēn aparchēn tou pneumatos echontes hēmeis kai autoi en heautois stenazomen hyiothesian apekdechomenoi*. Barth draws attention to the prominence of the *aparchē* ibid., 453. According to Rom. 8:16, the Spirit does indeed testify that believers are children of God. Starting with 8:17–18, however, particular attention is given to the "sufferings," and the witness of the Spirit seems not to correspond entirely to the conviction of the believers.

397. According to *CD* I/1, 468, the problem for humans as encapsulated in the Spirit revealing God the Lord as a Thou is that they, rather than God, must be the "following, obeying, imitating and serving" party. Thus, pneumatology is difficult especially "because the human person does not want the very thing that it states to be true."

398. See 8:17: *sympas'chomen—syndoxasthōmen,* 8:21: *phthora—eleuthēria tēs doxēs,* 8:23: *[hē] apolytrōsi[s] tou sōmatos hēmōn.*

399. *CD* IV/2, 233.

Yet not only is the idea of God speaking to the human person absent in Romans 8, but, according to Rom. 8:26, God does not even hear the call of the believers, so that the Spirit intercedes without words on their behalf. It is God's self who requires the mediation of another subject so that human persons can, as it were, reveal themselves to God. In this sense, the Spirit-filled call of the faithful rules out the unconditioned nature Barth attributes to God. Barth insists on the Spirit's nature as *donum*, "gift," making it seem more like an object, strictly following the activity of the *donator*, "giver,"[400] even if it is nothing less than God's own self-objectification. In Romans 8, by contrast, the Spirit appears as a subject vis-à-vis God on whose activity God even depends for God's own participation in the communion with the creature. The wordless communication of the Spirit is also in contrast to Barth's insistence on the literal, nonsymbolic meaning of *word* and *speech* in the communication between God and humanity.[401] Moreover, the simple objectified nature of the Spirit in Barth's notion of revelation corresponds to the passive role Barth attributes to the believers. Since together with the believers, the Spirit is not a free agent vis-à-vis God, the "unconditional" nature of God's freedom is the criterion of revelation.[402]

> The dogma of the Holy Spirit means recognition that in every respect man can be present at God's revelation only as a servant is present at his master's work, i.e., following, obeying, imitating and serving, and that this relation—as distinct from that of human servant and master—cannot be reversed in any way or at any point. This developed recognition of the unconditional nature and irreversibility of the lordship of God in His revelation is what makes the dogma of the Holy Spirit difficult.[403]

400. *CD* I/1, 471, 480, 489.
401. Ibid., 132–3; 135: "Reason communicates with reason and person with person." A sigh, by contrast, is an eminently physical phenomenon.
402. Ibid., 457.
403. Ibid., 468.

Since in Barth's concept, the Spirit is strictly God's act of self-giving, so that the Spirit does not engage in any activity vis-à-vis God, and since Barth highlights the "unconditionality" of the absolute God, we are dealing with a parallel to ancient modalism. This argument has also been made by John Webster.[404] In traditional modalism, God is conceived of as one hypostasis that is then, in a subsequent reflection, haphazardly identified with Father, Son, and Spirit, as God's modes of appearing. While modalism subordinates these three to God,[405] things are different in Barth's doctrine of revelation. Contrary to Barth's intentions, in effect the Son and the Spirit receive a lesser rank in relation to the Father. God is mediated in the work of the Son and the Spirit, yet the mediation also contributes to God's continuing hiddenness.[406] At this stage, the work of the Father is, at least for the most part, described in terms of superiority to creation and independence from it, while the work traditionally appropriated to the Father—the establishment, preservation, and guidance of God's

404. John Webster sees in Barth's doctrine of the Trinity an example of a "slow drift into modalism which is so common in western Trinitarian theology." Webster, "The Identity of the Holy Spirit," 6. Moltmann draws a parallel to modalism, to some extent based on Barth's designation of the Trinitarian persons as modes of being, which is an insufficient reason. He also highlights God's absoluteness as well as personalism. Jürgen Moltmann, *The Trinity and the Kingdom: The Doctrine of God*, trans. Margaret Kohl (Minneapolis: Fortress Press, 1993), 139–44.

405. On modalism see Christoph Markschies, "'... *et tamen non tres Dii, sed unus Deus*...' Zum Stand der Erforschung der altkirchlichen Trinitätstheologie," in *Alta Trinità Beata: Gesammelte Studien zur altkirchlichen Trinitätstheologie* (Tübingen: Mohr Siebeck, 2000), 286–309, at 293–4; Markschies, "Theologische Diskussionen zur Zeit Konstantins: Arius, der 'arianische Streit' und das Konzil von Nicaea," in *Alta Trinità Beata*, 99–195, at 106–7: *monarchianists* or *identification theologians* are better terms than *modalists*. With a view to Pannenberg's critique of Barth's doctrine of the Trinity as subordinatianism above, it should be added that *identification theologians* did not teach subordination among Father, Son, and Spirit, but distinguished the three from the proper God. In *CD* I, the Father takes on this role of the numinous, who is not revealed as Father in three modes, as "God" is in identification theology, but in two.

406. Karl Rahner criticizes the fact that the treatise *De Deo Uno* typically precedes the treatise *De Deo Trino*. This leads to an understanding of God's *essentia* as being a fourth entity that precedes the three persons. Karl Rahner, "Remarks on the Dogmatic Treatise *De Trinitate*," in *Theological Investigations: More Recent Writings*, trans. Kevin Smyth (Baltimore: Helicon, 1966), 77–102. See also Robert Jenson, *Systematic Theology: The Triune God* (Oxford: Oxford University Press, 1997), 96; Webster, "The Identity of the Holy Spirit," 6–7.

creatures—does not receive much attention.[407] The portrayal of the work of the Father differs from the account of the Son and the Spirit in that Barth's emphasis is on *how* the Father acts, but not on *what* the Father does. A substantial account of the Father thus remains elusive. A trinitarian revelation in the actualistic sense can never achieve more than a highly elusive, relative significance. Such actualism highlights both God's self-revelation and God's abiding hiddenness, but conceives of both aspects as total, thus insisting on restrictions on God's conveying God's self.[408] In all likelihood, there will always be aspects of God that remain hidden even in God's self-revelation, but a mere twofold totality of God's revealed and hidden state is too artificial a concept to impose on the living God.

Actualistic Ethics: The Lecture Cycle 1928–9, 1931–2

After this critique of marked dogmatic statements from 1924 to 1932, I turn to examine the ethical consequences of actualism. Indeed, actualism is a crucial concept in Barth's ethics lectures 1928–9 and 1931–2.[409] Barth completed this two-term lecture cycle both in Münster and in Bonn. Although edited in German in 1978 and 1981 (2 volumes) and in English in 1981, secondary literature has paid little attention to the lecture.[410] Presumably, the reason is that it is

407. *CD* I/1, 385.

408. This critique thus differs from the charges of modalism against which Dennis W. Jowers defends Barth in "The Reproach of Modalism: A Difficulty for Karl Barth's Doctrine of the Trinity," *Scottish Journal of Theology* 56 (2003): 231–46, at 241, 243–4.

409. Barth, *Ethics*. The translation was first published by Seabury Press (New York, 1981).

410. Webster, *Barth's Moral Theology: Human Action in Barth's Thought* (Edinburgh: T&T Clark, 1998), 2: The lectures, "curiously enough, have remained almost unnoticed in accounts of Barth." See Webster, "'The Great Disruption': Word of God and Moral Consciousness in Barth's Münster Ethics," in *Barth's Moral Theology*, 41–63, at 41. Busch comments that the lectures were "all the more exciting since various critics had lamented the lack of 'an' ethics in Barth" (Busch, *Barth: His Life from Letters*, 181). These contributions discuss the lectures: Thies Gundlach, "Theologische Ethik unter modernen Bedingungen: Zu den politischen Implikationen der Ethik Karl Barths von 1928/29," *Kerygma und Dogma* 37 (1991): 209–26; Nigel Biggar, *The Hastening That Waits: Karl Barth's Ethics* (Oxford: Oxford University Press,

conceptually less homogeneous than, say, *GD*. Barth himself called it "a ride through nothing but cliffs" and never published the lectures.[411]

Nonetheless, Barth held the lecture cycle twice, notably during a time that was crucial for the end of the Weimar Republic. After a period of consolidation in 1924–9, the agony of the Weimar Republic began when the grave psychological and economic consequences of the global economic recession began to take their toll in winter 1929–30. Gross income plummeted.[412] Unemployment, which had already been high, increased more than threefold between the fall of 1929 and the fall of 1931.[413] Starting in March 1930, President von Hindenburg resorted to the emergency measures provided in article 48 of the Weimar Constitution to keep three consecutive administrations in power against parliamentary majorities.[414] Supported also by bourgeois conservatives and the German army, the president rendered the parliament increasingly powerless, especially at the expense of the Social Democrats.

1993), 46–88; Hans-Richard Reuter, "Das Recht in der Auslegung des Glaubens: Über Rechtsbegriffe in der neueren systematischen Theologie," in *Rechtsethik in theologischer Perspektive: Studien zur Grundlegung und Konkretion*, Öffentliche Theologie 8 (Gütersloh: Gütersloher Verlagshaus/Kaiser, 1996), 93–120; Wolfgang Lienemann, "Gewalt, Macht, Recht: Gewaltprävention und Rechtsentwicklung nach Karl Barth," *Zeitschrift für Dialektische Theologie* 17 (2001): 153–69; Webster, "The Great Disruption"; David Haddorff, *Christian Ethics as Witness: Barth's Ethics for a World at Risk* (Eugene: Wipf & Stock, 2011), 75–86; Gregor Etzelmüller, *'... zu richten die Lebendigen und die Toten': Zur Rede vom Jüngsten Gericht im Anschluss an Karl Barth* (Neukirchen-Vluyn: Neukirchener, 2001), 123–6; Heinrich Assel, "Grundlose Souveränität und göttliche Freiheit: Karl Barths Rechtslehre im Konflikt mit Emanuel Hirschs Souveränitätslehre," in *Barth in Deutschland*, eds. Beintker et al., 205–22.

411. Busch, *Barth: His Life from Letters*, 181 (trans. rev.).
412. Eberhard Kolb, *Die Weimarer Republik*, 7th ed., Oldenbourg-Grundriß der Geschichte 16 (Munich: Oldenbourg, 2009), 124: in 1932, it was 40 percent below the level of 1929, as in the United States.
413. Ibid., 125: in Sep. 1929, 1.3 million people were unemployed, in Sep. 30, over three million, in Sep. 31, 4.3 million, in Sep. 32, 5.1 million. See ibid., 330: in Feb. 1932, 6.128 million people were unemployed. These numbers do not include the high, yet unknown number of those who worked part-time or had given up the job search.
414. Ibid., 131, 133.

> The ideologues of the 'conservative revolution' were particularly efficient in their journalistic support; their attacks on liberalism, democracy, and the parliamentary system were associated with an emphatic call for a strong leader and an authoritarian state.[415]

In the elections for the *Reichstag* in September 1930, the National Socialists achieved a dramatic increase in votes, ending up as the second strongest party. Despite heavy losses, the Social Democrats received the most votes, and the Communist Party came in third.[416]

In this explosive political situation, Barth's ethics lectures were, on the whole, dominated by the notion of repentance. To begin with, however, an essential point of Barth's is that no human person can judge right action; only God can. God issues God's command anew again and again in individual concrete situations.[417] A general rule, by contrast, does not constitute responsibility, as it depends on human interpretation, so that the ethical agent is first of all responsible to him- or herself. Such a 'commandment' would not amount to judgment. God's commandment, by contrast, does mean judgment, as human action again and again fails to live up to this standard.[418] God's commandment is an external factor vis-à-vis the human person, who must not doubt the reality, meaning, and significance of God's command. Ethics cannot "act as though God had not spoken, or perhaps had not spoken."[419] God commands anew again and again and is thus able to call into question what humans have heard God command before. Ethics is thus a positive science insofar as it does not ask critically how far God's command can be real and meaningful;

415. Ibid., 130.
416. Ibid., 129.
417. Barth, *Ethics*, 73, 76, 93–4. For the same concern, see also Dietrich Bonhoeffer, "Lecture in Ciernohorské Kúpele: On the Theological Foundation of the Work of the World Alliance," *Ecumenical, Academic, and Pastoral Work: 1931–1932*, eds. Victoria J. Barnett et al., trans. Anne Schmidt-Lange et al., Dietrich Bonhoeffer Works 11 (Philadelphia: Fortress Press, 2012), 356–69, at 359–60.
418. Barth, *Ethics*, 89.
419. Ibid., 40.

after all, the command constitutes the discipline of ethics itself.[420] As ethics can only provide an indication of the event of God's commanding, it relativizes its own rank in favor of the command in question.[421] Yet it must not only be critical of itself, but also of the addressee of the commandment, as Barth considers God's commandment primarily judgment, which calls for sacrifice.

According to *Rom* II, the cross implies uncompromising judgment, as the execution of Jesus revealed the contrast between the world and God. Barth's ethics lecture goes beyond this not only with the concept of the actualistic commandment, but also—at least in rudimentary fashion—by calling the law "the concrete form and voice of the gospel."[422] Is this the beginning of a development leading to the concept of "gospel and law"? Once the judgment of the law has happened, the "law of the Spirit of life" (Rom. 8:2) guides Christians into the moral dimension within the communion between God and creature. This concept is associated with God's preceding election. Vaguely, a new paradigm seems to emerge.[423]

However, there are two crucial differences in comparison with Barth's later concept of gospel and law. On the one hand, the commandment, which is supposedly guided by the gospel, turns out to consist in sacrifice and self-abnegation after all (see below). On the other hand, Barth calls the accusing law "only taskmaster (Gal. 3:24) according to Paul's polemic."[424] It does not merely change

420. Ibid. Webster, "The Great Disruption," 45: "Theological ethics is therefore positive, not because we can pretend to have 'its content in our pocket', but only as it emerges out of the judgment of God." See ibid., 48.

421. In a private letter, Barth seems to have relativized the ethics lectures, comparing it to a "lecture on Palestinian topography." See Barth's letter to Thurneysen (April 9, 1928), in *Barth-Thurneysen-Briefwechsel 1922–30*, 571.

422. Barth, *Ethics*, 91. Etzelmüller, '*... zu richten die Lebendigen und die Toten,'* 124. Barth's first seminar as a professor was about Calvin's *Institutes* (Münster, winter 1925–6) and his last seminar before the beginning of the ethics lectures dealt with the Galatians commentaries by Calvin and Luther (summer 1927); see McCormack, *Barth's Theology*, 378.

423. Gundlach, "Ethik," 212 comments that Barth comes close to his later position in "GL," but ends up only elaborating on the judgment of grace.

function, but it is "finished and done away with"[425] as soon as the law of the Spirit comes into its own. Any legitimate, constructive, and properly ethical role for the law must be questioned, and yet it seems to figure prominently. On the whole, the notion of judgment dominates the ethics lectures, so that communion with God is only anticipated in judging oneself.[426] For this reason, §6 (pp. 87–115), which is relevant here, indeed bears the title, "The Command of God as the Judgment of God."[427] Judgment, not the gospel, is the first word.[428] Characteristically, John Webster's analysis of the lecture is called by the name of the ethical chapter from *Rom* II, "The Great Disruption."[429] Barth insists that in actualistic ethics, Christians are far from having a say with regard to the content of the commandment. After all, this would mean that God was at one's disposal; having power over a command means not being judged by it. Barth states the priority of the law and its drastic extent succinctly: "Judgment *and* grace, condemnation *and* beatification—these are always the implications of this event, of God's command in its revelation. It encounters me thus, killing me and making me alive."[430]

424. Barth, *Ethics*, 91 (trans. rev.).

425. This statement from Barth's German text is missing from Barth, *Ethics*, 91. Barth, *Ethik: Vorlesung Münster, Sommersemester 1928, wiederholt in Bonn, Sommersemester 1930*, ed. Dietrich Braun, Barth-Gesamtausgabe (Zurich: Theologischer Verlag, 1973), 151.

426. Etzelmüller, '*...zu richten die Lebendigen und die Toten,*' 122–3, criticizes the notion of God's judgment in the actualistic commandment: A proper goal "beyond judgment" does not come into view. Indeed, Barth's idea of a "better or worse character of an action" (thus *GD* III, 380) is thus sacrificed to the principle of God's superiority.

427. Webster, "The Great Disruption," 45.

428. Ibid., 51; 52–3.

429. Gundlach, "Ethik," 213 reads like an analysis of *Rom* II: "Something utterly negative ... creation of a void . . . tremor . . . against any conceptualization as anything distinct [*Positivierung*] . . . harsh critique of religion."

430. Barth, *Ethik: Vorlesung Münster, Wintersemester 1928/1929, wiederholt in Bonn, Wintersemester 1930/31*, ed. Dietrich Braun, Barth-Gesamtausgabe (Zurich: Theologischer Verlag, 1978), 2 (from the chapter "Transition," which is not included in the translation of Barth's ethics lectures). See also Barth, *Ethics*, ed. Dietrich Braun, trans. Geoffrey W. Bromiley (Eugene: Wipf & Stock [2013]), 261.

On the positive side, Barth raises the metaethical question about the kind of commandment that can legitimately claim to command human action. It can be meaningful, even moral for a tragic hero to rebel against historical or natural forces:

> We can fail by them. They might crush us. But they could not put us in the wrong. They could not condemn us. For in the last resort we owe them no obedience. Even in the event of the severest collision with them we could still be deeply at peace with ourselves and with them, too, even confronting them as superiors [i. e., ourselves being superior]. . . . "If the vault of heaven broke and fell on him, the ruins would smite him undismayed."[431]

The emancipatory potential of this thought is not exploited, however. For the distinction between the command and a force of nature to acquire some leverage in the moral life, a closer description of the command must first be provided. Yet Barth does not specify any criteria above and beyond the divine origin of the true command, offering no help in distinguishing God's command from the projections of human license.[432] God's commandment does not require something of the person, but calls for the whole person; the authority lies in the mere authority of the commanding subject. The judgment of the command is a mere principle: at issue is not a better or worse form of obedience, but all or nothing, and everybody will be short on something.[433]

That precisely the totality of the commandment vouches for its authority is a dangerous thought. It is associated with the idea that only an unconditioned commanding can truly judge. The ideal of totality and an unconditioned nature seem to be the result of a projection. Barth even concedes that complete human passivity in

431. Barth, *Ethics*, 95 (trans. rev.), see 298–9, 300.
432. Ibid., 95.
433. Ibid., 94, 96.

hearing the commandment is bad epistemology.[434] Nonetheless, *Ethics* attempts to justify the metaphysical theistic assumptions of the total claim of the command and the unconditioned commanding in building a bridge from metaphysical theism to christological traditions. To begin with, §11, "The Command of Law," part of the chapter "The Command of God the Reconciler," seeks to show why a human epistemological contribution to the content of the commandment is sin. Especially in the central five pages, 314–8—in the chapter "The Command of God the Reconciler," of all places—the crucial concept is that of the Creator, while Barth does not even allude to Jesus Christ, the Reconciler.

As the author of the commandment, God remains Creator, and thus the Creator of reason.[435] Reason, however, must not treat its Creator like an object.[436] The Creator alone is unconditioned.[437] The human person thus does not recognize God's commandment like an object. "A pure acknowledgment would be of such a kind that I recognize indeed what I am told, but in this I am not at all creative, as that which I am told is clear to me purely *by itself* because it is *said* to me in a particular way, but not at all insofar as I am telling me the very thing myself."[438] Barth drives home his point: "'There is' no law of God, 'there is'—a terrible thing to say—indeed no God. What 'is there' can only be an object."[439] Nonetheless, Barth characterizes God as objective—in contrast to an illusion—insofar as God can be thought by the human person and since existence in

434. Ibid., 313–14.
435. Ibid., 314.
436. Ibid., 315.
437. Ibid.; see 65: "The question for the origin shows itself . . . to be . . . the question of superior, unconditional truth." The point is not merely unconditional obedience and the absolute authority of the commandment, but, by the same token, about God being unconditioned. On this characteristic of God, see ibid., 67, 69–70, 71–2, 73–5, 77, 79–80, 92, 95–6, 307, 311–12, 481, 483, 486–7.
438. Ibid., 316 (trans. rev.).
439. Ibid., 317 (trans. rev.).

thought alone, rather than also in existence, does not qualify for the concept of God at issue here.[440] The true, unthinkable God reveals God's self cloaked and thus hidden as this objective God. This is an indirect way of knowing God, for "by its very nature, knowledge of God the creator differs from the knowledge of objects."[441] Yet how might the true God and Creator be revealed in Christ? Rather than questioning the metaphysical theism of this thought, Barth asserts both nonobjectivity and objectivity. Surprisingly, Barth then asserts that these deliberations have implicitly been concerned with Christ all along: he contends that these presuppositions are met precisely—in Jesus Christ. He ends one paragraph with the statement, "The law of faith is the law of revelation of God." A paragraph break follows, and Barth continues immediately, "Let us now speak more plainly. It is the law of *Jesus Christ*."[442] The deeper meaning of Christology consists in a formal reconciliation of God's unconditioned command and human recognition of the command. The unconditioned nature of God and God's command seems to be Barth's prior concern.

As a result, the command that humans thus recognize in Christ calls for surrender. Barth explains that the commandment must be heard entirely passively, since in his days on earth, Jesus Christ commanded a strict obedience that must not flinch from consistent self-abnegation. The self-abnegation demanded in hearing the commandment is no different than the one practiced in Christ's passion. Ethics must thus hold fast to the fundamental Christian disposition of dying. When God's commandment took place historically, when God demonstrated the commandment to

440. Ibid., 315: "God has objectivity inasmuch as he has existence not only in our knowledge but also over against it, not in the understanding alone, but also in reality (Anselm)."

441. Ibid., 317. See 315: "Where the Creator himself is understood as an object, as that which stands over against all cosmic reality, the question unavoidably arises as to the Creator and Lord of the two new antitheses that arise in this way."

442. Ibid., 321 (italics added). Before this reference, the previous reference to Christ is on p. 310.

humanity in the most drastic clarity in Christ's passion, the objective operation of reason is reconciled with passive recognition of the commandment. This is a category mistake of Barth's, however, as the question of whether it is epistemologically consistent to think of the *mode* in which the commandment is recognized in terms of mere passivity is answered with the thesis that the *content* of the commandment consists in mere passivity. Only on this basis does Barth assert that passivity in hearing is even possible.

This theory of the actualistic commandment characterizes especially the first chapter, "On the Reality of the Divine Command," even if Barth explains important conceptual additions only in the following chapters. Together with the introduction, this conceptual foundation is 112 pages of the whole 516 pages. The remaining three chapters follow a Trinitarian structure.

The theological goal of these chapters results from the foundational chapter. The command will amount to self-negation on the whole, yet one must remain open to the shape this is going to assume. To answer this question ultimately remains up to the command itself. Barth explains in chapters 2–4, however, that it is subordination and self-negation that then require further instruction. Barth interprets different circumstances in which the human person is called into question as pointers to God's commanding. With such pointers, ethics fulfills its proper task. At the same time, ethics decisively contradicts any attempt to specify God's command, in order to let the contingent command speak for itself. In fulfilling this task it will "quietly re-open doors which were just about to fall shut, quietly shut doors again that were just about to open."[443] Apart from this destructive function, a potentially constructive aspect of the lectures will be part of the following discussion. This latter aspect must be

443. This is from an eight-page chapter, "Transition," that is missing altogether from the translation. Barth, *Ethik: Vorlesung Münster, Wintersemester 1928/1929*, 7.

distinguished from God's contingent commanding, however. In this respect, the major part of the lectures, which strives for the constructive aspect, only deals with the outer margin of ethics, from a conceptual point of view. This outer margin, however, constitutes 80 percent of Barth's text. This indicates, however, that the original concept is perhaps less clear than it would seem. Even in the supposedly outer margin, far-reaching decisions are made.

It is typical of the lecture that the calling into question of the human person is already the subject of the ethics of creation. The Creator's command calls on the human person to live, which needs to take place in the vocation or profession, in the orders, and in faith (chapter 2, §§7–10). The orders are work, marriage, and family.[444] State and church, by contrast, deal with fallen humanity; they are orders of preservation or emergency and thus they are not discussed in the ethics of creation.[445] Creaturely life always takes place in encountering others, so social claims and conflicts of interest are unavoidable.[446] In this, Barth sees the fundamental character of natural law: as creature, the human person is confronted with other human persons. Since this constitutes the commandment of the Creator, it is in accordance with natural law to subordinate oneself to others and to obey. However, persons continually fail to follow this command of the Creator; they are "in conflict with the life of others," they neglect their "calling" and do not comply with the orders of creation.[447]

With regard to specific action, the commandment of the Reconciler (chapter 3) does not differ much from the Creator's

444. Barth, *Ethics*, 216.

445. Ibid., 243–4. According to Gundlach, "Ethik," 214, Barth asserts a biblical foundation of ethics, but cannot make good on this due to the dominance of judgment. Thus he elaborates on orders of creation instead.

446. Barth, *Ethics*, 263–4.

447. Ibid., 266.

commandment. In retrospect, recognition of creation as such turns out to be, as it were, a *praeambula fidei* in disguise. For the commandment of the Reconciler, too, calls for sacrifice. Such sacrifice must be made in concrete personal encounters. Barth thus understands the most varied claims of others as pointers to Christ's commandment, which is characterized by a certain heteronomy, calling for self-negation.[448] This is the conclusion to a complex discussion of the relationship between law and gospel (§11,"The Command of Law").

In keeping with the Lutheran tradition, Barth argues that the believers are judged by the law. God's judgment is God's *opus alienum* (strange work), but justification, God's *opus proprium* (proper work), takes place in the "transition" from the *opus alienum* to the *opus proprium*.[449] The *opus alienum* already takes place as people hear the Creator's command and fail to fulfill it. Since the ethics of creation attribute value to certain institutions, it creates standards by which persons fail. Such failure serves as a reminder that persons cannot recognize and know God's commandment by themselves.

With regard to the orders themselves, however, an important decision has now been made. Although they are not God's commandment in themselves, they are nonetheless valid as they demand respect, thus preparing for God's commandment to happen. What needs to be done within these orders is only for God to specify. Yet subordination will be an important presupposition of God's commandment. This principle provides the precedence according to which God's judgment takes place. The constructive contribution of ethics is that it introduces people into that relationship within which God's *opus alienum* will give way to God's *opus proprium*. God's commandment can only be heard in doing what

448. Ibid., 330–31.
449. Ibid., 286.

is in accordance with being a creature and in subordinating to the orders. God's judgment, however, does not merely take place in the Creator's command, but even more so in looking at the crucified Christ: "Christ judges us, not 'also,' but 'precisely.'"[450] For "Christ's *vicarious suffering of the penalty*"[451] expiates all trespasses against the Creator. "This is also our judgment, for we have crucified this man who is God himself."[452] To highlight this, Barth draws emphatically on Luther's warning of the attempt to come to know God through an understanding of the world generally rather than in the crucified Christ.[453]

Such judgment, however, means salvation as well. In recognizing the punishment for one's own sin in Christ's suffering, one also becomes aware of the forgiveness of sin.[454] This is the "transition" from God's *opus alienum* to God's *opus proprium.* The cross is both the law that judges and the consolation of the gospel. The parallel to Barth's concept of revelation consists in God being the ineluctable Lord. God is the authority in the critical encounter with the person who receives the revelation, yet God reveals God's self personally, too, in the relationship between an I and a Thou. As a result, however, the gospel has moral authority. By justifying in Christ, God also imposes an obligation in Christ: "But it is about him as the law of faith, as the divine claim that goes forth concretely with the promise, that we have to speak in ethics."[455] Both the consolation and the demand are rooted in the cross. "This reconciling, this way of his to the cross for us, characterizes his *order* to us."[456] For Christ's

450. Ibid., 287.
451. Ibid.
452. Ibid., 322.
453. See ibid., 318–19, 322.
454. See ibid., 280: righteousness "comes to us only in the Word and . . . the word judges us even as it discloses grace. . . . For this word that faith believes as it hears it, and that acknowledges and accepts it as a word of judgment on us, is the word of *forgiveness*."
455. Ibid., 327.

commandment says, "Follow me!"[457] Thus, true obedience amounts to suffering. It remains up to God's free commandment to determine the constellation within which such suffering will take place. One thing, however, is certain: "Where man is negated, there is *iustitia* [justice, righteousness]."[458] For this reason, justifying faith is, as Barth puts it in the style of *Rom* II, "the creation of an empty space."[459] Barth follows Calvin in calling faith "our exinanition (abasement) (*Inst.* III, 11, 7). Faith is 'merely passive, bringing nothing of ours' (*Inst.* III, 13, 5)."[460] What the gospel brings into force is judgment rather than positive action.

Under the headings "Authority," "Humility," and "Love" (§§12–14), Barth discusses what shape the command of God the Reconciler will take. After the commandment of the Creator mainly had a judging function, the commandment of the Reconciler is supposed to give direction and call to action. Yet here the confrontation with fellow human beings is in the foreground as well. The notion of a confrontation with the neighbor as a Thou is particularly prominent. While the encounter between two persons as such must be distinguished from God's command itself, it nonetheless prepares the ground for the positive commandment. There may be cases in which Christ's free command cannot be heard without doubt. The preliminary indication of the shape Christ's command is going to take will thus become a momentous placeholder.

456. Ibid., 328 (trans. rev.).
457. Ibid.
458. Ibid., 284 (trans. rev.).
459. Ibid.
460. Ibid., 280.

The personal encounter that acknowledges the alterity of the other person, respecting him or her in self-restraint, is the next best correspondence to God's concrete commandment. "To follow Jesus, then, is not only to be sacrificed with him but to be sacrificed with him for the brethren, to be bound to men, to be bound to our neighbors as those to whom we owe our life."[461] The unconditional acknowledgment of the other person, the respect commanded by the alterity of the person, reflects the "otherness, strangeness, and supremacy," which characterizes the commandment of the Reconciler in its authority.[462] This is an important concern of §11, "The Command of Law."

Since only God's commandment can legitimately claim authority, §12 ("Authority") asks how it is encountered. Barth's answer is education, customs, and law. In effect, this amounts to orders of preservation, although Barth does not use the term. Church and state, which Barth names explicitly as orders of emergency, are discussed only in §13.4 ("Humility"). Yet the dimension of the state is already at issue when Barth's discussion of legal justice raises the fundamental question of the circumstances in which the state should use its monopoly on legitimate force. Thus, the ethics of reconciliation present two ethics of orders, one under the heading "Authority," one under the heading "Humility." Certain statements in Barth's discussion of legal justice and of the relation between church and state will turn out to be quite momentous.

According to §12, not only the legal system, but also custom and education are ambiguous: education can oblige people in someone else's name other than Christ's; the legal system can be perverted, and custom can in fact result in selfishness and hypocrisy. Nevertheless, representatives of custom, as well as of education and the legal system,

461. Ibid., 329.
462. Ibid., 332.

need to stay the course: "Here, too, we must not try to keep our fingers clean. . . . Our clean fingers regarding pharisaism could well be the worst pharisaism."[463] In all likelihood, potential evils in education, the legal system, or culture are the lesser evil in comparison to the hubris that may inspire attempts at reform. At the end of the day, education, custom, and law cannot help but confront people with authority.

Since repentance is important for Barth, it is necessary to consider how those supposed to embody authority are to practice repentance. Yet this is a blind spot in Barth's ethics of orders. Instead, he asserts, authority is "something which fundamentally and supremely is alien, which cannot be translated or appropriated, but only acknowledged."[464] Here, too, the message of *Rom* II reverberates, which had developed the cause of a blanket critique of anything temporal, motivated by Christ's cross, at the expense of the budding attempts to conceptualize a constructive ethos.[465] Due to the lecture's strong emphasis on subordination, its authoritarian ring is not a coincidence.[466] Especially in the discussion of legal justice, Barth's personalism and the dominance of humility and subordination *coram Deo* have far-reaching consequences.

Presumably, Barth was aware that his emphasis on authority and self-restraint could possibly work in favor of authoritarian political thought. Nonetheless, weakening the forces in favor of a constitutional democracy was not at all his intention. This is evident from the chapter on church and state, §13.4, which argues for a separation of powers, the principle that all power emanates from the

463. Ibid., 395.
464. Ibid., 355.
465. *Rom* II, 621–6.
466. Lienemann, "Gewalt, Macht, Recht," 160, thinks that the authoritarian tone of Barth's ethics of legal justice is merely superficial. Barth's constructive concern for the acknowledgment of the neighbor is crucial. Yet with this aspect Barth makes a case for a principle of subordination, which is untouched by the difference between legitimate and illegitimate subordination.

citizens, and the protection of minorities.[467] However, his abiding positive evaluation of heteronomy and coercive authority means that Barth's attempts to articulate a constructive role of the church in a liberal democracy do not carry the day, in effect remaining limited to a personal love ethos.[468] In addition, the basic subaltern structure of Barth's discussion is grist to the mill of political reactionaries. While it may be intended to curb the activities of those opposing the constitutional, democratic nature of the Weimar Republic, the balance Barth hopes to achieve may very easily tip in favor of those who think that the Weimar Republic, on account of its revolutionary beginnings and its pluralistic, democratic nature, is not the kind of state to wield authority and correspond to the judgment of God's wrath upon the sinner. Barth's statements arguing for the democratic heritage of the West appear rather incidental, while the fundamental theological drift of these lectures points in a different direction.

In both versions, the chapter on church and state is clearly dominated by the words *repentance* and *humility*, which Barth conspicuously retains in the reworked 1930–31 version. Indeed, this is only in keeping with the overall section, which is entitled "Humility" (§13). As will be argued in the section on legal justice, it is not the state that is called upon to be humble. To begin with,

467. Barth, *Ethics*, 448, 519. Pages 440–51 present the chapter "Church and State" according to Barth's 1930/31 manuscript. The 1929 text is known only from a student's lecture notes, translated in an appendix to *Ethics* (517–21). Barth reworked his original 1929 manuscript for the second presentation of the lecture cycle. He reworked the second version again in summer 1933, in order to publish it in *Zwischen den Zeiten*, but he did not follow through with this plan due to new political events.

468. Gundlach, "Ethik," 224–5, reflects positively on the fact that Barth does not relate the church's task to the political system as a whole because this reflects the late modern pluralization of society. By contrast, historical experience seems to speak in favor of Lienemann's doubt ("Gewalt, Macht, Recht," 164) about Kant's conviction that a reasonable, enlightened self-interest leads by necessity to a constitutional democracy with general equality before the law. See also Lienemann, "Gerechtigkeit und Versöhnung: Erinnerung erlittenen Unrechts im Kampf um ein neues Südafrika," in *Politik der Versöhnung*, ed. Gerhard Beestermöller and Hans-Richard Reuter, Theologie und Frieden 23 (Stuttgart: Kohlhammer, 2002), 197–230, 202.

Barth's stereotypical designation of the church is not, for example, the communion of word and sacrament, but the communion of "proclamation and repentance."[469] This may have been due to Barth's intention to restrain overly conservative and nationalistic leanings within the church, yet the trade-off is that, as in *Rom* II, a progressive, constructive stance of the church is equally discouraged. The insistence on repentance makes Barth's later statement in *Theological Existence To-day!* appear unlikely: theology and the church "are the natural limit of any state, even of the totalitarian one."[470] This may very well be the reason that Barth gave up his project to publish a reworked version of these theses on church and state in *Zwischen den Zeiten* in 1933, publishing *Theological Existence To-Day!* instead (June/July 1933).

When Barth does call Christians to responsibility for the state[471] and when he argues that Christians must obey God rather than human beings,[472] he does so against the backdrop of church and state sharing the task of service to one's neighbor, thus employing a theme from personal ethics.[473] Since Barth understands the Christian love ethos in personal rather than structural, systemic terms, and speaks highly of heteronomy, these incidental positive statements are unlikely to do real work. The chapter may acknowledge that the state

469. First version of the chapter: see, for example, Barth, *Ethics*, 517, 520, 521. Already the first short thesis references repentance three times and humility once. Approximately five pages mention repentance thirteen times and humility six times. See the second version: "proclamation of the Word and repentance" (ibid., 449, 450, similarly 441–2); in slightly more than one page, Barth speaks eleven times of repentance, sacrifice, and humility; on three pages, the nine theses on the church speak of repentance and humility eleven times.

470. Barth, Barth, *Theological Existence To-Day! (A Plea for Theological Freedom)*, trans. R. Birch Hoyle (Eugene: Wipf & Stock, 2012), 84 (trans. rev.). See 39: "The *principle* of leadership talked about is sheer nonsense."

471. Barth, *Ethics*, 520.

472. Ibid., 446, 519.

473. Ibid., 450; Heinz Eduard Tödt, "Karl Barth, der Liberalismus und der Nationalsozialismus: Gegendarstellung zu Friedrich Wilhelm Grafs Behandlung dieses Themas," *Evangelische Theologie* 46 (1986): 536–51, at 545.

must respect "the right of each,"[474] and Barth incidentally and vaguely advocates for an improvement of the political system.[475] But such liberal notions are rather isolated in comparison with the subaltern structure that insists on authority and repentance.

As regards the church itself, it should respond to Christ's call for humility in transferring all internal legal force to the state,[476] thereby expressing a fundamental difference between faith on the one hand and the business of politics with its legal dimension, on the other. If all legal dimensions of the church's life were to be sacrificed to the state, it is unclear how a group of theologians would even muster the will to mount a case against the introduction of the Aryan paragraph later on. The church's proper contribution to society is located at the level of individual action, consisting primarily in "the witness of free acts of love in [or by] the church."[477] Still, Barth asserts that the church can even "move on to protest against the state."[478] But Barth's recurring, stereotypical phrasing of the church's public ethos as "repentance before God" and "service to the neighbor"[479] reduces this potentially critical thought to a mere velleity. Barth may critique the particular Protestant focus on German nationalism,[480] but given his own attempts at a theology of orders, this remains ironically paradoxical.

474. Barth, *Ethics*, 519 ("each person's right to themselves").
475. Ibid., 446.
476. Ibid., 450, 521.
477. Ibid., 442. Interestingly, even Werner Elert, who later exhorted students to excel in faithfulness to the Führer, is said at the same time to have been kind to Jews on a personal level. Helmut Thielicke, *Zu Gast auf einem schönen Stern: Erinnerungen* (Bergisch Gladbach: Bastei Lübbe, 1987), 124.
478. Ibid., 450.
479. Ibid., 442–5.
480. Tödt, "Barth," 545.

The humble attitude of the church, its focus on the ethos of the individual, Barth's appreciation of heteronomy, and a vague, only haphazard protest against political injustice constitute the backdrop against which Barth's treatment of legal justice (§12) stands out: Christian repentance is practiced when the state's given coercive power is acted out with few restraints. This is where "authority" is encountered. Barth highlights the special authority of the legal system. He understands it only in the sense of punishment and views legal relationships mainly in correspondence to the encounter between God and the sinner.[481] For this reason, his case for a division of powers can no longer carry the day. Instead, the legal system must embody particular Christian convictions: "For on this ground I know of myself first, not of others, that I am wrong with my right, even my supreme right, that right must necessarily be set up against me and I must be made to conform to justice."[482] The Christian element in the legal system is not the distinction between right and wrong, but the supposedly humble acceptance of guilt. In prosecuting a crime against temporal law, the legal system points the sinner to his or her guilt before God. At the same time, Barth is not concerned with a constructive criticism of law for the sake of protecting particular values that are theologically significant. Not only is temporal justice understood as a symbol of God's just judgment; in addition the "neighbor," who prevails at court, is the concealed presence of God, no matter what his or her case is in fact about.[483] Indeed, "the dogma of original sin is much better preserved by the police than by teachers and even by modern pastors."[484] To follow this line of reasoning

481. Reuter, "Recht," 102 speaks of a "funeral of dialogism," by contrast.

482. Barth, *Ethics*, 381 (trans. rev.).

483. Ibid., 382: "*I* will then submit, not to my neighbor, nor to society, but to God, yet to God in submitting to my neighbor and society, in acknowledging that I have deserved and need that intrinsically very irksome and dubious claim of the monarch or the majority."

484. Ibid., 378. "Wittingly or unwittingly," police work rests on "a very theological presupposition."

consistently would mean to call for a totalitarian state. Correspondingly, Barth inverts the legal principle of the presumption of innocence: "It is well known that in the eyes of the law everybody is always a suspicious person, an unreliable citizen, until there is proof to the contrary, which needs to be produced at any moment."[485] To a considerable degree, Barth's coercive approach shows his sympathies with Luther's notion of the *usus civilis legis* (political use of the law), as he considers a given legal reality the fulfillment of a divine mandate—"for the state is a necessary remedy against corrupt nature."[486] Barth is against a legislative approach focused on a material norm, for example natural law, arguing that the legal system will not at all be harmed if indeed it is the product of a society of sinners. His approach is closer to legal positivism, which does not ask for a correspondence between the legal system and God's true, positive commanding. At the same time, Barth conflates the *usus politicus legis* and the *usus elenchticus legis*. Here we see Barth in the company of Emanuel Hirsch and F. Gogarten.[487] Especially since sinners are in the right against "me"—Barth repeatedly uses the exemplary first person—"I" am forced to realize that it is always "my" own sin, rather than sin in general, which is extraordinarily sinful.[488] This is especially true for the legal system of a "supremely neronic . . . authority."[489]

"In all who bear human face it [i.e., the police] sees necessary objects of innumerable regulations and ordinances, and possible objects of civil or penal proceedings" (ibid).

485. Ibid., 378.

486. Ibid., 444, quoting Luther (trans. rev.). Luther's *Temporal Authority: To What Extent It Should Be Obeyed*, 89–90, speaks of a twofold function of the law. See also Luther, *Lectures on Galatians 1535: Chapters 1–4*, 308–10.

487. Wilfried Joest, "Barth," 90: "The former *usus civilis*, now sublimated by ideology, takes over the role of the law as such and now, in outline, precisely that also of the *usus theologicus*: Lutheran theologians such as E. Hirsch and F. Gogarten thus claimed that in contrast to the demon of individualism, which has its origin in the Enlightenment and liberalism, the discipline and strictness of a form of life in the 'orders,' characterized by authority, must be regained, *in order that* human persons encounter God's law again."

488. Barth, *Ethics*, 381–2.

489. Ibid., 382 (trans. rev.). There are traditions that link Paul's death with Nero. Roughly around that time, Nero also blamed Christians for a large fire in Rome. In any event, however, Paul's

Indeed, a "supremely neronic . . . authority" would become reality soon enough.

Barth sometimes limits his positive notion of coercive state power with the expression that punishment "can" point toward God. Yet even this weak, ambiguous qualification is often absent in the rest of the lecture. The idea that temporal punishment, punishment *coram hominibus* (before human persons) is justified because punishment is justified spiritually, *coram Deo*, prevails.[490] Barth pays too little attention to the notion that punishment can be wrong *coram hominibus,* while guilt before God persists. Not every sin is a crime.

After Barth has charged the legal concept of guilt theologically by drawing on original sin, even appreciating the sinful state insofar as it completes "my" legitimate humiliation before God, he attempts to balance out this drastic statement, saying that the state can even be "the beast from the abyss,"[491] to which no obedience is due. This is in conflict with his statements about a "neronic authority." Primarily, however, Barth views the temporal fight for one's own right negatively in terms of self-righteousness.[492] Later on, Barth argues that Christians indeed render a service to their neighbors by taking them to court, and then "neither my personal sin and guilt, nor my insight into the human lack of sanctity of justice as such need hamper the resolution of my act."[493] Such conceptual

letters had already been written by that time. On the whole, Nero's notorious acts of injustice seem not to have reached as deeply into the life of the Christian churches as Barth's comparison of the legal system with Nero's rule implies. Lienemann, "Gewalt, Macht, Recht," 160 argues that the emphasis on the authorities is not sign of a pessimistic anthropology, as the human person is indeed "fundamentally ready for violence." Yet for this reason precisely it is fatal that the coercive approach replaces a theory of the justice of material law—even if Barth's discussion of legal justice does indeed offer a "sociological theory of justice based on conflict, a theory of intersubjective recognition, and a transcendental theory of justification" (ibid., 161).

490. See also Barth, *Ethics*, 387–8.

491. Ibid., 383.

492. Ibid., 381–2. See Barth's the example of Michael Kohlhaas, who, in Heinrich von Kleist's novel, is a victim of injustice turning into a violent fanatic pursuing his own right.

493. Ibid., 386 (trans. rev.).

contradictions result from the fact that the "neighbor" is just as much sinner as "I" am. Whoever ends up on the winning side in temporal justice represents God in "concealment."[494] If indeed original sin were the most significant fact in legal ethics, it would indeed make no difference who is taking whom to court and how the matter ends, as long as there is no compromise or even reconciliation. A legal war of everybody against everybody would be the logical result. By contrast, the call to "speak up for those who cannot speak for themselves, for the rights of all who are destitute" (Prov. 31:8) would be unthinkable in this legal ethics, which sacrifices the sober, material search for increasingly better forms of justice for the all-or-nothing approach encountered earlier in chapter 1.

The conflict with society or with an individual at court reflects, Barth argues, the relationship between "me" and God. And who has the right to boast before God? In this way, Barth focuses negatively on punishment rather than on the legitimacy of a legally protected good. In the continental legal system this denotes the legitimate protection of interests, such as physical integrity or property, relevant especially in criminal law. His reduction of the legal system to a reflection of the personal encounter with the divine ignores the relative social independence of the legal system, subordinating it to the religious system, which in turn is conceived of in individualistic, authoritarian terms.[495]

Due to this personalistic, coercive approach, Barth's question for the "*right* of our right,"[496] the question for proper justice in the legal system, cannot gain any leverage when faced with a totalitarian state. Neither can Barth's remark that the practice of the legal system

494. Ibid., 382.

495. Only later, when faced with the explosive character of a conservative theology of orders, did Barth reach a clearer distinction between the social systems of law and religion, which would eventually amount to the fifth thesis of the Barmen Declaration.

496. Ibid., 388 (or the moral legitimacy of our legal system).

must amount to a "*favor.*"[497] Is not punishment just that? Barth also speaks positively of equity, but that cannot make up for the damage done by the personalistic, coercive approach. Since "I" am a sinner, "I" must subordinate myself to the legal system of sinners, for "my sanctification takes place in this acknowledgment [of the legal system]."[498] "'Count, be hard'—not for your own sake, nor for the sake of the legal system or the order of society, but for the sake of God and therefore for the neighbor, who vitally needs your hard resistance."[499] Or, along the same lines, "Where man is negated, there is *iustitia* [justice, righteousness]."[500]

The section following the discussion of authority in education,[501] the legal system,[502] and custom[503] highlights again the confrontation with the neighbor, who represents God's commandment. No moral claims must be made. Instead, interpersonal difficulties and scandals are by necessity "the occasion for repentance on my part."[504] This repentance is the sacrifice that we owe to God anyway.[505] This is the gist of §13, "Humility," which also includes the chapter on church and state. Christian action can only consist in "a sacrifice of my life."[506] Section 14, "Love," adds that when I "bow to authority, and offer to God the sacrifice of humility that is a pleasure to him," this should be done in love.[507] Just as God's mercy is selfless concern for the human person in spite of everyone's unworthiness, so Christians should act toward others in gratuitous love, which again is a

497. Ibid.
498. Ibid., 382.
499. Ibid., 386 (trans. rev.).
500. Ibid., 284 (trans. rev.).
501. Ibid., 363–76.
502. Ibid., 376–90.
503. Ibid., 390–9.
504. Ibid., 424.
505. Ibid., 425–6.
506. Ibid., 399.
507. Ibid., 453 (trans. rev.).

confession of how little one deserves God's grace. All in all, this summarizes the third chapter, "The Command of God the Reconciler."

Contrary to the actualistic view that apart from God's contingent commanding, little can be said about concrete action, Barth makes momentous presuppositions about good human action. He cannot sustain his thesis that ethics must again and again question any course of action so as not to preempt God's specific commandment. In fact, this critical view is directed only against courses of action that constitute a fundamental alternative to a subaltern ethics of authority by claiming a positive right of the creature. Nonetheless, it is not a coincidence that actualistic ethics take this shape, as deep as the roots of actualism are in the utterly critical theology of *Rom* II. In consequence, God's revelation in Christ is reduced to a practical negation of the world. Thus, the hope for a commandment that relativizes the repressive preparation for the commandment is in vain. Precisely as Barth highlights the aspects of judgment and death in God's revelation, fundamentally questioning any theological foundation and assertion of a distinct positive ethics, the negative shape of life emerges in which God's judgment initiates a "transition"[508] to the moral obligation constituted by the gospel.

Due to its inner relatedness to *Rom* II, it is unlikely that Barth's ethics lecture amounts to an accidental misstep. On the contrary, he presented it again in its entirety soon after he first devised it. Barth certainly had always had a strong interest in ethical questions. The problem is, however, that the actualistic concept of revelation was supposed to lead beyond the negative ethics of *Rom* II, while remaining obliged to its theology of sacrifice. The prime concern in Barth's ethics lectures is therefore to give practical shape to the

508. Ibid., 286.

unconditioned nature of a worldless God in the midst of a fallen world. To put it mildly, this concern is problematic as it justifies and supports subaltern forms of life. John Webster, for example, overlooks this when commenting favorably on the supposed continuity of Barth's work ranging from the 1920s up to the "theanthropology" of the 1950s.[509] In turn, we must ask whether and how Barth's thought was able to overcome the fatal dominance of the theological notion of judgment.

The Concept of Sacrifice and Barth's Political Activism (1931–8)

For more than a decade after the publication of *Rom* II, Barth continued to assign theological importance to the notion of sacrifice. *GD* integrated the strong sense of judgment prevalent in *Rom* II into a larger synthesis, so the notion of God's contingent, incommensurate command sublated Barth's strong critique of any ethos. Yet the fundamental critique remained influential even if God's current command calls for concrete obedience.

Parallel to this strand in Barth's work, however, another line emerges in the 1920s that highlights a positive ethos rather than quietism and actualism. An ambiguity in Barth's political activity corresponds to this ambiguity in his theology. When both fascist and bourgeois middle-class circles increasingly sabotaged the crisis-torn Weimar Republic, Barth publicly defended moderate politics, holding fast to constitutional democracy.[510] Later on he stayed that course in opposition to National Socialist tendencies in the Protestant

509. Webster, *Barth's Moral Theology*, 3; Webster, "The Great Disruption," 42.

510. In addition to Barth's public activities (see below), he practiced the democratic virtue of rational political debate in regular meetings with students. See Angela Dienhart Hancock, "Training for a Serious Game: Theo-Political Deliberation as a Christian Practice," in *Theo-Politics? Conversing with Barth in Western and Asian Contexts*, ed. Markus Höfner (Minneapolis: Fortress Press, 2016).

church. By his own judgment, however, he was nonetheless exercising restraint in this.[511]

Due to the relationship between theological and political ambiguity, this section will discuss Barth's most relevant political pronouncements during the early 1930s. Since this area presents us with more hesitation and self-critique than a portrait of Barth as a single-minded fighter against the Aryan heresy may allow for, this account substantiates in practical terms the thesis that the hypercritique of *Rom* II continued to be influential, even if indirectly: "If an *ethics* is at issue, nothing else is possible than a *critique* of all ethos."[512] Yet to some extent, already in the years around 1930, Barth of course overcame both the paralyzing self-criticism of self-righteousness as well as the actualistic notion that beyond the particular moment of God's contingent revelation of God's command, nothing positive could be asserted about ethics. Both in *Rom* II and in *GD*, it is—not just historically, but also theologically—inconceivable that Barth would consider the military fight against a European nation, without reservation, a fight for Christ and his church, as he did in 1938 (see below). To the extent

511. See Günther van Norden, *Die Weltverantwortung der Christen neu begreifen: Karl Barth als homo politicus* (Gütersloh: Kaiser, 1997). Klaus Scholder, "Neuere deutsche Geschichte und protestantische Theologie: Aspekte und Fragen," *Evangelische Theologie* 23 (1963): 510–36, 522: "In those years, when the intellectual assault opened fire on the Republic, weakening it for storming," Barth was "on the attacking side, at least from the perspective of the wider public." Friedrich Wilhelm Graf, "'Der Götze wackelt'? Erste Überlegungen zu Karl Barths Liberalismus-Kritik," *Evangelische Theologie* 46 (1986): 422–41 articulates a similar critique. This is in contrast to the views of Tödt, "Barth," van Norden, *Weltverantwortung*; Holtmann, *Barth*, 302–25. John W. de Gruchy is convinced that in South Africa, Barth's theology had worked against the apartheid regime—see de Gruchy, "Racism, Reconciliation, and Resistance," in *On Reading Karl Barth in South Africa*, ed. Charles Villa-Vicencio (Grand Rapids: Eerdmans, 1988), 139; 140–41: in 1925 Barth declared a "fascist, racialist *nationalism*" a matter of *status confessionis*, a fundamental decision about faith or unbelief. See Barth, "Wünschbarkeit und Möglichkeit eines allgemeinen reformierten Glaubensbekenntnisses, 1925," in *Vorträge und kleinere Arbeiten 1922–1925*, ed. Holger Finze, Barth-Gesamtausgabe (Zurich: Theologischer Verlag, 1990), 604–43, 640.

512. *Rom* II, 576.

that Barth emerges as a determined opponent of National Socialism, however, a new theological inspiration must be identified. At this juncture between chapters 1 and 2, then, this concluding section hearkens back to the continuing influence of the overly critical theology of the early 1920s and looks ahead by noting a new theological position being foreshadowed also in practical terms. It is important to note that the function of this section is to elucidate the genesis of Barth's ethics and his politics. Far from pronouncing an overall verdict on the political Barth, it is not intended to detract from Barth's undoubted achievements in this area, which speak for themselves. Neither is the ensuing overview intended to be complete. The point is to shine a spotlight at particular points of Barth's public activity that turn out to be correlated with the heterogeneous theological factors present in his work during the 1920s and 30s.

In 1931, Barth made a clear-headed political diagnosis when he joined the German Social Democrats "due to the overwhelming terror from the right."[513] He expected Fascism and Bolshevism to fight Christianity relentlessly, as they pray to a different God. However, quite in the style of the universal criticism of *Rom* II, which may steal the thunder of any one particular critique, he adds that he expects the same of "Americanism."[514] In 1932, Barth again eschewed neutrality, self-critique, or even the affirmation of an authoritarian political order in declaring that "the church's proclamation is per se political, insofar as it must admonish the disorderly heathen polis to establish justice."[515] In an open letter published in a widely read newspaper in 1932, Barth took sides against the agitation of National

513. Barth's letter to Asmussen 1932, see van Norden, *Weltverantwortung*, 25.

514. Barth, "Fragen an das 'Christentum': 1931," in *Vorträge und kleinere Arbeiten 1930–1933*, ed. Michael Beintker, Michael Hüttenhoff, and Peter Zocher, Barth-Gesamtausgabe (Zurich: Theologischer Verlag, 2013), 141–55, at 146. Barth defines an inordinate concern for "health" and "coziness" in combination with "egoism," "optimism," and a naïve approach to "technology" as "Americanism" (ibid., 146–7).

515. Barth, "An Michael M. Hoffmann, Berlin, 1932," in Koch, *Offene Briefe 1909–1935*, 229–34,

Socialist students and professors—among them Emanuel Hirsch—in a much-noted affair. Günther Dehn, professor at Halle University, experienced much vilification since he had declared that the death of German soldiers should not be portrayed as similar to Jesus' death.[516]

In June 1933, Barth again took a prominent stance in a widely circulated pamphlet, *Theological Existence To-Day! A Plea for Theological Freedom.* To begin with, he argued for "carry[ing] on theology, and only theology, now as previously—perhaps in a slightly higher pitch, but without direct reference—and as if nothing had happened."[517] This seemingly less than dramatic response to National Socialism was prompted by the intense public debate about the face-off between Friedrich von Bodelschwingh and the "German Christian" Ludwig Müller for the newly created post of the Protestant imperial bishop.[518] Barth feared that all theological thought about the church might degrade into mere politicking. This led to the charge, however, that the German Christians were engaging only in a pseudotheology that was in fact dominated by current political affairs. Adopting the Aryan Paragraph in the church would seal its fate theologically.[519] Barth calls on the church to demand religious freedom from National Socialism: "Because of this, theology and the Church cannot accept any . . . 'assimilation' [*Gleichschaltung*]. They

at 233. What Barth means with justice, however, must be analyzed in dialogue with the legal ethics of Barth's ethics lecture.

516. "Warum führt man den Kampf nicht auf ganzer Linie?" (Why does the opponent not go for an all-out fight?) Barth, "An die Frankfurter Zeitung: 1932," in *Briefe 1909–35*, 170–83. See also Barth, "An den Rektor der Universität, Prof. Dr. Gustav Aubin, Halle, 1931," ibid., 158–64.

517. Barth, *Theological Existence To-Day!*, 9 (trans. rev.).

518. Introduction to "Theologische Existenz heute! 1933," in Beintker et al., *Vorträge und kleinere Arbeiten 1930–1933*, 271–363, at 274.

519. See Barth, *Theological Existence To-Day!* 52. Wilhelm Vischer felt thus encouraged to plan the Bethel confession; see Eberhard Busch, *Unter dem Bogen des einen Bundes: Karl Barth und die Juden 1933–1945* (Neukirchen-Vluyn: Neukirchener, 1996), 58. Karl Löwith judged in 1940 that Barth's pamphlet "was and remained the only serious expression of academic resistance against the raging time" (Löwith, *My Life in Germany*, 37). He argues that Heidegger thought favorably of National Socialism as his book was *Being and Time* rather than *Being and Eternity*.

are the natural limit of any state, even of the totalitarian one."[520] This marks a significant change of mind after Barth's ethics lectures had argued that the church should entrust all legal affairs—even those regulating internal church affairs—to the state government. Further, Barth's criticism of the totalitarian nature of National Socialism and its crimes against the Jews, uttered in dialogue with individual Protestant theologians in October 1933, contributed to his removal from his university post.[521]

Another event that is characteristic of the way Barth interrelated theology and politics in a progressive way is how in December 1933, he delivered a sermon on Romans 15, claiming Jesus' Jewish descent as highly relevant theologically. The sermon was published in two editions.[522] Better known of course is Barth's endeavor to bring about a religious disenchantment of the totalitarian state in the Barmen Declaration. Thesis 5, for example, reminds the church of the importance of its contribution to a just political system.[523]

Yet there was also a retarding force in Barth's stance toward National Socialism. This was the effect of Barth's message of sacrifice and repentance in *Rom* II and the actualistic synthesis of *GD*, which was also formative in the ethics lectures. While Barth was an astute and critical political observer, he initially tended, at least some of the time, toward a benevolent interpretation of the new German administration. In retrospect he argued that in the academic system,

520. Barth, *Theological Existence To-Day!* 84 (trans. rev.). See 39: "The *principle* of leadership talked about is sheer nonsense."

521. See Hans Prolingheuer, *Der Fall Karl Barth: 1934–1935: Chronographie einer Vertreibung* (Neukirchen-Vluyn: Neukirchener, 1977), 287–8.

522. See Barth, "Römer 15, 5–13: 10. Dezember 1933 (2. Advent)," in *Predigten 1921–1935*, ed. Holger Finze-Michaelsen, Barth-Gesamtausgabe (Zurich: Theologischer Verlag, 1998), 296–305, at 300. See Busch, *Unter dem Bogen*, 165; 165–174. Interestingly, Barth made a point of sending a copy to Hitler himself.

523. "The concept of the state present here is that of the liberal constitutional democracy (*liberaler Rechtsstaat*) as in all of Karl Barth's writings" (thus Paul Althaus in 1934 according to Tödt, "Barth," 549).

the "sabotage" of the Weimar Republic could hardly have been missed.[524] Nevertheless, at the time he did not expect Hitler's appointment as chancellor of the *Reich* "to beget spectacular news in any sense."[525]

In 1933, after the dreaded Aryan Paragraph took effect in the Prussian Union of Churches, Germany's largest Protestant church, Barth was approached by Dietrich Bonhoeffer. Lobbying for pastors to resign in unison and exploring the idea of creating a free church in opposition to the established Prussian Union of Churches, the young Berlin theologian asked if Barth would stand by his influential judgment in *Theological Existence To-Day!* Barth agreed that, as he had written in the pamphlet, the 'Aryan paragraph' constituted a *status confessionis* indeed, as one could no longer serve legitimately in a church that excluded Jewish-Christian pastors.[526] Already a day before Bonhoeffer's letter, Barth had received a letter from a Heidelberg professor who asked the same question.[527]

Although Barth considered Bonhoeffer's project basically right, he nonetheless counseled against the establishment of an independent church in rivalry to the established Prussian church. Public attention to the matter might have been an important argument for hesitating no longer. Yet Barth was afraid that the proponents of the good cause might be perceived as mere troublemakers, while the fascist

524. "In the years 1921–33, I found the professors . . . with only a few exceptions, preoccupied indeed with the fight against 'Versailles' that was customary in those days, and . . . with an attitude vis-à-vis the poor Weimar Republic that even today I can only call sabotage." Barth, "An Prof. Dr. Erich von Holst," 124. As illustrations he mentions five episodes from the 1920s (ibid., 125–6).

525. Barth, "An Anna Barth, 1.2.1933," in *Briefe des Jahres 1933*, ed. Eberhard Busch (Zurich: Theologischer Verlag, 2004), 48–9; "An Anna Barth, 25.2.1933," ibid., 72–5, at 73–4.

526. Editor's introduction to Barth's letter to Dietrich Bonhoeffer, Berlin (Sept. 11, 1933), in Barth, *Briefe des Jahres 1933*, 376–80.

527. Editor's introduction to Barth's letter to Renatus Hupfeld, Heidelberg (Sept. 11, 1933), in *Briefe des Jahres 1933*, 380–81. Barth's letter to his son Markus speaks of the two letters as written by "people from quite different corners who must be taken seriously" (Sept. 11, 1933, ibid., 381–2). Creating a free church would be legitimate only when "all else fails" (ibid.).

sympathizers might well overplay their hand even more drastically.[528] It seems that there was a certain amount of planning and studying behind the new piece of advice. Yet *Theological Existence To-Day!* —which had successfully attracted a lot of attention in rallying an opposition to the "German Christians"—had singled out the introduction of the Aryan Paragraph as the crucial event.[529]

What Barth was waiting for now, by contrast, remained vague. This makes it likely that Barth's critique of everything human, all too human in *Rom* II in fact tipped the balance for him. He hoped for the turnover to happen by itself, with no one hurrying it along in particular: "It is too great a responsibility that one might handle it somehow, wanting to 'get it started.'"[530] For Barth, a theological and spiritual orientation excluded practical and strategic concerns: "It will pay off if we decide by no means to act strategically now, but to think spiritually, as well as we can."[531] Thus, Barth did not take part when the *Pfarrernotbund* (Emergency Covenant of Pastors), an important predecessor to the Confessing Church, was founded the same month. Indeed, Barth feared the exaggeration of critique more than the lack of critique, for example when, in 1933, he branded a sermon that called Hitler the antichrist "itself a bit Hitler-like."[532]

At a synod of the Confessing Church in October 1934 he did argue for a more critical attitude toward the state.[533] On the other

528. Indeed, the convention of the German Christians in the Berlin *Sportpalast* two months later, which called for the removal of the Hebrew Bible from the Christian canon, was met with a greater public outcry than the Aryan Paragraph. But in contrast to Barth's prediction of a self-destruction of the German Christians, this led to their moderation.

529. Ironically, Barth even adduces the strong resonance that *Theological Existence To-Day!* had generated in favor of *waiting* since not all hope might be lost for the Protestant churches.

530. Barth, letter to Bonhoeffer (Sept. 11, 1933), 378.

531. Ibid. Barth does think strategically as well, arguing that one ought not to shoot one's bolt prematurely, but he does not make a case for why a certain point in time is the best to shoot one's bolt. Presumably, Bonhoeffer's suggestion of creating a free church in response to the Aryan paragraph was the best combination of a spiritual and a practical stance.

532. See Barth, "An Vikar Reinhard Busch" (Oct. 19, 1933), in *Briefe des Jahres 1933*, 454–8.

533. See Busch, *Bogen*, 243.

hand, he objected to the view that the church was now called to proclaim divine judgment over the state: "The church is not called to judge the state. It must proclaim the gospel, which implies judgment over everything worldly."[534] Preferring the wholesale, bland notion of judgment from *Rom* II to a precise message of judgment, Barth blurred important distinctions. Only by singling National Socialism out for critique and not by directing the charge of egregious misdeeds at itself as well could the church have avoided an innocuous, hackneyed message.

The SS, the notorious Nazi paramilitary organization, had meanwhile come to consider Barth a danger for the National Socialist state, as he contributed to the intellectual foundations of an opposition.[535] Yet in a letter from 1935, Barth wrote he had "even so" imposed "a certain restraint" on himself, "as my publications show." "It will be and remain an embarrassing recollection of the past two years that I have not advanced more vigorously in the necessary direction. Perhaps it was not my right as a Swiss citizen to do so."[536] In an even later letter Barth confessed to feeling guilty for not protesting publicly, for example, in the *Theological Declaration of Barmen*, against the discrimination against the Jews as Bonhoeffer had done. Yet he rightly submitted that an explicit pronouncement against the persecution of the Jews would not have achieved a majority in Barmen anyway.[537]

Barth's explicitly public pronouncements for a constitutional democracy before Hitler's appointment as chancellor (January 1933)

534. Wilhelm Niemöller, *Die Zweite Bekenntnissynode der Deutschen Evangelischen Kirche zu Dahlem* (Göttingen: Vandenhoeck & Ruprecht, 1958), 22 ("*Gericht über alles Irdische*").

535. See Busch, *Bogen*, 244.

536. Barth, "Brief an Hermann Hesse, 30.6.1935," in K. Immer, *Die Briefe des Coetus der reformierten Prediger: 1933–1937* (Neukirchen-Vluyn: Neukirchener, 1976), 73–4.

537. Barth, "To Rector Eberhard Bethge, Rengsdorf near Neuwied, May 22, 1967" in *Letters 1961–1968*, ed. Jürgen Fangmeier and Hinrich Stoevesandt, trans. Geoffrey W. Bromiley (Grand Rapids: Eerdmans, 1981), 250–2, at 250.

are in tension with his previous argument in the ethics lecture that was, in effect, in support of an authoritarian state. From this point on, Barth's activity against National Socialism certainly must be appreciated. Nonetheless, Barth's early cautionary statements are in contrast to Bonhoeffer's clear-sighted call from 1933 to confront the National Socialist persecution of the Jews, when he called on the church "not just to bind up the wounds of the victims beneath the wheel, but to seize the wheel itself."[538]

The overall picture of Barth's political activities resists a blanket evaluation. This overview is not a moral evaluation, but an attempt to understand why he acted the way he did and to reconstruct the theological factors at work. In the struggle for the Weimar Republic, the retarding element played by Barth's notion of sacrifice is problematic, in spite of his undoubted merits. At times it worked against Barth's commitment for a liberal democracy. The notion of sacrifice lost its prominence gradually. Barth's thinking about taking sides politically in unambiguous ways changed during the first years of National Socialist rule. Writing to Hromádka in 1938, he argues for a war between good and evil indeed: "Every Czech soldier who then fights and suffers will do so also for us—and today I am saying so without reservations: he will do so also for the church of Jesus Christ, which in the sphere of Hitler's or Mussolini's influence can only become either a laughing stock or be wiped out."[539] This quotation raises the question of whether Barth would have agreed with a clearer critique of National Socialism already in 1933, had he held the same theological views as in 1938. Indeed, a certain restraint in Barth's political activities began to decrease notably up to 1938, which was

538. Bonhoeffer, "The Church and the Jewish Question," in *Berlin: 1932–1933*, ed. Larry Rasmussen, trans. Isabel Best and David Higgins, Dietrich Bonhoeffer Works 12 (Minneapolis: Fortress Press, 2009), 361–73, at 365.

539. Barth, "Brief an Prof. Dr. Josef L. Hromádka, Prag 1938," in *Offene Briefe 1935–42*, ed. Diether Koch, Barth-Gesamtausgabe (Zurich: Theologischer Verlag, 2001), 107–33, at 114.

due to a clearer questioning of his previous message of sacrifice. The following considerations seek to reconstruct this process.

2

The Ethics of the Doctrine of God in *Church Dogmatics* II/2

"Judgment *and* grace, condemnation *and* beatification—these are always the implications of this event, of God's command in its revelation. It encounters me thus, killing me and making me alive."[1] As the ethics lectures highlighted especially the aspect of judgment in discussing God's command, the notion that moral obligation is constituted by the gospel did not attain full force—on the contrary. Even to the extent that the gospel rather than the law ultimately determined the sinner's status before God, Barth drew attention to this relation *coram Deo* rather than to the moral reality of an ethos, of actions and obligations that might be brought forth by the gospel.

1. Barth, *Ethik: Vorlesung Münster, Wintersemester 1928/1929, wiederholt in Bonn, Wintersemester 1930/31*, ed. Dietrich Braun, Barth-Gesamtausgabe (Zurich: Theologischer Verlag, 1978), 2 (from the chapter "Transition," which is not included in the translation of Barth's ethics lectures). See also Barth, *Ethics*, ed. Dietrich Braun, trans. Geoffrey W. Bromiley (Eugene: Wipf & Stock, 2013), 261. Whenever the footnote provides a German title for an English quotation, the translation is my own.

The ethics of the doctrine of God in *CD* II/2 chapter 8 (1942) sets a new tone by describing the gospel as prior to and more fundamental than the law. At the same time, *CD* II/2 is highly sensitive to a potential human encroachment on the authority of the divine judge, as Barth was in the ethics lectures. Where exactly lies the difference between this new constellation and the ethics lectures? Does the gospel lead to a moral obligation and claim human action as an important aspect of the relationship with God, or is the moral dimension again strictly subordinated to the encounter with the condemning and justifying God?

The Priority of the Gospel over the Law

Barth's lecture "GL" (1935), which presents the subordination of the law to the gospel as a new paradigm, features neither a contingent, elusive commandment nor personalist thought. By contrast, the ethical sections in *CD* II/2 will present a highly actualistic concept of God's command, which Barth prefaces, again, with the subordination of the law to the gospel. This seems to be at variance with the drift of the present work so far. My argument has been that the actualistic concept of God's revelation and command was necessary for forging a synthesis between a positive notion of revelation and God's abiding absoluteness. This results in the prominence of the aspect of judgment in all revelation. This clear prominence is associated with Barth's continuing preoccupation with a Lutheran concept of law and gospel. *CD* II/2, however, describes the relationship between gospel and law explicitly as a priority of the gospel. Does this mean that the reconstruction of the actualistic commandment so far is wrong-headed? Viewed from another angle, is the combination of the priority of the gospel with actualism in *CD* II/2 sound and straightforward? To get a better grasp on these questions, it is necessary to reconstruct the genesis of Barth's concept of "gospel and law."

Setting the Course: Lectures in the Early 1930s

Barth's lecture "Die Not der evangelischen Kirche" ("The Affliction of the Protestant Church," 1931)[2] offers a more differentiated take on claims to authority than the ethics lectures. It highlights Christ's cross, but does not refer to creation, God's preservation of creation, and respective social orders. Barth wishes to retain a sense of authority in the church, but notably, his emphasis is on fending off illegitimate claims to authority. The latter aspect describes the difference to the ethics lectures most succinctly.

The lecture laments that the church ignores the crucified Christ, who demonstrates human affliction and misery, even though it wishes to affirm faith in Jesus Christ. A confession to Christ avoids such an illegitimate abstraction, however, if one does not evade the claims of the neighbor within the church. The message of the cross is taken seriously only if one accepts obligations and responsibility. In accordance with the message of the cross, Christians need to embrace "lowliness and the concrete demands [*konkrete Zumutung*]" rather than fleeing the "scandal of the human, all too human,"[3] which is implied in the responsibility toward the brothers and sisters in the church. Claims to authority that do not grow out of this sobering reality must, however, be rejected. Further, the recognition of God's particularity in the cross must be associated with the affirmation of social particularity. In an ironic caricature: "God, however, or the divine . . . is great, true, good, and beautiful. Thus the visibility

2. Barth, "Die Not der evangelischen Kirche," in *Vorträge und kleinere Arbeiten 1930–1933*, ed. Michael Beintker, Michael Hüttenhoff, and Peter Zocher, Barth-Gesamtausgabe (Zurich: Theologischer Verlag, 2013), 64–122.
3. Ibid., 93.

of the church as such is a scandal. Ecclesial offices, ecclesial order and custom, the church's confession, even the church's authority—nothing but an embarrassment."[4] The theology of the cross is in contrast to a

> church that comes into being only now and again, at most in joint convictions, sentiments, and efforts. Such a church would lack bonds, obligations, or any forms other than those that anyone might just as well cast off at any time. A Church in which only the dear God and nothing else is above everyone, no matter if teaching or learning, a church in which, ultimately, everyone needs to negotiate the question of responsibility exclusively with himself or herself![5]

While the influence of the ethics lecture cannot be missed, Barth is differentiating between legitimate and illegitimate claims. Authority in the church presupposes the proclamation of the gospel, and apart from the social ties constituted by the gospel, faith would remain strangely abstract.

In contrast to the lack of commitment by church members, Barth asserts that in 1931, "today's affliction [*Not*], the current one," "the greater affliction"[6] than disregard for authority consists in unfounded claims to ecclesial authority, in the church's "escape into visibility." Barth's typical call for repentance and humility makes sense only when it is not inculcated as a categorical, exclusive principle that paradoxically presupposes authority without accounting for its potential legitimacy. The call for humility must also be empowering and allow expressly for critique of ill-founded claims to authority.

The critical edge of the lecture comes into sharper relief here as Barth expressly takes up again the subject of his polemical pamphlet "*Quousque tandem . . . ?*" (1930).[7] This essay initiated a widely noted

4. Ibid., 90.
5. Ibid., 91.
6. Ibid., 88, 94.
7. Barth, "*Quousque tandem . . . ?*" in *Vorträge und kleinere Arbeiten 1925–1930*, ed. Holger Finze,

controversy with Bishop Otto Dibelius,[8] in which Barth attacked an ecclesial presumption of privilege that was in contrast to both the church's proper message and social problems in society.[9] The proclamation of the gospel does not justify just any sort of authority, and in turn, grave social problems unmask ecclesial claims to authority as ill founded. The Protestant church extols institutional stability as well as social and political influence, Barth wrote, "as if there were no housing shortage and no unemployment in Germany."[10] Church officials in power turn a blind eye to the great skepticism the church encounters in society,[11] being concerned merely with securing petty bourgeois piety. In this situation, that amounts to offering "opium"[12] to society.

Barth sees the Protestant church pursuing privileges for itself,

Barth-Gesamtausgabe (Zurich: Theologischer Verlag, 1990), 521–35. The title quotes Cicero's First Catiline Oration: "How long (O Catiline, will you abuse our patience)?"

8. Eberhard Busch, *Karl Barth: His Life from Letters and Autobiographical Texts*, trans. John Bowden (Eugene: Wipf & Stock, 2005), 177–8, at 191.
9. Barth, "*Quousque tandem . . . ?*" 50. The pamphlet is directed against Otto Dibelius, *Das Jahrhundert der Kirche: Geschichte, Betrachtung, Umschau und Ziele*, 5th ed. (Berlin: Furche, 1928) (*The Century of the Church*) and statements by the president of the Rhineland synod Walther Wolff about the public role of the Protestant churches from 1930. Friedrich Wilhelm Bautz, "Dibelius, Otto," *Bibliographisch-Biographisches Kirchenlexikon* (Nordhausen: Bautz, 1990), 1:1281–3, at 1281–2. According to Wolfgang Huber, *Folgen christlicher Freiheit: Ethik und Theorie der Kirche im Horizont der Barmer Theologischen Erklärung*, Neukirchener Beiträge zur systematischen Theologie 4 (Neukirchen-Vluyn: Neukirchener, 1983), 137, Dibelius's *Jahrhundert der Kirche* is paradigmatic for a particular understanding of *Volkskirche* ("church of the people"): "The church claims to unite and integrate *society, the entire German people* as a prominent public agent [*Integrations- und Öffentlichkeitsanspruch*]. . . . This claim was associated with a new 'will for the public dimension' [*Öffentlichkeitswille*], which aimed at the implementation of 'Christian fundamentals' in politics."
10. Barth, "*Quousque tandem . . . ?*" 532. During the Great Depression, unemployment had risen from 1.3 million people in Sep. 1929 to over 3 million in Sep. 1930 and to 6.13 million in Feb. 1932. Eberhard Kolb, *Die Weimarer Republik*, Oldenbourg-Grundriß der Geschichte 16, 7th ed. (Munich: Oldenbourg, 2009), 125, 330.
11. Barth, "*Quousque tandem . . . ?*" 530.
12. Ibid., 531; see Karl Marx, *Critique of Hegel's "Philosophy of Right,"* ed. Joseph O'Malley, trans. Janette Jolin and J. O'Malley, Cambridge Studies in the History and Theory of Politics (Cambridge: Cambridge University Press, 2009), 131: "The wretchedness of religion is at once an expression of and a protest against real wretchedness. Religion is the sigh of the oppressed creature, the heart of a heartless world and the soul of soulless conditions. It is the opium of the people."

mostly blaming others for a decrease in loyalty to the church, and failing to fulfill its primary responsibility of proclaiming the gospel of undeserved justification. All in all, this amounts to hostility to the gospel.[13]

"Die Not der evangelischen Kirche" charges the Protestant church with the same faults and is clearly directed against the very same problem to which the ethics lectures were likely to contribute with their blanket approval of subordination. After all, an undifferentiated principle of subordination without a critique of illegitimate authority willy-nilly contributes to the problem it seeks to avoid, that is, authoritarian positions.

By contrast, the foundations of true ecclesial authority must lie in the theology of the cross, while the theology of the cross also contradicts an illegitimate presumption of ecclesial authority. "Is the visibility of the church, which must supposedly be emphasized again, indeed simply history, fate, reality, sociological necessity, community, *Gestalt*, order . . . and whatever else all the shibboleths of the new realism may be?"[14] The church must differ from the kind of authority presumed under the guise of these entities. According to the theology of the cross, Christians must not claim authority themselves, but are called to repentance in response to the undeserved forgiveness of sins.[15] That a Christian ascribes authority to brothers and sisters within the church is a consequence of this. But in contrast to *Rom* II, the ungodly character of church and world does not prevail here. On the contrary, Barth highlights not only God's judgment of sin, but even more strongly God's affirmation of the human person:

> What needs to come to the fore then in the church is the non-

13. Barth, "*Quousque tandem . . . ?*" 530.
14. Barth, "Die Not der Kirche," 101.
15. Ibid., 104–5.

> imputation of evil, the radical disbelief in godlessness, the free non-recognition of the human revolt, not the least of that in modern humanity. What needs to come to the fore then is that [the church] sees humanity, in spite of everything that [the church] holds against [humanity] . . ., on God's side, and resolutely so, without reserve and conditions.[16]

Barth charges the church with proclaiming a socio-religious moralism instead of its proper message:

> Struggle for religious renewal, moral purity, personal freedom, ethnic or social community . . . Is [the church's] proclamation not a thinly veiled, or even a naked proclamation of the law, precisely at that point where [the church] turns to the world, over which it is seemingly losing its influence, where it turns most emphatically and most explicitly to the educated ones, the workers, the youth? More precisely, is the church's proclamation not far from the proclamation of God's law, but rather the proclamation of a very human law . . . ?[17]

The critique of an abstract law is also the gist of Barth's polemic against Christian political parties in "CCCC" (1946): The gospel is made into "a law glued together from humanitarian philosophy and morality."[18] The reason is not that the gospel must be strictly kept separate from all forms of law; the problem is that God's law is inherently connected to the gospel, which is the condition of proper authority. As in 1931, Barth says in 1946 that if the church "has first to advertise its desire to play a part in public life, where it must first establish its claim to be considered a factor of public importance," then it is showing at the same time that inherently it does not deserve such public attention.[19] In 1931, Barth warns that the church's relation to authority vacillates between a blanket refusal

16. Ibid., 106.
17. Ibid.
18. "CCCC," 184 (trans. rev.).
19. Ibid., 167. See 166: "The divine purpose is therefore not at all that the State should itself gradually develop more or less into a church."

and a presumptuous overemphasis.[20] These are the two extremes that Barth already diagnosed in *Rom* I and "ChrSoc."[21] Along these lines, Barth would later present "alienation" and "self-glorification," or "secularization" and "sacralization," as the two great temptations of the congregation.[22] Barth's polemic here is directed against Dibelius's public claims when he opposed an implementation of "Christian principles" in politics and society in 1931, in a way reminiscent of "ChrSoc." Barth criticizes ecclesial claims for power, arguing that the church serves society best by focusing on its own message, trusting that this message is powerful enough to generate the potential for social change itself.[23] Here the primary issue is to avoid both a religious authoritarianism and an insensitivity to true Christian moral obligations. Crucially, it is now the *gospel* that creates moral *obligations.*

While "Die Not der evangelischen Kirche" rejects the principle of direct moral claims that are insufficiently justified in being merely official ecclesial pronouncements, the lecture only indicates vaguely with regard to church law and the church's teaching that God's claims on human action draw their obligatory character exclusively from the assurance of the gospel. Barth does not yet use the terminology of gospel and law in making this case. Rather, individual, explicit hints at a priority of the gospel over the law began to appear more and more frequently in the lecture "Das erste Gebot als theologisches Axiom."

In "Das erste Gebot als theologisches Axiom" ("The First Commandment as a Theological Axiom," 1933, henceforth "Das erste Gebot"),[24] two aspects show how Barth viewed the relationship

20. Barth, "Die Not der Kirche," 95–6.
21. *Rom* I, 517, "ChrSoc," 36, 38.
22. *CD* IV/2, 667–76.
23. Huber, *Folgen christlicher Freiheit*, 137.
24. The lecture was presented twice in Denmark in March 1933, published in *Zwischen den Zeiten*

between God's power and the authority of the gospel. In the first, Barth's exegesis must give us pause. In contrast to a subordination of the law to the gospel, Barth argues that the command of exclusive worship of God highlights "God's being the Lord":[25] "God not only *calls* God's self the Lord, God also behaves the way a lord does by claiming, commanding, and prohibiting."[26] The contrast between this claim and the findings of biblical exegesis is astounding. In the so-called historical books from Genesis to Job, God does not call God's self *Lord* even once. On the whole, the designation *Lord* for God, while never portrayed as a divine self-designation, occurs only thirty-one times there, so it is practically irrelevant in comparison with the proper name *YHWH*, which the Pentateuch on its own already uses more than one thousand times.[27] This confirms Wilfried Härle's thesis that Barth's one-sided emphasis on God's lordship and rule "determines the selection, emphasis, and interpretation of the testimonies to revelation."[28] In comparison to Barth's later subordination of the law to the gospel, it would have been more apposite for Barth to highlight how numerous biblical calls for social justice are based on the reference to God's liberating action, rather

in 1933, and reedited by Barth in 1957. Barth, "Das erste Gebot als theologisches Axiom," in *Vorträge und kleinere Arbeiten 1930–33*, 209–41.

25. Ibid., 221.

26. Ibid.

27. Presumably God's designation as *Lord* would have sounded too much like *Ba'al* (Hebrew: "Lord"). That might mean that the emphasis on God's sheer power and authority achieves what the First Commandment hopes to avoid, according to *CD* IV/3, 101–2: "The combination and admixture of [the worship of God], [God's] invocation and acknowledgment in practical obedience, with the adoration of the numina of Canaan and other surrounding peoples." In the Pentateuch, God is addressed eleven times as *Lord* (*'adōn*) and once designated as *Lord* by the narrator: Gen. 11:9, 15:2, 15:8, 18:3, 30, 32, Exod. 4:10.13, 5:22, 15:17, 34:9 (twice). The books Josh.—2 Kgs. call God *Lord* nineteen times: Josh. 7:7, Judg. 16:28, 2 Sam. 7:18–22 (five times), 7:28–9 (twice), 1 Kgs. 8:53, 22:6, 2 Kgs. 7:6, 19:23, 2 Chron. 30:17, Neh. 1:11, 4:7, 8:10, 10:30, Job 28:28. Even in Ezekiel's formula of recognition ("Recognize that I am YHWH," for example Ezek. 7:4.27, 11:10.12, 12:15–16, 25:5.7.11.17), God never calls God's self *Lord*.

28. Wilfried Härle, *Sein und Gnade: Die Ontologie in Karl Barths Kirchlicher Dogmatik*, Theologische Bibliothek Töpelmann 27 (Berlin and New York: de Gruyter, 1975), 29.

than to overemphasize simple claims to authority. George Hunsinger speaks of a "disjunction" between Barth's notion of certain orthodox articles of faith and the biblical emphasis on justice and mercy, to which Barth does justice only incidentally.[29]

At the same time, however, Barth draws particular attention to the fact that in the Decalogue, the command of the exclusive worship of YHWH follows God's self-description as the liberating God. Thus, the Decalogue justifies the authority of God's command with God's liberation of Israel out of slavery.[30] This is in clear contrast to a concept of God's alien and God's proper work in which God kills in order to make alive. In *CD* I as well, biblical witnesses to God's particular historical activity indicate that a new orientation is underway in comparison to *GD* and *MD*. In the lecture, Barth now emphasizes that God asserts God's self as the Lord not in an abstract act of commanding or in an event of sheer heteronomous power, but in a particular act of liberation. It is for this reason, according to Barth, that there must be no worship of other gods such as "the highest being" or the "absolute spirit" next to "the God who led Israel out of Egypt."[31]

This leads to a statement that is fundamental in metaethics, or, roughly, in the argument about the fundamental validity of norms and criteria in ethics: "The force of the commandment lies in God's mercy that has been demonstrated before."[32] Thus the condition of the validity of a commandment is that it corresponds to a previous act of grace. This definition of the authority of the commandment is a rival to the one offered in the ethics lectures: "Where man

29. George Hunsinger, "Karl Barth and Liberation Theology," in *Disruptive Grace: Studies in the Theology of Karl Barth* (Grand Rapids: Eerdmans, 2000), 42–59, at 55.

30. See Barth, "Das erste Gebot," 222.

31. Ibid., 226–7.

32. Ibid., 224. For further details on metaethics and related fields, see William Schweiker, *Responsibility and Christian Ethics*, New Studies in Christian Ethics (Cambridge: Cambridge University Press, 1999), 35–7.

is negated, there is *iustitia* [justice, righteousness]."[33] The lecture called authority "something which fundamentally and supremely is alien, which cannot be translated or appropriated, but only acknowledged."[34] God's liberating, gracious action is at issue when Barth argues that the commands from Sinai are essentially about Jesus Christ.[35] "Which command is recommended today as a 'pedagogue leading to Christ'? [Gal. 3:24] The law from Sinai? The law that is essentially one with the gospel? The law that leads to Christ, because Christ is also where it is *coming* from? Or is it a different one …?"[36] The ethics lectures had already explained, "As Christ's law the law is *incarnate* law."[37] However, while this might be understood as a call to act in a way that corresponds to God's affirmation of the creature in Christ, in *Ethics* this statement was meant as a call merely to imitate the suffering of Christ that amounts to an indictment of the world. In "Das erste Gebot," by contrast, the emancipatory history of the Hebrew Bible is in the foreground. The exodus becomes the new hermeneutical key for ethics.[38] God's liberative action in the world replaces the worldless image of God from *Rom* II and *Ethics*. This new image of God was already operative when Barth, in "Die Not der evangelischen Kirche," argued that the church must

33. Ibid., 284 (trans. rev.).
34. Ibid., 355.
35. Ibid., 224.
36. Ibid., 235.
37. Barth, *Ethics*, 121 (italics in the original).
38. See *CD* IV/2, 204: What is "proclaimed" in the New Testament is "the fulfilment of the lordship of God on earth" in Christ. "The same cannot be said either of the exodus from Egypt or the conclusion of the covenant with Abraham or at Sinai. These—and the whole history of Israel, and the divine Word spoken in and with it and repeated by Moses and the prophets—were not depreciated but given their true and supreme value when this event took place, i.e., they were shown to be one great promise which had found in this event its fulfilment." On the significance of the exodus in *CD* IV, see Bertold Klappert, "Die Rechts-, Freiheits- und Befreiungsgeschichte Gottes mit den Menschen: Zum Verständnis der Auferstehung in Karl Barths Versöhnungslehre," in *Versöhnung und Befreiung: Versuche, Karl Barth kontextuell zu verstehen*, Neukirchener Beiträge zur systematischen Theologie 14 (Neukirchen-Vluyn: Neukirchener, 1994), 118–37, at 128.

not believe in the godlessness of humanity. In *CD*, the doctrine of election will turn out to be the fundamental crossroads in the development of a different doctrine of God. It is not a coincidence that in chapter 8, an argument for the subordination of the law to the gospel will ensue.[39] But already in "Das erste Gebot," the change of perspective is of paradigmatic importance for ethics.[40] The negative commandment not to worship any other gods is only the consequence of the positive commandment to worship the true God as the liberator, and thus to act in correspondence with this liberation by God. God's commanding grace aims at a particular positive ethos in the world and not at a blanket negation of the world. The interpretation of Jesus Christ as the personification of God's command has changed meaning for Barth, leaving behind the one-sided emphasis on judgment in favor of liberation. The message of reconciliation is no longer also a message of the blanket negation of the world. Conceptually, the actualistic notion of God's command is no longer necessary now as its paradoxical function was to justify action in the world that witnesses to a worldless God.

It may seem to speak in favor of actualism that "Das erste Gebot" repeatedly speaks of an encounter between God and humanity as an *I* and *Thou*. But the relation between the prime importance of God's act of liberation and personalism is unclear. It might seem that the phrasing of God's self-presentation and the First Commandment

39. Thies Gundlach, *Selbstbegrenzung Gottes und die Autonomie des Menschen: Karl Barths Kirchliche Dogmatik als Modernisierungsschritt evangelischer Theologie*, Europäische Hochschulschriften Theologie 471 (Frankfurt am Main: Lang, 1992), 155n18.

40. Albrecht Peters, *Gesetz und Evangelium*, Handbuch Systematische Theologie 2 (Gütersloh: Mohn, 1981), 113, argues that Barth's "groping and searching" for the right relationship between gospel and law reaches an important landmark in this lecture. A change in Barth's outlook at this time is confirmed by André Demut, *Evangelium und Gesetz: Eine systematisch-theologische Reflexion zu Karl Barths Predigtwerk*, Theologische Bibliothek Töpelmann 145 (New York: de Gruyter, 2008), who sees the gospel set the tone of Barth's sermons in the 1930s a lot more often than during the 1920s. Demut interprets this as a "significant discontinuity" (ibid., 109). An implicit dominance of the law decreases significantly in the sermons of the 1930s (ibid., 290).

in Exod. 20:1–3 speak in favor of personalism. In fact, here is no need to reject personalism categorically. But given the prominent function in Barth's theology at the time, the present encounter with the divine Thou threatens to eclipse God's historical revelation. *GD* had argued that revelation culminates in communication between Spirit and spirit,[41] and *CD* later insists that God's word, the only proper mode of revelation, is not to be conceived of symbolically. This contradiction will become apparent when *CD* II/2 argues in actualistic manner that, of all texts, the Decalogue must not be understood as conveying a proper commandment, which Barth defines as highly definite.[42] On the other hand, God's history with God's people replaces any disembodied notion of a divine encounter and, by implication, the fundamental importance of an individualist personalism. This is in keeping with the fact that nine months after delivering the lecture, Barth's sermon on Romans 15 attributes fundamental importance to Jesus' Jewish identity.[43]

"Gospel and Law" (1935)

Pursuing the new development further, Barth focuses on the conceptual priority of the gospel over the law. In concise form it appears in "the basic text of Barth's theology,"[44] the second thesis of the Barmen Declaration of 1934: "As Jesus Christ is God's assurance

41. See Barth's love for an expression by Goethe, which he alters slightly: "The Spirit speaks to the spirit." *GD* I, 62, 225, 227, 237 (twice), 253, 308. See also *GD* II, 69 (§16: "God's Essence"), *GD* III, 415. See also Barth, *MD*, 88, 511, 578.
42. *CD* II/2, 686. Personalism might suggest a contrast with the Decalogue as a historical testimony mediated to the Israelites by Moses: in a proper command of God, "we are face to face with the person of God" (ibid., 676).
43. See Barth, "Römer 15, 5–13," in *Predigten 1921–1935*, ed. Holger Finze-Michaelsen, Barth-Gesamtausgabe (Zurich: Theologischer Verlag, 1998), 300 (December 1933, published in two editions at the time). See Eberhard Busch, *Unter dem Bogen des einen Bundes: Karl Barth und die Juden 1933–1945* (Neukirchen-Vluyn: Neukirchener, 1996), 165–74, at 165.
44. Eberhard Jüngel, "Barth's Life and Work," in *Karl Barth: A Theological Legacy*, trans. Garrett E. Paul (Philadelphia: Westminster John Knox, 1986), 22–52, at 43.

of the forgiveness of all our sins, so in the same way and in the same seriousness is he also God's mighty claim upon our whole life."[45] It is not a coincidence that the Barmen Declaration will go on to draw practical conclusions from this, which will be considered in one particular respect below.

Barth elaborates on the consequences of the new constellation of gospel and law in the lecture of the same name in 1935.[46] Jüngel rightly identifies it as a watershed in Barth's thought, calling it an "addition to the prolegomena" of *CD* I,[47] since the inner differentiation of the word of God into gospel and law is an aspect not yet touched on with Barth's doctrine of the threefold form of the word of God.[48] This confirms the significance of the new development in Barth's thought, and the revisions that would find their way into *CD* in volume II/2.

Like the Barmen Declaration, the lecture entirely lacks both any hint of dialogistic personalism or the actualistic concept of God's contingent, new commanding. Barth toned these elements down

45. Eberhard Busch, *The Barmen Theses Then and Now: The 2004 Warfield Lectures at Princeton Theological Seminary*, trans. Darrell Guder and Judith Guder (Grand Rapids: Eerdmans, 2010), 35.
46. Having just moved to Switzerland, Barth returned to Germany (Barmen/Wuppertal) in October with the lecture "Gospel and Law." The lecture was read in Barth's presence by pastor Karl Immer, as he was categorically forbidden to speak publicly in Germany (Busch, *Barth: His Life from Letters*, 266).
47. Eberhard Jüngel, "Zum Verhältnis von Kirche und Staat nach Karl Barth," in *Zur Theologie Karl Barths: Beiträge aus Anlass seines 100. Geburtstags*, ed. E. Jüngel, Zeitschrift für Theologie und Kirche Beiheft 6 (Tübingen: Mohr Siebeck, 1986), 76–135, at 77. "The programmatic importance of the lecture 'Gospel and Law,' published in 1935, must be considered very high since the volume of the *Church Dogmatics* that appeared two years before was still . . . able to present the doctrine of the word of God without elaborating on the distinction of law and gospel." In keeping with this is Wolf Krötke's judgment in "Die Summe des Evangeliums: Karl Barths Erwählungslehre im Kontext der Kirchlichen Dogmatik," in *Karl Barth im europäischen Zeitgeschehen (1935–1950): Widerstand—Bewährung—Orientierung*, eds. Michael Beintker et al. (Zurich: Theologischer Verlag Zürich, 2010), 67–82, at 70.
48. Jüngel, "Gospel and Law: The Relationship of Dogmatics to Ethics," in *Karl Barth: A Theological Legacy*, trans. Garrett E. Paul (Philadelphia: Westminster John Knox, 1986), 105–26, at 111, calls this a "startling conclusion."

entirely in order to hammer home a christological concentration. His question is how the gospel, on the one hand, and the law, on the other, relate to God's revelation in Christ. A crucial difference to *Rom* II is that the lecture ignores the docetic assumption that a "unity" of the world with God is real "only beyond birth and death."[49] Instead, the focus is on Jesus Christ, who is of utmost importance for the reality of gospel and law. The later lecture "CS," again without reference to personalism and actualism, will draw further consequences from this with respect to social ethics.

Barth begins his talk "GL" by acknowledging that to most theologians, the formula *law and gospel* suggests itself. By contrast, while gospel and law are distinct, he nonetheless argues that they constitute a unity in "peace in the one word of this Father."[50] Moreover, Barth sees the gospel having priority over the law. God's one word is always grace. It is in God's grace that the law is given. Barth defines it as being in conformity with "the occurrence of the will of God at Bethlehem, at Capernaum and Tiberias, in Gethsemane, on Golgotha and in the garden of Joseph of Arimathea."[51] Later on, more needs to be said about Barth's assertion that God's word is still grace even if God uses it to "judge us, punish us, and kill us" and if it means "judgment, death, and hell."[52] Nonetheless, the law is associated with God's promise that it will not be a heteronomous burden.[53] This allows Barth to dispute "a source of revelation bubbling forth independently of the gospel," which is directed against supposed orders of creation that manifest God's law independently of the gospel.[54] In keeping with "Das erste

49. *Rom* II, 60, 76.
50. "GL," 71, see the first Barmen Thesis: "Jesus Christ, as he is attested for us in Holy Scripture, is the one Word of God."
51. Ibid., 77–8.
52. "GL," 72.
53. Ibid., 78, 81–2.

Gebot," Barth assumes that God's covenant of grace with Israel had already taken on concrete shape in the commandments, the purpose of which is neither to provide a way to earn salvation nor to prepare believers for grace by leading them into despair about their works.[55] The unity of God's word and its gracious nature are fully revealed in Jesus Christ. That is also relevant for the judgment to which the law may amount. A critique of human behavior that is experienced as judgment can only be granted the dignity of God's law if indeed such judgment does not merely pave the way for God's revelation in Christ, but is rooted in God's revelation in Christ. This is also true for the practical guidance that the law provides: positive moral advice is authoritative only insofar as it can be understood as practical correspondence to the gospel.[56]

This is a metaethical statement of fundamental importance. The validity of moral claims depends strictly on whether the agent can be assumed to affirm the basis of such moral obligation. The gospel is the only source and basis of any true moral obligation. There are no legitimate moral claims that might constitute a wholesale obligation independently of the agent's fundamental ability to assent.

A crucial difference between this and the Lutheran concept of law and gospel is that in the latter, the gospel is not only a free, truly pleasant gift that liberates from any demand for action, but that the gospel liberates for the kind of action that occurs spontaneously and freely and that must never come close to being a demand.[57] If, by

54. Jüngel, "Zum Verhältnis von Kirche und Staat," 107, describing Werner Elert's assertion that the law confronts people relatively independently in the empirical orders.

55. "GL," 87, see 82: "All commandments are included in the *first* commandment and always must be understood and explained as especially emphasizing the first Commandment."

56. This is also emphasized by Reinhard Hütter, *Evangelische Ethik als kirchliches Zeugnis: Interpretationen zu Schlüsselfragen theologischer Ethik in der Gegenwart*, Evangelium und Ethik 1 (Neukirchen-Vluyn: Neukirchener, 1993), 269. See also 69.

57. See Jüngel, "Gospel and Law," 108–10, 122–3. "Luther took seriously Paul's description in Romans 4:5 of 'believing' as 'not doing works'" (122). Honecker, *Einführung*, 78 speaks of a

contrast, a legitimate command guides action, the Lutheran tradition often distinguishes this from the law as New Testament paraclesis. By contrast, Barth sees the gospel as constituting strict moral obligations. Thus, according to his notion of the priority of the gospel, the demand of the law can indeed support life and enhance life beyond harsh pedagogy. By contrast, the Lutheran distinction between law and gospel always includes a prominent element of competition, even if such competition ultimately results in spiritual edification. The Lutheran distinction asks whether it is the law or the gospel that constitutes the identity of the human person *coram Deo*.

By contrast, Barth's notion of the unity of gospel and law may well be due to Barth's lifelong respect for Immanuel Kant. The Enlightenment thinker called an action moral only if it is not merely objectively reasonable, but also if it is performed out of rational motives, for duty's sake.[58] Certainly, the notion of autonomous reason plays a much lesser role in Barth's thought. But by analogy, both thinkers are concerned with action that is in keeping materially with that which fundamentally characterizes human identity, and that is performed for the sake of that which fundamentally characterizes human identity. In Barth's thought, this is the gospel. In that sense, "Die Not der evangelischen Kirche," "Das erste Gebot,"

"struggle between law and gospel," as both Luther and Paul deal with the path to salvation (ibid., 79). Jüngel, "Gospel and Law," 110, speaks of "the wrathful God of the law."

58. Immanuel Kant, *Groundwork to the Metaphysics of Morals: A German-English Edition*, trans. and ed. Mary Gregor and Jens Zimmermann (Cambridge: Cambridge University Press, 2011), 29: "*Duty is the necessity of an action from respect for the law.*" Barth, *Die protestantische Theologie im 19. Jahrhundert: Ihre Vorgeschichte und ihre Geschichte*, tvz reprints (Zurich: Theologischer Verlag, 1981), 195, calls J.-J. Rousseau the "precursor of Kant in raising the ethical-anthropological problem" (see also 197–8) and quotes Rousseau as the mastermind of modern autonomy: "Obedience to the law one has prescribed to oneself is freedom." Jean-Jacques Rousseau, *"The Social Contract" and Other Later Political Writings*, ed. and trans. Victor Gourevitch, Cambridge Texts in the History of Political Thought 2 (Cambridge: Cambridge University, 1997), 54 (I, 8). Barth attributes to Rousseau the discovery of the self-experience that abstracts from sensual impressions and in which one is "immediately conscious both of oneself and of one's relation to the external world, prior to all behavior, prior to all knowledge and action" (ibid., 203).

and "GL" are all directed against a heteronomous ethics.[59] Any moral obligation is valid only due to its inner, material relation to the gospel.[60]

Later on, Barth will come to identify a grain of truth even in heteronomy. *CD* I/2, §§23–4 summarize Christian theology as theonomous in a way that transcends the binary of autonomy and heteronomy. This is yet another way to construe these terms. An element of autonomy is crucial for ethics insofar as a Christian perspective will be shaped by the gospel, so that the command will arise from a ground that is not at all foreign or even hostile to Christians. Heteronomy may even be involved to the extent that God's command will involve an element of novelty and discovery. Yet the harsh sense of subjection to a foreign law can by no means characterize the essence of God's command. Since God's command will transcend autonomy and heteronomy in this sense, it can indeed be called theonomous.[61] Yet to fill the vision of a theonomous command with life, one condition is that the ethical discourse steer a course between those aspects of heteronomy and autonomy problematic from the perspective of Christian ethics.

In spite of the difficulties arising in the theological appropriation of Kant's terms, this discussion is helpful in one respect: the overlap of God's command with autonomy will be greater than with heteronomy, to the extent that the gospel precedes the law. The aspect of subjection to a foreign law is essentially alien to God's command. By contrast, Barth's harsh reaction against all human participation in the emergence of God's command in the ethics

59. On Kant's concept of autonomy, see Kant, *Groundwork to the Metaphysics of Morals*, 109.

60. The notion of human autonomy remains too vague, however, in Gundlach, *Selbstbegrenzung*, 238–9, who argues that God forgoes an immediate implementation of God's will in acts of mercy or punishment, which is supposedly in keeping with the heritage of the Enlightenment and liberal theology.

61. See *CD* I/2, 911.

lectures, which amounted to a full-blown rejection of autonomy, rested on dubious notions of divine absoluteness vis-à-vis the creature.

As "Das erste Gebot" was already directed critically against orders of creation, this is also an important concern for "GL."[62] In the Lutheran concept of law and gospel, the gospel encourages spontaneous, voluntary action, while in public life, a general notion of reason that would be in harmony with creation guides action. Beyond the commission to preach, the gospel does not involve any responsibilities, which would turn the gospel into a demand. Indeed, the instructions for a love ethos in the Sermon on the Mount, if taken as a moral obligation, would put public safety at risk. By contrast, it is Barth's fear that the institutions of general reason, as reflected in the orders of creation, are not sufficiently immune to the harmful effects of sin, inviting an authoritarian takeover of public life. In turn, Barth is wary that the concept of law and gospel neglects the practical, life-enhancing significance of the biblical commandments.

Thus, the material content of the command of the law is morally obligatory insofar as it is in correspondence with the liberation through the gospel; "the Law is nothing else than the necessary *form of the gospel*, whose content is grace."[63] Jesus Christ fulfills God's will in his earthly ministry, in his passion and in his resurrection. "In this occurrence of the will of God, thus in the occurrence of God's grace being *revealed* to us, the *law* is revealed to us."[64]

Barth's description of how God's will becomes a reality in Christ highlights the cross, and in consequence he again emphasizes self-negation in the Christian life.[65] Nonetheless, the high importance of the Old Testament commands and the place names of Capernaum,

62. Busch, *Karl Barth: His Life from Letters*, 266.
63. "GL," 80.
64. Ibid., 78 (trans. rev.).
65. Ibid., 79.

Tiberias, and Joseph of Arimathea's garden[66] indicate that there is more to Jesus Christ's story than just the passion. While *Ethics* reduces Christ's command to the bearing of the cross, and while *CD* I widens the theological perspective over against personalist actualism by referring to God's involvement in the story of God's people, as in the exodus, "GL" resists reducing Jesus Christ to a principle of self-negation. Barth's increasing attention to story and history later reaches a watershed in the correspondence that *CD* II/2 sees at work between God's eternal act of election and Christ's ministry, his passion and the resurrection. *CD* IV/2 will again show how the focus on Christ shifts from a supratemporal principle of self-negation to a particular history:

> We must now attempt—and thus we are reaching the decisive point—to understand Jesus . . . in the act accomplished by him. It is in the *act of his life* that the distinctiveness of his existence and his likeness to God became actual and thus visible and comprehensible. His life was his act, and it has therefore the character of *history*. . . . The totality of his being in its scope for [the New Testament congregation] and the whole world was identical with the totality of his *activity*.[67]

In contrast to a one-sided attention to the cross, "GL" also argues that "this justification and acceptance of our humanity is really accomplished in the *resurrection* of Jesus Christ from the *dead*."[68] Certainly, Christ's cross is of particular importance for theology, and in a particular sense, we can even see Christ's entire life as a sacrifice.[69] But neither does this exclude the affirmation and enhancement of biological and social life throughout Jesus' ministry,[70] nor can Christ's

66. Ibid., 77–8.
67. *CD* IV/2, 193 (trans. rev.).
68. "GL," 74–5.
69. Kathryn Tanner, *Jesus, Humanity and the Trinity: A Brief Systematic Theology* (Minneapolis: Fortress Press, 2001), 29.
70. In "The Messianic Mission of Christ," as Jürgen Moltmann sees it, "The Gospel of the Kingdom of God to the Poor," "The Healing of the Sick," and "The Acceptance of the Outcasts" play

cross be reduced merely to self-abnegation and passivity.[71] The notion of a suffering acceptance is indeed far from dominating the Christian ethos when Barth asserts that "grace means the office of Moses and Elijah, of Isaiah and Jeremiah, the office of the Baptizer, of Paul, of James. Grace, by becoming the summons to grace, means the church which dares and must dare to speak with authority,"[72] "also for the world, for state and society."[73] This act must preserve the priority of the gospel, so that ecclesial authority does not degrade into authoritarianism. How such ecclesial witness is possible is Barth's concern in "Die Not der evangelischen Kirche."

Barth also asserts that God's word is still grace even if God uses it to "judge us, punish us, and kill us" and if it means "judgment, death, and hell."[74] This raises the question how consistent Barth's christological interpretation of the law is indeed, as Christ's ministry and passion are characterized exactly by a renunciation of punishment of others. The one thing that the "occurrence of the will of God at Bethlehem, at Capernaum and Tiberias, in Gethsemane, on Golgotha and in the garden of Joseph of Arimathea"[75] does not include is "judgment, death, and hell" being inflicted on Jesus' opponents. By contrast, when the risen Christ meets the disciples that

a crucial role. *The Way of Jesus Christ: Christology in Messianic Dimensions*, trans. Margaret Kohl (London: SCM, 1990), ch. 3, §§4–6. See also Moltmann's perceptive comment, ibid., 52: According to large strands of the ecclesial tradition, "the history of Christ is essentially the vertical history between God and human beings. . . . If the history of Christ is essentially this vertical history, then it is a fundamentally 'eternal history.' . . . Between his birth from a virgin and his death under Pontius Pilate, the dogmatic history tells us *almost nothing;* and the same may be said of the traditional confessions of the Christian faith. The Nicene creed says 'and became man'; the Apostles' creed, merely 'suffered.'"

71. The cross, which would be indiscernible apart from the resurrection, thus also reveals "the judging and saving God" in the person of Christ. Michael Welker, *God the Revealed: Christology*, trans. Douglas W. Stott (Grand Rapids: Eerdmans, 2014), 185. See also Paul Dafydd Jones, *The Humanity of Christ: Christology in Karl Barth's Church Dogmatics*, T&T Clark Theology (London and New York: T&T Clark, 2008), 157–62.
72. "GL," 80.
73. Ibid., 79.
74. Ibid., 72.
75. Ibid., 77–8.

had forsaken him, his greeting is "do not be afraid" and "peace be with you." "But God proves his love for us in that while we still were sinners Christ died for us" (Rom. 5:8). It is thus essential that the concept of gospel and law not only calls the gospel the original reason and motivation for God's activity in the law and that the gospel not only constitutes a moral obligation. Above and beyond that, the priority of the gospel can only be respected if the judgment of the law is consistently and strictly limited to proportions that are in keeping with the good news of the gospel. Moreover, in the light of the gospel of grace, God's transforming and redeeming action will become significantly more prominent than the negative character of judgment.

Consequently, if Barth affirms that God's word still inflicts severe punishment, the subordination of the law to the gospel has been suspended in favor of a *deus absconditus*, a reality of God that is quite different and distinct from God's revelation in Jesus Christ.[76] This severely restricts Barth's view that Jesus Christ "has borne the need, the curse, the punishment"[77] that is "God's answer to the sin of the human person," or that "he bore our punishment."[78] To subject sinful humans to punishment so that they may act in better agreement with this salvific event would be to reassert the principle of works righteousness. Such punishment runs the risk of being overly heteronomous, and Barth's emphasis on the gospel over the law denies that heteronomy constitutes any moral obligation. The only way in which the proclamation of salvation in Christ can coexist with divine judgment is the regret of the justified for their sin and their inspired striving for better divine guidance. The law may compel

76. See, for example, Gerhard Ebeling, "Karl Barths Ringen mit Luther," in *Lutherstudien: Begriffsuntersuchungen—Textinterpretationen—Werkgeschichtliches* (Tübingen: Mohr Siebeck, 1985), 3:428–573, at 571.

77. "GL," 73.

78. Ibid., 74.

confession and conversion insofar as it preaches "condemnation" (2 Cor. 3:9–10).[79] Yet such compulsion to conversion requires the prior gift of the Spirit, and terms like *punishment*, *killing*, and *hell* fail to convey God's abiding love, regardless of whether they are used figuratively or not.

The priority of the gospel to the law must mean that it is the consolation and encouragement through God's grace and the gift of the Holy Spirit that bring about conformity with God's word. The *usus elenchticus legis* is legitimate only under this condition. By contrast, if a person is so deeply enmeshed in sin that the quenched Spirit can no longer make the instruction of the law heard, it is unlikely that an escalation of punishment would be in keeping with New Testament christological traditions. Certainly, what is generally accepted as God's commandment can be perverted and wreak great havoc.[80] But under those circumstances, this is no longer God's own true command of grace. By contrast, the gravity of sin is revealed in those forces causing Christ to suffer. This is, in fact, very similar to a concept Barth was to pursue later on when arguing that sin is that which is primarily recognized in Christ's cross.[81] The contrast is to a supposed revelation of sin in the law's inflicting "judgment, death, and hell" on Christians.

"GL" thus perpetuates also a Lutheran understanding of law and gospel in which the law is, at least on occasion, a harsh force of

79. Ibid., 94.

80. Michael Welker, "Gesetz und Geist," in *"Gesetz" als Thema Biblischer Theologie*, Jahrbuch für Biblische Theologie 4 (Neukirchen–Vluyn: Neukirchener, 1989), 215–29, at 223–4.

81. Barth writes on the recognition of sin in *CD* III/3, § 50, 304–5: "That which rendered necessary the birth of God's son in the stable of Bethlehem and his death upon the cross of Calvary . . . is that which primarily opposes and resists God Himself, and therefore all creation. It is obvious that this neither can nor may be understood as something which God Himself has posited or decreed." What has been left out in this quotation is Barth's notion that sin in its entirety was defeated at the cross. The crucial point is now that God's judgment of sin, insofar as it exceeds the corrective instruction of the law, takes place at the cross. God does not "judge us, punish us, and kill us" in the judgment of the law—that would indeed detract from what Christ has achieved in the place of the sinner.

retribution rather than the shape in which human action replies to God's salvation. According to "GL," God asserts God's self against sin in the judgment of the law. As the law is given "into the hands of *sinners*,"[82] Barth now asks what will become of it. Will it be perverted through a works-righteousness interpretation, so that it is forced to serve self-justification? A conflict emerges in which, however, God will hold the upper hand, according to Barth. By revealing human sin, the law is judgment for those who rely on their own achievements. In the law, God now fights against the perversion of sin: "It is the Law, dishonored and emptied by sin's deception, which, with the power of the *wrath* of God, nevertheless is and remains *God's* law. If we serve *this* law, then there is no escape from God's judgment, and in the temptation in which this judgment is manifest, there is no counsel, no comfort, no help."[83]

If we wish to retain God's absolute, effective Lordship and God's self-assertion in history, however, the danger is that God's judgment is all too easily identified with various harrowing experiences in history. This was widespread not only in extreme, anti-Semitic forms of German Protestantism, but also in slightly more moderate, conservative, nationalistic Protestantism.[84] Under this premise, authoritarian orders of creation will again present themselves as a

82. "GL," 84, also 85. This aspect is also highlighted by Jüngel, "Zum Verhältnis von Kirche und Staat," 95, 103.
83. "GL," 94.
84. Paul Althaus, *The Theology of Martin Luther* (Minneapolis: Fortress Press, 1985), 177, explains that according to Luther, any true knowledge of the law reveals tribulation and misfortune as divine punishment. "God, through his law, forces man continually deeper into sin" (ibid., 176). God punishes such sin with "plague, famine, the sword, and other troubles" (Luther, quoted ibid., 173). This is an important part of "the dialectic of God's alien work and his proper work, of law and gospel" (ibid., 171). Such thinking was modified and used by fascist thinkers such as Wilhelm Stapel in his doctrine of the *Nomos Germanikos* (German divine law): "The *nomos* [i.e., divine law] is, as it were, the point at which God attacks the human person." Stapel, *Der christliche Staatsmann: Eine Theologie des Nationalismus* (Hamburg: Hanseatische Verlagsanstalt, 1932), 181.

legitimate theological option, and Barth's interpretation of custom, education, and law in the ethics lectures pursued this goal as well.

"Church and State" (1938)

The groundbreaking theological achievements of Barth's lecture "CS" ("Rechtfertigung und Recht," literally "Justification and Justice," 1938) are often overlooked. To begin with, however, even this text retains the notion of God's unconditioned nature, and there are problematic consequences to Barth's insistence on God's sovereignty. Barth does admit that demonic entities such as the totalitarian state are not entirely powerless in their rebellion against God. Yet ultimately, in a sovereign exercise of power and resilience, God uses those deeds that are directed against God for God's own purposes. Even when faced with the climax of rebellion, the execution of God's incarnate Son, God asserts God's own purposes against the sinful creature. In justification through grace, God does not tolerate any limitation of divine power in torture and murder, creating good through evil.[85]

To maintain God's absolute sovereignty nonetheless, Barth pays the steep price of calling God the ultimate subject of the crucifixion.[86] One might argue that God detests the cross, but is still able, in justification, to extract good out of evil. Yet such differentiations are absent in "CS." By contrast, Barth continues to maintain a crucial premise of the actualistic concept of revelation: the idea that God

85. This position should be distinguished from Bonhoeffer's more nuanced statement that "God can and will let good come out of everything, even the greatest evil." Bonhoeffer, "After Ten Years," trans. Barbara Rumscheidt and Martin Rumscheidt, in *Letters and Papers from Prison*, ed. John W. de Gruchy, trans. Isabel Best et al., Dietrich Bonhoeffer Works 8 (Minneapolis: Fortress Press, 2009), 37–52, at 46. ("For that to happen, God needs human beings who let everything work out for the best. . . . God . . . responds to sincere prayer and responsible actions.")

86. "CS," 110 (trans. rev.): "Precisely by allowing injustice to run its course (in the guise of justice, mind you! in the exercise of the authority given to him by God) Pilate was the human created instrument of that justification of sinful humanity that had to be completed in this crucifixion."

cannot be turned into an object unless God does it God's self. Ultimately, it is the heavenly Father himself who crucifies Jesus.

At this juncture Barth is at pains to argue that in the sovereignty of the state we are not dealing with an order of creation but "indirectly," though "in reality, with the authority of Jesus Christ."[87] Barth contests a blanket approval of authority and state power under the title of an order of creation. Yet the statement that, indirectly, Pilate's unjust rule is Christ's rule, puts Christ's rule into an uncomfortable proximity to tyranny. While it was sinful humans who crucified Christ, the assertion of God's sovereign power over history is a two-edged sword. If Christ's suffering on the cross means divine punishment, Barth's association of God with absolute grace and goodness as revealed in Jesus Christ, and the priority of the gospel over the law, is again compromised. If God is the ultimate subject of the crucifixion and humanity God's "created instrument,"[88] then God kills in order to make alive.[89] The two central dates of the Christian faith, Good Friday and Easter, would constitute the original event of "law and gospel," not of "gospel and law."[90] The priority of the gospel over the law stands in contrast to the notion that God, even if through creaturely agency, executes God's eternal son. Not even for the sake of reconciliation should this judicial murder be called grace.

If taken seriously, however, the priority of the gospel implies a revision of the concept of revelation in *CD* I/1 with its opaque

87. Ibid., 122.
88. Ibid., 110.
89. See Luther, *On the Bondage of the Will*, in *Career of the Reformer*, ed. and trans. Philip S. Watson, Luther's Works, vol. 33 (Philadelphia: Fortress, 1972), 3:62: "Thus when God makes alive he does it by killing."
90. Wilfried Joest, "Karl Barth und das lutherische Verständnis von Gesetz und Evangelium: Gedanken und Fragen zur Wiederaufnahme einer stehengebliebenen Diskussion," *Kerygma und Dogma* 24 (1978): 86–103, at 99. See Bertold Klappert, *Promissio und Bund: Gesetz und Evangelium bei Luther und Barth*, Forschungen zur systematischen und ökumenischen Theologie 34 (Göttingen: Vandenhoeck & Ruprecht, 1976), 111–13: This is the work of God's own anger in the face of humanity perverting the law. That the law kills is not merely a human misunderstanding.

affirmation of God's absolute lordship. Thus, Barth can also write, "Fundamentally and decisively God distinguishes God's self from the creature by His grace. Fundamentally and decisively His divinity consists and confirms itself in His grace."[91]

After these critical observations on "GL" and "CS", their positive contribution to Barth's ethics must be highlighted emphatically. In contrast to a merely negative ethics, it is an important merit of "GL" to embed repentance and self-negation into the wider theological context of gospel and law. Repentance, sacrifice, and self-negation, the lecture argues, are legitimate, indeed called for insofar as Christians repeatedly attempt to misuse God's good law for their self-justification. It must be noted that "GL" treats the classic problem of works righteousness only in the third of four sections. Barth's notion, moreover, that God's commandment gives concrete shape to the gospel in providing the corresponding form of life subverts the one-sided emphasis on repentance and sacrifice.

According to "CS," Christian faith implies Christian responsibility for legal justice. This notion is of utmost importance for Barth's ethics.[92] Already the fifth thesis of the Barmen Declaration called the church to task to remind the state of the divine ordinance to pursue justice and peace. It would be difficult to construe this categorical statement about God's will in actualistic terms. Neither does it express merely Barth's private political views, as "CS" now makes clear. The Reformers "owed us greater clarification"[93] when they described the relation between the organization of the political commonwealth and the great spiritual themes of Reformation doctrine only in terms of a compatibility of civil responsibility and justifying faith. In the relation between church and state, they emphasized the difference at the

91. *CD* II/1, 357.

92. See Michael Beintker, "Die politische Verantwortung der Christengemeinde im Denken Barths," *Zeitschrift für Dialektische Theologie* 12 (1996): 149–74, at 166, 168–9.

93. "CS," 102 (trans. rev.).

expense of the positive relation.[94] The theory of God's two kingdoms in the Lutheran tradition underestimates the danger that the state may be perverted to a demonic force.[95] In Barth's context, a positive relationship between the doctrine of justification and temporal justice was a burning issue.[96] "CS" was written four months after the German annexation of Austria in 1938. At the same time, public opinion in Switzerland became more favorable toward Nazi Germany.[97]

While temporal justice is not by itself the substance of Christian proclamation, a fundamental danger for legal justice nonetheless also implies a fundamental danger for Christian proclamation. Due to the inherent relationship between justification and legal justice, Christian proclamation cannot remain silent in the face of a fundamental threat to legal justice without betraying the gospel.

Presenting this intimate relationship between the two, Barth recounts the passion story with allusions to current events—"the harsh

94. Ibid., 103–4.
95. Ibid., 106–7.
96. According to William Werpehowski, "Justification and Justice in the Theology of Karl Barth," *Thomist* 50 (1986): 623–42, "CS" presents a Lutheran theory of two reigns, while the point of Barth's political ethics on the whole is an anthropology of fellow-humanity, which Barth worked out in the theology of creation. However, a Lutheran theory of God's two reigns is based on a particular distinction between law and gospel: just as the gospel does not create any obligations like the law does, so Christian love must not be conflated with the public ethos of political authorities. By contrast, "CS" is concerned less with the distinction between law and gospel than with bringing the law into an appropriate relationship with the gospel. See also Jüngel, "Gospel and Law," 110; Jüngel, "Zum Verhältnis von Kirche und Staat," 79; 93–4. See also *CD* II/1, 386–7.
97. Ibid., 105, see Busch, *Karl Barth: His Life from Letters*, 287. The Lutheran theory of two kingdoms relies strongly on the notion of natural law, which it understands as God's means in governing temporal affairs. As temporal affairs require a clear distinction from spiritual affairs, the law is thought of as clearly distinct from the gospel. Under the sway of National Socialism, however, natural law was conceived of in fundamentally nationalistic and racial terms. For this reason, "CS" works out an alternative theological scheme that seeks both spiritual and temporal orientation in reversing the Lutheran evacuation of the temporal realm from spiritual traditions relating to Christ, the cross, and justification. In a nutshell, "CS" thinks of Christ's work of reconciliation as constitutive for justice, a concept in which again the two dimensions—the spiritual ("righteousness") and the legal ("justice")—are inseparable, as reflected in the Latin *iustitia* and German *Gerechtigkeit*.

picture of the execution of Jesus Christ by the officials of the State"[98]—as a testimony to the suffering under an unjust state that executes Jesus without proper sentence. It is not only the monopoly on the use of force that made the Roman state a proper state, but its impartiality in administering justice. "In this encounter of Pilate and Jesus, the 'demonic' State is not the State that asserts itself too much, but the one that is too *little* of a State!"[99]

The demonic state is in contradiction to the essence of a state, which, according to Barth, can be seen clearly from a theological perspective. Revelation 21 presents the eschatological salvation of the end times in terms of a political order. A city of justice is the form of life in which salvation is operative: "Could the church of divine justification hold the human state of legal justice in higher esteem than when it sees in that very state, in its heavenly reality, into which its terrestrial existence will finally be absorbed, the final predicate of its own grounds for hope?"[100] The city of justice, for which the church hopes, is characterized by the presence of the crucified Christ. The justice of the eternal city is constituted by Christ's

> eternal right (*Recht*). It is His right (*Recht*), won by Jesus Christ in His death and proclaimed in His resurrection which constitute His eternal right (*Recht*) . . . Now this eternal right (*Recht*) of Jesus Christ constitutes precisely the content of the message of justification, in which, here and now, the task of the church consists.[101]

Crucially, Barth asserts, God constituted justice in Christ's cross and resurrection, and this is again the basis of both the church and politics. For this reason, the church cannot neglect temporal justice without betraying its own calling.

98. "CS," 107.
99. Ibid., 113.
100. Ibid., 124 (trans. rev.).
101. Ibid., 127 (trans. rev.: the German *Recht* includes both justice and righteousness and has been rendered as "right").

Barth also asserts that by far the best fulfillment of political justice is possible in a democracy. This may seem to be at variance with the fact that the New Testament, notably Romans 13, seems to legitimize an authoritarian state. However, Barth argues that 1 Timothy 2 subverts the legitimacy of any authoritarian state, and that only a state in which Christians can actively claim their stake has any theological authority at all. In praying for the state, Christians exercise their responsibility for a "*Rechtsstaat*,"[102] a state in which the rule of law warrants liberty and justice. Christians do not merely exercise responsibility for the state for its own sake, but also for the sake of Christian proclamation, which requires the state to respect religious freedom, and for the sake of temporal justice, which is a genuine theological concern. Should the state fail in this respect, however, Christians are bound by the theological nature of justice and must give to God what belongs to God.[103]

The theological account of justice does not mean, however, that the state must be a Christian state. The state should be neutral in religious matters,[104] as the state is not immune to the temptation of power abuse in striving for religious truth.[105] The state should forgo

102. At the heart of Barth's discussion is the concept of the *Rechtsstaat*, which is a legally ordered state that safeguards the liberties of its citizens, especially vis-à-vis centralized government, in preserving the option of legal recourse. An appropriate English equivalent is a "constitutional democracy." This concept, in turn, is best thought of in terms of a separation of powers, participatory democracy, the preservation of liberties and a just order by means of a constitution, as well as institutions for the administration of justice and the forming of public opinion in political matters. See Ernst Benda, "Rechtsstaat," in *Lexikon der Politik: Begriffe, Theorie, Methoden, Fakten: Politische Theorien*, ed. Dieter Nohlen (München: C. H. Beck, 1995), 515–18.

103. "CS," 145.

104. Barth fears that a legal privilege for Christian orientations in the midst of differences in worldviews creates an unjust moralism, especially given human fallibility. According to "CCCC," 152, the state must thus pursue only "external, relative, and provisional tasks and aims." The lecture describes a political competition that strives for a pragmatic consensus, which is unable, however, to reveal any objective order of nature. Barth thus argues for the rule of law in a basic constellation oriented towards freedom and social justice (173) with a separation of powers (175–6) and "certain spheres (the family, education, art, science, religion, culture), safeguarded but not regulated by law" (174).

any religious confession, but strive for justice and freedom. Since the church is aware of this necessity, it is the first advocate for a neutral state and must fight against any neglect of legal justice. "Just as divine justification is *the* continuum of right (*rechtliches Kontinuum*), so the church is *the* political continuum. And to be this is the church's first and fundamental service to the state."[106] The church knows that the human person is "a sinner in need of justification,"[107] so the church should also be committed to a defense of temporal justice, by violent means, if need be. In a thinly veiled call for a revolution against Hitler, Barth asserts that this includes the removal of blatant tyranny.[108] The goal of the church's support in this cause, however, can only consist in later focusing again on the activity for which the just state is the presupposition: the free discharge of its specific ecclesial tasks in proclamation and the administration of the sacraments.

With this discussion Barth has decisively turned his back on a fundamental, one-sided emphasis on sacrifice and repentance. "CS" spells out the political consequences of the case made in "GL," according to which God's commandment calls for a concrete form of life that corresponds to the liberation in the gospel.

Before concluding, it is worth asking whether the church's commitment for a constitutional democracy collides with Barth's reminder in "Die Not der evangelischen Kirche" that an implementation of Christian principles through the church's influence amounts to legalism, as people with other religious convictions may be unable to come to the same practical conclusions on the basis of the gospel.

In "CS," Barth urges that in matters not allowing for a clean

105. "CS," 132, 110.
106. Ibid., 141 (trans. rev.).
107. Ibid., 142.
108. Ibid., 145.

separation between politics and religion, state action should be utterly parsimonious. "CCCC" (1946) suggests how a "clericalization" of the world—or even a "war of the good against the evil"[109]—can be avoided. Public discourse needs to make decisions only for reasons that everybody involved can be presumed to accept, which may require the promotion of practical measures with reasons that, from a Christian perspective, may not have priority or be entirely appropriate. Thus politicians may depend on drawing "from the porous well of the so-called natural law."[110]

Election and the Doctrine of God in *CD* II/2

In "GL" and "CS," Barth argued that Christ's cross and resurrection constitute moral obligations for Christians and that reconciliation precedes any potential judgment on humanity. God's relation to the world still implies the potential for a critical Christian ethics that swims against the stream, but the fundamental thrust is constructive. In *Rom* II, by contrast, salvation for the creature paled in comparison to God's judgment, and even in the actualistic concept of revelation in *GD*, God's affirmation of the creature emerged from the shadows of judgment only for the evasive moment of contingent revelation within the church. Thus, "GL" and "CS" mark a watershed in Barth's thought both in theological and ethical respect.

In the face of these changes, the crucial importance of the doctrine of election *CD* II/2, particularly chapter 7, lies in Barth's refusal to continue maintaining the unconditioned, unworldly nature of God that was the driving force behind the critical judgment over the world in *Rom* II. Barth even pursues the notion that Christ's cross and resurrection constitute worldly justice further, arguing categorically

109. Ibid., 38, 40; *Rom* I, 43; *Rom* II, 653.
110. "CCCC," 170, see also 163–4.

that there is no hidden God who might again cast doubt on the validity of the gospel. The eighth chapter of *CD*, vol. II/2, with its subordination of the law under the gospel, has rightly been called an "addition to the prolegomena of the *Church Dogmatics*,"[111] but this addition goes hand-in-hand with the argument of chapter 7.

As the prolegomena saw the threefold form of the word of God rooted in God's Trinitarian nature, so *CD* II/2 sees the priority of the gospel rooted in the eternal act of election by the Triune God. The eternal decree of election does not say anything besides what is revealed in Jesus Christ.[112] Barth criticizes Reformed Orthodoxy for a disjunction between eternal predestination and the interpretation of the incarnate Son. For this reason, the electing and rejecting God potentially appeared as a different God than the one revealed in Jesus Christ. This, in turn, significantly reduced the importance of the doctrine of the Trinity.

> Now clearly if this view is taken, it is impossible to give a concrete answer to the question: Who is the electing God and elected man? The twofold obscurity in the doctrine of predestination is thus made inevitable. The triune God neither appears nor speaks to us except in the form of Jesus Christ, but He is always the unknown God. And if we do not know the electing God, where can we turn when it is a question of elected man? How can elected man be anything else but unknown?[113]

CD II/2, chapter 7, by contrast, argues that Jesus Christ is the electing God and the elected human person from all eternity. At the same time, we are facing the election of God the Father, the Son, and the Spirit in him.[114] In committing to communion with the creature from

111. Jüngel, "Zum Verhältnis von Kirche und Staat," 77.
112. Calvin's doctrine of predestination was not fundamentally particularistic, but was open to the possibility of universal mercy. Bertold Klappert, "Die Rezeption der Theologie Calvins in Karl Barths Kirchlicher Dogmatik: Einige vorläufige Überlegungen zu Barth als Schüler Calvins," in *Karl Barth und Johannes Calvin: Karl Barths Göttinger Calvin-Vorlesung von 1922*, ed. Hans Scholl (Neukirchen-Vluyn: Neukirchener, 1995), 46–73, at 63, 70.
113. *CD* II/2, 150.

all eternity, God determines God's own essence in Jesus Christ, so that God cannot be thought of in any other way than as revealed in the incarnate Son. In the Son as the *incarnandus*, the Son-to-be-incarnate, God's self is willing to undergo rejection in order to maintain the election of the creature.

Here Barth clearly rejects a crucial presupposition of the actualistic concept of revelation: God's very essence does not consist in freedom from humanity. God's affirmation of the creature does not stand against a dark backdrop of divine absoluteness, which otherwise asserts itself as judgment. In election from eternity, God's being is in relationship with humanity.[115] Might one, perhaps, assume that God was a free, absolute subject "before" election? Nothing valid or cogent can be asserted about a nonelecting God. "In a free act of determination God has ordained concerning Himself; He has conditioned Himself. Without any obligation, God has *put* Himself under an obligation to man."[116] God is unconditioned only insofar as God is not conditioned by anything other than God. It will no longer do to polemicize against the idea that God "is there" like an object. Even with eternal election, God is still not "there" like an object, but in a very particular way, God has made God's self available for the creature. God's conditioning of God's self is definite. God ruled out the possibility of libertarian unboundedness, even if it had again and again implied God's free decision in favor of the creature. Since there is no retreat into divine absoluteness, God no longer chooses to react either in mercy or in judgment if the creature claims God in Christ's name. The idea of unbounded power must be revised as well: "God Himself rules in a definite sphere and with a definite power. What makes Him the divine Ruler is the very fact that His

114. Ibid., 101.

115. Gundlach, *Selbstbegrenzung*, 150–53 with references from *CD* II/2, ch. 7.

116. Ibid., 101 (trans. rev.: "In freier Bestimmung hat Gott über sich selber verfügt, sich selber bedingt; ungeschuldet hat er sich selbst dem Menschen schuldig *gemacht*").

rule is determined and limited: self-determined and self-limited, but determined and limited none the less"[117] With the doctrine of election in *CD* II/2, Barth denies the Lutheran doctrine of a *deus absconditus* (hidden God), although the previous priority of the law over the gospel had implicitly affirmed such a notion with the prominence of the negation of the creature.[118] Now, by contrast, God's election is "not dialectical but non-dialectical."[119] "What *decretum absolutum* is there that secretly or openly can override or challenge this *decretum concretum*?"[120]

While the relation between God's electing and rejecting and time was arbitrary in *GD* §18, not creating any obligations on God's own part, God now commits God's own being to creation in a free choice from all eternity: "And the reality of this eternal being together of God and man is a concrete decree."[121] The rejection of the worldless image of God of *Rom* II is programmatic.

In addition, a merely spiritual doctrine of revelation as in *CD* I/1[122]

117. Ibid., 50.
118. See Krötke, "Die Summe des Evangeliums," 70. Barth's previous statement that God's being reconciles God's unconditioned and God's conditioned state, in which the duality of conditioned/unconditioned is again asserted (*CD* II/1, 303, see Härle, *Sein und Gnade*, 64–5), is now replaced by the view that God willingly gave up God's unconditioned state. Therefore, we may indeed affirm Luther's statement about the *Deus absconditus* (hidden God), *quae supra nos, nihil ad nos* (what is above us does not concern us), but—in contrast to Luther's opinion—the mystery of the *Deus absconditus* must not be "feared and revered" (Barth, *CD* II/1, 210). Luther asserts that rejection by the hidden God "is not to be inquired into, but reverently adored, as by far the most awe-inspiring secret of the Divine Majesty" (Luther, *Bondage of the Will*, in *Career of the Reformer*, 3:139). See Eberhard Jüngel, "Quae supra nos, nihil ad nos: Eine Kurzformel der Lehre vom verborgenen Gott—im Anschluss an Luther interpretiert," *Evangelische Theologie* 32 (1972): 197–240, at 201. See also Wolfgang Lienemann, "Das Gebot Gottes als 'Ereignis': Bibelgebrauch und freie Verantwortlichkeit in der Ethik Karl Barths," *Zeitschrift für Dialektische Theologie* 15 (1999): 155–77, at 169: "'Radical Autonomy' can no longer be attributed even to God as God determined God's self to be the creature's covenant partner—in freedom and love."
119. *CD* II/2, 13.
120. Ibid., 101 (trans. rev.). See Gundlach, *Selbstbegrenzung*, 154–5.
121. *CD* II/2, 158. According to Gockel, *Barth*, 196, *CD* II/2 implies a "fundamental" change in comparison to *GD*.
122. See *CD* I/1, 63, 133–5, at 183–4, 204. See Krötke, "Summe des Evangeliums," 74–5.

is now excluded in that the doctrine of election draws the Trinitarian consequences from Jesus Christ's *history*. Christ's embodied existence is now no longer excluded from the revealing presence of God. On the contrary, Christ's embodiment contributes to a particular story, which can no longer be excluded as nonspiritual. With history, as it were, inscribed into the eternal God, this story contributes fundamentally to God's identity.

This is also relevant for God's commanding, which can no longer take place in libertarian freedom.[123] As the communion with the creature characterizes God's eternal being, God is the way Christ reveals God. A statement like the one from *CD* I/1 could be no longer written now:

> [God] remains free in His working, in giving Himself. This freedom of His is the basis of the distinction of the essence of God as such from His essence as the One who works and reveals Himself. On this freedom rests the incomprehensibility of God, the inadequacy of all knowledge of the revealed God.[124]

In contrast to this, the doctrine of election points to Col. 2:9: In Christ "the whole fullness of deity dwells bodily."

Chapter 7 does not follow this trend entirely consistently, or at least without ambiguity, as when Barth comments that the Son's eternal being is independent from election, and that Jesus Christ is at the beginning of creation, but "not at the beginning of God."[125] This

123. See, for example, Rowan Williams, "Barth, War and the State," in *Reckoning with Barth: Essays in Commemoration of the Centenary of Karl Barth's Birth*, ed. Nigel Biggar (London/Oxford: Mowbray, 1988), 170–90, at 183.

124. Barth, *CD* I/1, 371. Barth's significant distinction between God's temporal action and God's eternal essence is the basis for Barth's distinction between the intratrinitarian and the extratrinitarian form that God's grace takes and that, in turn, questions all deductions from God's works to God's being. See Härle, *Gnade und Sein*, 37–8, 62–3.

125. Barth, *CD* II/2, 102. Barth's continuation, "for God has indeed no beginning," seemingly a truism, amounts in fact to a refusal of election, as it suggests an inert, lifeless eternity. See Härle, *Sein und Gnade*, 23–4n66. Jüngel also asserts ("Quae supra nos," 216): "As the hidden God works *alone* without any human presence and without any human cooperation, so the Triune God

may be in keeping with the notion of God's abiding absoluteness over against creation, as for example in *CD* II/1, and thus may be counted among "the theistic elements in Barth's theology."[126]

However, *CD* II/1 is also sometimes at variance with the notion of an unconditioned God. To begin with, Barth does assert that God's being is independent from creation and is not exhausted in God's works. However, Barth goes on to summarize this to the effect that God is indeed the way God reveals God's self and that God is, in God's self, by no means any different from God's being in God's works.[127] According to *CD* II/1, "the only begotten Son of God and therefore God Himself . . . does not exist as God's Son from eternity to eternity except in our flesh."[128] If *CD* II/2, by contrast, argues incidentally that the eternal Son retains his unconditioned state, while his being either as *incarnandus* or *incarnatus* is simultaneously conditioned, this is an inconsistency that opens up the possibility of isolating the eternal decree of election from the temporal revelation in Jesus Christ. If, however, the eternal God must potentially be distinguished more clearly from God's appearance in God's acts,[129] as, for example, with the distinction between an unconditioned and a conditioned state, the economic Trinity would not necessarily correspond closely to God's eternal being.[130] That is the problem with

[i.e., God revealing God's self] is without human presence alone by God's self." See also Jones, *Humanity of Christ*, 67.

126. Härle, *Sein und Gnade*, 23–4n66. Härle asserts, however, that these aspects of Barth's thought are of abiding relevance in Barth's theology. By contrast, Gundlach, McCormack, and Nimmo diagnose an inconsistency in *CD*. Gundlach, *Selbstbegrenzung*, 160; Bruce L. McCormack, "Grace and Being: The Role of God's Gracious Election in Karl Barth's Theological Ontology," in *The Cambridge Companion to Karl Barth*, ed. John B. Webster (Cambridge, UK: Cambridge University Press, 2000), 92–110, at 101 (in critique of *CD* I/1, 312); Paul T. Nimmo, *Being in Action: The Theological Shape of Barth's Ethical Vision* (Edinburgh: T & T Clark/London: Continuum, 2007), 12–13.
127. *CD* II/1, 257, 259.
128. Ibid., 151.
129. Härle, *Sein und Gnade*, 22 with reference to *CD* I/1 371.
130. Ibid., 191 argues that "primarily and originally the Word of God is undoubtedly the Word that

the previously prominent statement that God always also conceals God's self in revelation.

The task for now is to follow through also in the ethical corollaries with the idea that Jesus Christ is indeed at the beginning of God. The ethical significance of the statement that Jesus Christ is the electing God and humanity elect from all eternity can be seen from the change in the doctrine of election from *GD* to *CD*. The early lectures argued that God works judgment anew each time in order to bring about conversion in grace and repentance, while an ultimate rejection was not excluded. An important problem of this position consisted, however, in Barth's opinion that it was God's own choice anyway whether or not someone repents. As far as God as the Lord enjoys unconditional freedom of choice, and both options are conducive to God's glory, the choice between election and rejection must seem capricious, at least from a human perspective.[131] In consequence, the human question of whether the commandment of such a God constitutes a moral obligation cannot be answered in an ethically consistent way, either.

By contrast, *CD* chapter 7 describes a movement in God's eternal being—at the expense of an unconditioned absoluteness—because of which God's eternity is no longer a fundamental reservation over and against the temporal creature.[132]

The Ethics of Election and the Doctrine of God in *CD* II/2

After *CD* II/2, chapter 7 has rejected the notion of an absolute deity,

God speaks by and to Himself in eternal concealment." See also Bruce L. McCormack, "Barths grundsätzlicher Chalkedonismus?" *Zeitschrift für Dialektische Theologie* 18 (2002): 138–73, at 158–9n52.

131. *GD* II, 180.

132. See Bruce L. McCormack, *Karl Barth's Critically Realistic Dialectical Theology: Its Genesis and Development 1909–1936* (Oxford, UK: Oxford University Press, 1995), 372–3; Gregor Etzelmüller, *"... zu richten die Lebendigen und die Toten": Zur Rede vom Jüngsten Gericht im Anschluss an Karl Barth* (Neukirchen-Vluyn: Neukirchener, 2001), 110–11.

this must also be reflected in the ethical section of the doctrine of God, *CD* II/2, chapter 8. Sections 36–7 do so with an explicit prioritization of the gospel over the law. Indeed, God's commanding constitutes a moral obligation only under this assumption, while obedience to an arbitrary force requires an equally arbitrary act of will on the part of the moral subject. It is another question, however, if chapter 8 on the whole will pursue the insight consistently that a supposed absoluteness of God would undermine Christian ethics.

The Gospel and the Commandment (§§36–7)

While an argument has just been made that the doctrine of election invalidates the actualistic concept of revelation, obviously *CD* II/2 chapter 7 is followed not only by sections assigning the gospel priority over the law (§§36–7), but also by a decidedly actualistic ethics (§§38–9). Apart from the ethics of the doctrine of creation in *CD* III/4, the ethics of the doctrine of God in *CD* II/2 even constitutes Barth's main work in ethics. Thus, the present book can only advance one of its main theses successfully if there is a fundamental contradiction between the doctrine of election in *CD* II/2 chapter 7 and the actualistic ethics of *CD* II/2 chapter 8.

That there may be a contradiction between these two chapters is already indicated by the fact that Barth's ethics lectures were highly actualistic in 1928, while Barth's mature doctrine of election was an innovation from the late 1930s and early 1940s. This suggests that the link between election (chapter 7) and actualism (chapter 8) is not as strong as might be assumed. Indeed, *CD* chapter 8 will highlight, apart from a particular relation between gospel and law, God's absoluteness and unconditioned character. At various points it will draw on notions, and even phrases, to this effect that Barth developed in the ethics lectures.

God's commandment is portrayed in distinctly actualistic terms in §38, which attributes a conceptual key function to the unconditioned nature of God in any new act of revelation. While the doctrine of election chapter 7 conceives of eternal election strictly in light of the incarnate one's earthly life, chapter 8 answers the question whether God's constantly new, potentially discontinuous commanding in Scripture amounts to a disparate contents of a "note box"[133] without reference to God's eternal self-binding act of election in Jesus Christ, but instead by pointing to the abstract self-identity of God, who is universally efficacious in the most varied divine acts in history. Human disobedience must not infringe on the sovereignty of the God who "confronts [the human person] as lawgiver, judge, and avenger in the greatest things and in the smallest, openly and in secret."[134]

Hence, if the self-identity of power, or God's unconditioned nature rather than the consistency of grace, is key, Barth runs the danger of reintroducing the priority of the law over the gospel. Indeed, according to chapter 8 (§§38–9), God's commandment encounters the human person first as judgment. God's unconditioned nature requires pure passivity in the human act of attending to this commandment, in a way reminiscent of how the worldless depiction God in *Rom* II resulted in the condemnation of any particular, positive human position. In arguing for the validity of a certain command, Christians must not claim the story of Jesus Christ. On the contrary, "its validity for me must then consist in the fact that the very question of its validity is taken out of my mouth, out of my mind, and out of my heart."[135]

According to both the ethics lecture and *CD* chapter 8, God's

133. *CD* II/2, 705 (trans. rev.: "*Zettelkasten*"), 704: "lottery wheel" ("*Kasten mit Loszetteln,*" trans. rev.).
134. Ibid. (trans. rev.).
135. Ibid., 651. (trans. rev.).

authoritative command cannot consist in a general rule. It must not leave anything open to interpretation, as the commanding God is unconditioned, and only an unconditioned command is truly binding. Barth will thus articulate ideas very similar to the ones from the ethics lecture. A significant aspect of this conspicuous overlap between the two ethical texts is an actualistic ontology: "'There is' no law of God, just as—a terrible thing to say—'there is' no God either. What 'is there' is an object. . . . The law that 'is there' is never the law that is set up, that makes an absolute claim to our acknowledgment. God's law is the law of faith, i.e., the law that *God* gives . . . as he gives himself in his revelation."[136]

Barth fails to integrate ethics consistently into dogmatics, which his subordination of the law to the gospel set out to do. Thus the overall shape of Barth's ethics requires a reevaluation. Since this thesis has wide-ranging implications for Barth's ethical thought, it requires greater elaboration.

Barth's ethics of the doctrine of God follow his doctrine of election, as God's gracious election is the reason why Christians can and must be concerned with ethics. Sections 36–7 highlight the importance of the new obedience in a reappropriation of John Calvin's thought. "The goal of election is virtuousness of life (*Instit.* III, 23, 12). That which is future holiness among the elect had its beginning in election (ibid., 22, 3)."[137] Humanity was elected in God's grace, which promises both the merciful acceptance and the transformation of the sinner. As a continuation of the old life would not be in the best interests of the Christian, the new ethos will take shape so that reconciliation is not a mere abstraction. As the new Christian ethos is rooted in election, and since the obligation expressed in the commandment is constituted in no other way than in God's mercy,

136. Barth, *Ethics*, 317–8 (trans. rev.).
137. *CD* II/2, 512 (Barth's parentheses, translations from the study edition).

the new foundation of ethics in the priority of the gospel must indeed follow the doctrine of election. *CD* II/2 indeed integrates significant aspects of "GL":

> It is as He makes Himself responsible for man that God makes man, too, responsible. Ruling grace is commanding grace. The Gospel itself has the form and fashion of the Law. The one Word of God is both Gospel *and* Law. It is not Law by itself and independent of the Gospel. But it is also not Gospel without Law. In its content, it is Gospel; in its form and fashion, it is Law. It is first Gospel and then Law. It is the Gospel which contains and encloses the Law as the ark of the covenant the tables of Sinai.[138]

Barth not only took over the distinction of form and content from "GL" in *CD* II/2, but he also considers Christ's story the touchstone of Christian ethics, which he describes with the terminology from "GL":

> We must seek the command of God only where it has itself torn off the veil of all human opinions and theories about the will of God and manifested itself unequivocally. We must seek it only where He has revealed Himself as grace and therefore in His truth. We must seek it only in what happened in Bethlehem, at Capernaum and Tiberias, in Gethsemane and on Golgotha, and in the garden of Joseph of Arimathea. In this event God uttered His command.[139]

One crucial merit of §37 consists in Barth's insistence that the obligation imposed by the commandment is not constituted by

138. Ibid., 511.

139. Ibid., 559. In "GL," 77–8, Barth calls it "perverse to want to understand the Law of God on the basis of any other thing, of any event which is different from the event in which the will of God, tearing in two the veil of our theories and interpretations, is visible as grace, in both form and content. This event is, however, the occurrence of the will of God at Bethlehem, at Capernaum and Tiberias, in Gethsemane, on Golgotha and in the garden of Joseph of Arimathea. Because this occurrence of the will of God, therefore the occurrence of his grace, becomes *manifest* to us, the *Law* becomes manifest to us." Nielsen also points out that *CD* II/2 replaces "law" ("GL") with "command." Bent Fleming Nielsen, "Beten—und Kanonen kaufen: Evangelium und Gesetz im Zusammenhang von KD II/2 (§§ 36–9)," in *Karl Barth im europäischen Zeitgeschehen (1935–1950)*, ed. Michael Beintker et al., 109–36, at 127.

power or sheer authority, but by the gospel. "Power as power does not have any divine claim, no matter how imposing or effective it might be."[140] Written in 1942, with Nazi Germany at the peak of its geographical expansion, Barth emphasizes the fact that moral greatness can lie even, and precisely, in resisting an overwhelming physical power. Presumably this was also due to the influence of Kant's notion of transcendental freedom, in which reason abstracts from the power of sensuous incentives.[141] Kantian reason—or Christian liberty, in Barth's case—imposes its judgment as a new beginning of a causal chain in the sensuous realm, with the "causality through freedom."[142] Barth's reasoning corresponds to this even in the choice of Kantian terminology: "To reserve himself against power as power [i.e., for a different kind of power], even to his own undoing, is not merely a possibility for man. It is not merely the assertion of his right and dignity. It is the duty which he has to fulfil with his existence as man."[143] To bolster up his case for autonomy, Barth also adduces quotations by Horace and Goethe.[144] "Prometheus is justified against Zeus."[145] Against the backdrop of the Nazi regime of injustice, Barth marshals a row of distinguished advocates of autonomy who reinforce Barth's point that the gospel is the real source of humanism: "There is no humanity apart from the humanity of Jesus Christ."[146]

Discussing various justifications of authority and finding only the gospel capable of creating a moral obligation,[147] Barth invalidates the

140. *CD* II/2, 553. See also Nielsen, "Beten," 132.

141. See for example Kant, *Groundwork to the Metaphysics of Morals*, 36–7.

142. Kant, *Critique of Practical Reason*, trans. Werner Pluhar (Indianapolis: Hackett, 2002), 68.

143. *CD* II/2, 553 (trans. rev.). Autonomy involves a refusal of the claims sheer power makes on one's core loyalties, which must be reserved for the power of the gospel.

144. Ibid., 554: "*Si fractus illabatur orbis impavidum ferient ruinae*," "[Even] if the broken world-disc crashes, the ruins will strike him undaunted [nonetheless]." See also Barth, *Ethics*, 95.

145. *CD* II/2, 554.

146. *CD* II/1, 541.

147. *CD* II/2, 552–7 (§37.1: "The Basis of the Divine Claim").

notion that there is such a thing as authority in and of itself, sheer authority. By contrast, God's commandment is "permission—the granting of a very definite freedom."[148] But it is even more than that: "The command of God orders us to be free."[149] "Its seriousness and rigour are unconditional *just because* it imposes freedom on man."[150] The advantage for ethical theory is the categorical rejection of heteronomy: "Anything that in itself is really dark and accursed cannot possibly be the cross that we are ordered to carry."[151] Notably, this implies the rejection of the statement from "GL" that the law is grace even if it meant "judgment, death, and hell."[152] Due to the priority of the gospel to the law, Barth indeed presents a eudaemonism of a higher order:

> And when one of the widespread and constantly re-emerging moral systems—hedonism, utilitarianism or eudæmonism, the so-called ethics of value—tries to use these natural aims as a basis for its presentation of the ethical, Christian ethics must be careful not to adopt at once towards this system the well known and purely negative attitude of Kant and the Kantians. Where the obligatory is to be understood as the content of the divine command, we cannot refuse absolutely to interpret it also as that which is supremely pleasing and useful and valuable.[153]

This notion is highlighted especially in §38.3: "We understand by goodness the sum of all that is right and friendly and wholesome."[154]

148. Ibid., 585.
149. Ibid., 588.
150. Ibid., 596 (emphasis added by A. M.).
151. Ibid., 611.
152. "GL," 72. See also *CD* III/4, 513: "The prophecy of the community can be ten times right in substance and yet still be false prophecy if it is not the prophecy of grace and hope but of a wicked, scolding and quarrelsome community."
153. *CD* II/2, 650. Eudaemonism denotes the teleology toward human flourishing that is fundamental to virtue ethics. While the previous analysis has presented Barth's thought in proximity to Kant's, the point of contention between the two at this point is that Barth sees reason and faith as complementary to sensuous needs, while Kant tends to view reason and sensuous claims in competition.
154. Ibid., 708.

The commandment is an offer that the human person cannot reject, in the best possible sense of the expression, and thus an offer as a command. The command imposes itself with the motivating promise of the command.

> It will not compel man, but burst open the door of the compulsion under which he has been living. It will not meet him with mistrust but with trust. It will not appeal to his fear but to his courage. It will instil courage, and not fear into him. . . . Do this, because in so doing you may and will again live of and by My grace. . . . Do this . . . in the freedom to which you have been chosen and called, because in this freedom you may do this, and can do only this. For this, and not for any other reason, do it. You may do it. And: Do not do this . . . because it would not correspond to the grace addressed to you but contradict it, because you would have to do it as the captive which you certainly are not.[155]

Human conscience—as the leverage point of God's commandment, as it were—plays an important role here. It is certainly notable that Barth avoids the term. But when gospel and law are at issue as modes of divine action in the world, then the human mind and spirit in which the human person perceives and relates to gospel and law are also at issue. They become the stage on which the relationship with God takes on the shape of either freedom and joy or fear and bondage.[156]

An unexpected notion enters the picture, however, when Barth assumes that there is a general human awareness of moral duty. Not rooted in Christian proclamation, this general notion of duty amounts to self-righteousness. While it is vague, it will still lead to tribulation. This dark backdrop, in turn, contributes significantly to the resonance of the liberating message of the gospel, which transforms self-righteousness into thankful obedience.

155. *CD* II/1, 586, 587.

156. *CD* I/1 indeed opts against a natural character of the encounter with the divine and chooses instead a mental or spiritual one. If *CD* II/2, ch. 8 did not deal with conscience, God would have to approach the human person, as it were, naturally by sidestepping the mental and spiritual character of the human person.

> Certainly the existence of that general conception of ethics as an answer to the question of the good is an exceedingly instructive fact. It confirms the truth of the grace of God which as it is addressed to man puts the question of the good with such priority over all others that man cannot evade it and no other question can completely hide or replace it.[157]

We have already encountered this strategy in Barth's 1922 lectures "The Problem of Ethics Today" and "The Need and Promise of Christian Proclamation" as well as in the opening chapters of *GD* (§4: "Man and His Question"). The result was an *ordo salutis* that is characteristic of the priority of the law over the gospel in nineteenth- and twentieth-century German Protestant theology: God's guidance of the Christian life moves through different stages such as longing for fulfillment, crisis and despair, repentance and forgiveness. What unites Barth with the modern "revival of religion" at this point is that the personal sense of fulfillment serves as a compass guiding the search for religious truth.[158] In *CD* II/2, however, God does not win over the world for the church by means of an accusing law, but by means of the gospel and the instruction of how to live as a free person. This more positive account still presupposes the accusation of God's law, which is operative only at the level of a vague general moral

157. *CD* II/2, 518.

158. On this prominent intellectual history, see Wolfhart Pannenberg, "Theology and the Crisis in Ethics," in *Ethics*, trans. Keith Crim (Philadelphia: Westminster and London: Search, 1981), 57–70, at 62: "Above all, however, August G. Tholuck, the influential teacher not only of Ritschl and Herrmann, but also of Martin Kähler, was influenced by the early-nineteenth-century 'revival of religion' and presented the moral experience of mankind as the criterion of revelation. This experience was to resolve the moral discord that resulted from the experiencing of guilt: 'If [a person] finds a revelation that is successful in resolving the discord in his inner being, then this is for him the true revelation.'" Another strand of this tradition is the Luther Renaissance with Karl Holl and his students, among them Emanuel Hirsch. It is also in this context that Paul Althaus spoke of the "original revelation" (*Uroffenbarung*): *Grundriß der Dogmatik*, 4th ed. (Gütersloh: Bertelsmann, 1958, originally 1936), 21, 30. For Barth's later judgment on the concept, see *CD* IV/1, 45. See Gunther Wenz, "'...der Unterscheid des Gesetzes und Evangelii als ein besonder herrlich Licht' (BSLK 790, 21 f): Fallbeispiele zur Aufnahme des hermeneutischen Kriteriums der Wittenberger Reformation in der Dogmatik des 20. Jahrhunderts," in *Grundfragen ökumenischer Theologie: Gesammelte Aufsätze* (Göttingen: Vandenhoeck & Ruprecht, 2010), 2:116–59, at 127–8.

consciousness, however. The difficulty with this thought does not lie in the proposal that God's true command is in fact experienced as liberation. But it may appear as a novel discovery that is independent of wide-spread moral illusions, which in turn must not be attributed to God's commanding in such whole-sale fashion.

Once the gospel is proclaimed, anything that is not perceived as both liberating and obligatory cannot be God's gospel and command. Moral conscience has thus assumed the role of a "criterion of revelation."[159] It is for this reason that Barth insists, perhaps surprisingly: "Where the obligatory is to be understood as the content of the divine command, we cannot refuse absolutely to interpret it also as that which is supremely pleasing and useful and valuable."[160] The distinction between power as power and power being powerful in the gospel is the main point Barth is making in this section. As surprising as it may sound, the liberating experience of the gospel—even if deferred and highly subtle—is indispensable for Barth's argument. The motivational power of the commandment should be distinguished from the objective basis for the validity of the commandment, of course. The motivation to follow the command, which lies in the gospel itself, and the recognition of the objective validity of the commandment in God's eternal election coincide.

Barth's attention to the motivation for fulfilling the command plays an interesting role in the overall development of his ethical thought. In a sense, chapter 8 §§36–7 repeats a methodological step that Barth already took in 1925.[161] *GD* §29 forged a compromise between the power of the resurrection and the view that this power can work only as the power of death by highlighting God's action in Christ's royal office in the church. Apart from God's particular

159. See n158.
160. *CD* II/2, 650.
161. See the section "The Dogmatic Concept of the Actualistic Commandment 1924–32: Personalism and Lordship" in ch. 1.

act of revelation in the church, the gnostic worldview of *Rom* II was not fundamentally left behind; in God's elusive act of revelation in the church, however, Christ's power overcame human futility and fundamentally transformed Christians, quite in keeping with *Rom* I. *CD* §§36–7 share with this concept the emphasis on God's power. God overcomes the distinction between church and world by transforming the world powerfully in grace and commandment, thus gathering the church out of the world.[162] In this concept, God's power in the act of commanding plays a crucial role. Significantly, at least according to various strands in §§36–7, the human encounter with the commandment proper is not primarily God's act of judgment.

In issuing the command, God wins over the human person entirely for God's self. Before the human person might marshal an objection to God's commandment, God invalidates this objection preemptively. Judgment is replaced with transformation. The "seriousness and rigour [of the commandment] are unconditional just because it imposes freedom on man."[163] In consequence, a static face-off between church and world would be inappropriate. The commandment is not a heteronomous judgment, but is in accordance with the gospel: "There is no escaping the command of God because, when it confronts us, it immediately and at the same time places itself behind us. Pursuing the cause of God, it immediately and at the same time takes up also our most proper cause."[164] An important

162. This is one example of a way of thinking that is characteristic of Barth. Barth often does not refute positions that are originally in tension with his opinion, but integrates them dialectically. Barth's theory integrates the tension itself so that it can now play a constructive role. At this point, the concept of commanding serves the purpose of overcoming the tension between church and world. The appeal to conscience retains aspects even of the world, rather than merely dissolving the world into the church. Due to the actualistic character of the command, the tension is not eliminated, however. The basic pattern is described by Ingolf U. Dalferth, "Karl Barth's Eschatological Realism," in *Karl Barth: Centenary Essays*, ed. Stephen W. Sykes (Cambridge: Cambridge University Press, 1989), 14–45, at 35.

163. *CD* II/2, 596.

difference between §§36–7 and "GL" lies in the fact that according to the lecture, the law is directed against any disobedience, while according to §§36–7, disobedience is inexplicable in the first place. In divine omnipotence, God's commandment creates the corresponding obedience in tandem with the gospel. This does not happen through despair due to judgment, but because the law irresistibly wins over the human person.[165]

It may seem that such interest in the motivation to follow the command puts too much emphasis on human experience, which is, after all, that of a sinner.

> Man obviously thinks that he is particularly free and happy even in his fall. . . . It is in his free will that he is tricked . . . reducing himself to that servile state and service, however free and happy he thinks himself to be. . . . He is then oppressed and tormented by the law of that foreign lord and tyrant, . . . in whose service he can never be free and happy (whatever his consciousness, experiences and feelings may be), in whose service he can only be deceived even in this consciousness.[166]

However, the passage continues,

> The command of God rends this veil, and it does it by being and expressing the real permission given to man. It is in this that it is serious and rigorous, binding and committing us with a seriousness and rigour beyond the power of all other commands. The command of God sets itself against human free will, not because it does not wish man to be really free and happy, but on the contrary, because God does want this, because he cannot really be free and happy in his self-will.[167]

With the semantics of revelation and power, this passage sees God's command aligning human experience and God's eschatological reality. To preserve Barth's case for the "supremely pleasing and

164. Ibid.
165. By contrast, Nielsen, "Beten," 126 sees "GL" and *CD* ch. 8 in continuity on the whole.
166. *CD* II/2, 594.
167. Ibid.

useful and valuable" against heteronomy and divine caprice, we must indeed avoid an ethics of the commandment with merely a formal concept of responsibility. For the priority of the gospel to the law to retain its criteriological function, the eudaemonistic ethics of flourishing must not be considered simply illegitimate.[168] Statements to that effect can be found especially in §37.3, "The Form of the Divine Claim." This is the longest subsection in chapter 8 based on the word count.[169]

The propaedeutic status Barth attributes to a general human moral awareness requires further consideration. These remarks by Barth constitute an important development in comparison to "GL." Barth no longer maintains God's sovereignty and assertion in a decidedly harsh judgment of the law. The proper power God exercises in the gospel and the law is located in the obligatory force of the liberating gospel. This removes a notable problem of the lecture: as it called God's judgment "death and hell," seeing the law "judge us, punish us, and kill us," the lecture left few criteria to distinguish worldly powers of all stripes from God's judgment. The danger of granting theological legitimation to human injustice under the rubric of God's work through the law, which "GL" had not overcome, is no longer present in the law as it is proclaimed in conjunction with the gospel. This particular attention to subjection to foreign authority, which was characteristic of the ethics lectures, has been removed even in the remainder that was still present in "GL." What remains to be mentioned in this regard is the universal moral horizon on which §§36–7 draws.

Several aspects of this line of reasoning are helpful in §§36–7.

168. William Schweiker, *Responsibility and Christian Ethics*, 44 points out how a structure of "call-and-response" blocks out several aspects in ethics: "Concepts like virtue, happiness, and moral perfection, to name a few."

169. Subsection 37.3: 34,562 words in forty-eight pages; §38.2: 31,960 words in forty-eight pages; §36.1: 19,839 words in thirty-five pages. *Digital Barth Library* (Alexander Street Press).

Nonetheless, Barth's insistence on God's unconditioned sovereignty creates theological difficulties. To begin with, Barth lays out the scenario of God's powerful liberation, by means of gospel and commandment, from a universal moral awareness that other theologies mark more clearly as an attempt at self-righteousness.[170] In fact, the only purpose for which the much discussed passage Rom. 1 refers to the concept of a natural cognition of God is to convict human persons of their sin. Barth agrees that self-righteousness is a universal temptation, precisely because God's commandment creates the moral question in every person. At this point, Barth is in agreement with Paul Althaus' notion of an *Uroffenbarung*.[171] Barth fully acknowledges "the ethical question as the question of human existence," but adds that it does not lead to moral action by itself. Nor is it supposed to. "But in so far as this general conception of ethics seems to speak of an answer to the question which is to be worked out by man himself, it also confirms that man tries to escape the grace of God by which the question of the good is put."[172] On the other hand, the general human moral striving is the question to which God's more explicit command is the answer. A general moral inquiry recognizes in the divine command "an enigmatic knowledge of the Whence? and Whither? of all ethical enquiry and reply."[173] In turn, the general moral inquiry is an important prerequisite for the power of the divine command to convict the human person.

Hence the concept of a general moral consciousness takes on particular importance, even among those not yet exposed to the church's proclamation. The early lecture "The Problem of Ethics

170. See n158. In contrast to Barth's present model of a moral hermeneutic, theologies that perceive "the moral experience of mankind as the criterion of revelation" (n158) typically highlight human failure and God's consolation.

171. See n. 158.

172. *CD* II/2, 518.

173. Ibid., 519.

Today" (1922) presented the moral question, also experienced by non-Christians, as the basis for a negative philosophical recognition of God, which would make the question for God more pressing. According to *CD* II/2, §36, God's revelation exercises a powerful influence even on non-Christians by way of a non-Christian ethics. To be sure, this argument is followed by Barth's well-known polemics against general philosophical ethics: "Strange as it may seem, that general conception of ethics coincides exactly with the conception of sin."[174] After instrumentalizing the human moral quest apart from God's proper revelation, Barth tries to contain the problematic potential of a general moral awareness, lest the general moral question determine the content of God's command. Barth emphasizes that "'what is good' has been 'said' to man (Mic. 6:8), so that man has been forbidden to try to say it to himself, and bidden simply and faithfully to repeat what has been said to him."[175]

In criticizing attempts to answer the moral question on one's own, Barth may very well have had Christian support for Nazi politics in mind. Yet we may also ask if theological ethics can ever be entirely immune to such barbaric distortions if a secular ethics is not either.[176] When Barth polemicizes against a naive notion of autonomy, that tries to answer the moral question based on a mere whim, this is not only in contrast to the supposed omnipotence with which God's commanding already warrants proper obedience. It may also be the case that Barth is fighting against the consequences he had previously accepted when assigning a constructive role to the

174. Ibid.

175. Ibid., 537 (Barth's parenthesis).

176. On the problems of a secular ethics, see, for example, the notes the philosopher Karl Löwith took while fleeing from Nazi persecution: "Ruge's question . . . whether all people, also including the negroes, are human?! That is a very precarious question: And if it can be answered positively in abstraction from Christianity?" Löwith, *Von Rom nach Sendai: Von Japan nach Amerika: Reisetagebuch 1936 und 1941*, ed. Klaus Stichweh and Ulrich von Bülow (Marbach: Deutsche Schillergesellschaft, 2001), 31, 164.

universally human moral question that gave the answer of God's gracious commandment its compelling character.

Barth describes the ambiguity of a general moral consciousness—its importance in preparing the way for God's proper revelation and its abrogation by this revelation—with the metaphor of Israel's relation to Canaan. The promised land is not a new land for Israel, but it reaches its proper destiny in Israel's settlement. Canaanite religious traditions must be taken seriously, no more and no less, in their strict subordination to Israel's own worship of the true God:

> The concern of the apologetic school of theological ethics in its recourse to a general moral enquiry and reply can, of course, be recognised as justifiable upon one condition: that is, if in its annexation of the realm of general ethical problems theological ethics behaves as the Israelites did or should have done on their entry into Canaan. They had to invade Canaan, not as a foreign country which did not belong to them, but as the land of their fathers. Had it not for a long time belonged to Yahweh? . . . This means that theological ethics has to accept the fact that it must not believe in the possibility and reality of a general moral enquiry and reply which are originally and ultimately independent of the grace and command of God, which are not touched or affected by them and to that extent stand inflexible and inviolate in themselves.[177]

The notion that a general moral inquiry is ultimately dependent on God's grace and command is a two-edged sword. In vague, historically imprecise terms, it can denote both the influence Canaan has on Israel and Israel's impact on Canaan. The notion is related to Barth's understanding of natural theology, "i.e., the theology from which man comes when he starts from nature, from the nature which he has not lost even as a Christian."[178] This universal moral question is also the crucial factor in Barth's actualistic anthropology:

> By the decree of the divine covenant with man, the ethical question as

177. *CD* II/2, 522.
178. *CD* II/1, 142.

> the question of human existence is put from all eternity as the question to which, on the basis of revelation and the work of grace, man will himself in some way be the answer. That is why it is such a necessary, a burning question. And that is also why all possible attempts to answer it, all forms of ethics, are so pressing.[179]

Already in the ethics lecture cycle, Barth articulated an actualistic ontology:

> The ethical question is obviously not just one question among many others but is in an eminent sense the question of human *existence*. As we will, we *are*. What we do, we *are*. Man does not exist and also act. He exists as he acts. His action, his stepping forth or appearance (*existere*), is his existence.[180]

The practical quest inherent in every human life thus constitutes God's point of contact with every human being.[181] As the ethics lecture cycle had done already fourteen years before the doctrine of election, *CD* II/2 also views humanity in actualistic terms: "To exist as a man means to act."[182] It is only within the dialectics of revelation that the unthematic knowledge of God's revelation in natural conscience, the vague horizon of all human existence, turns out to be the problematic and yet indispensable *praeambula fidei* for the revelation of the gospel and its commandment. The priority of the law has thereby been transformed into the backdrop of a fundamental, universal, and vague judgment of the law, against which the thematic action of gospel and law plays out. *CD* II/2,

179. *CD* II/2, 516.
180. Barth, *Ethics*, 16–17.
181. Ibid., see Jüngel, "Gospel and Law," 121. A natural inclination supposedly makes a correspondence to God's word possible. Nimmo, *Being in Action*, 95 argues that action continues to play a constitutive role, as the election of humanity in Christ is the reason for humanity's existence. Jesus Christ's existence consists precisely in action. Barth, meanwhile, does not deduce the general statement, "To exist as a man means to act" (*CD* II/2, 535), from the doctrine of election but from a supposedly general, natural impulse to act.
182. Ibid., 535.

chapter 8 also argues for a particular way in which Barth seeks to avoid the trade-off—an abiding influence of Canaan on Israel, as it were—that he accepted in assigning universal moral striving a constructive role.

For now, however, Barth sees the answer of the gospel assert itself more clearly, independently, and forcefully than the universal human striving. The subtle side-effects of universal human moral striving remain to be dealt with, but Barth sees the gospel attaining priority over the law already. After the universal moral question has been raised in every human person, God asserts God's self successfully in gospel and commandment, since only God's grace and command provide an answer to this question. Barth sees the constructive function of a general moral consciousness in that it heightens the sense in which only God's gospel and commandment unite the objective validity of the commandment with the mature self-determination of moral agents.

> That is the majesty of His command, from which we in our self-will, our pride, our anxiety, our foolishness and wickedness, can certainly flee, but which we cannot evade. . . . The fact that God is gracious to us does not mean that He becomes soft, but that He remains absolutely hard, that there is no escaping His sovereignty and therefore His purpose for man. To know His grace is to know this sovereignty. And obviously to accept His grace can only be to acknowledge this sovereignty, and therefore the duty of obedience to Him, or, briefly, to become obedient to Him. . . . There is no escaping the command of God because, when it confronts us, it immediately and at the same time places itself behind us.[183]

In the gospel and the commandment, Jesus Christ "lives and reigns and conquers."[184] Barth's notion of the omnipotence of the divine word is closely related to the importance Barth assigns to the attempt

183. Ibid., 559, 560, 596.
184. Thus twice ibid., 568; twice 569; 570.

of a general, natural recognition of God.[185] Barth also articulated a fully developed notion of God's omnipotence in *CD* II/1 (1940). There he portrays God's love as that of the holy lord. "He seeks and creates fellowship, is always the Lord. . . . He condemns, excludes and annihilates all contradiction and resistance to it. . . . His favourable inclination overcomes and destroys this resistance."[186]

Such statements leave behind the nagging question of how this possibly related to current events in 1940 or 1942. It is doubtful at any rate if Barth's discussion of the omnipotence of God's command in chapter 8 retains the primary interest in what happened "at Bethlehem, at Capernaum and Tiberias, in Gethsemane, on Golgotha and in the garden of Joseph of Arimathea." Drawing on a universal moral striving, Barth attempts to combine God's grace with an abstract principle of omnipotence. This is strikingly at variance, however, with the narratives of Jesus, whose earthly ministry was not characterized by triumph over his enemies. At the cross, even his cry of godforsakenness gave occasion for renewed mockery. The New Testament very often describes the young church as a community in tribulation.

By contrast, another option would be to ascribe a certain degree of power to God's command that is, however, short of absolute power. This might not qualify for certain theistic notions of divine omnipotence. Still the command would exercise power by the attraction of true freedom. However, it is hard to conceive how the recognition of the commandment can completely leave behind the danger of distortions in human conceptions of freedom. In a similar way, it is doubtful how something like a universal human moral

185. See Barth, "The Need and Promise of Christian Proclamation, 1922," in *The Word of God and Theology*, trans. Amy Marga (New York: T & T Clark, 2011), 101–30, at 117; Barth, "The Problem of Ethics Today, 1922," in *Word of God and Theology*, 131–70, at 137, 157–8, *GD* I, 69, 84–5, *CD* I/1, 154–5.

186. *CD* II/1, 359, 360.

striving can fit into a grand salvific scheme so easily. In some cases, the gospel might not offer release from the perplexities of the moral life, but even provoke hostility.

Distortions in hearing the divine command are indeed the danger Barth is compelled to accept by assigning human conscience such a crucial mediating role. In *CD* II/2, conscience is no longer a fallible, precarious entity as in "GL," but the gear box, as it were, that transmits the sweep of God's omnipotent revelation into the moral realities of a finite human life.[187] Barth's own recollections about Hirsch's talk of conscience testify to the precarious potential of the notion.[188] Moreover, the commandant of the concentration camp in Auschwitz, Rudolf Höß, astounded the audience at the Nuremberg trials with his unconcerned descriptions of the atrocities he organized, while his autobiographical notes demonstrate, in some peculiar sense, an intact bourgeois morality.[189] Another controversial German figure, Hans Filbinger, was famously accused of a "pathologically clear conscience."[190] After the Second World War, he was president of the German state of Baden-Württemberg. Previously, however, as a judge and NSDAP member, he had given

187. The well-known metaphor of "point of contact" would also be appropriate. A more complex understanding of a "point of contact" is laid out by Michael Welker, *God the Spirit* (Minneapolis: Fortress Press, 1994), 179 in interpreting the vision in Ezekiel 37: The efficacious prophetic word creates a "point of contact" with the vision of dry bones that are not yet animated by the Spirit. This point of contact remains ambiguous, taken by itself. Without the activity of the Spirit, hope can very easily give way to despair. Barth's focus on God's omnipotence does not grasp the ambiguity of the point of contact.

188. See the section in ch. 1, "Sacrifice and Repentance after the Second Edition of the Romans Commentary."

189. "The case of Höß makes clear with all force that mass murder does not need to be associated with personal cruelty. . . . Höß's notes . . . reveal . . . a person . . . who is all in all . . . in his own way 'spiritually' inclined [*innerlich*] and even decidedly 'moral.'" Martin Broszat, "Einleitung," in Rudolf Höß, *Kommandant in Auschwitz: Autobiographische Auszeichnungen*, ed. M. Broszat, 20th ed. (München: Deutscher Taschenbuch-Verlag, 2006), 7–30, at 19. See also Hannah Arendt, *Eichmann in Jerusalem: A Report on the Banality of Evil*, 2nd ed. (New York: Viking Press, 1964).

190. Matthias Bartsch, Udo Ludwig, et al., "Pathologisch gutes Gewissen," *Der Spiegel* 61, no. 16 (2007): 36–8, http://magazin.spiegel.de/EpubDelivery/spiegel/pdf/51211746.

death sentences to defectors. In his later career, he argued that what was just or legal ("*rechtens*") in those days cannot be illegal today.

Such precarious constellations make less sweeping claims about wholesale concepts such as a general moral conscience, or God's relentless, sovereign dominance, advisable. Indeed, *CD* II/2 also displays more nuanced positions than the general argument Barth had laid out previously. Chapter 7 speaks of Christ's suffering and the "risk" God takes in the election.[191] Barth refers to the "danger-point of man's susceptibility to temptation."[192] This would imply an element of uncertainty about the course of history, and to some degree a forgoing of sovereign control. Taken by itself, this does not imply the necessity of suffering. Further, Barth does see the danger that in self-righteousness, the human person may feel "free and happy" in sin.[193]

The relation between a non-Christian ethics and God's commandment in Christ can also take on a more constructive appearance than the image of Israel's annexation of Canaan may suggest at first glance. Barth argues that considerations in a "general," or philosophical ethics, must be scrutinized carefully, as they might

191. *CD* II/2, 162. Ibid., 169: God "was foreordained to danger and trouble." Günter Thomas asks with respect to eternal election, "Suppose the history of the covenant or of Christ takes the risk of religion, then why is the incarnation, in which the Son enters the realm of endangered creation, not itself risky?" Thomas, "Das Kreuz Jesu Christi als Risiko der Inkarnation," in *Gegenwart des lebendigen Christus,* eds. Günter Thomas and Andreas Schüle (Leipzig: Evangelische Verlagsanstalt, 2007), 151–79, at 165. This is also suggested in 1 Cor. 2:8. This notion would defuse the suspicion of a belittling of Christ's suffering, which might seem *sub specie aeterni* as an element of a plan implemented with sovereign control. That suspicion fuels, on the other hand, Emil Brunner's impression that Barth's doctrine of election portrays Christ's story as a mere temporal reflection of an eternal state of affairs: Brunner, *Dogmatics: The Doctrine of God*, trans. Olive Wyon, Library of Theological Translations (Cambridge: Clarke, 2002), 347. In turn, Jones, *Humanity of Christ*, 90–91 takes issue precisely with this view. He understands election as a definitive supralapsarian decision, while its fulfillment depends on Christ's free historical action. To that extent, election is not exempt from the possibility of failure.

192. *CD* II/2, 169.

193. Ibid., 594.

witness, as it were, incognito to God's commandment.[194] "In all ages the will of God has been fulfilled outside the Church as well. Indeed, to the shame of the Church it has often been better fulfilled outside the Church than in it."[195] The standards of such scrutiny, however, must be genuinely theological.[196]

> Thanks to the wisdom and patience of God, and the inconsequential nature of men, it is quite possible in practice that Christian insights and deductions may actually exist where their Christian presuppositions are wholly concealed, or where a closer investigation would reveal all kinds of presuppositions that are only to a small extent Christian.[197]

Honecker's interpretation of Barth's line of reasoning is thus not cogent: "The divine answer is thus also in an inclusive relationship to the human question; but it is exclusive to the answer of any human ethics." Martin Honecker, "Das Problem des theologischen Konstruktivismus", *Zeitschrift für Evangelische Ethik* 24 (1980): 97–111, at 104. In the interest of a constructive, dialogical relationship between theological and philosophical ethics, Barth may even go too far to the other extreme, however. He writes that theological ethics

> has to take up the legitimate problems and concerns and motives and assertions of every other ethics as such, and therefore after testing them in the light of its own superior principle. It has to listen to all other ethics in so far as it has to receive from them at every point the material for its own deliberations. To that extent its attitude to every other ethics is not negative but comprehensive. But just because it is comprehensive, it is fundamentally critical and decidedly not one of compromise.[198]

194. David Fergusson, *Community, Liberalism and Christian Ethics*, New Studies in Christian Ethics (Cambridge: Cambridge University Press, 1998), 27–9 points to the constructive potential of non-Christian ethics in *CD* II/2, §§36–7.
195. *CD* II/2, 569.
196. Ibid., 523.
197. Ibid., 542.
198. *CD* II/2, 527.

The priority of grace over the law also plays a constructive role in ethics in another context. Barth portrays God's command as a liberating power offering guidance when *CD* II/1, §30.2 elaborates on "The Mercy and Righteousness of God" in the sense that God's "love and grace and mercy" call upon the human person to cease pursuing self-righteousness. God is not on the side of those who expand their own supposedly rightful share to the disadvantage of the disenfranchised.[199] By contrast, Barth highlights legal traditions from the Hebrew Bible in favor of the proverbial "widows and orphans" (see, for example, Exod. 22:21). Due to their lack of legal representation in a patriarchal system, their needs are often systematically ignored. The group for whom God takes sides in Barth's days is the "harassed and oppressed people of Israel, which, powerless in itself, has no rights, and is delivered over to the superior force of its enemies; and in Israel it is especially the poor, the widows and orphans, the weak and defenceless."[200] Indeed "a very definite *political* problem and task follows directly from faith in God's righteousness [*Gerechtigkeit Gottes*]."[201] This ethical reflection is closely linked to the priority of the gospel to the law. Especially in the face of the contemporary political context in 1940, the implications are clear. Moreover, these remarks go beyond the concerns of "CS" in highlighting not only legal justice, but also the importance of it conjunction with social justice.[202]

199. Johannes Fischer argues that God's action provides the motivation for Christian action without implying, however, what the content of such Christian ethics is. This may be right insofar as an attempt to act in correspondence with God's action can indeed short circuit a close analysis of the actual situation. However, it must also be asked why an extra motivation provided by faith is helpful at all if the reasonable content of moral action is evident anyway. Johannes Fischer, "Theologische Ethik und Christologie," *Zeitschrift für Theologie und Kirche* 92 (1995): 481–516, at 481–3.

200. *CD* II/1, 386.

201. Ibid., 387 (trans. rev.). See also Jüngel, "Verhältnis von Kirche und Staat," 79–80. The relation between God's righteousness and God's concern for justice, which is at the heart of this remark, is more evident in German, as both notions are expressed with the same term *Gerechtigkeit*.

202. Huber, *Folgen christlicher Freiheit*, 103–4, criticizes the fifth thesis of the Barmen Declaration for

A remaining question is how exactly Barth wishes to channel the ethical influence of a supposedly universal moral awareness into a constructive direction. While in Barth's view an anthropological moral drive constitutes an opportunity for God's command to appeal to human moral consciousness and thus to exercise power, Barth wishes to restrict the influence of moral traditions that are foreign to God's proper revelation. This potential conflict is played out especially in christological terms.

The interpretation of God's lowliness in Jesus Christ constitutes a difference between "GL" and *CD* II/2, chapter 8. "GL" says seven times that God has given the law "into the hands of sinners."[203] This phrase alludes to the scene in Gethsemane Mark 14:41: "The Son of Man is betrayed into the hands of sinners." *CD* chapter 7, §35 uses this phrase often with regard to God's revelation in Jesus Christ.[204] This is notable ethically as Barth considers Christ, the incarnate Word, the personification of God's gracious command and law. Repeatedly, chapter 7 draws attention to the scandal of Jesus' suffering at the cross.[205] Jesus Christ bears his rejection by the other human protagonists, thus sustaining the election of humanity: "And because the eternal divine predestination is identical with the election of Jesus Christ, its twofold content is that God wills to lose in order that man may gain. There is a sure and certain salvation for man, and

failing to mention social justice as well. See also Beintker, "Die politische Verantwortung der Christengemeinde," 169.

203. "GL," 84, 85 (twice), 89, 94, 100.

204. Jesus handed over into the hands of sinners: *CD* II/2, 461, 467, 481, 482, 490, 497, 500. "GL," 89–90 restricts the misuse of God's word, but still acknowledges it to a certain extent: "Sin triumphs also in respect to the Law only in its misuse, not, however (for good reason, not), in its abandonment! And, on the other hand, that deception cannot mean that though the Law be misused, desecrated, corrupted, the Gospel would be preserved intact. . . . No, the content falls and is corrupted with the form, the Gospel also falls with God's Law. Of the people of Israel . . . which finally crucified its Messiah, of this people, Isaiah said that they talk of nothing but 'covenant.' . . . One short and unessential step beyond them we bump into a Christianity which, with respect to the Law, has likewise fallen prey to sin's deception."

205. See Nimmo, *Being in Action*, 108.

a sure and certain risk for God."[206] Chapter 7 speaks drastically of the creature, which "nails the Messiah of God to the cross."[207]

By contrast, chapter 8 portrays Jesus Christ in much more sovereign and powerful terms than chapter 7 and "GL." The lecture does not speak of election, but mentions Christ's suffering thirteen times without reference to the resurrection. The opposite is the case only twice.[208] While the lecture speaks of humanity perverting the gospel,[209] §§36–7 present the gospel as the way in which the omnipotent God transforms the world. That the law as the form of the gospel is, contrary to its proper meaning, abused in the attempt of works righteousness, is no longer the problem it was in the lecture. Certainly chapter 8 considers self-righteousness a universal sin as well.[210] Yet chapter 8 does not pay nearly as much attention to this problem as "GL" did. According to "GL," faced with the human attempt at self-justification, "Jesus Christ becomes the indispensable companion, the useful lever arm, and finally and above all the stopgap for all our efforts toward out own justification! . . . This is what becomes of grace, of the Gospel . . . There grace is discarded, there Christ has died in vain."[211] "There we find sheer enmity against the cross." Our "godlessness" "crucified Christ and crucifies him again

206. See n. 191.

207. Ibid., 164 (trans. rev.).

208. Christ's suffering: "GL," 73–4, 76, 79, 81, 84, 86, 89–90, 91. Although the lecture sometimes speaks of Christ's suffering and resurrection in the same breath, "GL," 74–5 highlights Christ's suffering more strongly than the resurrection. Christ's triumph: ibid., 75, 79.

209. Ibid., 85: "Our autocracy attests and means our rejection of grace and our self-assertion against God, our separation from God." ". . . distorting precisely the good, precisely the best, into its opposite." The Christian "makes out of God's claim a claim of his own" (87). "*Sin* triumphs in this zeal" (ibid.). "With the help and to the honor of God, it is for our own godlessness—which crucified Christ and crucifies him again and again in the midst of Christendom" (89). "No, the content falls and is corrupted with the form, the Gospel also falls with God's Law" (ibid.). "There grace is discarded, there Christ has died in vain (Galatians 2:21)" (91).

210. *CD* II/2, 582.

211. "GL," 90–91.

and again in the midst of Christendom."[212] Religious zeal is indeed a precarious affair.[213]

By contrast, God's command "cancels out all this" according to *CD* II/2 chapter 8.[214] In contrast to "GL" and *CD* II/2 chapter 7, chapter 8 no longer uses the phrase that Jesus, the law, or the command is handed over "into the hands of sinners." On the whole, §§36–7 speak much less of Christ's passion. If the cross is mentioned, it is in the same breath as the resurrection.[215] From the perspective of the election from all eternity, chapter 8 presents the passion and Easter as an event consistently implemented by God's sovereignty. "By giving [away] His Son to rule and live and reign and conquer by His obedience," God remained paradoxically in control.[216] This hardly leads us to assume that the cross is associated with extraordinary hardship. In keeping with this, *CD* II/2 later on lends expression to a one-sided theology of glory in describing how God's judgment came upon Christ at the cross and how the Christian follows Christ:

> Far from treating man as alien and indifferent to Him, God treats him as His beloved Son, as He there allows the judgment of God's command to overtake Him. It was, indeed, the good-pleasure of God in the man who allowed this to overtake Him. Surely all the choirs of angels rejoiced when it happened. This event was, for the man who endured it, the entrance to everlasting glory. The man who is judged by God's command stands even now at the right hand of God the Father, and all the extremity and shame of the judgment are covered over by this glory. If God is a radiant King, so too is the One who is judged.[217]

212. Ibid., 89.
213. Ibid., 87, 89.
214. Ibid., 594, 595.
215. Ibid., 512, 524, 526, 536, 539, 541. Section 37 often mentions the cross together with the resurrection. Only in the small print section is the cross mentioned without the resurrection. Emphasis on Christ's triumph: "By giving His Son to rule and live and reign and conquer" (571). Passion and resurrection: 559, 581, 582, 587, 591, 607. Passion without resurrection: 574, 577. Resurrection without passion: 559, 592.
216. Ibid., 571.
217. Ibid., §39, 737.

There is no reference to Christ's cry of godforsakenness here.[218] In contrast to such belittling of the cross, Barth would later remark, "The truth is that Anselm's question: *quanti ponderis sit peccatum?* ['of what weight is sin?'] is given an answer either from the cross of Christ or not at all."[219]

The discussion of Christ's passion also raises another issue about the priority of the gospel over the law. This priority does not ignore the hardship of the cross. However, the fact that *CD* II/2 does not consistently subordinate the law to the gospel can also be illustrated in another way. In *CD* II/2, chapter 7, §34, even the doctrine of election itself attributes undue prominence to the judgment of the law.

Barth notably asserts that evil is not only a risk the electing God takes, but indeed a necessity. By virtue of the eternal election, evil "must" have "autonomous power." As God saves humankind from the tribulation that God brought about in the first place, this is indeed reminiscent of Luther's theology of law and gospel: "God cannot be God unless He first becomes a devil. We cannot go to heaven, unless we first go to hell."[220] Although the power of evil is real by necessity, its paradoxical ontological status is that of the impossible that has effects in history.[221] Although chapter 7, on the whole, gives priority to the gospel over against the law, the particular prominence of evil, or "Satan," will turn out to play a particular role in the relation between law and gospel.

As Jesus Christ elects for himself to suffer the consequences of the

218. That the ethics *CD* II/2 chapter 8 differs from the doctrine of election, chapter 7, with only a thinly veiled theology of glory is worth noting. By contrast, Nimmo, *Being in Action*, 108–9, responds to the critical question of whether Barth's concept of God's free command takes the human situation seriously precisely by saying that Barth points to nothing less than God's suffering. In addition to portraying Christ's cross in less than grave terms, however, §39 again attributes the crucifixion to God's agency.

219. *CD* IV/1, 412; see Barth's protest against a trivialization of sin, ibid., 381.

220. Luther, *The Exposition of the 117th Psalm (1530)*, in *Selected Psalms III*, ed. and trans. Jaroslav Pelikan, Luther's Works 14 (Saint Louis: Concordia, 1958), 32.

221. *CD* II/2, 170.

election of the sinful creature, Christ's cross appears as his "endurance of judgment,"[222] Christ's enduring self-determination for judgment. The considerations above have been critical of the moral legitimacy of "judgment, death, and hell" attributed to God's action. In *CD* II/2, such problems are mitigated as God's judgment on the cross makes God's grace for humankind stand out even more clearly: the electing God chooses "sure and certain salvation for man, and a sure and certain risk for God."[223]

In chapter 7, §34, however, this binary of judgment borne by Christ and grace for humanity is subverted in its strictness. The communion of the elect in its historic form is subdivided into "its form as Israel," which "has to serve the representation of the divine judgment," while "its form as the Church [has to serve] the representation of the divine mercy."[224] As the terms of judgment and mercy indicate, the relation of law and gospel is at the heart of §34. The section offers an extended commentary on Romans 9–11. Barth has certainly made a significant advance over *Rom* II in realizing that Romans 9–11 refers also and importantly to Israel and not simply to the church.[225] Nonetheless, both §34 and *Rom* II see the gospel emerge out of God's judgment, thus suggesting an inherent connection between the gospel and God's abiding judgment, between destruction and liberation.[226]

Barth's bold pronouncements about the essence of Israel and the

222. Ibid., 197–8.
223. See n. 191.
224. Ibid., 195 (Barth's thesis statement).
225. Ekkehard W. Stegemann, "Israel in Barths Erwählungslehre: Zur Auslegung von Röm 9–11 in KD II, 2, § 34," *Israel und Kirche* 20 (2005): 19–42, at 24, 27. Rudolf Smend reports how Barth said in an advanced seminar on the doctrine of election, "In their reviews [of *Rom* I], Adolf Jülicher and Adolf Schlatter held against me that Rom. 9–11 is not about the church, but about Israel. There had to be yet another Adolf to make me understand they were right." Smend, "Karl Barth als Ausleger der Heiligen Schrift," in *Bibel und Wissenschaft* (Tübingen: Mohr Siebeck, 2004), 199–229, at 208n64.
226. In *Rom* II, the respective chapters on Rom. 9, 10, and 11 are entitled, "The Tribulation of the Church," "The Guilt of the Church," and "The Hope of the Church."

church indicate that, in 1942, §34 tackles a highly charged issue.[227] It is relevant for a theological interpretation of the contemporary Nazi genocide. On the positive side, it is notable that Barth portrays church and synagogue as inseparably one, thus arguing that the Nazi genocide is directed immediately against God's word. For "in faith [the church] knows itself to be one with Israel."[228] The abiding mission God assigned to Israel "establishes positively the election of all Israel."[229] Israel and the church are the two aspects of the one "elected community," over which "the bow of the one covenant arches."[230] Within this community, Israel has a special privilege: the "Messiah" did not come "from Greece, not from Rome, not from Germany, but from Israel!"[231]

What, then, is the distinction between church and Israel within the deeper unity of God's congregation? Israel keeps the elect community from hubris by witnessing to the fact that God's mercy is in any case undeserved.

> The Israelite form of the community of God reveals that when in His eternal election of grace God elects fellowship with man He has Himself assumed in relation to man the indestructible position of Leader, Disposer and Giver. He does not choose the free, the wise and the rich. On the contrary, it is He who makes those whom He elects free, wise and rich by electing them.[232]

While there is no person whose achievements might prove him or her righteous as such, Israel's witness to the undeserved character of

227. For the grave ambiguity of Barth's treatment of Israel in §34, see also Stegemann, "Israel in Barths Erwählungslehre."
228. *CD* II/2, 201.
229. Ibid., 240, see 237.
230. Ibid., 200.
231. Ibid., 204. Moreover, Barth rightly points out that Romans 9–11 does not even mention a Christian mission among the Jews, considering Christ himself the subject who brings about a Jewish confession to Christ. Ibid., 284. See Stegemann, "Israel in Barths Erwählungslehre," 24, 29–30.
232. *CD* II/2, 234.

grace is especially poignant in Barth's analysis: God arranged for a witness to the undeserved character of grace—precisely by holding on to a people that openly refuses to believe God's word.

This certainly presents the Nazi genocide in a particular light: racist Germans, calling themselves Christians, cannot bear the message of judgment that is directed also against them. In their persecution of Israel, the personification of divine judgment within the congregation, they kill the messenger, as it were, in direct rebellion against God's word. It also was presumably for this reason that in 1942, a circle of persecuted Jews and their supporters in Berlin drew consolation from §34.[233]

In making this point, however, Barth displays highly problematic stereotypes, for example, of the crucifixion as carried out by "Israel" corporately. The Gentiles only had a "dependent share in the crucifixion. . . . They carried out only what as a decision was the sin of the chosen people."[234] As Ekkehard Stegemann points out, Barth is mistaken in supposing that Romans 9–11, which is at the heart of this section, holds the crucifixion against the Jews.[235] Moreover, Barth reduces Israel to "obduracy," a "stubborn" character, and "disobedience."[236] Israel "resists its election."[237] Barth even considers it characteristic of "the Church" that it "contests . . . the nationalist-legalistic Messiah-dream of the Synagogue."[238] Given that this was written in 1942, this is ironic, to put it very mildly.

233. Busch, *Unter dem Bogen*, 437. For Barth's portrayal of the Nazi genocide of the Jews as a rebellion against the human deficiency and sinfulness that is both implied in God's grace and visible especially in the Jews, see also Barth, "Verheißung und Verantwortung der christlichen Gemeinde im heutigen Zeitgeschehen," in *Eine Schweizer Stimme: 1938–1945* (Zollikon/Zurich: Evangelischer Verlag, 1945), 307–33, at 317–18.

234. Ibid., 282.

235. Stegemann, "Israel in Barths Erwählungslehre," 24, 32.

236. *CD* II/2, 200, 204, 237. For other anti-Semitic stereotypes, which Barth sees outweighed by Israel's virtues, see ibid., 236 (a mild translation of *KD* II/2, 260).

237. Ibid., 199.

238. Ibid., 204. Barth considers "Jewish nationalism" "the prototype of all bad nationalisms," ibid., 280. See Stegemann, "Israel in Barths Erwählungslehre," 31.

Why are the heinous crimes committed against the Jews throughout the centuries, very often in the name of Christianity, and particularly the unprecedented Nazi mass murder of the Jews, not an even stronger witness to the fact that *Christians*, rather than their victims, are undeserving of God's grace? After all, they not only hear the word of God's mercy, they even profess to believe the gospel. In turn, why does Barth single out the church as the community of those who not only hear God's word but also believe in it, precisely in a period in which the Christian churches in Germany tolerated, or even supported, Nazi politics?

Barth continues, by contrast, to suggest that "Israel suffers under this [i.e., Israel's] disobedience."[239] This is not merely a coincidence. Instead, it is Israel's mission "to reflect the judgment from which God has rescued man."[240]

> Israel is the people of the Jews which resists its divine election. It is the community of God in so far as this community has to exhibit also the unwillingness, incapacity and unworthiness of man with respect to the love of God directed to him. By delivering up its Messiah, Jesus, to the Gentiles for crucifixion, Israel attests the justice of the divine judgment on man borne by God Himself. Encountering the fulfilled promise in this way, it remains only its hearer without pressing on to faith in it. In its existence it can only *reveal the passing of the old man* who confronts God in this way. But Israel as the Jewish people resisting the divine election is at the same time the secret origin of the Church in which alone God's mercy can be praised only by faith in God alone, in which faith itself is simply obedience, the perfect hearing, in which the coming of the new man becomes true *only in the passing of the old.*[241]

A crucial question with Barth's notion of Israel's corporate testimony to God's rejection of sin is whether he sees the genocide of the Jews as in some way caused by God's rejection. Eberhard Busch

239. *CD* II/2, 237.
240. Ibid., 206. See also 195 (thesis statement).
241. Ibid., 198–9 (italics by A. M.).

answers this question in the negative.[242] On the other hand, Barth does not view the fact of Israel's suffering, which he portrays as parallel to Jesus' suffering, as a mere coincidence. Repeatedly, he highlights the perceived Jewish lack of faith in Christ in strong terms, even using anti-Semitic stereotypes. Barth's description of Israel as a "witness to God's judgment" is notoriously ambiguous. Even if God did not directly inflict the Holocaust on the Jews, according to Barth, he presents Jewish suffering at least as appropriate. The more disagreeable "the Jews" appear, the clearer is the undeserved nature of God's grace for the Jews, and the more clearly they also deserve hardship, and hardship is what they experience. "The question at issue in the whole context is surely that of the righteousness of God's mysterious guidance of Israel from the very first and in the present, and therefore of the meaning of the *divine bitterness* which Israel had and still has to experience."[243]

Certainly, it must give us serious pause that Barth sees even in the Holocaust, of all things, at least a faint reflection of God's own judgment. Even the most heinous human misdeeds are seen as capable of testifying positively to God's active rejection of sin. It is not only because of Christ's solidarity in suffering with the Jews, but also because of Barth's assumption of God's judgment that he argues, "To know Him always means to know the gracious God, even in sin and death, even under the dominion of the devil, even in the abyss of hell."[244]

The ambiguity of God's work is precisely the ambiguity of God's work in law and gospel. Wolf Krötke also criticizes Barth for giving attention, to a certain degree, to divine rejection for its own sake in §34.[245] One may object that it is theologically inconsistent to

242. Busch, *Unter dem Bogen*, 441–2; see also 439.
243. *CD* II/2, 230 (italics by A. M.).
244. Ibid., 92.
245. Krötke, "Summe des Evangeliums," 75.

portray what happened to Israel as the performative witness to God's judgment, as God's judgment was borne by Christ once and for all, and the performative witness to God's judgment is indistinguishable from a new instantiation of God's judgment. But, in fact, the ambiguity is inherent in Barth's theological interpretation of the cross as vicarious punishment. The notion that Christ personifies gracious election in bearing the judgment himself also perpetuates the strict binary of God's harsh demand and God's free gift. Vicarious punishment is not the only interpretation that allows Christians to see God's mercy enacted in Christ's cross. But the merciful character of the vicarious punishment of the cross can only be appropriated by believers if it is correlated with a sense of the gravity of the sin punished there. Thus the notion of vicarious punishment will always lend itself to a certain justification of misery. As helpful as Barth's doctrine of eternal election is in rearranging the priorities between gospel and law, this remains a problem at the heart of *CD* II/2. An interpretation of God's saving act in Christ that presents an alternative to substitutionary punishment will be developed in *CD* IV/1.

To be sure, in §34 Barth at times attributes an overarching importance to the gospel: "Faith and therefore the Church is already the goal and ground of Israel's election."[246] Yet the question is why the undeserved character of grace requires the abiding personification of judgment as such. There might have been other ways to point out the gracious, undeserved nature of God's grace apart from judgment, as with a saving or transforming act of God. Yet the thesis statement of §34 highlights Israel's corporate witness to judgment before the church's corporate witness to God's mercy, Israel's hearing—and its

246. *CD* II/2, 239.

failure to believe—before the church's believing, Israel's passing before the church's coming.[247]

The distribution of the two aspects, judgment and mercy, to two stable poles assigns value to divine judgment almost for its own sake.[248] The church is constantly dependent on Israel discharging its service of displaying the human unworthiness of God's grace, and only thus the church "arises from it and remains in need of its special auxiliary service."[249] God's judgment must continue to be manifested in the congregation, so that the true faith of the church flourishes. In other words, the law must continue to be preached in judgment so that the gospel may emerge from the condemnation of the law and shine. In turn, the independent value of the judgment of the law then allows for a negative theology of history that makes sense out of current events as witness to, or even an effect of, divine punishment.

Barth concedes that he deals with Israel and the church "synecdochically."[250] However, the fact that Nazi violence was directed against Jews regardless of whether or not they were baptized is one factor that upsets Barth's concept of an enduring personification of judgment within God's congregation. For all its appalling implications, Barth's theory might have been strangely plausible had the Nazis made a point of consistently sparing Christian Jews. After all, §34 portrays the unified congregation in which both Jews and Christians hear and believe as the goal God pursues in history. Barth's stereotypical portrayal of the Jews as rejecting Christ is in sharp contradiction to the fact that the looming Aryan Paragraph in the German Protestant *churches* was one of the first issues that made

247. Ibid., 195.
248. Krötke argues that an abiding interest in the fate of the rejected is operative here, which was characteristic of the traditional doctrines of predestination before Barth. Krötke, "Summe des Evangeliums," 75.
249. *CD* II/2, 238.
250. Ibid., 199.

Barth a prominent public opponent of Nazi racism.[251] In other words, since *Jewish Christians* were the first for whom Barth prominently took sides in the struggle against the Nazi infiltration of the churches, it is even more difficult to understand how §34 can argue that the Nazi genocide reflected God's punishment for a *lack* of faith in Christ. The rejection of the Nazi genocide must be strictly undialectical. The element that outweighed the great problems in §34 for Barth must have been the particular prominence of divine punishment still lingering in Barth's theology. In §34, the conviction that the punishment has been borne by Christ is ambiguous and thus tainted.

When Barth articulates his hope that faith does indeed flourish in the entire church, this remains vague, by contrast. God's judgment does not seem to have any other function than preparing for the proclamation of grace. A proper prioritization of the gospel would ask how the law contributes in more concrete, practical terms to shaping the living presence of faith. Judgment on human sin can or may be necessary under particular circumstances, but why "freeze" this aspect of judgment in time and speak only about a dualism of judgment and gift, rather than ask for moments of God's salvation and transformation of unjust constellations, both through divine mercy and divine guidance?

The difficulty of both the necessity of evil and its reduced ontological status is closely associated with Barth's supralapsarianism. Questions about Barth's supralapsarian scheme also raise doubts about the consistency of his views on gospel and law. To begin with, *CD* II/2 offers an extensive discussion of classical Reformed supra- and infralapsarian theologies.[252] Barth argues that, in contrast to

251. Barth, *Theological Existence To-day! (A Plea for Theological Freedom)*, trans. R. Birch Hoyle (Eugene: Wipf & Stock, 2012), 52; see above ch. 1.
252. *CD* II/2, 127–145, at 140–41.

infralapsarianism, God did not elect humanity—with all the implications election has for God—only once it had fallen. The object of election is thus not, in this sense, the *homo lapsus* (the fallen human person). This would present Christ's incarnation only as a response to a contingent emergency, which might not have taken place under different circumstances. Christ would not be the revelation of God's eternal being.[253]

Nevertheless, since supralapsarians argue that God elected and rejected certain parts of humanity from all eternity, and thus not human persons as fallen ones (*lapsi*) but as those able to fall (*labiles*), reconciliation in the Son of God appears only as the execution of another decision by God, which, however, seems to have been made independently of the Son.

Barth does not consider the incarnation to be a response to a contingent event (*lapsus*). That might speak for the supralapsarian perspective. The problem with the supralapsarianism designation of the *obiectum electionis, homo labilis* (the human person able to fall) is that the fall itself, as well as the incarnation of the Son, should not be considered merely a contingent possibility. Yet Barth is closer to the supralapsarian position in that he sees the deeper meaning of the fall, from all eternity, in God's glory and sovereignty. He does not conceive of this as God's sheer freedom of choice toward the creature, but as God's gracious action on behalf of the creature. God's will for the creature's salvation in Christ characterizes God in all eternity, and thus the fall is certain as it is implied in this eternal decision. Thus, the glory of God as redeemer presupposes the misery of sin. We might call the object of election in Barth's account the *homo lapsurus quia redemptus futurus*, the person bound to fall for the sake of future

253. If the *obiectum electionis* is only considered the way the infralapsarians do, Barth contends, the groundwork is laid for a "natural theology" which looks first at the human being as such and only after that in the light of Christology (ibid., 136, 137–8).

redemption. From all eternity the creature is bound to fall because Christ, whom we only and rightly know as the Reconciler, must as such be no less than the second person of the Trinity.

> The existence of this man, the predestined bearer and representative of the divine Yes and the divine No, foreordained to victory over sin and death but also to the bearing of the divine penalty, is the divine promise, the divine Word, in which the God who elects from all eternity confronts all humanity and each individual. . . . Such, then, is the Supralapsarian theory as detached and purified from the doubtful presuppositions of the older theology.[254]

Apart from this "purification," the God of the supralapsarians would take on "*the appearance of a demon,*" Barth contends.[255] God elected or rejected the creature for God's own glory, at the expense of some other creatures. But even if Barth sees God's glory fulfilled in the salvation of all creatures, "the appearance of a demon" has not entirely disappeared even from Barth's treatment. After all, for the sake of eternal election, evil "must" have "autonomous power."[256] Yet when writing about Israel and the church as two forms of God's elect congregation in 1942, Barth was aware of the gravity of evil. The praise of God by some of the saved will therefore be muted by the fact that God's election also assigned evil its harmful place in the world in order then to overcome it.

> God does not will and affirm evil and the fall and an act of sin on the part of this man . . . , but for the sake of the fulness of His glory, ... for the sake of the perfection of His love, He wills and affirms this man as sinful man, i.e., as man laden with sins and afflicted by their curse and misery, and He wills and affirms this man as one who stands like Himself in opposition to sin, as His companion in the necessity of repudiating it. . . . But for this purpose it was necessary that this man

254. Ibid., 142.
255. Ibid., 140.
256. Ibid., 170.

> should really be confronted with what God Himself repudiates. . . . And it is inevitable that this confrontation with what God repudiates, with evil, should mean for man, who is certainly not God and not almighty, that evil confronts him as a hostile power, a power which is, in fact, greater than his own power.[257]

In trying to forge a synthesis between the infralapsarians and the supralapsarians of the seventeenth century, Barth argues that we can neither be strictly neutral nor find either position truly convincing. Indeed, "on the ground on which it was fought out the controversy was one which could not be decided."[258] Barth himself, however, does not succeed either in providing the ground for a satisfactory answer. The extent to which the affliction is God's own doing remains hauntingly ambiguous. Barth called its arising in the first place inevitable for the sake of salvation by grace alone. The drama of salvation thus seems artificially set up. Can Barth himself avoid the charge that he brings against the supralapsarians, which is that they portrayed God as *auctor peccati*, the author of sin?[259]

The traditional scheme of law and gospel faces a similar difficulty. Luther asserted that "when God makes alive he does it by killing."[260] "God, through his law, forces man continually deeper into sin."[261] God punishes such sin with "plague, famine, the sword, and other troubles,"[262] in order to save through the gospel. *CD* II/2, §34 tends to evade the direct attribution of evil to God. Barth belittles God's relation to evil as mere permission.[263] When Barth portrayed the

257. Ibid., 141.
258. Ibid., 139.
259. Ibid., 138.
260. Luther, *Bondage of the Will*, 3:62.
261. Althaus, *Theology of Martin Luther*, 176.
262. Luther, quoted ibid., 173.
263. *CD* II/2, 127, 136, 138, 170. Luther, in Jüngel's presentation, seeks to reconcile divine universal efficacy with God's goodness in yet another way, attributing evil merely to a deficiency within the secondary causes (Jüngel, "The Revelation of the Hiddenness": "Die Offenbarung der Verborgenheit," 174). Since Jüngel and Luther would hesitate to detract from God's omniscience, and since this constitutes an exception from God's universal efficacy, which

power of evil as a power of "powerlessness" in 1942, the number of concentration camps north of the Alps was in the five-digit range,[264] and about fourteen thousand SS men and German special forces carried out the "Shoah by bullets" in the newly occupied territory in the East.[265]

It is unclear how Barth relates this dark side of God to the full-blown omnipotence of the divine command in chapter 8. He argues that only the command of grace can do that which other concepts are incapable of doing: "That it should confront him, his being and his existence with an absolute demand; that it should, with absolute sovereignty, dominate him and confront him with a claim; that it should have for him the character of majesty; that it should be able to hit him and concern him as a command of God."[266] Such power of the command is true if indeed "by God is meant the Lord who in Jesus Christ, by the decree of His mercy, controls man absolutely, without any option of preliminary questions or further inquiry."[267]

What would it mean under these premises that in 1942, at the time of Barth's writing, Nazi armies had just expanded the reach of German terror even deeper into Soviet territory, with a host of

Luther asserts vigorously (ibid., 173), this is less than convincing. Nonetheless this is instructive as it shows Jüngel in doubt that the work of divine wrath is justified due to its preparing the ground for God's work of mercy. Thomas Aquinas's *Summa contra Gentiles* makes an exception from God's universal efficacy: God allows for creaturely cooperation as an artisan may work with an instrument without determining the form with which it achieves its effect ("*tamen non dat formam*," *ScG* 3, 70). *ScG* 3, 71 makes the same point with regard to evil: "*Divina providentia non subtrahit a rebus fortunam et casum.*"

264. In 2013, the overall number of Nazi concentration camps from France to Russia was found to be at 42,500. Eric Lichtblau, "The Holocaust Just Got More Shocking," *New York Times*, March 3, 2013, p. SR3. Jüngel argues that Barth's take on God's involvement in evil in his doctrine of the *Nichtiges* fails. Jüngel, "Revelation of the Hiddenness": "Offenbarung der Verborgenheit," 178–80.

265. Antony Beevor, *The Second World War* (New York: Little, Brown & Co., 2012), 210–16. The regular army was also involved in these killings. This resulted in the murder of more than 1.35 million Jews by German mobile units by the end of 1942 (ibid., 216).

266. *CD* II/2, 532–3 (trans. rev.).

267. Ibid., 533 (trans. rev.).

European countries—Finland, Norway, Denmark, the Netherlands, Belgium, France, Italy, Austria, Poland, Czechoslovakia, Hungary, Greece, Romania, Bulgaria, the Balkans, the Baltic states, Belarus, and the Ukraine—either occupied by Germany or in control of its allies?[268]

A fundamental, groundbreaking achievement of chapter 8 so far consists in the realization that power as power, or sheer authority, is not a moral fact. From a theological perspective, Barth calls it a "duty" for the sake of humanity to rise up in defense of that which is "supremely pleasing and useful and valuable," which Christ's commandment emphatically supports. However, a problem arises once Barth portrays God's commandment as omnipotent, using such strong terms that anything but a strictly universal efficacy would detract from Christ's divinity. So how does Christ's commandment relate to the experience of a large scale, dramatic breach of justice in 1942? Has the promise of freedom in Christ's commandment been inefficient in the face of political turmoil?

The Ethics of the Actualistic Commanding (§§38–9)

Barth's prominent ethical actualism is introduced in §36 and fleshed out further especially in §38.[269] Section 36 explains briefly that God

268. It was not before winter 1941 that experts would have recognized that Germany's attack on Soviet Russia suffered from fundamental logistical and strategic problems. The outcome of the German invasion was basically decided in summer 1942 (Bauer, *Nationalsozialismus*, 382, 388). In the battle of Stalingrad, however, the tide would not turn against the Germans until the fall of 1942.

269. In their essays, William Werpehowski and Wolfgang Lienemann defend Barth against the charge of intuitionism or occasionalism. Werpehowski argues in "Command and History" and "Realism and Discernment" in *Karl Barth and Christian Ethics: Living in Truth*, Barth Studies Series (Farnham: Ashgate, 2014), 15–36, 57–69, that Barth's actualism attributes exclusive authority to arguments drawing on biblical narrative rather than on a general ontology. Any act of ethical deliberation needs to perceive the individual situation afresh every time as part of the relation to God's story and narrative (Werpehowski, "Command and History," 22, 27–8, 30–31). This ignores, however, Barth's harsh objection to a construal of the divine command in general terms that leaves specifics up to human judgment. On Barth's critical statements see below. Wolfgang Lienemann, "Das Gebot Gottes als 'Ereignis': Bibelgebrauch und freie

must always be thought of as a God in action, that God is active in God's commanding: "We do not know God Himself otherwise than as acting God."[270] Before ethics can address human action, it first witnesses to God's action, and ethics is "the theory of this practice."[271] Already before *CD* II/2, Barth's ethics lectures emphasized that ethics is not faced with a static God, but—corresponding to an actualistic anthropology—with God who acts by revealing God's word.[272] In fact, in writing *CD*, chapter 8, Barth often adopted the very phrasing he chose in the ethics lectures:

> The Word of God is only the Word of God in act. The Word of God is *decision.* God *acts.* Only with reference to this reality which is not general but highly specific can theological ethics venture to answer the ethical question. Its theory is meant only as a theory of this *practice.* But this practice presupposes that it is taking place and only on this presupposition does it dare to give an answer. In the same divine decision, in the same actuality, in the same knowledge of revelation, the knowledge which is itself revelation, the Christian church exists and there is faith and obedience in it.[273]

Already in the ethics lecture cycle Barth argued that action is fundamentally characteristic of God. Not only does God continue to be active; in addition, this must be correlated with the creature's receptivity and passivity.[274]

Verantwortlichkeit in der Ethik Karl Barths," *Zeitschrift für Dialektische Theologie* 15 (1999): 155–77 also defends Barth's ethics of the divine command by pointing out the character of the event as the crucial category in Barth's "fundamental ontology" (ibid., 165). However, the essay hardly discusses the main document of Barth's command ethics, *CD* II/2, chapter 8.

270. Ibid., 548.
271. Ibid.
272. Barth, *Ethics*, 20, 85. Barth, *Ethik: Vorlesung Münster, Wintersemester 1928/1929*, 3 (part of the chapter "Transition," which was omitted in Barth, *Ethics*).
273. Ibid., 50–51. See, for example, *CD* II/2, 704.
274. Barth, *Ethics*, 112: "The new life cannot be abstracted from the free, giving act of God. ... This life cannot be reinterpreted as a being, having, and doing of man distinguished from direct knowability from all his other being, having, and doing. We cannot be too cautious in handling all the concepts that might denote a third sphere between God and man and common to both. The Bible knows no such sphere. It knows only the event of the incarnate Word and the

> Yet God's command is not as an inert, objective truth that is written down somewhere or could be articulated somehow, which the human person might or might not know, might or might not acknowledge ... for it is God's command as an event that in no way is at my disposal or over which I have power, but that encounters me and that disposes of *me*, having power over me . . . for it is God's command, the event that will judge my action, my existing.[275]

Along these lines, *CD* II/2 also repeats the statements from the ethics lectures that deny any mere facticity of a divine command. In *CD* II/2, Barth writes,

> No, "*there is*" ["*es gibt*"] *no* command of God! What "is there" [*Was "es gibt"*] is not as such the command of God. But the core of the matter is that *God gives* [gibt] *His command*, that he gives Himself to be our Commander. God's command, God Himself, gives Himself to be known. And as He does so, He is heard. Man is made responsible. He is brought into that confrontation and fellowship with Jesus Christ. And his action acquires that determination.[276]

Already fourteen years before, the ethics lectures put it similarly:

> "There is" ["*es gibt*"] no law of God, just as—a terrible thing to say—"there is" no God [*es . . . gibt*] either. What "is there" [*Was "es gibt"*] is an object. . . . The law that "is there" is never the law that is set up, that makes an absolute claim to our acknowledgment. God's law is the law of faith, i.e., the law that *God* gives [*das Gott gibt*] . . . as he gives himself in his revelation.[277]

Barth contrasts the notion of the acting God with knowledge of God gleaned from the natural order or an immediate awareness in competition with God's activity in Israel and in Jesus Christ.[278]

quickening Spirit. In this event God is and remains the one who acts, of course, as the one who is."

275. Barth, *Ethik*, 2:1–2 (not included in the translation).
276. *CD* II/2, 548 (italics and punctuation from the original).
277. Barth, *Ethics*, 317–18 (trans. rev.).
278. *CD* II/1, 10–11; 18–19.

Since the command is a contingent, free revelation, believers are fundamentally needy and dependent on God's free grace—which is as dramatic as it is unforeseeable given the great gulf that separates creator and creation. This is the basic constellation of Barth's actualistic ethics. The development of Barth's mature doctrine of election in 1942 has not changed the fundamental outlook of Barth's command ethics. *CD* II/2 does not offer an ethics of orders in 1942, as Barth leaves this issue to be discussed as part of the doctrine of creation *CD* III/4. But regarding other parts of the ethics lecture, it was presumably an overstatement when Barth said that *CD* chapter 8 was "casting" the ethics lecture "radically anew."[279]

In *CD* chapter 8, §38, "The Command as the Decision of God" is the longest section, and §38.2, "The Definiteness of the Divine Decision," is among the longest subsections both in chapter 8 and in §38.[280] Barth asserts in §38.2 that God's command is heard in listening to the words of Scripture. God's revelation in Scripture was already a prominent concern in the ethics lecture,[281] but these lectures also attached great importance to the orders of creation and preservation as well as the personal encounter with the neighbor. By comparison, *CD* II/2 puts the emphasis much more resolutely on Scripture. Christians encounter God's command in the words of the Bible.[282] Christians must not try to establish some direct, immediate communication with God apart from Scripture. Barth's explicit statements on natural law, for example, are quite negative.[283]

279. Busch, *Barth: His Life from Letters*, 302 (trans. rev.). See Geoffrey Bromiley's description, "Translator's Preface," in Barth, *Ethics*, vi: "The lectures clearly came to serve as a first draft of the ethical section of the Church Dogmatics. . . . It will be seen that Barth also made considerable use of the contents of these early discussions."

280. In terms of the word count, §37.3 is the longest subsection in chapter 8. Based on the number of pages, §38.2 is as long as §37.3. Subsections in §38: §38.1: 18,653 words, thirty-one pp., §38.2: 31,946 words, forty-eight pp., §38.3: 16,732 words, twenty-four pp.

281. Barth, *Ethics*, 16, 53, 310–11, 346, 442–3.

282. *CD* II/2, 671.

283. Ibid., 712.

Barth's insistence that God's commanding takes place with absolute authority is again very much in keeping with the ethics lectures. As Barth did in the lectures, §§36–7 cast the authority of God's command in such sharp relief that hearing the command amounts to a dramatic alternative between faithfulness and idolatry:

> It belongs to the nature of all other commands that in face of them we necessarily have to come back again and again to ourselves, to our function of judging between good and evil, either conceding obedience to them from this position, or perhaps in the future confronting them with partial or complete disobedience.[284]

The lectures also highlighted the concreteness of God's command and the importance this has for its absolute authority.[285] In both texts, Barth elaborates on the relation between God's absolute command and a philosophical notion of the absolute good. According to *CD* II/2, §38.2, this philosophical notion may to some extent seem to correspond to the true command of God, who is after all "the unconditional ground of our being":

> There is an idea of the good . . . which may be identified with that of perfect being, and even of the original transcendent ground of all being. . . . The idea of the good is . . . the unconditional ground of our being, also makes an unconditional claim and passes an unconditional judgment on our will and conduct. Now, undoubtedly, the idea of the divine command is to some extent coincident with this thought.[286]

Remarkably, Barth identifies the true problem with this notion of the good with the fact that it fails to be *truly absolute*: "The idea of the good can obviously be a command only in so far as [man] himself, as he has conceived and planned and established it, gives it its concrete embodiment in particular cases according to his private judgment

284. Ibid., 595.
285. Ibid., 666.
286. Ibid., 665–6.

and discretion, so that *in concreto* he is his own lord and master."[287] By contrast, the "idea of the divine command is the idea of something which is incomprehensible to man of himself."[288]

This is also the critical point that the ethics lectures raise against a philosophical notion of the absolute good. The philosophical notion of the absolute good can never in fact rise above the realm of the relative.

> In believing in God the Christian faith does not believe in any of these antithetical and obviously mutually limiting things, in any of these things to which unconditionality can be ascribed only in relation to opposing conditioned things, and between which the relation can at any time be reversed and frequently enough has been reversed.[289]

The problem with the philosophical notion of the good is that it fails to be absolute, Barth submits. By contrast, the ethics lectures lay down a clear criterion under which God's command is indeed absolute: "The law of God *has been* set up *without* my doing it or even cooperating in doing it. Any law that *I* set up or even *cooperate* in setting up would *not* as such be God's law."[290] This corresponds closely to Barth's claim in *CD* II/2 about the authority of God's command that implements itself actively: "It must have authority and power to do so *in and through itself* [*in und durch sich selbst*], and not by my rendering it so."[291] The published translation fails to preserve Barth's clear distinction between the command and the moral agent. Barth envisions God's command as absolute indeed,

287. Ibid., 666.
288. Ibid. ("*Es ist der Begriff des Gebotes Gottes der Begriff des vom Menschen her Unbegreiflichen,*" *KD* II/2, 742).
289. Barth, *Ethics*, 315.
290. Ibid. (trans. rev.).
291. *CD* II/2, 651 (trans. rev., emphasis by A. M.), *KD* II/2, 725: "*Es* [the command] *muß dann* in und durch sich selbst *Autorität und Kraft dazu haben und nicht dadurch, daß ich sie ihm verleihe*" (emphasis by A. M.).

and in consequence he does *not* write about it that an "imperative to which I owe absolute obedience must necessarily come in the most radical sense from within."[292] On the contrary: "If there is an imperative to which I owe obedience, it must approach me from without in the most radical sense. Coming from there, it claims me within as well."[293] Hence, the command "does not need any interpretation, for even to the smallest and last detail it is already interpreted *by itself* [*durch sich selbst*]."[294] The ethics lecture highlights in just the same manner as *CD* II/2 the self-sufficiency and self-implementation of the command ("purely *through itself*" [*rein durch sich selbst*]):

> A pure acknowledgment would be of such a kind that I recognize indeed what I am told, but in this I am not at all creative, as that which I am told is clear to me purely *by itself* because it is *said* to me in a particular way, but not at all insofar as I am telling me the very thing myself.[295]

Already the ethics lecture cycle emphasized that the authority of the command depended on its unconditioned nature. The consequence is that God's act of commanding, the validity of the command, and the hearing and understanding of the command must not in the least depend on the Christian. From start to finish, it must strictly be God's unilateral act in which the human person realizes his or her responsibility.

> A general, formal, and abstract command is obviously *no* command but an object of theory like any other. If the good is indeed unconditioned and therefore not general and theoretical truth; if it is command, claim, a claim made upon us and not just a statement of our own thought

292. Ibid.
293. Ibid. (trans. rev.: *KD* II/1, 725).
294. *CD* II/2, 665 (trans. rev.), *KD* II/2, 741: "*durch sich selbst . . . interpretiert.*"
295. Ibid., 316 (trans. rev.).

> that is given the rank of claim; then it is a concrete, definite, individual command whose content is not under our control, but which *is* controlled with the same unconditionality as is proper to its form, a command which comes to us already filled and definite in content.[296]

As Barth's sense for God's unconditioned nature in God's command is highly acute and sensitive, it is no wonder that even *CD* III/4 is overly vigilant to the slightest stirring of what may seem like a usurpation of the throne of God the judge on the part of the human person.[297] So keen is Barth's suspicion of human hubris that he must see God's absoluteness as very fragile and urgently in need of protection. With Barth's warning systems set on the highest sensitivity level, the potential for conflict in the encounter between God and a human person is out of proportion. Given the absoluteness and unworldliness of the divine, God and the creature are on a collision course from the outset. This is the reason why Barth makes a point to name §39, almost 50 pages long, "The Command as the Judgment [*Gericht*] of God," while the subsection 38.3, "The Goodness of the Divine Decision," merely 25 pages long, only follows subsections titled "The Sovereignty of the Divine Decision" (§38.1, 30 pages) and "The Definiteness of the Divine Decision" (*Bestimmtheit*: specificity, which preempts all human interpretation—see below; §38.2, almost 50 pages). Conflict and judgment, rather than the gospel, are the key themes of §§38–9. Of course §§37–8 highlighted the priority of the gospel, but they did so based on a natural human moral striving, from which God's command only derives its power—which would be unthinkable if the perceived command did not also derive its orientation in content from the natural moral striving, to which it offers fulfillment and

296. Barth, *Ethics*, 77.

297. *CD* III/4, 10. Barth's overprotectiveness of God's absoluteness is in an inverse proportion to the degree in which *CD* II/2, ch. 8 acknowledges God's suffering on the cross. See below.

release. Sections §§38–9 cannot accept this as this renders human moral inclinations more fundamental than God's contingent command. If the resulting prominence of conflict and judgment should reflect Barth's situation while writing, with Nazi Germany at the peak of its power, this development is understandable. But then the degree to which Barth's ethics is primarily reacting to the opponent is astounding.

To be sure, *CD* §38 does not fail either to drive home the fundamental conditions impinging on the very constitution of moral obligation. Just as the philosophical notion of the absolute good falls short in being conditioned, so the unconditioned nature of God and the unconditional validity of God's command must be preserved absolutely intact: God's true command "must lay upon me the obligation of unconditioned truth—truth which is not conditioned by myself. Its authority and power to do so must be intrinsic and objective, and not something which I lend to it."[298] This is the reason why Barth rejects, for example, a eudaemonistic ethic: "How can that which seems desirable and useful and valuable justify its claim to validity for us apart from the fact that it is understood and felt and viewed and experienced and therefore asserted and affirmed by us as such?" This quotation immediately continues by drawing on the notion of a claim that is valid independently of any justification furnished by believers themselves: "What authority and power can its imperative have but that with which we ourselves are able to clothe it?"[299]

Already the ethics lectures emphasized that God's command is very concrete.[300] It is not up to the human person to furnish the particulars of what God demands.[301] An important point at which *CD* II/2 differs

298. *CD* II/2, 651.
299. Ibid., 650–51 (trans. rev.).
300. Barth, *Ethics*, 292–3, 305, 322 ("Here is special, concrete law, God's law, law which has come to us as such and can only be acknowledged by us. What is not acknowledgment in the pure

from the lectures is that *CD* chapter 8 does not see the concrete character of the command immediately in the social encounter to which God's law, according to the lectures, alerts Christians. In this sense *CD* only asserts the concreteness of the command without specifying further in what the concreteness consists. The very words of the Bible as the vehicle of God's command take the place that the lectures assigned to the encounter with the neighbor.

Since the words of the Bible have risen in prominence in comparison to the ethics lecture, the problem of how the authority of God's command is translated into the Christian's own understanding requires a more detailed treatment in §38. Barth now attempts to flesh out this statement with a view to basic hermeneutical questions. The title of §38.2, "The Definiteness of the Divine Decision," summarizes how Barth treats the hermeneutical problem. If the hearing of the command depends on the interpretation of Scripture, then the interpreters will have a share in determining the content of the command. Barth focuses especially on the notion that one might extract general moral rules from Scripture. The relevance of a rule, however, depends on its application in an individual case, which again depends unavoidably on new interpretations.

This injunction is also directed against Kant's categorical imperative[302] or the eudaemonistic concern for human flourishing.

sense, the acknowledgment which is the obedience of faith, is an illusion, i.e., nonknowledge." Trans. rev.).

301. Ibid., 77: "Then it is concrete, definite, individual command whose content is not under our control, but which *is* controlled with the same unconditionality as is proper to its form." Ibid., 80: "For what fills the empty concepts, the source of concreteness, and consequently the criterion of good and evil, is the freedom of human choice [*das liberum arbitrium*; cf. Luther, *On the Bondage of the Will/De servo arbitrio*], or, in other words, man himself. . . . We maintain, then, that the very unconditionality of the command does not, as a shortsighted understanding of Kant believes, exclude the specific and concrete determination of the content of the command. On the contrary, it includes it. In [the] moral decision it is a question of obeying or disobeying."

302. Kant's categorical imperative, "Act only according to that maxim through which you can at the same time will that it become a universal law," understands the universal as the truly rational. This yields an entirely formalized, general testing procedure for moral claims to which Barth's

In such schemes, those who are required to obey would become judges themselves. Barth calls this constellation illegitimate in the face of the authority of God's command. God's authority figures very prominently in the section at hand.[303] Hence, Barth wishes to discredit fundamentally the possibility of extracting general rules of conduct from Scripture. For this reason he interprets God's command in Scripture as a concrete individual command: "The command of God . . . does not need any interpretation, for even to the smallest details it is self-interpreting."[304] This point has not always received the attention it deserves, but Barth even repeats it, to some extent literally, in *CD* III/4.[305] The definiteness of the command rules out interpretation. This is the crucial point that Barth is careful to

notion of the divine command is directly opposed. Kant, *Groundwork of the Metaphysics of Morals*, 71.

303. See also Nimmo, *Being in Action*, 26.

304. *CD* II/2, 665. Nimmo's discussion of the ethical importance of Scripture is concerned with the question in how far two statements in §38 can be in keeping with each other: God's command can indeed deviate from the tendency of the biblical witnesses, and God commands indeed what God, according to Scripture, had commanded individuals before (*Nimmo*, Being in Action, 33). The definite words of Scripture can utter a command for us today, but the same words can amount to quite a different command each time (see ibid., 33–4, 35). However, it is not clear how the relation between the words and their meaning can be virtually equivocal. For example, Martin Buber asks the New Testament scholar and Nazi Gerhard Kittel in an open letter whether the commandments Num. 15:15–16, Lev. 24:22, 19:33–4 are also directed to non-Jews ("You and the alien who resides with you shall have the same law and the same ordinance"). Martin Buber, "Offener Brief an Gerhard Kittel," in *Schriften zum Christentum*, Buber-Werkausgabe 9, ed. Karl-Josef Kuschel (Gütersloh: Gütersloher, 2011), 169–72.

305. *CD* III/4, 12. See *KD* II/2, 740–43 (Barth's italics replaced to highlight agreements): We would be mistaken if the ethical task consists in "unser Wollen . . . durch jene *allgemeine Regel* ... begrenz[t] . . . [sein zu] lassen. . . . [God's command is not] erst noch der Auslegung und *Anwendung* auf den *besonderen* Fall *bedürftig* . . . *Es bedarf keiner Interpretation*: darum nicht, weil *es durch sich selbst bis aufs Kleinste und Letzte interpretiert ist*. . . . Die *'Idee des Guten'* kann diese bestimmte göttliche Entscheidung nicht sein . . . Ebenso steht es nun aber mit dem sogenannten *'kategorischen Imperativ.'*" *KD* III/4, 11: Casuistry falsely assumes "das Gebot Gottes sei eine *allgemeine Regel* . . . der *besonderen* konkreten speziellen Füllung durch die *Anwendung bedürftig*, um als Gebot in Kraft zu treten. Nun, die *'Idee des Guten'* oder der *'kategorische Imperativ'* oder ähnliche philosophische Inbegriffe des sittlichen Gesetzes mögen dessen in der Tat bedürfen. Das Gebot des lebendigen Gottes aber bedarf dessen nicht. . . . *Es bedarf* also, um in Kraft zu treten, *keiner Interpretation. Es ist bis ins Kleinste und Letzte durch sich selbst interpretiert.*"

highlight even in the title of the subsection §38.2. The authority of God's command to issue a binding imperative, its

> authority and power to do so must be intrinsic and objective, and not something which I lend to it. . . . On the contrary, it establishes its own validity by asking concerning my own . . . The essence of the idea of obligation is not that I demand something from myself but that, with all that I can demand of myself, I am myself demanded.[306]

The basic constellation of the sovereign, active God and the purely receptive believer entails fundamental problems for the act of scriptural interpretation.[307] In §38.2, the word *interpret/interpretation* is used negatively throughout as an evasion from true divine authority, if associated with a human subject.[308] If anything requires interpretation, it is human life that must be interpreted in the light of Scripture, and not the other way around.[309] Certainly, God's command must not be interpreted:

> The command is intrinsically concrete. It is already interpreted and applied to myself and my circumstances, to my position at the moment. There is nothing that I myself can add to it. I am asked only concerning my obedience or disobedience. I am not asked concerning my interpretation, but only my perception and the consequent practical recognition of the form in which it is given me.[310]

The secondary literature on Barth's ethics typically wishes to restrict his harsh reaction to scriptural interpretation merely to general rules

306. Ibid., 651.
307. In the same vein, *CD* III/4, 12 speaks of "direct instruction."
308. *CD* II/2, 664–5, 667–8, 671, 702 ("deceive ourselves . . . the interpreter of the divine norm and therefore to be his own judge"). Barth does discuss legitimate or illegitimate "interpretations" of the Sermon on the Mount and the Decalogue, but crucially he does not consider those texts to be mediating God's command. Section 38.3, 716 argues that norms that are interpreted are antisocial, while God's command unites.
309. *CD* II/2, 660. But even that is problematic—see below.
310. Ibid., 667.

that might be extracted from the Bible,[311] as in the prominent ethical schemes of eudaemonism or the categorical imperative.

But Barth's critique of a fundamental interpretive judgment cannot stop short of critiquing any act of ethical interpretation, even if Barth is less explicit in this regard. Both a reading from Scripture and the matching of a general rule and a specific case rest fundamentally on interpretation. The first unavoidable, yet momentous human judgment over Scripture is so basic that it is sometimes overlooked—the choice of which biblical text to read. The choice of a particular language or translation makes a difference as well. Moreover, Barth wishes for the faithful readers of Scripture to become "contemporaneous"[312] to a particular biblical text. Unavoidably, this implies that the reader identify particular features of his or her situation and recognize them within the particular concerns of Paul or Isaiah—in a way resembling a judge who explores the extent to which a case matches with an existing legal precedent, or, in continental law, subsumes a particular case under a general rule specified by a law. Indeed, it is unclear how Barth wishes to rule out a fundamental role of human judgment when he construes the divine command in the words of Scripture as detailed instruction for a particular situation today. Roughly two thousand years and a host of historical, political, economic, linguistic, and other cultural factors constitute a marked difference between the concerns the biblical texts had when written down and the ones we might ascribe to them with regard to today's situation. Yet Barth rules out the legitimacy of general rules in ethics because "there can be no question of an appraisal or judgment by man of what is required."[313] By the same logic Barth must rule out interpretation of Scripture across the board,

311. See Nimmo, *Being in Action*, 30–31, who does not discuss Barth's explicit invectives against interpretation.
312. *CD* II/2, 701, 706.
313. Ibid., 673.

as any act of interpretation can be described as some contribution to the message of the text. Many interpretive choices of which we may be unaware are conditioned by novel cultural conditions. The individualistic focus of §38 on the very particular situation of the individual Christian comes to mind: "God confronts man in an individual and solitary relationship when He gives him His command and prohibition, and again man stands before God in an individual and solitary relationship when he has to receive this command and prohibition."[314] Further, when Barth argues that general rules do not encapsulate God's command, he not only singles out the categorical imperative or eudaemonistic ethics for critique, he also has the strict prohibitions in the Sermon on the Mount in mind. Nonetheless, Barth objects to any significant judgments on God's command on the part of the reader:

> On the contrary, [the command] establishes its own validity by asking concerning my own: whether and how far I can satisfy it and be justified and stand before it. The essence of the idea of obligation is not that I demand something from myself but that, with all that I can demand of myself, I am myself demanded.[315]

Barth draws again on his manuscript of the ethics lectures, which also argued that the unconditioned God raises the fundamental question of the legitimacy of the moral agent, thus turning the tables on the ethicist who asks for the legitimacy of God's command:

> We are asking about the unconditional when we ask unconditionally as

314. Ibid., 710. Ibid., 682 singles out the "individual" person as the addressee of God's command no less than eighteen times. Further textual references in §38 highlighting the "individual" are not difficult to find: pp. 681, 703, 705, 711, etc. The focus on individuality is inherent already in the basic constellation of the actualistic concept of revelation. It was implicit when Barth quoted his beloved phrase from Goethe in the 1920s. See Goethe, *Wilhelm Meister's Apprenticeship*: "The person whom I am to speak with, I must see, because it is a *solitary man* . . . but, on the other hand, whoever sings to me . . . it is not *spirit speaking to spirit*" (italics added by A. M.). Thus in *GD* I, 62, 225, 227, 237, 253, 308, *GD* II, 69, *GD* III, 415, *MD* 88, 511, 578.

315. Ibid., 651.

> we do not do in general and theoretical asking, i.e., when our asking expresses the basic acknowledgment that we *are asked*. We see it as the question of the origin that precedes all being when we see it as being prior in order to the questions of our general and theoretical thinking.[316]

As a result, it is unclear how Barth's explicit invectives against Scriptural interpretation could be restricted to interpretations governed by ethical schemes such as the Categorical Imperative or eudaemonism.

How then does §38.2 envision moral discernment in reading Scripture? The theological vision from which Barth seeks to derive guidance is that of a humble, plain, and faithful human commitment to God's word, rather than a subjection of the biblical text to crude, mechanistic routines—as the subsumption of a case under general rules may have appeared to Barth. A humble concern for hearing God's word will eventually coincide with the self-evident reality of the commandment that God imparts out of sheer grace. Since Scripture interprets itself, the reader does not need to—and must not—contribute to the emergence of God's command.[317] Barth wishes to convey this vision in an eighteen-page small print interpretation of the Decalogue and the Sermon on the Mount.[318] When the secondary literature asserts the legitimacy of some form of scriptural interpretation in §38.2, it is typically with a view to this section. Barth argues that the general rules these two texts provide are not intended as commandments.[319] The Decalogue and the Sermon on the Mount merely summarize, Barth argues, the broad lines in accordance with which the command in Scripture will be issued

316. Barth, *Ethics*, 65.
317. Although Luther called Scripture *sui ipsius interpres* (its own interpreter), this by no means excludes the reader's interpretation for Luther.
318. *CD* II/2, 683–700.
319. The case these texts make is, according to Barth, the purely formal paradigmatic portrayal of the individual human person as standing before God, who addresses him or her—through other texts—with an absolute, definite command.

in other texts. Such broad lines may offer preliminary assistance in attending to God's command, but they are not specific and definite in the way God's command itself is. If Barth in fact arrives at this conclusion in establishing a mode of understanding that does not do violence to the text, but allows the text to let its own light shine, then this might render his categorical critique of human judgment on God's command understandable.

If the Sermon on the Mount and the Decalogue merely wish to convey the general human situation before God rather than to make a specific practical point, it constitutes a fundamental difficulty that they do so at least with a certain degree of specificity. In contrast to first impressions, the commandments of the Decalogue are fairly specific. They address free, land-owning adult male heads of families who participate in the legal and religious institutions of society.[320] That the prohibition of physical violence in the Sermon on the Mount is simply categorical does not mean it is unspecific. These texts may not always be tailored toward very particular, individual situations. But they clearly do forbid or command particular sorts of behavior. It is thus unclear why the texts at hand can be categorically subjected to the idea that God's command must explicitly reflect, by definition, the concrete situation of a particular individual. Moreover, the scale of the potential specificity in the fit between the text and the reader's situation is open-ended, as there is no limit to the detail within which the concrete human context of moral discernment can be described. What degree of specificity must a text exhibit precisely in order to be judged appropriate for conveying God's command?

320. Phyllis Bird, "Images of Women in the Old Testament," in *Religion and Sexism: Images of Women in the Jewish and Christian Traditions*, ed. Rosemary Radford Ruether (New York: Simon & Schuster, 1974, Eugene: Wipf & Stock, 1998), 41–88, at 49–50. Since almost all of these criteria applied to Barth himself, he may have been as unaware of them as a fish is of water. Nonetheless, his view that the Decalogue issues "general" commands constitutes a significant interpretive judgment.

The specificity of God's command can exclude ambiguity, contributing to the evident nature of a statement. The experience of an evident nature, however, is already an interpretation by itself, even if subconsciously so.[321] A state of affairs is obvious to the degree that it rests not only on perception, but also that it is in harmony with other perceptions and convictions in the absence of indications to the contrary. Even sense perception and a supposedly intuitive, prereflexive grasp of a statement are an interpretation.

There is also reason to assume that Barth's interpretation of the Decalogue and the Sermon on the Mount is influenced to a high degree by the long-standing political positions that Barth had already been advocating for several years. Many generations of Christians had construed these two texts, especially the Sermon on the Mount, in a pacifist sense. While in Switzerland conscription had existed at least since the creation of the federal state in 1848, there had also been a strong Christian influence among Swiss conscientious objectors. While ninety-two Swiss men were sentenced to prison for refusing military service between 1930 and 1939, in 1940 alone the number was at forty-six.[322] By contrast, Barth himself had signed up for the auxiliary military service, even insisting that he not be assigned a desk job, but train with a loaded rifle.[323] Although §38 argues that God gives God's command each moment anew, Barth had been consistent

321. The seemingly trivial observation that railroad tracks, for example, appear to move away from the observer into the distance is a subtle interpretation in which the human mind is not passive as it processes two-dimensional information as suggesting three dimensions. For such illustrations by Viktor von Weizsäcker, see Christian Link, "Die Erfahrung der Welt als Schöpfung: Ein Modell zum Dialog zwischen Theologie und Naturwissenschaft," in *Die Spur des Namens: Wege zur Erkenntnis Gottes und zur Erfahrung der Schöpfung* (Neukirchen-Vluyn: Neukirchener, 1997), 123–70, at 142.

322. Theodor Wyder, *Wehrpflicht und Militärdienstverweigerung: Entstehung, Gesetz, Arten und Sanktionen in der Schweizer Armee*, Europäische Hochschulschriften: Rechtswissenschaften 523, 2nd ed. (Frankfurt am Main et al.: Lang, 1988), 61–2; Christian Koller, "Der Lange Weg zum 'zivilen Ersatzdienst' in der Schweiz," in *Ich dien' nicht! Wehrdienstverweigerung in der Geschichte*, ed. Dierk Walter and Christian Th. Müller (Berlin: Winter, 2008), 227–42.

323. Busch, *Barth: His Life from Letters*, 306–7.

in advocating a particular political stance for several years. For at least four years previously, Barth had argued that the response to any Nazi act of military aggression must be armed resistance, rather than the pacifism of the Sermon on the Mount and the Sixth Commandment. It would thus appear that fear of high-handed judgment on biblical texts and attention to a highly specific command in a particular situation were probably not the primary motives for Barth's assertion that the Decalogue and the Sermon on the Mount are not themselves vehicles of God's command.

It should also be noted that Barth's criterion of a specific command directed to a specific individual situation excludes more than just the Decalogue and the Sermon on the Mount from the biblical candidates for vehicles of God's command. His insistence on the concrete situation of the individual rules out the large group of legal commands, for example.[324] Numbers 15:15–16, Lev. 24:22, 19:33–4 do not summon many people individually to grant the same rights to resident aliens, but demand the collective implementation of legal rules within a society. The constituent members of society cannot consult whether every individual has received the identical command whenever the equal rights of a resident alien are at stake. Later, Barth went on to question the fundamental restriction of ethics to an individual ethics, or the fundamental separation of "individual and social ethics."[325] He also critiqued the notion of a highly specific biblical commandment: "It is only infrequently . . . that [the New Testament writings] speak relatively concretely."[326] In chapter 8, however, the emphasis is on the concrete, individual command that

324. See also *CL*, 34: with reference to *CD* II/2, Barth asserts that in principle, ethics cannot foresee what God would command. In keeping with this undifferentiated, categorical form, no act could be ruled out categorically as contrary to God's command, such as involuntary euthanasia or nuclear warfare. Another difficulty lies in how we know which acts God has provided a commandment for and which are too trivial.

325. *CD* III/4, 465.

326. *CD* IV/2, 374.

must not be interpreted, that is, rendered dependent on human judgment.

This suggests that it is Barth who is making a less than straightforward, fundamental judgment about biblical texts. Nonetheless, he wishes to refute the hypothesis that God's authoritative command is issued in the Decalogue and the Sermon on the Mount.

In Barth's eighteen-page small-print interpretation of the Sermon on the Mount and the Decalogue, it is instructive to consider his statements about the Holy Spirit, which in §38.2 are highly concentrated at the end of this particular section. Of the fifteen references to the Spirit that occur in the forty-eight pages of §38.2, no less than eleven occur in about two pages of small print.[327] Christians can hear God's commandment only through the Spirit's guidance. In accordance with the Spirit's instruction, God's command "is as little foreshown in the Sermon [on the Mount] as in the Ten Commandments, and as far as the biblical witness is concerned, will have to be taken from other parts of the Old and New Testaments."[328]

Barth overwhelmingly portrays the divine activity as a hierarchical power relation, at the top of which is, according to *CD* II/2, the Spirit, or according to the wider context, Christ. The Spirit is said to "control," "rule," "impel," and "govern" readers of Scripture.[329] This is in keeping with a statement that explicitly excludes human participation in the work of the Holy Spirit: the "elucidation and application of the Word of the Sermon [on the Mount] . . . will *not* be their own concern *but* that of the Holy Spirit."[330] At this point, Barth

327. *CD* II/2, 698–700.

328. Ibid., 699 (trans. rev.).

329. Ibid., §38.2, 699. In addition, the unilateral control of the Holy Spirit ("Ausgießung . . . und ... Regiment": "outpouring . . . and . . . governing") is not captured by the translation.

330. Ibid. (emphasis added).

is thinking of the Holy Spirit and human agency in competitive terms. Thus §38.2 attributes exclusive control over the interpretive process to God.

However, this unilateral, hierarchical relation is at odds with the overall theological tenor of Barth's small print discussion *CD* II/2 (pp. 698–700). On occasion it is even in clear contrast to it. Barth depicts the Christian search for guidance as a strenuous, precarious affair. It depends on a constant, "tireless asking, seeking and knocking."[331] In just over two pages, Barth speaks of "asking, seeking and knocking" three times.[332] Thus, human cooperation plays a crucial role in coming to know the commandment. The congregation will even "have to recognise the voice of the Holy Spirit and to distinguish it from the voices of other spirits."[333]

Insisting categorically that God's command is not issued in the Decalogue and the Sermon on the Mount, Barth may seem to be "controlled" and "governed" by the Holy Spirit, but this complete certainty is something other than a "tireless asking, seeking and knocking." In addition, does the Spirit "control" the readers of Scripture or are Christians, by contrast, charged with the responsibility of judging which spirit is the Holy Spirit? Does the discerning reader depend on the Spirit, or does the effective working of the Spirit depend on the reader's judgment about the Spirit? Barth articulates the matter in terms of this binary. How do readers know they are choosing the Holy Spirit if indeed the question is whether to affirm or to reject the "spirit" of a particular interpretation of Scripture? Moreover, how can the discernment of spirits guide the

331. Ibid., 695.

332. Ibid., 695–6. Inspired by the Sermon on the Mount, the image is from Barth's early essay "Unerledigte Anfragen an die Theologie (1920)," in *Vorträge und kleinere Arbeiten 1914–1921*, ed. Hans-Anton Drewes, Barth-Gesamtausgabe (Zurich: Theologischer Verlag, 2012), 622–62, at 637: according to the Bible, Christians must ask God for an inspiration similar to that of Socialism; they must "hunger and thirst, seek, ask and knock."

333. *CD* II/2, 695–6.

understanding of Scripture if God's particular command in any given particular text must remain unconditioned rather than be subjected to the conditioning factor of human judgment? This is the hermeneutical circle in his interpretation of the Sermon on the Mount and the Decalogue: the unconditioned character of the commanding implies that biblical texts must not be made dependent on human interpretive judgment, but to tease precisely that out of the texts at hand, with Barth's concept of the individual specificity of the command intact, requires great interpretive artistry and maneuvering. The point at which Barth's hermeneutical circle ruptures, however, is the open contradiction between being controlled by the Spirit and discerning the spirits.

Eventually §38.2 no longer seeks a plausible resolution of the tension between divine unilateralism and human cooperation in understanding Scripture. In concluding §38.2 (pp. 700–8, regular print),[334] Barth undoes his ambiguous efforts in pneumatology by failing to mention the Holy Spirit at all and repeating the claim that the Bible's individual commandments must not be interpreted.[335]

Any act of interpretation would question "this definiteness" in which "the command is unconditional, leaving us no other choice than that between obedience and disobedience, . . . independently of our own views."[336] As the medium of God's command, Scripture brings us "face to face with the person of God, with the action and revelation of this person, with God Himself."[337] To safeguard the basic constellation of Barth's actualistic ethics, no interpretation must secure the human person against this confrontation and endanger

334. Ibid., 700–8.

335. Ibid., 702 ("But we also deceive ourselves . . .").

336. *CD* II/2, 669.

337. Ibid., 676. See also ibid., 682: God "will always and in all circumstances speak to each individual, and the one who is now man as the object addressed in these summaries will always and in all circumstances be face to face with God, whoever he may be."

God's authority and sovereignty in this direct encounter. If God's command is indeed highly definite, as the heading of the subsection emphasizes, if it is even a *mandatum concretissimum* ("most concrete order"), rather than merely a *mandatum concretum*,[338] then it is in the very nature of the command to defy interpretation. As a "most concrete" order, it excludes vagueness and ambiguity to a maximum degree. Any act of understanding, however, fundamentally rests on the ambiguity of symbols or signs by virtue of which, besides being themselves, they also refer to, or "stand for" entities other than themselves.

Does Barth's characterization of the command as "most concrete" thus imply that the referential relation is univocal? From a semiotics perspective, univocity is inconsistent,[339] but even apart from that, Barth's assumption that passages in Scripture convey God's command individually in very different situations through the centuries rules this out as well. Interpretation rests fundamentally on an open-ended degree of generality on the part of the signs. This is, however, what Barth wishes to rule out as he considers the command the way God makes God's self present[340] while remaining unconditioned.[341] "It is surely apparent at once that the concept of an unconditional truth of the divine command is incompletely grasped, or not properly grasped at all, if its definiteness is not taken into account."[342]

Since this discussion highlights the importance of an interpretation of God's command, which is not infallible, it is important to distinguish the argument that even the experience of an evident

338. Thus *CD* II/2, 662, 669, 670.

339. The notion of univocity rests on the structuralist code fallacy. Terrence Deacon, "The Symbol Concept," in *The Oxford Handbook of Language Evolution*, ed. Maggie Tallerman and Kathleen R. Gibson, Oxford Handbooks in Linguistics (Oxford: Oxford University Press, 2012), 393–405, esp. 394–6.

340. *CD* II/2, 669–70, 675, 676.

341. Ibid., 651, 652, 655, 656, 657, 659.

342. Ibid., 664.

state of affairs is an interpretation, from theological relativism. The opposite is the case. Realism must necessarily take into account that appearances can be true or deceiving. By contrast, to rule out fundamentally the possibility of an error in perception, as §38.2 does for hearing God's command, is Cartesianism. For Descartes, to question the reliability of clear and distinct perception is to question God.[343] For Barth, the question of God's existence is of course not an issue. What is at stake for him is the certainty that God issues a command in unambiguous terms.

In *CD* I/1, Barth had spoken out highly critically against a theological analogy to Cartesian thought, which he called "indirect Cartesianism."[344] In *CD* II/2, however, the situation has changed. As long as Christians stick to a few simple rules in reading the Bible, he denies the possibility of distorting God's word. As this section

343. René Descartes, *Meditations on First Philosophy: With Selections from the Objections and Replies*, trans. Michael Moriarty, Oxford World's Classics (Oxford: Oxford University Press, 1998), 32. See Eberhard Jüngel, *God as the Mystery of the World: On the Foundation of the Theology of the Crucified One in the Dispute between Theism and Atheism*, trans. Darrell L. Guder (Grand Rapids: Eerdmans, 1983), 116–17: "'To conceive very clearly and very distinctly' (*clare et distincte percipere*) may be taken as the criterion of certainty or of truth with regard to *all* things—*as long as it never occurs* that something conceived of in this way as clear and distinct should prove to be false. . . . There must be a *guarantee* that that which is clearly and distinctly conceived of cannot be proven false. This guarantee is provided through *doubting*. Therefore we must doubt that something clearly and distinctly conceived of cannot be proven false. This is where *God* is called into play." Doubt is fed by the awareness of human imperfection. Yet this cannot indicate an absolute imperfection, as the awareness of imperfection requires the correlate of divine perfection. Human imperfection is the driving force behind the method of doubt, and the promise of this method is based precisely on divine perfection. Descartes, *Meditations*, 32–3.

344. *CD* I/1 charges theologians who take pious feeling to be the foundation of theology with "indirect Cartesianism" (213, 217). The link between subjectivist theology and Descartes is Descartes's case for the innate idea of God (see *CD* I/1, 99–100, 211–12, Descartes, *Meditations*, 36–7), which fuels Descartes's endeavor to establish the reality of the world with the mind. Barth suggests in passing that Cartesianism is less than cogent on strictly philosophical terms (*CD* I/1, 195). On the theological side, *CD* I does not offer a match for the absolutely certain knowledge pursued by Descartes, as Barth argues that *divine revelation* is in danger of distortion and violation as such, even if Scripture will ultimately impose itself. *CD* I/2, §21 and Barth's previous hermeneutical remarks did not merely reflect the political and ecclesial turmoil of the times, but were indeed developed in parallel to the danger and risk that God accepted in the incarnation itself (ibid., 713).

will argue later on, this constitutes a significant change of mind in comparison with the hermeneutical position Barth took in *CD* I/1 and *CD* I/2, which considered the possibility of a serious distortion of God's word inherent in the incarnation itself.[345] In *CD* II/2, however, to doubt God's command or to cast it in ambiguous terms is to question fundamentally God's authority. God's lordship rules this out categorically.

In turn, when Barth invokes God's lordship especially vigorously, as he does at the end of §38.2 (see below) and at other places, it is worth examining an indirectly Cartesian motivation. As Descartes, in the face of radical doubt, tried to secure the continuity of the subject, whose clear and distinct perception he considered ineluctable,[346] so Barth tries, even if in an extreme situation and by extreme measures, to secure the moral agent—to be sure not by a foundationalist understanding of innate ideas or a general human pious sentiment, but by means of a particular understanding of divine revelation. As God, metaphysically conceived, safeguards human knowledge according to Descartes, so a strong sense of God's authority and power safeguards the reliability of God's command according to Barth.[347] *CD* II/2 chapter 8 protects this guarantee of Christian moral agency through heavy warnings of hubris and apostasy. Both in Descartes's and Barth's account, the unconditioned character of God safeguards the human stance vis-à-vis the world, allowing for

345. See, e.g., *CD* I/1, 106, *CD* I/2, 681, 684, 713. For further details, see below.

346. Descartes's reference to God secures the continuity of the ego, which is in danger as soon as radical doubt is directed not at the *cogito* of the very self, but at its recognition of something external. See Jüngel, *God as Mystery*, 112–16.

347. That Barth's notion of God is sometimes of a decidedly metaphysical character during this period can also be seen from a statement in *CD* II/1 (634–5) that criticizes the theology of *Rom* II as one-sided, but takes pains to specify God's relation to time in strictly exclusive terms (*CD* II/1, 631): "The conceptions of God's pre-temporality, supra-temporality, and post-temporality have all to be emphasised in their different ways. But they are not to be played off the one against the other, as if God could be better known and were to be taken more seriously under one of these forms and less so or not at all under another." See also *CD* II/1, 608.

absolute certainty. In turn, both *CD* II/2 chapter 8 and Descartes rule out that God—with regard to the incarnation in Barth's case—accepts fundamental risk and danger.

The plain perception of the command must neither be doubted nor obstructed by a high-handed act of human judgment. Barth boils down questions about the content of the command to the question of obedience or disobedience. Hence Barth's harsh, categorical pronouncement:

> We have vindicated ourselves as judges, i. e., as interpreters of that law, justifying our own will in the concrete situation. Strictly speaking, a general, formal, abstract command is not a command at all. . . . In this conception far too much devolves upon those who, in relation to a real command, can only be regarded as obedient or disobedient. . . . Whatever else it may be, a command whose truth is conditioned in this way is *no* command![348]

While *CD* II/2 chapter 7 singles out Jesus Christ as the divine determination of God's self, chapter 8 maintains that God gives God's self to be known every moment afresh. But why does Barth assign such prominence to the unconditioned nature of the word of God in chapter 8 after chapter 7 argued that God determined God's self to be conditioned by the creature in Christ?

In a nutshell, a likely reason why Barth attached such prominence to the unconditioned nature of God's word in 1942 is the fact that the deliberative, public realm of the Protestant churches in Switzerland and Germany required by his previous hermeneutical discussions had since become utterly perverted and corrupted. In 1938, in *CD* I/2, Barth already developed his biblical hermeneutics against the backdrop of the nationalist, racist crisis in the church.[349] His earlier

348. *CD* II/2, 664–5 (trans. rev.).

349. "To-day we have to defend against barbarians, and at the same time and above all to realise ourselves, the contingence of the divine revelation, that is, *in concreto*, the revelational character of the Old Testament on the one hand, and on the other, the independence of the Church and

section "The Word of God in Its Threefold Form," *CD* I/1, §4 (1932), had conceded that even the church's interpretation can do "violence" to the Bible. Ultimately, in being interpreted, the Bible itself must and will defend itself "against the encroachments of individual or total periods and tendencies in the Church."[350] Barth explained in a deft allusion to the incarnation, "Now, since God's Word in Scripture has taken the form of a human word, it has entered into the need of such interpretation. Our human responsibility is related to this need of interpretation."[351] It is for this deeply christological reflection that Barth's earlier discussions of biblical interpretation in *CD* I/1 (1932) and I/2 (1938) are much more in keeping with the later doctrine of election *CD* II/2, chapter 7 (1942) than the way *CD* II/2 chapter 8 envisions the absolute God using Scripture to convey God's absolute command. Speaking with a characteristic phrase of "GL" and *CD* II/2, chapter 7, Barth asks what will become of God's word once it has been given into the hands of sinners.

CD I had maintained that eventually, God's word will impose itself upon the readers and emerge victorious. For this end, however, it is necessary that Christians make interpretive decisions and judgments about the message of the Bible. If these turn out to be harmful, the properly theological question is not *if* they will be corrected, but *when*. The one thing that must not happen, by contrast, is that Christians abstain from interpretive judgments.

Thus Barth provides a remarkable interpretation of the classic Protestant doctrine of the properties of Scripture. With its emphasis

its message." Barth sees this in continuity with the church's historic fight against "Gnosticism" and the Reformation's defense of the gospel (*CD* I/2, 684). Barth names the fight against the "German Christians" explicitly as a fundamental concern of his theological work, ibid., 292, 611, 628–9, 654. The national prominence of the "German Christians" rose sharply in 1933.

350. *CD* I/1, 106.

351. *CD* I/2, 713 (trans. rev.).

on the sufficiency, perspicuity, and self-imposition of Scripture, the doctrine of the properties of Scripture[352] has argued, among other things, that Scripture can be understood by laypeople, that a privileged magisterium is neither necessary nor helpful, and that no special, extraordinary human efforts or powers are necessary for a faithful Christian life to result from plain attention to Scripture. Crucially, this concept of Scripture is inclusive of human interpretive efforts.

The nationalistic crisis in the German churches forced Barth to interpret the classic Protestant doctrine of Scripture in a striking way (*CD* I/2, §21). God's revelation is in fact impugned and disputed. To disregard this crisis would have meant to sacrifice the realism of revelation. Hearing the Christian proclamation would not necessarily result immediately, or even for a certain amount of time, in a faithful Christian life. This is indeed likely once the German Christians had thoroughly perverted Christian proclamation. If, however, God's revelation in Scripture is bound to remain victorious nonetheless, there was a special divine promise for the vigorous fight against the German Christians.

Unfortunately, the English translation distorts Barth's case when he argues that Scripture is to some degree, but certainly not entirely, exposed to human caprice and distortion. The passage should read,

> Why should it not be the case often [*auch immer wieder*] that the prophets and apostles are heard directly in the interpretation which the hearers themselves are enabled to give? And why should they not often [*auch immer wieder*] be in a position to offer an explanation themselves?[353]

The English translation, by contrast, misconstrues Barth's colloquial

352. On *sufficientia, perspicuitas,* and *efficacia* among the *affectiones Scripturae,* see Otto Weber, *Foundations of Dogmatics,* trans. Darrell L. Guder (Grand Rapids: Eerdmans, 1982), 1:278–86. The properties of Scripture include *auctoritas* as well.

353. *CD* I/2, 713 (trans. rev.: *KD* I/2, 799).

expression "*auch immer wieder*" (often, pretty much always)[354] as "always." Yet Barth concedes that there are even "ages and situations in which we perhaps have to speak more of the suffering than the effective working of God's Word—of its neglect and rejection, its non-recognition and distortion."[355]

After *CD* I/2 appeared early in 1938,[356] however, the "German Christian" crisis reached a climax in the same year after the leading circles of the Confessing Church decided to affirm an oath of allegiance to Hitler.[357] Already before, Barth had called the Confessing Church "a barely flickering light."[358] Now, however, he commented in anger that in Germany, a proper confession of faith could only be maintained precisely in opposition to the Confessing Church.[359] In the summer term of 1939, Barth devoted a seminar to the relations between the German Protestant Churches to the National Socialist regime.[360] So if indeed the last remaining theologically defensible foothold of the Reformation tradition in Germany has thus discredited itself, can one hear God's revelation at all in the German Protestant churches? And does this not invalidate core assumptions with which the Protestant doctrine of the properties of Scripture defended the Reformation? Can Christians put their

354. In particular situations, "auch immer wieder" can mean "(strictly) always." However, if it did so in this case, it would not make sense for Barth to say, "Holy Scripture [has] the *facultas semetipsam interpretandi* [ability to interpret itself] which at any rate means the power sooner or later to throw off every foreign sense attributed to it" (*CD* I/2, 681–2).

355. Ibid., 684. The epochs Barth names are the church's fight against Gnosticism, the Reformation, and the current fight against the Deutsche Christen.

356. Busch, *Barth: His Life from Letters*, 285. The publishing house Kaiser in Munich had just been forbidden to print Barth's books.

357. Ibid., 288 f. Busch (ibid., 272–3) notes Barth's increasing criticism of the Confessing Church after 1935.

358. Ibid., 273. See also Shelley Baranowski, "The Confessing Church and Antisemitism: Protestant Identity, German Nationhood, and the Exclusion of the Jews," in *Betrayal: German Churches and the Holocaust*, ed. Robert P. Ericksen and Susannah Heschel (Minneapolis: Fortress Press, 1999), 90–109.

359. Busch, *Barth: His Life in Letters*, 288 (trans. rev.).

360. Ibid., 292–3.

hope in God indeed, and does God's word offer any guidance for faithful action?

In addition, the German occupation of Europe had happened with such breathtaking rapidity that Barth's preface to *CD* II/2 from March 1942[361] makes a point of mentioning that he found himself on duty in the barracks of the Swiss army while correcting the galley proofs. He had presumably finished the manuscript during the preceding winter term, which began at the same time that Stalin and his Defense Committee fled from the German attack on Moscow, only to return aghast upon seeing that the chaos in the city was even worse than they feared.[362]

In 1938, half a year after the publication of *CD* I/2, Barth had publicly called on the Czech population to take up arms against Hitler, for theological reasons.[363] Leading circles of the Confessing Church promptly declared their disagreement with Barth formally.[364] A few days after that, the Munich agreement pushed forward the agenda of appeasement. While Germany celebrated Hitler as an advocate for peace, Barth wrote in his diary, "Catastrophe for European freedom in Munich."[365] Barth finished the manuscript of *CD* II/1 (published in 1940) at about the time that Germany invaded Poland (September 1939).[366] But even when France and Great Britain declared war on Germany in response, the Allied forces did not engage in significant military operations against Germany for another six months.[367]

361. Ibid., 315.
362. Beevor, *The Second World War*, 236–7.
363. Barth, "Brief an Prof. Dr. Josef L. Hromádka, Prag, 1938," in *Offene Briefe 1935–1942*, ed. Diether Koch, Barth-Gesamtausgabe (Zurich: Theologischer Verlag, 2001), 107–33, at 114: "Every Czech soldier who then fights and suffers will do so also for us—and today I am saying so without reservations: he will do so also for the church of Jesus Christ, which in the sphere of Hitler's or Mussolini's influence can only become either a laughing stock or be wiped out."
364. Busch, *Barth: His Life from Letters*, 289.
365. Ibid.
366. Ibid., 292.

In Barth's lectures and seminars, class size shrank considerably as many Swiss students were in active military service.[368] In spring 1940, Barth himself signed up voluntarily for the Swiss auxiliary military, training with the troops occasionally but regularly, keeping his helmet, uniform, a rifle, and a bayonet at the ready even in his civilian bedroom.[369] He also joined two civilian societies strengthening the Swiss defense effort.[370] Clearly, he perceived the situation as dire when the very first paragraph of the preface in *CD* II/2 comments explicitly, if with grim humor, on the 'Third Reich' and the struggle within the German churches.

In addition, the danger was not merely of an external kind. Barth's urgent call to attend to God's contingent command took place at the same time that the Swiss authorities had suspended the secrecy of letters and telecommunications with regard to Barth.[371] They engaged in censorship in general as well as with regard to Barth, in part due to direct German prompting.[372] Germany's Ministry of Foreign Affairs confirmed internally in June 1941 that Switzerland had dropped its economic neutrality vis-à-vis Germany. Barth knew that Switzerland helped refinance the German war effort.[373] All in all, it seemed that Barth was on to something when he argued in 1938 that "the church of Jesus Christ . . . in the sphere of Hitler's or Mussolini's influence can only become either a laughing stock or be wiped out."[374]

367. Beevor, *The Second World War*, ch. 3.
368. Busch, *Barth: His Life from Letters*, 299.
369. Ibid., 305–6. Barth's active duty was all in all limited to 104 days. Deemed unfit for service at age nineteen, he was now fifty-four.
370. Ibid., 307.
371. Busch, *Unter dem Bogen*, 341.
372. Ibid., 339 (Swiss censorship and collaboration with Germany early in 1941); Busch, *Barth: His Life from Letters*, 305.
373. Busch, *Unter dem Bogen*, 338; See Emil Brunner's letter to Barth from July 9, 1941, and Barth's reply from July 12, 1941, in *Karl Barth—Emil Brunner: Briefwechsel 1916–1966*, ed. Eberhard Busch, Barth-Gesamtausgabe (Zurich: Theologischer Verlag, 2000), 312–15, 316–19.
374. Barth, "Brief an Hromádka," 114.

In sum, when the disarray of the German churches had left its mark on the scriptural hermeneutics of *CD* I in 1932 and 1938, Barth had conceded that the German churches might perhaps be in one of the epochal "ages . . . of the suffering . . . of God's Word."[375] However, the advance of Nazi Germany had continued even after that, and while this meant—by the standards of *CD* I §§4, 21—that the self-assertion of God's word would become even less likely, this was also the situation in which the self-assertion of God's word mattered more than ever. It seems that the unfolding political and ecclesial events had proceeded to such a degree that Barth's revisions to traditional scriptural hermeneutics in the face of current events had reached a dead end. An about-face was called for if he still wanted to account for the current, abiding power of God's word in a realistic way.

Due to the dramatic climax of the crisis, Barth's biblical hermeneutics had to be modified, circumventing the dependence of God's word on human interpretation. In 1938, Barth argued that in interpreting Scripture, humans must open the door so that God's word can enter the church, even if a certain amount of chaos and confusion would thus slip in as well. God's word itself would eventually disperse those destructive forces. In the meantime, however, the destructive forces had turned out to be a massive flood. An entire political and religious system was making dramatic headway in its all-out rebellion against God's gracious command. With the Confessing Church waving the white flag, even those willing to undertake the labor of attending to the powerful self-imposition of God's word have entered into a pact with the forces of confusion. After Barth, in 1932, had warned of the "constant danger that the Bible will be taken prisoner by the Church,"[376] this seemed to have come true for the German churches ten years later.

375. Ibid., 684.
376. *CD* I/1, 106.

In 1942, Barth's argument for the unassailable absoluteness of God's word fleshed out a development that had already begun two years earlier. In *CD* II/1, Barth struck a new tone in answering the question of what happens to God's word if given into the hands of sinners. *CD* II/1 (1940) argued that believers can readily avoid the dangers of human encroachment on God's word. Barth strongly asserted that all distortion is put to an absolute end when we are convicted of the truth of God's revelation in a way that is *zwingend*, "excluding any doubt."[377] On a single page, *CD* II/1 highlights the compelling (*zwingend*) character of God's self-revelation no less than six times, in a way to which the English translation fails to do full justice.[378] By contrast, on a merely subjectivist basis we are "not led to the indisputable and definitive knowledge" of God for which Barth is looking.[379] His doubting is even more radical than Descartes's. Descartes asked if even subjective experience might be an illusion. He put an end to this doubt with the argument that subjective doubt cannot doubt itself. Proceeding onward from there to external entities, Descartes asked if the experience of reality was perhaps the work of a "deceitful God."[380] He negated this question in arguing for God as the metaphysical warrant of reality. Barth, by contrast, despaired of autonomous human subjectivity in his quest for absolute certainty about God. But especially against the backdrop of what *CD* I had said about the danger of distorting God's word inherent in biblical hermeneutics, Barth's search for absolutely unassailable knowledge in *CD* II is remarkably similar to Descartes's:

> Thus and only thus, in this *clarity and certainty* [*Klarheit und Gewissheit*,

377. *CD* II/1, 45–7.
378. *KD* II/1, 50: 473 words, no small print on this page. *CD* II/1 uses the word "forceful," which is too weak to convey the sense of *zwingend*. *CD* II/1, 46 omits one German use of *zwingend*: "Führt er [i.e., God] ihn [i.e., den Selbstbeweis] zwingend?"
379. Ibid., 47.
380. Descartes, *Meditations*, 26.

> i.e., as imparted by God] and in no other. . . . And *the clarity and certainty* in which we know Him are His and not ours. . . . We cannot understand anything at all in this matter except as deriving from God . . . neither the order in which it happens nor the fact that it happens in that *indisputable clarity and certainty*.[381]

The parallel to Descartes's endeavor becomes even clearer when Barth holds on quite resolutely to the necessity of well-founded subjective insight, contrasting insight with mere human decisionism. God's *absolutely compelling* self-revelation is both available and cogent for anyone who dares to expose to doubt the human relation to the world. "We thus need to ask ourselves whether it is true or not that He who speaks here is the One to whom we are indebted for everything, and still owe everything."[382] Whenever a human person asks this question, God's self-revelation will put an end to all human evasion.

The crucial divine attribute seems to be divine efficacy. The following discussion will argue that that is also the case in *CD* II/2, §38.2.[383] Indeed Barth seeks to fortify his case in *CD* II/1 with a truly remarkable, vigorous evocation of God's lordship. Among the 580 words on *CD* II/1, 47, the word *lord* occurs no less than twenty-two times, and the section pp. 45–8 (2,125 words)[384] almost keeps up this pace, with fifty-nine occurrences of the words *lord*/*lordship*.[385] This is despite the fact that the first sentence of this section, "But God speaks in His Word about Himself as the Lord" is demonstrably an inadequate characterization of Scripture.[386]

381. Ibid., 40, italics by A. M. Descartes himself holds human cognition accountable to the standard of *clare et distincte percipere*.
382. Ibid., 47 (trans. rev.).
383. See below on *CD* II/2, 705.
384. *CD* II/1, first full paragraph on p. 45 to the last full paragraph on p. 48.
385. Ibid., 47.
386. Ibid., 48. In the so-called books of history from Genesis to Job, God is not even once portrayed as calling God's self *Lord*. On the whole, the designation *Lord* for God occurs only thirty-one

Barth's interaction with Cartesianism during this period is also visible in his work on the theology of creation, which he began in the summer of 1942 (published as *CD* III/1 in 1945).[387] Barth argues that if it were not for the Christian faith in the Creator, our experience of reality might just as well be an illusion. Fergus Kerr has drawn attention to the fact that this constitutes a new take on the issue of Cartesianism as discussed explicitly in *CD* I.[388] Descartes, after all, argued that the experience of reality is not an illusion on account of God. While *CD* I/1 suggested in passing that Cartesianism might not be compelling even on merely philosophical grounds, Barth now assumes that Descartes's problem of doubt is even more trenchant than the French philosopher thought himself, for whom the existence God as a warrant of reality was a matter of a few simple deductions.[389] Barth conceives of Cartesian doubt in even more radical terms than Descartes did, while he agrees with Descartes's framing of the question insofar as he seeks absolute certainty and considers God as providing a readily available, absolute guarantee of the integrity and consistency of human knowledge. This is remarkable especially in comparison with the risk and danger that is, according to the biblical hermeneutics of *CD* I, implicit in the view of Scripture as witness to God's revelation in Christ.

It is thus in keeping with Barth's argument in *CD* II/1 that *CD* II/2, chapter 8 suggests a simple rule that safeguards certainty about God's true command, which is in sharp contrast to the danger that

times there, so it is practically irrelevant in comparison with the proper name *YHWH*, which the Pentateuch uses more than one thousand times. See above n28.

387. Busch, *Barth: His Life from Letters*, 315.

388. Fergus Kerr, OP, "Cartesianism according to Karl Barth," *New Blackfriars* 77 (1996): 358–68, at 365. Kerr argues that even philosophically, there is no need for external safeguards for the reality of the world (ibid., 368).

389. What is less clear in Kerr's essay is that the Cartesian aspects in *CD* III/1 are not congruent with Cartesianism proper, or even indirect Cartesianism, insofar as Descartes not only raises, but also refutes the Cartesian doubt by means of innate ideas.

the church take the Bible "prisoner" (*CD* I). If previously, in taking on the precarious task of interpreting Scripture, Christians needed to open the church door from inside so that God's word could enter, *CD* II/2 argues that there has never been a door that required opening in the first place. As Christians barely lay their hands on the doorknob, the word of God enters even through a closed door. There is thus no reason to lose faith in the very possibility that Christians can hear God's word, even if in a confused culture undermined by fascism, the Bible may appear to have been "taken prisoner by the Church."[390] It is not as if God had broken God's promise for those who attend to God's revelation.

By contrast, in the self-imposition of God's word, there is no room for true human cooperation that involves an interpretive judgment on the biblical text. Appearances suggest that the creaturely forces on which God's word might depend are in disarray, but in fact God's word has never depended upon them in the first place. Barth's categorical, vehement insistence on the reality and power of God's word are meant to project vigorously the message that God's word cannot be trifled with. Human subjectivist factors can never provide truth and certainty anyway. By contrast, God's powerful self-revelation provides absolute, unassailable certainty about the divine truth, independently of any human judgment. In contrast to the bleak appearances, opposition to Nazi Germany and the German Christians is not a lost cause. The only crucial thing is clear individual obedience to God's clear command.

After §§36–7 sought to base the omnipotence and authority of the command in a theology of conscience, §38 disputes the crucial importance of the active subject of recognition that is unavoidable in a theology of conscience. If the omnipotence and authority of the

390. Thus the danger Barth warns of in 1932: *CD* I/1, 106.

command are still maintained, however, this puts the priority of the gospel in peril. While §§36–7 argued that there is no such thing as sheer authority, §38.2 asserts the opposite, contradicting the answer that §37.2 gave to the question of how God's commandment achieves its omnipotence. In contrast to a priority of the gospel to the law, Barth now asserts an absolute commandment: "Its validity must then consist in the fact that the very question of its validity is taken out of my mouth, out of my mind, and out of my heart."[391]

This would locate the obligatory force of the command in its alien character and its power to impose itself, not in the gospel. This clear expression of heteronomy is again strongly reminiscent of the ethics lecture, which argues that authority is "something which fundamentally and supremely is alien, which cannot be translated or appropriated, but only acknowledged."[392] "Where man is negated, there is *iustitia* [justice, righteousness]."[393] Barth's vigorous insistence on the absolute, unconditioned authority of the command removes a criterion that would distinguish the command of the gospel from a totalitarian command.

Since §38 contradicts the priority of the gospel to the law, the question arises what else will now claim the place otherwise held by the gospel and where theological ethics should now find guidance. The subsection 38.2 makes a case for an abstract notion of totality and omnipotence. Especially the end of §38.2 is characterized by a vigorous assertion of God's constant efficiency, authority, and rule. On p. 705, this climaxes in a rhetorical intensity that may well be unrivaled in *CD*.[394] The rhetorical vigor of the passage in the German

391. *CD* II/2, 651 (trans. rev.).
392. Barth, *Ethics*, 355.
393. Ibid., 284 (trans. rev.).
394. Barth's urging is played out also on the rhetorical level of *CD* II/2, 705: In 566 words (no small print), Barth speaks ten times of God as *Lord/lordship*, eleven times of God's "work/working," no less than five or six occurrences of which speak of God in "fulfilment of (t)his work." Five times the words *act/action* is used. In the German edition, Barth speaks three times of a "handing

original is to some extent lost in translation. In German, the section corresponding to pp. 705–7 (regular print) contains no less than thirty-three cases of increased letter spacing, twelve of which are in the text to which p. 705 corresponds. The fact that this page—which Barth may well have proofread in the army barracks—uses the authoritarian term *Befehl* (order) three times instead of his typical, biblical *Gebot* is not evident from the use of "command" in both cases in the English translation. This page heightens the supposed objectivity of God's order using the term *Befehlsausgabe*, a handing out of orders, three times. Ten times this one page calls God *lord* or attributes lordship to God. The recipients of the orders cannot avoid obeying, even if they "fail to bend their backs."[395] Barth highlights the comprehensive character of the realm subjected to God's authority with multiple repetitions of the words *each*, *whole*, *every*, and *all* and a repeated use of contrasts that God's reign encompasses.[396] Barth calls God not only "Lawgiver and Judge,"[397] but also highlights divine retribution:

> For the Lord in fulfilment of this work is the Lord of the *whole* world and—whether He is recognised or not recognised, loved or not loved, honoured or not honoured—the Lord of *each* individual life, who is

out of orders." The English translation uses *command* nine times, including three cases where *order* would be the appropriate translation. God is called *judge* twice. Barth also uses the words *instruction* (twice), *decree* (once), and *decision* (once). In addition, the English translation omits one German use of *Anweisung* ("instruction"). Barth's blanket assertions use the words *all* (seven times), *every* (five times), *whole* (twice), and *each* (once).

395. Trans. rev. They stand under the truth of God, who, we are told, is maximally powerful and universally active.

396. "Who accepts the witness of the Bible, bends before the truth of the word . . . and those who do not bend, stand nonetheless—even if failing to bend their backs—under the truth of this word." "For the Lord in fulfilment of this work is the Lord of the whole world . . . whether He is recognised or not recognised, loved or not loved, and honoured or not honoured." " . . . in the greatest things and in the smallest, openly and also in secret." Similar notions occur in Barth's ethics lecture, see "'The Great Disruption': Word of God and Moral Consciousness in Barth's Münster Ethics," in *Barth's Moral Theology: Human Action in Barth's Thought* (Edinburgh: T&T Clark, 1998), 41–63 at 63.

397. *CD* II/2, 704. Terms like *gospel*, *reconciliation*, or *mercy* are absent.

> present with *every* man at *every* time and in *every* situation in life, and confronts him as lawgiver, judge, and avenger in the greatest things and in the smallest, openly and in secret. That is the witness and voice of the Bible: God the Lord in the fulfilment of His work.[398]

No less than six times, p. 705 affirms that God is the "Lord in the fulfillment of His work." In Luther's phrase, God is the *Deus semper ubique actuosus*, the God who is active always and everywhere, who "works all in all."[399] In Barth's words, God is "working in all things, in the whole space-time multiplicity of [everyone's] existence."[400]

Barth thus ascribes the metaphysical attributes of Luther's terrifying *deus absconditus* (hidden God) to the one true God. Barth's emphasis on God's actuosity is in contrast to the traditions of God's resting on the seventh day of creation and of God's revelation in the suffering of the cross.[401] But by definition, Barth seems to assume passivity would be in contradiction to God's divinity. This concept of God is merely a maximal notion of action. In addition, any human presuppositions about what God's word could or could not reveal need to be cast aside. In keeping with this, Barth coins the "hyperlative" that it must be our "most urgent concern . . . to prepare ourselves for more total [*sic!—völligerer*] openness . . . than before, really to ask ourselves more critically than before: *what* are we to

398. Ibid., 705 (trans. rev.).

399. Luther, *Bondage of the Will*, 3:175. Luther calls the notion of a deity that is less than universally efficacious "ridiculous" (ibid., 189). On the other hand, worship of a person executed on a cross has often been considered ridiculous, too.

400. *CD* II/2, 705.

401. *CD* III/1, 214 calls the Sabbath the conclusion of creation. In resting on the seventh day, God acted in such a way that God is no longer hidden from creation, categorically distinct from the world as its creative ground. Instead, God's being itself became temporal: "When He had created the world and man, [God] *made Himself temporal and human*, i.e., He linked Himself in a temporal act with the being and purpose and course of the world" (ibid., 216, italics added according to the German original). Thus the story of creation narrates a correspondence in God's activity to God's ontological decision as construed in Barth's doctrine of election. Since a *homo semper ubique actuosus* would correspond only to the illusion of a *Deus semper ubique actuosus*, *CD* III/4, §53.1 begins the ethics of creation with the command of the Sabbath rest.

do?"[402] Nonetheless, Barth says about this "lord in the fulfillment of his work," from whose command one cannot escape: "Who He is, and who man is who is subject to Him and has to obey Him, cannot be hidden here. . . . From God's side nothing at all is hidden at this point."[403]

The absolute efficacy of the omnipotent God is portrayed with so little reference to theologically substantial specifics that the concluding eight pages of §38.2 (pp. 701–8) do not mention the reality of sin, apart from the paradox that one might not subject oneself to the command of the omnipotent, universally efficacious God. This is in keeping with the way Barth speaks about God: seven times he mentions Jesus Christ, but speaks eighty times of "God." One looks in vain for terms like *Father*, *Son*, and *Holy Ghost*. Similarly, references to Jesus' incarnation and earthly ministry, or even the gospel are absent. Only at the very end does Barth gesture vaguely to Jesus' "death and resurrection."[404] This thinly veiled theism corresponds to how Barth's prohibition of scriptural interpretation robs the theological vision of these pages of any specificity, and all that is left is a vague notion of omnipotence and totality.

Barth himself is only too keenly aware that God's command appears random under these conditions. He tellingly asserts that the Bible is not merely a "register or arsenal containing all sorts of counsels, directions and commands." He takes special care to diffuse this impression, arguing that the Bible commands "not as a lottery wheel, not divided and dissolved into a multiplicity of timeless instructions and revelations of the divine will unrelated to history."[405] The biblical statements are not disparate artifacts of God's former commanding, but they are God's current commanding also today.

402. *CD* II/2, 647 (trans. rev.).
403. Ibid., 704 (trans. rev.).
404. Ibid., 708.
405. Ibid., 704–5 (trans. rev.).

Faced with the search for the unity and specificity of the innumerable commandments, however, which take on new shape in innumerable new ways in many new situations, Barth does not answer with reference to the story that took place in Bethlehem, Capernaum, Gethsemane, Golgotha, and the garden of Joseph of Arimathea. The unity of the disparate commands lies in their shared point of reference, which is a theistic concept of a God. This God does no less than everything. Since this vision of God does not exclude anything, it is ultimately trivial. "God the Lord in the fulfilment of His work, who constitutes the historical unity of the Bible, is rich over all and for all, abounding in counsels and purposes for all, and working in all things, in the whole space-time multiplicity of their existence."[406]

God's unconditioned character is the crucial link between the ethics lecture and *CD* §38. The unconditioned deity, with whom the creatures cannot cooperate at all in constituting the unconditioned, absolute command, is not the electing God Jesus Christ who, from all eternity, forsaking his unconditioned state, chooses rejection. In him, God allows God's self to be characterized by Jesus' own story for the sake of the creature's salvation. Accordingly, the encounter with God's command in §38.2 is a fundamental challenge to the human person, but the command is not the concrete shape of the gospel, as would be required by the priority of the gospel to the law. It is the command of the absolute deity that "exposes us totally to the free air, to the total divine claim and the total questioning by God."[407]

Conclusion

Due to the rhetorical vehemence Barth musters in *CD* II/2, chapter 8, the ethics of the doctrine of God is a prime example of Barth's actualistic concept of revelation. The task of ethics consists in

406. Ibid., 705.
407. *CD* II/2, 660 (trans. rev.).

teaching that Christian ethics must listen to God's contingent command again and again. General moral rules are contrasted with Christian moral discernment. However, the actualistic concept of revelation is in contrast to the concept of gospel and law, which also plays a prominent role in *CD* II/2, chapter 8. With the actualistic revelation of God's contingent command, Barth continues on the road laid out in the ethics lectures. It is only after these lectures, at the beginning of the 1930s, however, that the concept of gospel and law gains contours as it rises to fundamental importance in Barth's thought. Jesus Christ is the essence both of the gospel and of the law, with the gospel taking precedence over the law. It is thus not a coincidence that Barth's references to the history that took place in Bethlehem, Capernaum, Gethsemane, Golgotha, and the garden of Joseph of Arimathea ("GL," §37) is absent from his discussion of the highly specific, absolute command in §38.2. By contrast, the moral obligation of the command should not be based on the sheer authority or force of the unconditioned, absolute commander, but on the gospel. In yet another peculiar conceptual twist in §§36–7, this position culminates in Barth's notion of the omnipotence of God's commanding. As the law commands freedom, humans cannot maintain any reservations about it. It is the value of natural human moral striving and the actualistic ontology that safeguard this concept. Thus, the human person will not disregard God's commandment with indifference or distorted notions of freedom.

The emphasis on God's omnipotence, however, is associated with a trivialization of Christ's suffering. The trivialization of sin is in part in harmony with an undifferentiated esteem for a natural moral striving. That the word of God is given into the hands of sinners does not play a role in §§36–7. By contrast, Barth does not see a problem in asserting that the effectiveness of God's commanding is a consequence of the release it offers from the perplexities of a 'natural' moral instinct. In turn, Jesus' passion and resurrection no longer imply a risk for God's revelation, as "GL" still assumed when it drew a parallel between Jesus being given into the hands of sinners and God's law being perverted into a mere instrument in the human striving for works righteousness.

Sections 38–9, and especially §38.2, project a different message: God's commandment executes God's judgment, which human persons must not evade with an interpretation of the command. While in §§36–7, the commandment gains leverage by being interpreted in a liberative sense, §§38–9 locates the legitimacy of the command in God's sheer authority. The validity of the command "for me must then consist in the fact that the very question of its validity is taken out of my mouth, out of my mind, and out of my heart."[408]

By contrast, Barth's doctrine of election should be understood as a decisive negation of God's absoluteness. In Christ's election from all eternity, God determines that God's self is conditioned by the creature, whose rejection Christ alone is going to bear. This roots out the notion of God's absoluteness and worldlessness fundamentally, which has characterized Barth's ethics since *Rom* II—in the sense of a negative ethics and which thus necessitated the actualistic concept of revelation. Consequently, Barth fails to follow through with his wish to conceptualize the ethics of *CD* II/2 as a true part of his dogmatics.

In spite of this fundamental critique of *CD* II/2, chapter 8, the aspect that is of abiding value is that God's command does not occur primarily in judgment, but constitutes its authority for the addressee in liberation. Its power does not rest on sheer power or sheer authority in and of itself, but on the gospel. If judgment occurs, along with liberation and transformation, it must not be in competition with the joyful character of the gospel. For there is no

408. Ibid., 651 (trans. rev.).

pure, sheer authority, just as there is no sheer, merely eternal God. The Triune God is at the same time the temporal God, who is in covenant with God's creatures from all eternity. In asking what the conditions are of the obligation imposed by a command, Barth attaches great importance to the matter of motivation. Theological ethics should learn from this that its public articulation should not rest content with mere appeals and calls for action, which easily degrades into moralism.

3

The Ethics of the Doctrine of Creation in *Church Dogmatics* III/4

The discussion of *CD* II/2, chapter 8 detected a significant contradiction between ethical actualism on the one hand and the priority of the gospel over the law or the doctrine of election on the other. The ensuing volumes of *CD* III deal with the doctrine of creation. The subvolume discussing the ethical aspects of the doctrine of creation, *CD* III/4, discusses those ethical questions that arise with regard to God's work as Creator. In part, Barth explicitly retains the actualistic concept of ethics, especially at the beginning. Yet at the same time, he engages in the discussion of empirical phenomena, which provides more general moral guidance. This is at variance with the actualistic concept of revelation, however. The contradiction has been noted before.[1] At this point, the task is to show in greater detail how the influence of actualism declines in favor of a more

1. James M. Gustafson, *Ethics from a Theocentric Perspective*, vol. 2: *Ethics and Theology* (Chicago: Chicago University Press, 1992), 26: "There are strains in the system as ethics gets elaborated."

sustainable ethical model. A closer look at how Barth discusses the issues of the Sabbath rest, the termination of a pregnancy, of killing in the name of justice, and peace ethics will ensue. The question is whether a consistent method can be detected in Barth's ethical reasoning and how empirical insights contribute to Barth's ethical judgment. The thesis is that the priority of the gospel to the law will allow for particular sensitivity to empirical circumstances of moral conflicts. Trutz Rendtorff's assertion that Barth's reordering of gospel and law tends to "deduce the ethical questions both 'from above' and 'downwards,'" thus turning a blind eye to "these conflicts that arise in life,"[2] cannot be maintained in the face of several material sections in *CD* III/4.

Looking at Barth's doctrine of creation first, it should come as no surprise that Barth does not conceive of creation in abstraction from Jesus Christ and the covenant of grace, perhaps as an interpretation of natural experience that would eventually introduce us to the deeper mysteries of the Christian faith.[3] "The fact and the way that God has acted historically cannot be mistaken in creation when we have learned to know it, as we must, in the light of the atonement, and therefore of the person and work of Jesus Christ."[4] Christ himself is the creative word. In turn, reconciliation does not derive from creation, but creation "sets the stage for the story of the covenant

Paul T. Nimmo, *Being in Action: The Theological Shape of Barth's Ethical Vision* (Edinburgh: Clark/London: Continuum, 2007), 58, concurs.

2. Trutz Rendtorff, *Ethics: Basic Elements and Methodology in an Ethical Theology*, trans. Keith Crim (Philadelphia: Augsburg Fortress Press, 1986), 62. This statement is in contrast to an earlier characterization of Barth's theology by Rendtorff: "This basic motif of a critical unmasking and destabilization of all insight possible for humans is one of the most momentous motifs in Barth's theology on the whole. It can be found in the *Church Dogmatics* throughout." Rendtorff, "Radikale Autonomie Gottes: Zum Verständnis der Theologie Karl Barths und ihrer Folgen", in *Theorie des Christentums: Historisch-theologische Studien zu seiner neuzeitlichen Verfassung* (Gütersloh: Gütersloher Verlagshaus Mohn, 1972), 161–81, at 167.
3. On Barth's doctrine of creation, see Christian Link, *Schöpfung*, vol. 1, Handbuch systematischer Theologie 7 (Gütersloh: Mohn, 1991).
4. *CD* III/1, 27.

of grace."[5] This also implies that creation is ordered toward Christ—however subtle or vague the relationship may be.[6] Creation is the "external basis of the covenant,"[7] and the covenant is the "internal basis of creation."[8] It would not say a whole lot simply to speak of a correspondence between creation and covenant, as either entity is more complex than a relation of simple agreement or disagreement would imply. To the extent that Barth's terminology implies a mutually reinforcing relationship between creation and covenant, there is certainly some kind of positive correlation, but that does not rule out ambiguity involved in creation, nor does it determine the degree to which the covenant may imply novelty over against creation.

Nonetheless, it is helpful to see that Barth already views creation as God's condescension. This is also the point of Barth's seemingly

5. Ibid., 44 ("*Raum*"). Ibid., 63: "Creation and covenant, creation and history, belong together. . . . In and with his existence man is already the object of the electing grace of God . . . the heavens and the earth were not only ordained [*bestimmt*] to be the scene [*Schauplatz*] of the operations of this gracious God, but were originally created for this purpose." Upon first glance, the purpose of creation to be a stage or a scene may seem trivial, but this takes too much for granted. For example, variation and selection are basic for Darwinian evolution, which makes this dynamic seem harsh and cruel. However, cooperation is also a fundamental principle—and for mammals, perhaps empathy is as well. Martin A. Nowak, "Five Rules for the Evolution of Cooperation," in *Evolution, Games, and God: The Principle of Cooperation*, ed. Martin A. Nowak and Sarah Coakley (Cambridge, MA: Harvard University Press, 2013), 99–114. On the whole, see Christian Link's critical comments on a potential disjunction between creation and covenant: Link, *Schöpfung: Ein theologischer Entwurf im Gegenüber von Naturwissenschaft und Ökologie* (Neukirchen-Vluyn: Neukirchener, 2012), 27.

6. To perceive creation in Christ thus also means to perceive hints at Christ in creation—even if christology is not to be deduced from the experience of nature and culture. Barth thus depicts creation in making indirect reference to Christ and imbues creation with teleology: "Here, too, we may see the curiously named object of creation—'heaven and earth' and man in their centre. *Ecce homo*! is true in this respect [John 19:15]. Here is the *Son of Man*. Here is humanity at the heart of the cosmos: with its upper and lower aspects; with its whence and its whither; over the earth but destined to come under the earth and itself to become earth; under heaven but *destined* to be above all heavens; and in both respects limited by the creative will of God and *ordered* with reference to a new heaven and a new earth" (*CD* III/1, 28, italics by A.M.).

7. Ibid., 94.

8. Ibid., 228.

arcane discussion of whether the act of creation took place in time or not.

> But how can there be any possibility or actuality of the intercourse between God and the creature, and of the establishment and commencement of this intercourse, if not by God's graciousness to His creature, by His condescension to it, by His entrance into its form of existence, by His setting out on the way alongside with it, by the utterance of His Word and the accomplishment of His work in time?[9]

In contrast to Augustine's theology of creation, according to which the act of creating itself is not temporal, Barth argues that as Creator, God does not operate in a fundamentally different mode than when God acts in carrying out the history of the covenant. Creation and covenant share both the temporality of God's action and the activity of God's word, the activity of Jesus Christ. This undercuts a schematic opposition of a supratemporal being of God as well as a supratemporal act of creation.

Since creation is the presupposition of the covenant and since it already implies God's condescending into the creature's mode of being, the meaning of the doctrine of creation is that God *grants* the creature existence and *allows* it to be, that its existence is by itself a benefit.[10] This is a positive qualification of creation as a whole and a statement of value rather than a neutral description. As a result, Barth thinks of his doctrine of creation as an endeavor differing categorically from "*every* (not only every existent, but also every conceivable) worldview,"[11] with which theology can neither be in harmony nor in tension. Barth seems to understand worldviews and

9. Ibid., 68–9 (trans. rev.). See 68 (trans. rev.): "When God creates and therefore gives reality to another alongside and outside Himself, time begins as the form of existence of this other. It is itself, of course, the creation of God. . . . But it actually begins together with His creating, so that we have to say that His creating is the ground and basis of time. But we must also say that His creating takes place *in time* and therefore has a genuine history."

10. Ibid., 330.

11. Ibid., 343 (trans. rev.).

science as playing a more modest role in their relations to particular aspects of life. He may understand worldviews as overarching modes of orientation and perception characterizing particular communities, while the operative understanding of science seems to be the description of natural processes in time based on repeated observation. From the difference between the particular orientation of science and worldviews, with their limited descriptive and pragmatic scope, and the more encompassing, fundamentally evaluative role of faith, then, the view typically emerges that there cannot be anything at stake for Barth's doctrine of creation, should it ever engage worldviews or the sciences. Barth even says so explicitly: "There can be no scientific problems, objections or aids in relation to what Holy Scripture and the Christian Church understand by the divine work of creation."[12]

This neat separation between theology and the sciences, creation and nature is correlated with Barth's radical restriction of the doctrine of creation to anthropology (*CD* III/2).

> The Word of God is concerned with God and man. It certainly gives us an ontology of man, and we shall be concerned with this in the doctrine of the creature, i.e., with the ontology of man living under heaven and on earth. But the Word of God does not contain any ontology of heaven and earth themselves.[13]

This view—which is problematic from an exegetical point of view (see, e.g., Ps. 19:2, 42:7, Job 38–41)—turns out to be an apologetical effort, although the separation between creation and nature may originally have been devised to ward off apologetics.[14]

Of course belief in God as the Creator can be neither proved nor

12. Ibid., ix.
13. *CD* III/2, 6; see 11: "the Word of God speaks of God Himself and also of man, but does not contain either directly or indirectly any disclosure about an independent being and nature of the cosmos."
14. See Wolfgang Huber, "'Nur wer die Schöpfung liebt, kann sie retten': Naturzerstörung und

disproved. But this should not be taken to mean that the theology of creation on the one hand, and science and worldviews on the other, are incommensurate tout court. It is highly significant that in the same context, Barth explicitly takes into account the possibility that other worldviews encroach on theological territory.[15] For example, as part of the doctrine of creation, Barth also goes to great lengths to discuss Heidegger and Sartre. His analysis of their 'worldviews' includes—at least in Heidegger's case—the subtle, ambiguous question whether or not they are atheists.[16] In fact, a clean distinction between faith and scientific worldview would not only presuppose an essentialist distinction between spheres as multifaceted as well as historically and culturally variable as religious belief and the sciences. Neither can interpretation in the sciences be separated from value judgments as easily.[17] Due to Barth's assumption of a categorical break between fact and value, he considers the world good regardless of how bad the state of affairs in the world may be. One may find consolation in this, but viewed from another angle, this condemns the theology of creation to irrelevance.[18] By contrast, if God's act

Schöpfungsglaube," in *Konflikt und Konsens: Studien zur Ethik der Verantwortung* (Munich: Kaiser, 1990), 176–94, at 183–4.

15. A statement like Richard Dawkins's, for example, does require demythologization—certainly not for the sake of some creationist or "Intelligent Design" theology, but for the sake of both consistency of thought and a realistic Christian faith: "The universe we observe has precisely the properties we should expect if there is, at bottom, no design, no purpose, no evil and no good, nothing but blind, pitiless indifference. . . . DNA neither cares nor knows. DNA just is. And we dance to its music." Dawkins, *River out of Eden: A Darwinian View of Life* (London: Weidenfeld & Nicolson, 1995), 133.

16. *CD* III/3, 334–49 (small print). Barth concludes the discussion with a seemingly detached dismissal of the two, while he also diagnoses an ambiguous theological concern both in Heidegger and Sartre (343). Although he ultimately considers this concern below the standard of theology proper (344–5), it is not difficult to see that, for example, Heidegger's 1929 lecture on metaphysics is closely related to a particular Lutheran theology that places great emphasis on a law that is virtually separate from the gospel and precedes it. The clear distinction between theology and worldview is not as easily maintained as Barth may at times suggest.

17. John Hedley Brooke, *Science and Religion: Some Historical Perspectives*, The Cambridge History of Science Series (Cambridge: Cambridge University Press, 1991), Introduction (1–15). Brooke understands science and religion as preliminary terms that are very hard to define, as the social realities that they are typically taken to denote are in fact very often closely intertwined.

of creation truly sets the stage for reconciliation—as weak as even this metaphor portrays the mutual interrelationship between creation and reconciliation—and if reconciliation is not merely an eternal state of affairs in some isolated heavenly realm, then such neat separating out of clear-cut spheres of fact and value is unlikely.[19] No setting of the stage is ever entirely external and peripheral to the play thus performed.

One well-known, and rightly criticized example of a mutual influence between presuppositions about creation and reconciliation in Barth's work is his interpretation of the creation of humanity in God's image, which Barth understands as the endowment of humanity with the destiny of heterosexual relationship, which again mirrors the relationship internal to God.[20] This relationality involves a particular understanding of roles within heterosexual marriage, but it will culminate in Jesus' obedience to the heavenly Father, as laid out in *CD* IV. For this reason, Barth's sexual ethics will be discussed in the next chapter. To be sure, this indicates that resonances between creation and reconciliation are a precarious affair. To be on the safe side once and for all in this question, however, would require paying a very high price. The Scylla that needs to be avoided in this issue is a fatal watering down of the novelty of revelation in Christ, as reconciliation might be reduced to the premises laid out in a doctrine of creation. The Charybdis consists in a "Docetism in the doctrine

18. Ivan Karamazov, for example, is portrayed as saying, "It's not God that I don't accept, Alyosha, only I most respectfully return him the ticket." He does not doubt God's existence, but denies that God is worthy of worship as God does not seem to make a positive difference in the world. Creation should be considered a blessing only insofar as it indeed sets the stage for reconciliation.

19. For the intricate business of interpretation in the sciences, which is hermeneutically laden with various cultural and religious assumptions, see Andreas Losch, *Jenseits der Konflikte: Eine konstruktiv-kritische Auseinandersetzung von Theologie und Naturwissenschaft*, Forschungen zur systematischen und ökumenischen Theologie 133 (Göttingen: Vandenhoeck & Ruprecht, 2011); Philip Clayton, *Explanations from Physics to Theology: An Essay in Rationality and Religion* (New Haven: Yale University Press, 1989).

20. *CD* III/1, §41.2.

of creation"[21] that is unable to see the world as anything else than a foreign counterpart to which God's revelation can only relate in the mode of invasion.

> The absolute authority and power of the divine lordship and rule in this history rest on the fact that it does not take place on soil that is originally foreign to it, but in a sphere ordained and prepared for it and for it alone from the very beginning; in the humanity and universe which are God's creation and therefore His property, and as such the object, scene [*Schauplatz*] and instrument of His acts.[22]

In Barth's doctrine of creation, there are other ways, besides the heterosexual understanding of the image of God, in which created life involves, in some particular respect, a subtle precedent about God's command. Not that it does so always, in every respect, or even in an unambiguous way, but neither is it true that it never does. Due to Barth's vision of the weak coupling between creation and covenant, a course of action that is in conflict with a mature theology of creation is likely to be in conflict with Christology as well. One example will be discussed with regard to Barth's view that the creature Jesus with his particular posture vis-à-vis God is the revelation of created humanity in general (*CD* III/2, §44, III/4, §52). Another significant precedent is that the creation of life constitutes a precedent in favor of preserving life. Even if conflicts arise about such preservation, God does not issue a command that is unrelated to or random with regard to the context of creation and the world of experience, as the discussion of *CD* III/4, §55 will argue below. Barth begins to negotiate the difficult relationship between God's contingent command and the wider scope of God's "good" creation in the section that introduces the ethics of the doctrine of creation.

21. Wolfhart Pannenberg, *Systematic Theology*, trans. Geoffrey W. Bromiley (London and New York: T&T Clark, 1992), 2:60, quoting Edmund Schlink.
22. *CD* III/1, 44.

The Introduction to Special Ethics §52: Transformation and Development in the Ethics of Creation

To begin with, it is in keeping with actualism that Barth's introductory section, "Ethics as a Task of the Doctrine of Creation" (§52), rejects "casuistry." Barth is critical of deducing God's command from known rules, biblical commands in particular, as if God's current commanding were dispensable for true moral action.[23] By contrast, Christ commands anew in every moral situation. In this, actualism involves a critique of biblicism. Nevertheless, Barth considers biblical guidance necessary. The identification of God's word and God's command with Jesus Christ refers to particular events to which biblical traditions witness. This is in tension with an ethical actualism, however, with which Barth prefaces his discussion. He explicitly repeats his view that God's command excludes human interpretation, as God's command specifies every detail of a moral question.[24] Thus, Scripture must not be interpreted, as one's own interpretation replaces direct, exclusive responsibility to God with responsibility to oneself and one's own interpretive choices, so that "the moralist wishes to set himself on God's throne."[25]

Yet even at this point, Barth's stance is ambiguous: "The way of casuistry is fundamentally unacceptable. . . . It certainly has its *particula veri* [grain of truth]."[26] Without further commentary, the special ethics in *CD* III/4 will defy the introductory critique of casuistry again and again. To be sure, Barth will write in *CD* IV/

23. On casuistry, see Nigel Biggar, *The Hastening That Waits: Karl Barth's Ethics* (Oxford: Clarendon, 1993), 37–8; 40–41; Biggar, "A Case for Casuistry in the Church," *Modern Theology* 6 (1989): 29–51, at 41: "Principles and rules do not motivate us; but they do help us to explain why we acted as we did. . . . Casuistry can just as easily be rigorist as it can be lax; and it need be neither." According to Nimmo, *Being in Action*, 52, an enduring validity of moral rules is in contrast to Barth's actualistic ontology.
24. *CD* III/4, 12.
25. Ibid., 10.
26. Ibid., 8 (trans. rev.)

2 that the Holy Spirit's instruction is not a general rule requiring interpretation.[27] But when asked about this statement, Barth replied that Christian moral reasoning must not only include prayer, but that it must also arrive at a rational, empirical argument that is consistent with the situation at hand and that lives up to the standards of a wider responsibility—making a case "we can stand by."[28] Morality must not be subverted by the caprice of a supposedly direct spiritual inspiration.

> I hope nobody understood [the statement from *CD* IV/2] thus: that some honest man or a diligent woman is sitting there, hearkening, and *zoom!* the Holy Spirit is coming, demanding absolute, concrete obedience. . . . But [the Holy Spirit] must indeed be prayed for, and when one prays for it, then . . . work is to be done. And in this case the work consists in thus engaging in political reflection . . . while being very clear: we are not in heaven, but on earth, in the as yet unredeemed world, also with this entire [political] party system. But even then we are not entirely left to our own devices. Even there, there might be a whispering of the Holy Spirit, in obedience to which we then take steps, now to the left, now to the right, aware that this will not be anything perfect, but something we can stand by. After all, that is all politics can be about.[29]

In the "as yet unredeemed world," ethical reflection includes and excludes certain options, but is faced with ambiguity as well. The danger of the illusions of an ever renewed revelation must be reduced, even when a choice is to be made between alternatives that all seem rational. For now, how one may attend to the "whispering of the Holy Spirit" remains methodologically unclear in spite of Barth's

27. *CD* IV/2, 372.
28. Barth, "Gespräch mit der Kirchlichen Bruderschaft in Württemberg (15.7.1963)," in *Gespräche 1963*, ed. Eberhard Busch, Barth-Gesamtausgabe (Zurich: Theologischer Verlag, 2005), 42–109, at 83. Whenever the footnote provides a German title for an English quotation, the translation is my own.
29. Ibid., 82–3.

insistence on reflection and responsibility. This calls for further methodological clarification.

The introduction §52 already prepares for the demise of actualism. Barth inveighs explicitly against the notion of "direct and particular divine inspiration and guidance, and [efforts] to prepare oneself, to make and keep oneself fit and ready, for the reception of such guidance, perhaps by 'quiet times' or similar exercises."[30] By contrast, the possibility of categorical judgments about God's potential command is crucial here. One of Barth's critical words on this issue in §52 is that special ethics can judge neither positively nor negatively about God's real command.[31] Contrary to initial appearances, however, Barth does not at all reject the possibility of a binding, more general judgment about God's command in Christian ethics.[32] If Barth had abided by the concept of *CD* II/2, §38, by contrast, his discussions of the death penalty, the termination of a pregnancy, or the killing of an unjust ruler in §55 would only confirm the dramatic character of God's command and of human action, resulting in the demand that human attending to God's word must be entirely unbiased. Barth would be unable to dismiss involuntary euthanasia of the elderly and of people with a handicap categorically.[33] Such discussions would not provide any guidance as to the potential content of the command, which would then be revealed—in contrast to all general moral principles—entirely independently of the human

30. *CD* III/4, 15.
31. Ibid., 17–18.
32. By contrast, Nimmo, *Being in Action*, 51–2, argues that §52 rules out any categorical judgment about the material content of the command.
33. *CD* III/4, 425. This should be kept in mind considering the oft-repeated, but erroneous notion that, according to Barth's ethics, human moral reasoning can only be preliminary and cannot offer any definite guidance. See the reference, for example, in Matthew Puffer, "Taking Exception to the *Grenzfall*'s Reception: Revisiting Karl Barth's Ethics of War," *Modern Theology* 28 (2012): 478–502, at 491.

discourse about the situation at hand. The special ethics in *CD* III/4 would thus point to the commanding, but not to the command.

By contrast, the introduction of §52 demands that "the ethical reference [*Hinweis*: guidance, pointer, advice] becomes a formed reference," even a "sharply formed" reference.[34] The guidance (*Hinweis*) that an ethics provides should be "articulated, colourful and contoured" rather than "monotonous, colourless and formless."[35] "It is not just any power or lord who here commands,"[36] but the Trinitarian God who has not remained unknown. For this reason, ethics can and must give a "sharply formed" pointer (*Hinweis*) to God's command, "a description and attestation of the command of God and the good human action corresponding to it."[37] Barth delineates an ethics that tries to achieve greater familiarity with the

34. *CD* III/4, 23, 25, 26. Barth speaks repeatedly of a "formed reference" (*geformter Hinweis*), e.g., in 23–4. On the whole, §52 speaks twice of a "sharply formed" *Hinweis* and ten times of a "formed" *Hinweis*.

35. Ibid., 17. Nimmo argues that the individual, formed reference to God's commanding may also be wrong-headed (*Being in Action*, 33: "With this picture in view, the freedom of God in all its actuality dictates that 'Jesus may just as well command something different.'"). He quotes *CD* III/4 to the effect that a casuistic interpretation of a marginal case is prescriptive "only in general terms and in the sense of a guiding line" (*CD* III/4, 421 in Nimmo, ibid.). At this point, the translation of *CD* has contributed to a misunderstanding. Barth calls the "reference" to God's command valid "*nur in bewußter Allgemeinheit freilich, nur im Sinne einer ernstlich zu beachtenden Richtlinie*" (*KD* III/4, 480, "only in intentionally general terms however, only in the sense of a guideline that is to be seriously observed"). While a suggestion, a recommendation—or perhaps a hermeneutical orientation—may be general in the sense that one does not need to heed it strictly always, Barth states that the guideline in ethics is valid categorically, while it may not be very specific. Its general nature denotes the latter, not the former aspect. There may be alternative ways to follow a general guideline, but still there are clear criteria for compliance. By contrast, if the rule were not strictly valid, what would it be good for in the first place unless we knew the conditions in which it is invalid? The quotation in question occurs in Barth's discussion of abortion. In that context, the generality of the rule means that even a medical or a criminal indication does not warrant the morality of an abortion. At the same time, the categorical validity of the ethical rule means that in Barth's view, an abortion is certainly immoral in the absence of such an indication (see the section "The Termination of a Pregnancy (§55.2): Conditions of the Marginal Case in a Realistic Ethics" below). By contrast, to highlight the requirement of absolute openness to whatever God may command, regardless of rules, means to consider Christian ethics a private affair that does not allow for principled statements about anti-Semitism, racism, strategic nuclear warfare, and a host of other critical issues.

36. *CD* III/4, 25.

37. Ibid., 30 (trans. rev.).

potential content of the command and is "not simply exhausted in its reference to the event"[38] of the commanding itself. In this sense there is no methodological conflict to the introduction in §52 when §55 discusses in some detail the conditions under which the termination of a pregnancy or a war could or could not be justified theologically in the sense of a "marginal case."[39] The task of special ethics with regard to God's commanding is

> the investigation and representation of the character which this event will always take, of the standard by which the goodness or evil of human action will be decided, not by the moralist and his ethics, but by God the Commander. . . . A knowledge of the character which is always peculiar to this event, and of the standards which are always valid in the decisions made in it, is not only possible but is also demanded.[40]

How exactly a particular command will relate to a particular situation cannot be predicted by an ethical system. Yet it must offer more than to provide "a formless reference to . . . the Holy Spirit"[41] or an ethical occasionalism. Special ethics is concerned with the properties characteristic of the class of potential commandments. As it is concerned with an "instructional preparation"[42] of God's command, its contribution must be more than calling for the greatest possible openness in listening to God's command. On the one hand, an ethics can analyze between which courses of action God may choose and which ones God will rule out. On the other hand, the ethicist is unlikely to narrow down the potential plurality to a single command. Within the bounds of the general guideline that is oriented toward the history of God's Trinitarian revelation, God's commanding is free

38. Ibid., 17 (trans. rev.).
39. The term "exceptional case," which *CD* chooses to translate *Grenzfall*, is unhelpful as it implies that a rule is compromised rather than preserved. See *CD* III/4, 343; Puffer, "Taking Exception to the *Grenzfall*'s Reception," 484.
40. *CD* III/4, 18.
41. Ibid.
42. Ibid.

in a libertarian sense. Yet vis-à-vis God's history of revelation, God's commanding is free in a compatibilist sense. If Christian ethics is thus guided by reflection on God's revelation in Christ, it is unlikely to reject God's true commandment. However, Barth rightly insists, God's commanding cannot be considered free in a libertarian sense insofar as God will not disregard standards implied in the testimonies to revelation and in a cogent analysis of the empirical situation—or else revelation in Christ would cease to be binding for God's self.[43]

In the engagement of the biblical testimonies to God's revelation, however, the notion of a potential command of the exalted Christ, every moment anew (§38.2), raises the critical question whether these biblical witnesses are too particularistic. After all, *CD* II/2 argued that Christian ethics should again and again receive a new revelation, passively, without interpretation, rather than engage it theologically with exegetical and theological arguments.

This would give rise to the danger that a command of Christ that is issued anew each time seems unpredictable and arbitrary. Barth addresses the problem of an arbitrary command in not only speaking of a vertical dimension of God's command, which denotes the irreducible character of the event, but also of its horizontal aspect, in which God's commanding constitutes a continuity. The continuity of God's command consists in God's faithfulness as the Creator, Reconciler, and Redeemer. None of these three aspects can be played off against another one.

Barth goes on to lay out a methodological approach that draws fundamental aspects of a theology of creation from christological traditions. "But the Word of God in Jesus Christ, in whom man's humiliation and exaltation are resolve, event and revelation, tells

43. That God's revelation in Christ is essential for the eternal God is the point of the doctrine of election. On different notions of freedom, see Robert Kane, *A Contemporary Introduction to Free Will*, Fundamentals of Philosophy Series (Oxford/New York: Oxford University Press, 2005), chap. 2.3.

him about his *creaturely* being presupposed in this occurrence."[44] Barth thus pursues the identification of God's command with the incarnate Christ, whom he interprets in turn from the perspective of a theology of creation. While the resulting doctrine of creation will differ from many conventional accounts, Barth thus also hopes to flesh out the unity of gospel and law. In spite of the difference between nature and creation, a command that is thus in accordance with creation is unlikely to be perceived as heteronomous. This in in clear contrast to Barth's insistence in *CD* II/2, chapter 8, that any biblical passage—with two notable exceptions—reveals God's command without human interpretation and that God's command encounters Christians as foreign and unconditioned.

At the same time, §52 seeks to place the theology of creation on a more solid foundation than the one he perceives in Emil Brunner's and Dietrich Bonhoeffer's ethical works. He disagrees with a theology of orders, as he sees its identification of reality and creation as uncritical and naive.[45] Nonetheless, Brunner is right, according to Barth, in arguing that "the Divine Command is not a law which hovers above our actual existence without any connexion with it; it is the command of the God who has created our actual existence."[46] In Bonhoeffer's doctrine of divine mandates, Barth appreciates the attempt to articulate a doctrine of creation in drawing on God's word. Ultimately, however, Barth sees Bonhoeffer merely reduplicating a subaltern social reality by means of a doubtful biblicism.[47]

This demonstrates how Barth left behind doubtful premises of

44. *CD* III/4, 43.

45. Ibid., 20, 37.

46. Ibid., 20, quoting from Emil Brunner's *The Divine Imperative: A Study in Christian Ethics*, trans. Olive Wyon (London: Lutterworth Press, 1937), 93. For Barth's relative appreciation of certain aspects of a theology of orders, see also *CD* III/4, 23.

47. Ibid., 23.

his own ethics lectures. He seeks to reconcile a recognition of the command gained in creation with clear attention to the biblical witnesses to revelation by interpreting christological traditions for the sake of a doctrine of creation on the one hand, but also by announcing an empirical sensitivity in his methodological sketches on the other. This results in a significant, yet relative appreciation of empirical insights, which he calls "working hypotheses," "permissible and necessary hypotheses."[48] With a traditional theology of orders he shares the attempts at gaining empirical insight into the reality of experience, hoping to profit from this in gaining theological insight. Nevertheless, he critiques the theology of orders for an "obscure" notion of reality.[49] The status of empirical insight as a "working hypothesis" remains tentative, as it cannot answer the question for the human person in the sense that the human person stands as a sinner before a merciful God, as a christological reflection maintains. It is questionable whether christological traditions can indeed be reduced to such an abstract, binary notion. Nevertheless, it should be acknowledged that the ethical model sketched out in §52 is already more nuanced and promising than Barth's ethical actualism.

Although Barth attributes fundamental significance to the theological aspects toward which he gestures with concepts from a theology of justification, he does not see them in competition with empirical working hypotheses. Instead, these two aspects are complementary, with the theology of justification placing the empirical working hypotheses on "a firm basis."[50] It may well be argued that his theological reflection does not only run from Christology to empirical experience, but also the other way around (see below). For now it should be noted that a second aspect in which

48. Ibid., 41, see also 42.
49. Ibid., 37–8.
50. Ibid., 42.

Barth developed his thought in comparison to the ethics lectures comes to the fore. By means of his "working hypotheses," Barth lays out an anthropology that is supposed to describe God's revelation in Christ as creation. Barth highlights four aspects from this theology of creation by christological means: a) in historical life, the human person is responsible to God; b) the human person exists in a dialogical relationship between an *I* and a *Thou*; c) the human person is the soul of its body; and d) being human means being limited temporally.[51] These four theses structure the special ethics in *CD* III/4, with each sentence encapsulating the theme of one section: a) §53 "Freedom before God", b) §54 "Freedom in Fellowship", c) §55 "Freedom for Life", d) §56 "Freedom in Limitation."

These four constant features of Barth's theology of creation may—and indeed should—be criticized for their narrow focus on humanity and for the one-sided influence of a particular philosophy that they betray (see below). Nonetheless, Barth is striving to articulate four common features in Christology and empirical experience. This anthropology is the result of a dialogue Barth had been conducting with philosophical traditions of the nineteenth century. In turn, philosophical traditions assume a hermeneutical role in Barth's theological interpretation of Scripture. The choice of his four supposed anthropological constants, which may otherwise seem hard to account for, reflects his interaction with Ludwig Feuerbach.[52]

On the whole, Barth called Feuerbach's reduction of theology to anthropology trite.[53] Nonetheless, he considers it historically

51. Ibid., 43–4, *CD* III/2, 38–41.

52. Michael Welker, "Barth und Feuerbach," in *Theologische Profile: Schleiermacher—Barth—Bonhoeffer—Moltmann*, edition chrismon (Frankfurt am Main: Hansisches Verlagshaus, 2009), 157–81, at 172–3. In the following, see Barth, "Ludwig Feuerbach," in *Die Theologie und die Kirche: Gesammelte Aufsätze 2. Band* (München: Kaiser, 1928), 212–39. See also Jan Rohls, "Barth und der theologische Liberalismus," in *Karl Barth in Deutschland (1921–1935): Aufbruch—Klärung—Widerstand*, eds. Michael Beintker, Michael Trowitzsch, and Christian Link (Zurich: Theologischer Verlag, 2005), 285–312, at 293.

significant for blowing the cover off neo-Protestantism. If taken with a grain of salt, Feuerbach's thesis could be justified through the doctrine of incarnation, as it does not conceive of God in abstraction from humanity, but precisely in union with humanity.[54] Thus Barth saw in Feuerbach's philosophy a helpful counterbalance to an anthropological one-sidedness in theology. While neo-Protestantism highlighted human self-consciousness in a way that amounts to an "*apotheosis of the human person*," Feuerbach emphasized that only a *Thou* allows an *I* to emerge, and he insisted on the lived body and human sensuality.

Of course, Barth argues against Feuerbach that it is not the human person in general that fulfills the true human essence, but only Jesus Christ. Barth asserts about Jesus what Feuerbach ascribes to humanity in general: he articulates his *I* in contact with a *Thou.* With regard to the reality of the human person he considers "neither mental nor bodily existence by itself . . . but both in their unity together."[55] Idealism and neo-Protestantism, according to Barth, sublated "the divine being into reason by separating it from the human person," thus "isolating it even more strictly from the *sensuous* life, from the *world*, from the *human person.*"[56] God's true humanity, sociality, and corporeality in Christ is indeed opposed to a one-sided theology of consciousness.

On the other hand, Barth also critiques Feuerbach—drawing on Hans Ehrenberg's arguments—for not knowing death and harboring illusions about evil ("*Nicht-Kenner des Todes*," "*Verkenner des Bösen*").[57] By reducing the concept of God to an overly optimistic anthropology, Feuerbach does not sublate it in Hegel's sense, but

53. Barth, "Feuerbach," 220, 228, 236.
54. See also *CD* III/2, 47–8.
55. Barth, "Feuerbach," 232.
56. Ibid., 215–16.
57. Ibid., 237.

restricts it to relative, temporal affairs. By contrast, Barth attributes to Jesus sober knowledge about his death. Finally, responsibility before God figures prominently in Barth's discussion, but Feuerbach operates only with a general concept of humanity, which he then identifies with the concept of the divine.[58] In Barth's view, however, the uniqueness of existence is both greatness and burden, as it cannot be subsumed under a human essence, which the individual might use to justify himself or herself before God. Refusing to evade his responsibility before God, Jesus is the one who lives up to this mature insight. In reconciling the contrasts of existence, Jesus gives the answer that all anthropologies seek, if unwittingly.[59]

In drawing upon early existentialism in his Christology, Barth adopts certain hypotheses of a philosophical project that is not theological in the narrow sense. His existentialist borrowings commit him to the philosophy of a particular epoch with all its opportunities and limitations. Yet Feuerbach's insistence on human sensuality, for example, is characteristic of an attempt to assign empirical experience an important status in anthropology.

Since §52 assigns priority to theological insights into "the" human situation before God,[60] it is not clear to what extent Barth was aware of the mutual interdependence of philosophy and theology in writing this introduction. Nonetheless, this interrelationship can illustrate how Barth's emphasis on biblical traditions does "not contradict or render superfluous these working hypotheses of human self-consciousness."[61] God's word is revealed in a meaningful, comprehensible way. Although Barth argues that ultimate

58. Ibid., 237–8.
59. *CD* III/2, 47–8.
60. *CD* III/4, 42: the theology of grace gives a "firm basis" to hypotheses that are not originally theological.
61. Ibid., 41–2.

knowledge of the human person is inaccessible merely on empirical grounds, he nonetheless appreciates empirical working hypotheses:

> We do not need to reject them for this reason, or even to underestimate them. Even the understanding of man from the Word of God will always be effected in practice in the language, categories and framework of the possibilities of human self-understanding. In it we shall always and inevitably have before us the phenomena of the human, and to that extent make use of naturalistic, idealistic, existential, historical, psychological and similar thoughts and expressions.[62]

Barth's appreciation of nontheological endeavors in the humanities and the sciences in §52 is relevant at this point because of their hermeneutical function. They influence the interpretation of biblical traditions, contribute by raising issues in special ethics, and help clarify the true implications of the courses of action discussed. Barth's sketches in Christology and the theology of creation in §52 imply a casuistic procedure insofar as Barth wished to evaluate particular courses of action by relating them to a larger theological vision. In comparison to the actualism proposed at the outset of §52, the weights have shifted. The abiding truth in actualism now consists in the fact that a special ethics still cannot prescribe moral action for the very particular situation and that moral judgment remains a highly contextual affair.

Yet Barth's concept of attending to an incommensurate command that is given in radically new ways in every situation, and that assigns passivity to the Christian who faces the unconditioned commander, will pale even further when, for example, in §56.2 ("Vocation"), Barth provides particular indications for what God's command may consist in.[63] A meditation upon one's vocation can provide

62. Ibid., 44.

63. William Werpehowski, "Command and History," in *Karl Barth and Christian Ethics: Living in Truth* (Farnham: Ashgate, 2014), 15–35, at 22–3; Biggar, *Hastening That Waits*, 139.

"orientation" in grasping God's command.[64] Attention to one's vocation does not amount to occasionalism, as Barth repeatedly argues that vocation is not to be confused with an "inner call—even if one would regard this as the call of the Gospel."[65] If reflection upon one's vocation does provide orientation in attending to God's command, then human obedience must be meaningfully related to one's age,[66] one's "special historical situation,"[67] one's "specific endowment and inclination,"[68] and one's characteristic "sphere of operation"[69] in society.

In spite of the anthropocentric approach in the theology of creation in §52, on a positive note Barth's special ethics values empirical findings, interpreted as "working hypotheses," and a theology of justification more highly than the basic tenets of his existentialist Christology. The overly personalistic outline of his theology of creation does not keep him, for example, from attributing fundamental importance to questions of basic economic constellations in political ethics (§55). As Barth's ethical approach in §52 is inspired both by his constructive interest in an ethics of orders and his skepticism toward it, his concept of "working hypotheses" is not merely an ad hoc makeshift, but is rooted in a deeper methodological reflection that leads to a synthesis of a theology of orders and a fundamentally christological approach to theology. It is especially due to this respect for empirical experience that Barth's special ethics do justice, or at least come close to doing so, to the demand in §52 that ethics not be about letting "oneself be governed from moment to moment and situation to situation by a kind of

64. *CD* III/4, 607.
65. Ibid., 603 (trans. rev.).
66. Ibid., 607.
67. Ibid., 618.
68. Ibid., 623.
69. Ibid., 630.

direct and particular divine inspiration and guidance." The task of moral deliberation is not that, "like Goethe's mule," one "has to find his own way in the mist."[70]

The Holy Day (§53.1): Continuities in the Christian Life and Contextual Ethics

Barth begins the material section of the ethics of creation with the discussion of continuous practices that characterize the Christian way of life. Among them are the keeping of the holy day (§53.1), confession (§53.2), and prayer (§53.3). An important aspect of §53 lies in the fact that Barth points to continuous, more habitual practices, including those of a communal kind, while the actualistic focus on the concrete individual command implies a methodological restriction to individual situations in personal ethics.[71] While Barth emphatically affirmed the "Definiteness of the Divine Decision" in *CD* II/2, §38.2, which he contrasted with the supposedly general character of the Decalogue, Barth now highlights the fact that the command of the Sabbath is among the most extensive commands of the Decalogue. This is in tension with its neglect in Christian ethics.[72]

In the discussion of the Sabbath, Barth arrives at further fundamental decisions about a dimension of life characterized by the act of worship that also influence other questions of his special ethics, such as the section "The Active Life" (§55.3), in which the actualistic concept of revelation does not play a role. Further, Barth's

70. *CD* III/4, 15. This gives Goethe's first "Mignon" Lied an ironic twist: "Do you know the land where the lemons blossom? . . . Do you know the mountain and its cloudy path? The mule seeks its way in the mist." Johann Wolfgang von Goethe, *Wilhelm Meister's Apprenticeship*, trans. Eric A. Blackall (New York: Suhrkamp, 1989), 83–4.

71. According to the discussion of *CD* II/2, §38.2 above, Barth's exclusion of the Decalogue and the Sermon on the Mount from transmitting God's specific command is doubtful by the standards of that subsection.

72. Ibid., 49–50. The Sabbath command is the longest of the Ten Commandments, linking those referring to God with those referring to other persons. See Frank Crüsemann, *Bewahrung der Freiheit: Das Thema des Dekalogs in sozialgeschichtlicher Perspektive* (Munich: Kaiser, 1983), 53–4.

discussion of the command of the holy day helps identify a grain of truth encapsulated in the actualistic concept of revelation, in spite of all necessary critique. Even in §53, Barth occasionally follows an actualistic logic, which creates theological difficulties. At the same time, however, a partial aspect of this concept is legitimate in pointing to the contextual nature of the moral decision, the freedom of conscience, and a certain degree of openness in results in the search for moral truth.[73]

Barth regards the Sabbath as the anticipation of eschatological consummation and thus as a tentative realization of Christian freedom. In turn, in prayer the holy day radiates into the workweek.[74] The meaning of keeping the holy day is "to become free before God and for Him, and therefore free from and for ourselves, free from our work and free for divine service."[75] Worship in this respect denotes an aspect of the entire life.

Barth draws conclusions from this later as well when discussing "The Active Life" (§55.3). A closer look at that section allows us to appreciate the decisions made in the section on the holy day. In §55.3, Barth first asks how much the active life should be influenced by being a member of a congregation. He considers human cultural activity in the wider sphere of society only after that. Barth thus emphasizes that human life should be "service" precisely in the "freedom" before God. The human person is "called from the isolation and self-sufficiency of a life for life's sake."[76] On this basis, work and wider culture are to be relativized and appreciated at the same time: they are not purposes in themselves, but ambiguous

73. According to John de Gruchy, "Racism, Reconciliation, and Resistance," in *On Reading Karl Barth in South Africa*, ed. Charles Villa-Vicencio (Grand Rapids: Eerdmans, 1988), 139–55, at 140, the notion of a repristination of Barth's theology is self-contradictory; on its own terms, it presses on towards a contextual interpretation.

74. *CD* III/4, 89.

75. Ibid., 64.

76. Ibid., 477.

phenomena. Once this is granted, however, they must not be looked down upon. They are not God's command in themselves, but they can correspond to God's command.

By contrast, Karl Holl's depiction of Luther's ethics of work overestimates human achievement: "In the supreme sense all human work is simply the mask behind which God Himself works."[77] Indeed, if that were so, we would be ill advised to rest even on the Sabbath.

Human work and culture are "the production of his [man's] actual thinking, willing and feeling, the mirror of his striving for law and yet also of his caprice, of his dignity yet also his ignominy, his life yet also his death."[78] Only if human work is relativized with reference to its ambiguity—Barth mentions "the prophetic service of the community"[79]—is it also clear that all human work must follow its inherent rationality, contrary to all "dilettante or botched work."[80]

Building on the foundations laid in the chapter on the Sabbath, Barth can claim an argument he made in the Tambach lecture "ChrSoc" (1919) without running the danger inherent in a theology of history.[81] Barth's awareness of the ambiguity of human culture is not merely a happy coincidence, but a consequence of his understanding of the Sabbath command. In turn, it is important not to summarize the holy day merely negatively as a renunciation of work. To see the point of the holy day merely negatively in not working might even mean merely to suspend a quasireligious stance toward culture for twenty-four hours. By contrast, seeing the holy day as a positive testimony to and celebration of God's eschatological

77. Ibid., 522.
78. Ibid.
79. Ibid., 509.
80. Ibid., 508.
81. In §56.2 ("Vocation"), Barth criticizes Reformation theology not just for rejecting a spiritual elitism of withdrawal from the world, but for endowing the matters of everyday life as a whole with too great a spiritual dignity as well (ibid., 602).

consummation is to claim a vantage point that may allow for a full awareness of the ambiguity inherent in human culture.

Barth's sense of the holy day as a benefit is then brought to bear in the section on the active life as he first highlights the witness of the congregation. For the sake of the gospel, "the Christian community cannot be against the world; it can only be for it."[82] This rules out a wholesale pessimism about culture or an overly critical correction of the Tambach lecture in the style of *Rom* II. At the base of this is not a vague optimism, but the proclamation of forgiveness based on Jesus Christ's cross.[83] The cross inspires the congregation with a skepticism toward cultural phenomena such as the call for "Moral Rearmament."[84]

Further, as the mission of the congregation is not merely based on the work of the Creator, it is at times called to nonconformism as well.[85] This dynamic cuts both ways: even the church "is not infallible. It may well have things to learn or to correct."[86] To begin with, the church may constitute a realm of freedom over and against governing standards: "The community will sometimes have to call unrighteous what everyone regards as righteous, and to recognise a higher justice where everyone feels it incumbent to protest against a notorious injustice."[87] For now the question will remain open whether from the outside such freedom for nonconformism may appear as a freedom for caprice, or even whether this difference in evaluation may emerge within the congregation. It remains to be discussed in what sense the congregation will need to bolster up its ethical claims.

82. Ibid., 502.
83. Ibid., 503.
84. Ibid., 506–7.
85. Ibid., 504–5, 511–12.
86. Ibid., 520.
87. Ibid., 511.

The command of the holy day, at any rate, also implies a negative aspect in refusing to overrate work. To begin with, the negative dimension of sacrifice and renunciation, which was crucial in the actualistic concept of revelation, is overcome here in principle, as the *freedom* that may imply a certain degree of repentance and sacrifice is highlighted more clearly than in Barth's early work. This freedom is freedom before God and human beings, and thus also freedom for God and human beings. In this sense, Barth's later ethics of reconciliation will argue that the call for obedience is fundamentally "*anapausis*, sabbath refreshment, rest."[88]

Nonetheless, a crucial inconsistency emerges in Barth's discussion of the Sabbath command when he emphatically summarizes the meaning of the entire command with the notion of renunciation, thus highlighting the negative aspect in a one-sided way once again.

> The Sabbath commandment demands the *faith in God* which brings about the *renunciation* of man, his renunciation of himself, of all that he thinks and wills and effects and achieves. . . . This renouncing faith is the comprehensive content of the Sabbath commandment. . . . It carries with it two great benefits in which it may be seen that this same commandment is indeed the commandment of the gracious God. In the first place, by making man free from himself it makes him free for himself in a special way, temporarily absolving him from the care of his work. And secondly it makes him free for God in a special way.[89]

If the holy day, even the practice of renunciation on the holy day, has such positive implications, why sum it up nevertheless with the negative term of renunciation and call the benefit only an implication? Many academics may find it counterintuitive not to work on a Sunday, but a diligent Swiss housewife, for example, might find the command to abstain from work on Sundays and

88. *CL*, 31. The Greek term *anapausis* is from Matt. 11:29.
89. *CD* III/4, 59–60.

attend church quite welcome. But Barth's one-sided emphasis on renunciation corresponds to Calvin's view that "negatively at least our sanctification consists in the *mortificatio propriae voluntatis . . . ut propriis affectibus et operibus emortui, regnum Dei meditemur*" (killing of one's own will . . . so that we reflect on God's reign, having died to our own feelings and works).[90] In this sense, sanctification is primarily a negative occurrence. To begin with, humans are not given something, but something is taken away from them. The Sabbath command first appears as a command that kills ("*mortificatio . . . emortui . . .*").

By contrast, if the commandment truly is "*anapausis*, sabbath refreshment, rest," then the notion of *mortificatio* should be ranked second after the aspect of *vivificatio*. Insofar as the gospel has priority over the command, renunciation is justified only if it serves a greater, positive good in which the gospel takes practical shape.

Barth also agrees with Luther, Calvin, and the Heidelberg Catechism that the holy day should be characterized by participation in worship.[91] True enough, the Decalogue does not mention worship, and paradoxically, Barth even uses this as an argument to question the importance of a worship service.[92] However, the Sabbath rose to particular prominence in Judaism as the day of the synagogue service, and in today's Christian theology, it can be argued indeed that it is the appropriate form of claiming the proper reason for the Sabbath commandment,[93] which is God's eschatological rest on

90. Ibid., 58. See John Calvin, *Institutes in the Christian Religion*, ed. John McNeill, trans. Ford Lewis Battles (Louisville: Westminster John Knox, 2006) 1:396 (II, 8, 29): "Our sanctification consists in mortifying our own will" (*Sanctificatio nostra proprie voluntatis mortificatione constat*). Apart from *mortification*, killing off one's sinful drives, the Sabbath command aims at hearing the law, performing religious ceremonies, and providing rest for those under someone else's rule (II, 8, 28). The biblical text highlights physical rest, so that physical rest should not be considered merely serving another purpose.

91. *CD* III/4, 62.

92. Ibid., 63.

93. In Israel, the Sabbath was associated with religious service and the cult; see Werner H. Schmidt,

the seventh day, which itself prefigures Israel's worship,[94] or God's initiative in liberating Israel out of slavery in Egypt. Going beyond §53, Barth's reference to the worship service can be called a command that commands freedom. The motivating power of the command must lie in the fact that the worship service and the holy day of rest convey a sense of positive freedom granted in the gospel. This would be the crucial point with which Barth's one-sided attention to *mortificatio* is overcome.

Mortificatio, on the other hand, points to the ambiguity of human action. Why should everyone be burdened with the *mortificatio* of the worship service indeed if the holy day is truly about God's benefits? Worship services inspired by Barth's prioritization of *mortificatio* are likely to be a sad, even repressive affair. Barth realizes this, and interestingly, his emphasis on *mortificatio* leads to a surprisingly strong critique of worship services: it is "ultimately also only a very dubious and fragile human work subject to that question" whether it revolves indeed around the "great acts of God in Jesus Christ."[95] Certainly, worship services are often in danger of losing sight of their proper theological foundation. But if the congregation strives to do justice to this foundation, does not Jesus Christ's transforming presence make it more than "only a very dubious and fragile human work"? If not, then it should not be the subject of a commandment.

A good part of Barth's discussion is not in keeping with the fact that he emphasizes the aspect of *mortificatio* unduly himself. The worship service is especially prominent theologically as it does not imply an obligation, but because this is where God's word takes on

Die Zehn Gebote im Rahmen alttestamentlicher Ethik, Erträge der Forschung 281 (Darmstadt: Wissenschaftliche Buchgesellschaft, 1993), 92.

94. Bernd Janowski, "Tempel und Schöpfung: Schöpfungstheologische Aspekte der priesterschriftlichen Heiligtumskonzeption," in *Schöpfung und Neuschöpfung* (Neukirchen-Vluyn: Neukirchener, 1990), 37–69, at 46–7, 67.

95. *CD* III/4, 63 (trans. rev.).

a liberating shape. This is indeed in keeping with the priority of the gospel to the law, according to which a command is morally obliging only insofar as it lends concrete shape to the gospel. In this sense Barth argues that, because "it belongs to God and not to man, [the proper holy day] should be for man a day free from any compulsion."[96] Thus Barth belabors the problem that, on the one hand, the worship service cannot be called a commandment as it would be contrary to the gospel to make rigorous claims in God's name, to set up a sheer obligation. On the other hand, it is in the worship service that the gospel can be heard and embraced properly, yet this entails a certain degree of renunciation as well.

As Barth does not relate his characterization of the service as *mortificatio* properly to the character of the holy day as a benefit, the question of how to keep the holy day properly cannot overcome the tension between benefit and privation. The worship service should be benefit, *vivificatio*, but appears as privation, as *mortificatio*. Barth seeks to overcome this problem with an actualistic ethics. In order to prevent the theological problem of the worship service from being replaced by a seemingly unproblematic, yet secular activity, Barth first takes issue with the notion of a general command. He proceeds on a more general anthropological basis: making a particular activity a duty is in contrast to the fact that freedom and joy often elude careful planning and production. Even a well-intended instruction for joy easily achieves the opposite effect. Neither does a renunciation of planning, the decision for caprice, lead to freedom.[97] Human spontaneity cannot be regulated with a particular regimen: "*res severa verum gaudium*" (true joy is a strict affair).[98] In general, the meaning of

96. Ibid., 67.
97. Ibid.
98. Ibid., 68–9, quoting Seneca (*Epistulae morales*). "Can one really sleep or go for a walk on Sunday morning without on Sunday afternoon becoming in one way or another a real slave of Sunday?" (*CD* III/4, 67).

the holy day includes the worship service, but is not limited to it; in fact it cannot be called a command properly, Barth argues.[99] Rather than asking, "What is going wrong in the way worship services are conducted?," Barth argues that ethical analysis must necessarily withhold judgment on the details of keeping the holy day properly.

After Barth sums up the essence of the holy day under the rubric of renunciation and after raising the problem that renunciation does not always do justice to the properly joyful, spiritual meaning of the holy day, Barth does not challenge the prominence of renunciation, but resorts to the actualistic concept of revelation instead. "No ethics of the holy day can come between God and the individual, nor can the particularity of the Sabbath commandment, as God Himself proclaims it, be reduced to general rules, thus telling the individual indirectly what is his obedience to this commandment."[100] If indeed no "ethics of the holy day can come between God and the individual," then not even a soft, general guideline of attending the worship service can be asserted. Why should "the individual" not face both the gospel and the commandment as an individual, that is, not as part of the congregation?

These problems result from Barth's characterization of the holy day as renunciation, or *mortificatio*. To begin with, Sabbath rest is, according to the biblical commandment, not merely the negative flip side of a positive command. As the negation of another activity, such rest may at times imply the aspect of *mortificatio*. In the biblical traditions, however, rest itself is *vivificatio*. In the Hebrew text of the commandment, the verb *'bd* describes that one should not labor (*'bd*), as one used to be an *'ebed*, a slave laborer who was liberated. In contrast to Barth's and Calvin's opinion, the biblical command does not restrict physical rest to those in inferior social positions,

99. Ibid., 63–4.
100. Ibid., 65.

and even with a view to them, the rest should not be relativized as something that is not properly at the heart of the command.[101] At its heart, the Sabbath rest is *vivificatio*. If such rest appears primarily as an unwelcome sacrifice, *mortificatio*, the proper question is what is wrong with the way the gospel is proclaimed and enacted in worship.

By contrast, Barth also asserts that rest and the worship service are not of primary importance for the Sabbath command. Its primary purpose is to provide an occasion at which God's specific command should be received, which in turn replaces ethical deliberations.

> Whether it be activity or inactivity, what God requires of man as the sanctifying of the holy day, as the exercising of that renouncing faith, . . . [will] always [consist] in concrete action and abstention. As the Sabbath commandment, too, the commandment of God reaches and encounters each man in direct reference to his person, his situation, his ability, task and surroundings at this specific time and in these specific circumstances.[102]

Why does Barth not characterize this individualized receiving of a particular commandment the way he also characterizes the worship service, as "ultimately also only a very dubious and fragile human work subject to that question" whether it revolves indeed around the "great acts of God in Jesus Christ"?[103] Barth's attempt to surpass the worship service in a private, direct reception of God's command also does not answer the question of what to do on the holy day. The individualistic anthropology remains unaccounted for.[104]

But Barth then goes on to assert that the Sunday should be properly

101. Jürgen Ebach, "Zum Thema: Arbeit und Ruhe im Alten Testament: Eine utopische Erinnerung," *Zeitschrift für Evangelische Ethik* 24 (1980): 7–21, at 19–20: the two creation narratives in Genesis view work and rest in a complementary way. Thus the statement that God perfects creation by resting (Gen. 2:2, *šbt*) contradicts Barth's notion that resting is primarily *mortificatio*.

102. *CD* III/4, 65.

103. Ibid., 63 (trans. rev.).

104. Ibid., 65.

kept as part of the assembled congregation,[105] and that it is not "only a question of meeting [God] privately."[106] This in turn also calls into question the actualistic concept of revelation. Continuing the Reformation appreciation of the worship service, Barth holds on to a counterbalance of the actualistic concept of revelation. Close to Calvin's interpretation of the Sabbath command, however, is also Barth's valuable critique that in the time since Calvin, the casuistic interpretation of the command paid inordinate attention to the "claims of the ruling classes."[107] In this sense Barth does indeed highlight vivification and challenges his emphasis on renunciation. For the holy day

> is also the establishment and victory of a well-founded law of life and freedom. . . . It is one of the features of Calvin's explanation of the Fourth Commandment that he expressly states this aspect, especially in relation to those who are socially dependent (*Inst.*, II, 8, 28).[108]

Despite the present critique of actualism, Barth's search for the shape of the subjective experience of Christian freedom on the holy day also implies a positive aspect. A grain of truth in actualism is that under special circumstances, ethics cannot give a final and detailed answer about the proper way to keep the Sabbath. This would depend on too many individual and contextual factors. Insisting on mere rest in the abstract would contradict the political and economic dimensions of the command. Rest needs to include the creation of sustainable living conditions for those in socially inferior positions. The command is directed against conditions that are contrary to the liberation by God. After all, Israel is commanded not to forget, in all its work, the liberation from forced labor.

105. Ibid., 69–70.
106. Ibid., 70.
107. Ibid., 66.
108. Ibid., 60–61. See Deut. 5:14–5, Exod. 20:10.

Attending the worship service, physical rest, and social sensibility are meaningful guidelines as to how to keep the Sabbath, but this is valid only as long as they do not appear as a one-sided *mortificatio*. More extensive instructions may run the risk that under special circumstances, the command no longer appears to correspond to the gospel. For example, a congregant's efforts to have worship services highlight the gospel more clearly may suffer repeated setbacks, so that the general rule of church attendance may occasionally, and ironically, stand in the way of vivification. This relativization of the general rule differs from Barth's, however, who at this point tends to view the private encounter with God as being of equal rank with the communal worship service. The intention to be in accordance with the gospel and to allow for unforeseen, contingent factors also characterizes Jesus' attitude in the Sabbath controversies: "The sabbath was made for humankind, and not humankind for the sabbath" (Mark 2:27). This also allows for the freedom of conscience, which Barth highlights also in §52: "Ultimately each can only act for himself in a case of conscience."[109]

Once the relevance of the actualistic concept of the command is narrowed down to a particular function within a more general discursive ethics, it also wards off the attempt to relieve Christians of moral responsibility by playing off a valid, general command against the need to discern God's will at a particular moment. Barth thus reclaims the Enlightenment ideal of mature responsibility—which Kant put famously as, "If I have a book to have understanding in place of me, a spiritual adviser to have a conscience for me . . . I need not make any efforts at all."[110]

109. *CD* III/4, 9.

110. Immanuel Kant, "An Answer to the Question: 'What Is Enlightenment?'" in *Political Writings*, ed. Hans S. Reiss, trans. H. B. Nisbet, 2nd ed., Cambridge Texts in the History of Political Thought (Cambridge: Cambridge University Press, 1991) 54–60, at 54.

The Termination of a Pregnancy (§55.2): Conditions of the Marginal Case in a Realistic Ethics

Although the actualistic concept of revelation is problematic, it contradicts at least a rash categorical judgment about contextual circumstances of action, guarding freedom of conscience. In this sense *CD* III/4 often highlights the contextual dimension of ethics, allowing for a strong sense of the empirical. In order not to lose sight of human life lost and saved in Jesus Christ, it is also necessary to be sensitive to human experience in those dimensions of human action relating especially to the doctrine of creation.

Barth's §55.2, "The Protection of Life," discusses several ethical problems: suicide (pp. 400–15); the termination of a pregnancy (pp. 415–23); the killing of a supposedly unworthy life (pp. 423–7)—an analysis that includes even a gesture toward the possibility of voluntary or noninvoluntary euthanasia (pp. 427)—killing in self-defense (pp. 427–37); capital punishment, including the problem of tyrannicide (pp. 437–48, 448–50); as well as the ethics of war and peace (pp. 450–70). In these discussions, empirical observations are of great importance for Barth. His ethical method will be elucidated by discussing his views on some of these issues. The problematic section on gender relations will be deferred to the next chapter.

Barth's discussion of the termination of a pregnancy is the first extensive treatment in German in Protestant theology after the Second World War.[111] This is especially significant as an estimated two million German women had been raped during the Red Army's occupation of East Germany 1945–7.[112] Barth's discussion makes explicit reference to this humanitarian disaster.

111. Christiane Kohler-Weiß, *Schutz der Menschwerdung: Schwangerschaft und Schwangerschaftskonflikt als Thema evangelischer Ethik*, Öffentliche Theologie 17 (Gütersloh: Kaiser/Gütersloher, 2003), 37.

112. John Lewis Gaddis, *The Cold War* (London: Penguin, 2007), 24, 269n24.

In Nazi Germany, the termination of a pregnancy was categorically prohibited, with exceptions for mothers who had a disability. Under the Allied forces, the regulations preceding the Nazi era were again put in place in the West, and abortion due to health risks for the mother was permitted ("medical indication"), albeit not on an unambiguous legal basis. An illegal termination of a pregnancy meant a high risk both for the pregnant woman and the physician involved. In Switzerland, the law required a medical indication as well (1942–2002). In Eastern Germany, the termination of a pregnancy required a medical or an embryopathic indication until 1972, when restrictions were removed during the first trimester of the pregnancy. Ultimately, West Germany adopted this regulation as well in 1995. Only at that point was abortion due to rape no longer part of the legal gray area of the medical indication.

Barth's ethical discussion in 1951 begins with embryological observations on pregnancy, from which Barth concludes that the embryo is a human being "from the very first."[113] In consequence, in the termination of a pregnancy, a human being is killed.

> The embryo has its own autonomy, its own brain, its own nervous system, its own blood circulation. If its life is affected by that of the mother, it also affects hers. It can have its own illnesses in which the mother has no part. Conversely, it may be quite healthy even though the mother is seriously ill. . . . It may also continue to live after its mother's death, and be eventually saved by a timely operation on her dead body. In short, it is a human being in its own right.[114]

It is remarkable that Barth begins the ethical analysis with an empirical description. This description yields decisive consequences in ethical regard. Certainly, Barth's description must be criticized in that some of the observations must be differentiated from today's

113. *CD* III/4, 415.
114. Ibid., 416.

scientific perspective. While the embryo develops nervous tissue and nerve centers from very early on, we cannot speak of a proper brain before the neurons migrate to their later position in the mature central nervous system between the ninth and the sixteenth week after conception.[115] Further, Barth's presentation of empirical aspects may be selective in that there must be no complications in the embryo's nidation as well as in the continuous supply of nutrients for the embryo to develop normally.[116]

Yet these points represent questions of detail in comparison with a fundamental theological critique of Barth's mode of analysis. If Barth's theology is known for one thing, it is his polemics against any deduction of God's reality from wider human experience. This critique of "natural theology" may render the assumption of any fundamental importance of empirical knowledge in Barth's ethics suspect. Thus, the ethicist Christiane Kohler-Weiß comments that "in the context of Barth's presentation of the problem," it may seem

> as if insights from the natural sciences provided the reason for an equal ethical status of the fetus and a born human person. In the context of Barth's theology, however, this is entirely out of the question. What makes the human person a human person is, in Barth's view, the relationship with God.

This objection amounts to the critique that Barth, consciously or not, misuses the appearance of empirical science to establish a verdict that rests upon overly particularistic presuppositions. However, this critique suspends the relevant question for the termination of a

115. Wissenschaftlicher Beirat der Bundesärztekammer, "Pränatale und perinatale Schmerzempfindung: Stellungnahme des Wissenschaftlichen Beirates der Bundesärztekammer (1991)," *Deutsches Ärzteblatt* 88, no. 47 (1991): A 4157–A 4169 (95–107), A-4161 (99), https://www.aerzteblatt.de/pdf/88/47/a4157.pdf. Satoshi Kurosaka and Anna Kashina, "Cell Biology of Embryonic Migration," *Birth Defects Research Part C: Embryo Today: Reviews* 84 (2008): 102–22.

116. Kohler-Weiß, *Schutz der Menschwerdung*, 76 critiques Barth for, in her view, ignoring the "vital dependency of the embryo/fetus on the pregnant woman."

pregnancy of whether or not God's relationship to an embryo or fetus is theologically the same as that to a born child.[117] The theological argument that the relationship with God establishes human status, regardless of biological observations, does not answer the question whether human dignity should be attributed to an embryo and not to other forms of life. In this regard it is remarkable indeed that Barth does not refer to some incommensurate command of God in order to justify a critique of abortion, perhaps fortified with reference to ecclesial tradition. Moreover, Barth's introduction to special ethics, §52, argues that God does not issue God's command with regard to creation in isolation from creaturely processes. Thus, for Barth, empirical arguments constitute necessary working hypotheses in ethics.

In addition, the theology of justification, to which Kohler-Weiß alludes, is indeed of great importance for Barth. The relationship with God requires the protection of human life. Christ died even for the embryo, or for the guilt it will incur—as Barth can assert in accordance with his empirical observations. "The true light of the world shines already in the darkness of the mother's womb."[118] The theological statement about human status is crucial, yet it depends on the necessary working hypotheses from embryology. Once the question about the human status of the embryo arises, the working hypothesis from embryology turns out to be decisive.

Moreover, although the christological argument is unlikely to gain a large following outside of the church, the embryological working hypothesis does, at least in theory, allow for a constructive public debate that may involve both Christian and secular arguments. Although the findings of embryology on which Barth draws require

117. From fertilization onwards or from the first cell division, the fertilized egg cell is called an embryo. With the eighth week after conception, it is called a fetus. For the sake of simplicity, however, the following discussion will speak only of an embryo.

118. *CD* III/4, 416.

qualification, it is nonetheless significant that after the fertilization of the ovum, or at least after nidation, the embryo requires no more than a continuous nutrient supply in order to mature into a viable infant.[119]

While determining the point in time at which the incipient life is a human being is necessary for Barth's argument, this does not constitute its real nerve. The embryological case may speak for a precedent against the termination of a pregnancy, but in Barth's discussion, the last word is not yet spoken even then. The crucial question is whether it is acceptable, faced with the particular conditions of the individual constellation, to attribute to the pregnant woman the motivation to complete the pregnancy until birth. This line of reasoning introduces aspects of a theory of action into the question of God's command.

Above and beyond the empirical arguments from embryology, it is notable that Barth does not justify his presumption against the termination of the pregnancy with a timeless norm, but with the gospel. With a view to the pregnant woman in particular, he argues, "The command of God is based on His *grace*. He summons man to the freedom in which he *may* live instead of *having to* live."[120] The grace that speaks in favor of the embryo's life is the same grace that

119. The nidation of the blastocyst in the endometrium, the inner membrane of the uterus, begins roughly a week after ovulation, and is concluded after about another week. Moreover, the morally significant question whether the fertilized egg cell will give rise to multiples can be answered no sooner than three weeks after conception. See Fabian Kliesch, "Der Beginn des menschlichen Lebens aus medizinischer Sicht: Embryonalentwicklung als strukturierbares Kontinuum," in *Ethik im Kontinuum: Beiträge zur relationalen Erkenntnistheorie und Ontologie*, ed. Wilfried Härle (Leipzig: Evangelische Verlagsanstalt, 2008), 127–41, at 131–3. This might give rise to further questions about the status of the egg cell before that. Ontologically, the question of multiples is typically determined at fertilization or shortly thereafter. Fraternal multiples may not emerge immediately with fertilization, but one cannot conclude that the embryo is *not* a developing person because it is unclear if one or *more* persons are developing. Another question that is sometimes raised is whether the development of the polar body denotes the inception of human dignity. However, "then we would expect that with this moment, a qualitative leap would take place, as . . . in fertilization. . . . Yet this cannot be confirmed by observation." Günter Rager, "Präimplantationsdiagnostik und der Status des Embryos," *Zeitschrift für medizinische Ethik* 46 (2000): 81–9, at 87.

120. *CD* III/4, 418 (emphasis in the German original).

enables the pregnant woman to live and in which God reconciles her with God's self as well. Once she becomes aware how much she lives from this grace herself, there may be hope that she will be able, in spite of adverse circumstances, to experience the baby as supported by the same grace. The motivation not to terminate an unwanted pregnancy would have to derive from gratitude for divine mercy.[121] For the commanding God is after all

> our Father in Jesus Christ, in whom He has not rejected sinful man but chosen him for Himself and reconciled him to Himself, in whom He Himself has intervened for sinful man who has violated His command, in order that the latter may not be lost to him . . . Nor does it weaken the command . . . that He has given His Son, and in Him Himself, on its behalf, that [this sinful world] should not perish.[122]

This leads Barth to hold it against the Protestant churches that they have been unable to proclaim the gospel in a way that inspires trust.[123] Even the Protestant church often presented the rejection of abortion as an "abstract prohibition."[124] This would be more in keeping with the theology of the Roman Catholic church. Yet Barth also criticizes the Protestant tradition: "The proclamation of [abstract] law will, after all, be inefficient here as well!"[125]

In addition to reflecting on the individual moral problem, Barth also discusses the wider societal conditions of the conflict. Even if this is not where Barth's emphasis lies, he makes clear efforts to overcome a mere personal ethics. He submits that "a sound social policy might well be a most powerful weapon in the struggle against criminal abortion."[126] Looking not only at the church's influence on morals

121. Ibid., 419.
122. Ibid.
123. Ibid., 418.
124. Ibid., 417.
125. A sentence missing ibid. (*KD* III/4, 476).
126. *CD* III/4, 422.

and medical legislation, but also at economic and social politics, he gestures to a multisystemic argument.[127] Theological ethics, rather than addressing only the faithful, is also directed at a wider public. In analogy to Barth's theological point that both the obligation and the motivation to carry full term must be based on God's mercy, it can be argued in public debate that the summons to decide against a termination of the pregnancy should appeal to experiences in which life appears as an undeserved gift. Yet given the ambiguities of more general morals, the moral force of such experiences is likely to erode if society and politics do not provide the means that resonate with and support the will for a decisive protection of the embryo.

Another major aspect in Barth's treatment of the ethical problem is that his rejection of the termination of the pregnancy is not categorical. Instead, in close keeping with the logic behind the constitution of moral obligation, he also discusses a "marginal case" (*Grenzfall*).[128] A marginal case is, in Barth's usage, moral action that differs significantly from the expectations raised by a more general ethical analysis.[129] In the marginal case, action is faced with the challenge of following a command that may take an unusual form due to exceptional circumstances.[130] Barth argues that one cannot specify in general when exactly the marginal case is given.[131] The circumstances in which the moral question arises are contingent. Yet

127. Barth's discussion thus foreshadows the development that took place with reforms in German criminal law. In 1976, the respective law provided for different regulations depending on medical, criminal, or other reasons ("indications") for a termination of a pregnancy. The German Protestant churches no longer viewed the issue in terms of criminal law, either, but as a question of socio-politics. Simone Mantei, *Nein und Ja zur Abtreibung: Die evangelische Kirche in der Reformdebatte um §218 StGB (1970–1976)*, Arbeiten zur kirchlichen Zeitgeschichte B 38 (Göttingen: Vandenhoeck & Ruprecht, 2004), 573.

128. The term "marginal case" is more suitable to translate Barth's *Grenzfall* than "case of exception." It is sometimes translated as "borderline," "limit," or "extreme case." See also Puffer, "Taking Exception to the *Grenzfall*'s Reception," 485.

129. On the regular case, see Biggar, *Hastening That Waits*, 133–4.

130. On the marginal case see here and in the following ibid., 33–4; Clough, *Ethics in Crisis*, 94–7.

131. *CD* III/4, 411.

that does not mean that the marginal case strictly evades analysis.[132] This does not lead Barth to define when exactly a termination of a pregnancy should be carried out and when it should be resisted. Nonetheless, he describes necessary, albeit not sufficient, conditions in which the termination of the pregnancy is potentially moral, no more and no less.[133] This constitutes a minimum requirement that provides guidance as to when the marginal case is not given, yet his argument is insufficient to specify positively when the marginal case obtains.[134] His ethics provide a guideline that is general and in some specific cases indeterminate, but nonetheless binding.[135] Thus Barth respects the contextual conditions of the decision in the individual case as well as the freedom of conscience of the moral agent, without leaving the decision up to caprice. In specifying the necessary conditions for a *casus*, a "case" (German: *Fall*), Barth does indeed practice "casuistry."[136] In accordance with the critique articulated in §52, however, this casuistry does not argue normatively in a narrow,

132. John Howard Yoder, "Barth and the Problem of War," in *Karl Barth and the Problem of War & Other Essays on Barth*, ed. Mark Thiessen Nation (Eugene: Cascade/Wipf & Stock, 2003), 1–100, at 47, is suspicious of an overly systematical treatment of the marginal case: "The *Grenzfall* does not emerge unpredicted at a point where concrete problems turn out on inspection to be otherwise insoluble; the concrete cases are, rather, found to fit the place prepared for them by the systematic exposition." It is unclear how Yoder thinks of prediction here. If he thinks of predictions internal to Barth's analysis, this must not necessarily count against Barth. He does not invent moral conflicts at random, but reflects lived experience more generally.

133. On this distinction, see Biggar, *Hastening That Waits*, 37.

134. Marginal cases cannot be defined in terms of sufficient conditions. Importantly, however, this does not mean that they cannot be specified in advance at all (pace Nimmo, *Being in Action*, 55). William Werpehowski, "Hearing the Divine Command: Realism and Discernment in Barth's Ethics," *Zeitschrift für Dialektische Theologie* 12 (1996): 64–74, at 71, argues that in specifying conditions for the marginal case, one devotes too much attention to the marginal case already, thus distracting from the common shape of God's command. Yet the refusal to specify necessary conditions for the marginal case with reference to a potentially incommensurate character of God's commanding can in effect underwrite the practice of abortion that may be in contrast to the witness to God's regular command.

135. *CD* III/4, 420–21.

136. Thus John Howard Yoder, "The Pacifism of Karl Barth" (1963), in Nation, *Barth and the Problem of War*, 109–32, 123.

deterministic sense, as if the ethical judgment could be made in advance independently of contingent, morally relevant facts. Based on the possibility of a marginal case, Barth rejects a categorical condemnation of a termination of a pregnancy.

For the extraordinary constellation of a marginal case, Barth claims that grave conditions must be met: "These situations may always be known by the concrete fact that in them a *choice* must be made for the protection of life, *one life* being balanced *against another*."[137] Barth lacks sympathy for the Roman Catholic position that in such cases the life of the mother is the one to be sacrificed. The necessary condition of the marginal case is that the choice between one life and the other is not a random choice, but a forced choice medically. From a legal point of view, Barth argues for a "medical 'indication' in its full extent,"[138] which includes both the somatic and the psychiatric dimension. In the latter case Barth seems to have rape in mind.

> In the circumstances there is something almost horribly respectable in the attitude of the Roman Church. It has to this day remained inveterate and never changed its course an inch in this matter—never sparing in its extreme demands on women! In the encyclical *Casti connubii* of 1930 (Enc. 2242 f.), deliberate abortion is absolutely forbidden on any grounds, so that even Roman Catholic nuns raped when the Russians invaded Germany in 1945 were not allowed to free themselves from the consequences in this way.[139]

Barth's refusal of a "social 'indication'" is directed against counting

137. *CD* III/4, 421 (emphasis added according to the original). A variation of this case is an ectopic pregnancy, in which the embryo, due to nidation outside of the uterus, is not viable. "The insidious and potentially catastrophic nature of [an] E[ctopic] P[regnancy] has historically made it one of the most feared conditions to occur in women of reproductive age." Eric M. Heinberg, "Ectopic Pregnancy," in *General Gynecology*, ed. Andrew I. and Eric A. Sokol, The Requisites in Obstetrics and Gynecology (Philadelphia: Elsevier, 2007), 257–86, at 257. Its statistic likelihood in the United States amounts to 2 percent of all pregnancies or more.

138. *CD* III/4, 422 (trans. rev.).

139. Ibid., 417 (trans. rev.). Encyclical 2242–3 refers to Denzinger's *Enchiridion Symbolorum* (no. 3719–20 in the Denzinger/Schönmetzer edition). See Mantei, *Nein und Ja zur Abtreibung*, 32–3.

a loss in "freedom, honour or capacity"[140] as a valid reason for a marginal case. From a legal point of view, Barth argues that a "socio-medical 'indication'" should nonetheless be legal, since the social dimension of the conflict may involve a psychiatric dimension. Today, however, the problem has arisen that in fact a medical justification for the termination of a pregnancy has come to include the illegal "eugenic," or embryopathic "indication," which Barth does not discuss.[141]

Regardless of these legal questions, Barth insists on the crucial importance of God's commanding:

> Human life, and therefore the life of the unborn child, is not an absolute, so that, while it can be protected by the commandment, it can be so only within the limits of the will of Him who issues it. It cannot claim to be preserved in all circumstances, whether in relation to God or to other men, i.e., in this case to the mother, father, doctor and others involved. In His grace God can will to preserve the life which He has given, and in His grace He can will to take it again. Either way, it is not lost before Him.[142]

Since Barth declares God's contingent choice the ultimate criterion in this case, Barth's argument has sometimes been criticized as voluntaristic. Is God's commandment indeed understandable on grounds other than a divine voluntarism, even in the marginal case, so that human life can be protected effectively against caprice, as the thesis statement of §55 demands? Or is the insistence on God's particular command precisely a recipe for arbitrariness by subjecting

140. *CD* III/4, 422.

141. Austrian criminal law (§97) allows for an embryopathic indication, while according to German and Swiss law, a likely disability of the infant can only be a reason for the termination of a pregnancy insofar as it implies medical harm for the mother. In terms of actual practice, the difference between the two kinds of regulations is not very large due to fear of psychological pressure on the mother.

142. *CD* III/4, 420.

momentous decisions to a fideism or decisionism, which is inaccessible to a critical, intersubjective questioning, as critics argue?

> To make the content of ethical discernment depend entirely on the obedience to God's commanding is persuasive only within an ethics resting entirely on faith. Within today's Protestant ethics, however, the legitimacy of such an approach is only limited. . . . A contemporary Protestant ethics should at least be rationally comprehensible, and thus plausible, also for non-believers, if it wishes to hold on to its claims to provide orientation for action for everyone affected.[143]

With less restraint, Hendrik van Oyen calls an "individual listening to God's voice . . . which can be so free, so sovereign, but which can also imply such contradictions," as "fatal," equating Barth with the adherents of the "spiritualist sects of all ages."[144]

This critique assumes that Barth only refers to an absolute command without providing any rational guidance. That would exclude the specification of necessary conditions of the marginal case. By contrast, Kohler-Weiß draws attention to the development of the embryo, which leads her to criticize Barth's concept of life as too general, as he does not allow for any distinction between a fertilized egg, a viable fetus, and a born baby. Her particular attention to Barth's concept of life is indeed appropriate, as §55.2 deals with "The Protection of Life." On the face of it, Barth's main argument for such protection is that life is the Creator's "loan."[145] A theology of creation that makes reference only to the loan of life, however, has to "give the same answer basically to ethical problems as varied as . . . the termination of a pregnancy, infanticide, and homicide," as its concept of life does not allow for distinctions. For this reason, Kohler-Weiß argues, "the possibility of including the health of the

143. Kohler-Weiß, *Schutz der Menschwerdung*, 81.

144. Hendrik van Oyen, "Gibt es eine evangelische Ethik der Grenzfälle?" *Zeitschrift für evangelische Ethik* 1 (1957): 2–17, at 6–7.

145. On the notion of life as a loan in *CD* III/4, see especially 335–8.

pregnant woman within the ethical consideration in the conflict about the unborn life [remains] . . . basically incomprehensible" in Barth's discussion.[146] The only way to do justice to a more differentiated state of affairs would then consist in a retreat to the caprice of a command that can only be discerned by true faith.

However, an important aspect in Barth's discussion of the termination of a pregnancy is that his concept of creation is more specific than the mere notion of life as a "loan" seems to suggest. It is not only crucial for Barth that the difference between being and nonbeing rests on God's activity. By itself, this might allow for a voluntaristic act in which God freely disposes of God's own property. If the foundation of Barth's argument consisted merely in this notion of property and loan, then God's act that posits being would be the foundation of all responsibility to God in the creaturely realm.

By contrast, Barth insists on a close interrelationship between creation and Christology, or the theology of the cross; the notion of life as a loan is much less prominent than those traditions. In §55.2, the concept of loan only emerges in Barth's discussion of suicide. Even the notion of respect for life (*Ehrfurcht*, awe) plays only a minor role in the section on pregnancy.[147] Barth does emphasize in the preceding section §55.1 that life is a loan from God. But even there he fleshes out what respect for life implies from a christological perspective.[148] Creation is not an abstract positing of life by God, but is teleologically ordered toward the relation with Christ. Barth's doctrine of creation rests fundamentally on the idea that creation is

146. Kohler-Weiß, *Schutz der Menschwerdung*, 80. In Albert Schweitzer's case, this critique would be apposite.

147. The term *loan* occurs only twenty-four times in *CD* III/4, and only 3 times outside of §55. In the seventy-three pages of §55.2, however, the term only appears three times. Of the ninety-three occurrences of the term "respect" (*Ehrfurcht*) in *CD* III/4 (only six outside of §55), only ten are in § 55.2.

148. Barth adopts this term in *CD* III/4, §55.1 from Albert Schweitzer, yet crucially Barth differs from Schweitzer's understanding of it in not taking it in the categorical, "broad sense" (324).

"the external basis of the covenant"[149] and that the covenant is "the internal basis of creation."[150] The covenant, in turn, is fulfilled in Jesus Christ. Thus, the basis for respect for life is not merely that it is posited, in and of itself, by God. "We may confidently say that the birth of Jesus Christ as such is the revelation of the command as that of respect for life. This reveals the eternal election and love of God. . . . And therefore this makes it an object of respect."[151]

The introduction to §55.2 also highlights the importance of the incarnation for the dignity of the loan of life: "Human life . . . belongs to God. It is His loan and blessing. For God has unequivocally and fully accepted it in Jesus Christ, in the incarnation of His Word. Therefore respect is due to it, and, with respect, protection against each and every callous negation and destruction."[152] Barth's discussion of the termination of a pregnancy gives this christological dimension of creation clearer contours in a theology of the cross. Thus, Barth's arguments in the theology of creation cannot be appreciated in abstraction from Christology.

Certainly, it could be argued both in a theology of the cross and a theology of creation that God's unilateral activity, either as Reconciler or as Creator, imparts dignity to the embryo categorically. By contrast, in Barth's Christology and his theology of the cross, the gospel has priority over the law. A command constitutes an obligation only if it can truly be understood as a plausible way for life to correspond to God's grace. This is the crucial point in Barth's argument that *usually*, God's command is directed against the termination of the pregnancy.[153]

It is precisely for this reason, however, that the theology of the

149. *CD* III/1, §41.2.
150. Ibid., §41.3.
151. *CD* III/4, 339.
152. Ibid., 397.
153. Ibid., 418, 419.

cross itself is the foundation of a potential marginal case. By contrast, an argument from a theology of creation in abstraction from Christology is in no way obliged to interpret God's command as an act of grace. Ordinarily, in giving the loan of life, grace constitutes the obligation to protect life. If in extraordinary circumstances, however, the preservation of life cannot be understood as a consequence of grace, then the validity of a supposed command to preserve life must be questioned:

> The command of God is based on His grace. He summons man to the freedom in which he may live instead of having to live. At root, the man [*Mensch*] who thinks he must live cannot and will not respect life, whether his own or that of others, far less the life of an unborn child.[154]

Barth highlights this aspect strongly in discussing the ordinary case, which excludes a termination of the pregnancy. By the same token, however, this excludes an understanding of the command that, in virtually fanatical consistency, disregards extraordinary misery on the part of the pregnant woman. The "reference" (*Hinweis*, §52) to God's command that is among the tasks of Christian ethics amounts to the question whether there are compelling, medical reasons for which the pregnant woman can or will see a command to carry the embryo to term as a contradiction to God's liberating grace.[155]

It might be argued critically that Barth does not highlight the priority of the gospel over the law when discussing the marginal case of abortion. Yet since he makes the obligation of a command

154. Ibid., 418.

155. Hans-Joachim Kraus, an eventual successor of Barth's on the Göttingen chair for Reformed theology, interprets the priority that Barth assigns to the gospel in this sense: A categorical vote against the termination of the pregnancy "errs about the mother's fundamental predicament, in whose situation in life the 'medical indication' can only be an indication among others that are equally grave. Love and freedom will reign and will have to combat license both on the right and on the left. In the end, love and freedom will tend towards a temporally limited lack of restrictions on abortion [*Fristenlösung*]." Hans-Joachim Kraus, *Systematische Theologie im Kontext biblischer Geschichte und Eschatologie* (Neukirchen-Vluyn: Neukirchener, 1983), 171n9.

against the termination of the pregnancy dependent upon the gospel, it is unavoidable that a supposed consequence of the gospel loses its obliging force when it can only be experienced as judgment. "Anything that in itself is really dark and accursed cannot possibly be the cross that we are ordered to carry."[156]

The christological dimension in Barth's discussion allows comparisons of competing goods and weighs them against each other. Christians can refuse to suffer under a supposed command if it contradicts the priority of grace, even if this implies the loss of an embryo.

One might object that God's sovereign command should not be made dependent on mere human wishes. However, the decision about a termination of a pregnancy—as long as serious moral reflection takes place at all—is neither a sovereign disposing of God's command nor a mere whim. After all, Barth takes note both of the difficulties and the dignity in which the pregnant woman finds herself when she faces the decision about a termination of the pregnancy. She must live up to her responsibility before God in a "scrupulous consideration and yet also a resolute venture."[157] Since this precarious decision is "always so dangerous,"[158] it is impossible unless it is done in the confidence of God's forgiveness. Thus, the objection that the current interpretation unfortunately renders God's command dependent on a merely human decision must be turned around. If God's commanding took place in absolute sovereignty, regardless of the human situation, it would be abstract and questionable. Then, however, the decision would only seemingly be God's; ultimately, however, it would only be that of the pregnant woman, who in turn would be left to her own devices in terms of

156. *CD* II/2, 611.
157. *CD* III/4, 423, see 421.
158. Ibid., 423.

ethical guidance. Only once the priority of the gospel over the law receives criteriological function can God's command differ from the liberty of caprice.

Killing for the Sake of Justice (§55.2)? Capital Punishment

Barth begins his discussion of the death penalty with an empirical overview, as he did in the section on the termination of a pregnancy. In this case, the overview is more historical in nature, beginning with the early stages of legal evolution in the biblical book of the covenant. Jesus' crucifixion is then presented as a prominent case of capital punishment, in which the Roman state saw it necessary to proceed against its enemies. The argument of the high priest Caiaphas in John 11:49–50 illustrates that Jesus' crucifixion was justified as preventing greater evil: "But one of them, Caiaphas, who was high priest that year, said to them, 'You know nothing at all! You do not understand that it is better for you to have one man die for the people than to have the whole nation destroyed.'"[159] Barth considers this representative of a larger trend that also continued with the persecution of the Christians in ancient Rome.[160] It "was as a defensive act of the *state* against *its* enemies that capital punishment gained a new ascendancy in imperial Rome."[161]

This presents the death penalty disadvantageously. The soteriological interpretation of Jesus' death on the cross does not lead to an uncritical attitude toward state violence. For Barth, who published *KD* III/4 in 1951, the most recent historical experience

159. *CD* III/4, 437.

160. According to Wolf-Dieter Hauschild, *Lehrbuch der Kirchen- und Dogmengeschichte: Alte Kirche und Mittelalter* (Gütersloh: Gütersloher, 1995), 115–16, the Roman Empire did not justify its own existence in a way plausible to all its members. Thus it had to arrange for quiet and order within and without by military means. The outward performance of the state cult was intended to serve a unifying function.

161. *CD* III/4, 437 (emphasis added according to the original).

in Germany probably plays a role in this evaluation, although Barth does not make the connection explicitly before he comments on the question of tyrannicide. Yet the so-called People's Court (*Volksgerichtshof*) in Germany sentenced 1,662 people to death in 1943 alone, which amounts to almost 50 percent of the cases dealt with. In the Nuremberg trials, many of the judges at this court lacked an appropriate sense of guilt; they did not consider themselves fanatical National Socialists.[162] But even after the collapse of National Socialism and the abolition of capital punishment in West Germany in 1949, there were numerous prominent Protestant theologians who argued in favor of the death penalty. It is not as if recent abuses had inoculated Germans against the pitfalls of capital punishment. Empirical data even indicated at the time that the death penalty had no detectable deterrent effect.[163]

In the face of the harsh experience in National Socialist Germany, a theology of the cross seems to have provided Barth with the opportunity to discuss ethical issues in close contact with current experience. "CS" (1938) also portrays the crucifixion as the execution of an innocent person by an unjust state, in order then to issue an only slightly veiled call for a revolution against Hitler.[164]

While Barth treats the preservation of life in general as an issue in the theology of creation, it will become clear that in the debate about capital punishment, traditions about the reconciliation brought about by Jesus Christ loom large. If patterns of argument in favor of the

162. William Sweet, "The Volksgerichtshof: 1934–45," *Journal of Modern History* 46 (1974): 314–29, at 326. Thus, only 123 of 3,338 defendants were deemed innocent. "Although the court had been expanded considerably since the beginning of the war, it could not keep pace with this kind of overloading." "There is no need to assume that the Volksgericht's members were radical Nazis deliberately undermining traditional law. They were probably fairly conventional jurists following general trends'" (ibid., 321).

163. Max Grünhut, "Todesstrafe," in *Religion in Geschichte und Gegenwart*, 2nd ed. (Tübingen: Mohr, 1931), 5:1202–8. Grünhut was a legal scholar and criminologist at the University of Bonn and later became a well-known criminologist at the University of Oxford.

164. "CS," 145.

death penalty are still upheld in this debate, they may perhaps appeal vaguely to a regulation of moral relations by a seemingly more primal mechanism, and thus perhaps to creation, although these concepts seem rather nebulous.

By contrast, Barth's attention to the theology of the cross influences his presentation of relevant facts and the arrangement of his argument. By attributing such significance to Christ's cross in his discussion of capital punishment, Barth effectively reshapes the issue as one pertaining to the ethics of reconciliation, while the mere question of the preservation of life originally led him to treat the matter within the ethics of creation. This is only natural, given that the central symbol of the Christian faith is indeed the instrument with which capital punishment was inflicted on an innocent victim. This is significant as the rejection of capital punishment was by no means a foregone conclusion in the Protestant churches of postwar Germany.

The critical potential of the theology of the cross is not inherent in several other theological traditions, as they put less emphasis on the cross as God's judgment over the world, while *Rom* II does so very strongly. Thus Barth calls it a notable fact that during the Middle Ages and in the Reformation period, ecclesial and theological circles were supportive or at least tolerant of the death penalty. When individual Enlightenment thinkers criticized the death penalty, they found an opponent, among other groups, in the church.[165] This is not a surprise given the historically influential justification of the death penalty with the notion of the atonement. "Punishment is, as it were, a representation and proclamation in human and earthly terms of the retributive justice of God."[166] Barth calls this approach not necessarily

165. *CD* III/4, 438: "For example, in Switzerland, where [the critics of capital punishment] had to meet the resistance of the Catholic Conservative Party, which so intransigeantly refuses to agree to any legalisation of abortion." Among the supporters of the death penalty were, among others, Locke, Voltaire, Rousseau, and Kant as well (ibid.).

166. Ibid., 440.

wrong per se. But at the same time, it is precisely because of Christ's atonement that the death penalty is no longer legitimate: "From the point of view of the Gospel there is nothing, nothing at all to be said for its institution, and everything against it."[167] Punishment of the innocent cannot be justified with the idea that further atonement is necessary before God.

Barth's considerations played an important role in the discussions about criminal law and its resocializing function in the 1960s in West Germany.[168] On the one hand, Barth presupposes an interpretation of the cross in terms of atonement. More recent theological discussion has distinguished the atonement more clearly from penal substitution than Barth does.[169] Nonetheless, according to Barth, the atonement that took place in the cross once and for all rules out the legitimacy of any further atoning suffering:

> On the Christian view the retributive justice of God has already found full and final expression, the expiation demanded by Him for all human transgression has already been made. . . . Now that Jesus Christ has been nailed to the cross for the sins of the world, how can we still use the thought of expiation to establish the death penalty? . . . The Church, from which one might really expect faith and therefore an understanding of the decision made at Golgotha, still speaks as if that stripping of evil of all its rights, and therefore the killing of certain wicked men, were commanded and necessary in confession of God's retributive justice.[170]

167. Ibid., 446 (trans. rev.). Barth asserts this at least for the application of criminal law in the civilian realm.
168. On the German reform of criminal law in 1969, see Peter Borowsky, "Sozialliberale Koalition und innere Reformen," in *Zeiten des Wandels: Deutschland 1961–1974*, Informationen zur politischen Bildung 258 (Bonn: Bundeszentrale für politische Bildung [Federal Agency for Civic Education], 1998), http://tinyurl.com/p2lglrm. Barth's ethical concept and the German reform of criminal law amounted to similar conclusions: punishment must be oriented toward resocialization, while retribution does not offer an empirical basis for a just assessment for punishment.
169. Article four of the Augsburg Confession interprets Christ's cross as an act of satisfaction, which differs from an atoning sacrifice. Friederike Nüssel, "Die Sühnevorstellung in der Dogmatik und ihre neuzeitliche Problematisierung" in: *Deutungen des Todes Jesu im Neuen Testament*, ed. Jörg Frey and Jens Schröter (Tübingen: Mohr, 2007), 73–94, at 91.

One might perhaps respond that an affirmation of the concept of atonement allows for an affirmation of capital punishment under the condition that Christ's atoning death is valid before God, while in the human realm, atonement is still necessary. But it is a difficult notion at any rate that a perpetrator's death would effectively redress the moral balance. Then again the Old Testament notion of cultic atonement is not aware of such a precise distinction between the divine and the human realm.[171] God grants the atoning effect of the sacrifice, while humanity cannot effect the benefit, but only receive it.[172]

Moreover, Barth quotes the view of the exegete and theologian Adolf Schlatter, according to whom basic respect for justice depends fundamentally on the death penalty.[173] However, especially in the face of the most recent experience in Nazi Germany, Barth's objection is fully justified that authorities purporting to act in the name of God fundamentally underestimate the relativity of the legal order, which can tend toward harshness toward petty criminals or the innocent while being lenient toward grave offenses.[174] Moreover, to some extent, society as a whole shares in the guilt of the offender.

In addition, Barth argues, no society will succeed in persuading enough people that there is no escape from criminal prosecution.[175] In his earlier ethics lectures, by contrast, Barth seems to affirm capital punishment cautiously. In 1951, however, he sees capital punishment as spurring criminals on to greater ruthlessness in trying to evade prosecution. These considerations are in fact based on the

170. *CD* III/4, 442–3.

171. Hartmut Gese, "The Atonement," in *Essays on Biblical Theology*, trans. Keith E. Crim (Philadelphia; Augsburg Publishing, 1981), 93–116, at 95: Atonement responds to sin, a loss in cosmic integrity.

172. Ibid: the atonement is not due to God's demand. Instead, God grants a human wish.

173. *CD* III/4, 443.

174. Ibid., 442.

175. Ibid., 445.

comparative research of the time, according to which capital punishment does not lead to a decrease in felonies.[176] The idea that due to its deterrent effect, the means of capital punishment is justified by the ends, is based on an illusion: tolerating a potential, yet fatal miscarriage of justice is not going to win over potential criminals for the legal order; instead, it may even subvert the respect it commands so far.[177] Human judgment must be of such a kind that it can "be transcended and corrected."[178] Interestingly, Barth's argument against creating a deterrent by means of capital punishment and his insistence on judgments open to correction are also ethical modes of argument that are oriented toward defensible results.

In this discussion of capital punishment, Barth's interpretation of the cross serves as a hermeneutical key. For Barth it contributes significantly to a critical and constructive understanding of social realities. In approaching the issue of capital punishment descriptively, Barth leads to a reappraisal of whether the practice is tenable at all, given also that it led to the execution of the Son of God.

This leads to the question whether theologians, of all people, have not contributed to the toleration of violence, since they have largely considered the execution of Jesus Christ a good thing, even if a blessing in disguise. Barth notes in fact that theologians have reliably supported the death penalty. Even if the crucifixion happened once and for all, the theology of atonement may contribute to the specter of redemptive violence. The chapter on *CD* IV will tackle this grave issue in discussion with Barth. For now, suffice it to say that the primordial judicial murder, as it were, sensitized Barth to a larger

176. Ibid, with reference to Max Grünhut, "Todesstrafe", 1205–6. Grünhut's balanced discussion—by the standards of the times—tends toward a rejection of death penalty. According to Fritz Loos, "Todesstrafe: IV. Juristisch," in *Religion in Geschichte und Gegenwart*, eds. Hans Dieter Betz et al., 4th ed. (Tübingen: Mohr Siebeck, 2005), 8:451–3, at 452, there is consensus that based on today's comparative studies, a deterrent effect of capital punishment is an illusion.
177. *CD* III/4, 444–5.
178. Ibid., 444.

dimension of injustice. For Barth, universal reconciliation at the cross plays a central role. It is only after he rejects capital punishment based on the notion of Christ's atoning death that happened once and for all that he gives a definite answer to the question of deterrence, having left the question unanswered before.[179] It is not the case that two different strategies of argument are juxtaposed without an inherent relationship, a theological one and a more general, nontheological one that points to the necessity of infallible judgment and difficulties in deterrence.[180]

Nonetheless, Barth argues for two marginal cases. God might command the death penalty in order to preserve a state that is threatened in its very existence. The issues at hand are treason in times of war and tyrannicide. The death penalty as an instrument of criminal law as applied in a civilian context remains out of the question, however. Nevertheless,

> there is certainly a place for the killing of those whose existence threatens the state and its stability in such a way that a choice has to be made between their existence and that of the state. . . . What must be at stake in these cases is . . . the state . . . in *greatest* difficulties . . . when not just the *bene esse* [flourishing] but the very *esse* [being] of the state and its members is at issue, when "to be or not to be" is the question which it faces.[181]

Barth restricts even this marginal case. The demise of a state that must be at issue here must consist in more than a mere redrawing of the map or a change in cultural habits: it needs to amount to nothing less

179. Ibid., 440–41.
180. The comparison with Barth's ethics lectures (1928–9, 1939–1) confirms these observations on the role of the theology of the cross. Barth's discussion of capital punishment makes reference to Christ's cross only once in interpreting John 11:50 in the sense of deterrence. Barth, *Ethics*, ed. Dietrich Braun, trans. Geoffrey W. Bromiley (Eugene: Wipf & Stock, 2013), 153. Barth considers the guilt of a particularly cold-blooded mass murderer so grave that one cannot reject capital punishment entirely.
181. *CD* III/4, 446–7 (trans. rev.).

than an immediate threat to the very life of the population. This is the condition under which indeed—as Barth puts it with allusion to John 11:50—"it is better for one person to die, and thus to be rendered harmless and to serve as a deterrent to the rest, than that the whole nation should perish."[182]

This statement is notable for the fact that in the face of Christ's crucifixion, Barth neither argues for strict pacifism nor justifies the possible legitimacy of violence with a radical, libertarian freedom of God's command. Instead, Barth weighs different goods against each other in valuing the survival of a population and the defense against anarchy more highly than the preservation of the individual lives that endanger those goods.

Barth also specifies criteria for the legitimacy of tyrannicide. There must be a clear danger of imminent perishing, the failure of regular means in averting this evil, and clear signs of a notorious, fundamental breach of law on the part of the tyrant.[183] Basically, Barth weighs the principles of a constitutional democracy against the avoidance of violence. Already in "CS" (1938) and in *CD* II/1,[184] Barth gave a theological justification of the principles of constitutional democracy. God's *Gerechtigkeit*, his justice and righteousness, was "won by Jesus Christ in His death and proclaimed in His resurrection," and as a consequence, the state must "administer justice and protect the law."[185]

In *CD* III/4, §55, Barth doubts that those men who attempted the assassination of Hitler on July 20, 1944, had perceived a command by God. They did not consider their plans immoral, yet their hesitation showed that they were unwilling to venture their lives.[186] However, it

182. Ibid., 447.
183. Ibid., 448–9.
184. *CD* II/1, 386–7. See the chapter on *CD* II above.
185. "CS," 127, 119.
186. *CD* III/4, 449.

is problematic to speculate about other people's motives, and a fanatic may be under the impression of hearing a command by God in quite different circumstances.[187] It would have made more sense at this point to adhere to the method of weighing goods against one another and ask about the extent to which the killing of an individual will create a realistic chance of preserving just principles and due process in the legal system.

Peace Ethics (§55.2): Politics of Peace and the Marginal Case of War

Barth begins his discussion of peace and war[188] with observations on contemporary warfare (1951), which are still relevant today. His key point is that the ultimate cause of war is usually economics. The striving for economic power, especially for natural resources, drives bellicose politics. In addition, religious semantics have often dressed this up in terms of heroic sacrifice. Yet Barth argues critically that in war, "the economic power . . . is shown not so much to be possessed by man as to possess him."[189] In the question of war and peace, Barth gestures toward a multisystemic approach.

In all likelihood, Barth is influenced by socialist or communist thought, although he does not provide any references of the sort. In a 1914 lecture, Barth contended that the call not to share one's loyalty to God with Mammon (Matt. 6:24) implies the refusal of those capitalist interests that led to the First World War.[190] Already the Communist Manifesto regarded capitalism similarly,[191] and a year

187. See, for just one example, Monica Davey, "Doctor's Killer Puts Abortion on the Stand," *New York Times*, Jan. 29, 2010, A 1, http://nyti.ms/9wTEDb.

188. Lienemann, "Das Gebot Gottes als 'Ereignis,'" 173, counts this issue, together with political resistance, among the most important ethical themes in Barth's oeuvre.

189. *CD* III/4, 452.

190. Barth, "Krieg, Sozialismus und Christentum: Vortrag in der Sozialdemokratischen Partei Oftringen 6. XII. 14," in *Vorträge und kleinere Arbeiten: 1914–1919*, ed. Hans-Anton Drewes (Zurich: Theologischer Verlag, 2012), 86–93.

after Barth's lecture, Lenin's essay "Socialism and War" argued along similar lines. Lenin called the First World War an imperialist war driven by capitalist powers striving for greater economic power, although cloaked in the pathos of patriotism and liberty.[192] Pacifism is legitimate and likely to succeed only after a proletarian revolution, according to Lenin, while on the way there, it is counterproductive—a fact supposedly concealed by the Social Democrats.[193] By contrast, Barth argues in 1951 that measures in the spirit of Social Democracy are indispensable on the way to a sustainable peace—which he does not understand in the sense of the party politics of the day.[194]

Barth's thesis that economics is at the root of war is in agreement with the materialist view that the spirit that seems to guide action is in fact determined, at least to some degree, by the relations of production. This monocausal thesis is certainly one-sided; Barth's limited advocacy for just war will relativize this categorical statement. Nonetheless, the general drift of Barth's analysis is cogent and significant. On the one hand, war is often about natural resources; on the other, bellicose politics are propelled by the lobbyism of the arms industry. Barth thus diagnoses incipient forms of a military-industrial complex.[195] "War reveals the basically chaotic character already of the

191. Chapter 2 of the *Communist Manifesto*: "In proportion as the exploitation of one individual by another will also be put an end to, the exploitation of one nation by another will also be put an end to. In proportion as the antagonism between classes within the nation vanishes, the hostility of one nation to another will come to an end."

192. Vladimir Ilyich Lenin, "Socialism and War: The Attitude of the R[ussian] S[ocial] D[emocratic] L[abor] P[arty] Toward the War," in *August 1914–December 1915*, ed. Julius Katzer, Collected Works 21 (London: Lawrence & Wishart/Moscow: Progress Publishers, 1964), 295–338, at 303 (first published in 1915 in Geneva). Among others, one important difference between Barth's and Lenin's thought on war and the economy is Lenin's view that war can help along the development of the relations of production, which will eventually usher in the final stage of history. By contrast, Barth assumes that in capitalist economic expansion, humanity to a large extent exploits itself.

193. Lenin, "Socialism and War," 315, 328–9.

194. *CD* III/4, 526.

195. Comments on a) the global arms export, b) the example of Germany, and c) the concept

so-called peaceful will, efforts and achievements of man."[196] It is not that society's will and action bends toward violence only in war, for "obviously we want something quite warlike even in peacetime."[197]

Barth's ethics thus does not focus too narrowly on the symptoms of the crisis, asking instead for deeper causes of war. Neither does

of the military-industrial complex are in order here. a) Between 2004–8 and 2009–13, the international transfer of weapons increased by 14 percent, amounting to 2.4 percent of the international GDP (2014). This is despite knowledge about unsustainable financial politics in recipient states, the harmful effects of arms races, and widespread civilian casualties in current armed conflicts. India, China, and Pakistan stand out for strong increases in imports. With the United Arab Emirates and Saudi Arabia, two states standing accused of massive human rights abuses have reentered the list of top-five arms importers. Together they account for almost one-third of all arms imports. Seven of the ten largest arms producers are from the United States, and the United States, Russia, China, Germany, and France are the largest exporting countries. *SIPRI Yearbook 2014: Armaments, Disarmament and International Security* (Oxford: Oxford University Press, 2014), http://tinyurl.com/metgmfg (sec. 4 and 5). b) On the theological side, the Memorandum of the Council of the Evangelical Church in Germany, *Live from God's Peace—Care for Just Peace* (2007), Evangelische Kirche in Deutschland, http://tinyurl.com/qzkr9yy, ch. 4.3.1 (p. 53, para. 159) points out that Germany has, or at least sees, an economic interest in international rearmament, even in violent conflict. Indeed, in 2013, 30 percent of German arms exports with an individual export license were directed to countries receiving foreign aid (2011: 21 percent, 2012: 18 percent), and sixty-four of the importing countries were officially deemed problematic in their human rights affairs (2012, 2013: sixty-three). See the reports on German arms exports by the German Joint Conference on Church and Development for 2011–13: Gemeinsame Konferenz Kirche und Entwicklung (GKKE), Fachgruppe Rüstungsexporte: *Rüstungsexportbericht*, Bonn and Berlin, for 2012: GKKE-Schriftenreihe 58, 2013, http://tinyurl.com/k9wmzu3 /July 21, 2015); for 2013: GKKE-Schriftenreihe 59, 2013, http://tinyurl.com/lw9skbd; for 2014: 2013, http://tinyurl.com/o2y877l. Tabled exports to Saudi Arabia include tanks ("Boxer") suitable for street fighting, and indeed Saudi Arabia was involved in crushing the "Arab Spring" protests in Bahrain. In 2013, exports of small arms and tanks increased strongly. Although the German constitution forbids arms exports (article 26), the German constitutional court argued in 2014 that the administration needs to inform parliament about exports only after contracts have become effective. c) The influence of the military-industrial complex rests especially on the connection between the local economic significance of the arms industry and its political operation. See Rachel N. Weber, "Military-Industrial Complex," *Encyclopædia Britannica*, http://tinyurl.com/ok26uvl. A more recent example is provided by David Barstow, "Behind Analysts, the Pentagon's Hidden Hand," *New York Times*, April 20, 2008, http://nyti.ms/nSJFyM. On further points made above, see Amnesty International UK, "Repression and Injustice in the United Arab Emirates," Nov. 18, 2014, http://tinyurl.com/mcqnnee; Christoph Hickmann, "Opposition rügt möglichen Panzer-Deal," *Süddeutsche Zeitung*, Dec. 3, 2012, http://tinyurl.com/bqef8e5; "Regierung darf Anbahnung von Rüstungsexporten geheim halten," *Süddeutsche Zeitung*, Oct. 21, 2014, http://tinyurl.com/ksnewuj.

196. *CD* III/4, 452 (trans. rev.).

197. Ibid. (trans. rev.)

Barth merely ask whether a particular war is justified by traditional standards of just war ethics. To some extent, recent continental peace ethics has adopted this tendency by integrating peace studies and research into conflict resolution.[198] Nonetheless, Barth's discussion highlights a glaring deficiency in current academic moral deliberation.[199] War is not merely an issue for the politics of the day, but is played out against a particular structural backdrop. In effect, political pleas by themselves will only have a limited effect, especially if limited to military aspects. This is illustrated by how quickly the rejection of war in Germany after the Second World War gave way to support of rearmament, while critique in the tradition of the Confessing Church suffered from an isolated treatment of political aspects.[200]

With regard to the structural backdrop of bellicose politics, *CD* III/4 was incapable of suggesting a constructive role of capitalist economics in reducing the dangers of war.[201] In keeping with his

198. See especially Wolfgang Huber and Hans-Richard Reuter, *Friedensethik* (Stuttgart: Kohlhammer, 1990).

199. See Adam Roberts, "Against War," in *The Oxford History of Modern War*, ed. Charles Townshend (Oxford: Oxford University Press, 2000), 317–40. On the just war tradition, see especially Nigel Biggar, *In Defence of War* (Oxford: Oxford University Press, 2013). A striking aspect in this book is how single-mindedly Biggar frames the issue of war as an instrument for restoring peace without elaborating on other such instruments. But if war is indeed the last resort, one would like to know the other options first. In spite of its positive qualities, Biggar's book is part of a strong but one-sided tradition. Biggar names six or seven monographs in English proceeding this way, besides his own and Oliver O'Donovan's *The Just War Revisited* (ibid., 2–3). With one exception, all of them have appeared since 1997. The framing of the issue of war is not merely a question of specialization, however. Barth's emphasis on peaceful means of contributing to peace also serves a vital hermeneutical function in pointing to the role of concealed economic interest. Only by disregarding this dimension can one, for example, call Germany "virtually pacifist" (Biggar, *In Defence of War*, 7), although it has long been the third-largest (now being the fourth-largest) arms exporter of the world. This suggests, however, that the theory of just war is best discussed within the framework of an ethics of peace, which in turn is to be conceived of much more fundamentally than the goal pursued in just war.

200. On the historical issues in postwar Germany, see Wolfgang Lienemann, "Das Problem des gerechten Krieges im deutschen Protestantismus nach dem Zweiten Weltkrieg," in *Der gerechte Krieg: Christentum, Islam, Marxismus*, Friedensanalysen 12, ed. Reiner Steinweg (Frankfurt am Main: Suhrkamp, 1980), 125–62, at 134, 136–7.

201. By contrast, see Wolfgang Lienemann, "Verantwortungspazifismus (*legal pacifism*): Zum

thesis that to a large extent, war is caused by economic politics, Barth focused on a contrast between capitalism and humanism.[202] Nonetheless, heading in the direction of a multisystemic approach, *CD* III/4 steered the right course.

Barth's discussion of war and peace also argues against papering over the fact that war has always been plainly about killing. The Second World War, including the use of nuclear weapons, has rendered the insight inescapable that in "cold objectivity,"[203] war is "quite nakedly and brutally" about "the killing of as many as possible of the men who make up the opposing forces . . . with neither restraint nor consideration in any respect."[204] This statement lacks certain qualifications, which will entail problems in ethical theory. However, Germany's "total" warfare in the Second World War, the deliberate bombing of civilian targets by the German air force, RAF, and USAAF, as well as nuclear warfare do suggest indeed that the fundamentally cruel and destructive character of war unmasks much praise of chivalry as naive. In 1951, Barth feared the reemergence of a crusader's mindset[205] in the ideologically charged Cold War, in which few, if any, restraints are placed on the potential use of violence. Thus he insists that "the inflexible negative of pacifism has almost infinite merits."[206] The danger that lurks here is "a flat betrayal of

politischen Gestaltungspotential pazifistischer Bewegungen im Blick auf das Völkerrecht," in *Der gerechte Friede zwischen Pazifismus und gerechtem Krieg: Paradigmen der Friedensethik im Diskurs*, ed. Jean-Daniel Strub and Stefan Grotefeld (Stuttgart: Kohlhammer, 2007), 75–99, at 76. Strict pacifism in Western modernity has often had motives of trade. According to Immanuel Kant, the "*spirit of commerce* . . . cannot exist side by side with war." *Perpetual Peace: A Philosophical Sketch*, in *Political Writings*, ed. Hans S. Reiss, trans. H. B. Nisbet, 2nd ed., Cambridge Texts in the History of Political Thought (Cambridge: Cambridge University Press, 1991), 114.

202. *CD* III/4, 458–9.

203. Ibid., 453.

204. Ibid., 452, 453.

205. Barth, "An Pfarrer Wolf-Dieter Zimmermann, 'Unterwegs', Berlin(-West), 1950," in *Offene Briefe 1945–1968*, ed. Diether Koch, Barth-Gesamtausgabe (Zurich: Theologischer Verlag, 1984), 202–14, at 210.

206. *CD* III/4, 455.

the Gospel."[207] It should be added that today as well, moral motives, careful planning, and today's technological advances fail again and again in sparing civilian lives.[208]

The fundamental critique of war and the diagnosis of economic causes prompt Barth to adopt a new perspective in the question of just war. Rather than calling for peace only when a war is in the offing already, the churches and theological ethics need to make clear that "truly *peace* is the momentous case [*Ernstfall*, in contrast to mere preparation or inactivity]."[209] This involves more than the absence of hostilities. Basic constellations of justice, with respect to economics as well, are called for. Barth inverts the classic mantra of the politics of deterrence, *Si vis pacem, para bellum* (If you want peace, prepare for war), with *Si non vis bellum, para pacem!* (If you do not want war, prepare for peace!).[210] After Barth has been wary of a potential deterrent effect of capital punishment, he now argues against the politics of fear again.[211] He thus draws the conclusion from his assertion in *CD* II/2 that God's command "will not meet [man] with mistrust but with trust. It will not appeal to his fear but to his courage. It will instil courage, and not fear into him. This is

207. Ibid.

208. When the war in Iraq (2003–11) ended, the number of civilian casualties was well above estimates from 2006, which range from 400,000 to 650,000. John Tirman, "Why Do We Ignore the Civilians Killed in American Wars?" *The Washington Post*, Jan 6, 2012, http://tinyurl.com/7cwuq8h.

209. *CD* III/4, 459 (trans. rev.). *KD* III/4, 525: "Daß *der Friede* der Ernstfall ist." Biggar's presentation of this section ignores this significant statement, rendering Barth's peace ethics a just war ethics (Nigel Biggar, *Hastening That Waits*, 93).

210. *CD* III/4, 452. The original aphorism is from Vegetius's *Epitoma Rei Militaris*. The variation in this aphorism by the memorandum of the Evangelical Church in Germany, *Live from God's Peace* (p. 28, para. 159), "Si vis pacem, para pacem," is even more apt, as the intended goal is not merely the absence of armed violence.

211. While this may be criticized as a risky abandonment of a deterrent, Barth's thinking is more akin to Kant's realization that republics—and we might add constitutional democracies a fortiori—are peaceful since citizens with rights and responsibilities do not like being sent to war or to pay for it. Kant, *Perpetual Peace*, 100. Barth's rejection of the pacifist call to abolish compulsory military service (*CD* III/4, 466–7) is related to this idea.

the case because the command, as we have seen, is itself the form of the grace of God."[212] Thus the politics of fear must be replaced by constructive peace work.

Moreover, Barth's refusal of the politics of violence is also influenced by the Sermon on the Mount,[213] which *CD* II/2, chapter 8 sought to subvert with an actualistic ethics of the contingent divine command and his categorical assertion that the Sermon on the Mount does not witness to God's command. Yet the church needs to be "a small yet significant force for peace."[214] Already in times of peace, this tradition needs to keep its priorities straight: "Neither 'rearmament' nor 'disarmament' can be a first concern, but the creation of an order of life which is meaningful and just."[215]

The necessity of an active politics of peace is not necessarily new. This position had already been articulated by the representatives of so-called Organizational Pacifism, yet their influence had remained rather limited.[216] In addition, the notion of a politics of peace is even

212. *CD* II/2, 586.

213. Heino Falcke, "Aspekte der gegenwärtigen Friedensdiskussion beleuchtet durch Karl Barths Friedensethik," *Zeitschrift für Dialektische Theologie* 12 (1996), 175–91, at 182–3.

214. *CD* III/4, 456.

215. Ibid., 459 (trans. rev.). Bonhoeffer argued for a similar cause in 1932: a sustainable peace cannot be attained apart from truth and justice. Dietrich Bonhoeffer, "Lecture in Ciernohorské Kúpele: On the Theological Foundation of the Work of the World Alliance," *Ecumenical, Academic, and Pastoral Work: 1931–1932*, eds. Victoria J. Barnett et al., trans. Anne Schmidt-Lange et al., Dietrich Bonhoeffer Works 11 (Philadelphia: Fortress Press, 2012), 356–69. However, Bonhoeffer did not see the economic dimension pointed out by Barth in 1951. In 1934, Bonhoeffer argued in a less "realist" vein: "Peace is the opposite of security. To demand guarantees is to mistrust, and this mistrust in turn brings forth war. . . . Peace is to give oneself altogether to the command of God." "Address to the Fanø Conference: English Transcription" ["The Church and the Peoples of the World"], in *London: 1933–34*, ed. Keith Clements, trans. Isabel Best, Dietrich Bonhoeffer Works 13 (Minneapolis: Fortress, 2007), 307–10, at 309 (trans. rev.). Bonhoeffer does criticize rearmament for the sake of peace as an illusion, yet—understandably—the question of how peace can in fact be attained remains opaque. "If peace is the opposite of security, precisely how then does faith in the peace which God commands engage with the world which, like it or not, *does* work in and through the big banks, government offices, media barons and—yes—the armed forces?" Keith Clements, "Ecumenical Witness for Peace," in *The Cambridge Companion to Dietrich Bonhoeffer*, ed. John de Gruchy (Cambridge: Cambridge University Press, 1999), 154–72, at 170.

216. Walter Dignath, "Friedensbewegung," *Religion in Geschichte und Gegenwart*, 3rd ed. (Tübingen:

more striking before the backdrop of the economic factors propelling a bellicose politics. Thus, Barth should indeed be considered an early, prominent proponent of a new theological paradigm in international political ethics. Later on, the World Council of Churches picked up the connection between social justice and peace that Barth had pointed out, while expanding the diagnosis with an ecological dimension. Even though Barth's explicit discussion of these issues does not figure prominently in the ecumenical documents, the significance of his position also consists in the fact that at the ecumenical conferences in Oxford (Life and Work, 1937) and Amsterdam (1948), the two positions of a strict pacifism and a toleration of war based on a harsh view of human sin confronted each other head-on.[217]

Moreover, it follows from Barth's argument that he raises questions about the state as the agent in warfare. He argues against the view that the essence of the state is to wield power. Maintaining the monopoly on violence as the characteristic of the state[218] does not do justice to the ethical question of how to use the monopoly on violence. "According to the Christian understanding, it is no part of the normal task of the state to wage war; its normal task is to fashion peace in such a way that life is served and war kept at bay."[219] This

Mohr Siebeck, 1958), 2:1135–41, at 1138; Wolfgang Huber, "Frieden V: Kirchengeschichtlich und ethisch," *Theologische Realenzyklopädie* (Berlin and New York: de Gruyter, 1983), 9:618–46, at 631; Huber and Reuter, *Friedensethik*, 112–13; 199–200.

217. On the Oxford conference, see Lienemann, "Das Problem des gerechten Krieges im deutschen Protestantismus," 132–3 Barth uses the term *just peace* increasingly in 1939, while the mere absence of war might, under particular circumstances, even include hatred and injustice. Barth, "Ein Brief nach Frankreich, 1939," in *Briefe 1935–42*, 205–23, at 217; Barth's letter to Visser't Hooft, Oct. 7, 1939, in *Karl Barth—Willem Adolf Visser't Hooft Briefwechsel 1916–1966*, ed. Thomas Herwig, Barth-Gesamtausgabe (Zurich: Theologischer Verlag, 2006), 100–11, at 109; Barth's letter Feb. 21, 1940, ibid., 129–30, at 129.

218. Max Weber, *Economy and Society: An Outline of Interpretive Sociology*, eds. Guenther Roth and Claus Wittich (Berkeley et al.: University of California Press, 1978), 54: "A compulsory political organization with continuous operations (*politischer Anstaltsbetrieb*) will be called a 'state' insofar as its administrative staff successfully upholds the claim to the monopoly of the legitimate use of physical force in the enforcement of its order."

position of Barth's is in keeping with a view on war and the state proposed, for example, by Luther.[220] At the center of Barth's notion of the state is the creation of a "just order of life."[221] Already in "CS," Barth defined the real meaning of the state in this sense. At the root of this task he saw reconciliation in Christ.[222] Now he argues that the just political order must be a "social democracy."[223] Barth refers to Kant's treatise *Perpetual Peace*,[224] which critiques the authoritarian state in favor of a republic.[225]

Moreover, *CD* II/1 drew the conclusion from the biblical testimonies to God's covenant with Israel that God's mercy constitutes an obligation for partisanship in favor of the marginalized.[226] In Barth's reasoning, a social state is conducive to a just order of peace, while a one-sided, neoclassical orientation toward private enterprise increases the danger of an aggressive foreign policy.[227]

Barth's theological advocacy for social and legal justice is strongly influenced by his Christology, which thus has implications even for international political ethics.[228] At the same time, Barth's ethics of

219. *CD* III/4, 458.
220. "Worldly government has not been instituted by God to break the peace and start war, but to maintain peace and avoid war." Martin Luther, "Whether Soldiers, Too, Can Be Saved. 1526," in *The Christian in Society*, ed. Robert C. Schulz, trans. Charles M. Jacobs, Luther's Works 46 (Philadelphia: Fortress Press, 1967), 3:93–137, at 118.
221. *CD* III/4, 459.
222. In contemporary foreign politics, the task of nation building increases in prominence due to the importance of nongovernmental agents in wars. A just legal system requires "the security of human force" ("CS," 142, trans. rev.). From the task of democratization (see below) results the task of fostering the growth of civil society.
223. *CD* III/4, 459; see 451, 456.
224. Ibid., 450.
225. According to Kant, *Perpetual Peace*, 100, citizens of a republic are not in favor of being deployed in war, or are unwilling to pay for war.
226. *CD* II/1, 386–7.
227. *CD* III/4, 458–9; Wolfgang Huber, *Folgen christlicher Freiheit: Ethik und Theorie der Kirche im Horizont der Barmer Theologischen Erklärung*, 2nd ed., Neukirchener Beiträge zur Systematischen Theologie 4 (Neukirchen-Vluyn: Neukirchener, 1985), 265.
228. According to Nigel Biggar, the contribution of Barth's doctrine of reconciliation to the question of war is limited to the statements that pacifism cannot be categorical, that ultimately,

peace does not merely focus on the state, but also highlights the role of church and theology as well as of all citizens in constructive work for peace. He argues for an end to a fundamental separation "between individual and social ethics."[229] On an international level, Barth calls for new initiatives in diplomacy and legal relations, "for solid, legal agreements and alliances and their honest observance, for international courts and international associations"[230] With a pedagogy of peace, Barth thus also touches on another important concept of a peace ethics.

Peace ethics can thus help overcome the contrast with which an ethical and a legal discussion of just war is typically beset—in the terminology of international law, the opposition between a "discriminating" concept of war and a "fencing in" of war. On the one hand, war is subjected to moral scrutiny, which may, in a fanaticism of the good cause, lend moral justification to the most extreme measures.[231] On the other hand, if rational procedures and modes of conduct are conceived of independently of the unsteady "ebb and flow" of moral discourse, it may seem rational to suspend fundamental moral scruples against war in international law.[232]

war is not waged against, but for the benefit of the military opponent, and that it must not be waged for ideological purposes (Biggar, *Hastening That Waits*, 93). For a more substantial analysis of the christological dimension already operative in this section of the ethics of creation, see Marco Hofheinz, *"Er ist unser Friede": Karl Barths christologische Grundlegung der Friedensethik im Gespräch mit John Howard Yoder*, Forschungen zur systematischen und ökumenischen Theologie 144 (Göttingen: Vandenhoeck & Ruprecht, 2014).

229. *CD* III/4, 465, which highlights individual conscientious objection. By contrast, Beintker, "Verantwortung," 171–2, argues for a stronger notion of the social in comparison with the personal that he sees prevailing in Barth's work.

230. *CD* III/4, 460 (trans. rev.).

231. With a word of General Sherman, Walzer (*Just and Unjust Wars*, 32–3) points to the dangers of the "war is hell" doctrine, according to which war should be short und thus harsh in the means employed.

232. See Carl Schmitt, *Die Wendung zum diskriminierenden Kriegsbegriff* (Berlin: Duncker und Humblot, 1938, 2007); William Hooker, *Carl Schmitt's International Thought: Order and Orientation* (Cambridge: Cambridge University Press, 2009). See Niklas Luhmann's argument in a different context: "Only when law is differentiated from the ever-changing tidal flow of moral communication, and only when distinctions based on law's own criteria for validity can

Barth's criterion of a just order of peace also plays a crucial role in the marginal case. The strict pacifist refusal of war is only "almost" entirely right.[233] It is in this aspect that Barth relates constructively, if indirectly, to the classic just war tradition. While working on *CD* III/4, Barth commented in an open letter (1950), "In the Hromádka letter from 1938, for the sake of faith I called for armed resistance against Hitler's armed threat and aggression that was just taking place. I am not a pacifist and would do the same again today if in the same situation."[234] Thus, Barth writes also in 1951 that a just war can be possible and necessary if "responsibility for the whole physical, intellectual and spiritual life of the people comprising it, and therefore also their spiritual relationship to God" may be "bound up with the independent life of a nation."[235]

This statement—although rather vague—is the key to understanding the marginal case in the ethics of peace in *CD* III/4. The creation of an international balance of power, the integrity of

be made, is it possible to specify the facts which are legally relevant and distinguish them from a wholesale appraisal of the person that is at issue." Luhmann, *Law as a Social System*, ed. Fatima Kastner et al., trans. Klaus A. Ziegert (Oxford: Oxford University Press, 2004), 108 (trans. rev.).

233. *CD* III/4, 455.

234. Barth, "An Zimmermann," 208. See Barth, "Brief an Prof. Dr. Josef L. Hromádka, Prag 1938," in *Offene Briefe 1935–42*, ed. Diether Koch, Barth-Gesamtausgabe (Zurich: Theologischer Verlag, 2001), 107–133, at 114. In 1939, before the German invasion, Barth argued that Christians in Denmark need to do at least two things: "I cannot give you an itemized list. But I can give you the first bullet point: *Pray!* And the last one: *Buy guns!* What is in between these two items, you need to discern yourselves." Bent Fleming Nielsen, "Beten—und Kanonen kaufen: Evangelium und Gesetz im Zusammenhang von KD II/2 (§§ 36–39)," in *Karl Barth im europäischen Zeitgeschehen (1935–1950): Widerstand—Bewährung—Orientierung*, ed. Michael Beintker and Christian Link (Zurich: Theologischer Verlag, 2010), 109–36, at 116. As Nielsen states (ibid., 134), "There is also something like a distanced reflecting and choosing here." According to John Howard Yoder, "Barth and the Problem of War," 81, and David Clough, *Ethics in Crisis*, 97, the structures preparing for the marginal case of war subvert Barth's fundamental position tending against war. Yet both Yoder and Clough fail to take sufficiently into account the proper emphasis of Barth's peace ethics, which puts a premium on constructive peaceful work for peace. Neither do they do justice to Barth's christological arguments for legitimate violence for the sake of the rule of law. Both points have most recently been highlighted by Hofheinz, "*Er ist unser Friede,*" especially 422–65, 610–26.

235. *CD* III/4, 462 (trans. rev.).

political borders and state sovereignty, even the very preservation of a state are not necessarily a justification of war, much less defamation or a striving for hegemony.[236] An act of aggression as a reason for war still requires further qualification.[237] The preservation of a just legal system including freedom of religion as its root—see Barth's account of legal justice in "CS"—seems to be decisive. In the question of killing in the name of justice (§ 55.2), Barth considers the killing of a ruler potentially moral if the ruler systematically subverts the rule of law. Later on, Barth explained the vague statement cited above.

> Of course, speaking of the "spiritual relationship to God," I meant something slightly different than a threat to religious education [i.e., in state schools] and such things. Instead, as I indicated in the following three and a half lines, I thought quite concretely of what it would be like now if we gave in here in Switzerland. That is, to the pressure of the Hitler state during the Second World War. After all, there were people in Switzerland who wanted to give in. There were even Swiss National Socialists.[238]

Indeed, Barth wrote in 1938 that in the fascist state, an intact Christian confession would be impossible.[239] Thus, freedom of religion is, as it were, the canary in the coal mine. If it is systematically restricted, the rule of law and social justice are in danger on the whole. As Barth considers Christ's reconciling work the foundation of a realist ethics, and thus of a just legal system,

236. Ibid., 461. Yoder's critique that Barth lapses back into the ethnic theology that he criticized himself ignores Barth's view that the proper vocation of a state consists in the preservation of the rule of law and thus in protecting life from license; under this condition the use of force can be legitimate. Yoder, "Barth and the Problem of War," 57–9.

237. Since Barth thinks that it "can sometimes happen that the time of a state in its present form of existence has expired" (*CD* III/4, 461), he also questions Walzer's communitarian assumption that the sovereignty of a people in the face of aggression is the criterion of a just peace (Walzer, *Just and Unjust Wars*, 55).

238. Barth, "Gespräch mit der Kirchlichen Bruderschaft in Württemberg (15.7.1963)," in *Gespräche 1963*, ed. Eberhard Busch, Barth-Gesamtausgabe (Zurich: Theologischer Verlag, 2005), 42–109, at 75.

239. Barth, "An Hromádka," 114.

a decrease in religious freedom goes hand in hand with reduced chances for reform in legal and social justice.

As practical respect for life, the prohibition to kill must be weighed against the good of protection from license by the rule of law. During the Second World War, Barth considered asylum for the persecuted as well as freedom of speech and of religion a crucial difference between Switzerland and Germany. In his view, traditional Swiss neutrality thus had to prove its moral worth in preserving these goods rather than in a merely external neutrality in military questions.[240] Wars must be waged only for the sake of a worldly rule of law that includes protection of basic rights. There are no directly religious reasons for a potentially just war apart from the preservation of religious freedom.[241] Barth considered a worldly order of war capable of justification in secular terms, although he regarded its religious justification as fundamental, albeit compatible with a secular account. The action that may thus be morally demanded can even comprise a military intervention by a third state.[242]

Barth speaks repeatedly of the peaceful initiative for social and legal justice as the "proper work" (*opus proprium*) and violence and war as the "foreign work" (*opus alienum*) of the state. Only in extraordinary cases can violence serve the peaceful mission of the state. The "foreign work" is legitimate only under the condition that it is necessary for the sake of the proper work. After *CD* II/2, chapter 8 argued that power as such cannot constitute moral obligation, Barth now makes the moral status of the use of force dependent on a further

240. Eberhard Busch, *Unter dem Bogen des einen Bundes: Karl Barth und die Juden 1933–1945* (Neukirchen-Vluyn: Neukirchener, 1996), 336–7.

241. Barth, "Bruderschaft," 75–6.

242. *CD* III/4, 462. In the face of the conflict with National Socialism, Barth doubted the meaningfulness of Bonhoeffer's interest in Gandhi. "To Rector Eberhard Bethge, Rengsdorf near Neuwied, May 22, 1967," in *Letters 1961–1968*, ed. Jürgen Fangmeier and Hinrich Stoevesandt, trans. Geoffrey W. Bromiley (Grand Rapids: Eerdmans, 1981), 250–52, at 250.

moral purpose. He does not, however, harbor illusions about its great destructive potential and the danger of economic interest.

However, Barth's differentiation between the state's proper and foreign work is sometimes not understood in a logical, but in a temporal sense, as if politics could sometimes make an exception to its first priority, the creation of peace, without exhausting all peaceful means of doing so.[243] This misunderstanding conceives of politics not according to the unity between the gospel and the law, but sees Barth arguing for a correspondence between state politics and a diastasis between the hidden and the revealed God. However, it is due to the inner unity of gospel and law, and the priority of the former, that Barth suspects the state of a "flat betrayal of the Gospel,"[244] wary that war might not serve the cause of peace. Barth's terminology is infelicitous, however, insofar as God's "foreign work" is considered by certain Lutheran theologians legitimate, indeed necessary and indispensable, in preparing the way for God's "proper work." If state politics were to reflect a theological concept like this, there would be no reason to assume that peaceful ways of stabilizing peace must take priority over bellicose ones. Since this is Barth's position, however, Oliver O'Donovan's interpretation in the sense of a more traditional Lutheran theology of gospel and law is not to the point. After all, a theology of a *deus absconditus* (hidden God) or a theology of orders might justify a politics of war that seems enigmatic like a *deus absconditus* with a "Janus head."[245]

When faced with God's command in extraordinary circumstances, however, it is precisely the "preaching of the Gospel"[246]—rather than

243. Oliver O'Donovan argues that Barth, driven by the inner dynamics of his theology, came out sometimes in support, sometimes in critique of war without being able to provide clear criteria. Oliver O'Donovan, "Karl Barth and Ramsey's 'Uses of Power,'" *Journal of Religious Ethics* 19 (1991): 1–30, at 3.

244. *CD* III/4, 455.

245. Ibid., 458.

246. Ibid., 453.

of an independent law—that constitutes an obligation to wage war. But since economic reasons will often tempt toward war, the church needs to employ a hermeneutics of suspicion against the justification of war.[247] Barth's international political ethics not only tends toward the critique of war due to its prior commitment to a peaceful politics of peace, but also by attributing the burden of proof to a case for just war. If this proof has been furnished, however, the church is obliged to support military action. On the whole, Barth's peace ethics share much with a consequentialism that is after just and peaceful relations in the long run[248] and that has also learned the hard lesson provided by the repeated abuse of just war semantics.

Barth's views about a just war also single him out as one of the few Protestant voices in postwar Germany arguing that the classic doctrine of just war is one-sided, but not necessarily wrong.[249] Interestingly, convictions about the moral demerits of war united traditional Lutherans and the former leaders of the Confessing Church. Between these two groups, however, the conclusions drawn with regard to Germany's rearmament were diametrically opposed. Is war unavoidable and must it thus be tolerated in faith, or does faith call for categorical protest? By contrast, Barth draws precisely

247. Ibid., 460.

248. According to Nigel Biggar, just war theory is more properly deontic than consequentialist (*In Defence of War*, 29). From another perspective, however, one of its basic intuitions is the restoration of a certain political order that outweighs concomitant evils and that, in the choice of its means, must in certain cases be in strict proportion to the chances of success. See, for example, ibid., 32. In certain circumstances, this consequentialist intuition can certainly be relativized by deontic ethical principles.

249. Cf. Lienemann, "Das Problem des gerechten Krieges im deutschen Protestantismus," 138; 140. Hans Joachim Iwand argued that a just war would be possible in principle, while in fact nuclear rearmament would prepare an unjust war. He points to Kant's statement that those means in warfare are illegitimate that destroy the basis for a future peace accord. Hans Joachim Iwand, "Das geschichtliche Phänomen der Atomwaffe und die Angst: Ein Versuch ihrer Überwindung [1955]", in *Frieden mit dem Osten: Texte 1933–1959*, ed. Gerard C. den Hertog (Munich: Kaiser, 1988), 97–124, at 107; Kant, *Perpetual Peace*, 95–6 (article 6); Lienemann, "Das Problem des gerechten Krieges im deutschen Protestantismus," 137. Lienemann argues "that the price for abandoning any doctrine of just war can be high, for this doctrine aimed after all primarily at a limitation of war" (139).

on the traditional doctrine of just war when tending toward a pacifist position that included notable room for exceptions (see below).

Barth's discussion of the marginal case, however, suffers from a lack of precision. Certainly Barth is right in viewing war as targeted killing with few restraints and in calling for peaceful means to contribute to peace. Yet in the question of the potential morality of war itself, the aspect of the *ius ad bellum* (right to go to war), the determination of legitimate reasons for going to war, dominates. By contrast, *CD* III/4 implicitly tends to view the question of *ius in bello* (justice in war), or legitimate conduct in war, as a naive romanticization of systematic injustice.[250] The relative merit of this view is that Barth implicitly transforms the question of *ius in bello* (justice in the conduct of war) into a *ius contra bellum* (right against war), as it were.[251] Certainly his overwhelming interest is in peace, which he now presents as a richer concept than the absence of armed conflict.

Moreover, the nihilistic ideology and the criminal energy of the National Socialists indeed disregarded fundamental rules and conventions of war, especially in the war of extermination against the USSR.[252] This gruesome endeavor stands out for its terrors, but it should not be considered the representative of warfare.[253] If the Second World War is taken as the paradigm of war, on the other

250. *CD* III/4, 453: in war, "whole nations as such are out to destroy one another by every possible means." Barth will in effect distance himself from this statement later on. See also William Werpehowski, "Karl Barth and Just War: A Conversation with Roman Catholicism," in *Commanding Grace: Studies in Karl Barth's Ethics*, ed. Daniel L. Migliore (Grand Rapids: Eerdmans, 2010), 60–82, 69–70.

251. The memorandum of the Evangelical churches in Germany, *Live from God's Peace*, also argues for a *ius post bellum*, which reduces the risk of the current conflict to incite a future crisis. The implementation of human rights and a lively interaction with the past, also from a legal perspective, are meant to serve that goal (p. 47, para. 133).

252. Bauer, *Nationalsozialismus*, 381; 384; Antony Beevor, *The Second World War* (New York: Back Bay, 2012), 207–18.

253. Biggar, *In Defence of War*, 200.

hand, it is unclear to what extent Barth's thesis about economics as the most significant driving force behind war can still stand. This raises the question of *ius in bello* again. The concept gains in importance if an extreme conduct of war is not the rule after all. In times of globalization, especially due to more strongly distributed economic networks and the creation of a wider, more quickly responsive international public, perhaps a systematic removal of the constraints in killing imposed by conventional warfare seems not only immoral, but, in the longer run, imprudent as well.

On the other hand, a suspension of the *ius in bello* question leads to the fatal effect that Michael Walzer describes as the doctrine of "war is hell."[254] If in the marginal case war is potentially moral, the question also arises whether the potential morality of war includes all that is usually abhorrent in war. In the marginal case, should a military operation indeed aim at "the killing of as many as possible of the men that make up the opposing forces,"[255] and perhaps even more than that? There may be a temptation to the effect due to the proverbial importance of winning, but also in the efforts to limit the amount of bloodshed temporally.[256] The question is especially pertinent as any treatment of war in the 1950s should have included the issue of nuclear warfare. Strangely enough, Barth's treatment of peace and war does not comprise this crucial question, although it was especially virulent in postwar Germany.

What is most significant from an ethical point of view here is that an act of military aggression that threatens to get rid of the rule of law may force the victims to go to war and thus to imitate the wicked action of the aggressor. Within the bounds of conventional warfare, such imitation is potentially moral. Above and beyond these bounds,

254. Michael Walzer, *Just and Unjust Wars: A Moral Argument with Historical Illustrations*, 4th ed. (New York: Basic, 2006), 32–3.

255. *CD* III/4, 452.

256. See n230.

however, the use of nuclear weapons in an escalation of the Cold War would have made it unlikely to fill an order of legal and social justice with life (in both senses of the word) after it has been reestablished.

In a self-critical look back to §55, Barth judged in 1963 that the marginal case must be ruled out ethically when nuclear weapons are likely to be used in warfare. "Properly speaking, nuclear warfare is the end of all things from the first moment! That is when warfare itself and as such loses all meaning. Nuclear warfare means: total destruction."[257] Barth concluded, "Nuclear warfare as such cannot be a just war. If that [i.e., the use of nuclear weapons] is certain, then there is nothing but unjust wars, and in concrete terms, then there will actually be nothing left to do for Christians than—here's the point!—conscientious objection."[258] In Switzerland, conscientious objection was decriminalized only in 1992, while in Western Germany, the refusal to serve in the military was still highly contentious, although it has been a constitutional right since 1949.[259]

Barth thus adopted the position of so-called just war pacifism. Indeed Barth called the question of *ius in bello* indispensable in the discussion of war:

> For even the classic theologians of the sixteenth and seventeenth centuries discussed "just war" . . . and said: there are certain rules . . . this and that must not happen even in war, e.g., killing prisoners or women and children, etc. . . . And I should have taken up that lead: "just war"

257. Barth, "Bruderschaft," 72. This is true for both the operative and the deterrent use of nuclear weapons, due to potential accidents. Barth reproached himself "that I did not write there [i.e., in *CD* III/4, § 55.2] what can now be read in a quite different place: in the encyclical *Pacem in Terris* [by Pope John XXIII, 1963], and unfortunately not in the *Church Dogmatics*: 'Thus, in this age which boasts of its atomic power, it no longer makes sense to maintain that war is a fit instrument with which to repair the violation of justice.' That is the point that I missed there, in 1951—which was of course already six years after Hiroshima." Barth, "Bruderschaft," 69.

258. Barth, "Bruderschaft," 73.

259. West Germany has never been in possession of nuclear arms, yet as a NATO member, it has been obliged to assist allies with nuclear weapons since 1955. While Switzerland has neither been a NATO member nor has had nuclear weapons of its own, there have repeatedly been heated discussions about nuclear armament in the formally neutral country.

> not only with a view to the cause or the meaning of the war, but "just war" also with a view to its being carried out.[260]

Here Barth justifies his rejection of nuclear weapons, even of war itself, precisely with just war theory. Ultimately, a categorical refusal of war evades ethical dialogue and public decision making, as it cannot draw on the notion of the proportionality of means or *ius in bello*. This was significant also in the debate about German rearmament, around the time that the West German army was reestablished in 1955, four years after Barth wrote *CD* III/4. When arguing against the influential position that war should be rare but, in particular constellations, moral, many Christians were in fact helpless for lack of a doctrine of just war. This was true both for a Lutheran war fatalism, based on a strong doctrine of sin, and a strict Christian pacifism, sometimes based on the argument that God had knocked the weapons out of German hands.[261]

But can we justify the proposal that a particular course of military action must be called immoral on account of the extra-conventional means it employs, even if it appears justified in terms of its cause (*ius ad bellum*)? If certain goals justify conventional warfare, which is violent nonetheless, how can the choice and the use of means be restricted? Even if the people killed are combatants, they are still God's creatures. Above and beyond that, even in conventional war, the killing of civilians seems virtually unavoidable. Walzer argues that nuclear weapons are not even legitimate as a deterrent.[262] In a "supreme emergency," however, he considers the targeted killing of civilians legitimate if carried out with conventional weapons.[263] Since the recent wars in Afghanistan and Iraq, locally restricted wars

260. Barth, "Bruderschaft," 72–3.
261. Thus the position of the later secretary of justice and federal president Gustav Heinemann. See Lienemann, "Das Problem des gerechten Krieges im deutschen Protestantismus," 136.
262. Walzer, *Wars*, 274.
263. Ibid., 254.

without the use of weapons of mass destruction has become increasingly realistic. What counts against the extraconventional use of conventional weapons, as in the killing of civilians, is that the conventional use of conventional weapons offers a way of preserving at least a certain degree of moral integrity in not yielding entirely to the aggressor's coercion to use force.[264] By contrast, torture or the killing of prisoners or civilians can corrupt the will to restore the rule of law by eliminating the respect for life entirely, and this respect alone can justify a war. Thus the continued, targeted bombing of civilians by the Allied forces in the Second World War can be considered a decisive precedent that eventually lowered the threshold for the use of nuclear weapons.[265] To single out only one example, today a particular problem consists in the use of land mines, which are relatively easily available but quite difficult to remove. Thus, the civilian damage often surpasses the military use by far.[266] The international community needs to articulate a morally sustainable, practicable *ius in bello* that clearly restricts the civilian damage done by land mines. Before that has happened, the possibility of a *ius in bello* with regard to land mines must be viewed critically.

Barth's rejection of nuclear weapons shows that his question is less whether one can judge the morality of a course of action, and more in what way this should be done. This is confirmed by Barth's later affirmation of a *ius in bello*. This problem is also at issue in

264. Ibid., 257.

265. Cf. ibid., 255. On the whole, the bombing of civilian targets both by the R. A. F. and the German air force strengthened the will for resistance. Hermann Knell, *Untergang in Flammen: Strategische Bombenangriffe und ihre Folgen im Zweiten Weltkrieg* (Würzburg: Schöningh, 2006), 289; 293–6; Rolf-Dieter Müller, *Der Zweite Weltkrieg: 1939–1945*, 10th ed. (Stuttgart: Klett-Cotta, 2004), 91; 258; 262–4. The proclamation of a supreme emergency and the sense of mission associated with it may make an objective appreciation of military measures unlikely, especially if there is little experience in similar situations upon which to draw.

266. *Naturwissenschaft—Rüstung—Frieden: Basiswissen für die Friedensforschung*, ed. Jürgen Altmann and Ute Bernhardt (Wiesbaden: VS Verlag für Sozialwissenschaften, 2007), 135. See the website of the organization *People Against Landmines*, http://www.mgm.org/en.

another aspect of his discussion of peace and war that is crucial for Barth's method in ethics. Barth is of the opinion that, from a Christian view, a state must go to war even if defeat is likely, although the effort seems just. This would be in contradiction to the consequentialist element of the present discussion. Barth, in turn, may even appear to propose a fanaticism of justice. "A distinctively Christian note in the acceptance of this demand [of war] is that it is quite unconditional. That is to say, it is independent of the success or failure of the enterprise, and therefore of the strength of one's own forces in comparison with those of the enemy."[267]

So far it seemed that Barth would make a *ius ad bellum* depend on the likely results, such as the preservation of a just political system. In this passage, his reasoning seems principle based instead. Either there is a proper cause calling for war or there is not; the state must choose categorically between war or restraint based on this occasion, regardless of whether such war is likely to lead to a just peace. Yet it is also notable that Barth, in contrast to some interpretations of his argument,[268] still does not argue for the possibility of a just war based on a contingent command of God. Instead, a just war is legitimate in that without it, a society "would also have to yield something which must not be betrayed."[269] On this basis it is inconsistent of Barth to distinguish how a war is waged from the questions of its consequences. Nonetheless, this does not invalidate Barth's

267. *CD* III/4, 463. See also David Clough, "Fighting at the Command of God: Reassessing the Borderline Case in Karl Barth's Account of War in the *Church Dogmatics*," in *Conversing with Barth*, ed. John C. McDowell and Mike Higton, Barth Studies (Aldershot: Ashgate, 2004), 214–26, at 219–20.

268. *Pace* William Werpehowski, "Karl Barth and Politics," in *The Cambridge Companion to Karl Barth*, ed. John B. Webster (Cambridge: Cambridge University Press, 2000), 228– 42, at 238–9; Heino Falcke, "Aspekte der gegenwärtigen Friedensdiskussion beleuchtet durch Karl Barths Friedensethik," *Zeitschrift für Dialektische Theologie* 12 (1996): 175– 91, at 179. The latter (ibid., 180), however, lays out a critique of a consistent actualism, highlighting instead Barth's letter to Hromádka.

269. *CD* III/4, 462.

distinction between regular and irregular means of state politics. There is even a grain of truth in the inconsistency just criticized. For in particular circumstances it can make sense to endanger the life of soldiers, to some extent even of civilians, even if the preservation of the rule of law by military means is unlikely. Barth seems to think of a long-term war that transcends the regional realm, in which a regional defeat can and must be tolerated in the short term. It makes good sense to assume that Barth has the appeasement policy of the Munich agreement of 1938 in mind, in the wake of which Germany annexed a large part of Czechoslovakia without a fight. While working on *CD* III/4, Barth argued that it was wrong for the Western Allies to avoid military conflict with Germany in 1938. Barth had been moved quite strongly by the events of that year.[270] Barth felt isolated in his conviction of the overwhelming harm done by the Munich agreement. He thought the general sentiment was to consider appeasement the "realist" option. Nonetheless, to a considerable degree, Barth rejected appeasement for its likely consequences. As a result, the moral choice was not between an absolute, principle-based command (contra appeasement) and a consequentialist choice between rival goods (pro appeasement), but different views on the particular consequences entailed by a policy of appeasement. On the whole, to be entirely consistent, Barth's argument would have to be for a more consistent, consequentialist choice between rival goods. For the question at hand—the suggestion of a seemingly "fanatical" fight for a lost cause—this implies that low chances of success can be tolerated in *tactical* or operative regard, that is, in a short-term consideration, if indeed this constellation is part of a larger *strategic* scenario in the long run that implies better chances of success.

270. Barth, "An Hromádka," "An Zimmermann", 206–7.

Indeed the opinion that in certain conditions one can and should accept defeat in operative or tactical matters—but not in the long run, in strategic matters—would have been realistic in 1938. Had Czechoslovakia sternly insisted on national sovereignty in 1938, with the implication of military resistance, France would have had much greater difficulty ignoring its pact of mutual assistance with Czechoslovakia, and the United Kingdom would have been likely to reconsider the policy of appeasement sooner. The German attack on Czechoslovakia, which Hitler planned for that case,[271] would have revealed the German striving for hegemony to be even less of a conventional kind than in Wilhelmine times, but of a much stronger aggressive, ideological kind.[272]

By contrast, a British interest in a balance of power, including a stronger Germany facing the USSR, was based on the assumption of a more conventional German striving for hegemony, which would avoid overly daring military operations.[273] The fallacy of these considerations was revealed when in 1939, the pact between Hitler and Stalin undercut all hopes that the two totalitarian powers would neutralize each other. After the United Kingdom and France had failed, in a "fundamental error" of state craft,[274] to consult with Stalin before the Munich agreement, the Soviet leader suspected that the Western powers were not committed to joint action with the Soviet Union in confronting Hitler, but that the West closed ranks with

271. Beevor, *Second World War*, 9.
272. Joachim Fest, *Staatsstreich: Der lange Weg zum 20. Juli* (Berlin: Siedler, 1994), 61–2; 72.
273. A more conventional striving for hegemony, which would eventually lead to saturation, is the backdrop for Carl von Clausewitz's dictum that war is the continuation of politics by different means, i.e., the violent margins of an enterprise that is nonetheless more or less rational, that is, interested in long-term results and taking precautions in case of short-term failure. While Wilhelmine politics were not a prime example of political rationality, politics had become fundamentally irrational under Hitler's reign. See, for example, von Clausewitz's vote in Biggar, *In Defence of War*, 323n243: military risk can or must be proportionate to the urgency of the moral impetus, which is strong in strict self-defense.
274. Beevor, *Second World War*, 8.

Hitler in order to confront the Soviet Union. Rather than establishing a balance of powers, the Munich agreement played a major part in bringing about the pact between Hitler and Stalin.

By contrast, in 1938, German military experts did not consider Germany capable of quick success in a war on two fronts, facing both Czechoslovakia and France. Perhaps this situation would have provided the occasion for which General Ludwig Beck hoped in planning a coup d'état.[275] Hitler had indeed forced a rapid rearmament, rendering Germany a significant threat to a European peace in any case. Yet deferring armed conflict still improved the military perspectives for Germany. Hitler frantically sought to make up for the narrow confines that the Versailles treaty had imposed on German rearmament for almost a decade and a half.[276] So to return to the question of waging war regardless of the chances of success: while a Czechoslovakian defeat would have been likely in 1938, an earlier beginning of the war would have made a significant difference in the ensuing larger war.

Thus there were clear facts in favor of Barth's rejection of the

275. In an exercise in the German war academy, German forces were unable to defeat Czechoslovakia within eleven days, by which date a withdrawal behind the Rhine upon facing the French had become necessary in the west. Peter Hoffmann, *Stauffenberg und der 20. Juli 1944*, Beck'sche Reihe, 2nd ed. (Munich: Beck, 2007), 26; 52. After the Munich agreement, chief of general staff Beck canceled his plans for a coup d'état since Hitler had gained major public support, appearing now as an advocate for peace. Jürgen Schmädeke, "Militärische Umsturzversuche und diplomatische Oppositionsbestrebungen zwischen der Münchner Konferenz und Stalingrad," in *Widerstand gegen den Nationalsozialismus*, ed. Peter Steinbach and Johannes Tuchel (Bonn: Bundeszentrale für politische Bildung, 1994), 294–318, at 294, 303.

276. Since the beginning of Hitler's rearmament in October 1933, the generals had been reluctant as quantity took clear priority over efficiency (Hoffmann, *Stauffenberg und der 20. Juli 1944*, 34–5; Müller, *Weltkrieg*, 57). Hitler's goal was to win time before the western powers would intervene. At the same time, he could not hold out too long for fear of an end to Soviet neutrality and a US entry into the war (Müller, *Weltkrieg*, 77). In addition, Germany was in ruins economically already at the end of 1937 (Aly, *Hitler's Beneficiaries*, 41, 51). The annexation of Czechoslovakia, by contrast, gave Hitler weapons, industrial resources, and foreign currency (Müller, *Weltkrieg*, 58). He also won a vantage point from which to start the war in the east. The defeat of France, in turn, was due to the great risks Hitler ran in opting for rapid advances of German tank units as well as to bad French planning (Müller, *Weltkrieg*, 79–85).

politics of appeasement. He does not go into the historical details in 1951 when arguing against an overly narrow, opportunistic orientation toward results in the ethics of peace and war. However, this was presumably due to the fact that in the meantime, his letter to Hromádka was used to argue for the remilitarization of Germany around 1950. The German army was then reconstituted in 1955. The major factor in this course of events was of course the conflict between the USSR and the capitalist West,[277] which led to a proxy war in Korea (1950–53) during the time Barth was working on *CD* III/4.

In an open letter Barth gave his opinion on current affairs at the time. He did not want *CD* to be mostly a reaction driven by fear and thus attempted to abstract from pressure to act rashly.[278] Using his letter to Hromádka in 1950, Barth argued, would have amounted to preaching a "crusade against Russia and communism."[279] In 1950, Barth considered rearmament the greater danger for peace, while he did not see all means for deescalation exhausted, whereas in 1938 war could no longer have been averted.

Conclusion

On the whole, this discussion of Barth's introduction to his special ethics, §52, and of his discussion of the Sabbath command, the termination of a pregnancy, capital punishment, and peace and war argued that Barth draws on the Christian faith in a way that provides guidance in thorny moral problems. In doing so, he draws to a

277. After conferences in 1954 paved the way for the integration of West Germany into NATO, the Warsaw pact was constituted in 1955. That Germany was thus part of the escalation of the Cold War is indeed perplexing given the massive atrocities committed by German troops during the operation Barbarossa.

278. Barth, "An Zimmermann," 207–8. On the conventional character of the Korean War, see Walzer, *Wars*, 117–20; 119.

279. Barth, "An Zimmermann," 210.

significant degree on empirical research but does not replace dialogue between different conceptions of the Christian life and faith with fideism. In the notoriously difficult marginal case, the oft-repeated idea that ethical discernment does not, according to Barth, result in ethical guidelines turns out to be wrong, although Barth does not engage in detailed casuistry either. Instead, he offers necessary criteria for conditions in which God's command can take a particular, if unexpected shape, while he does not provide sufficient criteria for what God's command will, in fact, say. The latter qualification notwithstanding, this does not leave the ultimate decision up to an erratic, incommensurate pious emotional state. Another result that may seem surprising is that there is a clear consequentialist element in Barth's ethical reasoning.

Barth's special ethics in *CD* III/4 include, in Max Weber's terminology, a value-rational attitude (*wertrational*), insofar as the good of legal and social justice—which Barth sees morally constituted in Christ—plays an important role in guiding action. With this dimension of justice, Barth integrates the large sphere of human responsibility into his ethics. Barth also agrees with the view of instrumental rationality that the purposes of action can justify certain means—although certainly not all means. From this perspective, there is good reason to view Barth's ethics as close to Max Weber's description of an ethics of responsibility:

> But there is a profound opposition between acting by the maxim of the ethic of conviction [*gesinnungsethische Maxime*] (putting it in religious terms: "The Christian does what is right and places the outcome in God's hands") and acting by the maxim of the ethic of responsibility which means that one must answer for the (foreseeable) *consequences* of one's actions. . . . If evil consequences flow from an action done out of pure conviction, this type of person [i.e., someone acting out of conviction, a *Gesinnungsethiker*] holds the world, not the doer, responsible. . . . A man who subscribes to the ethic of responsibility,

> by contrast, will make allowances for precisely these everyday shortcomings in people. . . . He will say, "These consequences are to be attributed to my actions." The person who subscribes to the ethic of conviction feels "responsible" only for ensuring that the flame of pure conviction (for example, the flame of protest against the injustice of the social order) is never extinguished.[280]

Weber goes on to argue that pursuing seemingly moral goals may sometimes require morally doubtful action. Moreover, no ethics can define in advance what this walk on a tight rope should look like.[281] This leads Weber to draw a stark contrast between an ethics of conviction and an ethics of responsibility. Yet he also submits that the two must not be played off against one another as exclusive contrasts: "It is not that the ethic of conviction is identical with irresponsibility, nor that the ethic of responsibility means the absence of principled conviction—there is of course no question of that."[282]

What is notable in Barth's ethics at this point is that the purposes that moral action should pursue responsibly do not result from a sacrifice of Christian commitments at the altar of political realism. There is both a deep spiritual maturity as well as a certain worldly wisdom in Barth's case that, for example, God's commandment in a conflict about a pregnancy cannot be of such a kind that the fundamental goods and interests of a pregnant woman are strictly relegated to second rank, and the overarching political goods that may justify a war are based on Christ's work of reconciliation.

280. Max Weber, "The Profession and Vocation of Politics," in *Political Writings*, ed. Peter Lassmann, trans. Ronald Speirs, Cambridge Texts in the History of Political Thought (Cambridge: Cambridge University Press, 1994), 309–69, at 359–60.
281. Ibid., 360.
282. Ibid., 359.

4

The Foundations of Ethics in the Doctrine of Reconciliation in *Church Dogmatics* IV

Barth's doctrine of reconciliation in *CD* IV highlights the contingent event of reconciliation as the "centre of all Christian knowledge." Barth announces that no other topic is of such crucial importance; all theology stands or falls with the fundamental decisions made at this point: "To fail here is to fail everywhere. To be on the right track here makes it impossible to be completely mistaken in the whole."[1] This implies that Barth's theological interpretation of the reconciliation in Christ is fundamental also for his ethics. It will turn out, however, that matters are not as simple as Barth suggests when saying that the one right fundamental decision makes everything else fall more or less into place. This chapter will fathom both the ethical implications of Barth's decisions in the doctrine of reconciliation as

1. *CD* IV/1, Foreword.

well as potential alternatives. The consequences for ethics will be far-reaching indeed.

God's Revelation in the Passion of Christ

What Barth has in mind when highlighting the significance of the right basic approach to the doctrine of reconciliation is not only that God is properly recognized in Christ. Moreover, Barth insists that the incarnate Son of God is perceived appropriately especially in the testimonies to Christ's *passion*. Jesus Christ is true to his divine majesty precisely in the lowliness of his suffering. Barth thus sees God as

> the One who as the Creator and Lord of all things is able and willing to make Himself equal with the creature, Himself to become a creature; the One whose eternity does not prevent but rather permits and commands Him to be in time and Himself to be temporal, whose omnipotence is so great that He can be weak and indeed impotent, as a man is weak and impotent. . . . He is God in the fact that He can give Himself up and does give Himself up not merely to the creaturely limitation but to the suffering of the human creature, becoming one of these men, Himself bearing the judgment under which they stand, willing to die and, in fact, dying the death which they have deserved.[2]

Jesus Christ's lowliness is of more than incidental importance: his passion not only describes something about God's relationship to humanity, but characterizes God's self. According to Barth, we can only speak of God in speaking of "death, even the death of the cross."[3] What *deity* means can be seen first of all in the passion narrative:[4] "When it is a matter of knowing what is truly divine there can be no evading . . . the man on the cross of Golgotha."[5] God's very

2. Ibid., 129–30.
3. Ibid., 199.
4. Ibid., 129.
5. *CD* IV/2, 96.

being is characterized by this particular history, so that the traditional order of being and action must be inverted: *esse sequitur operari* (being follows action). The history of the world is inscribed, as it were, into God's being: "But this participation of the world in the being of God [in Jesus Christ] implies necessarily His participating in the being of the world, and therefore that His being, His history, is played out as world-history and therefore under the affliction and peril of all world-history."[6] According to Barth, "all the fulness of the Godhead" is "not changed" in the incarnation of the Son and the passion of Jesus Christ, but it "is given concrete form in Him."[7] At various points Barth gives expression to Christ's suffering in the passion.[8]

The Ethics of Cruciform Discipleship

The fundamental theological significance of Christ's passion is essential for ethics in *CD* IV, although these volumes deal with theology, being not primarily a presentation of an ethics. While Barth was unable to prepare the ethics of the doctrine of reconciliation for publication, he nonetheless presented them as lectures, which were published posthumously as *The Christian Life*. Nonetheless, the doctrine of reconciliation already makes important ethical decisions. Among these, for example, is the close relationship between Christ's exaltation on the cross and an ethics of cruciform discipleship: "In many of the New Testament records the call to discipleship closes with the demand that the disciple should take up his cross. This final order crowns, as it were, the whole call, just as the cross of Jesus crowns the life of the Son of Man."[9] "As the bearing

6. *CD* IV/1, 215.

7. *CD* IV/2, 86–7. Paul Dafydd Jones, *The Humanity of Christ: Christology in Karl Barth's Church Dogmatics*, T&T Clark Theology (New York: T & T Clark, 2008), 80, argues, "God wills, in fact, that the concrete life of Christ should *transform* God's life."

8. *CD* IV/1, 458: "The One who was really and finally humbled, who was thrust into the deepest darkness, who went for us to the cross and death and the grave." See *CD* IV/2, 349, 487–8.

of the cross was and is for Jesus Christ His coronation as the one Son of Man, the royal man, so for the Christian the cross which he has to suffer is his investiture with the distinction, glory and dignity proper to him as a Christian."[10] On account of this close relationship between theology and ethics already in the published volumes of *CD* IV, the current presentation will draw especially on these, adding material from *The Christian Life* mainly where it goes beyond what Barth himself published in *CD*.

As God's commandment in person, Jesus Christ is at the center of ethics in *CD* IV. The fact that God reveals God's self in the lowliness of the cross has far-reaching consequences for ethics. In the event of reconciliation, Christ proves his majesty precisely in his lowliness, Barth argues. This is the result of his uncompromising obedience to God's command, which implies misery and suffering for him. Barth's view that Christ's obedience to God's command manifests Christ's majesty precisely in his suffering is the foundation for an ethics of cruciform discipleship, which is especially prominent in *CD* IV.

At some points in his oeuvre Barth reacts critically against the notion of repeating Christ's work or of actively seeking out the misery he experienced.[11] Yet he also portrays cruciform discipleship in the sense of the *imitatio Christi* as a necessary manifestation of Christian freedom. In Christ's humility and his bearing of his suffering, Barth argues, we are faced with "a binding law" for all Christians,[12] referring to Scriptures such as Phil. 2:6–7 and Mark 8:34. Barth even heightens the emphasis on an ethos of subordination. For Christians, to follow Christ means

> that they should deny themselves . . . yield [their lives] freely to this

9. Ibid., 552.
10. Ibid., 599.
11. *CD* IV/2, 189, 546, 612–13.
12. *CD* IV/1, 189 (trans. rev.).

> total service. And this means concretely that each of them should take up his own 'cross,' not fearing or hating or avoiding or evading or trying to escape by force or subtlety the affliction that falls on him, but freely accepting it and taking it up and carrying it. . . . This is not the primary *theologia crucis* [theology of the cross] of the Gospels, but it is certainly the secondary.[13]

The subsection "The Dignity of the Cross" (*CD* IV/2, §66.6) breathes this affirmation of suffering as well. The subsection concludes section §66, "The Sanctification of Man." Dealing with the issue of discipleship, Barth writes that the Christian life culminates in bearing one's own cross.[14] Barth thus devotes an entire subsection to the topic. There Barth calls the cross "the most concrete form of the fellowship between Christ and the Christian."[15]

To a large extent, an evaluation of such strong, ambiguous statements depends on context. It constitutes a fundamental problem nonetheless that Barth calls such suffering "the rod of [God's] fatherly love."[16] By contrast, it appears strangely out of proportion that Barth's first example of carrying the cross appears rather prosaic. We may simply be dealing with an "ordinary toothache."[17] This does not exactly seem to be the kind of Christ-oriented suffering that one should not seek to evade. Does Barth thus try to tone down the overall strong rhetoric on the cost of discipleship? On the whole, Christians must not understand themselves "with a seriousness which has no place for criticism or humour."[18] Barth hints at smaller and lesser evils when speaking of being a social outsider, about creaturely limitations and existential doubts.[19] In a similar vein, cruciform

13. *CD* IV/2, 264.
14. Ibid., 552, see also 599.
15. Ibid.
16. Ibid, 608.
17. Ibid., 607.
18. Ibid.
19. Ibid., 610–12.

discipleship appears less dramatic when Barth argues in §59 that Jesus' love for his enemies confers obligations on Christians as well:

> Compared with that what is the bit of forbearance or patience or humour or readiness to help or even intercession that we are willing and ready to bring and offer in the way of loving our enemies? But obviously when we look at what Jesus Christ became and was for us, we cannot leave out some little love for our enemies as a sign of our recognition and understanding that this is how He treated us His enemies.[20]

In contrast to the strong general rhetoric, Barth downplays the concrete shape of bearing the cross. On the one hand, he compares Christ's suffering with that of others: "It might even be suggested that many men have perhaps suffered more grievously and longer and more bitterly than did this man in the limited events of a single day. Many . . . have been treated no less and perhaps more unjustly than this man." But even here Barth does not perceive suffering in all its terror, for notably he understands the suffering of others in "its hidden divine justification."[21] Christ's suffering, by contrast, is of a fundamentally unique nature,[22] for despite his innocence, he faced God as an enemy.[23] Barth can indeed view Jesus' cry of dereliction on the cross as an expression of utter misery, but he asserts at the same time that after Good Friday, there is no longer such misery.[24] It can then be supposed even more clearly that Christians should be prepared to suffer in faith.

Barth's most resolute case for an ethics of bearing the cross, however, is found in his section on man and woman, which he presented in *CD* III/4, §54.1, before he justifies and boldly reaffirms

20. *CD* IV/1, 244.
21. Ibid., 246 (trans. rev.: "*in ihrer . . . göttlichen Begründung*").
22. Ibid., 246–7.
23. Ibid., 264–5.
24. *CD* IV/2, 487.

it in the doctrine of reconciliation. An analysis of Barth's ethics would be incomplete without this notorious subsection. The current discussion will thus present Barth's christological foundation of the *tolerantia crucis* in order to describe then how Barth admonishes wives to be subordinate to their husbands. This illustrates the difficulties inherent in the tradition of cruciform discipleship, which can easily replace the liberating and empowering gospel with religious repression. This danger increases when suffering and hardship is portrayed, contrary to appearances, as exaltation and dignity. The critical potential of this analysis derives from Barth's own assertion that we can only speak of God in speaking of "death, even the death of the cross,"[25] that we can see first of all in the passion narrative what *deity* means—rather than in the legitimization of marginalization or against the backdrop of supposedly general gender relations.[26] Does Barth take his own statement seriously that "when it is a matter of knowing what is truly divine there can be no evading . . . the man on the cross of Golgotha,"[27] or does he fail to acknowledge the hardship of the passion by turning it into a blueprint and justification of marginalization, perhaps even under a contemporary conventional, bourgeois Christian morality?

To begin with, however, Barth's views on bearing the cross. According to *CD* IV it is decisive that, in fulfilling God's command, Jesus maintains his dignity as a moral subject even under the most difficult conditions. Jesus Christ's extraordinary obedience corresponds to his being as the divine Son, although Barth does not extrapolate the latter from the former. Others, by contrast, would likely have been scared off by the terrible suffering of the cross. Jesus understands his activity and his passion as repentance, in which

25. Ibid., 199.
26. Ibid., 129.
27. Ibid., 96.

he considers nothing good but the will of God, following him unconditionally, even regardless of his own vital interests:

> What distinguishes the man Jesus as the Son of God is that which apparently stands in the greatest possible contradiction to the being of God: the fact that in relation to God—and therefore to the world as well—this man wills only to be obedient—obedient to the will of the Father, which is to be done on earth for the redemption of man as it is done in heaven.[28]

While *CD* IV/1 depicts "The Obedience of the Son of God" (§59), *CD* IV/2 highlights that the Son's obedience is the obedience of the human person Jesus at the same time, who thus participates in the Son's majesty. This obedience consists in the repentant attitude to which Jesus commits in his baptism.[29] This stance eventually results in Jesus' cross. Jesus' obedience is illustrated especially by his temptation in the desert and in Gethsemane, which *CD* IV/1 interprets extensively. If Jesus had left the way of repentance, acknowledging Satan's reign—which would have been "a simpler and more practical and more realistic approach" without the need to "renounce God or to go over to atheism"—Jesus' way would not have led to the cross. At the same time, the world would not have been reconciled, and everything would have remained "as it had been."[30] Jesus' obedience was not blind obedience to a command of license, which based its claim to validity only on the abstract authority of a legislator and judge. Instead, the temptation narrative points to a lively relationship

28. *CD* IV/1, 164.
29. Barth adopts Calvin's position in considering Jesus' baptism the beginning of the obedience that leads to the work of reconciliation. John Calvin, *Institutes of the Christian Religion*, ed. John T. McNeill, trans. John L. Battles, The Library of Christian Classics (Louisville: Westminster John Knox, 2006), 1:507 (II, 16, 5). On the shape of Christ's obedience see *CD* IV/1, 270: "But He only prays. He does not demand. He does not advance any claims. He does not lay upon God any conditions. He does not reserve His future obedience. He does not abandon His status as a penitent. He does not cease to allow that God is in the right, even against Himself. He does not try to anticipate His justification by Him in any form, or to determine it Himself."
30. Ibid., 262.

between Father and Son. Its moral dimension is binding due to the shared will for reconciliation.

As the obedience of the Son led to the misery of the cross, Jesus' participation in the Son's majesty seems paradox. Barth's theological judgment that Jesus Christ proves his majesty precisely in suffering is not only based on particular biblical traditions, but also on John Calvin's theology as well as certain philosophical traditions. Barth puts a premium on Jesus' sovereignty in which he chooses obedience in the face of the gravest consequences. His determination in choosing humility is highest freedom in that he remains unmoved both by rival goals or the suffering his path implies. The more the implications of his obedience suggest that Jesus might wish to forego such a path, the more Jesus' inner freedom stands out in which he holds on to humility. His *oboedientia passiva* (obedience in suffering) is based on an active choice as well.[31]

Calvin also highlighted the voluntary nature of Christ's obedience.[32] In his lecture about the Reformer from Geneva, Barth describes Calvin's ethics again and again with the term *obedience*, which he understands in such a way, however, that he summarizes Calvin's ethics on the whole with the concept of freedom.[33]

The concept of freedom realized in freely chosen obedience is the point at which Barth's theological interests merge with his philosophical ones. Kant's concept of autonomy attributed great prominence to the idea that freedom consists in following a

31. Ibid., 244–56.

32. "And truly, even in death itself his willing obedience is the important thing because a sacrifice not offered voluntarily would not have furthered righteousness." Calvin, *Institutes*, 1:508 (II, 16, 5).

33. The occurrences of the word *obedience* in Barth's lectures on Calvin are part of characteristic descriptions of Calvin's ethics. On the whole, however, Barth considers the notion of freedom even more typical, which is not to be understood as incommensurate. Barth, *The Theology of John Calvin*, ed. Hans Scholl, trans. Geoffrey W. Bromiley (Grand Rapids: Eerdmans, 1995), 195–6.

reasonable law rather than acting in accordance with nonrational, sensual constraints. That voluntary, free obedience to a command is a point Barth shares both with Kant and Calvin. Doing good must not rest on inclination and requires, in certain cases, self conquest.[34] It is due to the prominence of the conflicts of introspection and moral resolve that §59.2 will present the Gethsemane scene, rather than Golgotha, as the climax of the passion. Moral freedom stands out—thus especially Kant—when obedience does not correspond to inclination, but implies particular sensual discomfort. The autonomous, or self-legislating, power of reason is clearer the more acute the opposing sensual promptings are. This notion helps explain why according to Barth, Jesus' obedience in suffering is the paradigm of Christian moral action, although moral freedom is not necessarily dependent on discomfort[35] and although, in Jesus' case, the freely respected law is not Kant's law of reason. In his interpretation of the Gethsemane story, Barth repeatedly emphasizes Christ's horror and struggle.[36] Jesus' will to obey overcomes all restrictions:

> He was not bound by any man, by any power of nature of history, by any destiny, by any orders, by any inner limits or obstacles. He did not stand or fall with any of these things, nor did He need to fear them. For Him there was only one imperative. Subject to this one imperative, and therefore not arbitrarily if not under any outward compulsion or constraint, He came and went with absolute superiority, disposing and controlling, speaking or keeping silence, always exercising lordship. This was no less true when He entered and trod to the end the way of

34. Calvin, *Institutes*, 1:508 (II, 16, 5): "And the Gospel history relates that he . . . met the soldiers. . . . Not, indeed, without a struggle; for he had taken upon himself our weaknesses, and in this way the obedience that he had shown to his Father had to be tested!" Kant also highlights the aspect of struggle in morality. Immanuel Kant, *Critique of Practical Reason: Including the First Introduction*, trans. Werner Pluhar (Indianapolis and Cambridge: Hackett, 2001), 109, 184–6.
35. Friedrich Schiller quips, "Gladly I serve my friends, but alas I do it with pleasure. / Hence I am plagued with doubt that I am not a virtuous person. / Sure, your only resource is to despise them entirely, and then with aversion to do / what your duty enjoins you."
36. *CD* IV/1, 264–5, 267–8.

> His death and passion. Indeed, to those who looked back, it was even more plainly true on this way.[37]

In good Kantian fashion, Barth appreciates the radical transcendental freedom in suffering, in which Jesus, ultimately, follows "only one imperative," abstracting from all sensual constraints.[38] Thus Barth is part of the European intellectual tradition that highlights transcendental freedom. He does not understand Jesus Christ's humiliation and exaltation as a linear sequence, but understands them as two aspects of one event: "He, the true God, is the One whose Godhead is demonstrated and plainly consists in essence in the fact that, seeing He is free in His love, He is capable of and wills this condescension."[39]

Christ's obedience as such is not all that is of theological importance to Barth. Its deeper meaning is that it is instrumental in God's reconciliation with the world, which constitutes the "centre of all Christian knowledge."[40] Moreover, it is characteristic of Barth's interpretation of reconciliation in *CD* IV that it even includes the destruction of evil. In being obedient to the will of the Father in his passion, Christ executes God's covenant with nullity (*das Nichtige*, or evil),[41] which calls for Jesus Christ's own death, but leads precisely to

37. *CD* IV/2, 164.
38. In this case, Kant speaks of *dignity* and *inner freedom*. On dignity: Immanuel Kant, *Groundwork to the Metaphysics of Morals*, ed. Mary Gregor, Cambridge Texts in the History of Philosophy (Cambridge: Cambridge University Press, 1997), 42–3. On inner freedom: "Two things are required for inner freedom: being one's own *master* in a given case (*animus sui compos*), that is, subduing one's affects, and *ruling* oneself (*imperium in semetipsum*), that is, *governing* one's passions." Kant, *The Metaphysics of Morals*, ed. and trans. Mary Gregory, Cambridge Texts in the History of Philosophy (Cambridge: Cambridge University Press, 1991), 208.
39. *CD* IV/1, 130.
40. Ibid., Foreword.
41. Barth's "*Nichtiges*" is often translated as nothingness, which would denote mere negativity without the destructive tendencies, however. The translation "nullity," which is taken from what is presumably the original source of Barth's German term: Martin Heidegger, *Being and Time*, trans. John Macquarrie and Edward Robinson, 6th reprint (Oxford: Basil Blackwell, 1985), seems most appropriate.

the destruction of nullity. Christ's obedience, Barth argues, defeated evil and "made an end" of sin.[42]

This understanding of the passion is the foundation on which *CD* IV builds an ethics of cruciform discipleship—notwithstanding the fact that discipleship is of course not charged with defeating evil as Christ did. Such an ethics of discipleship can only be convincing if Christ's cross is the symbol of triumph, not of failure. The hardship that must be endured in bearing the cross requires the call for discipleship to clarify that all hardship simultaneously implies particular dignity, which is participation in Christ's even greater glory. The fact that Jesus' obedience, even in utter misery, constituted no less than the epoch-making turning point toward salvation characterizes his extraordinary greatness. Thus it is also of great ethical importance that Jesus' passion created a new reality, amounting to no less than an apocalyptic intervention into the world:

> In Him a new human subject was introduced . . . beside and outside whom the other being of man, that old being which still continues to break the covenant, can only be a lie, an absurd self-deception, a shadow moving on the wall—the being of that man who has been long since superseded and replaced and who can only imagine that he is man, while in reality he is absolutely nothing.[43]

According to §59.2, this fulfillment takes place as Jesus Christ, "who is in the one person the electing God and the one elect man, is as the rejecting God, the God who judges sin in the flesh, in His own person the one rejected man."[44] This statement, hearkening back to the doctrine of election *CD* II/2, is now expanded by the dimension

42. Barth uses this terse expression, for example, ibid., 253, 280, 294, 344. Its repetition in 296–7 sounds slightly helpless: "The end . . . Judgment is judgment. Death is death. End is end. . . . judgment, death and end . . . judgment, death and end have come to us ourselves once and for all . . . the end . . . final and absolute."

43. Ibid., 89, see 502, *CD* IV/2, 400.

44. *CD* IV/1, 237, see also 408.

of an ontological change. Section §59.2 rests fundamentally on the idea that sin is destroyed by being entirely concentrated in one person, a collective person, after which this person is killed, and with him sin itself. Jesus Christ "made an end of us as sinners and therefore of sin itself by going to death as the One who took our place as sinners."[45]

In the question of how Christ defeated nullity (*das Nichtige*, or evil), already *CD* III/3, §50 points to the cross.[46] At that point, however, Barth discusses divine providence, so he goes into the details of the *how* only in the doctrine of reconciliation. In the question of cruciform discipleship, the doctrine of creation, *CD* III, thus dovetails with the doctrine of reconciliation, *CD* IV. The tenet that Christ defeated nullity is the subject of §50; Barth calls it the "final and decisive insight that nullity has no perpetuity."[47] Barth even defines evil as precisely that which Christ has defeated in the cross.[48] In the cross God's *opus alienum* takes place, which betrays the betrayer.[49] Since then, nullity only has the power of a "dangerous illusion."[50] "Under the control of God world-occurrence is even threatened and actually corrupted by nullity."[51] Notwithstanding the fact that Barth considers evil to happen at God's just disposal, but also to be an illusion, only five years after the liberation of Auschwitz,[52] the logical problem of §50 is that after Jesus' victory at Golgotha, there should be

45. Ibid., 253.
46. *CD* III/3, 363.
47. Ibid., 360 (trans. rev.).
48. Ibid., 420.
49. See also *CD* IV/1, 267: "In this world Satan can have only the power which is given and allowed him as he is powerfully upheld by the left hand of God."
50. Ibid., 367 (trans. rev.).
51. Ibid., 289 (trans. rev., part of the thesis statement of §50).
52. Wüthrich comments on God's relation to *das Nichtige*: "This is more than mere permission, which has been taught traditionally." Matthias D. Wüthrich, *Gott und das Nichtige: Zur Rede vom Nichtigen ausgehend von § 50 der Kirchlichen Dogmatik Karl Barths* (Zurich: Theologischer Verlag, 2006), 35. Whenever the footnote provides a German title for an English quotation, the translation is my own.

no evil at all to which God might respond in punishment by allowing evil to run it course.[53]

In the ensuing volumes, especially *CD* IV/1, Barth attempts to show in §59 ("The Obedience of the Son of God") how Christ defeated evil in the cross. Jesus' death is portrayed as unavoidable once he identifies with the sin of the world, in accordance with God's command. After all, God had decided to punish sin once and for all.[54] For this purpose, God uses human actors as "instruments" according to God's plan.[55] Interpreting the story of Jesus' temptation, Barth describes how Jesus' utter faithfulness to God provokes the enmity of evil. At the same time, Barth understands the enmity of evil itself as God's executing God's own judgment over sin. For in committing himself to God alone, Jesus also accepts that God concentrates all sin on Jesus himself, exposing him to the aggression of nullity. In destroying Jesus, evil thus destroys itself. Insofar as Jesus is obedient to God, Jesus' cross is—indirectly but certainly—God's work as well. In this sense, Barth argues, it "was a matter of God Himself obviously making a covenant with death and being about to keep it."[56]

In this event, the Gethsemane scene appears as the climax of the passion. Satan attempts to deter Jesus from obedience, as Satan had done in the temptation narratives. If Jesus remains faithful to God, who considers Jesus the personification of sin, evil itself will kill Jesus, like a virulent parasite killing its own host. The irony of nullity

53. Does Barth follow the logic of the war that ends all wars—which of course provokes new wars, as ruthlessly as it has to be conducted in order to eradicate evil? Another difficulty consists in Barth's paradox of generative rejection, according to which nullity is neither created nor exists independently of God; rather, its privative, albeit real character results from God's rejection of nullity in creation. As an aspect of rejection, it gains independent existence. Günter Thomas asks critically, "Then how can a divine rejection ever be conceived of that does not 'create' [*schaffen*] but that 'uncreates' [*abschaffen*, to abolish] nullity, so that it no longer 'is'?" Günter Thomas, "Der für uns 'gerichtete Richter': Kritische Erwägungen zu Karl Barths Versöhnungslehre," *Zeitschrift für Dialektische Theologie* 18 (2002): 211–25, at 217n14.

54. *CD* IV/1, 271–2.

55. Ibid. 239. See "CS," 110: the torturers are God's "created instruments."

56. *CD* IV/1, 271 (trans. rev.: *KD* IV/1, 298), see also *CD* IV/1, 271–2.

consists in the notion that evil tries to dissuade Jesus from obedience in suffering—although it would result in the evil fact of the death of the Son of God—in order to preserve itself. One problem in this reading is that in the Gospels, Satan does not play nearly as prominent a role as Barth assumes. According to Luke 22:3, Satan had even taken possession of Judas, so that, in direct contrast to Barth's portrayal, Satan's attempt is precisely not to prevent Jesus' execution, but to hasten it along. In Barth's telling of the story, Satan presented the perspective of cruel death on the cross to Jesus, in which his faithfulness would result, as a deterrent. This makes Jesus' obedience in Gethsemane both uncertain and precious.

> He saw that in so doing He would not only be alone but would necessarily have them all against Him: those who had not resisted temptation, but constantly gave way to it. . . . This was the world which in His own person He was to reconcile and willed to reconcile with God. He saw this world as it was. He saw what it was that dominated it and was fulfilled in it. He saw and felt the "great burden of the world." He saw what even the greatest of Christian and other martyrs did not see: that this burden is overwhelming, that in the last resort it can only overwhelm and crush Himself and other men.[57]

To his prayer in Gethsemane—"Take away this cup from me"—"Jesus does not, in fact, receive any answer, any sign from God,"[58] at least no answer that would have offered consolation. In this situation, God seems not to be on Jesus' side, but on Satan's. God's answer

> came in the same language in which Satan now spoke with Him. . . . The will of God was done as the will of Satan was done. The answer of God was identical with the action of Satan. That was the frightful thing. The coincidence of the divine and the satanic will and work and word was the problem of this hour, the darkness in which Jesus addressed God in Gethsemane.[59]

57. Ibid., 266.
58. Ibid., 268.
59. Ibid.

In praying, "your will be done," he chooses to obey God's will, although it corresponds to Satan's. Barth attaches great importance to Jesus' prayer, but if God responds to it in Satan's language with the terrifying prospect of suffering, the prayer cannot have conveyed God's consolation, and the power in which Jesus chose the path of suffering can have come neither from this prayer nor God's response. This makes implausible Barth's notion that "one thing is clear. In the power of this prayer Jesus received . . . His freedom to finish His work"[60] and to prove his obedience in suffering.

Examining the sources of Barth's theory of God's "covenant with death" is also instructive. While it resembles the older *Christus victor* motif, a key influence was Luther's *Commentary on Galatians.*[61] Barth explicates his notion of the destruction of sin in the death of its bearer by referring to Luther's commentary on Gal. 3:13:

> And in substance Luther's drastic commentary on this exchange is quite right, that God the Father said to God the Son: " . . . You are to be the one person of all men who has committed the sins of all men ... a blasphemer etc., greater than whom no-one has ever been in the world . . ." And it is the secret of what took place in Jesus Christ that in Him there met and clashed, "the highest, greatest, and only sin" and "the highest, greatest and only righteousness," but in such a way that there could be no doubt as to the outcome: "In Christ, the sin of all is conquered, put to death, and buried, and righteous remains the victor and ruler for eternity."[62]

60. Ibid., 271.
61. Barth held a seminar on the interpretation of Paul's Letter to the Galatians by the Reformers in summer 1948, two years before the publication of *CD* III/3, §50. Eberhard Busch, *Karl Barth: His Life from Letters and Autobiographical Texts*, trans. John Bowden (Eugene: Wipf & Stock, 2005), 352. Etzelmüller, *"...zu richten die Lebendigen und die Toten": Zur Rede vom Jüngsten Gericht im Anschluss an Karl Barth* (Neukirchen-Vluyn: Neukirchener, 2001), 183n505, argues for an influence of Luther's lecture on Galatians (1535) on *CD* §50 as well; according to Luther, *Lectures on Galatians: 1535: Chapters 1–4*, trans. Jaroslav Pelikan, Luther's Works 26 (Saint Louis: Concordia, 1963), 281, Sin attacks Christ, but is defeated.
62. *CD* IV/1, 238. Quotation marks have been added to indicate Barth's quotations from Luther. Barth's Latin quotations from Luther have been replaced with the translations from the *CD*

There are indeed remarkable parallels between Luther's and Barth's thought. According to Luther, the execution of the paradigmatic—even the sole—sinner is the work of the law, which Luther sees acting independently of God, but nonetheless in accordance with God's intention. Luther envisions God saying to Jesus,

> "be the person of all men, the one who has committed the sins of all men. And see to it that You pay and make satisfaction for them." Now the Law comes and says: "I find Him a sinner, who takes upon Himself the sins of all men. I do not see any other sins than those in Him. Therefore let Him die on the cross!" And so it attacks Him and kills Him.[63]

Barth's scenario runs along these lines as well when he argues for God's "covenant with death," in which God proclaims Jesus an outlaw—so that nullity can execute precisely the only one who truly fulfills God's will—and creates the legal fiction with which the judicial murder is justified, by burdening Jesus with sin itself.

Thus, when Barth speaks of God's "covenant with death," this is only a variation on God's punishment through the law. According to this theory, punishment is meted out on the basis of a fiction. Would this not strain the realism of the gospel? That God made a "covenant with death" is in contradiction to the priority of the gospel to the law, which refuses a Janus-headed God in favor of the God of the gospel. To dispense with this view precisely at the epoch-making event of reconciliation is to give up on the priority of the gospel. Already in those days, argues §59, the Sanhedrin and the Roman state were God's instruments in the fight against evil. By the same token, it would be very difficult to object to the view that even today, an alliance of authoritarian politics and authoritarian religion do their

Study Edition. Luther's quotations are originally from Martin Luther, *2. Galatervorlesung (cap. 1–4) 1531*, ed. Karl Drescher, Weimar Edition 40/I (Weimar: Böhlau, 1911), 435–9.

63. Luther, *Lectures on Galatians*, 280.

work as a legitimate expression of God's wrathful action in the law. If this were so, many questions from Barth's special ethics in *CD* III/4 would require fundamental reconsideration.

According to Barth's view, the notion of God's "covenant with death"[64] also clarifies Jesus' cry of dereliction at the cross. Indeed, this cry might be suitable to undermine the call to follow Christ in taking up one's cross.[65] For this reason, Barth must show how this cry is compatible with his assertion of Jesus' obedience in suffering, even his extraordinary majesty precisely in the lowliness of the passion. The death of Jesus, who, according to Barth, has become the personification of evil, may constitute salvation, as it amounts to no less than the self-destruction of evil. Yet the death of the one who carried all evil can only be terrible. This was a lonely death in which God was not an ally, but an enemy. And yet this death is the paradox triumph over evil. In this sense Barth interprets Jesus' cry of godforsakenness.[66] Since this death is the climax in God's fight against evil, this dramatic climax makes Jesus' death both terrible and triumphant. Before this chapter considers Barth's interpretation of Jesus' cry of abandonment, however, the close ties between *CD* III and *CD* IV require further consideration. I have already argued that Barth's doctrine of providence in *CD* III/3, § 50 dovetails with the depiction of the Gethsemane scene and Christ's passion in *CD* IV/1, § 59. What requires further examination is that Barth's concept that the wife's marital subordination to the husband is not simply an aberration occurring in his doctrine of creation that might be contrasted with Barth's doctrine of reconciliation. Instead, *CD* III and *CD* IV reinforce each other in this issue. Barth indicates as much already when he highlights a certain kind of cruciform discipleship in

64. *CD* IV/1, 271 (trans. rev.), see also 271–2.

65. For further details see below.

66. *CD* IV/1 §59, 185, 215, 239, 306; the disciples forsake Jesus as well (225).

CD IV. Interestingly, his gender ethics in the doctrine of creation is set on track by a particular christological reflection.

Gender Ethics: Unilateral Subordination

CD IV/1 repeatedly points out the relationship between obedience and moral dignity[67] when discussing the relation between man and woman, husband and wife.[68] It amounts to "a far-reaching consideration in New Testament ethics"[69] that suffering not only does not contradict God's essence, but that God is capable of "supremely asserting Himself and His deity"[70] precisely in the misery of the cross. As Jesus' suffering is of particular importance for Christian faith, the New Testament call to humility is a "binding law."[71] Barth then concludes,

> Hence *hypotagē* [subordination] as the basic concept in the Christian attitude to the civil powers (Rom. 13:1 f.), but also in the attitude of wives to their husbands (Col. 3:18), and also according to Eph. 5:21 in the attitude of all Christians one toward another. Hence the *hypakoē* [obedience] of children to their parents (Col. 3:20) and servants [i.e., slaves] to their masters (Col. 3:22). Hence the *timē* [honor], the respect in which, according to Rom. 12:10, all Christians are to prefer one another.[72]

Subordination, obedience, and honoring others gain their moral dignity, according to Barth, precisely in the face of the discomfort they imply. Without disadvantage and personal cost, subordination would be abstract and trivial. Barth points out four specific relationships in which the Christian ethos should follow the

67. Ibid., 188–92.
68. Ibid., 189, 201, 202.
69. Ibid., 188.
70. Ibid., 187.
71. Ibid., 189.
72. Ibid.

traditional patriarchal power asymmetry. He addresses relationships of *mutual* subordination with only one less specific example (all Christians) twice. As Jesus proved his majesty in subordination, so the Christian ethos should also manifest its moral dignity in affirming powerlessness.

In the two ensuing discussions of gender relations, Barth no longer takes into account that all Christians are supposed to serve each other, and not only the women the men. Barth argues that Jesus' obedience to the heavenly Father corresponds to the obedience of the eternal Son to the eternal Father. In God there is "an above and a below, a *prius* and a *posterius* [a *before* and an *after*], a superior and a junior and subordinate. Obedience as a possibility and actuality in God Himself seems at once to compromise the unity and then logically the equality of the divine being."[73] According to Barth, this is only an appearance, however. For God is revealed especially in the crucified one. His obedience does not question, but affirm the full divinity of Jesus Christ and his equal dignity in relation to the Father.[74] This allows it for Barth to have his cake and eat it, to affirm both equality and subordination, emancipation and repression. While this does not help when one seeks moral guidance in the first place, this strategy—unwittingly—gives a maximum of flexibility and control to those who already seem to know what is right. In interpreting the cross as the Son's subordination to the Father, Barth has his notion of God's "covenant with death"[75] against Jesus Christ in mind. If we consider how the Gospels define God's self in Jesus Christ's ministry,

73. Ibid., 195.
74. Ibid., 199–200. An important alternative would have been to highlight the mutual self-restraint for the benefit of the other person that characterizes all three divine persons. See the corresponding section below, which draws on Wolfhart Pannenberg, *Systematic Theology*, trans. Geoffrey W. Bromiley (Grand Rapids: Eerdmans, 1994), vol. 1 (for example, pp. 309–15).
75. *CD* IV/1, 271 (trans. rev.), see also 271–2.

however, the cross does not stand out as an example of Jesus Christ's equality with God.[76]

In ethical regard, the conclusion is that when Christian action corresponds to Jesus', there is equal dignity between husbands and wives as wives choose one-sided subordination, according to Barth. The one-sided subordination of wives to husbands no longer constitutes any loss in dignity, asserts Barth—who was himself a husband. Further differentiations, such as the call upon all Christians to be humble toward each other, are underrepresented. Barth adduces Col. 3:18, 20, 22; Eph. 5:21 in support, yet he does not mention that even so, Col. 3:18–25 summons husbands to love their wives and fathers to be lenient toward their children. Barth's reminder of respect between all Christians seems vapid, given that his only specific, explicit instruction to subordination is directed at women. Ironically, in Eph. 5:22–5, the cross does not seem to be intended as a moral example for women, but for men.[77] Ephesians 5:25 does not thereby make up for the patriarchal ethos of the household codes—see Eph. 5:33—but there is greater inner differentiation even in patriarchy than Barth would allow for.

76. Rowan D. Williams notes the stilted logic of the passage. "Barth on the Triune God," in *Karl Barth: Centenary Essays*, ed. Stephen W. Sykes (Cambridge: Cambridge University Press, 1989), 147–93, at 175. The problem is not solved by Paul Nimmo's observation that God is Lord of God's own being and that such obedience is freedom. Paul T. Nimmo, "Barth and the Christian as Ethical Agent: An Ontological Study of the Shape of Christian Ethics," in *Commanding Grace: Studies in Karl Barth's Ethics*, ed. Daniel L. Migliore (Grand Rapids: Eerdmans, 2010), 216–38. Wilfried Härle, *Sein und Gnade: Die Ontologie in Karl Barths Kirchlicher Dogmatik*, Theologische Bibliothek Töpelmann 27 (Berlin/New York: de Gruyter, 1975), 324, explains that according to *CD* I/1, God's oneness depends on God's universal rule. God's rule is fundamental to God's divinity, so that it cannot merely extend to creation, but must already be real within God's self. Only once God's revelation in the Son is revealed in the Spirit are both God's unity and God's rule complete. Paradoxically, once the Triune God is envisioned as Creator, the obedience of the Son in creation is fundamental to the eternal divinity of the Son.

77. According to Richard B. Hays, *The Moral Vision of the New Testament: Cross, Community, New Creation* (San Francisco: Harper Collins, 1996), 197, Eph. 5:25 is the only unambiguous New Testament verse that points to the cross as the reason for relinquishment of power and privilege in marriage. The verse addresses "*husbands* (not wives)."

Moreover, from an exegetical point of view, the reason for the subordination of wives in the deuteropauline tradition is not the cross. Such calls were already issued by the traditional, patriarchal pagan literature on the household ethos.[78] In Eph. 5, by contrast, the cross plays an ambiguous role in both softening the edges of and thus stabilizing patriarchal hierarchy.

Barth discusses gender relations in greater detail in *CD* III/1, §41.2–3; *CD* III/4, §54.1.[79] Here the cross plays a significant role as well, so that these chapters should indeed be discussed in the context of *CD* IV. With his doctrine of reconciliation, the eventual trajectory of Barth's gender ethics has been outlined.[80] Since the passages from

78. Exegetes have identified Greek economics/household literature as the most important cultural and literary background for the NT household codes. Jürgen Becker and Ulrich Luz, *Die Briefe an die Galater, Epheser und Kolosser*, 18th ed. (Göttingen: Vandenhoeck & Ruprecht, 1998), 234–5. This body of literature assumes "that men and women, free citizens and slaves, fathers and children differ in their endowment of reason, their natural characteristics, and their education." The analogy between the relations Christ—congregation and husband—wife (Eph. 5:23–4) comes "close to a causal relationship," but the husband is not called the wife's savior (ibid., 172).

79. Daniel Migliore's observations speak against taking these thoughts of Barth lightly: "The super-/ subordination theme in Barth's theology would thus appear to have several phases: [a] absent in the Göttingen Dogmatics; [b] considered a result of the fall in CD I/2; [c] presented as part of the meaning of being created in the image of God in CD III/2 and III/4; [d] grounded in the trinitarian being of God in CD IV/1." Migliore, "Karl Barth's First Lectures in Dogmatics: Instruction in the Christian Religion," in *The Göttingen Dogmatics: Instruction in the Christian Religion*, by Karl Barth, ed. Hannelotte Reiffen, trans. Geoffrey W. Bromiley (Grand Rapids: Eerdmans, 1991), 1:xv–lvii, at xlvii–xlviii.

80. For Barth's views on gender, see Katherine Sonderegger, "Barth and Feminism," in *The Cambridge Companion to Karl Barth*, ed. John B. Webster (Cambridge: Cambridge University Press: 2000), 258–73, at 260, 267. She argues that Barth's gender ethics implies both repressive and liberative aspects. Barth's theology can liberate from essentialist notions of gender, such as the affective/rational binary.

CD III are bypassed or downplayed[81] in some treatments of Barth's ethics, they will be discussed at this point.

Barth's gender ethics in *CD* III does not differ substantially from his assertions in *CD* IV/1, yet a few developments are worth noting. *CD* IV/1 argues that the sacrificial action of wives should be in correspondence to the cross. *CD* III/1, by contrast, quotes Eph. 5:31–2. This analogy of relations does not compare the relation between husband and wife with that between God the Father and Jesus Christ, but with that between Christ and the congregation. As Eph. 5:31 looks back to the second account of creation, from the vantage point of faith in Christ, Barth argues that creation already foreshadows faith in Christ.[82] Yet Barth argues with a questionable typological exegesis. That the woman was created from Adam's rib constituted a sacrifice on the part of the man, which takes place because "in and with Israel's election God has from the very first offered, surrendered and sacrificed no less than something of Himself, in some sense hazarding Himself."[83] The deep sleep of mythological Adam corresponds to the death sleep of the crucified one.[84] This typology ignores specific aspects of the Gospels: Jesus' ministry leading up to the passion and the inner connection between these two narrative complexes; Christ's premonition of his death and his commitment to his destiny in spite of it; the religious, political, and

81. For example, Timothy Gorringe argues that Barth's gender ethics as they are must not be tolerated. By contrast, his views on the Trinity, Christ's passion, and gender relations can be accepted provided that husband and wife are distinct but indeed truly equal. The relationship between humanity and God as presented in Christ must not be projected onto gender ethics. This, however, disregards the deep-seated connections between Barth's gender ethics (*CD* III, IV), his interpretation of the creation (*CD* III) and passion narratives (*CD* IV), and cruciform discipleship that embraces obedience and suffering (*CD* IV). Timothy Gorringe, *Barth: Against Hegemony*, Christian Theology in Context (Oxford: Oxford University Press, 1999), 207.
82. *CD* III/1, 190, 320–21.
83. Ibid., 318.
84. Ibid., 321.

social dynamic of Jesus' crucifixion, as well as the aspect of his drastic suffering.[85]

Nonetheless, with the excuse of this dubious typology, Barth views the husband as more important for the wife than vice versa. She is taken from him and is intended for him: "She is human as the completion of *his* humanity."[86] This is the "supremacy of man," that is, of the male.[87]

CD III/4 continues along these lines: "A precedes B, and B follows A. Order means succession. It means preceding and following. It means super- and sub-ordination."[88] The husband is his wife's "inspirer, leader and initiator,"[89] he takes the lead, so that she is condemned to passivity, at least in some important respect. While he has the duty to serve her, she cannot claim the right that he in fact carry this duty out.[90] If she perceives an illegitimate willfulness on

85. Barth continues the typology. According to Gen. 2:23, in recognizing Eve, Adam elects her. "The goal of the whole supremacy shown at this point is his subordination to this arrangement. It is only in this arrangement . . . that he alone is the one who elects" (*CD* III/1, 306, trans. rev.). This corresponds to Christ's exclusive agency in electing the congregation (ibid., 322, 325–6). That the man leaves his parental home for the sake of the woman (Gen. 2:24), rather than vice versa, "is because God has so irrevocably united Himself with His people" (ibid., 318). The traces of matrilocal tradition in Gen. 2:24 should not be burdened with overly refined theories (ibid., 368). According to Carol Meyers, *Discovering Eve: Ancient Israelite Women in Context* (New York and Oxford: Oxford University Press, 1988), 37–8, matrilocal societies have presumably not granted economic or social advantages to women. Sarah B. Hrdy, *Mothers and Others: The Evolutionary Origins of Mutual Understanding* (Cambridge, MA: Belknap, 2011), suggests otherwise, however. According to Meyers, the verse implies that "a couple's union supersedes the parent-child relationship" (86). In Barth's theological typology between Adam and Christ, there is no equivalent to this social dynamic. In another interpretation of Gen. 2:24, Barth flatly contradicts the biblical text: "He can and should go ahead of the woman by affirming her, taking her in [*aufnehmen*] and taking her along [*mitnehmen*], by doing (v. 31 f.) exactly what man (Gen. 2) did at the climax of his creation: 'Therefore shall a man leave his father and mother, and shall cleave unto his wife.'" (*CD* III/4, 175, trans. rev.).

86. *CD* III/1, 353 (trans. rev.).

87. Ibid., 301, 304, 306, 308, 309.

88. *CD* III/4, 169.

89. Ibid.

90. For Barth, such practical humility on the husband's part would amount to great respect for the wife when a decision about contraceptives is made. The wife is the weaker part, as a pregnancy has more dramatic consequences for her (*CD* III/4, 276).

his part, she must know that her protest can become legitimate only if it can be carried out in cooperation rather than in opposition to him. If this implies hardship for her, she "has the privilege to attest and express the incomparable lowliness of Christ"[91] and takes comfort in Christ having endured even greater hardship. The husband should take the initiative in imitating Christ. Patriarchalism can thus take the form of a love patriarchy, which may perhaps alleviate—and perpetuate—the problem.[92] Barth allows for such alleviation to be reversed, however, since he inculcates only the husband, not the wife, with the fact that Christ's sacrifice requires and permits no repetition.[93] By no means can the husband insult or humiliate his wife; for her part, however, any protest against such behavior would already be sin.[94]

In essence, Barth sees the equal dignity of the genders unharmed by her lack of certain rights. Her duties are impressed more vigorously upon the reader than his. *CD* IV/1 follows this example. Equal dignity is thus reduced to a farce.

Barth's artificial exegesis of the second creation account notwithstanding, Barth fails to do justice to a Scripture verse as important as Gal. 3:28. The verse objects to the gender binary of Genesis 1. Sharing in the problems of major Bible translations, Barth misrepresents the wording, saying "that in Christ Jesus all are one—Jew and Greek, bond and free, and male and female."[95] Crucially, Gal. 3:28 says that in Christ, there is "neither Jew nor

91. Ibid., 173 (trans. rev.: "*so darf sie . . . die unvergleichliche Tiefe des Christus bezeugen*").
92. On love patriarchalism in early Christianity, see Gerd Theissen, "Social Stratification in the Corinthian Community: A Contribution to the Sociology of Early Hellenistic Christianity," in *The Social Setting of Pauline Christianity: Essays on Corinth*, trans. John H. Schütz, 2nd ed. (Minneapolis: Fortress Press, 1989), 69–119, at 106–10: according to Theissen, the significance of love patriarchalism was due to the integration of members of the most diverse social strata.
93. *CD* III/4, 175.
94. Ibid., 171.
95. *CD* III/4, 156, similarly 164.

Greek [*ouk—oude*], neither slave nor free [*ouk—oude*], neither man and [*sic! ouk—kai*] woman." Thus the latter pair, used with a notably different particle, is a quotation from Gen. 1:27. Paul negates sex or gender as a basic distinction, at least as far as the congregation is concerned. He thus disputes that a woman lives up to her proper role only in marriage—that is, in the patriarchal household.[96] This is in contrast to a rash coordination of creation—as experienced in patriarchal, seemingly natural relations—and reconciliation as well as to Barth's view that the distinction between man and woman, husband and wife is ethically fundamental.[97]

There is yet another crucial point to Barth's gender ethics in *CD* III. The relation between husband and wife is, according to Barth, a proper, indeed the fundamental, dialogical relationship between an *I* and a *Thou.* In this relationship, unity and difference are correlated. According to *CD* III/1, this dialogical relationship between husband and wife is no less than necessary for salvation. Only in this framework can one appreciate fully how God in Christ offers God's self up to the congregation.

> It is in this way that God Himself will confront man, have intercourse with and act for him. Man's own existence must thus correspond to this mode if it is to be good for God; if it is to be serviceable for God and to qualify for interaction with God. . . . In virtue of his nature man must be formally prepared for grace.[98]

According to *CD* III/2, in the personal encounter between husband

96. Nils A. Dahl, *Studies in Paul* (Minneapolis: Fortress Press, 1977), 133; Elisabeth Schüssler-Fiorenza, *In Memory of Her: A Feminist Theological Reconstruction of Christian Origins* (New York: Crossroad, 1983), 211.

97. The assumption that women had to subordinate themselves to men also contradicts the fact that in New Testament congregations, women held leadership positions and that they held greater social and economic power than some contemporary views on gender ethics, or the call to subordination, suggest. Charles B. Cousar, *The Letters of Paul* (Nashville: Abingdon, 1996), 68.

98. *CD* III/1, 290 (trans. rev.: "*verhandlungsfähig*" *sein*, i.e., to have standing).

and wife, between I and Thou, no less than a "revelation" takes place.[99] Thus, Barth's gender ethics can be seen as a particular application of the Thomist adage *gratia non destruat, sed supponit et perficit naturam.* Human nature is thus a positive, albeit to some extent variable, human quality, which is a necessary condition for revelation and salvation. Thus it also has a key function for any knowledge of God.[100] Nonetheless, in 1933 Barth took Gogarten's affirmation of the Thomist formula as the occasion to sever ties officially.[101] As a result, the projection of human relations of authority and obedience into the eternal deity is also part of this natural theology laid out in *CD* III.

CD III/4 relativizes this problematic concept by presenting gender relations as a correspondence to revelation rather than its condition.[102] Nonetheless, *CD* III/4 maintains an analogy between divine and marital life, with leads Barth to characterize God according to the standards of particular creaturely social relations. On the one hand, in the creaturely realm, the shared life of husband and wife is "the prototype of all I and Thou, of all the individuality in which human persons differ from and yet belong to each other."[103] This is where subordination in equality is portrayed as a reality. On the other hand, Barth's understanding of the Trinity is shaped precisely by this interpersonal experience in the creaturely realm. Barth's assertion that

99. *CD* III/2, 316.

100. Thomas Aquinas, *Summa theologiae* I, 1 a.8 ad 2. In 1933, Barth broke off relations with Friedrich Gogarten in rejection of this statement. Barth, "Abschied," in *"Der Götze wackelt": Zeitkritische Aufsätze, Reden und Briefe von 1930 bis 1960*, ed. Karl Kupisch (Berlin: Vogt, 1961), 63–70. Barth is appreciative of Thomas's adage in his lecture "Die Kirche und die Kultur" (1926), which he came to regard very critically later on. In *Vorträge und kleinere Arbeiten 1925–1930*, ed. Hermann Schmidt, Barth-Gesamtausgabe (Zurich: Theologischer Verlag, 1994), 10–40. On the history of the adage, see ibid., 22. In his mature work, Barth calls the adage "dangerous," but, all things considered, not wrong (*CD* II/1, 411).

101. Barth, "Abschied," 64.

102. *CD* III/4, 175.

103. Ibid., 150 (trans. rev.).

God is the cause, and not a reflexion of such social relations, begs the question. Thus he calls God's Trinity "the original [*Urbild*] and source of every I and Thou,"[104] and as the wife is subordinate to the husband, so is the Son to the Father.

Barth's ethics of bearing the cross can thus take on a repressive shape indeed. Its theological foundation is Barth's assertion that the eternal Son affirmed his role in the passion as unilateral subordination under the Father, which, however, did not question his equality with the Father. In this respect, Catherine Keller's judgment is right: Barth's "doctrine of 'Man and Woman' can regrettably not be by-passed like some embarrassing, time-bound accident."[105]

The Crucifixion of Jesus in the Gospels

The preceding discussion of Barth's interpretation of the cross has pointed out its ethical relevance for Barth's ethics of cruciform discipleship. Indeed, Barth highlights the connection between the passion narratives and Christian ethics:

> New Testament ethics is an *indirect* and additional attestation of the true *Godhead of Christ*. True Godhead in the New Testament is being in the absolute freedom of love, and therefore the being of the Most High who is high, almighty, eternal, holy, righteous and glorious not *also* but *precisely* in His lowliness.[106]

It is likely that a comparison between Barth's interpretation of the passion and the biblical traditions offers the chance to phrase a critical and constructive contribution to ethics in dialogue with Barth. For that purpose, the ensuing analysis will not focus on the Gethsemane

104. *CD* III/2, 318.
105. Catherine Keller, *Face of the Deep: A Theology of Becoming* (New York: Routledge, 2003), 95.
106. *CD* IV/1, 191 (trans. rev.).

scene, as Barth does in §59, but on the culmination of the passion, the scene of Jesus' crucifixion.

The Crucifixion and Death of Jesus in the Gospel according to John (John 19:16–37)

Arguing for a defeat of nullity (*das Nichtige*) at the cross, Barth points especially to Jesus' last word on the cross according to the Gospel of John. To begin with, it is in keeping with Barth's view of the passion that John portrays the crucifixion with a double entendre as a "lifting up" (John 3:14, 8:28, 12:32). This not only denotes the fastening of Jesus to a torture instrument a certain distance above the ground, but also the particular dignity that Jesus manifests in his atoning suffering. Some exegetes thus confirm Barth's view of the simultaneity of humiliation and exaltation.[107]

Occasionally, John presents Jesus as king, which is also in agreement with Barth's argument that the cross manifests Jesus' majesty. The crowd in Jerusalem calls for Jesus' execution, arguing that it knows no king except the Roman emperor (19:15). This, however, leads precisely to Jesus' multivalent designation as king in the inscription on the cross. That Jesus' investiture takes place with a crown of thorns can be seen as a paradoxical coronation, a veiled expression—or travesty—of his majesty.

Yet Barth finds his strongest indication for his interpretation of the cross as a triumph in Jesus' last word in 19:30: *Tetelestai*, "it is accomplished," or "it is finished." Jesus' "sacrifice" has been carried out.[108] As John the Baptist announced (1:29), the lamb "takes away" the sin of the world.[109] Jesus' statement after drinking the vinegar,

107. Thomas Knöppler, *Die theologia crucis des Johannesevangeliums: Das Verständnis des Todes Jesu im Rahmen der johanneischen Inkarnations- und Erhöhungschristologie*, Wissenschaftliche Monographien zum Alten und Neuen Testament 69 (Neukirchen-Vluyn: Neukirchener, 1994), 154.

108. *CD* IV/1, 281.

tetelestai, may also be an allusion to his word in Gethsemane, "Am I not to drink the cup that the Father has given me?" (18:11)

As will be argued later,[110] Barth depicts Jesus' exaltation at the cross in such a way that the scandal of suffering seems to be papered over. Even this is, to some extent, in keeping with different aspects of the Johannine passion. This constitutes a problem, however: given his circumstances, Jesus would seem to suffer harshly, and his physical being is not a mere appearance. This is in contrast, however, to the impression that he seems to suffer misery only to a limited degree.[111] That Jesus, on the way to the crucifixion, carries the cross "himself" or "for himself" (*heautō,* John 19:17), says that nobody is there to serve him. But on the other hand, he is so sovereign that he needs no help.[112] If an entire cohort, several hundreds of men, along with their leader and the aides of the high priests and scribes, are said to fall on the ground at Jesus' word *ego eimi*, "I am" (18:3–6.12),[113] this raises the question how this exalted figure can be touched by suffering at all. Jesus is indeed portrayed as deciding freely for death, yet the aspect of misery recedes strongly into the background. In contrast to the Synoptics, the Gospel of John does not use the word *pas'chein* (to suffer) and related forms, and it does not include Jesus' prayer in

109. *CD* IV/2, 140, 207. According to Knöppler, *Die theologia crucis des Johannesevangeliums*, 84, the Passover rite was understood as an act of atonement in New Testament times. Further, according to the chronology of the Fourth Gospel, Jesus died during the slaughter of the Passover lambs (ibid., 121).

110. See the section *The New Testament Depictions of the Crucifixion and Barth's Interpretation of the Cross*.

111. On this problem, see Jörg Frey, "Die '*theologia crucifixi*' des Johannesevangeliums," in *Kreuzestheologie im Neuen Testament*, ed. Andreas Dettwiler and Jean Zumstein (Tübingen: Mohr Siebeck, 2002), 169–238, at 221–2.

112. That nobody serves Jesus in his misery would contradict a royal interpretation of the scene. *Pace* Knöppler, *Die theologia crucis des Johannesevangeliums*, 260–61. Raymond E. Brown, *The Death of the Messiah: From Gethsemane to the Grave: A Commentary on the Passion Narratives in the Four Gospels*, Anchor Bible Reference Library (New York: Doubleday, 1994), 2:917 interprets this as a sign of Jesus' sovereignty, although he does not consider the scene a royal enthronement.

113. Gerhard Barth, *Der Tod Jesu Christi im Verständnis des Neuen Testaments* (Neukirchen-Vluyn: Neukirchener, 1992), 140.

Gethsemane, in which Jesus articulates his unwillingness to suffer, subordinating it to the painful will of the Father.[114] Moreover, that the crucified expresses the physical need for a drink is portrayed as happening for the sake of the fulfillment of Scripture. A comparison with the Synoptics shows that the Gospel of John highlights Jesus' own initiative even in this, rather than portraying Jesus as being given to drink passively.[115] Again in contrast to the Synoptics, John does not mention the bystanders mocking Jesus. Thus the cross is portrayed as the climax of exaltation, yet occasionally it also appears as merely a transitional stage to full glory.[116] That Jesus' end implies his glory is noted in 12:28, 13:31-32, 17:1.5.

Jesus' last word, *tetelestai* (19:30), is ambiguous, which corresponds to a literary strategy in the Gospel of John. It may refer to the "accomplished" atonement or Jesus' completion of his mission as a whole.[117] Barth typically follows the common German translation ("*Es ist vollbracht*"), understanding Jesus' death mostly as an "accomplishment." The expression may also mean that Jesus is done drinking, but Jesus may thus also announce his dying.[118] The word

114. Frey, "Die '*theologia crucifixi*,'" 173; G. Barth, *Der Tod Jesu Christi*, 140.

115. Manfred Lang, *Johannes und die Synoptiker: Eine redaktionsgeschichtliche Analyse von Joh 18–20 vor dem markinischen Hintergrund*, Forschungen zur Religion und Literatur des Alten und Neuen Testaments 182 (Göttingen: Vandenhoeck & Ruprecht, 1999), 234, considers the drink of vinegar an act of euthanasia intended to shorten the pain. In an antidocetic intention, this would imply that Jesus suffered. But that Jesus died shortly after drinking does not exclude that the drink was for refreshment. After all, Jesus did not utter an inarticulate death cry, and "gave up his spirit," probably purposefully. On the drink of refreshment, see Brown, *Death of the Messiah*, 2:1063–4.

116. See John 12:32–3. Thus also in the prominent view of Jesus going to the Father (7:33; 13:1; 14:1–2, 12, 28; 17:13). Becker and Kümmel interpret the cross as a transitional stage. Jürgen Becker, *Das Evangelium nach Johannes*, 3rd ed. (Gütersloh: Gütersloher Verlagshaus Mohn, 1991), 144, and Werner Georg Kümmel, *Die Theologie des Neuen Testaments nach seinen Hauptzeugen: Jesus—Paulus—Johannes*, 4th ed. (Göttingen: Vandenhoeck & Ruprecht, 1980), 265. Knöppler's textual evidence for the notion that Jesus' glorification reaches its climax at the cross is not cogent at times: Knöppler, *Die theologia crucis des Johannesevangeliums*, 64: John 2:4c; 11:4, 40; 12:41; 17:1, 4–5, 19. According to John 11:4–5, the glory of the Son of God is not manifested in his death, but in his overcoming of death, at first of Lazarus' death (11:43–4).

117. The first occurrence of the expression, the accomplishment of the work, 4:34, does not allude to atonement. See also 5:36; 17:4.

may also reference further salvation history with a view to Jesus' sending of the Spirit. For in 16:7 (see also 14:15; 15:26), Jesus' death implies the gift of the Spirit for the congregation, and in 19:30, the narrator says in an ambiguous way that Jesus bowed his head and "gave over the Spirit" (*paredōken to pneyma*, or, "gave up the Spirit/spirit").[119] "It is this post-Easter experience of salvation that prompts the Gospel of John to evaluate Jesus' departure as a gain for the disciples."[120]

Occasionally, Barth also argues that Jesus' last word according to John also describes the cross as the accomplishment of reconciliation independently of the resurrection.[121] Yet it is questionable that one could call Jesus' suffering an exaltation independently of the resurrection, even according to John. Christina Hoegen-Rohls argues that the Gospel of John portrays the earthly Jesus as the risen Jesus. Thus one aspect of the narrator's time, or the future of narrated time, is presented as the present of narrated time. In that sense it is the already exalted Jesus who says in 17:4 that he has accomplished everything.[122] This peculiar modification of temporal dimensions results from John's view of the activity of the Spirit, in which the "pre-Easterly word is reconstructed and comprehended after Easter in the activity of the Spirit, which makes the pre-Easterly

118. Lang, *Johannes und die Synoptiker*, 235: "'it is finished!' But for the congregation, which is external to the text, the evangelist's phrase allows for another, wider meaning." This ambiguity is preserved in the King James Version, New King James Version, New International Version, Revised Standard Version, and New Revised Standard Version.

119. Lang, *Johannes und die Synoptiker*, 237, 312–13, highlights Jesus' activity in giving up the Spirit, which he does not understand to refer to the Holy Spirit, however.

120. Christina Hoegen-Rohls, *Der nachösterliche Johannes: Die Abschiedsreden als hermeneutischer Schlüssel zum vierten Evangelium*, Welt und Umwelt des Neuen Testamentes II 84 (Tübingen: Mohr Siebeck, 1996), 309.

121. *CD* IV/1, 281, 306, *CD* IV/2, 257.

122. Hoegen-Rohls, *Der nachösterliche Johannes*, 247. See Frey, "Die '*theologia crucifixi*' des Johannesevangeliums," 191: "Since proclamation is guided by the Spirit, the post-Easter congregation can, in faith, see the glorified one in the crucified one, in the earthly Jesus, in the incarnate one."

word present and comprehensible."[123] In this respect, Jesus Christ before Easter is already the post-Easter Christ, due to a "close entanglement of Christology and Pneumatology."[124] As a consequence, there is no abstract cross without resurrection and the gift of the Spirit according to John. Barth's view that regardless of the resurrection, the cross is already the accomplishment of salvation, requiring no addition, cannot be based on John 19.[125] This is presumably also the key to the problem that Jesus' suffering is noticeably toned down in the Johannine passion, although he endures tremendous hardship. Faced with the resurrection, which is already presupposed in John's telling of the passion, Jesus' suffering and misery is real, but it carries less weight vis-à-vis the majesty of the risen one.[126]

The Gospel of John highlights the stark contrast that Christ's exaltation follows the shameful, miserable death on the cross and that dramatic iniquity is followed by an act of unilateral reconciliation, by projecting the majesty of the risen one onto the lowliness of the cross and, by implication, free forgiveness onto the low point of guilt. Although the effect can be drastic, the literary strategy also has its risks, for there is the danger that the contrary aspects will no longer be visible as distinct. To that extent, the well-worn debate over whether the Christology of the Fourth Gospel is docetic

123. Hoegen-Rohls, *Der nachösterliche Johannes*, 309.

124. Ibid., 310.

125. On difficulties in seeing the cross as the perfect event of salvation, see Knöppler, *Die theologia crucis des Johannesevangeliums*, 157. Frey observes that the terms *theology of the cross* and *theology of glory* create difficulties in exegesis, for the alternative of contemplating God either in the glory of God's invisible essence or in the misery of the cross contradicts the glorious presentation of the cross in the Gospel of John. See Martin Luther, *Heidelberg Disputation*, in *Career of the Reformer*, ed. and trans. Philip S. Watson, Luther's Works, vol. 33 (Philadelphia: Fortress, 1972), 1:53 (thesis 20).

126. Frey's interpretation continues to imply a dualism of cross and exaltation in the Gospel of John, as he speaks of the *theologia crucifixi*, but not of the *theologia crucifixi et resurrecti*. "In the Gospel of John, cross and glory are associated not in a theology of glory, but in a *theology of the cross*" (Frey, "Die '*theologia crucifixi*,'" 191).

or antidocetic is not a surprise. The misery of the cross is indeed a necessary condition for perceiving the glory of God's salvation from death, yet if misery and death are portrayed already in the light of salvation and redemption, the fact can become blurred that such redemption is precisely redemption from misery and death. The coincidence of opposites is in danger of collapsing the opposites. In that case, misery and death may seem much less dramatic, and the triumph of Easter may seem like an easy victory.

In consequence, the same dynamic obtains for Barth's interpretation of the simultaneity of Christ's humility and majesty. His thesis gains some strong support from the passion narrative in the Gospel of John. To the same degree, however, Barth's thesis participates in the striking ambiguity inherent in the Gospel of John. After all, in the debate about the Christology of the Fourth Gospel, the positions of a docetic Christology and a clearly antidocetic view of Christ have been articulated, both with good reasons. Thus, Barth's portrayal of Christ's glory climaxing precisely in the misery and shame of the cross is certainly a powerful theological vision, but it is unlikely to shake off entirely the suspicion of taking the suffering of the cross less than seriously. The ethical import of this conclusion remains to be discussed at the end of the survey of the passion narratives.

The Crucifixion and Death of Jesus in the Gospel according to Luke (Luke 23:33–49)

Barth's view that the cross of Jesus Christ contributes decisively to his majesty seems, at least at first, borne out by an interpretation of the Gospel of Luke. The third Gospel paints a glorious, virtually heroic portrait of Jesus.[127] Luke eliminates the statement from Matthew and

127. Textual criticism makes it uncertain whether the tradition of Jesus sweating blood and water (Luke 22:43–4) should be considered part of the Gospel of Luke.

Mark that in Gethsemane, Jesus was "anguished to death" (Mark 14:34/Matt. 26:38). Although Jesus faces "the power of darkness" (Luke 22:53), he walks his path with his head raised high. On the way to the crucifixion, he defies the wailing women that woe is unto *them*—Jerusalem will face a worse fate a fortiori, since this is done "when the wood is green."[128] In turn, the cross appears as a damning event, rather than as salvific.

That Jesus, in a sovereign way, holds intercession for the torturers is peculiar to Luke. In Mark/Matthew, the authorities do not distinguish between Jesus and two so-called criminals, who, as miserable as they are, even go on to mock him (Mark 15:32, Matt. 27:44). By contrast, Luke has one criminal recognize Jesus' innocence, upon which he asks him to redeem him the way a ruler would ("your kingdom"). Jesus, unshaken by the torture, replies to this criminal that he will join Jesus in paradise.[129] The depiction of Jesus receiving vinegar for drink is modified, so it no longer appears as the allusion to Ps. 69:22 that it is in Mark 15:23.36 and especially Matt. 27:34.48.[130] Jesus' last word at the cross is an expression of complete trust in God, a quotation from Ps. 31:6, to which Luke adds an address of partiality, "father." Thus Jesus does not "cry" (Mark/Matt.: *boan*), but "shouts" (*phonēsas*). In contrast to Mark 15:37, Matt. 27:50, no further inarticulate cry of death ensues. Instead, bystanders beat their chests in repentance,[131] that is, recognizing the perversion that the righteous one is executed—again Lukan *Sondergut*, i.e., a tradition not found in the other gospels. A centurion gives voice to

128. Luke 23:31: *Sondergut*, a tradition unique to Luke.

129. This is Jesus' sovereign, and indirect, reply to the other criminal's exclamation, "Save yourself, and us!"

130. Brown, *Death of the Messiah*, 2:1059. In referring to the drink, the psalm describes the mockery of the righteous one. The point of the allusion to Ps. 22:16 in John 19:28 was not the kind of drink, but the fulfillment of Scripture.

131. Gerd Theissen and Annette Merz, *The Historical Jesus: A Comprehensive Guide*, trans. John Bowden (Minneapolis: Fortress Press, 1998), 453; Brown, *Death of the Messiah*, 2:1168.

the moral contrast between Jesus' dignity and his treatment,[132] and the onset of darkness "over the whole earth" indicates an undoing of creation.[133]

These aspects of the Lukan crucifixion scene may seem to speak in favor of Barth's interpretation that highlights Christ's majesty. For Luke, Jesus' majesty consists especially in his righteousness, which is in contrast to the cross. He proves his complete trust in God in that he bears the suffering in an exemplary way, even condescending to do good to others. Thus the Lukan Jesus maintains his existence for others, which also characterized his ministry previously. In this, the particulars of his death are a consequence of his life, although he suffers unjustly.[134]

That the misery of suffering even heightens Jesus' majesty, as Barth argues, is not in keeping with the Lukan passion, however. Luke eliminates expressions of Jesus' physical, psychological, and social misery, partly even turning them into their opposites. This is in keeping with the wider Lukan tendency to reduce Jesus' emotions, thus portraying him as the true Stoic sage.[135] The Lukan Jesus does not even suffer thirst and thus endures torture with virtually superhuman tranquility. This creates a tension to Barth's view that Jesus' sovereignty and freedom stand out precisely in adversity and suffering. In the Lukan crucifixion scene, Jesus' majesty seems to elevate him above suffering.

Another tension consists in the fact that Luke avoids the

132. Theissen and Merz, *Historical Jesus*, 454: Antipas and Pilate confirm Jesus' innocence (Luke 23:6–12).

133. Luke 24:44: *Skotos egeneto eph' holēn tēn gēn*, Gen. 1:2 LXX: *skotos*. Günter Thomas, *Neue Schöpfung: Systematisch-theologische Untersuchungen zur Hoffnung auf das Leben 'in der zukünftigen Welt'* (Neukirchen-Vluyn: Neukirchener, 2009), 458.

134. Christfried Böttrich, "Proexistenz im Leben und Sterben: Jesu Tod bei Lukas," in *Deutungen des Todes Jesu im Neuen Testament*, ed. Jörg Frey and Jens Schröter (Tübingen: Mohr Siebeck, 2007), 413–36, at 415.

135. David G. George, "Jesus' Lack of Emotion in Luke: The Lukan Redactions in Light of the Hellenistic Philosophers," PhD diss., University of Notre Dame, 2009, http://bit.ly/oKgHhU.

interpretation of Jesus' death in terms of atonement or penal substitution.[136] In Jesus' prayer for the torturers (Luke 23:34), it is their ignorance, not the atonement even for unintentional sin, that speaks in their favor. What is more, if even the righteous one is tortured to death, others will face a worse fate a fortiori. The bystanders comprehend this, beating their chests in an implicit request for mercy.[137] This is in keeping with the contrastive scheme in Acts 2:23–4.36, 3:15, 4:10, 5:30, 10:39–40, 13:28–30. According to the apostolic proclamation, Jesus' innocence contributes to the guilt incurred by those involved in the execution. This implies, contrary to Barth's theory of God's "covenant with death,"[138] that God was not indeed complicit in this crucifixion. By contrast, the human actors alone bear full responsibility.

The Crucifixion and Death of Jesus in the Gospels of Mark and Matthew (Mark 15:20–41, Matt. 27:31–56)

The Lukan image of the noble Jesus, who remains unchallenged by physical suffering, gains shape in discussion with the crucifixion scene in the Gospel of Mark.[139] With the cry, "My God, my God, why have you forsaken me?" (Mark 15:34), Mark chooses a contrast to the form of address in other prayers attributed to Jesus, "Father," which may presume a greater degree of partiality. It is remarkable that this cry is found in the Gospel of Matthew as well, as according to Matthew, the passion is usually rooted in Jesus' sovereign will. This is the case, for example, in Jesus' announcement of his suffering Matt.

136. Alfons Weiser, *Theologie des Neuen Testaments: Die Theologie der Evangelien* (Stuttgart: Kohlhammer, 1993), 145–6; Böttrich, "Proexistenz im Leben und Sterben," 413–14: the only two unambiguous references to the atonement, Luke 22:19–20; Acts 20:28 are controversial in textual criticism.

137. Brown, *Death of the Messiah*, 2:1168.

138. *CD* IV/1, 271 (trans. rev.), see also 271–2.

139. Brown, *Death of the Messiah*, 2:1067.

26:1–2 and Jesus' statement that he might avert his death by calling heavenly legions in aid (Matt. 26:53).[140] With the cry of dereliction at the cross, Jesus turns to the God whom he addresses, as it were, as the personal God who is ready to help. Nonetheless, he perceives his misery as so extreme that he interprets it paradoxically as dereliction precisely by this God.

Jesus' cry of dereliction on the cross is the one scriptural verse Barth most often refers to in *CD* IV/1. This is significant. Yet it would be inadequate to interpret the cry merely as an abstract expression of misery. What is the point of Jesus' question?[141]

Barth's repeated references to the verse are remarkable in that they are often suggestive of larger theological themes. On the whole, however, Barth's interpretations are heterogeneous and incidental, rather than carefully argued exegetical analyses. For example, Barth argues that God might have abandoned the world after the crucifixion and undone it:

> The reconciliation of the world with God which took place in Jesus Christ had therefore the meaning that a radical end was made of Him and therefore of the world. And that might have exhausted its meaning. The saying: "My God, my God, why hast thou forsaken me?" (Mark 15:34) shows how close was this frightful possibility. It might have been that God turned away His face finally from us. . . . He might have given death and nullity the last word in relation to the creature. He would still have been in the right.[142]

Yet an act of reconciliation does not deserve the name if an ensuing destruction is a legitimate option. If Barth interprets the cry of godforsakenness as a sign that an annihilation of the world would

140. Theissen and Merz, *Historical Jesus*, 452.

141. On Ps. 22:2 see Eva Harasta, *Lob und Bitte: Eine systematisch-theologische Untersuchung über das Gebet* (Neukirchen-Vluyn: Neukirchener, 2005), 76–111. On Jesus' cry of dereliction, see also Peter K. Stephenson, "The Crucified God: Mark 15:25–39," *Direction* 41 no. 1 (2012): 148–64.

142. *CD* IV/1, 306.

have been legitimate, then the cross does not warrant peace between God and creation. In direct contrast to his wider intention, he indicates that the crucifixion is not Jesus' coronation and triumph. Jesus appears as a victim, and the cross constitutes God's claim against the world.

Barth understands the cry as "the despairing question."[143] It appears as an expression of extreme social isolation, yet in the same breath Barth asserts that Jesus is the royal reign in person, *autobasileia*.[144] The assertion of the Christ as *autobasileia* is in contrast to the crucifixion scene in Mark and Matthew, given that in the Synoptics, God's *basileia*, or kingdom, is associated with healing and social integration. In a sense it would fit better with the royal allusions of John.[145]

At a different place, Barth interprets the cry to say that by his own choice, Jesus has undergone no less than the greatest hardship. It is precisely the suffering that presents Christ's *oboedientia passiva* (obedience in suffering) as anything other but trivial. Especially since his obedience becomes "passion," it remains "action."[146] In this sense already Jesus' prayer in Gethsemane was

> a remarkable historical complement to the eternal decision taken in God Himself, one which was not taken easily but with great difficulty, one to which He won through, which He won from Himself. And, of course, the question of the Crucified: Had God forsaken Him? (Mark 15:34), points even more strongly in the same direction.[147]

The call thus marks God's affirmation of hardship. This raises the

143. *CD* IV/2, 250.
144. Ibid., 168: the term has been eliminated in the published translation.
145. This is true in terms of Jesus' sovereignty, even though the *basileia* does not play an important role in John. In Luke 23:42–3, Jesus' entry into the kingdom means redemption from suffering rather than sovereign rule in suffering.
146. *CD* IV/1, 238. This is also Barth's interpretation of the cry of abandonment, ibid., 185 ("He acts as *Lord* over this contradiction even as He subjects Himself to it." Emphasis in the original). Ibid., 566–7, Barth argues that the cry reflects God's punishment of sin.
147. *CD* IV/1, 238–9.

question of whether Jesus' cry of godforsakenness allows for the notion that the crucified Jesus still affirms this course of events, in spite of all the misery.

In another instance, Barth argues that the cry expresses the depth of the communion between God and Jesus. Jesus paradoxically addresses God, asking why God had "forsaken" him; again paradoxically, Barth concludes "that God has not abandoned the world and man in the unlimited need of his situation."[148] This interpretation may perhaps be in keeping with the fact that Jesus still addresses God—unless in fact it presses that aspect too much. But the paradox must not be resolved too easily: the question of *why* God *had* forsaken Jesus, which may imply indignation at a lack of faithfulness, would otherwise simply mean that God had *not* forsaken Jesus. Jesus' suffering would then mean the deepest, albeit concealed, fellowship in suffering. Without explication, the meaning of communion with God has then changed, however. Jesus seems to understand such communion as God's *opposition* to suffering, yet its deeper meaning would then be communion *in* suffering. If this were the intention of Mark and Matthew, would they indeed make a point of reporting Jesus' inarticulate cry of death (Mark 15:37, Matt. 27:50), a difficult detail not present or—in Luke's case—even purposefully purged by the other Gospels? That such deepened understanding of communion with God would remain concealed precisely for Jesus, and that Jesus' notion of communion with God would then remain rather limited, precisely at the supposed climax of salvation history, would be peculiar.

At a different place Barth argues that Jesus' cry indicated not only the drastic extent to which Jesus "could not . . . dispose even of the help of God," but even the extent to which he "would not,"

148. Ibid., 215.

did not wish to, "dispose even of the help of God."[149] Does Barth here follow a theistic tradition, according to which one should not even attempt to influence the ineffable, absolute God, who is not at anyone's disposal?[150] That the crucified Jesus was unable to force God's hand into a divine intervention is clear enough from this question. Yet that he did not even wish for God to intervene seems to be in clear contrast to the question. In this case, Barth's reading seems anachronistic in that, far from wanting to be saved from suffering and death, all Jesus asked for was moral support.

In the interpretation of Mark 15:34, sometimes the opinion is voiced that the question, taken from Ps. 22:2, is at the same time an articulation of the hope of the one thus praying, in keeping with the continuation of the psalm (see Ps. 22:23).[151] Barth neither mentions this view, nor is it a fortunate interpretation as it transforms an expression of misery into its opposite. Taking the intertextual approach seriously, it would make more sense to locate the indirect, intertextual reference of the question on the level of the narrating, rather than on that of the narration. The author would thus provide the readers with a very indirect reference to the possibility of divine intervention, which, however, in all harshness still remains hidden for Jesus. Otherwise we would not do justice to the despair of the one thus crying.

Mark 15:34 expresses the contradiction within the situation: Jesus

149. Ibid., 458 ("*Die Tiefe der völligen Hilflosigkeit, des gänzlichen Nichtverfügenkönnens und Nichtverfügenwollens auch über die Hilfe Gottes*").

150. That Barth raises the question of "disposing," of a presumptuous sense of control over the events, is peculiar in the case of Mark 15:34. According to Patrick D. Miller, *They Cried to the Lord: The Form and Theology of Biblical Prayer* (Minneapolis: Fortress Press, 1994), 114, it is characteristic of the Psalms to move God to action. Psalm 22:6–8 presents God with the impression "that God's way is not consistent unless the psalmist is helped and also that the taunting of the psalmist is at the same time a mockery of God that God should set to rest" (ibid., 115). There is nothing illegitimate in such lament.

151. Holly J. Carey, *Jesus' Cry from the Cross: Towards a First-Century Understanding of the Intertextual Relationship between Psalm 22 and the Narrative of Mark's Gospel*, The Library of New Testament Studies 398 (London and New York: T&T Clark, 2009).

turns to God precisely in the conviction that the experience of suffering is in contrast to his trust in God. It would not do justice to the story simply to choose one horn of the dilemma, emphasizing the aspect of trust at the expense of the aspect of despair, or the other way around. Nonetheless, the aspect of bitter despair is indeed in keeping with the overall depiction of the crucifixion in Mark and Matthew. After all, the cross was notorious as one of the most shameful and 'excruciating' methods of execution.[152] The cry from the cross presents a fundamental protest against the crucifixion. The narrator also demonstrates this in setting up a contrast between Jesus' lament and the mockery of the witnesses of the crucifixion. It is rarely noted that the presentation of this mockery is unusually extensive. After the derision by the soldiers was already described in some detail in Mark 15:16–20, verses 29–32 report the mockery of the crucified one, using almost as many words as verses 22–26 do, which state Jesus' being led off, crucified, and given to drink, as well as the casting of the lot for Jesus' clothes and the account of the inscription on the cross. Going beyond that, Matt. 27:39–44 describes the mockery of the crucified one even more extensively.

The mockers cynically highlight the contrast to Jesus' previous authoritative ministry. In depicting them as shaking their heads over Jesus, Matt. 27:39, Mark 15:29 use the same expression as Ps. 22:8 LXX (*kineō kephalēn/tas kephalas*). To some extent, the crucifixion and Psalm 22 are moving in synchrony now. In Ps. 22:9, the mockers torment the afflicted one even further by drawing up a caricature of their victim's intimate relationship to God: "Commit your cause to YHWH; let him deliver—let him rescue the one in whom he delights!" In Matt. 27:40, 43; Mark 15:29–32 the mockers similarly

152. Martin Hengel, *Crucifixion in the Ancient world and the folly of the message of the cross*, trans. John Bowden, 2nd ed. (Minneapolis: Fortress Press, 1978), characterizes the cross with Origen's description, *mors turpissima crucis*, "the utterly vile death of the cross."

assume that only a divine intervention could set the one thus suffering into the right. Yet such a miracle would not take place. Matthew 27:43 even quotes Ps. 22:9, but Mark 15:29–32 also reports the derision by three groups of people. They highlight the contrast between Jesus' claims to higher authority and his help for others in need, on the one hand, and his own drastic misery on the cross, on the other. Thus the gospel narratives give ample room to the portrayal of the cross as the practical refutation of Jesus' ministry.

To this Jesus responds in turning to God. Like the psalmist in Ps. 22:2, he addresses God as "my God." The psalm, on the other hand, further develops the relationship between the psalmist and God. After the psalmist called on God, his enemies denied his relationship to God. Yet then Ps. 22:20 describes an "opening towards the future,"[153] since the psalmist now uses God's name, the tetragrammaton, addressing God directly rather than in the third person as before. In contrast to the mockery, the psalmist claims the personal relationship with God, and thus turns the lament of 22:2 into a positive summons: "But you, YHWH, do not be far away! O my help, come quickly to my aid!"[154] This is indeed the point of the cry of abandonment, to the extent that it implies trust: in spite of the experience of being forsaken by God, Jesus still calls on God to help him.

It is at this point, however, that the trajectories of the psalm and the crucifixion scene strikingly diverge. At Golgotha, the relationship between the one praying with Psalm 22 and God does not develop as the relationship in the psalm does. On the contrary, the mockers deny Jesus' relationship with God, even distorting Jesus' address to God (*'elî*, "my God," Ps. 22:2) in their sarcastic mockery of Elijah (Mark

153. Harasta, *Lob und Bitte*, 90, 96.

154. Hermann Spieckermann, *Heilsgegenwart: Eine Theologie der Psalmen,* Forschungen zur Religion und Literatur des Alten und Neuen Testaments 148 (Göttingen: Vandenhoeck & Ruprecht, 1989), 251: "In the petition, the psalmist wrenches the name of Yahweh from the enemies, which they quoted in mockery, and appropriates it."

15:36; Matt. 27:47): "Listen, he is calling for Elijah. . . . Wait, let us see whether Elijah will come to take him down." For the knowing reader, the bleak outlook of the passage is even compounded by the fact that Jesus said in Mark 9:9–13 and Matt. 17:9–13 (no parallel in Luke and John) that "Elijah"—that is, John the Baptist, from Jesus' perspective—had already come, "and they did to him whatever they pleased."[155]

The very genre of lament may imply trust, but crucially, such trust is only implied in lamenting that the trust has been disappointed. The mockers declare even such an indirect sign of trust absurd, even refute it practically. In some respect, Jesus' inarticulate death cry confirms their bitter diagnosis. At Golgotha, all appearances indicate that Jesus' authoritative ministry can only be relieved from the charge of presumption by an effective intervention of God, which does not take place, however. As things stand on Good Friday, Jesus experiences in bitter consequence that his unique relationship with God seemed to be a pretension—not only in the supposedly dull eyes of the disciples, but ultimately even to him. Barth's view that Jesus had himself consciously decided for an accursed death[156] conceals this dramatic conflict that is enacted between Jesus and the mockers. Jesus' lament expresses the contradiction between an ongoing relationship with God, on the one hand, and bitterness and indignation, on the other, yet he seems unable to muster confidence

155. Brown, *Death of the Messiah*, 2:1063, on the Elijah-motif, ibid., 1058–66. In Matthew's *Sondergut*, apocalyptic events of nature confirm the outrageous character of the scenario.

156. See also Paul Dafydd Jones, "Karl Barth on Gethsemane," *International Journal of Systematic Theology* 9 (2007): 148–71, at 162, 168. Jones asks why Jesus does not protest the impending sentence unless he consents to the crucifixion. See Gerd Theissen, *The New Testament: History, Literature, Religion*, trans. John Bowden (New York: T&T Clark, 2007), 107: Due to his monotheistic belief, Jesus was unable to claim divine authority explicitly. Rather than standing up for the truth himself, he would have expected his extraordinary status to be confirmed by no lesser authority than God. This is typical of societies in which a patriarchal system confers status upon a person, in contrast to the modern Western ideal of a person claiming his or her merits. For the current passage such confirmation would have implied divine salvation from the cross.

and articulate the disappointed trust directly as a petition. For God as the addressee of the lament, it would be appropriate to understand the lament as a desperate challenge to prevent the catastrophe in the last moment.

That lament is not only about spiritual and moral support in suffering is characteristic for the theology of the Psalms. According to a characteristic view in the Psalms, God proves God's faithfulness in saving from the lamented situation.[157] Thus, as an abstract expression of suffering or a plea for moral support in suffering, the cry of dereliction would not be interpreted properly. The most natural explanation of the cry is that according to Mark and Matthew, Jesus did not wish to die, at least not in this way, at least not in the last moment. As far as the cry also conveys a sense of trust, Jesus hopes, even at the cross, for salvation from imminent death. That God had forsaken the one thus praying would be in contradiction to the fact that the Psalms often confess God's faithfulness. God's faithfulness, or grace, *hæsæd*, is mentioned over seventy times in forty-five psalms, playing a very prominent role in this biblical book. "Most frequently associated with *hæsæd* is a plea for deliverance from enemies (e.g., Ps 17:7; 143:12) or thanksgiving for such deliverance (e.g., Ps 138:2)."[158]

If the cry implies an indirect performative aspect, what would be an appropriate response to the cry on the part of the addressee? A hope of resurrection may not have been uncommon among first-century Jewish martyrs. However, in Jesus' case, resurrection into God's eschatological realm would have implied a dilemma. On the one hand, Jesus would have been justified before God. But the actors

157. This is illustrated by Ps. 22:6; 13:4. See Bernd Janowski, *Konfliktgespräche mit Gott: Eine Anthropologie der Psalmen* (Neukirchen-Vluyn: Neukirchener, 2003), 54–5, 56–7, 61. According to Miller, *They Cried to the Lord*, 86, biblical texts of lament are primarily concerned with receiving help from God.

158. Katharine Doob Sakenfeld, "Love," in *The Anchor Bible Dictionary*, ed. David Noel Freedman (New York: Doubleday, 1996), 4:375–81, at 380, on *hæsæd* and on statistics, ibid., 377–80.

in the passion narratives would still have felt that Jesus' extraordinary claims to personify the reign of God were dashed at the cross. Neither does the parable of the wicked tenants in Mark 12:1–12 include a resurrection.[159] If Jesus told the parable as a warning to keep his adversaries from using lethal force, the cry from the cross faces the imminent failure of this attempt. The main problem in interpreting the cry as an articulation of Jesus' hope for the resurrection, however, is that such hope contradicts the lament of being abandoned by God. If Jesus' cry implies an ongoing relationship with God, it articulates Jesus' chagrin about the fact that the situation has come this far. If a performative aspect is implicit, the point would be that it is not necessarily too late yet for a public, effective, miraculous divine intervention.

In a post-Enlightenment world, or at least in a more introspective culture, a petition for divine intervention into the historical flow of events is presumably less common than in the ancient world. In abstraction from such intervention, the Psalms do not typically ask for consolation, comfort for the restless conscience, or a sense of divine solidarity. By contrast, the role of prayer in Old Testament congregations has been described thus:

> It is the cry of the innocent and the poor, the weak and the helpless, in a world where the strong, the rich, and the powerful, use those characteristics as weapons against others. . . . Extrication from the distress, God's help to alleviate the situation, is the primary aim of all these prayers.[160]

159. The quotation from Ps. 118:22–3 (Mark 12:10) seems to refer to divine vengeance. By contrast, in Ps. 118:18, the psalmist thanks God for saving him or her from death (see Carey, *Jesus' Cry from the Cross*, 86). But this is in contrast to story of the wicked tenants (Mark 12:8), so the indirect mode of intertextual reference should not be pressed. Beyond this particular pericope, the strongest point in favor of Carey's case is that Mark indeed places various references to Jesus' resurrection on his lips. The crucial question is if they relate meaningfully to the particular genre of Jesus' cry, that of lament, and to the ever bleaker development of the mockery scene, in which Jesus' inarticulate cry of death represents the absolute low point.

160. Miller, *They Cried to the Lord*, 105; Harasta, *Lob und Bitte*, 91.

While Mark 15:34 is a lamentation, Ps. 22:2 turns it into an explicit petition in verses 12 and 20. In comparison to this petition, the lament in verse 2 also includes an aspect of indignation about God keeping a distance. Thus, Jesus' lament also has a declarative aspect. This declarative aspect not only shows that Jesus experiences his situation as suffering, but also that in his trust in God, he is unable to accept this suffering. Thus, the declarative aspect should not be played off against a performative aspect: "Lament is directed toward the petition, that is, it preserves a sense of trust, which past experience has inspired. But it cannot yet ask for the future of such trust—as the petition will do."[161] The trust of the one thus lamenting implies the possibility that the focus will shift from the declarative to the performative aspect. Thus it is imperative to preserve also the performative aspect in Mark 15:34. The verse is not about some abstract moral support in suffering, so that God would merely change the circumstances in which the miserable death on the cross would seem more tolerable to Jesus.

In a rare passage, Barth interprets Jesus' cry from the cross in a related way: only in the resurrection did God answer the cry of dereliction.[162] But while the cry seems to be about divine intervention indeed, the most natural interpretation would not assume that Jesus appealed to God to raise him from the dead. After the contrast between Jesus' lament of abandonment and the Elijah mockery, the final inarticulate death cry seems to conclude this episode. It seems that the hope articulated in Ps. 22 was dashed with Jesus' death. In turn, Jesus' resurrection will appear like an entirely unexpected, new turn of events that snatches victory from the jaws of defeat, even after defeat has been accomplished. One important point in this

161. Ibid., 78–9.

162. *CD* IV/1, 307 (trans. rev.). Whether Jesus indeed hoped for the resurrection in yearning for deliverance is another question; it seems more likely that he wanted God to avert death in the first place.

interpretation is that Jesus' resurrection will be manifested publicly and that the rebuttal of Jesus' claims to special authority in the cross is itself publicly reversed.

At another instance, Barth captures the worrisome fear of failure inherent in the cry of abandonment: Jesus died "with that last despairing question on His lips, as One who was condemned and maltreated and scorned by men and abandoned by God."[163] Indeed, the drama of life and death at Golgotha should not be resolved too easily by assuming that Jesus hoped for life after death in the first place. On the whole, Barth did not share this interpretation, but Jesus' cry does appear to point to a vague, paradoxical hope that God might prevent this death in the first place.

According to this overall interpretation of the conflict at Golgotha, the resurrection rather than the crucifixion is the salvific event proper. Barth still understands the cry in the sense of this theory that in Jesus' passion, God carries out his "covenant" with evil undeterred, although at Jesus' expense. Thus Barth still does not take fully into account the scandal of the cross, which comes to the fore in the cry of abandonment.

The scandal of the cross is in contrast to Jesus' majesty manifested previously in the affliction in Gethsemane. Here Jesus' faithfulness to his vocation does indeed surpass his fear of suffering. Had Jesus fled from his arrest, he would have flinched from the ultimate identification with his proclamation and his ministry. From the perspective of historical research as well, there is good reason to assert Jesus' awareness that in his activity, God's reign was taking place.[164] By contrast, a refusal to affirm this reality in daring his own life might have virtually amounted to recanting.

As the dawning of God's reign in Jesus' ministry was *oboedientia*

163. *CD* IV/2, 252.
164. Theissen and Merz, *Historical Jesus*, 529.

activa, active obedience, the beginning of the passion meant Jesus proved his obedience even in suffering, in *oboedientia passiva*; Jesus tolerates the consequences of his abiding affirmation of the eschatological claims tied to his own person. In this respect Barth's thesis is justified that Jesus Christ manifested his divinity in the affliction of Gethsemane. In a certain sense, even the cross amounted to an act of divine majesty, since Jesus accepted arrest, not reneging on his authoritative ministry.

If the passion narratives, however, proceed from Jesus' expectation of conflict toward the cry from the cross, the relationship between exaltation and suffering is transformed. Jesus perceives suffering and death as the rejection of his eschatological self-awareness. Here lies the problem with interpretations of the passion as an unbroken *oboedientia passiva*. When in the cry of dereliction Jesus interprets his misery in such a way that God has indeed forsaken him, or is about to do so, he sees the death on the cross as the failure of his mission. Had God remained faithful to his Son, God would have averted such an end, at least in the last moment. In the expectation of such a turn of events, Jesus said his prayer in Gethsemane, and in this sense he trusted in his divine vocation, allowing the captors to take him prisoner. This interpretation disputes the climax of the supposed triumph at the cross, of Jesus' *oboedientia passiva*. As the crucifixion scene according to Mark and Matthew does not indicate imminent resurrection, it seems that Jesus' death on the cross answers the question whether Jesus had failed. The last thing that the bystanders hear from him is an inarticulate cry of death.

The New Testament Depictions of the Crucifixion and Barth's Interpretation of the Cross

The analysis of the crucifixion scene of the four Gospels suggests different understandings of Jesus' misery and exaltation. A presentation of Barth's view on the relationship will raise the question, however, whether he emphasizes Jesus' glory at the expense of a realistic sense of Jesus' suffering. He may argue that on Good Friday, the crucified one is already the risen one of Easter Sunday. This is the view of the Fourth Gospel. This is also related to Barth's statement that the resurrection reveals Christ's majesty, which was only hidden before. He creates the impression, however, that it was almost a mere formality that Christ "could now be seen, and was actually seen"[165] in his majesty. True enough, in the resurrection and the ascension, Jesus "did not become a different person."[166] But Barth continues, "How could He become anything different or better or higher" than at the cross?[167] This prompts the question in return whether suffering and death were only a mere illusion.

> The humiliation of God and the exaltation of man as they took place in Him are the completed fulfilment of the covenant, the completed reconciliation of the world with God. His being as such (if we may be permitted this abstraction for a moment) was and is the end of the old and the beginning of the new form of this world even without His resurrection and ascension. He did not and does not lack anything in Himself.[168]

Barth certainly wishes to refute the idea that only the resurrection made Jesus the Son of God. Following this legitimate concern, however, he falls into another extreme, according to which even the most drastic events of history are irrelevant within the existing communion between God and the creature that is enacted in Jesus Christ. This is in tension with a fundamental concern of *CD* IV: the reconceptualization of the classic doctrine of Jesus Christ's two

165. *CD* IV/2, 133.
166. Ibid. (trans. rev.).
167. Ibid.
168. Ibid., 132–3.

natures in terms of a history, or its "actualization."[169] If an event in history that transforms Jesus' miserable death at the hands of humanity into new and exalted life does not say anything fundamental about the relationship between God and creation, how does Barth's view of the communion between God and Jesus at the cross as entirely unharmed not result in a trivialization of soteriology? If the resurrection is not a dramatic turning point in Jesus' lot—although it is certainly not an adoption into the Trinity—if it was nothing but "simply a lifting of the veil,"[170] the preceding misery appears harmless, and the proper point of Barth's historical interpretation of the doctrine of Jesus Christ's two natures gets lost.

Yet at different points, Barth not only conceals the scandal that the tortured and maltreated one succumbs to the power of death on the cross; occasionally, he even purports that the opposite is the case. Since Christ manifested his obedience in the passion, Barth calls the cross a "triumph," to which the disciples were merely blind when they looked at the cross.[171] The fascination with paradox should not conceal how the victory over the destructive forces is much clearer in the resurrection than when an innocent, despairing victim is tortured to death. Disappointment at the cross was not merely due to the dullness of the disciples. Barth, however, portrays the matter differently.

> Jesus was not led to this place . . . in contradiction of the fact that He was the royal man. On the contrary, it was in a sense His *coronation* as this man. . . . What we have said finds its true *climax* and *glory* in the fact that—however hard this may sound—He finally hung on the gallows as a criminal between two other criminals, and died there, with that last despairing question on His lips, as One who was condemned and maltreated and scorned by men and abandoned by God.[172]

169. *CD* IV/2, 105.
170. Ibid., 133.
171. Ibid., 254.

Barth thinks especially of Jesus' obedience, but also of God's "covenant with death"[173] and finally Jesus' vicarious suffering for the sake of sinners when he writes equivocally, "In His passion the name of the God active and revealed in Him is conclusively sanctified; His will is done on earth as it is done in heaven; His kingdom comes."[174]

Barth's goal is to express the contrast between two extremes in the one event of the crucifixion: "Where and when is He not both humiliated and exalted, already exalted in His humiliation, and humiliated in His exaltation?"[175] The coincidence of opposites may even be legitimate to some extent. The cross results from the fact that Jesus refuses to negate his calling, and if even the execution of the Son of God does not result in God's abandonment of creation, this indicates radical love and forgiveness and is indeed good news. But this already presupposes, as shall be argued in more detail later, the resurrection as the decisive turning point, and this way of putting things involves a one-sided approach to the cross.

Barth's own version of this argument even heightens the one-sidedness. The event of the crucifixion cannot bear the weight that Barth's extreme intensification of this interpretation lays on it: "But in dying [Jesus Christ] is superior to death, and at once and altogether rescued from it."[176] A statement like this makes Christology appear docetic. This is the classic pitfall for those confronted with the gruesomeness of the cross.[177] On the whole, Barth's treatment of the matter is more mature than a straightforward denial of the embodied presence of God in Christ, attempting to do justice to Jesus' majesty in the midst of misery. But this is not evident from some of the points

172. Ibid., 252 (emphasis in the original).
173. *CD* IV/1, 271 (trans. rev.), see also 271–2.
174. *CD* IV/2, 252.
175. *CD* IV/1, 133.
176. Ibid., 131.
177. Hengel, *Crucifixion in the Ancient World*, 15–21.

he makes. In Barth's view, the gospels "describe the man Jesus as the One who is afflicted and tempted as King, suffers and dies, masters all of this as King, and thus passes through the midst of all others as King."[178] In suffering, Jesus was "*already* the secret Lord of death to which He subjected Himself."[179]

Barth expresses Jesus' exaltation in and through suffering in part even more strongly, but certainly more often, in *CD* IV/2, especially in §64, which deals with Christ's royal office. For example, Barth calls the cross simultaneously Christ's "descent into hell" and his "triumphant coronation."[180] Too often, misery does not appear unconcealed in its one-sided terror, but is seemingly canceled out by assertions of Christ's triumph. "His resurrection revealed Him as the One who reigns in virtue of His death, from the cross (*regnantem in cruce*)."[181] The crucified one was "never greater as Lord than in this depth of His servanthood!"[182]

> Subject to this one imperative [of doing the will of the Father], and therefore not arbitrarily if not under any outward compulsion or constraint, He came and went with absolute superiority, disposing and controlling, speaking or keeping silence, always exercising lordship. This was no less true when He entered and trod to the end the way of His death and passion. Indeed, to those who looked back, it was even more plainly true on this way.[183]

The occurrences of such problematic statements are legion; they paper over the fact that the one thus maltreated at the cross was slowly and miserably tortured to death.[184]

178. *CD* IV/1, 132 (trans. rev.).
179. Ibid., 307 (trans. rev.).
180. *CD* IV/2, 141.
181. Ibid., 291.
182. Ibid., 150 (trans. rev.: exclamation point by Barth).
183. Ibid., 161.
184. *CD* IV/1, 131–2, 134–5, *CD* IV/2, 152, 252, 254, 256, 257–8, 290, 299, 326, 349, 352, 353–4, 358 ("triumphantly alive even, and especially, in His death"), 467–8, 484, 486, 552, 583, 599,

Barth's views about Jesus' majesty in suffering show fundamental tensions in Barth's dogmatic method. On the one hand, he argues for exegetical support in interpreting the passion narratives, which supposedly amounts to Jesus' defeat of nullity. Barth thus strives to derive his discourse about God only from the christological traditions of Scripture: "What is to be understood by 'Godhead,' is something which—watchful against all imported ideas . . . —we must always learn from Jesus Christ."[185] Yet does Barth actually live up to this standard? Barth adds a little later, "Again, what is the exaltation of Jesus Christ? To say that as God He is transcendent, free, sovereign, above the world, and therefore above the limitation and suffering of the human situation is again a tautology which does not help us to understand His exaltation."[186]

That the incarnate Son of God is sovereign and superior is a tautology precisely from the perspective of classic theism. This is in tension with an unconcealed view on the Son of God dying on the cross, and this is what Barth has been struggling with as well. His attempt to bolster up his thesis of Christ's triumph in misery is an attempt to reconcile the metaphysical predicate of divine omnipotence with a theology that derives its basic convictions from biblical traditions.

Barth's interpretation of the *extra Calvinisticum*[187] points to the significance of metaphysical predicates of the divine as well.[188] Barth

765 ("His death as the crowning"), 796–7 ("the coronation of the royal man completed in His death"), *CD* IV/3, 390 ("the Victor of Gethsemane and Golgotha . . . the . . . unsightly *Imperator* [emperor] and *Triumphator* [triumphant one] who enters, rules and triumphs," trans. rev.). A similar view is expressed by John H. Yoder, *The Politics of Jesus: Vicit Agnus Noster* [Our lamb has conquered], 2nd ed. (Grand Rapids: Eerdmans, 1994), 51: "The cross is not a detour or a hurdle on the way to the kingdom, nor is it even the way to the kingdom; it is the kingdom come."

185. *CD* IV/1, 129, see 186.

186. Ibid., 134.

187. Barth notes the polemical origin of the term. He illustrates the doctrine with a quotation from Calvin's *Institutes* (1:481, II, 13, 4): "The Son of God descended from heaven in such a way that, without leaving heaven, he willed to be borne in the virgin's womb, to go about the earth,

agrees with a prominent statement of Calvin's: although the Son is incarnate in Jesus Christ, he is also God in the full sense, "and therefore omnipotent and omnipresent (and to that extent *extra carnem* ['outside of the flesh,' i.e., existing alongside Jesus of Nazareth], not bound and thus altered by its limitations)."[189] Barth thus interprets the view that the incarnate Logos has not ceased being God in the sense that the eternal Son is not ultimately affected by Jesus' death on the instrument of torture. Along these lines, he asserts, Christ was "triumphantly alive even, and especially, in His death."[190] If this holds indeed, what could it mean for the doctrine of election to assert that in Christ, God chose eternally to bear the consequences of the creature's sin?

Occasionally, however, Barth also shows considerable skepticism toward the *extra Calvinisticum*. The doctrine of the *logos asarkos* (the nonincarnate word) could be misused, he warns, in arguing for positions insufficiently grounded in the biblical witnesses to revelation.

> We may concede that there is something unsatisfactory about the theory, in that right up to our own day it has led to fatal speculation about the being and work of the *logos asarkos*, or a God whom we think we can know elsewhere, and whose divine being we can define from elsewhere than in and from the contemplation of His presence and activity as the Word made flesh. And it cannot be denied that Calvin himself (and with particularly serious consequences in his doctrine of predestination) does go a good way towards trying to reckon with this "other" god.[191]

and to hang upon the cross; yet he continuously filled the world even as he had done from the beginning" (*CD* IV/1, 180).

188. On the *extra Calvinisticum* see Christian Link, "Die Entscheidung der Christologie Calvins und ihre theologische Bedeutung: Das sogenannte Extra-Calvinisticum," *Evangelische Theologie* 47 (1987): 97–119.

189. *CD* IV/1, 181. This holds in spite of Paul D. Jones's perceptive comments on related questions in *Humanity of Christ*, 91–6.

190. *CD* IV/2, 358.

191. *CD* IV/1, 181.

Barth refutes the validity, or at least the relevance of the doctrine of a nonincarnate word of God, fearing that the projection of human wishes is passed off as divine revelation.[192] The only legitimate source of revelation is that form "which God Himself has given, willing to reveal Himself and to act outwards."[193]

If, by contrast, the true extent of Jesus' suffering is not eclipsed by a theological instinct that holds on to Jesus' abiding control and majesty as a matter of principle, even when faced with Jesus' utter misery, the ethical consequences are far-reaching. Among the immediate consequences are a clearer sensitivity to the scandal of suffering as well as clearer limits on how far an affirmation of an ethics of cruciform discipleship should be willing to go.

Moreover, Barth's view of Christ's sovereignty in suffering is also associated with assumptions about a dark side in God. Barth portrays Christ's cross as the result of God's "covenant with death."[194] If Barth did indeed take Christ's suffering on the cross entirely seriously, presumably he would also realize that this makes God complicit in torture. Both shortcomings are closely related to a lack of sensitivity for extraordinary violence. This is relevant in ethics in different ways. One can be illustrated by a recent exchange about just war theory. Nigel Biggar submits in an argument against categorical Christian nonviolence, "If (with [Richard B.] Hays) we take death to be the effect of divine wrath on sinners, then, notwithstanding God's active desire that they should be saved, [God] nevertheless ends up 'killing' those who do not participate 'in Christ' [in eschatological judgment]."[195] While the present discussion is not concerned with the postmortem fate of unbelievers, there is a connection between Biggar's views on eschatological consummation and the supposedly

192. Ibid., 52.
193. Ibid. (trans. rev.). See *CD* IV/3, 396–7, 724.
194. *CD* IV/1, 271 (trans. rev.: "*Bund mit dem Tode*").
195. Nigel Biggar, *In Defence of War* (Oxford: Oxford University Press, 2013), 51.

eschatological violence on Good Friday.[196] Seen from the opposite angle, Barth considers the universal range of Christ's atonement an important argument against capital punishment in *CD* III/4, §55.2. Whether or not Christ's cross is asserted to exhaust divine wrath entirely, that the bearer of sin must meet a violent fate is at the heart of Barth's interpretation of the passion narrative in §59. This contributes to the noble purpose of penal substitution in Christ's death, which supposedly characterizes his suffering as noble as well. Does violence therefore have an inherently redemptive dimension?

In an ethics of responsibility, by contrast, both a greater urgency in reducing suffering and a greater reluctance to tolerate suffering for ulterior purposes results.[197] Portraying the cross as a symbol of Christian discipleship, Barth justifies his ethics of cruciform discipleship in *CD* IV with fundamental christological assertions that appear hard to surpass. That in this endeavor he sometimes succumbs to the danger of papering over unjust suffering, or even of justifying it, is demonstrated by his gender ethics. There are other traditions in Barth's *Church Dogmatics*, however, which operate with a different notion of violence and reconciliation. It is to these that the next section will turn.

Justification through Cross and Resurrection: *Theologia Crucis et Gloriae*

CD IV/1, §59.2 presents Christ's cross as the effective destruction of sin and evil, and other statements in *CD* IV likewise focus on the

196. Note Barth's view in *CD* III/3, § 50, 289 that Christ's atoning work allows even for a continuation of retributive violence under divine direction. This has critical implications for the validity and the range of Christ's atoning sacrifice.

197. It is crucial for an ethics of responsibility not to disregard the increased suffering of others in pursuit of its own goals. In ethical discernment, the consequences for "the least of these" (Matt. 25) play a prominent role. See Wolfgang Huber, "Sozialethik als Verantwortungsethik," in *Konflikt und Konsens: Studien zur Ethik der Verantwortung* (Munich: Kaiser, 1990), 135–57, at 152, 153–4.

cross in the discussion of justification.[198] But in spite of these passages, *CD* IV on the whole tends to attribute reconciliation not to the cross alone, but to the interrelationship between Christ's cross and his resurrection. The cross does not dominate the account when Barth presents the resurrection as a "*different*, a new act of God" compared to the cross, which is even "superior" to the cross.[199] Here Barth judges things differently than when he calls Christ "already exalted in His humiliation"[200] and asks how he could "become anything different or better or higher" than at the cross.[201] Now, moreover, he argues that the significance of sanctification as God's claim on the human person is also, and crucially, rooted in the resurrection.

Barth's argument in §59.2 is especially consistent in portraying the cross as the completed event of salvation, requiring no additions in range or effectiveness.[202] In a lopsided way, he speaks of the "the good news of Good Friday."[203] The subsection highlights the perfection of salvation wrought in Jesus' death by adding a discussion of the sacrificial theology of the Letter to the Hebrews.[204] Barth explicitly appreciates Nikolaus Zinzendorf's "theology of blood."[205] The cross not only creates and perfects Christian justification, but based on Heb. 10:9, Barth also sees sanctification becoming reality in the cross: "It is now learned how to do good. Regard is now had for right. …

198. For example, see *CD* IV/2, 132–3.

199. *CD* IV/1, 298 (trans. rev.).

200. *CD* IV/2, 110.

201. Ibid., 133. To be precise, Barth raises the question of Christ's divinity here. Nonetheless he suggests that there is no essential difference between being tortured to death, even as an incarnate God, and not being so maltreated.

202. Was the resurrection necessary? "Certainly not in the sense that at Golgotha everything had not taken place which had to take place for the reconciliation of the world with God." *CD* IV/1, 306.

203. Ibid., 251.

204. Ibid., 274–83, small print. By contrast, the widespread view of the sufficiency of the cross in Hebrews, apart from the resurrection, is challenged by David M. Moffitt, *Atonement and the Logic of the Resurrection in Hebrews*, Novum Testamentum Supplementa 141 (Leiden: Brill, 2011).

205. *CD* IV/1, 275.

All these things are now taking place: 'by the which will [that was enacted in the sacrificial action of Jesus Christ] we are sanctified.'"[206]

Barth gestures toward fissures in this interpretation of the cross as penal substitution already in §59.2, however, in relativizing the motto, *crux—unica spes!* (the cross—the only hope).[207] Such predominant attention to the cross "cannot and must not be the totality of what we have to say on this matter."[208] Accordingly, Protestant theology must be *theologia crucis* (theology of the cross) indeed, but not in an exclusive sense. At a different place, Barth argues even that "a monism of the *theologia crucis*" cannot justify the necessity of good works.[209] In retrospect, "GL" already shifted the focus to Jesus' resurrection when speaking of God's proper work of salvation.[210]

Moreover, why is a subsection with the title "The Verdict of the Father" (§59.3) even necessary after a subsection called "The Judge Judged in Our Place" (§59.2)? After all, §59.2 argues that the Son, in precarious cooperation with the Father, executes the verdict of the Father by applying it to himself. Yet while §59.2 deals with the execution of the verdict at the cross, the ensuing subsection speaks of the resurrection. How do the two verdicts relate?

Barth describes the resurrection as a "*different*, a new act of God" compared to the cross, which is even "superior" to the cross. This is in direct contrast to Barth's presentation of the resurrection as "simply

206. *CD* IV/1, 281–2 (Barth's parentheses; trans. rev.). Based on Hebrews, Barth emphasizes the abolition of the temple sacrifices with Christ's sacrifice (ibid., 276).

207. *CD* IV/1, 250 ("O cross—my only hope!"). See *Rom* II, 418–19: "The child of God . . . finds hope in this hopelessness—*ave crux unica spes mea*!" The salutation of the cross is attributed to Venantius Fortunatus: Guido M. Dreves, *Hymnographi Latini: Lateinische Hymnendichter des Mittelalters*, Analecta Hymnica Medii Aevi 50 (Leipzig 1907), 74–5.

208. *CD* IV/1, 250.

209. *CD* IV/2, 504. Karl-Heinz zur Mühlen helpfully distinguishes between a soteriological and an ethical necessity for good works, rejecting the former and affirming the latter: *Reformation und Gegenreformation*, Kleine Reihe (Göttingen: Vandenhoeck & Ruprecht, 1999), 2:88.

210. "GL," 95, 98.

a lifting of the veil."[211] The resurrection is not "some predicate, or adjunct, or closer definition of the first," not "an extending or deepening or manifesting" of the cross. Remarkably, he calls the cross "an end," "a question," and a "riddle," arguing that the resurrection is "a beginning where the first is an end, an answer where the first is a question, and solution where the first is a riddle."[212] After referring to 1 Cor. 15:14, 17,[213] he describes the resurrection as

> an *autonomous*, *new* act of God. It is not, therefore, the noetic converse of it! Nor is it merely the revelation and declaration of its positive significance and relevance. . . . The *theologia resurrectionis* [theology of the resurrection] does not and must not absorb the *theologia crucis*, nor vice versa. The event of Easter in its indissoluble connexion with the event of the cross is an event which has its *own* content and its *own* form.[214]

Romans 4:25 plays an important role for Barth as well.[215] Christ's resurrection is not only a necessary condition for salvation, and it is more than an appendix or the noetic revelation of the cross. It even changes the meaning of the cross. At this point, Barth shows his awareness of the problem of violence in the cross. One of the results of Good Friday is that sinners are not punished de facto. But de jure, they are not acquitted of their guilt. There is a clear tension: viewed by itself, penal substitution—and atoning violence as well—creates as many problems soteriologically as it is intended to solve.[216] "The '*for* us' [*pro nobis*] of His death on the cross includes and encloses

211. *CD* IV/2, 133.
212. *CD* IV/1, 298 (trans. rev.).
213. Ibid., 299, 352.
214. Ibid., 304 (trans. rev.).
215. Ibid., 306–7, 310, 555.
216. Ibid., 245–7. Bertold Klappert, *Die Auferweckung des Gekreuzigten: Der Ansatz der Christologie Karl Barths im Zusammenhang der Christologie der Gegenwart* (Neukirchen-Vluyn: Neukirchener, 1971), 312, speaks of a "*relation of an implication between the contra nos and the pro nobis.*"

this terrible '*against* us.'"[217] Even in that part of *CD* IV/1 that argues for the sufficiency of the cross for reconciliation, Barth notes that the destruction of the entire world would have been an appropriate response to the crucifixion. God could have held judgment in an act of annihilation. God would not have infringed anyone's rights had God, "by the same eternal Word by which as Creator He gave being to man and the world . . . now willed to take away that being from them, to let them perish with all their corruption and sin."[218] If the mere cross, apart from the resurrection, had removed all guilt without ambiguity, such annihilation would be unjust license. This thereby constitutes a break with Barth's theory of the self-destruction of evil in God's "covenant with death." After all, if the evil forces that conspire to kill Jesus thus pronounce their own verdict, their co-conspirator who makes a "covenant with death" would share in their guilt. In contrast to the highly ambiguous moral relations in §59.2, Barth now sees both Jesus and God strictly in the role of the injured party, but the rest of humanity strictly on the opposing side. The strength of this notion is that it highlights the injustice of Jesus' execution. The "*against* us" loses its validity only in the resurrection. It is the "fulfilment of the *sentence* of the Father on the way which [Jesus Christ] had gone—His judicial sentence that the action and passion of Jesus Christ . . . in our place was not futile but *valid*, that it was not to our destruction but to our salvation."[219]

According to Barth, the cross implies the *pro nobis* ("for us"), as Christ pursued the atonement in his passion, even though the atonement, and thus reconciliation, was not perfected in the cross. This implies a marked transformation of Old Testament atonement theories, which do not imply a restitution of the animal as

217. Ibid., 296 (emphasis in the original).
218. Ibid., 306.
219. Ibid., 305 (trans. rev.).

instrumental in atonement. Thus, it is best to view the atonement interpretations of Christ's death as an extended metaphor, which does not do justice to all essential aspects of reconciliation.[220] If, however, Jesus' cry of dereliction suggests that we cannot attribute an unbroken *oboedientia passiva* (obedience in suffering) to Jesus throughout the entire passion—but that, according to Mark and Matthew, Jesus was unable to reconcile death on the cross with his mission—then Jesus' death highlights a harsh conflict with the human agents involved, which is only resolved, unilaterally, in the resurrection.

Admittedly, Paul occasionally abstracts from Christ's resurrection,

220. For example, in cultic atonement, animals are slaughtered exclusively, in a ritual way, typically by authorized personnel who have undergone proper cleansing rituals. The spilled blood is effective if applied to certain cultic instruments in the temple. The notion of atonement is not concerned with a resurrection of slaughtered animals. Nonetheless, the New Testament often interprets Jesus' death in terms of atonement through sacrifice (esp. Rom. 3:25, perhaps 8:3, 1 Cor. 2:2, 2 Cor. 5:19–21, Gal. 3:1.13. Luke is a notable exception). The achievement of this mode of thought consists in making "the scandalous riddle of Jesus' death comprehensible in soteriological terms, . . . leading beyond the so-called contrastive scheme in Acts 2:36, 10:39 f." Peter Stuhlmacher, *Biblische Theologie des Neuen Testaments: Grundlegung: Von Jesus zu Paulus*, 2nd ed. (Göttingen: Vandenhoeck & Ruprecht, 1997), 295. Otfried Hofius explains—in his article "Sühne IV: Neues Testament," *Theologische Realenzyklopädie* (Berlin and New York: de Gruyter, 2001), 32:342–7—that in the death of the sacrificial animal, "the death of the sinner, or of the people of God, takes place both truly and symbolically. The ensuing blood rite exposes the blood, which is viewed as the carrier of life (Lev. 17:11), to the sanctuary (Lev. 4:5 ff. 25.30.34) or to the *kapporæt* (the 'place of expiation') as the place of God's presence (Lev. 16:14f.). Thus the life of the guilty person or of the guilty people is abandoned to God. Cultic atonement is thus an event of substitutionary, complete abandonment, in which the sinner approaches God in 'bearing God's judgment of death' (Gese). In this event, the forfeited life is created anew, the forgiveness of sins takes place as the regeneration of the human person." Already according to the Old Testament, Hofius argues, God is not conceived of as passive, so that God's wrath would be appeased. Yet although the atonement is rooted in God's mercy, the concept shares the notion that justification requires violence with Anselm's theory of satisfaction. While the cross differs from Old Testament atonement traditions in many respects, Hofius sees the main difference in the eschatological, definitive meaning of the cross, as no one other than God takes the position of the sacrificial animal. The fact that Ingolf U. Dalferth, *Der auferweckte Gekreuzigte: Zur Grammatik der Christologie* (Tübingen: Mohr Siebeck, 1994) also focuses strongly on the cross (chs. 2, 5), is in tension with the fact that the confession of Christ's resurrection was "the core statement already of the earliest Christian proclamation," however (ibid., 61). In this sense the theology of sacrificial atonement must be considered limited in the face of the epochal meaning which the New Testament attributes to the resurrection at various places.

portraying death itself as the proper cause of salvation (Rom. 3:25, perhaps 8:3, 1 Cor. 1:13.18.23, 2:2, 2 Cor. 5:19–21, Gal. 3:1.13). At other places, however, he speaks of the resurrection only or of both cross and resurrection as achieving salvation (Rom. 4:17.25, 2 Cor. 15:15.17; Rom. 1:4, 10:5–9, Gal. 1:1, 1 Thess. 1:10, Rom. 8:34, Gal. 2:20). Romans 5:9 is also typical of this complex state of affairs. Proponents of the theology of atonement rightly point out that it is not God, but human persons who require the atoning sacrifice (2 Cor. 5:19), yet when Rom. 5:9–10 speaks of reconciliation through the blood of Christ, God's wrath also plays an important role (see Rom 2:5–8). The congregation is thus spared from God's wrath due to Jesus' death, which reveals God's love (Rom 5:8), yet verse 10 adds that, "much more surely, having been reconciled, will we be saved by his life."

Due to its salvific meaning according to Rom. 3:25, for example, as well as the cultic terminology used there, Christ's death can be understood metaphorically as salvific atonement. Yet the concept of atonement does not capture all significant aspects inherent in Paul's view of the salvation worked by Christ. If this concept is made absolute, the misunderstanding is close at hand that the cross causes God to be merciful, that the cross is necessary for God to overcome wrath in mercy. The impression results that violence has inherently salvific power. This is related to the problem of papering over Christ's suffering. Although there are clear tendencies in this direction in *CD* IV, one clear strength of Barth's treatment is, among others, that he emphasizes not only the aspect of the *pro nobis* (for us) in the cross, but also that of the *contra nos* (against us). Moreover, he argues that the "for us" comes into full effect only with the resurrection.

Yet how does the *pro nobis* come to dominate eventually, invalidating the *contra nos*? By asking this question explicitly, Barth is seeking for the meaning of the resurrection.[221] Barth's juridical metaphors can sometimes suggest that the difference between cross and resurrection amounts to the difference between an act proper and a mere statement of fact,[222] between a performative and a descriptive act. Yet in juridical terminology, Barth describes the resurrection also in performative terms as bringing about reconciliation (*Vollzug*: the fulfillment, execution of a sentence).

Barth's use of the terms *bringing into force* and *giving effect to* the salvific death[223] presents the resurrection in such a way that its relation to the death on the cross is more than noetic and descriptive. What happens in the resurrection is not anything new that is entirely independently of Jesus' death on the cross, but something new happens *to the cross*. While the cross implies both the *pro nobis* and the *contra nos*, the judicial force of the *contra nos* is abrogated in the resurrection. The resurrection, the verdict of the Father, is the creative event that transforms the past. With the resurrection, God's act corresponds to the *pro nobis* of the cross, which, however, is something new vis-à-vis the cross, insofar as the resurrection not only refuses to endorse the culpable destruction of life, but, on the contrary, creates new life. To that extent, the events of the passion only achieve reconciliation on the basis of the resurrection.[224]

Thus, there is a tension between subsections 2 and 3 in §59 about whether the cross by itself already implies salvation. Section 61 ("The Justification of Man") confirms this in favor of §59.3.[225] To begin

221. *CD* IV/1, 297.
222. Ibid., 228 (trans. rev.): "We keep to the Easter story as the commentary on the Gospel story ... to the statement of fact [*Feststellung*, declaration] made in the event of Easter . . . this Gospel story is the story of redemption." 305: The resurrection "was the expression and fulfilment [*Vollzug*: execution] of the sentence of the Father on the way which He had gone—His judicial declaration [*Feststellung*] that the action and passion of Jesus Christ were . . . according to His good and holy will."
223. Ibid., 157, 305.
224. That the resurrection, in addition to the cross, is the condition of justification, is highlighted in ibid., 321: The resurrection is the "validity" of the right established in the cross.

with, §61.2 describes Jesus' death in an ambiguous way, implying both the *pro nobis* and the *contra nos.*[226]

Even here Barth remains attached to the idea that the cross is the targeted destruction of sin in the destruction of its bearer, calling Christ's death "delectable."[227] Yet the result of Good Friday is ambiguous: "Our wrong and we ourselves as the doers of it are really and truly terminated."[228] As God punishes sin with death, human persons experience a "*crisis*" and "*division*,"[229] even if death does not befall the actual sinner. Thus, Good Friday by itself, God's action "on the left hand,"[230] means death as well as life. This is the effect of the "first and negative side" of justification.[231] In the sense of penal substitution, which subordinates the gospel to punishment in the law, Barth first of all speaks of the destructive "wrath of God" that is directed at sin and breaks forth against Jesus; yet "what rules finally and properly is grace, the divine Yes deeply buried under the divine No."[232] Here it seems that—contrary to Paul's presentation of the matter in 2 Cor. 5:19—it is primarily God, rather than the world, who requires reconciliation.

In spite of this problem inherent in this theory of penal substitution, Barth then gives full weight to the affirmation of the world *beyond* the cross. Barth calls the resurrection "the establishment of his right, the introduction of the life of a new man who is righteous before God."[233] While the cross included blatant injustice—and thus

225. Klappert, *Die Auferweckung des Gekreuzigten*, disputes such a tension; in essence he draws on §59 (ibid., 85) and hardly refers to §61.
226. *CD* IV/1, 543.
227. Ibid., 553 (trans. rev.: *köstlich*).
228. Ibid., 554 (trans. rev.). If this were the whole story of justification, the adage *operation successful, patient dead* would summarize the result. See 535.
229. Ibid., 541, see 543.
230. Ibid., 542.
231. Ibid., 554.
232. Ibid., 537.
233. Ibid., 554.

a *contra nos*—the resurrection defuses the *contra nos* and brings the *pro nobis* alone into effect. The resurrection "took place for our sake, for our justification (Rom. 4:25). It was for us that He received what He did receive in it."[234] This constitutes the "second and positive side of our justification as it has taken place in Jesus Christ."[235] On "the right hand,"[236] God confirms Jesus' innocence, to the benefit of humanity.[237] Jesus' righteousness is valid not only for him, but for everyone, "representatively . . . 'Jesus lives, and I with Him.'"[238] The resurrection thus modifies the meaning of Good Friday; it is only true since Easter that Jesus Christ has died only "for us," and not, simultaneously, "against us."

Not only justification is rooted in the resurrection, but sanctification as well. The resurrection is the establishment of righteousness and justice,[239] and to claim the benefit of this right is to enter into the obligation to live up to it as well.

Barth draws conclusions from the new emphasis on the resurrection in the theology of justification by arguing for a new understanding of the terms *theologia crucis* and *theologia gloriae* (theology of the cross, theology of glory). The latter concept he also calls *theologia resurrectionis* (theology of resurrection). In *CD* IV, the two terms denote the theological account of the contribution made by the cross and the resurrection to salvation. They imply that God

234. Ibid., 555.

235. Ibid.

236. Ibid., 542.

237. Johannes Fischer, for example, rejects the traditional notion of a salvific death and with it the justification for the sinner. He presupposes, however, that the justification of the sinner is solely dependent on Christ's death on the cross. Johannes Fischer, *Theologische Ethik: Grundwissen und Orientierung*, Forum Systematik 11 (Stuttgart: Kohlhammer, 2002), 145.

238. *CD* IV/2, 271.

239. "CCCC," 172 (trans. rev.): "The Church is witness of the divine justification, that is, of the act in which God in Jesus Christ established and confirmed his original *right* (*Recht*) to the human person and thus the *right* (*Recht*) of the human person himself and herself against sin and death."

revealed God's self fundamentally in the cross and, respectively, the resurrection.

In arguing that, to some extent, theology needs to be a theology of glory, he deviates from the classic text of the theology of the cross,[240] Luther's Heidelberg Disputation. According to Luther, *theologia gloriae* denotes the attempt to recognize God through the works of creation, which results in an attempt of works righteousness. By contrast, Barth does not see God's glory in the works of creation as such, but in the glory of the resurrection. Obviously, the latter concept is much less likely to engage in attempts to recognize God apart from biblical testimonies to revelation. Thus, Barth suggests a complementary relationship between the two concepts.[241] Both the cross and the resurrection are highly significant in theology, and it does not suffice to focus on just one of them.

> A *theologia gloriae*, the praise of what Jesus Christ has received for us in His resurrection, of what He is for us as the risen One, can have no meaning unless it includes within itself a *theologia crucis*, the praise of what He has done for us in His death, of what He is for us as the Crucified. But an abstract *theologia crucis* cannot have any meaning either. We cannot properly praise the passion and death of Jesus Christ unless this praise includes within itself the *theologia gloriae*—the praise of the One who in His resurrection is the recipient of our right and life, the One who has risen again from the dead for us.[242]

The traditional Protestant view, by contrast, is strongly influenced by Luther's nineteenth thesis of the Heidelberg Disputation: "That person does not deserve to be called a theologian who looks upon

240. Michael Korthaus, *Kreuzestheologie: Geschichte und Gehalt eines Programmbegriffs in der evangelischen Theologie* (Tübingen: Mohr Siebeck, 2007), 158. Luther, *Heidelberg Disputation*, 1:52–4 (theses 19–22). Jürgen Moltmann, *The Crucified God: The Cross of Christ as the Foundation and Criticism of Christian Theology*, trans. R. A. Wilson and John Bowden (Minneapolis: Fortress Press, 1993), 207.

241. *CD* IV/1, 304 (trans. rev.).

242. *CD* IV/2, 558 (trans. rev.).

the invisible things of God [through the created things]."[243] Thesis twenty-one articulates the theological alternative: "God can be found only in suffering and the cross."[244] The only beneficial rather than harmful recognition of God can take place "in the humility and shame of the cross" (thesis twenty).[245] Walther von Loewenich concluded, "Theologia crucis is not a chapter in theology, but a particular kind of theology."[246] With the criterion of the cross, proper theology is distinguished from unhelpful forms of theology. It must be noted, though, that Barth and Luther presuppose a different understanding of potential knowledge of God through God's glory.

Barth's critique of an "abstract theology of the cross" is not directed against the extreme statement of Luther's nineteenth thesis, the refusal of knowledge of God gained from the work of creation, as Barth agrees with Luther's suspicion against works righteousness. What Barth's critique is directed against is the one-sided view that "God can be found only in suffering and the cross." The categorical phrasing of thesis twenty-one needs to be taken with a grain of salt, as it is also due to the genre of the disputation. To some extent, the pithy, provocative phrasing of the theses is less about theological nuance than the display of rhetorical skill in a competitive setting. Thus the fact that the Heidelberg Disputation mentions the resurrection only once—not Christ's, but that of believers—while speaking nineteen times of the "cross" and ten times of Christ's "passion" should not be pressed.[247] The thrust of Luther's argument

243. Luther, *Heidelberg Disputation*, 1:52.

244. Ibid., 53; see Alister E. McGrath, *Luther's Theology of the Cross: Martin Luther's Theological Breakthrough*, Oxford 1985, 161–2.

245. Luther, *Heidelberg Disputation*, 53.

246. Walther von Loewenich, *Luther's Theology of the Cross* (Minneapolis: Augsburg Publishing House, 1976), 18.

247. Luther, *Heidelberg Disputation*, 50 (thesis 16): "But . . . place your hope in Christ in whom is our salvation, life, and resurrection." Nineteen occurrences of *crux* include one use of the word *crucifixio* and *cucifigo* each. Further significant terms are *humilitas* and *gloria*.

is directed against forms of theology in which Christ's ministry, passion, and resurrection do not figure prominently. According to thesis twenty, Christ argued against "seeing God elsewhere and led him to himself, saying, 'Philip, he who has seen me has seen the Father.'" The one-sided attention to the cross is directed against particular attention to the resurrection insofar as it can be associated with a one-sided metaphysical approach in theology. This does not at all mean, however, that particular attention to the resurrection implies works righteousness and a metaphysical approach in theology by necessity.

By contrast, seeing the resurrection as a "*different*, a new act of God" in comparison to the cross is both helpful and necessary theologically.[248] Restricting God's revelation to taking place in misery only, rather than also taking place in the liberation from suffering, should not be made normative. Redemption from suffering should not be limited to being a paradoxical implication of God's revelation in suffering.

Barth's interpretation of the theology of the cross and of the resurrection has been met with criticism, however, by theologians with loyalties to a particular interpretation of the theology of the cross in the Lutheran tradition, such as Pierre Bühler and, more recently, Michael Korthaus. They object that Barth does not see how the theology of the cross is about the very grammar of theology: one aspect in theology functions as the criterion in theology as a whole. By contrast, Barth is said to understand the theology of the cross only as denoting the "chapter" about the passion, the theology of glory only the "chapter" about the resurrection. If this charge against Barth's theology were to the point, however, Barth's polemics

248. *CD* IV/1, 298 (trans. rev.).

against a one-sided theology of the cross would imply that he sees the opponents of a theology of glory rejecting the resurrection itself.[249]

Barth's discussion of the relation between the theology of glory and the theology of the cross cannot be meant to deal with particular "chapters" or *loci*. When Barth makes a case for a balanced relationship between the two traditions, he argues that an appreciation of the resurrection only as an implication of the passion underrates the significance of the resurrection. Indeed, the idea that the crucifixion already implies the resurrection, or that God's agency must first of all and fundamentally be described in terms of suffering, does not do justice to the drastic injustice lamented in Jesus' cry of dereliction. Korthaus's point that "the God who can create new life out of death was revealed *in Christ's cross*"[250] is highly paradoxical indeed. Barth's case would be more properly described with the statement that God created new life out of death on Easter Sunday, revealing God's self as the God of salvation in overcoming death.

Barth thus excludes a one-sided theology of humility and cruciform discipleship. This way, Barth has indeed overcome the principle of sacrifice and self-abnegation from *Rom* II. For that reason it is now legitimate for *CD* IV/1 to pick up a prominent notion from that book. *Rom* II warned of a crusader's mindset that has forgotten about its own relativity and deals with political differences by demonizing its opponents. Faced with the universal, categorical judgment in the cross, *Rom* II asserted that the "warfare between good and evil" had outrun its course.[251] Along these lines, *CD* IV

249. Bühler criticizes Barth for a supposedly trivial misunderstanding: "If one defines things in such a way that the theology of the cross deals with the cross, and the theology of glory, by contrast, with the resurrection, then it does not make any sense indeed to pursue one concept without the other. . . . [The theology of the cross] comprises all of theology, including the resurrection and the glory." Pierre Bühler, *Kreuz und Eschatologie: Eine Auseinandersetzung mit der politischen Theologie* (Tübingen: Mohr Siebeck, 1981), 74. Thus also Korthaus, *Kreuzestheologie*, 160.

250. Korthaus, *Kreuzestheologie*, 158 (emphasis added by A. M.).

251. *Rom* II, 653.

critiques that as a "judge of good and evil, man wants to stand at God's side in defence of the cosmos . . . maintaining the *causa Dei* [God's cause] and the cause of man."[252] It should be noted that the emphasis on the *absolute* authority of the actualistic command of Christ in *CD* II/2, to which the creature must in no way contribute, is equally likely to spur on the battle of the good against the evil. By contrast, *CD* IV/1 warns against a "hypermorality." Those who take on the moral life with particular zeal run the risk of a particular "form of sin (perhaps the most stately one)."[253] Contrary to all moral indifference, morality stands up "against the invasion of chaos and disorder and wrong." "And there begins the whole misery of the moral battle of everyone against everyone else."[254] This hubris is unmasked in the passion narratives, as Jesus does not insist on his righteousness, but allows himself to be arrested. His faithfulness to his vocation is disarming in its universal judgment: "To be a man means in practice to want to be a judge, to want to be able and competent to pronounce ourselves free and righteous and others more or less guilty."[255]

This view by itself, however, does not yet lead to the point toward which Barth gestured already in *Rom* II: "The convulsions of revolution have thus been substituted by calm reflection—calm, because *final* assertions and final complaints have been ruled out, because a prudent reckoning with reality has outrun the insolence of warfare between good and evil."[256] Both *Rom* II and some sections in *CD* IV react to the danger of the ideological struggle with a one-sided recommendation of humility or carrying the cross. This, however, does not yet penetrate the more subtle forms of ideological

252. Ibid., 450.
253. *CD* IV/1, 389 (trans. rev.).
254. Ibid., 451, see 445–6.
255. Ibid., 231.
256. *Rom* II, 653.

struggle, as the questions for whose benefit and with what right humility is exercised—at least as far as proximate, temporal matters are concerned—are merely suspended.

But Christian ethics will only do justice to the theological importance of justice, at which the quotation from *Rom* II points, with an active commitment to a just social and legal system, to which the interpretation of cross and resurrection summons. Can an ethics, weighing off goods against one another, in some circumstances even recommend the use of force in the interest of justice (see esp. *CD* III/4)? This question should be affirmed, as can be defended with a christological reflection by Barth that fleshes out the majesty of Christ in other terms than a victory over sin and evil in the cross. To this task the next section will turn.

Transformations in Barth's Understanding of Christ's Majesty

After Barth argued for a more nuanced account of the theology of the cross, emphasizing the soteriological significance of the resurrection as well, *CD* IV/2, §64 ("The Exaltation of the Son of Man") tends to paper over Jesus' suffering by portraying the cross as a triumphant coronation. It is remarkable, however, that the same section also highlights other aspects of Christ's ministry. These allow for a new interpretation of the notion that Christ manifests his highness in his lowliness. At various places, §64.3 sees the aspect of Christ's majesty fulfilled in Christ's ministry in a way other than in suffering. Thus he undertakes it anew to present Christ's ministry under the assumption that God's being takes place in Jesus Christ in an event of history: "We must now attempt, in a third and decisive discussion, to understand Jesus in the act accomplished by Him. . . . The totality of His being in its scope for [the congregation] and the whole world was identical with the totality of His activity."[257]

In describing this activity, Barth emphasizes that the kingdom of God dawned especially in Jesus' miracles.[258] Jesus liberated the sick person in his or her misery, in "his physical existence, his existence as it is determined by the external form and force of the cosmos to which he belongs."[259] Barth underscores that Jesus' ministry does not deal merely with sin. Jesus neither convicts the sick of their guilt, nor is the forgiveness of sins usually the point of the healing. Instead, Jesus fights physical suffering as such.[260] As Barth pointed out previously already, Jesus took sides for the maltreated creature also in the economic sense: "In fellowship and conformity with this God who is poor in the world the royal man Jesus is also poor, and fulfils this transvaluation of all values, taking sides with those who (without necessarily being better) are in some sense *poor*."[261] This, however, does not lead to a romantic view of poverty. Jesus was hostile to anything contributing to the creature's suffering: "The shame which comes on man is primarily a violation of His own glory."[262] Precisely in the dawning of the kingdom of God, the destruction of created life is halted in all its forms. Moreover, Christ's work reflects the social justice dimensions of the Old Testament proclamation of covenant, exodus, and Torah:

> The fulfilment of the lordship of God on earth . . . [this] cannot be said either of the exodus from Egypt or the conclusion of the covenant with Abraham or at Sinai. These—and the whole history of Israel—were not depreciated but given their true and supreme value when this event took place, i.e., they were shown to be one great promise which had found in this event its fulfilment.[263]

257. *CD* IV/2, 193.
258. Ibid., 209–47.
259. Ibid., 222. See Etzelmüller, *"...zu richten die Lebendigen und die Toten,"* 213–15.
260. Ibid., 223.
261. Ibid., 169 (trans. rev.).
262. Ibid., 225.
263. Ibid., 204. On the importance of the exodus in *CD* IV see Bertold Klappert, "Die Rechts-, Freiheits- und Befreiungsgeschichte Gottes mit den Menschen: Zum Verständnis

Jesus' ministry serves not only proclamation, but it is also directed against the forces of marginalization. Jesus' miracles are "*military actions*" of "a mercy which is *active*, and therefore fundamentally *hostile* to that power on behalf of poor man!"[264] In contrast to Barth's depiction of the Gethsemane scene, now Christ's highness does not consist in suffering. Jesus' activity is in contrast to physical evil in particular. Barth even wonders how the Reformation and all of Protestantism could overlook the aspect of "*phthora* [physical corruption], death and wrong as the power of evil."[265]

To some extent, already *CD* III/3, §50 called Jesus' struggle against physical evil a sign of his Messianic authority. His miracles and healings are "manifestations of His character as the Conqueror not only of sin but also of evil and death, as the Destroyer of the destroyer, as the Saviour in the most inclusive sense."[266] Barth goes on to criticize the theologian Julius Müller for ignoring the *malum afflictionis* (or *malum naturale/physicum*, the evil of affliction or natural/physical evil) in favor of the *malum peccati et culpae* (or *malum morale*, i.e., the evil of sin, or moral evil).[267] Ironically, however, Barth does not continue to pursue this case in §50. Rather than making up for the shortcomings of the theological tradition, the section shows the same lack of sensitivity for physical evil. Christ's victory over nullity, with which §50 deals, took place when Jesus was tortured to

der Auferstehung in Karl Barths Versöhnungslehre," in *Versöhnung und Befreiung: Versuche, Karl Barth kontextuell zu verstehen*, Neukirchener Beiträge zur Systematischen Theologie 14 (Neukirchen-Vluyn: Neukirchener, 1994), 118–37, 128.

264. *CD* IV/2, 232.

265. Ibid., 233. See Barth's portrayal of Jesus struggle for the dead Lazarus, ibid., 227. Moreover, Barth argues that ultimately, in his miracles Jesus did not face the entire human person, even as he fought bodily evil. He did not attack the social and economic evil as rigorously as the physical one (ibid., 174, 222).

266. *CD* III/3, 311.

267. Ibid., 354; 359. Thomas, "Der für uns 'gerichtete Richter,'" 214–15n10.

death in obedience. Supposedly, the defeat of evil was complete when in fact evil was triumphing physically.

According to §64, however, Christ's ministry before the passion is already notable for his fight against physical evil. The ethics of the doctrine of reconciliation, *CL*, starts with the invocation of Father, similar to the pneumatology of *CD* I/1, §12. But this time, this approach includes a vigorous call for the "Struggle for Human Righteousness" (§78). In this case, the prayer for God's new heaven and earth empowers human responsibility for justice, freedom, and peace.

Jesus' majestic status in his fight against physical and social evils corresponds to another dimension in his ministry that Barth discusses as part of Jesus Christ's proclamation.[268] Barth observes how Jesus calls the reign of God his own reign.[269] The event that was foreshadowed and began in the Old Testament became a reality in his proclamation.[270] In Jesus' proclamation of the kingdom of God, "we have more than participation. We have coincidence and identity."[271]

In Barth's portrayal of Jesus' ministry, the relationship between the incarnate Son and God the Father takes on a particular form. While not commenting explicitly on Barth, Wolfhart Pannenberg pointed out along similar lines that this relationship is in fact richer and more differentiated than §59 portrays it with its insistence on Jesus' unilateral subordination to the Father. Even in §64, the relationship between Father and Son might be characterized as obedience, but by itself this term does not convey Jesus' special authorization by the heavenly Father. This, however, is at the heart of Christ's particular dignity: God's reign takes shape as it takes place in Jesus Christ's ministry. He personifies the kingdom. It is his action in which

268. *CD* IV/2 §64.3, 194–209.
269. Ibid., 197.
270. Ibid., 200.
271. Ibid., 204.

"*military actions*" of God's "power on behalf of poor man" take place.[272] In this vein, *CD* IV/3 depicts "the deed that his life was"[273] not only as his proclamation, but also as "acts of power and aggression and assistance set up as signs in the midst of sinful and suffering humanity."[274]

One may perhaps speak of Jesus' subordination under the will of the Father, whose recognition and glorification Jesus serves in these acts as well.[275] To speak only of a subordination would be too narrow, however. After all, Barth emphasizes that Christ is God's reign in person.[276] "According to the great voice from heaven in Rev. 12:10, the *basileia* [kingdom] of God and *exousia* [authority] are given to His Christ."[277] Jesus' ministry is exalted in the sense that he fights physical evil powerfully. While Barth speaks of Christ's *autobasileia*, of him being the kingdom in person, in interpreting Jesus' cry of dereliction on the cross, the Gospels associate the kingdom of God more closely with Jesus' ministry before his passion. In this context, Barth speaks again of Christ's *autobasileia*.[278]

Beyond Barth's thoughts about Christ's majesty in suffering, the New Testament portrays Jesus' fight against physical and spiritual suffering as a manifestation of the kingdom of God, which becomes a reality in the Holy Spirit, as in Matt. 12:28: "But if it is by the Spirit of God that I cast out demons, then the kingdom of God has come to you."[279] God has made the proclamation and the dawning of the

272. Ibid., 232.
273. *CD* IV/3, 862 (trans. rev.).
274. Ibid.
275. "Precisely by . . . subjecting himself to his will as his creature, by thus giving place to the Father's claim to deity as he asked others to do in his proclamation of the reign of God, he showed himself to be the Son of God." Wolfhart Pannenberg, *Systematic Theology*, 1:310 (trans. rev.).
276. *CD* IV/2, 198: "*In Evangelio est Dei regnum Christus ipse*," also ibid., 657–8.
277. Ibid., 198.
278. Ibid., 163, 198.
279. The association of Spirit and healing is found, for example, in Luke 4:18–19; that of healing

kingdom dependent on Jesus Christ's activity, and it is not a matter of course that Jesus claims this vocation indeed. In this sense, God's reign depends on him, and we may even speak of a subordination of the Father to the Son.

This notion does not necessarily contradict the view that Jesus proved his majesty precisely in his humiliation. The crucial question is how to understand Jesus' humility. One should not merely think of Christ's suffering in the passion at this point. Jesus' family background not only lacked in social prestige; his proclamation even alienated him further from this social background. Already this made his ministry a humiliation, as in the ancient Mediterranean world, the social rank of an individual depended to a high degree on his or her participation in social structures.[280] Jesus' fellowship with persons of culturally dubious rank contributed to his humiliation. His contact with the impure and outcast damaged his reputation among the religious elites even more, as did his healings on the Sabbath.[281] The social integration of tax collectors and prostitutes equally contradicted contemporary expectations.[282]

Such humiliation is not devoid of power, however. It instigates transformation. In a different context, Barth argues, "Coming from the table of the Lord, [the church] must not resist following His example and to sit down at table with the rest, with all sinners."[283] Thus, Jesus' own activity prompts the church to act in solidarity with the world.[284] A new interpretation of Barth's thesis about exaltation in humility thus suggests itself. This new interpretation should focus less

and God's kingdom in Luke 9:2.11, 10:9. The Gospels associate Jesus' birth and baptism closely with the Spirit. Exorcisms and healing characterize the dawning of the kingdom of God.

280. Bruce Malina and Richard Rohrbaugh, *Social-Science Commentary on the Synoptic Gospels*, 2nd ed. (Minneapolis: Fortress Press, 2003), 379.

281. See ibid., 151, on Mark 1:35–45; ibid., 395–7 on the issue of ritual purity.

282. Ibid., 415, Theissen and Merz, *Historical Jesus*, 221.

283. *CD* IV/3, 775 (trans. rev.).

284. Ibid., 779–83.

on the most drastic suffering in the passion than on Jesus' preceding ministry. His ministry involved acts of power and influence, even if the custodians of cultural standards frowned at them. If in this way an idealization of drastic suffering is avoided, an ethics of discipleship is christologically justified, even commanded.

Along similar lines, Pannenberg suggests that the Father confers the reign to the Son, so that the Son fulfills it in glorifying the Father.[285] The Son's rule is thus manifest in Christ's proclamation and acts of healing.[286] Accordingly, the correspondence between Father and the incarnate Son can be understood as mutual subordination and empowerment, and as joint participation in reigning and suffering. At this point, it is legitimate to speak of a certain degree of powerlessness, for the Father's entrusting the reign to the Son is highly precarious in that the Father thus enters into dependency on the Son. In a different context, Barth even suggests what the Father gains from this: "All the fulness of the Godhead" is "not changed" in the incarnation of the Son and the passion of Jesus Christ, but it "is given concrete form in Him."[287]

The particular dramatic potential of the temptation narratives and of the Gethsemane scene consists in the fact that Jesus might have renounced his divine mission, as §59.2 hauntingly emphasizes. On the other hand, Pannenberg refers to Barth in arguing that God cannot be conceived of apart from God's effective reign.[288] This means that in Jesus' passion and resurrection, nothing less than God's essence was at stake. Thus Barth also speaks legitimately of the

285. According to Pannenberg, ultimately the Son transfers the reign to the Father (1 Cor. 15:28).

286. "The lordship of the Son is simply to proclaim the lordship of the Father, to glorify him, to subject all things to him." Pannenberg, *Systematic Theology*, 1:313.

287. *CD* IV/2, 86–7.

288. Ibid., 313, with reference to Barth, *CD* I/1, 349, II/1, 461. Härle, *Sein und Gnade*, 21n55, made this observation already: Barth's doctrine of God results "seamlessly" from the three premises that revelation is exclusively God's self-revelation, that God's word is one, and that God's divinity is identical with God's rule.

suffering of the Father during the Son's passion.[289] It is against this backdrop that Barth's statement that God might have abandoned the world to nonbeing on Good Friday should be understood: the assault against the Son of God was an assault on God's self. This is also implied in the motto *esse sequitur operari* (being follows action) in Barth's ontology: "But this participation of the world in the being of God implies necessarily His participating in the being of the world, and therefore that His being, His history, is played out as world-history and therefore under the affliction and peril of all world-history."[290]

If the divine nature is given concrete form in Jesus Christ[291]—if the ontological significance of the incarnation for God thus consists in the fact that without it, God would have remained abstract in God's self—then it requires correction to speak only of the subordination of the Son to the Father. Moreover, Wolfhart Pannenberg points out that the meaning of this subordination consists in a mutual exaltation. Barth also speaks of a "self-giving of the Father to the Son and the Son to the Father which is accomplished in the fact that He is not merely the Father and the Son but also the Holy Spirit, and therefore as the Father is wholly for the Son, and as the Son wholly for the Father."[292]

The relevance of these considerations for ethics consists in the fact that Jesus' exaltation gains shape in authoritative acts of liberation in word and deed. God's activity amounts primarily to the good news of the gospel, not to affliction. Moreover, Barth views evil as physical evil, too, and not only as guilt before God. This makes it significantly more difficult to consider a humble tolerance of suffering as such as the event of Jesus' exaltation. Moreover, this new emphasis on

289. *CD* IV/2, 357: "A *particula veri* in the teaching of the early Patripassians."
290. *CD* IV/1, 215.
291. *CD* IV/2, 87.
292. Ibid., 757.

physical evil, based on Christology, increases the weight of the good that may be harmed. The importance of physical integrity may require that greater emphasis is placed on the consequences of action.

The Pneumatological Dimension in Ethics

When *CD* IV/2, §64 speaks of God's commitment to the integrity of life, Barth's emphasis on the unrivaled effectiveness and power of Christ's commanding can be surprisingly strong. This may echo his statements about the majestic, sovereign command of Christ in *CD* II/2, which portray Christ as the absolute ruler in the fulfillment of his work, highlighting authority and power in a one-sided way.[293] Yet in spite of the statements about the crucified Christ, which in §64 sometimes seem triumphalistic, this is not the main trend in the foundations of ethics in *CD* IV. On the whole, the development of *CD* points in another direction. This is already indicated by the fact that Barth's thesis statements in §§62, 67 point to the Holy Spirit and use metaphors that do not highlight absolute authority, but speak of the Spirit as the "awakening" and "quickening" power. In this context, Barth asserts that the Spirit neither imparts some occult, "supposed higher wisdom" to the Christian, nor does it "subject him to the yoke of a supposed power."[294]

Barth still considers the command the powerful command of Christ, but now he phrases this decisively in pneumatological terms. For example, Jesus Christ is said to give "direction." "But in the relationship between the man Jesus and other men, in the exercise of His power and lordship, and *therefore in the operation of the Holy Spirit*, this is not one possibility among many, nor is it merely the norm, but it is the only reality."[295]

293. *CD* II/2, 705.
294. *CD* IV/1 647.
295. *CD* IV/2, 361–2 (emphasis added).

A comparison of this section with *CD* II/2, §38 demonstrates a transformation in the understanding of Christ's commanding. In proportion to the overall word count, in §64, the occurrence of *(Holy) Spirit* and closely related terms is more than three times as high as in §38.[296] Compared with the longest subsection in §38, §38.2, the count is even five times as high in §64. When Barth describes the Spirit as participating in the event of the commanding, he continues along lines that deviated from the main trend of his discussion already in §38.2. As argued in the chapter on *CD* II/2, §38, isolated passages in §38.2 notably emphasize human discernment of the command to a much greater extent than the wider context, and in doing so, they lay out a different pneumatology than the context does. *CD* IV/2, §64 continues along these lines in not portraying God's commanding in the Spirit as a monohierarchical power structure.

While §38.2 saw God's command mediated exclusively through the letters of Scripture, Barth now argues that Scripture alone does not suffice in discerning God's command. Although the direction of the Spirit cannot be understood apart from the Bible, the "New Testament writings . . . can reflect the positive instruction of the Holy Spirit . . . in some sense only *imperfectly*."[297] In contrast to prohibitions, the positive instruction is typical of the Spirit, however. While *CD* II/2 emphasized strongly that God's command is highly concrete[298] and that in Scripture, God's command does not articulate general instructions or rules, in §64 Barth presents the issue rather differently.

> It is only infrequently (except in the First Epistle to the Corinthians)

296. The count rests on the digital version of *KD*; all instances of the words *Geist, geistlich, Pneumatiker, pneumatisch, pneyma, pneymatikos* were included insofar as they clearly refer to the Holy Spirit. Instances per one hundred words: §38: 0.072; §38.2: 0.046; §64: 0.24. *CD* IV/2 is the only volume of *CD* in which Barth's foreword mentions the Holy Spirit.
297. Ibid., 374 (trans. rev.).
298. §38.2: "The Definiteness of the Divine Decision."

> that [the New Testament writings] speak relatively concretely and authoritatively of specific phenomena and problems of the life of the community. When they do so, it is mostly in the form of prohibitions, and not of the positive commands which are our present concern. Even their commands—the exhortations to love and humility and peace and chastity and patience—have in the main the form of general direction rather than the particular or highly particularised indication in which we may recognise directly the distinctive operation and commandment of the Holy Spirit.[299]

That the aspect of the unambiguous, hierarchical rule of Christ in the Spirit is not absent from *CD* IV/2 is understandable from a historico-genealogical perspective and against the backdrop of *CD* II/2, §38. There is still a tendency to highlight God's omnipotence and absoluteness with the actualistic concept of revelation. The published translation conceals the militaristic imagery with which Barth introduces an authoritarian element into pneumatology, but at the same time there is a peculiar ambiguity in that the omnipotence of the Spirit depends on the openness with which Christians prepare themselves to receive the Spirit:

> It is He who calls them into the battlefield and gives them His orders and commissions. It is He who directs and controls their activities. It is He who gives them the power to execute them. Without Him, His creating, giving, commissioning, governing, empowering there can be no Christian, no community, no Christian word or act! All these things are from Him and by Him, and from Him and by Him alone! One does have to pay attention to their *defenceless state* in which [the Christians] present themselves, which they confess when at this decisive point they dare to count on this and only on this presupposition: with the Holy Spirit.[300]

299. *CD* IV/2, 374.
300. Ibid., 319–20 (trans. rev.: the call into the battlefield, *das Feld*, should not be translated merely as a "call into action." After using the term, Barth refers to "orders" being given. Just ten years before this was written, millions lost their lives in the *Feld*).

On the whole, there is a peculiar wavering between very strong notions of the Spirit's power and its subtle entry into the Christian life, in which the Spirit renders itself dependent on the Christian response. Along these lines, Barth sees the Spirit's guidance falling "straight down from above,"[301] but he modifies this well-known metaphor by depicting it as the falling of a seed. The Spirit's direction gains momentum, unfolds its "creative power"—the translation "divine power" fails to convey the subtlety—in the growing of the seed.

However, this still does not necessarily seem to be the Spirit of which Paul writes, "Do not quench the Spirit" (1 Thess. 5:19), with regard to which John summons the congregation not to believe every spirit, but to test the spirits (1 John 4:1), or which figures prominently in Isa. 42:1–3: "Here is my servant. . . . I will put my spirit on him. . . . He will not cry or lift up his voice, or make it heard in the street; a bruised reed he will not break, and a dimly burning wick he will not quench." In spite of hints at the subtlety of the Spirit's activity, Barth can still associate the Holy Spirit with brute force:

> Thus, unlike any direction which one man may give to others, it falls, as it were, vertically into the lives of those to whom it is given. It is thus effective with creative power. It is the sowing and the developing seed of new life. It crushes and breaks and destroys that which resists it. It constitutes itself the ruling and determinative factor in the whole being of those to whom it is given.[302]

Nonetheless, even in this ambiguity, Barth's notion of the direction of the Spirit differs from his earlier affirmation of Christ's rule in the sense of a "handing out of orders."[303] Barth points out that neither the image of a destructive force not that of the growing seed sufficiently

301. Ibid., 341, 340, 523. On Barth's use of the metaphor, see Barth, *MD*, 248–9n6.
302. *CD* IV/2, 523 (trans. rev.).
303. *CD* II/2, 705 (trans. rev.).

describes the Holy Spirit, as both of them rely on the notion of a mere force that does not treat the human person as a person. The Spirit must be distinguished from "the idea of a power which either mechanically pushes, propels, thrusts or draws, or organically produces; from a higher force of nature."[304] The Holy Spirit "is operative in the world, but not as one of its forces, working neither mechanically nor organically."[305] Instead, Barth portrays the work of the Holy Spirit as involving human activity.

> No doubt: this power may be very great and wonderful, but it has a clear affinity with sound reason. It puts this in its right limits. It stops its roving and raving. But it also sees that there is no laziness in its use. It thus releases it as well and sets it in an appropriate and beneficial movement. It brings it about that man can think and say with absolutely unshakable confidence that two by two make four and will never make five.[306]

The Holy Spirit demands no sacrifice of the intellect, but is sensitive to context: "It is certainly part of His instruction to cause or summon us to test ourselves and our situation, to consider most carefully our possibilities and choices."[307] Such rational discernment is not antithetical, but complementary to prayer: "The Holy Spirit is rather more than a professor of theological ethics."[308] This corresponds to Barth's emphasis on empirical working hypotheses in *CD* III/4. In a different context, Barth describes the union of the Christian with

304. Ibid., 309. Such a force of nature seems to be at issue when David Clough, *Ethics in Crisis: Interpreting Barth's Ethics*, Barth Studies Series (Burlington, VT: Ashgate, 2005), 116, summarizes Barth's understanding of the divine commanding with the metaphor of a roaring lion.

305. Ibid., 310 (trans. rev.). These are Barth's categories especially in *Rom* I. *CD* IV/2 310–14 also characterizes the Spirit, without further specifics, as "unmistakeably light" (in opposition to darkness), "joyfulness," "conversion," "obedience," "peace," not *mysterium tremendum et stupendum*.

306. Ibid., 313–14 (trans. rev.). See also *CD* III/4, 511.

307. *CD* IV/2, 372.

308. Ibid.

Christ as involving an active component on the part of the Christian as well: "In the reality and power of the union of Christ with the Christian, however, their fellowship has also the meaning and character of a union of the Christian with Christ. Their fellowship would not be complete if their relationship were actualised only from above downwards and not also from below upwards, if it were not reciprocal."[309] On the whole, this view of human participation in receiving the instruction of the Spirit leads Barth to a notable critique of Calvin: "It cannot be denied . . . that the doctrine of Calvin obviously suffers from a curious over-emphasizing of *mortificatio* [self-mortification] at the expense of *vivification* [quickening]."[310] This critique is pertinent in the present context, as the Spirit does not work on the human person as an impersonal force does. This would resemble too much a subjection to a heteronomous view. Nonetheless, an authoritarian, violent tone sometimes entered even into Barth's own description of the work of the Spirit. Such passages would be in continuity with those aspects of Barth's work for which the present work has critiqued Barth for too strong an emphasis on *mortificatio*, despite his programmatic subordination of the law to the gospel.[311]

Barth's characterization of the work of the Spirit in *CD* IV/2 suggest that ethics should be a process in which Christians also take part according to standards open to rational communication and discursive evaluation. Yet Barth is also afraid that Christian ethics might take place in the absence of God, as it were. Ethical

309. *CD* IV/3, 543.

310. *CD* IV/2 651; See Luther, *On the Bondage of the Will*, in *Career of the Reformer*, 3:62: "Thus when God makes alive he does it by killing."

311. Barth, *Ethics*, 280 draws on Calvin in calling faith an "exinanition (abasement)." Calvin, *Institutes*, 1:733 (III, 11, 7). On Barth's relationship to Calvin, see Barth, "Gespräch mit Wuppertaler Studenten (1.7.1968)," in *Gespräche 1964–1968*, Barth-Gesamtausgabe, ed. Eberhard Busch (Zurich: Theologischer Verlag, 1996), 472–521, at 489.

discernment in the power of the Spirit receives clearer contours in the witness to Christ: "What the Holy Spirit positively wills and effects—that to which He awakens and calls—is always a human existence that deserves to be called a life to the extent that it is lived in the light of the royal man Jesus."[312] Section 64 thus points to the importance of biblical traditions and their theological reception in moral discernment. This certainly rules out eclectic attention to individual biblical commands in the sense of "consulting Holy Scripture apart from the centre."[313]

Jesus Christ himself is revealed in the work in the Spirit. Based on pneumatology, ethics cannot disregard the counsels of reason,[314] both because this would introduce an illegitimate element of heteronomy into pneumatology and because of Jesus' own full humanity. At the same time, however, ethical discernment is not exhausted in rational and empirical discussions, since "the Holy Spirit is rather more than a professor of theological ethics,"[315] but also because there is no simple, unambiguous "human rationality." This is further in keeping with the fact that Barth does not present the Christian life simply in a subaltern relationship to Jesus. The Holy Spirit testifies to Jesus Christ the Reconciler; it "does not subject [Christians] to the yoke of a supposed power."[316]

Instead, it activates Christians themselves. At first the Spirit is faced with the sin of sloth or lethargy (*Trägheit*), in which the human person does not apprehend the direction of the Spirit. The Spirit does not do away with this sin at once, and even Christian believers are not free of it: "To describe their sanctity—in view of the fact that they are undoubtedly *still* sinners—we must first use a very modest and

312. *CD* IV/2, 375.
313. *CD* IV/1, 368, see 374–5.
314. By contrast, see *CD* III/4, 511.
315. *CD* IV/2, 372.
316. *CD* IV/1 647.

restrained, yet quite significant expression. They are *disturbed* sinners. Their sleep as such is broken. Their course as such is slow and lame and halting."[317] But there is already more than that: the Christian person "now lives as one who seeks God in his activity."[318] Through the direction of the Spirit, which refers to Christ, all "other men ... are already startled out of [their place]. They are already alarmed. They are already summoned to make the movement within which they too are put in virtue of the exaltation of this One."[319]

The precarious nature of human understanding is indicated by the fact that in his passion, Jesus is misjudged and maltreated. In spite of the "disturbance" caused by the Holy Spirit—Barth resumes a prominent theme from *Rom* II[320]—those who do not hear the voice of the Holy Spirit have the dubious capability of calming themselves again.[321] The human person is able "to pursue his sleep and course and activity, . . . in peace and harmony with himself."[322]

The supposed power of the Spirit to crush and to work with violent force is fundamentally relativized here, but Barth does not declare the Spirit powerless. The activity of the Spirit is ignored again and again, but it will not ultimately be suppressed. The Spirit does not eliminate human sloth at once,[323] but it works continuously in the human person who fights against sloth and indolence, so that eventually obedience results, "in the midst of disobedience: highly unsatisfactory obedience, which stands in constant need of forgiveness. But it is obedience."[324]

317. *CD* IV/2, 524 (emphasis in German original).
318. *CD* IV/1, 104.
319. *CD* IV/2, 382.
320. See *Rom* II, on Rom. 12: "The Great Disturbance: The Problem of Ethics."
321. *CD* IV/2, 524.
322. Ibid.
323. Michael Welker, *God the Spirit* (Minneapolis: Fortress Press, 1994), 58: God's Spirit empowers people for service, but it does not turn them into superhuman agents that transcend all moral ambiguity.
324. *CD* IV/2, 530 (trans. rev.).

Shortly after the ambiguous description of the Spirit as both destroyer and sower of a mere seed, Barth portrays the awakening of the human person to mature activity in faith without the violent expressions, only as the sprouting of a seed: in spite of abiding sinfulness, "it is obedience. To that extent there is the sowing seed of new life in the field which is the world."[325] The seed is sown "from above." This modifies the well-known phrase of God acting "straight from above": in the direction of the Spirit, God does not intervene into human affairs directly, "from above," but accommodates to creaturely processes, in order to work from within.[326] This vision is close to the biblical tradition of the "pouring out of the Spirit."[327] Thus, the pertinent human reaction to the activity of the Spirit is to engage one's own sinfulness in the power of the Spirit. In this process, both rational and transrational aspects will provide guidance—not irrational ones, though.

Barth also describes a struggle within the Christian with the metaphor of a current in a river and the wind that blows in the opposite direction.[328] This metaphor is deficient as well, as it makes the work of the Spirit appear ultimately inefficient. Nonetheless, it is clear that Barth is opposed to the notion that the direction of the Spirit dominates a passive person heteronomously. While the dynamic at work is not merely the work of human reason, the notion of autonomy is important here. Barth's work with the metaphors of seed, wind, and sleep show how he searches for appropriate images, beginning anew again and again to portray the work of the Spirit neither in a one-sided dominance nor in a merely immanent human moral discernment taking place in God's absence.

In addition, there is the image of the search, which Barth adopts

325. Ibid.
326. Ibid.
327. Welker, *God the Spirit*, ch. 5.
328. *CD* IV/2, 530.

from Phil. 3:12–13. Barth describes the Christian ethos as a "movement of seeking, of setting our affection, of walking and praying."[329] The human person is intimately involved in the quest for the direction of the Spirit, which requires great discipline and permits no evasion from the search for good and right action. "The positive instruction of the Holy Spirit consists always in a gathering and mobilising and concentrating of the *whole* man who is instructed."[330]

In effect this amounts to a new conception of repentance, which is primarily positive and constructive. As an act of repentance, Christian action takes place between the poles of abiding sin and new righteousness in turning away from sin.[331] The Spirit not only guides action, but also motivates for a positive, new ethos. Thus, true repentance should not be confused with a simple "humbly proud boasting of [one's] corruption and lost estate."[332]

The attitude of searching, looking, and praying is, in the words of Rom. 12:1, "a living sacrifice, holy and acceptable to God." This notion of sacrifice is directed toward an attitude of "a constant ... testing and critical examination" of the will of God.[333] This way Barth highlights the discernment (*dokimazein*) to which Rom. 12:2 summons. The concept of sacrifice, which has played an important role in Barth's ethics, is conceived of anew. It is not about principles such as self-restraint and a sacrifice of one's wishes, foregoing critique or self-assertion.

Despite all the criticism involved, essentially this new ethos is about a vivification, as the new, positive action is to be pursued single-mindedly. As the direction of the Spirit puts an end to all "laziness"

329. Ibid., 375.
330. Ibid., 376.
331. *CD* IV/1, 242–3, 769–71, *CD* IV/2, 529–30.
332. CD IV/1, 594.
333. *CD* IV/2, 376.

in the use of "sound reason,"[334] this notion of sacrifice is no longer dominated by bearing the cross in suffering, but by activity and focus.

The Activity of the Spirit and the Life of the Community: Church Law (§67.4)

The notion that the activity of the Spirit does not merely work in organic terms, transcending an ethics that operates as if God were absent, is not given very specific shape in *CD* IV/2 §64. It is crucial, however, that Barth sees the Spirit as the driving force in the work of Jesus Christ. At this point, the coincidence of lowliness and exaltation may be helpful ethically, as long it does not result in understanding Christ's death by torture as Christ's triumph. A mutual interdependence of humility and heightened dignity gains shape in a chapter that associates ethics and pneumatology with ecclesiology. Barth draws this conclusion from the notion that the Holy Spirit does not merely awaken individual persons.[335] In *CD* IV/2, §67, Barth calls the Spirit the "quickening power" of the body of Christ. Here Barth overcomes the Spirit's cerebral influence on the individual person, highlighting instead the irreducibly social nature of the Spirit's work, in which the new sociality is more than the sum of its parts.

In the power of the Spirit, the body of Christ also finds orientation in the head of the body as far as its legal constitution is concerned (*CD* IV/2, §67.4: "The Order of the Community").[336] Thus the church should not consider church law a mere formality, which would need to be sharply distinguished from the spiritual essence

334. Ibid., 313–14.

335. By contrast, see *CD* II/2, 682: God "will always and in all circumstances speak to each individual, and the one who is now man as the object addressed in these summaries will always and in all circumstances be face to face with God, whoever he may be."

336. Barth uses the more hierarchical image of Christ as the head of the body in Eph. 1:20–23, which projects Christ's rule onto gender hierarchies in 5:22–4. Rom. 12:3–8, 1 Cor. 12:12–31 would have been an alternative, as in this more functionally differentiated image, the entire congregation is the entire body of Christ.

of the church. As "*spiritual* law" throughout,[337] church law urges Christians to be more faithful in their service to the neighbor. Barth does not refuse legal demands within the church as a deviation from the proper essence of the church, but attributes to them a legitimate function within the body of Christ.[338] The problem is, of course, that they may end up being instrumentalized for individual competitive gain. It is for this reason that some strands in German Lutheranism were in favor of delegating all executive power within the church to state authorities. Rudolph Sohm, the most representative thinker of this tradition, saw this arrangement as most faithful to the notion that the church is governed *sine vi humana sed verbo* ("not with human force but with the word," Augsburg Confession, art. 38). By contrast, Barth argues that the regulations of church law must allow for demands of personal interest only insofar as such personal interest coincides with a better mutual service among brothers and sisters.[339]

Section 67.4, which continues along the lines of §64, is also highly instructive for ethics in the wider sense. Barth appreciates "sound reason," although he is not uncritical of monolithic or lopsided notions of reason. This is also reflected in the fact that Barth charges the church with learning from the craft of the jurist in temporal law. Barth even presents the effect of reason on law in wider society as

337. *CD* IV/2, 682.

338. On the wide-ranging implications of CD IV/2, §64.4, see the contribution by Kristopher Norris on the relationship of Karl Barth and John Howard Yoder to basic procedures and virtues involved in a democratic organization of society, in *Theo-Politics? Conversing with Barth in Western and Asian Contexts*, ed. Marcus Höfner (Minneapolis: Fortress Press, forthcoming). Jeffrey Stout's case that churches should be among the communities in civil society that nurture democratic virtues also hinges on the extent to which churches consider fundamental political procedures alien or congenial to their own core beliefs. See Jeffrey Stout, *Democracy and Tradition* (Princeton: Princeton University Press, 2004).

339. Interestingly, the conditions for individual privilege are very similar to John Rawls's "difference principle": "Social and economic inequalities are to be arranged so that they are both (a) to the greatest expected benefit of the least advantaged and (b) attached to offices and positions open to all under conditions of fair equality of opportunity." John Rawls, *A Theory of Justice*, 2nd ed. (Cambridge: Belknap, 1999), 65–72.

a shape that the reign of Christ adopts outside of the church. In this sense, the section on church law anticipates a basic assumption from Barth's doctrine of lights (*CD* IV/3, §69.2).[340]

The activity of the Holy Spirit is not exhausted, however, in the activation of a vague notion of reason that has evolved in wider society and congealed in its legal culture. Church law differs from worldly law in that it makes claims and demands dependent on the duty to serve. This in turn reflects the interrelationship between lowliness and heightened dignity for which *CD* IV argues. A church member may thus profit individually from legal recourse, thus heightening his or her reputation and influence, under the condition that this advantage is used for the benefit of everybody involved. Personal interest is by no means always harmful to the community, nor does it always have to be rejected based on a commitment to cruciform discipleship.

Barth also highlights the flexible character of church law. He wishes for provisions that are convincing and rational, but do not depend on the notion of absolute truth. Holding on to the notion of the omnipotence of the Spirit,[341] by contrast, might very well result in a rank of church law as divine law.[342] That church law is preliminary by nature is also important for Barth's statement in §67.4 that church law should be oriented toward the communal practices of proclamation, confession, sacrament, and prayer. Reinhard Hütter, for example, criticizes Barth's pneumatology for failing to take

340. Barth argued in retrospect, "Later I re-integrated natural theology by way of Christology." "Gespräch mit Vertretern der Herrnhuter Brüdergemeinde (12.10.1960)," in *Gespräche 1959–1962*, ed. Eberhard Busch, Barth-Gesamtausgabe (Zurich: Theologischer Verlag, 1995), 124–57, at 132.

341. See above; see *CD* IV/2, 319–20, 523.

342. On divine and human law, see Christoph Strohm, "Ius divinum und ius humanum: Reformatorische Begründung des Kirchenrechts," in *Das Recht der Kirche: Zur Geschichte des Kirchenrechts*, eds. Gerhard Rau and Hans-Richard Reuter (Gütersloh: Gütersloher Verlagshaus, 1995), 115–73.

seriously that God bound God's self in the Holy Spirit to ecclesial practices.[343] Yet Hütter's presentation of §67 does not mention Barth's case for the preliminary nature of church law.[344] The notion of a self-binding of God to ecclesial practices would result in even greater problems with Barth's earlier notion of a hierarchical exercise of power by the Spirit. This assumes too direct a relationship between God and church, as when Hütter asserts that God's activity in the church is "free but in fact obtains *always*."[345] This does not allow for the possibility that God eludes a church that may legitimize sinful acts with reference to God's self-binding.

The pneumatological reflections in §64, by contrast, delineate a differentiated activity of the Spirit that is more subtle than the notion of a "binding" allows for. Barth's emphasis on a "movement of seeking, of setting our affection, of walking and praying"[346] insists on the possibility of God's hiddenness. His suggestion that the Spirit can be present in continued service does not run the risk of granting a one-sided privilege to the authority of ordained office, as the notion of God's self binding to ecclesial practices does.

343. With these practices, Hütter means "at least word and sacrament." Reinhard Hütter, *Evangelische Ethik als kirchliches Zeugnis: Interpretationen zu Schlüsselfragen theologischer Ethik in der Gegenwart*, Evangelium und Ethik 1 (Neukirchen-Vluyn: Neukirchener, 1993), 55. On God's self-binding, see 47, 67, 91. On the whole, Hütter's book is after a Protestant virtue ethics. In speaking of God's self-binding to ecclesial practices, however, the importance of an empirical analysis of ethical problems is not sufficiently valued. Indications of empirical problems can easily be suppressed with reference to cruciform discipleship, which Hütter repeatedly highlights (72, 79, 87–8).

344. Ibid., 64–70.

345. Ibid., 56, interpreting Barth's statement that the church is "continually confronted with His presence as the Holy One, it is continually exposed to His activity, it is continually alarmed by him" (*CD* IV/1, 700, trans. rev.). However, if the more subtle pneumatological approach in §64 is combined with the notion of God's self-binding to ecclesial practices, the basis is lost on which recourse to the church's apostolicity can still be understood as a "*defense against a false ecclesiality*," as Barth does (*pace* Hütter, 58).

346. *CD* IV/2, 375.

Conclusion

Barth's doctrine of reconciliation, *CD* IV, is guided by the sense that God's involvement in history, especially in Jesus Christ, fundamentally shapes who God is. In ethics, Barth draws the conclusion from this that cruciform discipleship, involving the acceptance of suffering, is imperative. This dovetails seamlessly with Barth's inculcation of a wife's subservience to her husband, which he laid out in *CD* III. Rather than correcting this point of view, and if only by admonishing husbands to practice humility in relation to their wives, *CD* IV reinforces female subordination in its interpretation of Christ's obedience to the Father. Christ thus does not shy away from the passion, which eventually leads to torture and death. Meanwhile, Barth portrays God as making a "covenant with death," in which God concentrates all evil on Jesus, whom evil then, paradoxically, goes on to kill, thus executing judgment over evil by itself (*CD* IV/1, §59.2). This construal of Christ's passion in terms of both penal substitution and change in the ontological status of sin is a direct appropriation of Luther's theory of the priority of the law over the gospel. Not only does this seem to attribute an inherent redemptive potential to violence, but it also results in Barth's strong affirmation of Christ's utter majesty precisely in the midst of suffering. If, however, attention to Christ's passion and death on the cross is not balanced by a focus on the resurrection, this scheme is likely to result in a justification of suffering rather than in opposition to injustice and hope for liberation by God's action. This chapter argues that the primary meaning of Jesus' cry of abandonment on the cross in the Gospels of Mark and Matthew is that Jesus did not wish to be tortured to death on the cross.

However, this largely critical overview is not representative of *CD* IV on the whole. Barth's groundbreaking accomplishment in

CD IV, both from a theological and from an ethical point of view, begins with his case that the crucifixion amounts to the revelation of human sinfulness, rather than to justification. In a creative act of restorative justice, only the resurrection cancels out this guilt and justifies humanity alongside with Jesus. The past of the cross is transformed creatively. Along similar lines, *CD* IV portrays Jesus not only as heroic in enduring suffering, but, in contrast to that, as heroic in his combat against suffering and physical evil. This chapter also argues that under these premises, tolerating certain hardships can be the ethical course to follow if indeed this amounts to a testimony to the constructive and liberating action of God. In addition, rather than to think in terms of the Son's unilateral "obedience" to the Father, as Barth does at the beginning of *CD* IV/1, it is more helpful to think in terms of the multiple acts of free mutual self-restraint that all three divine persons exercise in their work in history for the benefit of the other two, as laid out by Wolfhart Pannenberg. Barth also explores the work of the Spirit further, which he distinguishes from sheer acts of power and interventions that impose a certain course of action in bypassing considerate, rational, and prayerful Christian ethical discernment. These distinctions gain clearer shape with Barth's call to have church law make individual privileges dependent on service to the larger congregation. In contrast to his unbalanced depiction of the misery of the cross as absolute glory, in this case Barth provides a helpful and constructive interpretation of the notion that in Christology—but also in reflection on the other divine persons, as one should add—humiliation and exaltation coincide.

5

Perspectives: Responsibility and Faith in the Triune God

After discussing Barth's the ethical dimension of Barth's works from *Rom* I to *CD* IV, the task of this chapter is to look back, recall some of the main results, and feed them into a constructive effort to learn from Barth's ethical reflections for today's Christian ethics.

The Concept of Gospel and Law in Public Dimensions of Moral Action

The historico-genealogical and systematic reconstruction of Barth's concept of gospel and law has been a continuing theme in this discussion. Referencing "GL" and *CD* II/2, chapter 8, Barth himself called it "the basic substance" of *CD*.[1] An important question pursued in the current interpretation was if this subordination of the law is authoritarian, as it attributes great authority to church proclamation,

1. *CD* IV/3, 370.

but little importance to empirical analysis of moral options. One of the results is that until the early 1930s, Barth repeatedly argues in favor of a subordination of the gospel to the law, attaching great importance to God's judgment and devoting significantly less energy, at least in a rigorously theological way, to constructive work on human action.

This trend continues to some extent even in *CD* II/2, chapter 8, although Barth saw the point of this section precisely in the subordination of the law to the gospel. First of all, in §§36–7 Barth argues that the power and the moral obligation of the command consist in God's liberating power. The gospel exercises power by addressing a general human moral striving.[2] Conscience functions as the interface between God and the human person, and this is where an actualistic anthropology dovetails with an actualistic doctrine of God. These latter concepts already date from Barth's ethics lectures (1928/29, 1930/31),[3] which Barth wrote about a decade before he fundamentally reshaped his doctrine of election (*CD* II/2, chapter 7).

Human conscience cannot resist liberation, Barth argues, as the command is truly in one's best interests. However, according to "GL," "The Gospel as well as the Law . . . have been given into *our* hands, the hands of *sinners*."[4] In 1935, Barth saw a parallel in how Jesus Christ and God's command are both vulnerable to abuse. For all their moral striving, the Romans and the Jewish elites crucified Christ. In "GL," Barth was deeply worried about this problem,[5] and *CD* II/2, chapter 7, also takes seriously the "danger for God"[6] that results from the fact that "the Son of Man" was "given over (*paradidotai*) into the hands of sinners" (Mark 14:41).[7]

2. *CD* II/2, 596.
3. Barth, *Ethics*, 16, 20, 85, 371–2, *CD* II/2, 516.
4. "GL," 84 (trans. rev.: "*gegeben*"). See also 85, 94.
5. "GL," 84–94.
6. *CD* II/2, 162 (trans. rev.: "*Gefahr*"), 499 ("danger in which God again placed Himself").

If, according to *CD* chapter 8, God's command resonates so powerfully with universal human moral striving, is there a danger that general moral orientations influence or distort the way God's command is perceived? Barth's view is that God asserts God's command powerfully against any potential resistance. But is this truly in keeping with the danger God entered into with the incarnation and with Barth's previous conviction that "since God's Word in Scripture has taken the form of a human word, it has entered into the need of such interpretation"?[8] In this context, CD chapter 8 highlights the sovereignty of Christ in the cross and the resurrection.[9] There is a striking difference between the emphasis "GL" and *CD* chapter 7 placed on the danger and affliction of Jesus' passion and the absence of this aspect in chapter 8.

In *CD* II/2, chapter 8, Barth then amends the argument he made in "GL," according to which God imposes God's command, if necessary by force and harsh punishment. These texts are heterogeneous, but §§36–7 rightly perceive a tension between such use of force and the priority of the gospel over the law. What authority can mere punishment command, as it attempts to convert the opposing moral agent with something other than the good news? Since "GL," however, highlighted Christ's affliction on the cross much more clearly than *CD*, chapter 8, the claim from the latter text that the promise and the command of freedom are irresistible and powerful must be viewed critically from the perspective of the lecture. On the positive side, however, nothing can be said about objective authority according to §§36–7 apart from the question whether the subjective conviction of the authority of a command is rooted in the gospel rather than in judgment.

7. Quotations of and allusions to Mark 14:41 and parallels: ibid., 460, 461, 467, 482, 497.
8. *CD* I/2, 713 (trans. rev.).
9. See especially *CD* II/2, 737 (§39).

The present work diagnosed the tendency not to take Jesus' suffering on the cross utterly seriously in *CD* IV as well. An interpretation of Jesus' cry of abandonment at the cross indicated that greater sensitivity for the scandal of suffering would be more apposite.

While in §§36–7, in spite of theological difficulties, Barth maintains the priority of the gospel to the law, this is in turn contradicted by §38.2. This subsection claims explicitly that God's commandment must not be interpreted. "An imperative to which I owe absolute obedience must necessarily come in the most radical sense from without."[10] The command "does not need any interpretation, for even to the smallest details it is self-interpreting. ... Only [thus] do we stand in a relation of responsibility, of obedience or disobedience, to Another, to a transcendent Commander and Judge."[11] Such statements still reflect the influence of Barth's early theology, in which an absolute, worldless God figured prominently and that argued passionately for a clear-cut, rigid distinction between transcendence and immanence. One result is that Barth, keenly aware that God's absoluteness is easily compromised, couches the encounter between God and the human person strongly in terms of conflict and judgment.

GD modified this with the notion of an elusive, actualistic command, which left fundamental views about the nature of God unchanged, however. *CD* II/2, chapter 8, continues in the tradition of an absolute, worldless God. On the other hand, in the doctrine of election *CD* II/2, chapter 7, Christ's eternal decision to bear the consequences of the sin of the creatures fundamentally undercuts

10. *CD* II/2, 651 (trans. rev.: not "from within"!). The quotation continues, ". . . in order that it may claim me most radically within." Ibid., 641: The validity of the command depends on its "absolute transcendence."

11. Ibid., 665.

the assertion of God's absoluteness and the resulting primacy of judgment.

The constructive suggestion advanced here is that the priority of the gospel to the law should be conceptualized in keeping with *CD* II/2, section 7 rather than in terms of an incommensurate command that resists interpretation and encounters us, in the first instance, as judgment. Moral action is of such a kind that it does not subject Christians to harsh demands. It lends practical shape to the way Christians articulate their embrace of the gospel. This is in fact what constitutes moral obligation.

These considerations indicate that an appreciation for Barth's concept of gospel and law, if conceived of properly, does not lead back into the polarized debate between proponents of a Lutheran theory of God's two reigns and of Christ's royal reign (*Königsherrschaft Christi*).[12] Having gained wide currency in German Protestantism during the National Socialist reign, the latter concept refuses to allow natural law concepts to predominate in Christian reflection on social ethics, often drawing both on the concepts of Christ's royal and his prophetic office. Thus, often describing

12. See Christian Walther, "Königsherrschaft Christi," in *Theologische Realenzyklopädie* (Berlin and New York: de Gruyter, 1990), 19:311–23. Shortly after the Second World War, the two concepts were considered fundamental in intraprotestant controversies. Herbert Lindenlauf, *Karl Barth und die Lehre von der "Königsherrschaft Christi": Eine Untersuchung zum christozentrischen Ansatz der Ethik des Politischen im deutschsprachigen Protestantismus nach 1934* (Spardorf: Wilfer, 1988), 81. Several articles have declared the controversy settled, but they presuppose a Lutheran position, not taking the possibility seriously that God might influence action in the public realm by means aside from natural law. Wilfried Härle, "Luthers Zwei-Regimenten-Lehre als Lehre vom Handeln Gottes," *Marburger Jahrbuch Theologie* 1 (1987): 12–32, at 13; Härle, "Zwei-Reiche-Lehre II: Systematisch-Theologisch," *Theologische Realenzyklopädie* (Berlin and New York: de Gruyter, 2004) 26:784–9, at 786 with reference to Hans-Walter Schütte, "Zwei-Reiche-Lehre und Königsherrschaft Christi," in *Handbuch der Christlichen Ethik*, ed. Anselm Hertz and Wilhelm Korff (Freiburg et al.: Herder and Gütersloh: Gütersloher Verlagshaus Mohn, 1978), 1:339–53. See also Gottfried Voigt, "Barmen II in lutherischer Sicht," in *Zum politischen Auftrag der christlichen Gemeinde (Barmen II): Votum des Theologischen Ausschusses der Evangelischen Kirche der Union*, ed. Alfred Burgsmüller (Gütersloh: Gütersloher, 1974), 81–93.

themselves as prophetic, proponents of this tradition vigorously advocated for alternative politics in postwar West Germany. After the Second World War, German Protestant churches were steering toward the brink of a schism over the debate between proponents of a Lutheran theory of God's two reigns and Christ's royal reign.[13] *Christ's royal reign* functioned as a "*slogan for the theological-political struggle.*"[14] The implications of this controversy clearly extend beyond mere historical interest. Essentially, the notion that God's *one* word encounters us in Christ was pitted against the notion that God's word is clearly *differentiated* into that of the Creator and that of the Reconciler, into God's law as reflected in natural law and the gospel proclaimed in the church. Proponents of "Christ's royal reign" traced the roots of this concept to the Confessing Church and Barth's theology, which seemed to give them the moral high ground. Among the Protestant theologians supporting National Socialism, certain adherents of a theory of two reigns had stood out.[15] Critics of *Christ's royal reign*, typically from the Lutheran tradition or liberal theologians, argued that the direct justification of such claims with God's will left no room for settling differences of opinion with reference to empirical expertise. One cannot deny the merits of either position—with one party arguing for a theologically reflected worldly realism and one for the contemporary, critical significance of God's eschatological righteousness. To put it this way, however, already indicates the tensions as well. Issues of contention included

13. Wolfgang Lienemann, "Das Problem des gerechten Krieges im deutschen Protestantismus nach dem Zweiten Weltkrieg," in *Der gerechte Krieg: Christentum, Islam, Marxismus*, ed. Reiner Steinweg, Edition Suhrkamp 1017 (Frankfurt am Main: Suhrkamp, 1980), 125–62, at 137–41.
14. Lindenlauf, *Königsherrschaft*, 84. Whenever the footnote provides a German title for an English quotation, the translation is my own.
15. Well-known names include Emanuel Hirsch, Friedrich Gogarten, Paul Althaus, and Werner Elert. This does not mean, however, that a theory of God's two reigns, or even a Lutheran theological background, automatically amounted to a pious and passive stance toward power. In Denmark, for example, the theory was used to critique Nazi ideology.

especially military and foreign policy during the Cold War, such as the so-called NATO double-track decision (1979), as well as social policy. These were especially controversial as the border between NATO and the Warsaw pact separated Germany into two states. But the debate touched on other subjects as well.

After National Socialist aggression and its atrocities, many Germans became more sensitive to the militaristic aspect of the Cold War, even more so as the destructive potential had increased even more with nuclear warfare. Many believed that a lack of concern for civic responsibility had contributed to National Socialist crimes, and so it was ever more urgent to bring faith and political responsibility into a meaningful relationship. Thus, the public debate about West German NATO membership,[16] rearmament, and the stationing of nuclear weapons in Germany became increasingly intractable, eventually wearing out the ethical argument that developed along the lines of *two reigns* and *Christ's royal reign.*

I have not analyzed Barth's ethics under the title of *Christ's royal reign.* The notion that God's word is one rather than twofold—a claim often used to subvert the sharp distinction between law and gospel operative in a Lutheran theory of God's two reigns—is of course associated with Barth's name. In addition, his actualistic concept of revelation emphasizes the relationship between Christ's royal office and the utter contingency of the event of Christ's commanding. Proponents of Christ's royal reign often referred to Barth's theology and typically shared his political orientation toward the left. His actualistic ethics, however, presupposes a marked difference between

16. The question of NATO membership raised the ethical question of nuclear weapons, as Germany would enter into treaties with nuclear powers. A German army outside of NATO would have been unrealistic, however. "With the decision for rearmament, the most important decision [about nuclear arms] had in fact taken place, and the debate in the churches about nuclear arms was only an affair of the rear guard, which hardly touched on the most difficult questions, i.e., their strategic use." Ibid., 141.

church and world. If Christians turn Christ's command into a public claim vis-à-vis wider society, they objectify the event of revelation, which fundamentally contradicts the notion of God's abiding status as the exclusive subject in revelation.[17]

While Barth's concept of gospel and law was repeatedly articulated in one-sided ways, the basic idea can serve as a resource for subverting the dualism of a theory of God's two reigns and the ethical concept of Christ's royal rule. For it rests on an emancipatory potential that can, unless distorted by false assertions of divine omnipotence and absoluteness, make a constructive contribution to ethical discourse. In various cases, Barth articulates the potential of the Christian faith to provide orientation without falling into fideistic isolation.

One example is Barth's discussion of the termination of a pregnancy. In the assurance of the gospel, the pregnant woman is not condemned to live, but allowed to live, Barth argues. He draws on embryology in affirming that the embryo deserves protection. But the pregnant woman's will to affirm the life of the embryo can and will only be rooted in her affirmation that her own life is a free gift in the first place. The ethical argument hinges on her own mature self-understanding. In consequence, however, ethics cannot simply discount empirical facts if they render impossible the affirmation of the embryo as a gift of the Creator. Such tragedy cannot be ruled out, but on the other hand, society can and must respect it only if it rests on compelling facts, such as a biological conflict between life and life. The social and ecclesial context in which this decision is

17. See also *CD* II/2, 710: "God confronts man in an individual and solitary relationship when He gives him His command and prohibition, and again man stands before God in an individual and solitary relationship when he has to receive this command and prohibition." Lindenlauf, *"Königsherrschaft Christi,"* 474–5, argues that rigorous public claims are a danger indeed for proponents of the concept of Christ's royal reign, but he negates the idea that Barth is among them. He is thinking of Oscar Cullmann, Alfred de Quervain, Dietrich Bonhoeffer, and Ernst Wolf (ibid., 79–80; 437–8; 465–8). Barth inspired the concept strongly, however (76–7).

made of course has repercussions for the decision itself as well. So the church and wider society have a responsibility in offering support to the pregnant woman and creating an environment in which the pregnant woman will sense that the message of life as a free gift can resonate meaningfully.

Barth's concept of the relationship between gospel and law also played an indirect, constructive role in the German reform of criminal law (1969). His involvement in Cold War political questions resonated strongly with German politicians and eventually influenced the German détente with the Warsaw pact.[18] All of this is closely related to Barth's fundamental case for social and legal justice, which he saw as based on Christ's work of reconciliation.

In the Lutheran concept of God's two reigns, on the other hand, Christian faith often plays a greater role in politics than is usually acknowledged. In the two reigns, Christian public action is typically described as following natural law. In negotiating the ambiguities of this concept, however, Luther also invoked Christ's example in recommending the principle of equity.[19]

In current ethics, this ambiguity reemerges with a subtle distinction. The Christian contribution to public action is sometimes identified as a liberation for the discovery of those secular norms that provide orientation in real world situations. Christian faith can motivate or even liberate agents to follow secular reason, ethicists

18. Barth's lecture "The Church between East and West"—"Die Kirche zwischen Ost und West," in *"Der Götze wackelt": Zeitkritische Aufsätze, Reden und Briefe von 1930 bis 1960*, ed. Karl Kupisch (Berlin: Vogt, 1961), 124–43—impressed the later politician and churchman Erhard Eppler, who was involved in Willy Brandt's politics of détente. Barth's lecture argued against the call for Christians not to meddle with politics, against an understanding of the state as divinely ordained, and against any demonization of Communism. The new direction in German *Ostpolitik* reflects Barth's influence only indirectly, but resonates, for example, with his statement that God's command, shaped by the gospel, will "not compel man. . . . It will not meet him with mistrust but with trust. It will not appeal to his fear but to his courage. It will instil courage, and not fear into him" (*CD* II/2, 586).

19. Hans Graß, "Luthers Zwei-Reiche-Lehre," *Zeitschrift für Evangelisches Kirchenrecht* (1986): 146–78, at 150–51, 162–3, 174–5.

argue, but faith does not provide norms for the case at hand.[20] If the motivating or liberating force is not trivial, however, then non-Christian thinkers seem to have difficulties in living up to the full potential of secular rationality. The distinction between the gospel and worldly affairs then appears less clear-cut than is often assumed.

In West Germany, the influence of Barth's ethics was most prominent in the political debates of the Cold War, and there were few other countries in which Barth's theology was as strongly represented in public debates. When the fall of the Iron Curtain changed the German political landscape, the theopolitical debates changed as well. The debate between the proponents of a theory of two reigns and of Christ's royal reign ran out of steam. At that time, Nigel Biggar concluded that "the English-speaking world has not been generous with the attention it has paid to the ethical thought of Karl Barth."[21] Interestingly, this was the point at which a surprising amount of literature on Karl Barth's ethics started to appear in English.

This scenario is indicative of the potential chances and pitfalls of an American reception of Barth's ethics. The ethical concept of Christ's royal reign cannot be equated with Barth's ethics; nonetheless, there was a connection during the German Cold War debates. By contrast, in the United Kingdom and the United States, the NATO politics of military deterrent were less controversial than in West Germany, provoking less opposition from Christians appealing to a command of Christ that is radically free over against political necessities.

Meanwhile, in the United Kingdom and the United States, the sense of mission that contributed to a coherent, relatively

20. Martin Honecker, "Vernunft, Gewissen, Glaube: Das spezifisch Christliche im Horizont der Ethik," *Zeitschrift für Theologie und Kirche* 77 (1980): 325–44, at 339; Johannes Fischer, "Theologische Ethik und Christologie," *Zeitschrift für Theologie und Kirche* 92 (1995): 481–516, at 481–3; Schütte, "Zwei-Reiche-Lehre," 352.

21. Nigel Biggar, *The Hastening That Waits: Karl Barth's Ethics* (Oxford: Clarendon, 1993), 1.

homogeneous political vision during the Cold War has become less relevant. While the United States especially has never been a homogeneous society, fissures within society have been on display more openly since the sense of responsibility in the fight against Communism has abated. In this scenario, an important question is how British and American theologians drawing on Barth's ethics are likely to do so. For example, some see the promise of a distinct ecclesial profile in a constructive dialogue with Barth. For some, Barth's ethics go well with social progressivism, and sometimes the two groups overlap.[22] If there is renewed attention being paid to Barth's ethics, what shape does this take?

In this context, it would be unfortunate to follow common misconceptions of Barth's ethics. John Howard Yoder, for example, argued that, with his notion of the marginal case, Barth excuses himself from disciplined theological reasoning. According to the Mennonite thinker, Barth's ethics of peace and war relapses into arbitrary personal judgments that might take the form of particularistic ethnic causes, perhaps under the illusion of orders of creation.[23] By contrast, Yoder hoped to defend substantial New Testament traditions against large-scale cultural and political aberrations.

The discussion of Barth's thoroughly christological case for legal justice and a *Rechtsstaat* (constitutional democracy, rule of law) has

22. George A. Lindbeck describes Barth as a proponent of the "cultural linguistic" paradigm. He closes his most prominent book with the words, "Only in some younger theologians does one see the beginnings of a desire to renew in a posttraditional and postliberal way the ancient practice of absorbing the universe into the biblical world. May their tribe increase." Lindbeck, *The Nature of Doctrine: Religion and Theology in a Postliberal Age* (Louisville: Westminster John Knox, 1984), 24, 135. See George Hunsinger, "Postliberal Theology," in *The Cambridge Companion to Postmodern Theology*, ed. Kevin J. Vanhoozer (Cambridge: Cambridge University Press, 2003), 42–57, at 43, 45–6.

23. John Howard Yoder, "Karl Barth and the Problem of War," in *Karl Barth and the Problem of War and Other Essays*, ed. Mark Thiessen Nation (Eugene: Cascade/Wipf & Stock, 2003), 1–104, at 59.

argued that this critique is unjustified. For it is this aspect, which prominently includes religious freedom, that drives Barth's concern for the marginal case of war. On the other hand, Barth's ethics are often held to be too ecclesial to be compatible with public discourse in the pluralism of late modernity. This is in tension not only with Barth's sustained case for legal and social justice, which is deeply committed to the church's share in public responsibility. His insistence on empirical "working hypotheses" (*CD* III/4, §52) also indicates that Barth identifies factors that can serve as bridges for public dialogue. This presupposes, of course, the argument that was made in the section on *CD* II in this book: Barth's vigorous prohibition of even the least human contribution to God's contingent, specific command—including even the interpretation of biblical texts—is indebted to the concept of an absolute God rather than to the Trinitarian God who commits God's self to creation in eternal election. For this reason, the command theory in *CD* II/2, chapter 8 should not distract from the constructive potential Barth's ethics holds.

In arguing for a practical commitment to practices of a constitutional democracy in civil society, Heinrich Bedford-Strohm also points to the priority Barth assigns to the gospel, arguing that to some extent, the commanded action is already part of one's own experience, albeit in the shape of a benefit. "Reference to the normative dimensions of life together in the democratic state loses the moralistic aftertaste once society can convey the sense that the *responsibility* for freedom is a dimension of the freedom *given freely*, by necessity and as a matter of course."[24] The extent to which a certain course of action can be experienced as practical correspondence to

24. Heinrich Bedford-Strohm, "Geschenkte Freiheit. Von welchen Voraussetzungen lebt der demokratische Staat?" *Zeitschrift für Evangelische Ethik* 49 (2005): 248–65, at 260.

the gospel amounts to a criterion for whether, from a Christian perspective, it is indeed commanded.

Ethics and the Theology of Creation

In his ethics of the doctrine of creation, Barth argues that empirical working hypotheses are fully legitimate, even necessary, while retaining a christological focus.[25] The significance of empirical working hypotheses has been illustrated in the discussion of Barth's treatment of the termination of a pregnancy, capital punishment, and of peace and war. In the articulation of ethical guidelines, Barth's interpretation of the theological tradition takes a shape complementary to empirical findings. Moral action does not depend on an individual piece of biblical direction, which would then require application. Instead, worldly affairs with their worldly justifications and motivations can even become parables of the kingdom of God. Barth can interpret the theological significance of empirical findings as reflecting the fact that God is the Creator of our world. This is not played off against christological arguments, however. Instead, he seeks a complementary relationship,[26] in which nature can, to some extent, indirectly reflect the mercy of God in Christ,[27] or in which natural law may even, although in no more than makeshift fashion, appear as the concealed rule of Christ.[28]

25. For this reason, *CD* III/4, §52, 20, sees a grain of truth in an ethics of orders: "What seems to be Brunner's basic idea is sound and must not be rejected: 'The Divine Command is not a law which hovers above our actual existence without any connexion with it; it is the command of the God who has created our actual existence.'"
26. This is the basic constellation of Barth's doctrine of creation, which considers creation "the external basis of the covenant" (*CD* III/1, §41.2), while the covenant is "the internal basis of creation" (§41.3).
27. For example, if the termination of a pregnancy is pondered, the pregnant woman's task of moral discernment is to fathom the extent to which she can understand her life, together with a new baby, as a reflection of God's mercy, which would come to the fore more clearly as this life matures into an explicit relationship with God in Christ. See also "ChrSoc," 52.
28. "CCCC," 169–70, 172, 183.

Nonetheless, Barth has reservations about a stronger, independent notion of creation. He argues that the attempt at a natural recognition of God in philosophical theology establishes a worship of a God of its own making[29] and seeks recourse to dubious orders of creation. This implies the danger of authoritarianism, in the most extreme case a nationalistic theology. While these are very categorical assertions, it should be acknowledged that the theology of creation can "naturalize" worldviews and moral orientations, or declare them created, and imbue them with greater moral dignity than warranted.

On the other hand, Barth may go to extremes in avoiding difficulties in the theology of creation. In Barth's doctrine of the Trinity in *CD* I/1, the Creator remains somewhat obscure due to an existentialist interpretation. That God the Father is the *Creator* means that God is Lord, the absolutely superior one, who nonetheless—and precisely as such—addresses Christians as a *Thou*.[30] In the formalistic concept of revelation of *CD* I/1, the Son and the Spirit correspond to the act and the result of revelation, but in addition, they are characterized more closely by their proper work vis-à-vis creation. To be sure, the Father does not remain unknown as the Father is mediated in the work of the Son and the Spirit. But this dynamic cuts both ways: a closer description of Son and Spirit also renders the Father more distant by comparison.

The highly formal concept of the Father from *CD* I/1, however, is in keeping with the notion of an unknown God that retains a certain independence from God's self-definition in other modes of being. The work of the Creator requires greater theological attention, while

29. According to *CD* II/1, 135, the attempt at a natural recognition of God is "arrogation, preservation and affirmation of the self-sufficiency" of the human person. On the history of the concept of "natural theology," see Wolfhart Pannenberg, *Systematic Theology*, trans. Geoffrey W. Bromiley (London and Lew York: T&T Clark, 1994), 1:107–18.

30. *CD* I/1, §10, 384.

at the same time the theology of creation must not be taken to legitimize authoritarian notions.

In an interpretation of the opening sections of Calvin's *Institutes*, Michael Welker has drawn attention to a fundamental ambiguity that may assert itself powerfully in the theology of creation. According to Calvin, the human person has an "awareness of divinity."[31] The ambiguity of the natural intuition of the deity, however, is evident in that it is confirmed even in idolatry. In religious error, the religious inclination may even assume paranoid forms in its sensitivity to the numinous. This confirms that a natural religious sensitivity should not simply be negated. "Rather it is extremely important to recognize that this vague, futile, and fleeting knowledge, this instinctive sense is *extremely powerful*, in spite of its constitution, which tends to provoke trivialization, denigration, and reduction to indifference."[32]

Precisely for this reason, a closer reflection upon the theology of creation is also required in ethics. In Barth's work, the ambiguity of the natural religious intuition plays out in various ways: in "GL"; *CD* II/2, chapter 8; and *CD* III/4, the "awareness of divinity" eludes clearer perception in different ways.

a) According to "GL," religious delusion and the abuse of God's law lead to divine judgment, which forces sinners to repent. Abuse of the law has indeed been characterized as a typical expression of a natural religious intuition.[33] The damage done by such misuse can be considerable, but ultimately, it is less than tragic or disastrous,

31. John Calvin, *Institutes of the Christian Religion*, ed. John T. McNeill, trans. John L. Battles, The Library of Christian Classics (Louisville: Westminster John Knox, 2006), 43 (I, 3, 1).

32. Welker, *Creation and Reality*, trans. John Hoffmeyer (Minneapolis: Fortress Press, 1999), 24–5. On Calvin see also Derek S. Jeffreys, "How Reformed is Reformed Epistemology? Alvin Plantinga and Calvin's 'Sensus Divinitatis,'" *Religious Studies* 33 (1997): 419–31.

33. See Martin Luther, *Heidelberg Disputation*, ed. and trans. Harold J. Grimm, in *Career of the Reformer*, Luther's Works 31 (Philadelphia: Muhlenberg Press: 1957), 1:35–70, 55 (thesis 24): "Yet that wisdom is not of itself evil, nor is the law to be evaded; but without the theology of the cross man misuses the best in the worst manner."

according to "GL." It even serves salvation in a paradoxical way, as God turns human sin against the sinner: "It is this Law, dishonored and emptied by sin's deception, which, with the power of the *wrath* of God, nevertheless is and remains *his* If we serve *this* Law, there is no escape from God's judgment . . . there is no counsel, no comfort, no help."[34] The way God works salvation for the sinner is paradoxical. Humiliated by God's wrath in the law, the once so proud sinner is now ready to accept God's mercy gladly, no longer resenting the idea that he or she is the recipient of undeserved mercy. The natural religious intuition, which abuses God's law, turns out to be part of the dialectics of salvation.

b) *CD* II/2, chapter 8, §§36–7 denies the possibility of a misunderstanding of revelation in natural theology in the long run. The difference from "GL" is that God overcomes human resistance not in judgment, but in winning over a person's conscience in the power of the gospel. The command of freedom also exerts an irresistible urge on the "natural" person. Barth seeks to bolster this claim with an actualistic anthropology that accords great significance to universal moral striving. In §38.2, by contrast, the repressed dark side of God returns with a vengeance, as it were, to "judge and avenge not only in the greatest things but also in the smallest, not only openly but also in secret."[35]

c) *CD* III/4 argues for a christological influence on the understanding of creation. In §54, this leads to a repressive gender ethics, as a natural theology is backed up with christological concepts. The sovereignty with which the incarnate Son undergoes suffering is reflected in the subordination of the wife, while Christ's divine status is reflected in male superiority and responsibility. This demonstrates the danger implied in a natural religious intuition as particular

34. "GL," 94.
35. *CD* II/2, 705. Trans. rev.: a *Vergelter* "avenges."

cultural constellations are first portrayed as natural and created and then, by a teleological argument from creation to reconciliation, imbued with christological authority. This would be much less convincing if Jesus' passion, which to some extent is projected onto the moral life as well, were fully recognized as horrendous torture and suffering.

Due to the dangers inherent in these developments, the neglect of the theology of creation in Barth's theology, or indeed its problematic forms, must be criticized. The theology of creation should not simply be usurped by Christology. God's self-determination in election does not mean the Creator's abdication, and the difficulties with supposedly natural or created human behaviors should be reduced not by the avoidance of a proper theology of creation, but by a more sober, open, and critical, if preliminary, theology of creation.

The theology of creation is also the typical place where science and theology intersect. The question of legitimate or illegitimate "naturalization" of the given social order is raised, for example, when a conservative secretary of education argues that new scientific research on the biological evolution of cooperation demonstrate that institutions "work best when small enough."[36]

While a theology of creation must be critical, it should also be constructive in conducting a dialogue between human experience and scientific interpretations. Christian Link, for example, comments on this dialogue, "If faith has indeed lost congruence with [scientific] insight, or at least the fruitful tension with it, it has lost touch with the grounds on which it claims commitment."[37] If the connections

36. David Willetts, "The Invisible Hand That Binds Us All," review of *SuperCooperators: Altruism, Evolution, and Why We Need Each Other to Succeed* by Martin Nowak and Roger Highfield, *The Financial Times*, April 24, 2011, http://tinyurl.com/knlzg6u.

37. Christian Link, "Die Erfahrung der Welt als Schöpfung: Ein Modell zum Dialog zwischen Theologie und Naturwissenschaft," in *Die Spur des Namens: Wege zur Erkenntnis Gottes und*

between faith and the various scientific endeavors is weakened, theology is in danger of losing its realism. It would also be unrealistic to assume that the sciences simply take stock of objective reality in a positivistic, seemingly neutral way.[38] Instead, the realism of the sciences is best thought of as a "hermeneutical realism," in which researchers interpret reality and discover it at the same time.[39]

This is also relevant in ethics in a wider sense. In the debate about a Lutheran theory of God's two reigns and the ethical theory of Christ's royal reign, proponents of the former concept argued that the logic inherent in reality cannot be disposed of according to religious preference. A Lutheran theory of God's two reigns contends that God's law, operative in nature and society as natural law, and the gospel, operative in the church, should not be conflated. The reference to particular dynamics inherent in nature and society makes a valid point, but it does not mean that all decisions in the social sciences are as strongly constrained as Max Weber's postulate of value-free science suggests in using the metaphor of the "iron cage."[40] In the words of the philosopher and physician Viktor von Weizsäcker, the sciences should acknowledge the "introduction of

zur Erfahrung der Schöpfung (Neukirchen-Vluyn: Neukirchener, 1997), 123–70, at 125 ("*büßt er seine Verbindlichkeit ein*"). Ibid., 121: "The trace of the Name is embossed not only in history, but also in nature—certainly in a less obvious way. In order to recognize it, we need to perceive the world as creation. . . . In systematic respect, this attempt is an offer of a 'natural' theology that is enlightened about itself, in Biblical terms: a wisdom argument."

38. Ibid., 137, 145.
39. William Schweiker, *Responsibility and Christian Ethics*, New Studies in Christian Ethics (Cambridge: University of Cambridge, 1999), 112–14. See also Paul Ricoeur, *The Rule of Metaphor: The Creation of Meaning in Language*, Routledge Classics (London: Routledge, 2003), 283: "It would seem that the enigma of metaphorical discourse is that it 'invents' in both senses of the word: what it creates, it discovers; and what it finds, it invents." There are parallels between Ricoeur's thought and critical realism in the philosophy of science. See Andreas Losch, *Jenseits der Konflikte: Eine konstruktiv–kritische Auseinandersetzung von Theologie und Naturwissenschaft*, Forschungen zur Systematischen und Ökumenischen Theologie 133 (Göttingen: Vandenhoeck & Ruprecht, 2011).
40. Max Weber, *The Protestant Ethic and the Spirit of Capitalism*, trans. Talcott Parsons, Routledge Classics (London and New York: Routledge, 2001), 123.

the subject into the object."[41] Certainly when attending to questions raised in the sphere of creation, ethics must respect constraints and dynamics obtaining in specific functional spheres of society. It will thus honor a point raised by the theory of God's two reigns. It should also be noted, however, how such constraints are constituted, what factors influence our perception of them, and in what ways both aspects may vary or allow for some leeway. In that sense, a clearer perspective on the importance of participation and of particular, historical traditions in knowing can be helpful.

Along these lines, Link argues that Barth's rejection of "natural theology" is valuable in rejecting Cartesian reductionism, which trusts in the supposed neutrality of observation and subjects theology to its methods as well.[42] This reductionism does not do justice to a multiperspectival approach to reality, or even to standards in the natural sciences.[43] Link argues that the biblical traditions should be taken seriously as an expression of a particular experience of the world,[44] rather than subjecting them to the standards of a "doubting

41. Link, "Erfahrung der Welt," 141. See Ingolf Dalferth, "'Was Gott ist, bestimme ich!' Theologie im Zeitalter der 'Caféteria-Religion,'" in *Gedeutete Gegenwart: Zur Wahrnehmung Gottes in den Wahrnehmungen der Zeit* (Tübingen: Mohr Siebeck, 1997), 10–35, at 22–3: the problem with the post-Enlightenment stance that declares religion a private affair, while considering reason a universal matter, is that the position of the unconcerned spectator is a fiction. Instead, Dalferth advocates a "participant's perspective," for theology must be "answerable in public for the Christian faith and not a substitute paraphrased in philosophical terms" (24). Truth is accessible only in an ineluctable act of participation (26).

42. Christian Link, "Bleibende Einsichten von Tambach," in *Karl Barth in Deutschland (1921-1935): Aufbruch—Klärung—Widerstand*, ed. Michael Beintker et al. (Zurich: Theologischer Verlag, 2005), 333–46, at 339; Link, "Die Einführung des Subjekts: Ein methodischer Umbruch in Medizin und Theologie," in *Zur Aktualität Viktor von Weizsäckers*, Beiträge zur medizinischen Anthropologie, ed. Rainer-M. E. Jacobi and Dieter Janz (Würzburg: Königshausen & Neumann, 2003), 227–45, at 240–42.

43. Link, "Bleibende Einsichten von Tambach," in *Karl Barth in Deutschland (1921–1935): Aufbruch—Klärung—Widerstand: Beiträge zum Internationalen Symposium vom 1. bis 4. Mai 2003 in der Johannes a Lasco Bibliothek Emden*, eds. Michael Beintker, Christian Link, and Michael Trowitzsch (Zurich: Theologischer Verlag, 2005), 333–46, at 339 discerns a comparable epistemological stance in "ChrSoc."

44. Link, "Erfahrung der Welt," 130.

ego which—*pace* Descartes's Meditations—reflects itself out of the world."[45]

Acting and being acted upon are influenced, of course, by external conditions and possibilities. Such conditions are unlikely to be deterministic. It is the point of the concept of creation that God's creative act is conducive to life as it has enabled contingent and free contributions to a mature life. Creation is a free expression of divine mercy, although such possibilities are not the same in all of human experience. The world as creation is concealed to experience where conditions conducive to life are lacking.

> The possibility referred to here is—in terms of physics—even in a precise sense an impossibility: . . . it is not causally determined, cannot be planned or predicted. . . . If one's thinking on the logic of this matter is resolute, one can hardly choose a weaker term: this possibility is "always a miracle."[46]

Creation does not denote the result of a process that happened once and for all, while the further story of the creatures would be part of a new reflection. Thinking of creation as a fixed state of affairs rather than an ongoing process is also the problem with a certain notion of divine preservation. The task of a doctrine of creation is more than a mere etiology of heaven and earth.[47]

Even theologians and ethicists favorable of Barth voice the view that a greater incorporation of empirical knowledge is necessary than is typically warranted by standard accounts of Barth's theology.[48]

45. Ibid., 140.
46. Ibid., 156, 165–6.
47. Ibid., 156 with reference to *CD* III/1.
48. Apart from Link's arguments, see Wolf Krötke, "Die Schöpfungsordnungen im Lichte der Christologie: Zu Karl Barths Umgang mit einem unabweisbaren Problem," in *Barmen—Barth—Bonhoeffer: Beiträge zu einer zeitgemäßen christozentrischen Theologie*, Unio und Confessio 26 (Bielefeld: Luther-Verlag, 2009), 155–78, at 178; Michael Beintker, "Die politische Verantwortung der Christengemeinde im Denken Barths," *Zeitschrift für Dialektische Theologie* 12 (1996): 149–74, at 171. Ronald Thiemann, "The Significance of Karl Barth for Contemporary Theology," *Thomist* 50 (1986): 512–39, at 536–7, appreciates Barth's skepticism

How can this be squared exactly with Barth's warnings of attempts at a natural recognition of God?[49] Link's suggestion is a natural recognition of God that is "enlightened about itself," that is, that knows its own limits.[50] This approach would indeed be faithful to both concerns. It excludes reductionist attempts that deduce—or abduct—Christian faith from experience that is conceived of as neutral. And yet, in the dialogue with the sciences, theology contends that Christian faith is at least not intellectually dishonest or nonrational. At the same time this does not yet prove religious skepticism to be an illusion.

I have argued for Barth's efforts to make Christian ethics plausible in dialogue with nontheological academic endeavors. Nonetheless, some of Barth's presuppositions in this attempt are based on dubious assumptions. Barth's empirical support for ethical decisions notwithstanding, Barth thought that God's word creates the faith itself in the proclamation of the word, and by no other means. This is of course a common claim in Protestant theology.[51] But Barth ascribes not only unrivaled, but even unlimited "power," or indeed "force" (*Gewalt*) to the word.[52] In God's word, God disposes of the human person. Due to the lordship of Jesus Christ, the "force (*Gewalt*) of the Word of God in itself and as such is absolute force (*Gewalt*)."[53]

In the evolution of Barth's theology, however, the notion of the

of a general natural knowledge of God in that such knowledge does not help in dialogue in a society with a plurality of worldviews.

49. See Pannenberg, *Systematic Theology*, 1:76: beginning in Middle Stoicism, the term *natural theology* denoted the philosophical attempt to gain insight into the true "nature" of the deity—in contrast to *mythological* and *political* theology. See also Jürgen Moltmann, *The Crucified God: The Cross of Christ as the Foundation and Criticism of Christian Theology* (Minneapolis: Fortress Press, 1993), 65.

50. Link, *Die Spur des Namens*, 121.

51. See, for example, question 65 of the Heidelberg Catechism and article 5 of the Augsburg Confession.

52. *CD* I/1, 150.

53. Ibid., 153 (trans. rev.), see 152–4.

unlimited force of God's word takes over the function that Barth's own forays in natural theology have had before. In essays and lectures, Barth argued for a universal religious sense that forms the backdrop against which alone Christian proclamation can unfold its own dynamic.[54] Both the concept of a point of contact with a general moral sense and that of the omnipotence of God's word pursue the notion of God's effective self-assertion and reject the possibility of a divine lack of power. Eventually, the human "point of contact" for God's revelation seems to become obsolete, but not because the supposed event of such contact can at times be illusory, but because the function in question is now entirely attributed to God's forceful revelation that is not mediated by human religious background assumptions. In effect, this is the separation of natural theology from anthropology and its integration into the concept of God.

Moreover, the interpretation of Christ's cry of abandonment in the present work suggests that Barth asserts God's absolute power at the expense of biblical traditions. *CD* IV/1 returns to Mark 14:45 again and again. Although Barth seems disturbed by the radical expression of suffering, he cannot bring himself to an undialectical acknowledgment of Jesus' powerlessness and humiliation on Good Friday.

Related to this is also the problem of Barth's actualistic ethics. The current, incommensurate commanding of God replaces the revelation in the incarnation with a present revelation, for which the proclamation of Scripture provides merely the occasion. One of the longest subsections of *CD* II/2, chapter 8, §38.2 ("The Definiteness of the Divine Decision")[55] inculcates the utter specificity of God's

54. Barth, "The Need and Promise of Christian Proclamation" and "The Problem of Ethics Today," in *The Word of God and Theology*, trans. Amy Marga (New York, T&T Clark: 2011), 101–29 and 131–69. *GD* I, §4 ("Man and His Question"), *CD* II/2, §§36–7 (universal moral striving).

command. Its definiteness forecloses the possibility of an interpretation that consists in breaking the command down in accordance with the current specific situation. As Barth's early work at first answered the question of how God's word develops its power with the human search for meaning, but then replaced the key position of human subjectivity with the notion of God's own absolute power, so *CD* II/2, chapter 8 insists that the power of God's command requires human passivity.[56] The command is not answerable to the judgment of a human person, but places the human person under judgment instead. In a human interpretation, "far too much devolves upon those who, in relation to a real command, do not enter in except as the obedient or disobedient."[57] The hallmark of any true commandment is the fact that it reflects the absoluteness of God. This rules out human interpretation, for "a command whose truth is conditioned in this way is not a real command."[58]

By contrast, it would follow from a more consistent orientation toward God's revelation in Jesus Christ that Barth should have developed a stronger, more honest concept of dialogue with voices from outside Christian theology.[59] In theology, Barth eliminated the key position he initially attributed to a more general human search for meaning, presumably in order to immunize his theology against ideological dangers inherent in such endeavors of meaning making. Yet the trade-off is significant, for by the same token, theology

55. §37.3: 34,562 words in forty-eight pages; §38.2: 31,960 words in forty-eight pages; §36.1: 19,839 words in thirty-five pages. *Digital Barth Library* (Alexander Street Press).
56. In this respect the key function of a general human moral striving in §§36–7 is in contrast to §38. The fact that human subjectivity first makes a crucial contribution to God's power (§37) but is replaced by God's unilateral activity in revelation (§38) strangely replicates Barth's early development in dogmatics.
57. *CD* II/2, 665.
58. Ibid.
59. It may seem that Barth pursues this cause in §§36–7, but this attempt would be convincing only if Barth acknowledged the contribution of wider moral orientations on Christian ethics.

can claim commitment and obligation only to the extent that proclamation has already resulted in commitment.

By contrast, it is not a coincidence that empirical aspects do contribute significantly to ethical judgments in *CD* III/4. This is also where the ethical argument proceeds in more discursive ways, contrary to ethical actualism, as Barth sets out to test the extent to which his theology leads to realistic moral judgments. It is, of course, possible that Christian proclamation and Christian ethical reasoning remain unheeded or follow false leads, but theologians and ethicists should not draw the conclusion that reasonable argument is futile or even dangerous for that reason. An immunization of ethics against reasonable discourse beyond the boundaries of the congregation increases the problem of subjective religious license.[60]

Further, the reference to reasonable argument does not imply an unambiguous, simple objective notion of rationality. This much is already clear from the "introduction of the subject into the object" argued for above.[61] By contrast, in the sections on freedom for life, Barth does justice to a desideratum of the theology of creation. He seeks to "honour . . . life . . . as a loan, and to secure it against all caprice."[62] In contrast to his gender ethics, this section deals with experiences of suffering that are destructive of life, and draws on empirical circumstances contributing fundamentally to the conditions and possibilities of the protection of life.

The task of an ethics of creation does not consist in "neutrally" taking stock of empirical facts. Embryology cannot confirm the

60. See Dalferth, "Was Gott ist," 17. Dalferth criticizes postliberal theology for a continuing lack of critical judgment (19).

61. By contrast, Honecker, "Vernunft, Gewissen, Glaube," 339, tends toward a unified concept of reason, which he separates from faith. "For a theological ethics, faith does not add anything in ethical insight." Along similar lines Fischer, "Theologische Ethik und Christologie," 481–3. Honecker and Fischer hope that an appeal to universal secular reason would allow for ethical communication beyond differences in faith; they attribute to faith a liberation for an open-minded use of reason. It is unclear how the latter point relates to the evident nature of reason.

62. *CD* III/4, 324.

beginning of human life as a given state of affairs. On the other hand, the task of an ethics of creation does not consist in arguing for a universal teleology open to insight regardless of questions of worldview. In the terminology of Barth's doctrine of creation, the reality of creation as the external ground of the covenant would remain abstract unless it could be understood as the contingent possibility of undeserved divine mercy, which in turn constitutes God's claim on the creature. In the discourse about protecting unborn life, the theology and ethics of creation point to contingent possibilities of life that can be discovered beyond the routine strategies of self-preservation and that provide motivation to protect life. In the marginal case, however, such contingent possibilities of life may be absent in a tragic way. In forging a consensus beyond the boundaries of one's religious group, Christians can seek for new possibilities of life that resemble the gospel and may even constitute a "parable of the kingdom of God" in secular shape. If they can indeed be identified, they also constitute a Christian moral duty.

That Barth does not view war as the regular use of a privilege accorded to the state by natural law is also consistent with the image of creation as a contingent, merciful possibility to enhance life. By contrast, he uncovers contingent options for responsible action through which people can influence the conditions of their future in creative ways. The classic doctrine of just war, on the other hand, conceives of ethics mainly retrospectively, asking for prevailing conditions rather than doing creative work with regard to these conditions themselves.[63] Even where it is used to evaluate potential courses of action, it does not transcend the situation of crisis.

CD IV also highlights traditions of social and physical liberation

63. This is in contrast, for example, to Nigel Biggar's view that a *ius post bellum* does not require special treatment in the just war tradition, as it is already implied in the notion of *ius ad bellum*. Nigel Biggar, *In Defence of War* (Oxford: Oxford University Press, 2013), 3.

in Jesus' earthly ministry. Short of the creation of new eschatological life, such traditions are not about a mere restitution of the old life,[64] but certainly about an enhancement of life that is in contrast to arbitrary dangers to life such as disease and ostracism. The natural context of life becomes a vision of the fulfilled life of the kingdom of God that may be anticipated in analogous ways. At this point, Barth's notion of Christ's triumph at the cross obscures the ambiguity of creation. By contrast, §61 does not see the cross, but salvation being brought out of death, the resurrection, as the central salvific event. God creates anew as forces of destruction rule out human flourishing. From the perspective of Easter, a salvific aspect of the cross can be identified in the fact that Jesus did not renounce his divine mission. A stronger soteriological emphasis on the cross, especially in terms of penal substitution, is problematic in different ways. Yet there are indications that, among others, it can compound things with a more positive moral view of violence.[65]

An Ethics of Responsibility and a Theory of Goods

Barth's lecture "GL" had already focused on the resurrection, rather than on the cross, as God's salvific act that defies human sinful destruction.[66] This aspect is closely linked with a reordering of the relationship between gospel and law, which denies a relatively

64. The concept of creation and not only of nature already includes ambiguity. Konrad Schmid, "Jenseits von Verfügungswissen und Orientierungswissen: Evangelische Ethik und das Evangelium," *Zeitschrift für Evangelische Ethik* 49 (2005): 190–7, at 194 with reference to Gen. 8:22.

65. This is Susan B. Thistlethwaite's interpretation of a significant survey by the Pew Forum. The survey found greater support for torture among Caucasian evangelical Protestants than among Caucasian, non-Hispanic Catholics and mainline Protestants (The Pew Forum, "The Religious Dimensions of the Torture Debate," April 29, 2009, Pew Research Center, http://tinyurl.com/nnmf45a). Thistlethwaite points to Mel Gibson's movie "The Passion of the Christ" (2004). "Why the Faithful Approve of Torture," originally in *The Washington Post*, January 5, 2009. On faith: http://tinyurl.com/phfycvh.

66. "GL," 95–6, 98 ("God is for us . . . precisely in the form of an awakening from the dead").

independent dimension in God's action that is supposedly salvific, but retributive. But the emancipatory aspect inherent in the precedence of the gospel over the law raises the question of the extent to which there is a problem of a kind of hedonism that only recognizes as a command that which appears to be liberative in terms of individual convenience.[67] Some commentators deplore "the culture of free religious constructions in the present," both inside and outside of the churches.[68] Some of this may seem like mere heteronomy even from a Kantian view. On the other hand, Kantian autonomy in the strict sense should not be treated uncritically from a theological perspective, either, as human reason may participate in the ambiguities of creation.

The hedonist tradition surfaces, for example, in literary allusions in Barth's critique of economic power, "which in war is shown not so much to be possessed by man as to possess him, and this to his ruin."[69] This statement inverts the hedonist maxim *I possess, I am not possessed*;[70] it is directed against the willingness to tolerate or even pursue economic dynamics that entail bellicose consequences.[71]

67. Dalferth, "Was Gott ist," 17, is directed against a "hedonistic subjectivism." On hedonism, see Gordon Graham, *Eight Theories of Ethics* (London: Routledge, 2004), 32–3; 40–3.
68. Dalferth, "Was Gott ist," 13, 34.
69. *CD* III/4, 452, see *CL* 224.
70. Aristippus of Cyrene: *Habeo, non habeor* (Cicero, *Epistulae ad familiares*, 9, 26, 2); *Et mihi res, non me rebus subiungere conor* (Horace, *Epistulae*, 1, 1, 19).
71. In a text originally called *Gelassenheit*—or equanimity, the Epicurean *ataraxia*—Martin Heidegger drew on hedonism as well when warning of the technological progress of the nuclear age in 1955—mostly referring to nuclear power plants rather than the nuclear bomb. *Discourse on Thinking*, trans. John M. Anderson and E. Hans Freud, Harper Torchbooks 1459 (New York: Harper & Row, 1966). In the technological age, the self-enslavement of calculating thought is the major problem, against which Heidegger plays off a traditionalist, provincial commitment to one's agrarian home—or "autochthony" (49)—that is required in order to rise above it, to sound the depths of meditative thought, and to fasten one's moorings in defense against calculating thought. When he reminds the listeners that many Germans have lost their homeland (48), his reflection is again strangely apolitical. His fear that "everything [can] now fall into the clutches of planning and calculation, of organization and automation" (49) is not new; Franz Kafka, Max and Alfred Weber jointly shared the same concern more than a generation before—see Jürgen Kaube, *Max Weber: Ein Leben zwischen den Epochen* (Berlin: Rowohlt, 2014), ch. 16. Heidegger's recommendation of Epicurean equanimity (54) also echoes

To gain a better sense of the relation between the emancipatory potential of the gospel and potential problems inherent in hedonism, an ethical theory of goods is needed. For this purpose, William Schweiker's ethics of responsibility is helpful. It discusses a contemporary ethos of authenticity and personal fulfillment, which is relevant here. Although it is critical of attributing a particularly high value to authenticity and fulfillment, it deals constructively with these aspects. This is of particular interest for my discussion of Barth's ethics as well, as I have repeatedly critiqued a one-sided category of cruciform discipleship. It would be unfortunate to fall into an opposite extreme.

Schweiker discusses the relation between those goods pertaining to human well-being and the ethical orientations of action. Along similar lines, the present work has also raised the question of the relationship between creation and reconciliation in Barth's ethics. Schweiker devises a natural theory of goods that differentiates between premoral goods—that is, bodily and affective needs—and moral ones—social and reflective goods.[72] While premoral goods follow a descriptive realism individually, they are interpreted and prioritized differently in different cultures. An element of a "descriptive relativism" is involved.[73] Contrary to fundamental relativism, however, these goods are perceived to rely on facts. At the same time, perception of these facts depends on a particular hermeneutical stance, which allows for cultural variation.[74] Another

Paul's summons to buy as if one had no possessions (1 Cor. 7:30 f.). Heidegger is quite confident that on the technological side, nuclear power will be harnessed safely (51). Since existential estrangement is the only—or at least by far the most acute—danger, he calls on the readers to cultivate an "openness to the mystery" that we encounter in technology (55). In comparison with Barth's view of the lordless powers, Heidegger's critique of technology is rather innocuous.

72. Schweiker, *Responsibility and Christian Ethics*, 117–9.

73. Ibid., 2; 118.

74. See n72. Dalferth, "Was Gott ist," 13, criticizes radical constructivism for subverting responsibility.

factor is the imperative of responsibility, which prompts a realistic interpretation and a particular prioritization of premoral, social, and reflective goods and calls for respect and the enhancement of life before God. This imperative describes the ethical good, which constitutes a metalevel in relation to the other three goods. It entails a moral paradox, which again implies a modified understanding of the use of power in that it cannot be pursued directly. By contrast, we are faced with the task of acting justly with regard to premoral, social, and reflective goods; abstaining from the immediate pursuit of power; and, in honoring other lives, foregoing the attempt to maximize our own goods directly.[75] This notion corresponds, Schweiker argues, to Jesus' word, "For those who want to save their life will lose it, and those who lose their life for my sake . . . will save it" (Mark 8:35).[76]

Notably, this also implies a critique of extraordinary sacrifices, even for the sake of responsible action. The ethical good refers to respect of life before God. A dramatic sacrifice for Christ's sake is a matter of personal vocation, but it should not be a matter of ethical prescription. In Barth's idiom, in election God has committed God's self to a communion with the creature that does not require sacrifice. Indeed, Schweiker's ethical imperative can be seen to give expression to the priority of the gospel to the law and thus to testify to Christ.

In Barth's marginal case, on the other hand, it is particularly clear that not only the justification of the agent, but also the immediate moral status of an action is beyond the influence of the moral agent. Moral intuitions about nonviolence, for example, remain valid, but in extraordinary cases, they cannot be pursued directly when responsible action requires the use of force. Neither can force be

75. Schweiker, *Responsibility and Christian Ethics*, 225.
76. Ibid., 215.

used lightly, however, since the ethical imperative is directed toward respecting life.

Barth draws on Dostoevsky's Grand Inquisitor to critique an ethic of responsibility that sanctifies all means to an end. This raises both the question of legitimate uses of force and an unbridled hedonism in the maximization of one's own power. There might be something heroic even about the sacrifice the Grand Inquisitor himself makes in devoting his life to a higher cause. But he claims responsibility in compromising truth, while in fact his own interest in power constitutes the relativity of his position. Thus he subjects truth to his own cause and distorts it.[77] A vague notion of responsibility, in which the end justifies the most diverse means, may easily collide with another one. In addition, some sacrifices are so great that they undermine moral action on the whole, especially in the face of human fallibility.[78]

> And there begins the whole misery of the moral battle of everyone against everyone else, in which, whatever position we take up or line we adopt or banner we follow, we are always deceived about our friends as well as our enemies, wronging the former just as much by our affirmation as the latter by our negation, sowing and reaping discord as the children of discord.[79]

But this does not invalidate Barth's case for responsibility when he contends that the preservation of a basic system of rights may require violence. Barth does not play off an ethic of conviction against an ethic of responsibility. Convictions about the dignity of life or the dignity of justice are both rooted in Christ's work of reconciliation.

77. *CD* IV/3, 436: "He will not negate [the truth]. On the contrary, he will confirm it emphatically. But he will confirm it only in the sense in which he can regard it as tolerable and useful . . . only in a character in which it seems to be brought under his control, and promises to become his willing and powerful servant, consoler and helper. This is how falsehood speaks. This is the view of the man of sin."

78. Ibid., 437–8.

79. *CD* IV/1, 451.

An infringement on either good may have to be tolerated, unless the damage is so severe that the question of the marginal case arises. Responsible action is characterized by a paradox, but the paradox must not become the formative principle.

The relationship between the premoral, reflective, and social goods, on the one hand, and the moral paradox of the ethical good, on the other, results in a question about authenticity and personal fulfillment.[80] The two terms denote influential values not only of the contemporary Western ethos, but also in the academic discipline of ethics.[81] They are relevant in the present discussion as they raise the question of whether the priority of the gospel over the law paves the way for a simple hedonism. However, authenticity can be conceived of—more objectively—as correspondence to more widely shared moral standards or—more subjectively—to individual values and projects.

An ethics of responsibility, however, will have difficulties in calling a consistent pursuit of personal fulfillment authentic while conceiving of fulfillment in self-referential terms.[82] This would amount to striving for ever more power. At the same time, modernity is characterized by a continuous extension of human power, while the complexity of society increases with pluralism and the division of labor. An increase in power may seem feasible, yet the use of power is associated with a loss in coherence. "The radical extension of human power in our time threatens to overwhelm moral reason."[83]

Barth articulates a comparable view with a warning against a simple-minded hedonism: Economic power "is shown not so much to be possessed by man as to possess him."[84] Barth's lectures on the

80. Schweiker, *Responsibility and Christian Ethics*, 12.
81. Ibid., 12n7.
82. Ibid., 27–8.
83. Ibid., 27.
84. *CD* III/4, 452.

Christian Life had the ambiguity of power firmly in view. Moreover, *CD* II/2, chapter 8 is helpful in noting that the priority of the gospel to the law prompted Barth to note that power does not constitute what is right. Human moral dignity can consist even in protest against overwhelming power.

To react appropriately to the risks inherent in the modern extension of power, Schweiker conceives of ethics as an ethics of responsibility. A merely self-referential understanding of authenticity and fulfillment undermines responsibility. Nonetheless, he interprets authenticity and fulfillment constructively in an ethics of responsibility. A striving for personal fulfillment should be respected in the attempt to integrate many goods of different kinds—notably including the moral good. "The ideas of authenticity, or truthfulness to some basic commitment, and of human wholeness, or fulfillment, are basic to a Christian ethics of responsibility."[85] With a view to the present interpretation of Barth's ethics, this means that if life is lived with a respect for life before God—including of course the lives of others, and of the marginalized especially—Barth's prioritization of the gospel cannot be misunderstood as a simple hedonism.

Schweiker fleshes out this conflict in terms of three kinds of goods and the call to respect and enhance life before God. This even offers the advantage of a descriptive apparatus that is more fine grained than the binary of gospel and law.

Barth's Christological Contributions to a Theory of Responsibility

In spite of similarities in Barth's and Schweiker's ethics, Schweiker highlights the theological tradition of creation more strongly than Barth. This does not mean that Schweiker's ethics is simply one of natural law. Then again, even Barth calls, in a passage rarely given

85. Schweiker, *Responsibility and Christian Ethics*, 225.

sufficient attention, for a new approach to the orders of creation.[86] Nonetheless, even in Barth's ethics of creation, Christology plays a significant role. The significance of Christology is not limited to the theory of the actualistic command, which should be viewed critically for reasons internal to Barth's theology. Goods such as political participation and a constitutional democracy, which Schweiker conceives of as social goods, are clearly appreciated in the christological parts of Barth's writings.

It is remarkable that Barth gives prominence to the concept of responsibility precisely in reflecting on the cross and the resurrection. At the very beginning of the lecture "CS," he raises a question which he goes on to answer in the affirmative: "Is there an inward and vital connection by means of which in any sense human justice, as well as divine justification, becomes a concern of Christian faith and Christian responsibility, and therefore also a matter which concerns the Christian confession?"[87] Among the members of the Christian congregation, "each one of them is responsible for the character of the State as a constitutional democracy [*Rechtsstaat*]."[88] Based on the New Testament call to pray for the state, the congregation "knows that it is responsible for the State and for Caesar."[89] The church is responsible not to the unjust state, but shares in responsibility for legal justice within the state.[90] "The [principle of a] just state requires, not love, but a simple, resolute, and responsible attitude on the part of its citizens."[91] "For us the fulfillment of political duty means rather [than outward conformity] responsible choice of authority, responsible decision about the validity of laws, responsible care for their

86. *CD* III/4, §52.
87. "CS," 101.
88. Ibid., 146.
89. Ibid., 107: The church exercises this responsibility in praying for the state.
90. Ibid., 136.
91. Ibid., 143.

maintenance, in a word, political action, which may and must also mean political struggle."[92]

Not only in the struggle against National Socialism, but also in 1946, before the foundation of the Federal Republic of Germany, Barth spoke repeatedly of the Church's "share of political responsibility"[93] for a constitutional democracy. According to Barth, responsibility to God implies responsibility for temporal justice, because Christ's act of reconciliation constituted justice, and the perfect justice in redemption will not abolish but affirm the legal form of social life.[94] The gospel entails the duty of entering into relationships of social responsibility. Barth's work refers to the responsibility of the Christian congregation especially in questions of church order, economic and social affairs, political questions of a constitutional democracy, and peace.

The aspect of social justice receives clear expression in *CD* II/1. The Christian congregation is called to solidarity with the poor as an analogy obtains between their social and economic status in society and Christ's solidarity with every Christian as sinner.

> As a matter of fact, from the belief in God's righteousness there follows logically a very definite political problem and task. But seen and understood *in abstracto*, the latter—i.e., the connexion between justification and law in all its relevance for that between Church and state—cannot really be evident and necessary of itself. It becomes so when we appreciate the fact that God's righteousness, the faithfulness in which He is true to Himself, is disclosed as help and salvation, as a saving divine intervention for man directed only to the poor, the wretched and the helpless as such . . . When we encounter divine righteousness we are all like the people of Israel, menaced and altogether lost according to its own strength. We are all widows and orphans who cannot procure right for themselves. . . . The connexion between God's righteousness

92. Ibid., 144.
93. "CCCC," 160.
94. "CS," 122–3.

> and mercy now becomes clear. The righteousness of the believer consists in the fact that God acts for him . . . . Faith grasps this full intervention on the part of God and it is therefore *eo ipso* faith in God's mercy, the faith of those who are poor and wretched before God. According to the Gospel of Luke and the Epistle of James, as also according to the message of the prophets, there follows from this character of faith a political attitude, decisively determined by the fact that man is made responsible to all those who are poor and wretched in his eyes, that he is summoned on his part to espouse the cause of those who suffer wrong.[95]

Barth's reference to widows and orphans follows an Old Testament ethos that can be found in legal traditions and narrative, cultic, and prophetic literature.[96] Barth sees Jesus' concern for the marginalized in continuity with this tradition. The Gospel of Luke in particular highlights Jesus' care for the poor, women, tax collectors, and sinners. "CCCC" points to such traditions in arguing for the Christian commitment to social justice: "The Church is witness of the fact that the Son of man came to seek and to save the lost."[97] This concern culminates in Jesus' reconciling passion and finds its continuation in the call for an inclusive ethos in the early congregations. Such an economic and social dimension of Christian action reflects the priority of the gospel to the law, as social action corresponds to the liberation by God, as responsibility for and to the marginalized corresponds to Christ claiming responsibility for the sinner. The justification of such action is analogous to the biblical justification for the care of another typical group of marginalized, which Barth does not mention: "The alien who resides with you shall be to you as the citizen among you; you shall love the alien as yourself, for you were aliens in the land of Egypt: I am YHWH your God" (Lev. 19:34).[98]

Barth's lecture "Die Not der evangelischen Kirche" (1931)

95. *CD* II/2, 377–8.

96. Exod. 22:21, Ps. 10:14, 27:10, 68:6, 146:9, Prov. 23:10–11, Isa. 1:17, Jer. 7:5–6.

97. "CCCC," 173. See Luke 19:10, 5:27–32, 6:20–22, 8:1–3.

98. Bedford-Strohm, "Geschenkte Freiheit," 261. Citation of Lev. altered from NRSV.

emphasizes mutual Christian responsibility. Here Barth attaches great importance to the theology of the cross. He distinguishes between two dangers: an evasion from the visibility of the church and a retreat into visibility, that is, the temptation to shy away from public obligation, on the one hand; and the lure of a disproportionate institutional influence, in which ecclesial demands on others are in contrast to the Christian duty to serve, on the other. "ChrSoc" called this dichotomy a secularization of Christ and a clericalization of society. The distinction reappears in *CD* IV/2, §67.3,[99] after which §67.4 insists that church law should reflect the duty of mutual service among church members according to Christ's example. Barth's conviction that freedom cannot be isolated from social responsibility is now carried over into legal considerations. Barth makes this case not only with a view to the church, but also to wider society.

Many of Barth's views are committed to a pluralistic, constitutional democracy that is oriented toward freedom. "ChrSoc" makes a case for the particular dynamics of individual social systems, arguing against a hegemony of the religious system or the civil association of the church.[100] Due to its legal order, the church is committed to the cultivation of a just legal system in wider society. According to its own abilities, theology should contribute to the dialogue with the culture undergirding the legal system. For example, the church should be sensitive to the potential need for legal reform in church and society and make the case for taking such steps if necessary.

99. *CD* IV/2, 776: alienation/secularization and self-glorification/sacralization.

100. Apart from "ChrSoc" and "Die Not der evangelischen Kirche," in *Vorträge und kleinere Arbeiten 1930–1933*, ed. Michael Beintker et al., Barth-Gesamtausgabe (Zurich: Theologischer Verlag, 2013), 64–122, see also "CCCC," 185–6. Paul Althaus wrote in 1934 with regard to Barth's political ethics: "The concept of the state we are dealing with here is that of the liberal constitutional democracy (*liberaler Rechtsstaat*) as in all of Karl Barth's writings." Heinz Eduard Tödt, "Karl Barth, der Liberalismus und der Nationalsozialismus: Gegendarstellung zu Friedrich Wilhelm Grafs Behandlung dieses Themas," *Evangelische Theologie* 46 (1986): 536–51, at 549.

Christian responsibility for social commitment includes not only responsibility within the church and wider society for the marginalized and the culture of a constitutional democracy. The church also cannot reject its share of responsibility for critical and constructive attention to a peaceful foreign policy. Of course, this became especially crucial for Barth in the wake of the Second World War. In the marginal case, the church may even be called to advocate for a war that serves a genuine order of peace. Before reaching that point, however, the duty of the church must be to work for relationships conducive to peace.

In arguing for a legal order within the church, constitutional democracy, social justice, and peace, Barth goes beyond the boundaries of a more conventional ethics of responsibility that considers individual Christians to be responsible vis-à-vis God and the individual neighbor. At the same time, Barth's critique of theologies of orders of creation can be understood as a critique of such an ethics of responsibility that sees the Christian duty especially in respecting established social roles.[101]

In sharing responsibility for premoral and moral goods, Christians hold each other responsible publicly and even seek accountability toward the wider public, which will measure the churches by the own moral standards thus established. A church that shares responsibility in filling a constitutional democracy with life and in supporting social justice exercises a political function in civil society.[102] That is "the nature of the service which the church, as the organ of divine justification, owes to the State, as the organ of human law, which the State has a right to expect from it, and by which, if it remains obedient, it will actually assist the State."[103]

101. On agent-centered, dialogical, and social theories of responsibility, see Schweiker, *Responsibility and Christian Ethics*, 41.

102. On the concept, see Michael Welker, *Kirche im Pluralismus* (Gütersloh: Kaiser/Gütersloher, 1995), 16–17.

In the area of peace ethics, Barth's lectures on the ethics of reconciliation, published posthumously, observe that economic interest can further peace, but that it can also work against it.[104]

> Money is a flexible but powerful instrument which, supposedly handled by man, in reality follows its own law. . . . It can cause the market to rise and then to fall again. It can arrest this crisis and cause another. It can serve peace yet pursue cold war even in the midst of peace. It can make ready for a bloody war and finally bring it about. It can bring provisional paradise here and the corresponding provisional hell there.[105]

Unfortunately, Barth does not follow up with this train of thought. Certainly there is more than a grain of truth in interpreting this seeming paradox of economics as an expression of money as a mythological entity. But do economics only contribute to the problem of the military-industrial complex, is the effect of economics on politics ultimately random, or can it possibly help in dissolving the link between bellicose politics and aggressive economics? Interestingly, among the early radical pacifists there were merchants whose advocacy of peace involved their own economic interests.[106]

Barth speaks in broad terms of economics as an autonomous system as if he were dealing with an "iron cage" that would rule out alternative courses of action within the capitalist sphere.[107] Yet even before Barth presented these thoughts, the European Coal and Steel

103. "CS," 139–40. (trans. rev.).

104. *CL* 222–4.

105. *CL*, 224.

106. Wolfgang Lienemann, "Verantwortungspazifismus (*legal pacifism*): Zum politischen Gestaltungspotential pazifistischer Bewegungen im Blick auf das Völkerrecht," in *Der gerechte Friede zwischen Pazifismus und gerechtem Krieg: Paradigmen der Friedensethik im Diskurs*, ed. Jean-Daniel Strub and Stefan Grotefeld (Stuttgart: Kohlhammer, 2007), 75–99, at 76. According to Immanuel Kant, the "*spirit of commerce* . . . cannot exist side by side with war." *Perpetual Peace: A Philosophical Sketch,* in *Political Writings*, ed. Hans S. Reiss, trans. H. B. Nisbet, 2nd ed., Cambridge Texts in the History of Political Thought (Cambridge: Cambridge University Press, 1991), 114.

107. Weber, *Protestant Ethic and the Spirit of Capitalism*, 123.

Community had been founded in 1951, a precursor to the European Economic Community and, eventually, the European Union. Serving economic interests also, this association united European states by means of communal interests, making economically motivated wars ever more unlikely. In consequence, rather than being suspicious of economic activity across the board, it would have made sense also to make plans for the taming of the mythological entity by differentiating between the constructive and antagonistic potential of economic politics and to argue at least for more research on such effects.

At least until recently, the relation between democratic deficits and economic politics can be seen more clearly in the area of energy politics. Thomas L. Friedman articulated the "first law of petropolitics," according to which the importance of crude oil for entire economies develops in an inversely proportionate way to the levels of freedom offered in societies that profit from trade in fossil fuels.[108] The possibility of enormous value creation independently of developments in a pluralistic civil society creates a dramatic temptation to engage in "systems paternalism."[109] Certainly this common problem is not limited to political power resting on large oil resources. While gaps in economic and social justice are not to be tolerated lightly, economic progress, on the other hand, is not inherently good from an ethical point of view. Widespread

108. Thomas L. Friedman, "The First Law of Petropolitics," *Foreign Policy* 154 (2006): 28–36, at 31. The question is to what extent this theory will remain valid in times of the low oil prices secured through "fracking."

109. Jürgen Habermas, *Between Facts and Norms: Between a Discourse Theory of Law and Democracy*, trans. William Rehg, 2nd ed. (Cambridge, MA: MIT, 1996), 351. The concept denotes an "integration" of a society "in a manner that bypasses the communicative power of the public of citizens" (352). See Welker, *Kirche im Pluralismus*, 21. Apart from Russia, Saudi Arabia, and Iran, Venezuela and Azerbaijan are to be named. Marina Ottaway concluded in 2003, "Semi-authoritarian regimes are becoming increasingly common: indeed, they are one of the most noticeable outcomes of more than a decade of efforts to promote democracy by the international community." Marina Ottaway, *Democracy Challenged: The Rise of Semi-authoritarianism* (Washington: Carnegie Endowment for International Peace), 2003, 133.

economic and social security can be used to legitimize authoritarian politics. At the same time, however, political action relating to the economic sphere can provide instruments that serve greater degrees of liberty and peace. If an ethics affirms with Barth that Jesus Christ's act of reconciliation is the creation of justice and righteousness, it will commit itself to responsibility in "The Struggle for Human Righteousness" (*CL*, §78). As a result, it must not rest content with denouncing the sphere of economics in mythological terms, but seek greater clarity about the political effects of specific economic constellations.

God's Differentiated Presence in the Spirit

There is a peculiar ambiguity in Barth's work that urges for obedience to God's command and yet considers the most significant work to have been done already. In ethics, this can lead to a helpful stance of a "hastening that waits." God's achievement in Christ provides orientation and motivation for sober action.[110] It is difficult, however, to specify what conditions must be met so that sober, relative action does indeed result from the tension between the all-important divine initiative and human duty. This was a problem in *Rom* II:

> We boast not only *in* tribulation, but we boast *about* it. We can say 'Yes' to the negation of the issues in our lives that are determined by chance, as surely as we can and must negate their 'Yes' very often. . . . Because . . . this way or the other we see through the realities and important issues of the moment . . . . Mere human suffering is now seen as the work of God the creator and redeemer, the inhibition of life as preparation for the victory of life, demolition as edification, disappointment and setback as hastening and waiting for the future of the Lord.[111]

110. *CD* IV/3, 470–41.
111. *Rom* II, 214–15.

Even later in his work, Barth occasionally subverts the precarious situation of human agency with emphatic affirmation of God's omnipotence, as in *CD* IV/3, §69.3, "Jesus is Victor."[112] Theologians who do not share such an emphatic sense of divine omnipotence are likely to bring the notion of responsibility to the fore more clearly. Bonhoeffer, for example, writes that in Christ, "God consents to be pushed out of the world and onto the cross. God is weak and powerless in the world, and in precisely this way, and only so, is at our side and helps us."[113] Bonhoeffer's notion of a Christianity without religion may have led to the misunderstanding of a Christianity without God. But while indeed the creature is certainly not thrown back onto itself, its practical contribution is indispensable. For in order to transform historical reality, "God needs human beings who let everything work out for the best," as God "waits for and responds to sincere prayers and responsible action."[114]

Eberhard Jüngel underscores parallels in Barth's and Bonhoeffer's construal of the exclusive and the complementary aspects in the relationship between God and the creature. Barth's mature theology rejects both the notion that God's being excludes humanity and that the human person can be ontologically godless.[115] A relative godlessness is possible, however. Jüngel sees in this description the possibility of overcoming the duality of atheism and theism. Modern

112. See Matthias D. Wüthrich, *Gott und das Nichtige: Zur Rede vom Nichtigen ausgehend von § 50 der Kirchlichen Dogmatik Karl Barths* (Zürich: Theologischer 2006), 303, 333–5.

113. Dietrich Bonhoeffer, *Letters and Paper from Prison*, ed. John de Gruchy et al., trans. Isabel Best et al., Dietrich Bonhoeffer Works 8 (Minneapolis: Fortress Press, 2010), 479.

114. Ibid., 46. By contrast, according to Hans Jonas, God has withdrawn from the world; in God's absence, only a vague notion of a goal entices human commitment to responsibility in the cosmic process. Hans Jonas, "The Concept of God after Auschwitz: A Jewish Voice," *The Journal of Religion* 67 (1987): 1–13, at 12. On Jonas's *The Imperative of Responsibility* and Bonhoeffer's ethics of responsibility, see Wolfgang Huber, "Sozialethik als Verantwortungsethik," in *Konflikt und Konsens: Studien zur Ethik der Verantwortung* (Munich: Kaiser, 1990), 135–57, at 141–7.

115. "For we must not forget that, while there is a godlessness of the human person, according to the Word of reconciliation there is no humanlessness of God." *CD* IV/3, 119 (trans. rev.).

atheism is reacting against a concept of God that sees God as an absolute entity in radical independence and freedom from the human person, while metaphysical theism supposedly defends such a concept. Yet both views fail to appreciate the true depth of the Christian concept of God, which Barth maintains with the true presence of God in Jesus Christ.[116] Jüngel also indicates that Barth's concept of a relative godlessness—which contrasts with an absolute godlessness—is open to misunderstanding.

This is the point at which the theological construal of the relationship is relevant for the relationship between human and divine action. To speak of an "indestructible community"[117] between God and the human person, as Jüngel understands Barth, suggests a fundamentally mutual communion that is not only potentially communion on the human side. In moral terms, this might distract from the ethical need to distinguish between better or worse courses of action, however.

Jüngel warns against von Balthasar's interpretation that sees in Barth's mature theology an argument not merely for a contingent human possibility for communion, but even for a natural human teleology toward the divine.[118] A blanket assertion of human godlessness would nevertheless portray the human person as a devil, in Jüngel's words.[119] What Jüngel does not discuss, however, is the possibility of the contingent sinful isolation of the human person from the divine, even if it takes place in direct contrast to God's

116. Eberhard Jüngel, ". . . Keine Menschenlosigkeit Gottes . . .: Zur Theologie Karl Barths zwischen Theismus und Atheismus," in *Barth-Studien*, Ökumenische Theologie 9 (Zurich and Cologne: Benziger/Gütersloh: Gütersloher Verlagshaus Mohn, 1982), 332–47, at 344.

117. Ibid., 345.

118. Hans Urs von Balthasar, *The Theology of Karl Barth: Exposition and Interpretation*, Communio Books, trans. Edward T. Oakes, SJ (San Francisco: Ignatius, 1992), 165. Jüngel, "Keine Menschenlosigkeit," 345.

119. Ibid.

seeking out the human person. Yet the utterly bleak moments of human history seem to require this possibility.

Certainly, Jüngel is in dialogue with Barth's and Bonhoeffer's views on the cross, which the three understand as the moment of the most intimate communion between God and humanity—in concealed shape, however. Jüngel sees Bonhoeffer in critical and constructive discourse with modern atheism, which leads Jüngel to ask, "How is this then to be done: not to think God without the world which, for its part, is to be thought without God?"[120]

Interpreting Bonhoeffer, Jüngel argues, "The crucifixion of Jesus is the actual element of persuasion in the knowledge that we must live and know in a world even 'if there were no God.'"[121] But what does it mean that God does not want to be without the human person and that the godless human person turns to God—by the help of the Holy Spirit?

Jüngel argues that "the 'Father in heaven' above us was among us through the crucified Son of God and in the Holy Spirit is united not only for himself but as one absent is present with us."[122] Trinitarian Christian faith consists not only in belief in the eternal Father, which "means to find delight in God as the Lord." It also means "to believe in God the eternal Son," which "thus means to take delight in God as the Lord in such a way that we take delight in ourselves."[123] The work of the Holy Spirit consists essentially in creating this reality.[124]

120. Eberhard Jüngel, *God as the Mystery of the World: On the Foundation of the Theology of the Crucified One in the Dispute between Theism and Atheism*, trans. Darrell Guder (Grand Rapids: Eerdmans, 1983), 57 (trans. rev.).

121. Ibid., 60.

122. Ibid., 63.

123. Ibid., 380, 382.

124. Ibid., 388–9. David Congdon's lucid discussion shows how Jüngel's pneumatology clearly goes beyond human subjectivity. "The Spirit of Freedom: Eberhard Jüngel's Theology of the Third Article," in *Indicative of Grace—Imperative of Freedom: Essays in Honour of Eberhard Jüngel in His 80th Year*, ed. David Nelson, T&T Clark Theology (London and New York: Bloomsbury T&T Clark, 2014), 13–28. But as Jüngel typically places the emphasis on the Spirit's role in the spiritual relation between God and the individual human person, it is also characteristic that

The work to be done here is to overcome the "pure demand" of the law.[125]

> There is no gospel here apart from the hardness of the law which emphasizes the difference between God and God as the *wrath* of God over the sinner. This hardness of the law, of course, is there only for the sake of the joy of the gospel; the wrath of God is only for the sake of his love.[126]

According to Jüngel, God asserts God's self in God's wrath. This foreign work prepares the way for the gospel, just as Christ endured the punishment of the law and won salvation in the midst of suffering. The primary salvific event is the cross, not the resurrection.

By contrast, according to Barth, in the resurrection the Spirit manifests God's faithfulness to creation: "But the body of Jesus Christ was not a body abandoned by the Holy Spirit. The Holy Spirit has shown Himself to it as the life-giving Spirit. The body of this One who was slain has become a body which is alive by the Spirit: *sōma pneymatikon* [spiritual body] (1 Cor. 15:44)."[127] The Holy Spirit did not abandon Christ, Barth says. On the contrary, he views the resurrection as the continuation of the relationship between the Son and the Spirit. According to Luke 4, Jesus is anointed with the Spirit to proclaim the gospel to the poor, freedom to prisoners, and vision to the blind. In enabling this work, the activity of the Spirit no longer takes place primarily in granting sinners participation in justifying faith, as *CD* I/1, §12 had argued. To begin with, with

he defers hope for the physical dimension of the Spirit's work to an end times consummation. Accordingly, Jüngel's influential schematic overview of the structure of *CD* IV in his Barth studies passes over Christ's work of physical and social transformation in silence.

125. Ibid., 366.

126. Ibid., 373.

127. *CD* IV/1, 664. Rowan D. Williams, "Barth on the Triune God," in *Karl Barth: Centenary Essays*, ed. Stephen W. Sykes (Cambridge: Cambridge University Press, 1989), 147–93, at 171n21 takes issue with Jüngel's subjectivity approach and critiques "the near total lack of reference to the Spirit in Jüngel's book."

the Spirit's activity on Easter, pneumatology transcends the classic doctrine of the *application* of grace by the Spirit. According to §61, the resurrection created justice for Christ, in which the creature participates. Moreover, in the power of the Spirit, Jesus fulfilled God's command in salvific acts of preaching and healing. In keeping with §64, the exaltation of the Son of God in the resurrection is strongly in keeping with the sovereign acts Christ performed in ministering to the sick and the outcast and proclaiming the forgiveness of sins. As the Spirit is the Spirit of Christ, justified Christians will not be left with only a vague ideal of love, but will be on the side of those who are systematically excluded from society.

Often it is not clear what such action will look like concretely. In the power of the Spirit, a search for the best course of action is set in motion, in an ever new praying, seeking, and asking. Christians will thus also attend to the structural dimensions of legal and social justice. The establishment of righteousness and justice in the resurrection constitutes a Christian share in responsibility for just conditions in society, which Barth conceives of both in terms of social justice and a constitutional democracy.

The work of the Spirit also includes the gathering of Christians as a congregation. Church law serves the continuity of mutual service in the congregation, which Barth highlights especially in *CD* IV/2, §67, "The Holy Spirit and the Upbuilding of the Christian Community." Appropriate care for the institutional dimension of the church, support for the spiritual edification of the congregation, a commitment to civil society, and support of diaconal work cannot be separated as dimensions of church law. Interestingly, at this point the work of the Spirit gives shape to a Christian social dynamic that defies the binary *coram Deo*/*coram hominibus* and overcomes the concept of a "vertical history."[128] This work of the Spirit is not merely a consequence of the individual's justifying faith; it gives expression to a richer, more fundamentally social soteriology.

Barth presents his views on church law, after §66 eagerly seeks new metaphors to describe the work of the Spirit. On the one hand, he holds on to powerful, even brutal images.[129] On the other hand, the images of a seed, of the wind moving a body of water, and a continued wake-up call from lethargy are more subtle, thereby subverting the binary of omnipotence and impotence. Barth seeks to articulate the work of the Spirit as a more nuanced way of God's working in the world. It mediates between the truth that God is neither a worldless God in isolation from humanity and that human persons may fundamentally contradict the fact that they have been elected from eternity, that they are God's creatures, that Christ bore their sins, and that the Spirit continues to beckon and empower them. At times, this mediation of the Spirit may even take on a very plain yet distinct appearance that is effective in its own subtle way. This work can take on various forms. Not to be neglected in comparison with the very social fabric of the church, of course, if the classic role of Christian testimony. In the "great and critical moments," the Christian congregation has again and again given true witness—"in the power of the Word of the true Witness again received by man, and therefore in the power of the Holy Spirit."[130]

128. Jürgen Moltmann, *The Way of Jesus Christ: Christology in Messianic Dimensions*, trans. Margaret Kohl (London: SCM, 1990), 52.

129. See *CD* IV/2, 523: the Spirit "crushes and breaks and destroys that which resists it."

130. *CD* IV/3, 440.

Bibliography

Works by Karl Barth

"Abschied. 1933." In *"Der Götze wackelt": Zeitkritische Aufsätze, Reden und Briefe*. Edited by Kupisch, 63–70.

"An Dietrich Bonhoeffer, Berlin" (Sept. 11, 1933). In *Briefe des Jahres 1933*. Edited by Busch, 376–80.

"An Markus Barth" (Sept. 11, 1933). In *Briefe des Jahres 1933*. Edited by Busch, 381–2.

"An Professor Dr. Renatus Hupfeld, Heidelberg" (Sept. 11, 1933). In *Briefe des Jahres 1933*. Edited by Busch, 380–81.

"Biblical Questions, Insights, and Vistas." In *Word of God and Theology*, 71–100.

"Brechen und Bauen: Eine Diskussion." In *"Der Götze wackelt": Zeitkritische Aufsätze, Reden und Briefe*. Edited by Kupisch, 108–23.

Briefe des Jahres 1933. Edited by Eberhard Busch. Zurich: Theologischer Verlag. 2004.

Briefe 1961–1968. Edited by Jürgen Fangmeier and Hinrich Stoevesandt. Barth-Gesamtausgabe. Zurich: Theologischer Verlag, 1979.

"The Christian Community and Civil Community." In *Community, Church, and State*. Edited by Haddorff, 149–89. ("CCCC")

"The Christian in Society." In *Word of God and Theology*, 31–70. ("ChrSoc")

The Christian Life: Church Dogmatics IV,4; Lecture Fragments. Edited by Hans-Anton Drewes and Eberhard Jüngel. Translated by Geoffrey W. Bromiley. Grand Rapids: Eerdmans, 1981. (*CL*)

"Church and State." In *Community, State, and Church.* Edited by Haddorff, 101–48. ("CS")

Church Dogmatics. Edited by Geoffrey W. Bromiley and Thomas F. Torrance. Translated by Geoffrey W. Bromiley et al. Edinburgh: T&T Clark, 1936–1969. (*CD*)

Community, State, and Church: Three Essays; With a New Introduction. Edited by David Haddorff. Translated by Will Herberg (Eugene: Wipf & Stock, 2004).

"Das Erste Gebot als theologisches Axiom." In *Vorträge und kleinere Arbeiten 1930–1933.* Edited by Beintker et al, 209–41.

"Das Halten der Gebote (1927)." In *Vorträge und kleinere Arbeiten 1925–1930.* Edited by Schmidt, 99–139.

Das Wort Gottes und die Theologie: Gesammelte Vorträge. 5th edition. Munich: Kaiser, 1929.

"Der Christ in der Gesellschaft." In *Vorträge und kleinere Arbeiten 1914–1921.* Edited by Drewes, 546–98.

"Der Götze wackelt": Zeitkritische Aufsätze, Reden und Briefe von 1930 bis 1960. Edited by Karl Kupisch. Berlin: Vogt, 1961.

"Der Heilige Geist und das christliche Leben (1929)." In *Vorträge und kleinere Arbeiten 1925–1930.* Edited by Schmidt, 458–520.

Der Römerbrief (Erste Fassung): 1919. Edited by Hermann Schmidt. Barth-Gesamtausgabe. Zurich: Theologischer Verlag, 1985. (*Rom* I)

Der Römerbrief (Zweite Fassung): 1922. Edited by Cornelis van der Kooi and Katja Tolstaja. Barth-Gesamtausgabe. Zurich: Evangelischer Verlag, 2010. (*Rom* II)

"Der römische Katholizismus als Frage an die protestantische Kirche. 1928." In *Vorträge und kleinere Arbeiten 1925–1930.* Edited by Schmidt, 303–43.

Die christliche Dogmatik im Entwurf: Die Lehre vom Wort Gottes: Prolegomena zur christlichen Dogmatik 1927. Edited by Gerhard Sauter. Barth-Gesamtausgabe. Zurich: Theologischer Verlag 1982. (*MD*)

Die christliche Lehre nach dem Heidelberger Katechismus: Vorlesung an der Universität Bonn im Sommersemester 1947. Zurich: Evangelischer Verlag, 1948.

"Die Deutschen und wir. 1945." In *Eine Schweizer Stimme: 1938–1945*. Zollikon/Zurich: Evangelischer Verlag, 1945, 334–70.

"Die Kirche und die Kultur. 1926." In *Vorträge und kleinere Arbeiten 1925–1930*. Edited by Schmidt, 10–40.

"Die Kirche zwischen Ost und West." In *Der Götze wackelt": Zeitkritische Aufsätze, Reden und Briefe*. Edited by Kupisch, 124–43.

Die Kirchliche Dogmatik. Vols. I/1–IV/4. Munich: Kaiser; Zurich: Theologischer Verlag, 1932–81.

"Die Menschlichkeit Gottes." *Theologische Studien* 48. Zollikon-Zurich: Evangelischer Verlag, 1956.

"Die Not der evangelischen Kirche." In *Vorträge und kleinere Arbeiten 1930–1933*. Edited by Beintker at al., 64–122.

Die protestantische Theologie im 19. Jahrhundert: Ihre Vorgeschichte und ihre Geschichte. 4th edition. Zurich: Theologischer Verlag, 1981.

Die Theologie Calvins 1922. Edited by Hans Scholl. Zurich: Theologischer Verlag, 1993.

Digital Karl Barth Library. Alexander Street Press, Alexandria, VA. http://solomon.dkbl.alexanderstreet.com.

"Ein Brief aus der Schweiz nach Großbritannien (durch J. H. Oldham und A. R. Vidler). 1941." In *Offene Briefe 1935–1942*. Edited by Koch, 268–303.

Ethics. Edited by Dietrich Braun. Translated by Geoffrey W. Bromiley. Eugene: Wipf & Stock, 2013.

Ethik: Vorlesung Münster, Sommersemester 1928, wiederholt in Bonn,

Sommersemester 1930. Edited by Dietrich Braun. Barth-Gesamtausgabe. Zurich: Theologischer Verlag 1973.

Ethik: Vorlesung Münster, Wintersemester 1928/1929, wiederholt in Bonn, Wintersemester 1930/31. Edited by Dietrich Braun. Barth-Gesamtausgabe. Zurich: Theologischer Verlag 1978.

Fides quaerens intellectum: Anselms Beweis für die Existenz Gottes, 1931. Edited by Eberhard Jüngel and Ingolf U. Dalferth. Barth-Gesamtausgabe. Zurich: Theologischer Verlag, 1981.

"Fragen an das 'Christentum.'" In *Theologische Fragen und Antworten: Gesammelte Vorträge 3: 1927–1942.* 2nd ed. Zurich: Theologischer Verlag 1986, 93–9.

"From Karl Barth, Oberrieden, September 11, 1933." In Dietrich Bonhoeffer, *Berlin 1932–1933.* Edited by Carsten Nicolaisen and Ernst-Albert Scharffenorth, translaed by Isabel Best and David Higgins. Dietrich Bonhoeffer Works 12. Minneapolis: Fortress Press, 2009, 166–9.

"Gespräch mit der Kirchlichen Bruderschaft in Württemberg (15.7.1963)." In *Gespräche 1963.* Edited by Busch, 42–109.

Gespräche 1959–1962. Edited by Eberhard Busch. Barth-Gesamtausgabe. Zurich: Theologischer Verlag, 1995.

Gespräche 1963. Edited by Eberhard Busch. Barth-Gesamtausgabe. Zurich: Theologischer Verlag, 2005.

Gespräche 1964–1968. Edited by Eberhard Busch. Barth-Gesamtausgabe. Zurich: Theologischer Verlag, 1996.

The Göttingen Dogmatics: Instruction in the Christian Religion. Edited by Hannelotte Reiffen. Translated by Geoffrey W. Bromiley. Grand Rapids: Eerdmans, 1991. (*GD* I)

"Gospel and Law." In *Community, State, and Church.* Edited by Haddorff, 71–101. ("GL")

"Interview von H. Lichtenstein, Westdeutscher Rundfunk (24.2.1964)." In *Gespräche 1964–1968.* Edited by Busch, 21–7.

Karl Barth—Emil Brunner Briefwechsel 1916–1966. Edited by Eberhard Busch. Barth-Gesamtausgabe. Zurich: Theologischer Verlag, 2000.

Karl Barth—Eduard Thurneysen Briefwechsel: 1913–1921. Edited by Eduard Thurneysen. Barth-Gesamtausgabe. Zurich: Theologischer Verlag, 1973.

Karl Barth—Eduard Thurneysen Briefwechsel: 1921–1930. Edited by Eduard Thurneysen. Barth-Gesamtausgabe. Zurich: Theologischer Verlag, 1974.

Karl Barth—Eduard Thurneysen Briefwechsel: 1930–1935. Edited by Caren Algner. Barth-Gesamtausgabe. Zurich: Theologischer Verlag, 2000.

Karl Barth—Willem Adolf Visser't Hooft Briefwechsel 1916–1966. Edited by Thomas Herwig. Barth-Gesamtausgabe. Zurich: Theologischer Verlag, 2006.

"Ludwig Feuerbach." In *Die Theologie und die Kirche: Gesammelte Vorträge 2. Band.* Munich: Kaiser, 1928, 212–39.

"The Need and Promise of Christian Proclamation. 1922." In *Word of God and Theology*, 101–29.

"No! Response to Emil Brunner." In *Natural Theology: Comprising "Natural Theology" by Emil Brunner and the Reply "No" by Karl Barth.* Edited by and translated by Peter Fraenkel. Eugene: Wipf & Stock, 2002.

Offene Briefe 1909–1935. Edited by Diether Koch. Barth-Gesamtausgabe. Zurich: Theologischer Verlag, 2001.

Offene Briefe 1935–1942. Edited by Diether Koch. Barth-Gesamtausgabe. Zurich: Theologischer Verlag, 2001.

Offene Briefe 1945–1968. Edited by Diether Koch. Barth-Gesamtausgabe. Zurich: Theologischer Verlag, 1984.

On Religion: The Revelation of God as the Sublimation of Religion. Edited and translated by Garrett Green. Bloomsbury Revelations. London: Bloomsbury Academic, 2013.

Predigten 1921–1935. Edited by Holger Finze-Michaelsen. Barth-Gesamtausgabe. Zurich: Theologischer Verlag, 1998.

Predigten 1954–1967. Edited by Hinrich Stoevesandt. Barth-Gesamtausgabe. Zurich: Theologischer Verlag, 1979.

"The Problem of Ethics Today. 1922." In *The Word of God and Theology*, 131–69.

"*Quousque tandem* . . . ?" In *Vorträge und kleinere Arbeiten 1925–1930*. Edited by Schmidt, 521–35.

"Rechtfertigung und Heiligung (1927)." In *Vorträge und kleinere Arbeiten 1925–1930*. Edited by Schmidt, 57–98.

"Reformierte Lehre, ihr Wesen und ihre Aufgabe, 1923." In *Vorträge und kleinere Arbeiten 1922–1925*. Edited by Finze, 202–47.

"Römer 15, 5–13. 10. Dezember 1933 (2. Advent)." In *Predigten 1921–1935*. Edited by Finze-Michaelsen, 296–305.

Theological Existence To-day! (A Plea for Theological Freedom). Translated by R. Birch Hoyle. Eugene: Wipf & Stock, 2012.

"To Rector Eberhard Bethge, Rengsdorf near Neuwied, May 22, 1967." In *Letters 1961–1968*. Edited by Jürgen Fangmeier and Hinrich Stoevesandt, translated by Geoffrey W. Bromiley. Grand Rapids: Eerdmans, 1981, 250–52.

"Unerledigte Anfragen an die Theologie (1920)." In *Vorträge und kleinere Arbeiten 1914–1921*. Edited by Drewes, 622–62.

Unterricht in der christlichen Religion: Die Lehre von der Versöhnung/Die Lehre von der Erlösung 1925/26. Edited by Hinrich Stoevesandt. Barth-Gesamtausgabe. Zurich: Theologischer Verlag, 2003. (*GD* III)

Unterricht in der christlichen Religion: Die Lehre von Gott/Die Lehre vom Menschen 1924/25. Edited by Hinrich Stoevesandt. Barth-Gesamtausgabe. Zurich: Theologischer Verlag, 1990. (*GD* II)

Vorträge und kleinere Arbeiten 1914–1921. Edited by Hans-Anton Drewes. Barth-Gesamtausgabe. Zurich: Theologischer Verlag, 2012.

Vorträge und kleinere Arbeiten 1922–1925. Edited by Holger Finze. Barth-Gesamtausgabe. Zurich: Theologischer Verlag, 1990.

Vorträge und kleinere Arbeiten 1925–1930. Edited by Hermann Schmidt. Barth-Gesamtausgabe. Zurich: Theologischer Verlag, 1994.

Vorträge und kleinere Arbeiten 1930–1933. Edited by Michael Beintker, Michael Hüttenhoff, and Peter Zocher. Barth-Gesamtausgabe. Zurich: Theologischer Verlag, 2013.

The Word of God and Theology. Translated by Amy Marga. New York, T&T Clark: 2011.

"Wünschbarkeit und Möglichkeit eines allgemeinen reformierten Glaubensbekenntnisses, 1925." In *Vorträge und kleinere Arbeiten 1922–1925*. Edited by Finze, 604–43.

Further Literature

Althaus, Paul, *Grundriss der Ethik: Neue Bearbeitung der "Leitsätze."* Erlangen: Merkel, 1931.

——. *Die Theologie Martin Luthers*. 2nd ed. Gütersloh: Gütersloher Verlagshaus Mohn, 1963.

Altmann, Jürgen, Ute Bernhardt et al. *Naturwissenschaft—Rüstung—Frieden: Basiswissen für die Friedensforschung*. Friedens- und Konfliktforschung 9. Wiesbaden: Verlag für Sozialwissenschaften, 2007.

Aly, Götz. *Hitler's Beneficiaries: Plunder, Racial War, and the Nazi Welfare State*. Translated by Jefferson Chase. New York: Holt/Metropolitan, 2009.

Amnesty International UK, "Repression and Injustice in the United Arab Emirates." November 18, 2014. http://tinyurl.com/mcqnnee.

Anselm von Canterbury. *Cur deus homo—Warum Gott ein Mensch geworden: Lateinisch und deutsch*. Edited and translated by Franciscus Salesius Schmitt OSB. Bibliothek klassischer Texte. 5th ed. Darmstadt: Wissenschaftliche Buchgesellschaft, 1993.

Anzinger, Herbert. *Glaube und kommunikative Praxis: Eine Studie zur 'vordialektischen' Theologie Karl Barths*. Beiträge zur evangelischen Theologie 110. Munich: Kaiser, 1991.

Arendt, Hannah. *Eichmann in Jerusalem: A Report on the Banality of Evil*. 2nd ed. New York: Viking Press, 1964.

Assel, Heinrich, "Grundlose Souveränität und göttliche Freiheit: Karl Barths Rechtslehre im Konflikt mit Emanuel Hirschs Souveränitätslehre." In *Karl Barth in Deutschland (1921–1935): Aufbruch—Klärung—Widerstand*. Edited by Beintker et al. Zurich: Theologischer Verlag, 2005, 205–22.

Baranowski, Shelley. "The Confessing Church and Antisemitism: Protestant Identity, German Nationhood, and the Exclusion of the Jews." In *Betrayal: German Churches and the Holocaust*. Edited by Robert P. Ericksen and Susannah Heschel. Minneapolis: Fortress Press, 1999, 90–109.

Barstow, David, "Behind Analysts, the Pentagon's Hidden Hand." *The New York Times*, April 20, 2008. http://nyti.ms/b5UoIS.

Barth, Gerhard. *Der Tod Jesu Christi im Verständnis des Neuen Testaments*. Neukirchen-Vluyn: Neukirchener, 1992.

Bauer, Kurt. *Nationalsozialismus: Ursprünge, Anfänge, Aufstieg und Fall*. UTB 3076. Vienna: Böhlau, 2008.

Bautz, Friedrich Wilhelm, "Dibelius, Otto." *Bibiographisch-Biographisches Lexikon* I (1990), 1281–3.

Becker, Jürgen. *Das Evangelium nach Johannes*. Ökumenisch-Theologischer Kommentar NT 4,1. 3rd ed. Gütersloh: Gütersloher Verlagshaus/Mohn, 1991.

Becker, Jürgen and Ulrich Luz. *Die Briefe an die Galater, Epheser und Kolosser: Übersetzt und erklärt von Jürgen Becker und Ulrich Luz*. Neues Testament Deutsch 8/1. 18th ed. Göttingen: Vandenhoeck & Ruprecht, 1998.

Bedford-Strohm, Heinrich. "Geschenkte Freiheit: Von welchen Voraussetzungen lebt der demokratische Staat?" *Zeitschrift für Evangelische Ethik* 49 (2005): 248–65.

———. "Öffentliche Theologie in der Zivilgesellschaft." In *Politik und Theologie in Europa: Perspektiven ökumenischer Sozialethik*. Edited by Ingeborg Gabriel. Mainz: Grünewald, 2008, 340–66.

Beevor, Antony. *The Second World War.* New York: Little, Brown & Co., 2012.

Beintker, Michael. *Die Dialektik in der 'dialektischen Theologie' Karl Barths.* Beiträge zur evangelischen Theologie 101. Munich: Kaiser, 1985.

———. "Krisis und Gnade: Zur theologischen Deutung der Dialektik beim frühen Barth." In *Krisis und Gnade: Gesammelte Studien zu Karl Barth.* Edited by Stefan Holtmann and Peter Zocher. Tübingen: Mohr Siebeck, 2013, 22–39.

———. "Die politische Verantwortung der Christengemeinde im Denken Barths." *Zeitschrift für Dialektische Theologie* 12 (1996): 149–74.

Beintker, Michael, Christian Link, and Michael Trowitzsch, eds. *Karl Barth in Deutschland (1921–1935): Aufbruch—Klärung—Widerstand: Beiträge zum Internationalen Symposium vom 1. bis 4. Mai 2003 in der Johannes a Lasco Bibliothek Emden.* Zurich: Theologischer Verlag, 2005.

———. *Karl Barth im europäischen Zeitgeschehen (1935–1950): Widerstand—Bewährung—Orientierung. Beiträge zum Internationalen Symposion vom 1. bis 4. Mai 2008 in der Johannes a Lasco Bibliothek, Emden.* Zurich: Theologischer Verlag, 2010.

Beiser, Frederick, *Schiller as Philosopher: A Re-Examination.* Oxford: Clarendon, 2005.

Benda, Ernst, "Rechtsstaat." In *Lexikon der Politik: Begriffe, Theorie, Methoden, Fakten: Politische Theorien.* Edited by Dieter Nohlen. Munich: Beck, 1995, 515–18.

Berkouwer, Gerrit C. *Der Triumph der Gnade in der Theologie Karl Barths.* Neukirchen: Verlag der Buchhandlung des Erziehungsvereins, 1957.

Bethge, Eberhard. *Dietrich Bonhoeffer: Eine Biographie.* Kaiser Taschenbücher 69. 8th ed. Gütersloh: Kaiser/Gütersloher Verlagshaus, 1994.

Biggar, Nigel, "Barth's Trinitarian Ethic." In *Cambridge Companion to Karl Barth.* Edited by Webster, 212–27.

———. "A Case for Casuistry in the Church." *Modern Theology* 6 (1989): 29–51.

———. *In Defence of War.* Oxford: Oxford University Press, 2013.

———. *The Hastening That Waits: Karl Barth's Ethics.* Oxford: Clarendon, 1993.

———. "Hearing God's Command and Thinking About What's Right: With and Beyond Barth." In *Reckoning With Barth,* 101–18.

———. *Reckoning With Barth: Essays in Commemoration of the Centenary of Karl Barth's Birth.* London: Mowbray, 1988.

Bird, Phyllis, "Images of Women in the Old Testament." In *Religion and Sexism: Images of Women in the Jewish and Christian Traditions.* Edited by Rosemary Radford Ruether. Eugene: Wipf & Stock, 1998, 41–88.

Blanford, Nicholas, "Gibson's Movie Unlikely Box-Office Hit in Arab World." *Christian Science Monitor.* April 9, 2004. http://bit.ly/blWL1z.

Blasius, Rainer A., "Appeasement und Widerstand 1938." In *Widerstand gegen den Nationalsozialismus.* Edited by Steinbach and Tuchel, 280–93.

Blass, Friedrich, and Albert Debrunner. *A Greek Grammar of the New Testament and Other Early Christian Literature.* Translated by Robert W. Funk. Chicago: Chicago University Press, 1961.

Bonhoeffer, Dietrich, "Address to the Fanø Conference: English Transcription" ["The Church and the Peoples of the World"]. In *London: 1933–34.* Edited by Keith Clements, translated by Isabel Best. Dietrich Bonhoeffer Works 13. Minneapolis: Fortress, 2007, 307–10.

———. "After Ten Years." Translated by Barbara and Martin Rumscheidt. In *Letters and Papers from Prison.* Edited by John W. de Gruchy, translated by Isabel Best, Lisa Dahill, et al. Dietrich Bonhoeffer Works 8. Minneapolis: Fortress Press, 2009, 37–52.

———. "The Church and the Jewish Question." In *Berlin: 1932–1933.* Edited by Larry Rasmussen, translated by Isabel Best and David Higgins.

Dietrich Bonhoeffer Works 12. Minneapolis: Fortress Press, 2009, 361–73.

———. "Lecture in Ciernohorské Kúpele: On the Theological Foundation of the Work of the World Alliance." In *Ecumenical, Academic, and Pastoral Work: 1931–1932*. Edited by Victoria J. Barnett et al., translated by Anne Schmidt-Lange et al. Dietrich Bonhoeffer Works 11. Minneapolis: Fortress Press, 2012, 356–69.

Borowsky, Peter. "Sozialliberale Koalition und innere Reformen." In *Zeiten des Wandels: Deutschland 1961–1974*. Edited by Bundeszentrale für politische Bildung. Informationen zur politischen Bildung 258. Bonn: bpb, 1998. www.bit.ly/JrG5iC.

Böttrich, Christfried. "Proexistenz im Leben und Sterben: Jesu Tod bei Lukas." In *Deutungen des Todes Jesu im Neuen Testament*. Edited by Jörg Frey and Jens Schröter. UTB 2953. Tübingen: Mohr Siebeck, 2007, 413–36.

Brakelmann, Hans. *Hans Ehrenberg: Ein judenchristliches Schicksal in Deutschland: Leben, Denken, Wirken 1883–1932*. Schriften der Hans Ehrenberg Gesellschaft 3. Waltrop: Spenner, 1997.

Brooke, John Hedley. *Science and Religion: Some Historical Perspectives*. The Cambridge History of Science Series. Cambridge: Cambridge University Press, 1991.

Brown, Raymond E., SS. *The Death of the Messiah: From Gethsemane to the Grave; A Commentary on the Passion Narratives in the Four Gospels*. Vol. 2, Anchor Bible Reference Library. New York: Doubleday, 1994.

Brunner, Emil. *The Divine Imperative: A Study in Christian Ethics*. Translated by Olive Wyon. London: Lutterworth Press, 1937.

———. Letter to Barth (July 9, 1941). In *Karl Barth—Emil Brunner: Briefwechsel 1916–1966*. Edited by Eberhard Busch. Barth-Gesamtausgabe. Zurich: Theologischer Verlag, 2000, 312–15.

———. "Natural Theology." In *Natural Theology: Comprising "Natural*

Theology" by Emil Brunner and the Reply "No" by Karl Barth. Edited and translated by Peter Fraenkel. Eugene: Wipf & Stock, 2002.

Buber, Martin. "Offener Brief an Gerhard Kittel." *Theologische Blätter* 12 (1933): 4–6.

Bühler, Pierre. *Kreuz und Eschatologie: Eine Auseinandersetzung mit der politischen Theologie, im Anschluss an Luthers theologia crucis.* Hermeneutische Untersuchungen zur Theologie 17. Tübingen: Mohr Siebeck, 1981.

Bühling, Kai Joachim and Wolfgang Friedmann. *Der Intensivkurs: Gynäkologie und Geburtshilfe.* Munich and Jena: Urban & Fischer, 2004.

Burchardt, Rainer. "Vom Minister zur Galionsfigur der Friedensbewegung: Zeitzeugen im Gespräch: Erhard Eppler." *Deutschlandradio.* November 27th, 2008. http://tinyurl.com/nskt4c2.

Burgsmüller, Alfred, ed. *Zum politischen Auftrag der christlichen Gemeinde (Barmen II): Votum des Theologischen Ausschusses der Evangelischen Kirche der Union.* Gütersloh: Gütersloher Verlagshaus/Mohn, 1974.

Busch, Eberhard. "Antworten, die zu Fragen wurden. Die Bedeutung des Tambacher Vortrags für K. Barths eigenen Weg." In *Der Christ in der Gesellschaft: Tambach 1919—1994.* Edited by Wilhelm Ebting. Tambach-Dietharz 1994, 9–21; http://wwwuser.gwdg.de/~ebusch/tambach.htm.

———. *The Barmen Theses Then and Now: The 2004 Warfield Lectures at Princeton Theological Seminary.* Translated by Darrell Guder and Judith Guder. Grand Rapids: Eerdmans, 2010.

———. *Die Anfänge des Theologen Karl Barth in seinen Göttinger Jahren.* Göttinger Universitätsreden 83. Göttingen: Vandenhoeck & Ruprecht, 1986.

———. *Karl Barth: His Life from Letters and Autobiographical Texts.* Translated by John Bowden. Eugene: Wipf & Stock, 2005.

———. *Karl Barth und die Pietisten: Die Pietismuskritik des jungen Karl Barth und ihre Erwiderung.* Beiträge zur evangelischen Theologie 82. Munich: Kaiser, 1978.

———. *Unter dem Bogen des einen Bundes: Karl Barth und die Juden 1933–1945.* Neukirchen-Vluyn: Neukirchener, 1996.

Calvin, John, *Institutes of the Christian Religion.* Edited by John T. McNeill, translated by John L. Battles. The Library of Christian Classics. Louisville: Westminster John Knox, 2006.

———. *Institutio Christianae Religionis: In libros quatuor nunc primum digesta ...1559.* Edited by Wilhelm Baum and Eduard Cunitz. Corpus Reformatorum 29. Braunschweig: Schwetschke, 1963.

Camus, Albert. *The Myth of Sisyphus.* Translated by Justin O'Brien. Penguin Great Ideas. London: Penguin, 2005.

Carey, Holly J. *Jesus' Cry From the Cross: Towards a First-Century Understanding of the Intertextual Relationship between Psalm 22 and the Narrative of Mark's Gospel.* The Library of New Testament Studies. New York: T&T Clark, 2009.

Clayton, Philip. *Explanations from Physics to Theology: An Essay in Rationality and Religion.* New Haven: Yale University Press, 1989.

Clements, Keith. "Ecumenical Witness for Peace." In *The Cambridge Companion to Dietrich Bonhoeffer.* Edited by John de Gruchy. Cambridge Companions to Religion. Cambridge: Cambridge University Press, 1999, 154–72.

Clough, David. *Ethics in Crisis: Interpreting Barth's Ethics.* Barth Studies Series. Aldershot and Burlington, USA: Ashgate, 2005.

———. "Fighting at the Command of God: Reassessing the Borderline Case in Karl Barth's Account of War in the *Church Dogmatics.*" In *Conversing with Barth.* Edited by John C. McDowell and Mike Higton. Barth Studies. Aldershot: Ashgate, 2004, 214–26.

Congdon, David. "The Spirit of Freedom: Eberhard Jüngel's Theology of the Third Article." In *Indicative of Grace—Imperative of Freedom: Essays in*

Honour of Eberhard Jüngel in His 80th Year. Edited by David Nelson. T&T Clark Theology. New York: Bloomsbury/T&T Clark, 2014, 13–28.

Council of the Evangelical Church in Germany. *Live from God's Peace—Care for Just Peace* (2007). Evangelische Kirche in Deutschland. http://tinyurl.com/qzkr9yy.

Cousar, Charles B. *The Letters of Paul*. Interpreting Biblical Texts. Nashville: Abingdon, 1996.

Craig, Gordon A. *Deutsche Geschichte 1866–1945: Vom Norddeutschen Bund bis zum Ende des Dritten Reiches*. Munich: Beck, 1996.

Crüsemann, Frank. *Bewahrung der Freiheit: Das Thema des Dekalogs in sozialgeschichtlicher Perspektive*. Kaiser Taschenbücher 78. Munich: Kaiser, 1983.

Dahl, Nils A. *Studies in Paul*. Minneapolis: Augsburg Fortress Press, 1977.

Dalferth, Ingolf U. *Der auferweckte Gekreuzigte: Zur Grammatik der Christologie*. Tübingen: Mohr Siebeck, 1994.

———. "Karl Barth's Eschatological Realism." In *Karl Barth: Centenary Essays*. Edited by Stephen W. Sykes. Cambridge: Cambridge University Press, 1989, 14–45.

———. "'Was Gott ist, bestimme ich!' Theologie im Zeitalter der 'Caféteria-Religion.'" In *Gedeutete Gegenwart: Zur Wahrnehmung Gottes in den Wahrnehmungen der Zeit*. Tübingen: Mohr Siebeck, 1997, 10–35.

Dannemann, Ulrich, *Theologie und Politik im Denken Karl Barths*. Gesellschaft und Theologie: Systematische Beiträge 22. Munich: Kaiser and Mainz: Grünewald, 1977.

Davey, Monica. "Doctor's Killer Puts Abortion on the Stand." *New York Times*, January 29, 2010, A1. http://www.nytimes.com/2010/01/29/us/29roeder.html.

Deacon, Terrence, "The Symbol Concept." In *The Oxford Handbook of Language Evolution*. Edited by Maggie Tallerman and Kathleen R.

Gibson. Oxford Handbooks in Linguistics. Oxford: Oxford University Press, 2012, 393–405.

De Gruchy, John, "Racism, Reconciliation, and Resistance." In *On Reading Karl Barth in South Africa*. Edited by Villa-Vicencio, 139–55.

Demut, André. *Evangelium und Gesetz: Eine systematisch-theologische Reflexion zu Karl Barths Predigtwerk.* Theologische Bibliothek Töpelmann 145. New York: de Gruyter, 2008.

Dibelius, Otto. *Das Jahrhundert der Kirche: Geschichte, Betrachtung, Umschau und Ziele.* 5th ed. Berlin: Furche, 1928.

Dignath, Walter. "Friedensbewegung." In *Religion in Geschichte und Gegenwart.* 3rd ed. Tübingen: Mohr Siebeck, 1958, 2:1138.

Dreves, Guido Maria. *Hymnographi Latini: Lateinische Hymnendichter des Mittelalters. Analecta Hymnica Medii Aevi* 50. Leipzig: N.N., 1907.

Drewes, Hans-Anton. "Die Auseinandersetzung mit Adolf von Harnack." In *Karl Barth in Deutschland (1921–1935): Aufbruch—Klärung—Widerstand.* Edited by Beintker et al., 189–204.

Ebach, Jürgen. "Zum Thema: Arbeit und Ruhe im Alten Testament: Eine utopische Erinnerung." *Zeitschrift für Evangelische Ethik* 24 (1980): 7–21.

Ebeling, Gerhard. "Karl Barths Ringen mit Luther." In *Lutherstudien: Begriffsuntersuchungen—Textinterpretationen—Werkgeschichtliches.* Tübingen: Mohr Siebeck, 1985, 3:428–573.

Ehrenberg, Hans. "Geleitwort." In "Der Christ in der Gesellschaft: Eine Tambacher Rede. Mit einem Geleitwort von Hans Ehrenberg," by Karl Barth. Der Bücher vom Kreuzweg erste Folge. Würzburg: Patmos-Verlag, 1920, iii–vi.

Elert, Werner. "Dialektik der Offenbarung." In *Gesetz und Evangelium: Beiträge zur gegenwärtigen theologischen Diskussion.* Edited by Ernst Kinder and Klaus Haendler. Erträge der Forschung 142. Darmstadt: Wissenschaftliche Buchgesellschaft, 1968, 159–65.

Encyclopaedia Britannica Inc. "Theobald von Bethmann Hollweg,"

Encyclopaedia Britannica Online Academic Edition, 2014. http://academic.eb.com.ubproxy.ub.uni-heidelberg.de/EBchecked/topic/63463/Theobald-von-Bethmann-Hollweg (subscription required).

Etzelmüller, Gregor. *". . . zu richten die Lebendigen und die Toten": Zur Rede vom Jüngsten Gericht im Anschluss an Karl Barth.* Neukirchen-Vluyn: Neukirchener, 2001.

Falcke, Heino. "Aspekte der gegenwärtigen Friedensdiskussion beleuchtet durch Karl Barths Friedensethik." *Zeitschrift für Dialektische Theologie* 12 (1996): 175–91.

———. "Was hatte die Barmer Theologische Erklärung den Kirchen in der DDR zu sagen?" *Ökumenische Rundschau* 58 (2009): 28–37.

Fergusson, David. *Community, Liberalism and Christian Ethics.* New Studies in Christian Ethics 13. Cambridge: Cambridge University Press, 1998.

Fest, Joachim. *Staatsstreich: Der lange Weg zum 20. Juli.* Berlin: Siedler, 1994.

Fischer, Johannes. *Theologische Ethik. Grundwissen und Orientierung.* Forum Systematik 11. Stuttgart et al.: Kohlhammer, 2002.

———. "Theologische Ethik und Christologie." *Zeitschrift für Theologie und Kirche* 92 (1995): 481–516.

Frei, Hans W. *Theology and Narrative: Selected Essays.* Edited by George Hunsinger and William Placher. New York: Oxford University Press, 1993.

Frey, Jörg. "Die '*theologia crucifixi*' des Johannesevangeliums." In *Kreuzestheologie im Neuen Testament.* Edited by Andreas Dettwiler and Jean Zumstein. Wissenschaftliche Untersuchungen zum Neuen Testament 151. Tübingen: Mohr Siebeck, 2002, 169–238.

Friedman, Thomas L. "The First Law of Petropolitics." *Foreign Policy* 154 (May–June 2006): 28–36.

Gemeinsame Konferenz Kirche und Entwicklung (GKKE), Fachgruppe Rüstungsexporte. "Rüstungsexportbericht 2012." GKKE-Schriftenreihe 58. Bonn and Berlin, 2013. http://tinyurl.com/ouq3h8a.

———. "Rüstungsexportbericht 2013." GKKE-Schriftenreihe 59. Bonn and Berlin 2014. http://tinyurl.com/lw9skbd.

———. "Rüstungsexportbericht 2014." Bonn and Berlin 2014. http://tinyurl.com/lflmqdw.

Gockel, Matthias. *Barth and Schleiermacher on the Doctrine of Election: A Systematic–Theological Comparison*. Oxford: Oxford University Press, 2006.

Gockel, Matthias, and Martin Leiner. "Kritik und Versöhnung. Karl Barth und die DDR." In Leiner and Trowitzsch, *Karl Barths Theologie als europäisches Ereignis*, 79–119.

Goebel, Hans Theodor. "Trinitätslehre und Erwählungslehre bei Karl Barth: Eine Problemanzeige." In *Wahrheit und Versöhnung: Theologische und philosophische Beiträge zur Gotteslehre*. Edited by Dietrich Korsch and Hartmut Ruddies. Gütersloh: Gütersloher Verlagshaus, 1989, 147–66.

Goethe, Johann Wolfgang von. "Die Geheimnisse. Ein Fragment." *Werke* 1:16. Edited by Erich Schmidt and Wilhelm Fielitz, et al. Weimar: Böhlau, 1894, 173.

———. *Wilhelm Meister's Apprenticeship*. Translated by Eric A. Blackall. New York: Suhrkamp, 1989.

———. Zahme Xenien VI. *Werke* 1:3. Edited by Gustav von Loeper, 363. Weimar: Böhlau, 1890, 1766–73.

———. "Zu den Leiden des jungen Werther." *Werke*. Edited by Gustav von Loeper and Bernhard Suphan. Weimar: Böhlau, 1981, 1:4.

Gogarten, Friedrich. "Karl Barths Dogmatik." *Theologische Revue* 1 (1929): 60–80.

Gorringe, Timothy J. *Karl Barth: Against Hegemony*. Christian Theology in Context. Oxford: Oxford University Press, 1999.

———. "Karl Barth on Romans." In *The Oxford Handbook of the Reception History of the Bible*. Edited by Michael Lieb, Emma Mason, and Jonathan Roberts. Oxford: Oxford University Press, 2011, 590–608.

Graf, Friedrich Wilhelm. "'Der Götze wackelt'? Erste Überlegungen zu Karl Barths Lieberalismus-Kritik." *Evangelische Theologie* 46 (1986): 422–41.

Graham, Gordon. *Eight Theories of Ethics*. New York: Routledge, 2004.

Graß, Hans. "Luthers Zwei-Reiche-Lehre." *Zeitschrift für Evangelisches Kirchenrecht* 31 (1986): 146–78.

Grewe, Wilhelm G. *Epochen der Völkerrechtsgeschichte*. Baden-Baden: Nomos, 1984.

Grünhut, Max. "Todesstrafe." *Religion in Geschichte und Gegenwart*. 2nd ed. Tübingen: Mohr Siebeck, 1931, 5:1202–8.

Gundlach, Thies. *Selbstbegrenzung Gottes und die Autonomie des Menschen: Karl Barths Kirchliche Dogmatik als Modernisierungsschritt evangelischer Theologie*. Europäische Hochschulschriften Theologie 471. Frankfurt am Main et al.: Lang, 1992.

———. "Theologische Ethik unter modernen Bedingungen: Zu den politischen Implikationen der Ethik Karl Barths von 1928/29." *Kerygma und Dogma* 37 (1991): 209–26.

Gustafson, James M. *Can Ethics Be Christian?* 2nd ed. Chicago: University of Chicago Press, 1977.

———. *Ethics from a Theocentric Perspective: Ethics and Theology*. Chicago: University of Chicago Press, 1992.

———. "The Sectarian Temptation: Reflections on Theology, the Church, and the University." In *Moral Discernment in the Christian Life: Essays on Theological Themes*. Edited by Theo A. Boer and Paul E. Capetz. Library of Theological Ethics. Louisville: Westminster John Knox, 2007, 142–54.

Habermas, Jürgen. *Between Facts and Norms: Between a Discourse Theory of Law and Democracy*. Translated by William Rehg. 2nd ed. Cambridge, MA: MIT Press, 1996.

Hancock, Angela Dienhart. "Training for a Serious Game: Theo-Political Deliberation as a Christian Practice," in *Theo-Politics? Conversing with*

Barth in Western and Asian Contexts. Edited by Markus Höfner. Minneapolis: Fortress Press, 2016.

Harasta, Eva. *Lob und Bitte: Eine systematisch-theologische Untersuchung über das Gebet*. Neukirchen-Vluyn: Neukirchener, 2005.

Härle, Wilfried. "Der Aufruf der 93 Intellektuellen und Karl Barths Bruch mit der liberalen Theologie." *Zeitschrift für Theologie und Kirche* 72 (1975): 207–24.

———. "Luthers Zwei-Regimenten-Lehre als Lehre vom Handeln Gottes." *MJTh* I (1987): 12–32.

———. *Sein und Gnade: Die Ontologie in Karl Barths Kirchlicher Dogmatik*. Theologische Bibliothek Töpelmann 27. New York: de Gruyter, 1975.

———. "Zwei-Reiche-Lehre II: Systematisch-Theologisch." *Theologische Realenzyklopädie*. New York: de Gruyter, 2004, 36:784–9.

Haspel, Michael. "Einführung in die Friedensethik." In *Friedens- und Konfliktforschung: Eine Einführung mit Quellen*. Edited by Peter Imbusch and Ralf Zoll. 2nd ed. Opladen: Leske + Budrich, 1999.

Haudel, Matthias. "Das Verhältnis von Gesetz und Evangelium als innerprotestantische und interkonfessionelle Herausforderung." *Kerygma und Dogma* 53 (2007): 230–49.

Hauschild, Wolf-Dieter. *Lehrbuch der Kirchen- und Dogmengeschichte: Alte Kirche und Mittelalter*. Gütersloh: Kaiser/Gütersloher Verlagshaus, 1995.

Hays, Richard B. *The Moral Vision of the New Testament: Cross, Community, New Creation; A Contemporary Introduction to New Testament Ethics*. San Francisco: Harper Collins, 1996.

Heidegger, Martin. *Being and Time*. Translated by John Macquarrie and Edward Robinson, 6th reprint. Oxford: Basil Blackwell, 1985.

———. *Discourse on Thinking*. Translated by John M. Anderson and E. Hans Freud. Harper Torchbooks 1459. New York: Harper & Row, 1966.

Heinemann, Gustav Walter. *Einspruch: Ermutigung für entschiedene Demokraten*. Edited by Diether Koch. Bonn: Dietz, 1999.

Hengel, Martin. *Crucifixion in the Ancient World and the Folly of the Message of the Cross*. Translated by John Bowden. 2nd ed. Minneapolis: Fortress Press, 1978.

Hertz, Anselm and Wilhelm Korff. *Handbuch der christlichen Ethik*. Vol. 1. Freiburg: Herder and Gütersloh: Gütersloher Verlagshaus Mohn, 1978.

Hickmann, Christoph. "Opposition rügt möglichen Panzer-Deal." *Süddeutsche Zeitung*. Dec. 3, 2012. http://tinyurl.com/bqef8e5.

Hirsch, Emanuel. "Kurzer Unterricht in der christlichen Religion." In *Das kirchliche Wollen der Deutschen Christen*, Schriftenreihe der Deutschen Christen. 2nd ed. Berlin: Grevemeyer, 1933, 17–20.

Hoegen-Rohls, Christina. *Der nachösterliche Johannes: Die Abschiedsreden als hermeneutischer Schlüssel zum vierten Evangelium*. Welt und Umwelt des Neuen Testaments II 84. Tübingen: Mohr Siebeck, 1996.

Höffe, Otfried. *Gerechtigkeit: Eine philosophische Einführung*. Beck Wissen, Beck'sche Reihe 2168. Munich: Beck, 2001.

Hoffmann, Peter. *Stauffenberg und der 20. Juli 1944*. Beck Wissen, Beck'sche Reihe 2102. 2nd ed. Munich: Beck, 2007.

Hofheinz, Marco. *"Er ist unser Friede": Karl Barths christologische Grundlegung der Friedensethik im Gespräch mit John Howard Yoder*. Forschungen zur systematischen und ökumenischen Theologie 144. Göttingen: Vandenhoeck & Ruprecht, 2014.

Hofius, Otfried. "Sühne IV: Neues Testament." *Theologische Realenzyklopädie*. New York: de Gruyter, 2001, 32:342–7.

Höfner, Markus, ed. *Theo-Politics? Conversing with Barth in Western and Asian Contexts*. Minneapolis: Fortress Press, 2016.

Holl, Karl. "Die Geschichte des Wortes Beruf." In *Gesammelte Aufsätze zur Kirchengeschichte: Der Westen*. Tübingen: Mohr Siebeck, 1928, 189–219.

———. *What Did Luther Understand by Religion?* Edited by James L. Adams and Walter F. Bense. Translated by Fred W. Meuser and Walter R. Wietzke. Minneapolis: Augsburg Fortress Press, 1977.

Holtmann, Stefan. "Dialektische Theologie im Streit um die Neuzeit: Zur Auseinandersetzung zwischen Karl Barth und Friedrich Gogarten." *Zeitschrift für Dialektische Theologie* 23 (2007): 246–62.

———. *Karl Barth als Theologe der Neuzeit: Studien zur kritischen Deutung seiner Theologie.* Forschungen zur systematischen und ökumenischen Theologie 118. Göttingen: Vandenhoeck & Ruprecht, 2007.

Hong, Liang. "Leben vor den letzten Dingen." PhD dissertation. Tübingen: 2015.

Honecker, Martin. *Einführung in die theologische Ethik: Grundlagen und Grundbegriffe.* De Gruyter Lehrbuch. New York: de Gruyter, 1990.

———. *Grundriss der Sozialethik.* De Gruyter Lehrbuch. New York: de Gruyter, 1995.

———. "Das Problem des theologischen Konstruktivismus." *Zeitschrift für evangelische Ethik* 24 (1980): 97–111.

———. "Vernunft, Gewissen, Glaube: Das spezifisch Christliche im Horizont der Ethik." *Zeitschrift für Theologie und Kirche* 77 (1980): 325–44.

———. "Weltliches Handeln unter der Herrschaft Christi: Zur Interpretation von Barmen II." *Zeitschrift für Theologie und Kirche* 96 (1972): 72–99.

Hrdy, Sarah Blaffer. *Mothers and Others: The Evolutionary Origins of Mutual Understanding*. Cambridge, MA: Belknap, 2011.

Hubatsch, Walter C. "Alfred von Tirpitz," *Encyclopaedia Britannica Online Academic Edition*, 2014. http://academic.eb.com.ubproxy.ub.uni-heidelberg.de/EBchecked/topic/596876/Alfred-von-Tirpitz (subscription required).

Huber, Wolfgang. "Anspruch und Beschaffenheit theologischer Ethik als Integrationswissenschaft." In Hertz and Korff, *Handbuch der christlichen Ethik*, 1:391–406.

———. *Folgen christlicher Freiheit: Ethik und Theorie der Kirche im Horizont der Barmer Theologischen Erklärung.* Neukirchener Beiträge zur

Systematischen Theologie 4. 2nd ed. Neukirchen-Vluyn: Neukirchener, 1985.

———. "Frieden V. Kirchengeschichtlich und ethisch." *Theologische Realenzyklopädie*. New York: de Gruyter, 1983, 11:618–46.

———. *Gerechtigkeit und Recht: Grundlinien christlicher Rechtsethik*. Gütersloh: Kaiser/Gütersloher Verlagshaus, 1996.

———. "'Nur wer die Schöpfung liebt, kann sie retten': Naturzerstörung und Schöpfungsglaube." In *Konflikt und Konsens: Studien zur Ethik der Verantwortung*. Munich: Kaiser, 1990. 176—94.

———. "Sozialethik als Verantwortungsethik." In *Konflikt und Konsens: Studien zur Ethik der Verantwortung*. Munich: Kaiser, 1990, 135–57.

———. "Streit um das rechte Handeln: Zwischen persönlicher Vergewisserung und gemeinsamer Aktion." In *Konflikt und Konsens: Studien zur Ethik der Verantwortung*. Munich: Kaiser, 1990. 272-90.

Hunsinger, George. *Disruptive Grace: Studies in the Theology of Karl Barth*. Grand Rapids: Eerdmans, 2000.

———. "Justification and Justice: Toward an Evangelical Social Ethic." In *Karl Barth im europäischen Zeitgeschehen (1935–1950)*. Edited by Beintker et al., 457–70.

———. "Karl Barth and Liberation Theology." In *Disruptive Grace*, 42–59.

———. "Postliberal Theology." In *The Cambridge Companion to Postmodern Theology*. Edited by Kevin J. Vanhoozer. Cambridge Companions to Religion. Cambridge: Cambridge University Press, 2003, 42–57.

———. "What Can Evangelicals and Postliberals Learn from Each Other? The Carl Henry/Hans Frei Exchange Reconsidered." In *Disruptive Grace*, 338–60.

Hütter, Reinhard. *Evangelische Ethik als kirchliches Zeugnis: Interpretationen zu Schlüsselfragen theologischer Ethik in der Gegenwart*. Evangelium und Ethik 1. Neukirchen-Vluyn: Neukirchener, 1993.

Iwand, Hans Joachim. "Das geschichtliche Phänomen der Atomwaffe und die Angst—Ein Versuch ihrer Überwindung (1955)." In *Frieden mit dem Osten: Texte 1933–1959*. Edited by Gerard C. den Hertog. Kaiser Taschenbuch 28. Munich: Kaiser, 1988, 97–124.

———. *Tod und Auferstehung: Christologie II. Vorlesung*, Bonn 1959. In *Christologie: Die Umkehrung des Menschen zur Menschlichkeit*. Edited by Eberhard Lempp and Edgar Thaidigsmann. Nachgelassene Werke, Neue Folge 2. Gütersloh: Gütersloher Verlagshaus, 1999, 291–433.

Janowski, Bernd. "Er trug unsere Sünden: Jes 53 und die Dramatik der Stellvertretung." In *Der leidende Gottesknecht. Jesaja 53 und seine Wirkungsgeschichte; mit einer Bibliographie zu Jes 53*. Edited by Bernd Janowski and Peter Stuhlmacher. Tübingen: Mohr Siebeck, 1996, 27–48.

———. "'Hingabe' oder 'Opfer'? Zur gegenwärtigen Kontroverse um die Deutung des Todes Jesu." In *Das Kreuz Jesu. Gewalt—Opfer—Sühne*, by Rudolf Weth. Neukirchen-Vluyn: Neukirchener, 2001, 13–43.

———. *Konfliktgespräche mit Gott: Eine Anthropologie der Psalmen*. Neukirchen-Vluyn: Neukirchener, 2003.

———. "Tempel und Schöpfung: Schöpfungstheologische Aspekte der priesterschriftlichen Heiligtumskonzeption." In *Schöpfung und Neuschöpfung*. Jahrbuch für Biblische Theologie 5. Neukirchen-Vluyn: Neukirchener, 1990, 37–69.

Jeffreys, Derek S. "How Reformed Is Reformed Epistemology? Alvin Plantinga and Calvin's 'Sensus Divinitatis.'" *Religious Studies* 33 (1997): 419–31.

Jehle, Frank. *Ever against the Stream: The Politics of Karl Barth, 1906–1968*. Translated by Richard Burnett and Martha Burnett. Eugene: Wipf & Stock, 2012.

Jenson, Robert. *Systematic Theology: The Triune God*. Oxford: Oxford University Press, 1997.

Joest, Wilfried. "Karl Barth und das lutherische Verständnis von Gesetz und Evangelium: Gedanken und Fragen zur Wiederaufnahme einer stehengebliebenen Diskussion." *Kerygma und Dogma* 24 (1978): 86–103.

Jonas, Hans. "The Concept of God after Auschwitz: A Jewish Voice." *The Journal of Religion* 67 (1987): 1–13.

———. *Gnosis und spätantiker Geist: Die mythologische Gnosis: Mit einer Einleitung zur Geschichte und Methodologie der Forschung.* Forschungen zur Religion und Literatur des Alten und Neuen Testaments 51, Neue Folge 33. 3rd ed. Göttingen: Vandenhoeck & Ruprecht, 1964.

Jones, Paul Dafydd. "Karl Barth on Gethsemane." *International Journal of Systematic Theology* 9 (2007): 148–71.

———. *The Humanity of Christ: Christology in Karl Barth's Church Dogmatics.* T&T Clark Theology. New York: T&T Clark, 2008.

———. "The Rhetoric of War in Karl Barth's Epistle to the Romans: A Theological Analysis." *Journal for the History of Modern Theology/ Zeitschrift für Neuere Theologiegeschichte* 17 (2010): 90–111.

Jowers, Dennis W. "The Reproach of Modalism: A Difficulty for Karl Barth's Doctrine of the Trinity." *Scottish Journal of Theology* 56 (2003): 231–46.

Jüngel, Eberhard. "Barth's Life and Work." In *Karl Barth: A Theological Legacy*, 22–52.

———. "Die Offenbarung der Verborgenheit Gottes: Ein Beitrag zum evangelischen Verständnis der Verborgenheit des göttlichen Wirkens." In *Wertlose Wahrheit: Zur Identität und Relevanz des christlichen Glaubens.* Theologische Erörterungen III. Munich: Kaiser 1990, 163–82.

———. *God as the Mystery of the World: On the Foundation of the Theology of the Crucified One in the Dispute between Theism and Atheism.* Translated by Darrell L. Guder. Grand Rapids: Eerdmans, 1983.

———. "Gospel and Law: The Relationship of Dogmatics and Ethics." In *Karl Barth: A Theological Legacy*, 105–26.

———. *Karl Barth: A Theological Legacy*. Translated by Garrett E. Paul. Philadelphia: Westminster John Knox, 1986.

———. ". . . keine Menschenlosigkeit Gottes . . .: Zur Theologie Barths zwischen Theismus und Atheismus." In *Barth-Studien.* Ökumenische

Theologie 9. Zurich and Cologne: Benziger/Gütersloh: Gütersloher Verlagshaus Gerd Mohn, 1982, 332–47.

———. "Quae supra nos, nihil ad nos: Eine Kurzformel der Lehre vom verborgenen Gott—im Anschluss an Luther interpretiert." *Evangelische Theologie* 32 (1972): 197–240.

———. "The Revelation of the Hiddenness of God: A Contribution to the Protestant Understanding of the Hiddenness of Divine Action." In *Theological Essays* II, translated byArnold Neufeldt-Fast. New York: Bloomsbury/T&T Clark, 2014, 120–44.

———. "Zum Verhältnis von Kirche und Staat nach Karl Barth." In *Zur Theologie Karl Barths: Beiträge aus Anlass seines 100. Geburtstags*. Zeitschrift für Theologie und Kirche Beiheft 6. Tübingen: Mohr Siebeck, 1986, 76–135.

Kane, Robert. *A Contemporary Introduction to Free Will.* Fundamentals of Philosophy. New York: Oxford University Press, 2005.

Kant, Immanuel. "An Answer to the Question: 'What Is Enlightenment?'" In *Political Writings*. Edited by Hans S. Reiss, translated by H. B. Nisbet. Cambridge Texts in the History of Political Thought. 2nd ed. Cambridge: Cambridge University Press, 1991, 54–60.

———. *Critique of Judgment*. Translated by Werner S. Pluhar. Indianapolis: Hackett, 1987.

———. *Groundwork to the Metaphysics of Morals*. Edited and translated by Mary Gregor. Cambridge Texts in the History of Philosophy. Cambridge: Cambridge University Press, 1997.

———. *The Metaphysics of Morals*. Edited and translated by Mary Gregory. Cambridge Texts in the History of Philosophy. Cambridge: Cambridge University Press, 1991.

Käsemann, Ernst. *An die Römer*. Handkommentar zum Neuen Testament 8a. Tübingen: Mohr Siebeck, 1973.

———. "Worship and Everyday Life: A Note on Romans 12." In *New*

Testament Questions of Today, translated by W. J. Montague. London: S. C. M., 1969, 188–95.

Kaube, Jürgen. *Max Weber: Ein Leben zwischen den Epochen*. Berlin: Rowohlt, 2014.

Keller, Catherine. *Face of the Deep. A Theology of Becoming*. 2nd ed. New York: Routledge, 2005.

Kerr, Fergus. "Cartesianism according to Barth." *New Blackfriars* 77 (1996): 358–68.

Klappert, Bertold. *Die Auferweckung des Gekreuzigten: Der Ansatz der Christologie Karl Barths im Zusammenhang der Christologie der Gegenwart*. Neukirchen-Vluyn: Neukirchener, 1971.

———. *Promissio und Bund: Gesetz und Evangelium bei Luther und Barth*. Forschungen zur systematischen und ökumenischen Theologie 34. Göttingen: Vandenhoeck & Ruprecht, 1976.

———. "Die Rechts-, Freiheits- und Befreiungsgeschichte Gottes mit den Menschen: Zum Verständnis der Auferstehung in Karl Barths Versöhnungslehre." In *Versöhnung und Befreiung: Versuche, Karl Barth kontextuell zu verstehen*. Neukirchener Beiträge zur Systematischen Theologie 14. Neukirchen-Vluyn: Neukirchener, 1994, 118–37.

———. "Die Rezeption der Theologie Calvins in Karl Barths Kirchlicher Dogmatik: Einige vorläufige Überlegungen zu Barth als Schüler Calvins." In *Karl Barth und Johannes Calvin: Karl Barths Göttinger Calvin-Vorlesung von 1922*. Edited by Hans Scholl. Neukirchen-Vluyn: Neukirchener, 1995, 46–73.

Klemm, David. "Towards a Rhetoric of Postmodern Theology: Through Barth and Heidegger." *Journal of the American Academy of Religion* 55 (1987): 443–69.

Kliesch, Fabian. "Der Beginn des menschlichen Lebens aus medizinischer Sicht: Embryonalentwicklung als strukturierbares Kontinuum." In *Ethik im Kontinuum: Beiträge zur relationalen Erkenntnistheorie und Ontologie*.

Edited by Wilfried Härle. Marburger Jahrbuch Theologie 97. Leipzig: EVA, 2008, 127–42.

Knell, Hermann. *Untergang in Flammen: Strategische Bombenangriffe und ihre Folgen im Zweiten Weltkrieg*. Würzburg: Schöningh, 2006.

Knijff, Henri W. de. "Vom Korrektiv zum Ganzen der Dogmatik." *Verkündigung und Forschung* 46 (2001): 49–54.

Knöppler, Thomas. *Die theologia crucis des Johannesevangeliums: Das Verständnis des Todes Jesu im Rahmen der johanneischen Inkarnations- und Erlösungschristologie.* Wissenschaftliche Monographien zum Alten und Neuen Testament 69. Neukirchen-Vluyn: Neukirchener, 1994.

Köckert, Matthias. *Leben in Gottes Gegenwart: Studien zum Verständnis des Gesetzes im Alten Testament.* Forschungen zum Alten Testament 43. Tübingen: Mohr Siebeck, 2004.

Kohler-Weiß, Christiane. *Schutz der Menschwerdung: Schwangerschaft und Schwangerschaftskonflikt als Thema evangelischer Ethik.* Öffentliche Theologie 17. Gütersloh: Kaiser/Gütersloher Verlagshaus, 2003.

Kolb, Eberhard. *Die Weimarer Republik.* 7th ed. Oldenbourg Grundrisse der Geschichte 16. Munich: Oldenbourg, 2009.

Koller, Christian. "Der Lange Weg zum 'zivilen Ersatzdienst' in der Schweiz." In *Ich dien' nicht! Wehrdienstverweigerung in der Geschichte*. Edited by Dierk Walter and Christian Th. Müller. Berlin: Winter, 2008, 227–42.

Koopman, Nico N. "Status confessionis im Blick auf Apartheid, processus confessionis zu Fragen der ungerechten Weltwirtschaft: Zur Rezeption der Barmer Theologischen Erklärung in Südafrika." *Ökumenische Rundschau* 58 (2009): 167–80.

Korthaus, Michael. *Kreuzestheologie: Geschichte und Gehalt eines Programmbegriffs in der evangelischen Theologie.* Beiträge zur Historischen Theologie 142. Tübingen: Mohr Siebeck, 2007.

Kraus, Hans-Joachim. *Systematische Theologie im Kontext biblischer Geschichte und Eschatologie.* Neukirchen–Vluyn: Neukirchener, 1983.

Kreck, Walter. "Das Verständnis von Barmen II unter dem Stichwort 'Königsherrschaft Christi.'" In *Zum politischen Auftrag der christlichen Gemeinde*. Edited by Burgsmüller, 65–80.

Krötke, Wolf, "Das Problem 'Gesetz und Evangelium' bei W. Elert und P. Althaus." *Theologische Studien* 83. Zurich: Evangelischer Verlag, 1965.

——. "Die Schöpfungsordnungen im Lichte der Christologie: Zu Karl Barths Umgang mit einem unabweisbaren Problem." In *Barmen—Barth—Bonhoeffer: Beiträge zu einer zeitgemäßen christozentrischen Theologie*. Unio und Confessio 26. Bielefeld: Luther-Verlag, 2009, 155–78.

——. "Die Summe des Evangeliums: Karl Barths Erwählungslehre im Kontext der Kirchlichen Dogmatik." In Beintker, *Karl Barth im europäischen Zeitgeschehen (1935–1950)*, 67–82.

——. *Sünde und Nichtiges bei Karl Barth.* Neukirchener Beiträge zur Systematischen Theologie 3. 2nd ed. Neukirchen-Vluyn: Neukirchener, 1983.

Kümmel, Werner Georg. *Die Theologie des Neuen Testaments nach seinen Hauptzeugen: Jesus—Paulus—Johannes.* Grundrisse zum Neuen Testament 3. 4th ed. Göttingen: Vandenhoeck & Ruprecht, 1980.

Lang, Manfred. *Johannes und die Synoptiker: Eine redaktionsgeschichtliche Analyse von Joh 18–20 vor dem markinischen Hintergrund.* Forschungen zur Religion und Literatur des Alten und Neuen Testaments 182. Göttingen: Vandenhoeck & Ruprecht, 1999.

Lazier, Benjamin. *God Interrupted: Heresy and the European Imagination between the World Wars*. Princeton: Princeton University Press, 2008.

Leiner, Martin and Michael Trowitzsch. *Karl Barths Theologie als europäisches Ereignis*. Göttingen: Vandenhoeck & Ruprecht, 2008.

Lenin, Vladimir I. "Socialism and War: The Attitude of the R[ussian] S[ocial] D[emocratic] L[abor] P[arty] Toward the War." In *August 1914–December 1915*. Edited by Julius Katzer. Collected Works 21.

London: Lawrence & Wishart/Moscow: Progress Publishers, 1964, 295–338.

Lessing, Eckhard. *Das Problem der Gesellschaft in der Theologie Karl Barths und Friedrich Gogartens.* Studien zur Evangelischen Ethik 10. Gütersloh: Gütersloher Verlagshaus Mohn, 1972.

Lichtblau, Eric. "The Holocaust Just Got More Shocking." *The New York Times*, March 3, 2013. SR3.

Lienemann, Wolfgang. "Das Gebot Gottes als 'Ereignis': Bibelgebrauch und freie Verantwortlichkeit in der Ethik Karl Barths." *Zeitschrift für Dialektische Theologie* 15 (1999): 155–77.

———. "Das Problem des gerechten Krieges im deutschen Protestantismus nach dem Zweiten Weltkrieg." In *Der gerechte Krieg: Christentum, Islam, Marxismus.* Edited by Reiner Steinweg. Edition Suhrkamp 1017. Frankfurt am Main: Suhrkamp, 1980, 125–62.

———. "Gerechtigkeit und Versöhnung: Erinnerung erlittenen Unrechts im Kampf um ein neues Südafrika." In *Politik der Versöhnung.* Edited by Gerhard Beestermöller and Hans-Richard Reuter. Theologie und Frieden 23. Stuttgart: Kohlhammer, 2002, 197–230.

———. "Gewalt, Macht, Recht: Gewaltprävention und Rechtsentwicklung nach Karl Barth." *Zeitschrift für Dialektische Theologie* 17 (2001): 153–69.

———. "Verantwortungspazifismus (*legal pacifism*): Zum politischen Gestaltungspotential pazifistischer Bewegungen im Blick auf das Völkerrecht." In *Der gerechte Friede zwischen Pazifismus und gerechtem Krieg: Paradigmen der Friedensethik im Diskurs.* Edited by Jean-Daniel Strub and Stefan Grotefeld. Stuttgart: Kohlhammer, 2007, 75–99.

Lindbeck, George A. *The Nature of Doctrine: Religion and Theology in a Postliberal Age.* Louisville: Westminster Knox, 1984.

Lindenlauf, Herbert. *Karl Barth und die Lehre von der "Königsherrschaft Christi": Eine Untersuchung zum christozentrischen Ansatz der Ethik des*

Politischen im deutschsprachigen Protestantismus nach 1934. Spardorf: Wilfer, 1988.

Link, Christian. "Bleibende Einsichten von Tambach." In *Karl Barth in Deutschland (1921–1935): Aufbruch—Klärung—Widerstand*. Edited by Beintker et al., 333–46.

———. "Die Einführung des Subjekts: Ein methodischer Umbruch in Medizin und Theologie." In *Zur Aktualität Viktor von Weizsäckers*. Edited by Rainer-M. E. Jacobi and Dieter Janz. Beiträge zur medizinischen Anthropologie. Würzburg: Königshausen & Neumann, 2003, 227–45.

———. "Die Entscheidung der Christologie Calvins und ihre theologische Bedeutung: Das sogenannte Extra-Calvinisticum." *Evangelische Theologie* 47 (1987): 97–119.

———. "Die Erfahrung der Welt als Schöpfung: Ein Modell zum Dialog zwischen Theologie und Naturwissenschaft." In *Die Spur des Namens: Wege zur Erkenntnis Gottes und zur Erfahrung der Schöpfung: Theologische Studien*. Neukirchen-Vluyn: Neukirchener, 1997, 123–70.

———. *Schöpfung*. Vol. 1. Handbuch systematischer Theologie 7. Gütersloh: Mohn, 1991.

———. *Schöpfung: Ein theologischer Entwurf im Gegenüber von Naturwissenschaft und Ökologie*. Neukirchen-Vluyn: Neukirchener, 2012.

Loos, Fritz, "Todesstrafe: IV. Juristisch." In *Religion in Geschichte und Gegenwart*. Edited by Hans Dieter Betz et al., 4th ed. Tübingen: Mohr Siebeck, 2005, 8:451–53.

Losch, Andreas, *Jenseits der Konflikte: Eine konstruktiv–kritische Auseinandersetzung von Theologie und Naturwissenschaft*. Forschungen zur systematischen und ökumenischen Theologie 133. Göttingen: Vandenhoeck & Ruprecht, 2011.

Luther, Martin. *2. Galatervorlesung (cap. 1 –4) 1531*. Edited by Karl Drescher, Weimar Edition 40/I. Weimar: Böhlau, 1911.

———. *Heidelberg Disputation*. In *Career of the Reformer* 1. Edited and translated by Harold J. Grimm. Luther's Works 31. Philadelphia: Muhlenberg Press: 1957, 35–70.

——. *Lectures on Galatians 1535: Chapters 1–4.* Edited and translated by Jaroslav Pelikan. Luther's Works 26. Saint Louis: Concordia Publishing: 1963.

——. *On the Bondage of the Will.* In *Career of the Reformer* 3. Edited and translated by Philip S. Watson. Luther's Works 33. Philadelphia: Fortress, 1972.

——. *Temporal Authority: To What Extent it Should be Obeyed.* In *The Christian in Society* 2. Edited by Walther I. Brandt, translated by J. J. Schindel. Luther's Works 45. Philadelphia: Muhlenberg Press, 1962, 75–130.

——. "Whether Soldiers, Too, Can Be Saved. 1526." In *The Christian in Society* 3. Edited by Robert C. Schulz, translated by Charles M. Jacobs. Luther's Works 46. Philadelphia: Fortress Press, 1967, 93–137.

Malina, Bruce J. and Richard L. Rohrbaugh. *Social-Science Commentary on the Synoptic Gospels.* 2nd ed. Minneapolis: Fortress Press, 2003.

Mantei, Simone. *Nein und Ja zur Abtreibung: Die evangelische Kirche in der Reformdebatte um § 218 StGB (1970–1976).* Arbeiten zur kirchlichen Zeitgeschichte B 38. Göttingen: Vandenhoeck & Ruprecht, 2004.

Markschies, Christoph. *Alta Trinità Beata: Gesammelte Studien zur altkirchlichen Trinitätstheologie.* Tübingen: Mohr Siebeck, 2000.

——. *Die Gnosis.* Beck Wissen, Beck'sche Reihe 2173. Munich: Beck, 2001.

——. "'. . . et tamen non tres Dii, sed unus Deus . . .': Zum Stand der Erforschung der altkirchlichen Trinitätstheologie." In *Alta Trinità Beata*, 286–309.

——. "Theologische Diskussionen zur Zeit Konstantins: Arius, der 'arianische Streit' und das Konzil von Nicaea, die nachnicaenischen Auseinandersetzungen bis 337." In *Alta Trinità Beata*, 99–195.

Marquardt, Friedrich-Wilhelm. *Der Christ in der Gesellschaft: 1919–1979:*

Geschichte, Analysen und aktuelle Bedeutung von Karl Barths Tambacher Vortrag. Theologische Existenz Heute 206. Munich: Kaiser, 1980.

———. *Theologie und Sozialismus: Das Beispiel Karl Barths.* Gesellschaft und Theologie: Systematik 7. Munich: Kaiser and Mainz: Grünewald, 1972.

Marx, Karl. *Critique of Hegel's "Philosophy of Right."* Edited by Joseph O'Malley. Translated by Janette Jolin and J. O'Malley. Cambridge Studies in the History and Theory of Politics. Cambridge: Cambridge University Press, 2009.

Marx, Karl and Friedrich Engels, *The Communist Manifesto.* Translated by Samuel Moore, Penguin Classics Deluxe Edition. New York: Penguin, 2011.

Matošević, Lidija. *Lieber katholisch als neuprotestantisch: Karl Barths Rezeption der katholischen Theologie 1921–1930.* Neukirchen-Vluyn: Neukirchener, 2005.

Mattmüller, Markus. *Leonhard Ragaz und der religiöse Sozialismus: Eine Biographie.* Vol. 2. Zurich: Evangelischer Verlag, 1968.

Maurer, Ernstpeter. "Barth-Rezeption bei lutherischen Theologen in Deutschland." In *Karl Barths Theologie als europäisches Ereignis.* Edited by Leiner and Trowitzsch, 367–86.

McCormack, Bruce L. "Barths grundsätzlicher Chalkedonismus?" *Zeitschrift für Dialektische Theologie* 18 (2002): 138–73.

———. "Grace and Being: The Role of God's Gracious Election in Karl Barth's Theological Ontology." In *Cambridge Companion to Karl Barth.* Edited by Webster, 92–110.

———. *Karl Barth's Critically Realistic Dialectical Theology: Its Genesis and Development 1909–1936.* Oxford: Clarendon Press, 1995.

McDougall, Walter A. "20th-Century International Relations." *Encyclopaedia Britannica Online Academic Edition,* 2014. http://academic.eb.com.ubproxy.ub.uni-heidelberg.de/EBchecked/topic/291225/20th-century-international-relations/ (subscription required).

Meyers, Carol. *Discovering Eve: Ancient Israelite Women in Context.* New York: Oxford University Press, 1988.

Migliore, Daniel L., ed. *Commanding Grace: Studies in Karl Barth's Ethics.* Grand Rapids: Eerdmans, 2010.

———. *Faith Seeking Understanding: An Introduction to Christian Theology.* 2nd ed. Grand Rapids: Eerdmans, 2004.

———. "Karl Barth's First Lectures in Dogmatics: Instruction in the Christian Religion." In *The Göttingen Dogmatics: Instruction in the Christian Religion,* by Karl Barth. Edited by Hannelotte Reiffen, translated by Geoffrey W. Bromiley, xv–lvii. Grand Rapids: Eerdmans, 1991.

Miller, Patrick D. *They Cried to the Lord: The Form and Theology of Biblical Prayer.* Minneapolis: Fortress, 1994.

Moffitt, David M. *Atonement and the Logic of the Resurrection in Hebrews.* Novum Testamentum Supplementa 141. Leiden: Brill, 2011.

Moltmann, Jürgen. *The Crucified God: The Cross of Christ as the Foundation and Criticism of Christian Theology.* Translated by R. A. Wilson and John Bowden. Minneapolis: Fortress Press, 1993.

———. *The Trinity and the Kingdom: The Doctrine of God.* Translated by Margaret Kohl. Minneapolis: Fortress Press, 1993.

———. *The Way of Jesus Christ: Christology in Messianic Dimensions.* Translated by Margaret Kohl. London: SCM, 1990.

Müller, Klaus-Jürgen. "Über den 'militärischen Widerstand.'" In *Widerstand gegen den Nationalsozialismus.* Edited by Steinbach and Tuchel, 266–79.

Müller, Rolf-Dieter. *Der Zweite Weltkrieg: 1939–1945.* Gebhardt: Handbuch der deutschen Geschichte 21. Stuttgart: Klett-Cotta, 2004.

Munzinger-Biographie. "Foerster, Friedrich Wilhelm." *Munzinger-Biographie: Internationales Biographisches Archiv.* http://tinyurl.com/lcplojs.

Nielsen, Bent Fleming. "Beten—und Kanonen kaufen: Evangelium und Gesetz im Zusammenhang von KD II/2 (§§ 36–39)." In *Karl Barth im europäischen Zeitgeschehen (1935–1950).* Edited by Beintker et al., 109–36.

Niemöller, Gerhard. *Die erste Bekenntnissynode der Deutschen Evangelischen Kirche zu Barmen: Geschichte, Kritik und Bedeutung der Synode und ihrer Theologischen Erklärung.* Arbeiten zur Geschichte des Kirchenkampfes 5. 2nd ed. Göttingen: Vandenhoeck & Ruprecht, 1984.

Niemöller, Wilhelm. *Die Zweite Bekenntnissynode der Deutschen Evangelischen Kirche zu Dahlem.* Arbeiten zur Geschichte des Kirchenkampfes 3. Göttingen: Vandenhoeck & Ruprecht, 1958.

Nimmo, Paul T. "Barth and the Christian as Ethical Agent: An Ontological Study of the Shape of Christian Ethics," in *Commanding Grace.* Edited by Migliore, 216–38.

———. *Being in Action: The Theological Shape of Barth's Ethical Vision.* Edinburgh: T&T Clark/Continuum, 2007.

Norden, Günther van. *Die Weltverantwortung der Christen neu begreifen: Karl Barth als homo politicus.* Kaiser Taschenbuch 153. Gütersloh: Kaiser and Gütersloher Verlagshaus, 1997.

Norris, Kristopher, "Barth and Yoder on Democratic Practice." In *Theo-Politics? Conversing with Barth in Western and Asian Contexts.* Edited by Höfner. Minneapolis: Fortress Press, 2016.

Nowak, Martin A. "Five Rules for the Evolution of Cooperation." In *Evolution, Games, and God: The Principle of Cooperation.* Edited by Martin A. Nowak and Sarah Coakley. Cambridge, MA: Harvard University Press, 2013, 99–114.

Nüssel, Friederike. "Die Sühnevorstellung in der Dogmatik und ihre neuzeitliche Problematisierung." In *Deutungen des Todes Jesu im Neuen Testament.* Edited by Jörg Frey and Jens Schröter. Tübingen: Mohr Siebeck, 2007, 73–94.

O'Donovan, Oliver. "Karl Barth and Ramsey's 'Uses of Power.'" *Journal of Religion* 19 (1991): 1–30.

Ottaway, Marina. *Democracy Challenged: The Rise of Semi-Authoritarianism.* Washington, DC: Carnegie Endowment for International Peace, 2003.

Otto, Rudolf. *The Idea of the Holy: An Inquiry into the Non-Rational Factor in the Idea of the Divine and its Relation to the Rational.* Translated by John W. Harvey. 7th ed. Oxford: Oxford University Press, 1936.

Pannenberg, Wolfhart. "Die Subjektivität Gottes und die Trinitätslehre: Ein Beitrag zur Beziehung zwischen Karl Barth und der Philosophie Hegels." In *Grundfragen systematischer Theologie: Gesammelte Aufsätze.* Göttingen: Vandenhoeck & Ruprecht, 1980, 2:96–111.

———. *Systematic Theology.* Translated by Geoffrey W. Bromiley. 2 vols. New York: T&T Clark, 1992.

Pauck, Wilhelm. *Karl Barth: Prophet of a New Christianity?* New York: Harper, 1931.

Peters, Albrecht. *Gesetz und Evangelium.* Handbuch Systematische Theologie 2. Gütersloh: Mohn, 1981.

Peterson, Erik. *Der Monotheismus als politisches Problem: Ein Beitrag zur Geschichte der politischen Theologie im Imperium Romanum.* Leipzig: Hegner, 1935.

Pew Forum. "The Religious Dimensions of the Torture Debate." April 29, 2009. http://www.pewforum.org/2009/05/07/the-torture-debate-a-closer-look/6.

Pfleiderer, Georg. *Karl Barths praktische Theologie: Zu Genese und Kontext eines paradigmatischen Entwurfs systematischer Theologie im 20. Jahrhundert.* Beiträge zur historischen Theologie 115. Tübingen: Mohr Siebeck, 2000.

Prolingheuer, Hans. *Der Fall Karl Barth: 1934–1935: Chronographie einer Vertreibung.* Neukirchen-Vluyn: Neukirchener, 1977.

Puffer, Matthew. "Taking Exception to the *Grenzfall*'s Reception: Revisiting Karl Barth's Ethics of War." *Modern Theology* 28 (2012): 478–502.

Rager, Günter. "Präimplantationsdiagnostik und der Status des Embryos." *Zeitschrift für medizinische Ethik* 46 (2000): 81–9.

Rahner, Karl. "Bemerkungen zum dogmatischen Traktat 'De Trinitate.'"

In *Schriften zur Theologie: Neue Schriften*. Einsiedeln: Benziger, 1960, 103–33.

Rawls, John. *A Theory of Justice*. 2nd ed. Cambridge: Belknap, 1999.

Rendtorff, Trutz. *Ethics: Basic Elements and Methodology in an Ethical Theology*. Translated by Keith Crim. Philadelphia: Augsburg Fortress Press, 1986.

———. "Karl Barth und die Neuzeit." In *Theologie in der Moderne: Über Religion im Prozess der Aufklärung*. Troeltsch-Studien 5. Gütersloh: Gütersloher Verlagshaus Gerd Mohn, 1991, 127–45.

———. "Radikale Autonomie Gottes: Zum Verständnis der Theologie Karl Barths und ihrer Folgen." In *Theorie des Christentums: Historisch-theologische Studien zu seiner neuzeitlichen Verfassung*. Gütersloh: Gütersloher Verlagshaus Mohn, 1972, 161–81.

Resis, Albert. "Vladimir Ilich Lenin." *Encyclopaedia Britannica Online Academic Edition*, 2014. http://www.britannica.com/Ebchecked/topic/335881/Vladimir-Ilich-Lenin (subscription required).

Reuter, Hans-Richard. "Das Recht in der Auslegung des Glaubens: Über Rechtsbegriffe in der neueren systematischen Theologie." In *Rechtsethik in theologischer Perspektive: Studien zur Grundlegung und Konkretion*. Öffentliche Theologie 8. Gütersloh: Gütersloher Verlagshaus, 1996, 93–120.

Ricoeur, Paul. *The Rule of Metaphor: The Creation of Meaning in Language*. Routledge Classics. London: Routledge, 2003.

Ringeling, Hermann. "Kritik der Moderne und kritische Modernität: Evangelische Ethik heute." *Zeitschrift für evangelische Ethik* 40 (1996): 23–37.

Roberts, Adam. "Against War." In *The Oxford History of Modern War*. Edited by Charles Townshend. Oxford: Oxford University Press, 2000, 317–40.

Ruschke, Werner M. *Entstehung und Ausführung der Diastasentheologie in Karl*

Barths zweitem 'Römerbrief.' Neukirchener Beiträge zur Systematischen Theologie 5. Neukirchen-Vluyn: Neukirchener, 1987.

Sakenfeld, Katharine Doob. "Love." In *The Anchor Bible Dictionary*. Edited by David Noel Freedman. New York: Doubleday, 1996, 4:375–81.

Schiller, Friedrich. "Concerning the Sublime." In *Essays*, translated by Walter Hinderer and Daniel O. Dahlstrom. The German Library. New York: Continuum, 1993, 70–85.

Schlak, Stephan. "Ordnung und Revolte: Helmut Schelsky und Jean Améry." *Deutschlandfunk*, May 24, 2009. Intellektuelle Gegenpole 4. http://tinyurl.com/mb3r8pm.

Schleiermacher, Friedrich. *The Christian Faith*. Edited by Hugh R. MacKintosh and James S. Stewart. New York: T&T Clark, 1999.

Schmädeke, Jürgen. "Militärische Umsturzversuche und diplomatische Oppositionsbestrebungen zwischen der Münchner Konferenz und Stalingrad." In *Widerstand gegen den Nationalsozialismus*. Edited by Steinbach and Tuchel, 294–318.

Schmid, Konrad. "Jenseits von Verfügungswissen und Orientierungswissen: Evangelische Ethik und das Evangelium." *Zeitschrift für evangelische Ethik* 49 (2005): 190–97.

Schmidt, Kurt Dietrich. *Die Bekenntnisse und grundsätzlichen Äußerungen zur Kirchenfrage des Jahres 1933*. Göttingen: Vandenhoeck & Ruprecht, 1937.

Schmidt, Werner H. *Die Zehn Gebote im Rahmen alttestamentlicher Ethik*. Erträge der Forschung 281. Darmstadt: Wissenschaftliche Buchgesellschaft, 1993.

Schmitt, Carl. *Die Wendung zum diskriminierenden Kriegsbegriff*. Berlin: Duncker & Humblot, 2007.

———. *Political Theology: Four Chapters on the Concept of Sovereignty*. Chicago: University of Chicago Press, 1985.

Scholder, Klaus. "Neue deutsche Geschichte und protestantische Theologie: Aspekte und Fragen." *Evangelische Theologie* 23 (1963): 510–36.

Schuhmacher, Wolfgang. *Theologische Ethik als Verantwortungsethik: Leben und Werk Heinz Eduard Tödts in ökumenischer Perspektive*. Öffentliche Theologie 20. Gütersloh: Gütersloher Verlagshaus, 2006.

Schüssler-Fiorenza, Elisabeth. *In Memory of Her: A Feminist Theological Reconstruction of Christian Origins*. New York: Crossroad, 1983.

Schütte, Hans-Walter. "Zwei-Reiche-Lehre und Königsherrschaft Christi." In *Handbuch der Christlichen Ethik*. Edited by Hertz and Korff, 1:339–53.

Schwager, Raymund. *Der wunderbare Tausch: Zur Geschichte und Deutung der Erlösungslehre*. Munich: Kösel, 1986.

Schweiker, William. *Responsibility and Christian Ethics*. New Studies in Christian Ethics. Cambridge: Cambridge University Press, 1999.

Schwöbel, Christoph. "Theology." In *Cambridge Companion to Karl Barth*. Edited by Webster, 17–36.

Simon, Christine. "Erhard Epplers Deutschland- und Ostpolitik." PhD dissertation. Bonn University, Germany, 2004. http://hss.ulb.uni-bonn.de/2004/0337/0337.htm.

Simon, Helmut, "Die zweite und die fünfte These der Barmer Erklärung und der staatliche Gewaltgebrauch." In *Bekennende Kirche wagen: Barmen 1934–1984*. Edited by Jürgen Moltmann, Kaiser Traktate. Munich: Kaiser, 1984, 199–222.

Smend, Rudolf. "Karl Barth als Ausleger der Heiligen Schrift." In Bibel und Wissenschaft. Tübingen: Mohr Siebeck, 2004, 199–229.

Smit, Dirkie, "Paradigms of Radical Grace." In *On Reading Karl Barth in South Africa*. Edited by Villa-Vicencio, 17–43.

Sonderegger, Katherine, "Barth and Feminism." In *Cambridge Companion to Karl Barth*. Edited by Webster, 258–73.

Spieckermann, Hermann. *Heilsgegenwart: Eine Theologie der Psalmen*. Forschungen zur Religion und Literatur des Alten und Neuen Testaments 148. Göttingen: Vandenhoeck & Ruprecht, 1989.

Spieckermann, Ingrid. *Gotteserkenntnis: Ein Beitrag zur Grundfrage der neuen*

Theologie Karl Barths. Beiträge zur evangelischen Theologie 97. Munich: Kaiser, 1985.

Spiegel, Der. "Friedrich Wilhelm Foerster," *Der Spiegel* 20, no. 4 (1966): 90. http://tinyurl.com/pydj2wa.

Stalla, Bernhard Josef. "Foerster, Friedrich Wilhelm." In *Bibliographisch-Biographisches Lexikon.* Edited by Traugott Bautz. Nordhausen: Bautz, 2007, 27:445–51.

Stapel, Wilhelm. *Der christliche Staatsmann: Eine Theologie des Nationalismus.* Hamburg: Hanseatische Verlagsanstalt, 1932.

Stegemann, Ekkehard W. "Israel in Barths Erwählungslehre: Zur Auslegung von Röm 9–11 in KD II, 2, § 34." *Israel und Kirche* 20 (2005): 19–42.

Steinbach, Peter and Johannes Tuchel, eds. *Widerstand gegen den Nationalsozialismus.* Schriftenreihe 323. Bonn: Bundeszentrale für politische Bildung, 1994.

Stephenson, Peter K. "The Crucified God: Mark 15:25–39." *Direction* 41, no. 1 (2012): 148–64.

Stoellger, Philipp. "Barth und die Postmoderne: Perspektiven auf eine prekäre Konstellation." In *Karl Barths Theologie als europäisches Ereignis.* Edited by Leiner and Trowitzsch, 397–432.

Stoevesandt, Hinrich. "Barths Calvinvorlesung als Station seiner theologischen Biographie." In *Karl Barth und Johannes Calvin: Karl Barths Göttinger Calvin-Vorlesung von 1922.* Edited by Hans Scholl. Neukirchen-Vluyn: Neukirchener, 1995, 107–24.

———. "Die Göttinger Dogmatikvorlesung: Grundriss der Theologie Barths." In *Karl Barth in Deutschland (1921–1935): Aufbruch—Klärung—Widerstand.* Edited by Beintker et al., 77–98.

Stout, Jeffrey. *Democracy and Tradition.* Princeton: Princeton University Press, 2004.

Strohm, Christoph. "Ius divinum und ius humanum: Reformatorische Begründung des Kirchenrechts." In *Das Recht der Kirche: Zur Geschichte des Kirchenrechts*. Edited by Gerhard Rau et al. Forschungen und Berichte der Evangelischen Studiengemeinschaft 50. Gütersloh: Kaiser and Gütersloher Verlagshaus, 1995, 115–73.

Strub, Jean-Daniel and Stefan Grotefeld, eds. *Der gerechte Friede zwischen Pazifismus und gerechtem Krieg: Paradigmen der Friedensethik im Diskurs*. Stuttgart: Kohlhammer, 2007.

Stuhlmacher, Peter. *Biblische Theologie des Neuen Testaments: Grundlegung: Von Jesus zu Paulus*. 2nd ed. Göttingen: Vandenhoeck & Ruprecht, 1997.

Sweet, William. "The Volksgerichtshof: 1934–45." *Journal of Modern History* 46 (1974): 314–29.

Sykes, Stephen W. *Karl Barth: Studies of His Theological Method*. New York: Clarendon/Oxford University Press, 1979.

Theissen, Gerd. *The New Testament: History, Literature, Religion*. Translated by John Bowden. New York: T&T Clark, 2007.

———. "Social Stratification in the Corinthian Community: A Contribution to the Sociology of Early Hellenistic Christianity." In *The Social Setting of Pauline Christianity: Essays on Corinth*. Edited and translated by John H. Schütz. 2nd ed. Minneapolis: Fortress Press, 1989, 69–119.

Theissen, Gerd, and Annette Merz. *The Historical Jesus: A Comprehensive Guide*. Translated by John Bowden. Minneapolis: Fortress Press, 1998.

Thiemann, Ronald. "The Significance of Karl Barth for Contemporary Theology." *Thomist* 50 (1986): 512–39.

Thistlethwaite, Susan B. "Why the Faithful Approve of Torture." *The Washington Post*. January 5, 2009. http://tinyurl.com/phfycvh.

Thomas, Günter. "Das Kreuz Jesu Christi als Risiko der Inkarnation." In *Gegenwart des lebendigen Christus: Festschrift für Michael Welker zum 60. Geburtstag*. Edited by Günter Thomas and Andreas Schüle. Leipzig: Evangelische Verlagsanstalt, 2007, 151–79.

———. "Der für uns 'gerichtete Richter': Kritische Erwägungen zu Karl

Barths Versöhnungslehre." *Zeitschrift für Dialektische Theologie* 18 (2002): 211–25.

———. *Neue Schöpfung: Systematisch-theologische Untersuchungen zur Hoffnung auf das Leben 'in der zukünftigen Welt.'* Neukirchen-Vluyn: Neukirchener, 2009.

Tirman, John. "Why Do We Ignore the Civilians Killed in American Wars?" *The Washington Post.* January 6, 2012. http://tinyurl.com/7cwuq8h.

Tödt, Heinz Eduard. "Karl Barth, der Liberalismus und der Nationalsozialismus: Gegendarstellung zu Friedrich Wilhelm Grafs Behandlung dieses Themas." *Evangelische Theologie* 46 (1986): 536–51.

van der Kooi, Cornelis. *Anfängliche Theologie: Der Denkweg des jungen Karl Barth (1909–1927).* Beiträge zur evangelischen Theologie 103. Munich: Kaiser, 1987.

———. "Karl Barths zweiter Römerbrief und seine Folgen." In *Karl Barth in Deutschland (1921–1935): Aufbruch—Klärung—Widerstand.* Edited by Beintker et al., 57–75.

Van Oyen, Hendrik. "Gibt es eine evangelische Ethik der Grenzfälle?" *Zeitschrift für Evangelische Ethik* 1 (1957): 2–17.

Villa-Vicencio, Charles, ed. *On Reading Karl Barth in South Africa.* Grand Rapids: Eerdmans, 1988.

Voigt, Gottfried. "Barmen II in lutherischer Sicht." In *Zum politischen Auftrag der christlichen Gemeinde.* Edited by Burgsmüller, 81–93.

Von Balthasar, Hans Urs. *The Theology of Karl Barth: Exposition and Interpretation.* Translated by Edward T. Oakes, SJ. Communio Books. San Francisco: Ignatius, 1992.

von Loewenich, Walther. *Luther's Theology of the Cross.* Minneapolis: Augsburg Publishing House, 1976.

Vorländer, Karl. *Geschichte der Philosophie: Altertum, Mittelalter und Übergang zur Neuzeit.* 5th ed. Leipzig: Meiner, 1919.

Walther, Christian. "Königsherrschaft Christi." In *Theologische Realenzyklopädie*. Berlin and New York: de Gruyter, 1990, 19: 311–23.

Walzer, Michael. *Just and Unjust Wars: A Moral Argument with Historical Illustrations*. 4th ed. New York: Basic Books, 2006.

Weber, Max. *Economy and Society: An Outline of Interpretive Sociology*. Edited by Guenther Roth and Claus Wittich, translated by Ephraim Fischoff et al. Berkeley, CA: University of California Press, 1978.

———. "The Profession and Vocation of Politics." In *Political Writings*. Edited by Peter Lassmann, translated by Ronald Speirs. Cambridge Texts in the History of Political Thought. Cambridge: Cambridge University Press, 1994, 309–69.

———. *The Protestant Ethic and the Spirit of Capitalism*. Translated by Talcott Parsons. Routledge Classics. New York: Routledge, 2001.

Weber, Rachel N. "Military-Industrial Complex." *Encyclopædia Britannica: Academic Edition*. http://tinyurl.com/ok26uvl.

Webster, John B. *Barth's Ethics of Reconciliation*. Cambridge: Cambridge University Press, 1995.

———. *Barth's Moral Theology: Human Action in Barth's Thought*. Edinburgh: Clark, 1998.

———, ed. *The Cambridge Companion to Karl Barth*. Cambridge Companions to Religion. Cambridge: Cambridge University Press, 2000.

———. "'The Great Disruption': Word of God and Moral Consciousness in Barth's Münster Ethics." In *Barth's Moral Theology*, 41–63.

———. "The Identity of the Holy Spirit: A Problem in Trinitarian Theology." *Themelios* 9 (1983): 4–7.

Weiser, Alfons. *Theologie des Neuen Testaments II: Die Theologie der Evangelien*. Kohlhammer Studium Theologie 8. Stuttgart et al.: Kohlhammer, 1993.

Welker, Michael. "Barth und Feuerbach." In *Theologische Profile:*

Schleiermacher—Barth—Bonhoeffer—Moltmann. Edition Chrismon. Frankfurt am Main: Hansisches Veragshaus, 2009, 157–81.

———. "Gesetz und Geist." In *"Gesetz" als Thema Biblischer Theologie.* Jahrbuch für Biblische Theologie 4. Neukirchen-Vluyn: Neukirchener, 1989, 215–29.

———. *God the Revealed: Christology.* Translated by Douglas W. Stott. Grand Rapids: Eerdmans, 2014.

———. *God the Spirit.* Translated by John Hoffmeyer. 2nd ed. Minneapolis: Fortress Press, 2004.

———. *Kirche im Pluralismus.* Kaiser Taschenbuch 136. Gütersloh: Kaiser/Gütersloher Verlagshaus, 1995.

———. *Creation and Reality.* Translated by John Hoffmeyer. Minneapolis: Fortress Press, 1999.

Werpehowski, William, "Command and History." In *Karl Barth and Christian Ethics: Living in Truth*, 15–35.

———. "Hearing the Divine Command. Realism and Discernment in Barth's Ethics." *Zeitschrift für Dialektische Theologie* 12 (1996): 64–74.

———. "Justification and Justice in the Theology of Karl Barth." *Thomist* 50 (1986): 623–42.

———. *Karl Barth and Christian Ethics: Living in Truth.* Farnham: Ashgate, 2014

———. "Karl Barth and Just War: A Conversation with Roman Catholicism." In *Commanding Grace.* Edited by Migliore, 60–82.

———. "Karl Barth and Politics." In *Cambridge Companion to Karl Barth.* Edited by Webster, 228–42.

———. "Narrative and Ethics." In *Karl Barth and Christian Ethics: Living in Truth*, 37–56.

Willetts, David, "The Invisible Hand That Binds Us All." Review of *SuperCooperators: Altruism, Evolution, and Why We Need Each Other to*

Succeed, by Martin Nowak and Roger Highfield. *The Financial Times.* April 24, 2011. http://tinyurl.com/knlzg6u.

Williams, Rowan D. "Barth on the Triune God." In *Karl Barth: Centenary Ethics.* Edited by Stephen W. Sykes. Cambridge: Cambridge University Press, 1989, 147–93.

———. "Barth, War and the State." In *Reckoning With Barth.* Edited by Biggar, 170–90.

Wissenschaftlicher Beirat der Bundesärztekammer. "Pränatale und perinatale Schmerzempfindung: Stellungnahme des Wissenschaftlichen Beirates der Bundesärztekammer" (1991). *Ärzteblatt.* https://www.aerzteblatt.de/pdf/88/47/a4157.pdf.

Wright, Jonathan. *Germany and the Origins of the Second World War: The Making of the Twentieth Century.* New York: Palgrave Macmillan, 2007.

Wüthrich, Matthias D. *Gott und das Nichtige: Zur Rede vom Nichtigen ausgehend von § 50 der Kirchlichen Dogmatik Karl Barths.* Zurich: Theologischer Verlag, 2006.

Wyder, Theodor. *Wehrpflicht und Militärdienstverweigerung: Entstehung, Gesetz, Arten und Sanktionen in der Schweizer Armee.* 2nd ed. Europäische Hochschulschriften: Rechtswissenschaften 523. Frankfurt am Main et al.: Lang, 1988.

Yoder, John H. "Karl Barth and the Problem of War." In *Karl Barth and the Problem of War.* Edited by Nation, 1–104.

———. *Karl Barth and the Problem of War and Other Essays on Barth.* Edited by Mark Thiessen Nation. Eugene: Cascade/Wipf & Stock, 2003.

———. "The Pacifism of Karl Barth (1963)." In *Karl Barth and the Problem of War.* Edited by Nation, 109–32.

———. *The Politics of Jesus: Vicit Agnus Noster.* 2nd ed. Grand Rapids: Eerdmans/Paternoster, 1994.

Zentralrat der Juden in Deutschland, Deutsche Bischofskonferenz, and EKD.

"Gemeinsame Stellungnahme zum Film 'Die Passion Christi' vom 18.3.2004." Evangelische Kirche in Deutschland. http://bit.ly/4rMKMF.

Zur Mühlen, Karl-Heinz. *Reformation und Gegenreformation.* Vol. 2. Kleine Reihe V&R. Göttingen: Vandenhoeck & Ruprecht, 1999.

Index of Names